BOOK OF
COMMON
WORSHIP

Book of Common Worship

PREPARED BY

The Theology and Worship Ministry Unit

FOR THE

Presbyterian Church (U.S.A.)

AND THE

Cumberland Presbyterian Church

PUBLISHED BY

WESTMINSTER/JOHN KNOX PRESS
LOUISVILLE, KENTUCKY

Inquiries concerning rights and reproductions not herein authorized should be directed to Westminster/John Knox Press, 100 Witherspoon Street, Louisville, KY 40202-1396.

For Acknowledgments, see pages 1099–1106.

Published by Westminster/John Knox Press
Louisville, Kentucky

This book is printed on acid-free paper that meets the American National Standards Institute Z39.48 standard. ∞

Book design by Susan E. Jackson

Interior illustrations by Aavidar Design Inc.

PRINTED IN THE UNITED STATES OF AMERICA

2 4 6 8 9 7 5 3 1

Library of Congress Cataloging-in-Publication Data

Presbyterian Church (U.S.A.)
    Book of common worship / prepared by the Theology and Worship Ministry Unit for the Presbyterian Church (U.S.A.) and the Cumberland Presbyterian Church.
       p.   cm.
    ISBN 0-664-21991-8
    1. Presbyterian Church (U.S.A.)—Liturgy—Texts.   2. Cumberland Presbyterian Church—Liturgy—Texts.   3. Presbyterian Church—United States—Liturgy—Texts. Presbyterian Church (U.S.A.) Theology and Worship Ministry Unit.   II. Cumberland Presbyterian Church.   III. Title.
BX8969.5.P74   1993a
264'.5137—dc20

93-20269

CONTENTS

PREFACE

WORSHIP IS AT THE VERY heart of the church's life. All that the church is and does is rooted in its worship. The community of faith, gathered in response to God's call, is formed in its worship. Worship is the principal influence that shapes our faith, and is the most visible way we express the faith.

In worship, through Word and Sacrament, the church is sustained by the presence of Christ. Joined in worship to the One who is the source of its life, the church is empowered to serve God in the world.

Because of the centrality of worship in the church's life, the continuing reform of worship is of primary importance in maintaining the integrity of the people of God. In an age dominated by individualism and secularism, it is particularly important to embrace forms of worship that are firmly rooted in the faith and foster a strong communal sense of being united with God, with the community of faith in every time and place, and with a broken world in need of God's healing touch. In other words, the concern for the reform of worship is, above everything else, a concern for the renewal of the church.

This conviction has informed every stage of the development of this edition of the *Book of Common Worship*, the fifth service book to be published in this century to serve American Presbyterians. As with each of its four predecessors, this edition of the *Book of Common Worship* was prepared with the intention of seeking a liturgical expression that is faithful to the tradition of the church catholic, truly reformed, rooted in scripture, and related to life.

The purpose of this preface is to provide an overview of the place a service book has within the Reformed tradition, and to describe aspects of this book that will contribute to its usefulness in shaping worship in Presbyterian congregations.

THE SERVICE BOOK AND THE DIRECTORY FOR WORSHIP

American Presbyterians have both a directory for worship and a service book. There is often a confusion over the distinction between the two, and over the role of each.

A Directory for Worship is a part of the constitution of the church and thus has the authority of church law. It provides the theology that undergirds worship, and includes appropriate directions for worship. It sets forth the standards and the norms for the ordering of worship. It does not have fixed orders of worship or liturgical texts.

The church's service book, on the other hand, provides orders and texts for worship. It is in harmony with the directory and is approved for voluntary use.

Where both a directory and a service book coexist, as in those churches served by this book, the service book sets forth, in orders of services and in liturgical texts, the theology and norms described in the directory. Service books have a longer history in the Reformed tradition than directories, and most churches in the Reformed community do not have directories but do have service books.

THE SIXTEENTH AND SEVENTEENTH CENTURIES

Reformed churches in the sixteenth century used service books. Ulrich Zwingli, Martin Bucer, and John Calvin all prepared worship forms for use in the congregations. John Knox, following Calvin, prepared *The Forme of Prayers* and subsequently a service book, the *Book of Common Order*, for use in Scotland. Liturgical forms were in general use in Switzerland, Germany, France, Italy, Holland, England, and Scotland.

However, the Reformation in England and Scotland after the death of Thomas Cranmer was formed in a very different context from that on the continent, where entire political entities were Reformed. The Reformed were thus able to prepare their own service books without interference. In England and Scotland those seeking to carry the reform from the continent had the difficult task of re-forming within a state church hostile to Genevan-inspired reform. Even after the Scottish kirk was reformed under John Knox, it continued to endure English political and religious pressures, resulting in bitter conflict with the English crown.

As the contending party in a state church, the Puritans were vulnerable. The liberty of the church to order its life and worship in harmony with the Word of God was threatened. The Puritans felt under attack by both church and nation. It was in worship that the conflict raged.

The Puritans' struggle for liberty put them in direct conflict with those who had power to legislate the content of the service book and to require its use. Initially, the Puritan conflict was not about opposition to the propriety and use of a service book. The Puritans proposed their own service books. Rather, the conflict was about a service book that was being imposed upon the Puritans that did not reflect their concerns.

The struggle ultimately drove the Puritans to join forces with the separatists. As a result, both the English Puritans and the Scots were forced into a more radical liturgical position than that of the reform on the continent, which did not have to face such issues. Whereas the Reformers were in a position to *reform* the forms of worship, the political and ecclesiastical situation compelled the Puritans, for the sake of liberty, to *reject* the forms thrust upon them.

It was in this context that the Westminster Directory for the Publique Worship of God, devoid of liturgical text, was created in 1644, under the influence of Puritans and separatists. This directory was destined to play the dominant role in shaping the worship of American Presbyterians.

It was at this moment in history that Puritans and Scots settled in the New World. They were the nucleus that initially shaped American Presbyterianism. Puritan views thus dominated the way the church took root in American soil. Opposition to service books continued even though the Puritans were no longer engaged in a struggle for liberty. The agenda remained, even though the context had changed. American Presbyterians soon forgot why they opposed service books. What began as a struggle for liberty turned into a new legalism.

In keeping with their Puritan legacy, Presbyterians who settled in the New World chose to be served by a directory for worship rather than a service book. Colonial Presbyterians had the 1644 Westminster Directory available to them until, in 1788, the Westminster Directory was revised for use in the United States and subsequently adopted by the first General Assembly. Two generations after the first General Assembly, things began to change.

THE NINETEENTH CENTURY

In the middle of the nineteenth century a movement emerged among American Presbyterians and other Reformed churches that sought to restore a liturgical tradition that was both Reformed and catholic, and thus to recover the values associated with use of a service book.

Individuals began to write service books for use by Presbyterians. Toward the end of the century, demand for such resources prompted the publishing house of the northern Presbyterians to produce collections of liturgical forms.

But it was the southern General Assembly that first extended official sanction to liturgical forms. In 1894 a directory for worship was adopted for use in the southern church that contained liturgical formulas, and liturgies for marriages and funerals were appended to it.

Nine years later, the northern General Assembly was ready to respond positively to overtures calling for a book of services.

BOOK OF COMMON WORSHIP—1906, 1932, 1946

In 1903, in response to the growing expression of need for worship forms, the General Assembly of the Presbyterian Church in the U.S.A. (northern) approved overtures calling for the preparation of a book of services. The result was that the first *Book of Common Worship* was published in 1906. In approving this book, the church embraced the growing concern for the reform of Presbyterian worship. Although American Presbyterians had a directory for worship to guide them in liturgical matters, the approval of a service book gave official recognition to the value of liturgical orders and texts in shaping worship.

The 1906 book was therefore a significant milepost in the reform of Presbyterian worship. It included orders with liturgical texts for both morning and evening Lord's Day worship. It provided for celebrating Holy Communion, and included an exemplary eucharistic prayer (in this book called "great thanksgiving"). Texts were provided for some festivals and seasons of the liturgical calendar. There were orders and liturgical texts for Baptism and for Confirmation of Baptismal Vows. A treasury of prayer, with family prayers, was included, as well as a selective psalter and a collection of ancient hymns and canticles. Congregational participation was encouraged with the provision of responses and unison prayers. This service book included prayers drawn from a wide range within the church catholic and from across many centuries.

By 1928, the book began to appear dated. Responding to popular demand, the General Assembly appointed a committee to revise the *Book of Common Worship*. The revised edition appeared in 1932. This edition was an expanded version of the 1906 book. Texts for additional festivals and seasons were added. A rudimentary lectionary was included. It is significant that the southern General Assembly approved it for use by its congregations.

Nine years later the northern General Assembly established a permanent committee on the revision of the *Book of Common Worship* to monitor the liturgical needs of the church and to periodically propose revisions. This underscores the importance that the Office of the General Assembly gave to the service book at that time.

A thoroughgoing revision of the *Book of Common Worship* resulted in a new edition being published in 1946. Those who prepared this book had the advantage of increasing ecumenical liturgical scholarship and of more knowledge about the worship of the Reformers. This edition of the service book provided for still greater congregational participation. It contained expanded resources for Sunday morning and Sunday evening worship and for the celebration of the Lord's Supper. The reading of scripture in worship was given emphasis by the addition of a complete two-year lectionary from the Church of Scotland's *Book of Common Order*, published in 1940. The liturgical year also received increased emphasis, with prayers included from the service books of other churches.

THE WORSHIPBOOK—1970

In 1955 the northern General Assembly called for another revision. As the committee appointed to revise the *Book of Common Worship* began its work, it was confronted with the great disparity between the Directory for Worship and the *Book of Common Worship*. The committee reported back to the assembly that it could not proceed until a new directory was adopted to replace the existing one, which for the northern church had remained virtually unchanged since its adoption nearly one hundred and seventy years earlier.

The southern Presbyterians joined with the northern church to produce the new service book but decided to prepare their own directory. Also joining the project was the United Presbyterian Church in North America, which in 1947 had published a book entitled *The Manual for Worship*, which included general guidelines for worship with some orders and liturgical texts. Before the new service book was completed, the United Presbyterian Church in North America had merged with the Presbyterian Church in the U.S.A. to form the United Presbyterian Church in the U.S.A. The Cumberland Presbyterian Church also joined in the project to produce the new service book. The Cumberland Presbyterians later engaged in preparing a new Directory for Worship, which was approved by their General Assembly in 1984. Other Reformed churches participated in early phases of the development of a new *Book of Common Worship*.

Work resumed on a revised *Book of Common Worship* when in 1961 the United Presbyterian Church in the U.S.A., and in 1963 the Presbyterian Church in the U.S., adopted new directories.

The committee distributed two trial use pieces prior to publication: one in 1964, another in 1966. In 1970 the service book was published with the title *The Worshipbook—Services*. Two years later it was published as part of *The Worshipbook—Services and Hymns*.

The contributions of *The Worshipbook* are noteworthy. As the first of a wave of new service books among American denominations, it broke new ground. It departed from Elizabethan English and began the search for a suitable contemporary style of language appropriate for the worship of God. It set forth with clarity that the norm of Christian worship on the Lord's Day is a service of the Word *and* Sacrament. Although six years earlier the committee had proposed a new lectionary, it recognized that the lectionary then being completed by the Roman Catholic Church was superior to the lectionary it had prepared. The committee therefore modified the Roman lectionary for use by Presbyterians and included it in the final publication of *The Worshipbook*. Other denominations also made revisions of the Roman lectionary.

But with all of its contributions, *The Worshipbook* was vulnerable. Following Vatican Council II there was a great resurgence of liturgical reform that continues unabated in virtually every branch of the church. Service book revision was begun by every church that had a service book. Presbyterians began to recognize the need to go beyond *The Worshipbook*. It was therefore no surprise that a new service book was soon called for.

BOOK OF COMMON WORSHIP—1993

In 1980 the General Assembly of the United Presbyterian Church in the U.S.A. approved an overture from the Presbytery of the Cascades calling for "a new book of services for corporate worship." In adopting the overture, the General Assembly expressed the fervent hope that the new book would be "an instrument for the renewal of the church at its life-giving center." Immediately the Presbyterian Church in the United States and the Cumberland Presbyterian Church approved participation in the project.

The process leading to a new service book called for the publication of trial-use resources prior to the finalization of the service book itself. Between 1984 and 1992 seven trial-use resources were published, each including proposed text for a portion of the service book. The trial-use volumes were published under the series title: Supplemental Liturgical Resources. Each volume was prepared by a task force chosen for the task. From fifty to one hundred congregations were invited to review testing drafts of each of these resources prior to its approval for publication. Suggestions received from these evaluations greatly contributed to the preparation of the final drafts, and thus to their usefulness in the church. Following the publication of each volume, evaluations and suggestions were received. These responses, based on their use, were carefully considered and were a valuable aid in revising the liturgical texts for inclusion in this book. In revised form the liturgical texts of the seven trial-use resources are included in this book.

During the course of the development of this service book, the reunion in 1983 of the Presbyterian Church in the U.S. and the United Presbyterian Church in the U.S.A. to form the Presbyterian Church (U.S.A.) occurred. This resulted in the preparation of a new Directory for Worship. In the years that followed reunion, until the adoption of the new Directory for Worship in 1989, the preparation of the directory and the development of the service book followed parallel tracks. Because the work was concurrent, there was a creative exchange between the two tasks. Each influenced the other. Appearing four years after the adoption of the Directory, the final *Book of Common Worship* is consistent with the provisions of the Directory.

FORM AND FREEDOM

This book honors the Reformed approach to worship, freedom within order, and thus provides a great variety of options and alternatives. Unlike other service books this book welcomes free prayer by providing guidelines for preparation of prayers for public worship.

The forms of worship included here thus provide for a wide spectrum of styles ranging from free and spontaneous prayer to the use of prayer texts. It is envisioned that while the style of praying will vary from one locale to another, the shape of the service will remain the same.

Each service is provided with an outline that gives the minister and those involved in the preparation and actual celebration a clear overview of the content and flow of the service.

Local pastoral concerns will determine the appropriate way to use the texts and services. Some will find strength and a sense of unity in the prayers shared in common with the whole church and so will use the liturgical texts as they appear in this book. Others will find it more appropriate to adapt the prayers for use in a particular setting. Others will be prompted to follow the structure of the services as they are outlined and use the texts as models for a free and more spontaneous style of prayer. Each of these styles is appropriate within the provisions of the directories for worship, and it is the intent of the *Book of Common Worship* to provide the necessary resources.

ECUMENICAL CONVERGENCE

The reform of worship in our time is the fruit of a movement that is now over one hundred and fifty years old. Beginning early in the nineteenth century the liturgical movement emerged as a force for the renewal of the Christian faith. While its early expressions tended toward romanticism, it matured into a vital force for renewal. It is now a major force directed toward the renewal of the Christian faith, both in its life together in worship and in its engagement in the world as a sign of the reign of God. While the movement started outside church bureaucracies and ecclesiastical councils, the churches have now embraced the central convictions of the movement. The liturgical reforms set in motion by Vatican II are the primary example.

During the past thirty years the Christian churches throughout the world have seen a reformation in worship unequaled in any other century. While styles vary between traditions, the shape of the liturgy among the various Christian traditions is witnessing a remarkable convergence. An example of such a convergence is the work of the World Council of Churches in *Baptism, Eucharist and Ministry* and its related documents.

The preparation of the 1993 edition of the *Book of Common Worship* has had the advantage of the continuing liturgical work in all branches of the Christian church, and it reflects these emerging areas of convergence.

We are beginning to recognize that our true unity begins at the baptismal font. Baptism is now recognized as fundamental to the life of faith, forming Christians in faith and service.

The centrality of the scripture read and proclaimed is being recovered due in large measure to the use of the lectionary. Since the publication of a lectionary that is embraced in whole or in part by a variety of traditions, we are recognizing our unity as we gather as one around the Word. We also share a common liturgical calendar. In celebrating the festivals and seasons, we find a certain unity as together we draw our life from the saving events of God in history.

We are moving toward unity at the table, as we are beginning to recognize that in belief and practice there is more that unites us in the Eucharist than divides us. The Eucharist is increasingly recognized as central to the liturgy on the Lord's Day, and there is a steady movement toward weekly celebration. The continuing barriers that separate us from one another at the table stand in grievous contrast to the growing sense of unity we understand in our baptism, and as we hear the Word.

We are learning that unity at the font, pulpit, and table is the true road to healing the brokenness of Christ's church.

It is important to recognize that as Christians we share much of our history in common with other parts of the church. While the sixteenth-century reforms and events of later centuries are very important in shaping the particular way we worship, we share in common with other Christians fifteen centuries of pre-Reformation history.

Churches are beginning to recognize that the context in which we are called to witness to the gospel today is increasingly a missionary situation. This awareness is causing churches in a variety of traditions to go back to the sources, to find their roots in scripture and in the formative period of the church's life. As we are reawakened to our common origins, liturgical reform results. It is in this search for renewal, which we share in common with other traditions, that convergence begins to take shape. In a variety of ways this book reflects this increasing convergence.

The ecumenical contributions to this book include the revised Common Lectionary and liturgical texts prepared by ecumenical consultations. It should be no surprise that the book draws freely from various portions of the body of Christ, given the commitment that the Reformed tradition has to the ecumenical movement. The book seeks to rise above sectarian limitations in embodying the prayer of the church ecumenical.

REFORMED AND CATHOLIC

This book is offered to the church as a resource that is fully Reformed and truly catholic.

In being Reformed, it embodies dominant characteristics of worship within the Reformed tradition. An important characteristic of worship in the Reformed tradition is that it centers on God rather than ourselves and our feelings. Our attention is drawn to the majesty and glory of the triune God, who created all things and by whose power all things are sustained, who was revealed in Jesus Christ raised from the dead to rule over all things, and who is at work as the giver of life in and among us by the power of the Holy Spirit. The focus of the forms in this book is fully theocentric.

True to the Reformed tradition, this book is thoroughly biblical, expressing the faith proclaimed in scripture. Its texts are rooted in the story of God's calling and redeeming a people in the death and resurrection of Jesus Christ, and of God's sending them in the power of the Holy Spirit to minister in the world. Liturgical texts make much use of biblical language and metaphor. The centrality of the proclamation of the Word through the reading of scripture and preaching is preserved.

This service book also honors the Reformed conviction that God is acting in history. God is not only the creator of all things, but rules over all things, and is involved in the affairs of the world to the end that the purposes of God may be embraced in all creation. In a variety of ways, the orders and forms contained in these pages underscore that liturgy and life, worship and mission belong together. The book therefore seeks to be in touch with the concerns of our times. Its prayers focus on the living issues in the world that confront us as we seek to be faithful disciples.

As stated above, this book honors the blend of freedom within form that characterizes Presbyterian worship. True freedom does not do away with form. On the contrary, form enables freedom to be truly free. Without structure, freedom can degenerate into license. The liturgical directions throughout the book are carefully worded to give direction without being mandatory.

While it is thoroughly Reformed, this book, like its predecessors, is also an expression of worship that is fully catholic. Indeed one could say that we are not truly Reformed unless we are truly catholic. This book is an expression of the church catholic, both in the faith that it expresses and in the liturgical practice it provides.

As with the sixteenth-century Reformers, the forms in this book are rooted in the earliest liturgical traditions that have characterized Christian worship throughout history. In keeping with the directories for worship, this book, like its 1970 predecessor, sets forth the Service for the Lord's Day as a service of Word and Sacrament. The variety of eucharistic prayers in this book should serve the church well as it moves toward recognizing the centrality of the Lord's Supper in its worship.

The celebrations of days and seasons that are provided for in these pages are those that have been at the heart of the way Christians keep time, centering most especially on the resurrection of Jesus Christ.

In being catholic, the book is universal in scope. It is informed by the way Christians have worshiped since earliest times, and so it reflects the growing convergence in liturgical theology and practice that characterizes our time.

COMMON WORSHIP

This book restores the title *Book of Common Worship*, long associated with Reformed service books. True to its title, the book embodies "common" prayer. While hundreds of contemporary prayers are included, prayers are also drawn from the ancient church and from across the centuries of Christian worship. Prayers and forms shared in common with the church from other times and places give a sense of our unity with the people of God throughout time. This book is faithful to the long tradition of Christian worship because the foundation of its orders is worship that centers on Word and Sacrament.

Prayers shared in common may be compared with the vast collection of hymns we share in common. In reality hymns are sung prayers. Just as hymns through familiarity are cherished and are a source of strength in daily life, so prayers in the liturgical treasury become familiar and greatly loved through repeated use. Set within our minds and hearts, they provide a rich reservoir of devotion available when needed in the varying circumstances of life.

LOCAL AND UNIVERSAL

The book seeks to keep both the local and the universal in focus. It is essential that worship express the burdens and concerns of the time and place in which we live. Forms are provided to help a congregation express its deepest concerns in its prayers. At the same time, the universal dimensions of Christian worship are essential. When both the local and the universal are thus held together, it becomes clear, in the ordering of prayer and in the prayers we pray, that the congregation in this place is a living expression of the church universal.

LANGUAGE

Care was taken in the development of the *Book of Common Worship* that its language be inclusive, not only in reference to the people of God but also in language about God and address to God. Guidelines for inclusive language adopted by the General Assembly in 1975, 1979, 1980, and 1985 were implicitly followed in the preparation of the texts. The result is that a richer biblical imagery is employed than was the case in prior service books.

It was a goal in the preparation of this book that the language of the prayers be eloquent and rhythmic, contemporary in language and comprehended with ease, believing that well crafted prayers engage the ear and are remembered by the worshiper.

The book also recognizes that language involves more than what we hear. The language of the visual and the tactile are also included in suggestions for actions that engage the whole person in the worship of God.

MORE YET TO BE PUBLISHED

This book does not include some liturgical resources that ordinarily are included in the service book, namely, ordinations, installations, and occasional services such as dedications. At the time of its publication, a major study on ordination is before the Presbyterian Church (U.S.A.). This has precluded the finalization of an ordination rite. The decision was made to do as other churches have done and produce a book of occasional services separate from this book, to include additional liturgical resources needed by the church, such as ordinations, installations, dedications, and other occasional services, and liturgies needed by presbyteries to fulfill their responsibilities.

THOSE WHO SHARED IN THE CREATION OF THIS BOOK

Development of this service book has involved more people and a broader spectrum of the church than any of its predecessors. This is appropriate to the development of a book that helps form and express the prayer of the church.

Seven task forces worked on portions of the book. Collectively, this work spanned ten years. Each task force produced a trial-use resource of an assigned section of the service book, published as Supplemental Liturgical Resources. Until the Presbyterian Church (U.S.A.) was restructured in 1988, the Administrative Committee of the Joint Office of Worship (Office of Worship after reunion) appointed the task forces and monitored the work of each task force. The Cumberland Presbyterian Church also appointed members to some of the task forces. Until restructuring, the Advisory Council on Discipleship and Worship through its Worship Committee was also responsible for reviewing the testing drafts of the work of the task forces prior to the completion of final drafts.

Since 1988, all of these functions have been the responsibility of the Theology and Worship Ministry Unit.

Those who served on one of the task forces were: Horace T. Allen, Jr., Martha Blunt, Peter C. Bower, Lewis A. Briner, Donald K. Campbell, Thomas D. Campbell, David Dyer, Karmen Van Dyke, William R. Forbes, Catherine Gunsalus Gonzalez, Lucile L. Hair, Jung Han, Cynthia A. Jarvis, Judith Kolwicz, J. Michael Krech, Thomas G. Long, William P. Lytle, Ross Mackenzie, Thomas Mainor, Roger A. Martin, Neddy Mason, James Hastings Nichols, Thomas E. Pass, Betty Peek, David H. Pfleiderer, Howard L. Rice, V. Bruce Rigdon, David W. Romig, Robert E. Shelton, Robert M. Shelton, Sue Spencer, Donald Wilson Stake, Juan Trevino, Jesse Truvillion, Jeannette Wessler. Staff to each task force: Harold M. Daniels.

Those who served on the Administrative Committee of the Joint Office of Worship or the Office of Worship during the period when the Supplemental Liturgical Resources were developed were: Melva W. Costen, Arlo D. Duba, Lucile L. Hair, Helen Hamilton, Collier S. Harvey, Jr., Robert H. Kempes, James G. Kirk, Wynn McGregor, Ray Meester, Robert D. Miller, Clementine Morrison, David C. Partington, Betty Peek, Dorothea Snyder, Robert Stigall, Darius L. Swann, James Vande Berg, John Weaver. Staff: Harold M. Daniels (Director), Marion L. Liebert (Administrative Associate).

Those who served on the Worship Committee of the Advisory Council on Discipleship and Worship during the development of the Supplemental Liturgical Resources were: Moffet Swaim Churn, Jay Dee Conrad, Melva W. Costen, Craig D. Erickson, Francis M. Gray, Robert S. Moorhead, Irene Overton, Franklin E. Perkins, J. Barrie Shepherd, Harriet Smith, Donald Wilson Stake, Helen Wright. Staff: James G. Kirk, Elizabeth Kirk. Adjunct staff: Harold M. Daniels.

Those who served on the Theology and Worship Ministry Unit during the completion of the Supplemental Liturgical Resources series were: Ruben P. Armendariz, José H. Bibiloni, Muriel Brown, Sandra Hanna Charles, Harland Collins, Melva W. Costen, Margery Curtiss, Donna Frey DeCou, Joseph G. Dempsey, Burnette W. Dowler, Gershon B. Fiawoo, Richard Fiete, Daniell C. Hamby, Roberta Hestenes, Thomas L. Jones, Clements E. Lamberth, Jr., Daniel W. Martin, William McIvor, Raquel Montalvo, Lewis Mudge, Deborah Mullen, Peter Ota, Douglas Ottati, Heath K. Rada, Marilee M. Scroggs, James C. Spalding, R. David Steele, Benjamin M. Weir, Mary Jane Winter, May Murakami Nakagawa (Presbyterian Association of Musicians Representative), Gordon Turnbull (Theological Institutions Advisory Member), Helen Wright (Presbyterian

Association of Musicians Representative). Staff: George B. Telford, Jr. (Director of the Unit), Joseph D. Small (Associate Director of the Unit). Staff of the worship function were: Harold M. Daniels, Janet Wolfe, Nalini Jayasuriya.

Those serving on the Worship Sub-Unit of the Theology and Worship Ministry Unit during the completion of the Supplemental Liturgical Resources series were: Ruben P. Armendariz, Melva W. Costen, Donna Frey DeCou, Gershon B. Fiawoo, Daniell C. Hamby, Daniel W. Martin, May Murakami Nakagawa, R. David Steele, Mary Jane Winter, Robert T. Henderson (consultant), Fred Holper (consultant), Donald Wilson Stake (consultant). Staff: Harold M. Daniels, Janet Wolfe, Nalini Jayasuriya.

Administrative details during the completion of the Supplemental Liturgical Resources series were provided by Valerie Hofmann (Associate for Administration), Cindy Ohlmann Stairs (Worship Administrative Assistant), Regina J. Noel (first as Worship Secretary and then as Worship Administrative Assistant).

Throughout the entire process of preparing the Supplemental Liturgical Resources, valuable editorial assistance was provided by Patrick Byrne, who provided detailed critique of each manuscript.

In 1991 work began on editing the liturgical material published in the Supplemental Liturgical Resources series. Harold M. Daniels, who served as project director and editor of the Supplemental Liturgical Resources series, also had responsibility for final editing of the material. To assist him, a group of editorial advisors was appointed in the fall of 1991. This network gave guidance to the editor at each phase of final editing. Communication was principally by computer.

In addition, four consultants were appointed to work with the Worship Sub-Unit to assist in overseeing the completion of the manuscript and recommending it to the Unit for publication. The Worship Sub-Unit, or a working group of the sub-unit, met four times during the spring and summer of 1992 to complete the task.

Those serving actively as editorial consultants were: Fred Anderson, John Burkhart, Cynthia Campbell, Melva W. Costen, Alan Detscher, Arlo Duba, Patricia Fort, Stanley Hall, Daniell C. Hamby, Duncan Hanson, Dennis Hughes, Paul Huh, James H. Logan, Jr., Deborah McKinley, D. Cameron Murchison, Elizabeth Nordquist, David Partington, K. C. Ptomey, Jr., Donald Wilson Stake, Diane Karay Tripp, Karmen Van Dyke, Marney Wasserman, Steven Yamaguchi. Bryan Hoover, Donald Wilson Stake, Diane Karay Tripp, and Marney Wasserman accepted and fulfilled major responsibilities in completing portions of the manuscript. Alan Detscher provided valuable assistance most particularly in formatting the book and making certain that the rubrics were succinct and clearly stated.

The Worship Sub-Unit responsible for overseeing the completion of the final draft and recommending it to the Theology and Worship Ministry Unit for its approval included Melva W. Costen, Donna Frey DeCou (chair), Gershon B. Fiawoo,

Daniell C. Hamby, May Murakami Nakagawa, K. C. Ptomey, Jr., Larry Rhoades. Consultants: Stanley Hall, Fred Holper, James Logan, Marney Wasserman. Staff: Deborah McKinley, Harold M. Daniels.

Membership of the Theology and Worship Ministry Unit Committee at the time the manuscript was approved for publication was: Melva W. Costen (chair), Donna Frey DeCou, David Eicher, Daniell C. Hamby, James B. Harper, John W. Larson, Sr., Daniel W. Martin, William McIvor, Lewis Mudge, Deborah Mullen, D. Cameron Murchison, Peter Ota, K. C. Ptomey, Jr., Ruth Sauter, Mary Elva Smith, Jack L. Stotts, Carol Wehrheim, Barbara Van Ark Wilson, Karmen Van Dyke, William C. Yeager, Martin Shelton-Jenck (theological advisor), Casper Glenn (missionary advisor), Larry Rhoades (Presbyterian Association of Musicians Representative). Staff: George B. Telford, Jr. (Director), Joseph D. Small, III (Associate Director). Worship staff: Harold M. Daniels, Deborah McKinley. Administrative assistance was provided by Valerie Hofmann (Associate for Administration), Regina Noel (Administrative Assistant for Worship), and Denise Williams (Secretary for Worship).

The Theology and Worship Ministry Unit also greatly appreciates the strong continued support of Robert D. McIntyre, Publisher of Westminster/John Knox Press, who has given enthusiastic support for this project from its inception, and especially for the completion of the *Book of Common Worship*. The competency of the staff of Westminster/John Knox Press has been invaluable to the success of the project. While many shared in tasks related to its completion, gratitude is extended especially to all who devoted careful attention to every detail in producing a quality book, and who evidenced strong commitment by working long hours to complete the project in a timely manner. Thanks especially to Danielle Alexander and Carl Helmich, who were responsible for copyediting, and to Maureen O'Connor, Director of Creative Publishing Services, and staff: Susan Jackson, designer, who also participated with Laura Lee, Drew Stevens, and Ron Sharpe in the composition of the book.

The *Book of Common Worship* is offered to the church with a fervent prayer that it may be an effective aid to congregations as they worship God, and that it may further the renewal of the church's faith and life.

THEOLOGY AND WORSHIP MINISTRY UNIT

ABBREVIATIONS

PH *The Presbyterian Hymnal: Hymns, Psalms, and Spiritual Songs.* Louisville, Ky.: Westminster/John Knox Press, 1990.

PS *The Psalter—Psalms and Canticles for Singing.* Louisville, Ky.: Westminster/John Knox Press, 1993.

. . . (in prayers) indicates a pause for silent prayer.

[ ] Square brackets, or horizontal brackets extending the width of the page, are used to designate optional elements or sections.

PREPARATION
FOR
WORSHIP

PREPARATION FOR WORSHIP

PRAYERS FOR USE BEFORE WORSHIP

The following prayers may be used by worshipers as they prepare for the
service.

1

Eternal God,
you have called us to be members of one body.
Join us with those
who in all times and places have praised your name,
that, with one heart and mind,
we may show the unity of your church,
and bring honor to our Lord and Savior,
Jesus Christ.   **Amen.**   [1]

2

Everlasting God,
in whom we live and move and have our being:
You have made us for yourself,
so that our hearts are restless
until they rest in you.
Give us purity of heart and strength of purpose,
that no selfish passion may hinder us from knowing your will,
no weakness keep us from doing it;
that in your light we may see light clearly,
and in your service find perfect freedom;
through Jesus Christ our Lord,
who lives and reigns with you and the Holy Spirit,
one God, now and forever.   **Amen.**   [2]

3

Almighty God,
you pour out the spirit of grace and supplication
on all who desire it.
Deliver us from cold hearts and wandering thoughts,
that with steady minds and burning zeal
we may worship you
in spirit and in truth;
through Jesus Christ our Lord.   **Amen.**   [3]

4

God of grace,
you have given us minds to know you,
hearts to love you,
and voices to sing your praise.
Fill us with your Spirit,
that we may celebrate your glory
and worship you in spirit and in truth;
through Jesus Christ our Lord.   **Amen.**   [4]

5

O Lord our God,
you are always more ready to bestow your good gifts upon us
than we are to seek them.
You are more willing to give
than we desire or deserve.
Help us so to seek that we may truly find,
so to ask that we may joyfully receive,
so to knock that the door of your mercy may be opened for us;
through Jesus Christ our Lord.   **Amen.**   [5]

6

Almighty God, you built your church
upon the foundation of the apostles and prophets,
with Jesus Christ himself as the cornerstone.
Join us together by their teaching,
so that we may be a holy temple
in whom your Spirit dwells;
through Jesus Christ our Lord.   **Amen.**   [6]

7

Almighty God, we pray for your blessing
on the church in this place.
Here may the faithful find salvation,
and the careless be awakened.
Here may the doubting find faith,
and the anxious be encouraged.
Here may the tempted find help,
and the sorrowful comfort.
Here may the weary find rest,
and the strong be renewed.
Here may the aged find consolation
and the young be inspired;
through Jesus Christ our Lord.   **Amen.**   [7]

8

O God,
light of the minds that know you,
life of the souls that love you,
strength of the thoughts that seek you:
Help us so to know you
that we may truly love you,
so to love you
that we may fully serve you,
whose service is perfect freedom;
through Jesus Christ our Lord.   **Amen.**   [8]

9

Bless us, O God,
with a reverent sense of your presence,
that we may be at peace
and may worship you with all our mind and spirit;
through Jesus Christ our Lord.   **Amen.**   [9]

10

God of mercy,
grant that the Word you speak this day
may take root in our hearts,
and bear fruit to your honor and glory,
for the sake of Jesus Christ our Lord.   **Amen.**   [10]

11

O Jesus, our great high priest,
be present with us
as you were present with your disciples,
and make yourself known to us in the breaking of bread.   **Amen.**   [11]

12

We do not presume to come to your table, merciful Lord,
trusting in our own goodness,
but in your all-embracing love and mercy.
We are not worthy even to gather up the crumbs under your table,
but it is your nature always to have mercy.
So feed us with the body and blood of Jesus Christ, your Son,
that we may forever live in him and he in us.   **Amen.**   [12]

13

Loving God,
you have so made us that we cannot live by bread alone,
but by every word that proceeds from your mouth.
Give us a hunger for your Word,
and in that food satisfy our daily need;
through Jesus Christ our Lord.   **Amen.**   [13]

14

To your name, Lord Jesus,
help me to bow the knee
and all its worshiping,
bow the head
and all its thinking,
bow the will
and all its choosing,
bow the heart
and all its loving.   **Amen.**   [14]

15

We praise you, we worship you, we adore you.
You hold the heavens in your hand,
all stars rejoice in your glory.
You come in the sunrise and the song of morn
and bless the splendor of the noonday.
The stars in their courses magnify you,
day and night tell of your glory.
Your peace blows over the earth
and the breath of your mouth fills all space.

Your voice comes in the thunder of the storm
and the song of the wind whispers of your majesty.
You satisfy all things living with your abundance
and our hearts bow at your presence.
Accept us, your children, Eternal Father,
and hearken to our prayer.
Bend over us, Eternal Love, and bless us.   **Amen.**   [15]

16

Eternal God,
you are the power behind all things:
behind the energy of the storm,
behind the heat of a million suns.

Eternal God,
you are the power behind all minds:
behind the ability to think and reason,
behind all understanding of the truth.

Eternal God,
you are the power behind the cross of Christ:
behind the weakness, the torture and the death,
behind unconquerable love.

Eternal God,
we worship and adore you.   **Amen.**   [16]

17

Grant unto us, O God, the fullness of your promises.
Where we have been weak, grant us your strength;
where we have been confused, grant us your guidance;
where we have been distraught, grant us your comfort;
where we have been dead, grant us your life.
Apart from you, O Lord, we are nothing,
in and with you we can do all things.   **Amen.**   [17]

18   *Christina Rossetti (1830–1894)*

As the wind is your symbol, so forward our goings.
As the dove, so launch us heavenwards.
As water, so purify our spirits.
As a cloud, so abate our temptations.
As dew, so revive our languor.
As fire, so purge out our dross.   **Amen.**   [18]

19   *Desiderius Erasmus (1466–1536)*

O Lord Jesus Christ,
the Way, the Truth, and the Life:
Do not let us stray from you, the Way,
nor to distrust you, the Truth,
nor to rest in anything other than you, the Life.   **Amen.**   [19]

20

Come, O Holy Spirit.
Come as Holy Fire and burn in us,
come as Holy Wind and cleanse us within,
come as Holy Light and lead us in the darkness,
come as Holy Truth and dispel our ignorance,
come as Holy Power and enable our weakness,
come as Holy Life and dwell in us.
Convict us, convert us, consecrate us,
until we are set free from the service of ourselves,
to be your servants to the world.   **Amen.**   [20]

21   *John Henry Newman (1801–1890)*

Give me, O my Lord,
that purity of conscience
which alone can receive your inspirations.
My ears are dull,
so that I cannot hear your voice.
My eyes are dim,
so that I cannot see the signs of your presence.
You alone can quicken my hearing
and purge my sight,
and cleanse and renew my heart.
Teach me to sit at your feet
and to hear your word.   **Amen.**   [21]

22   *Dag Hammarskjöld (1905–1961)*

Great and good God,
give us pure hearts that we may see you,
humble hearts that we may hear you,
hearts of love that we may serve you,
hearts of faith that we may live in you,
reverent hearts that we may worship you,
here and in the world out there,
through Jesus Christ our Lord.   **Amen.**   [22]

William Temple (1881–1944)

ighty and eternal God,
draw our hearts to you,
guide our minds,
ill our imaginations,
control our wills,
t we may be wholly yours,
rly dedicated unto you;
then use us, we pray, as you will,
  always to your glory
the welfare of your people,
ough our Lord and Savior, Jesus Christ.   **Amen.**   [27]

William Laud (1573–1645)

acious God,
  pray for your holy catholic church.
it with all truth in all peace.
ere it is corrupt, purify it;
ere it is in error, direct it;
ere in any thing it is amiss, reform it.
ere it is right, strengthen it;
ere it is in want, provide for it;
ere it is divided, reunite it;
  the sake of Jesus Christ your Son our Savior.   **Amen.**   [28]

Attributed to Benedict of Nursia (c. 480–547)

gracious and holy God,
e us diligence to seek you,
dom to perceive you,
patience to wait for you.

ant us, O God,
ind to meditate on you;
s to behold you;
s to listen for your word;
eart to love you;
a life to proclaim you;
ough the power of the Spirit
esus Christ our Lord.   **Amen.**   [29]

Alcuin of Tours (c. 735–804)

rnal Light, shine into our hearts;
rnal Goodness, deliver us from evil;
rnal Power, be our support;

PREPARATION FOR WORSHIP

23

Thanks be to you, Lord Jesus Christ,
for all the benefits which you have won for us,
for all the pains and insults which you have borne for us.
O most merciful Redeemer, Friend and Brother,
may we know you more clearly,
love you more dearly,
and follow you more nearly,
day by day. **Amen.** [23]

24

Lord, open unto me
Open unto me—light for my darkness.
Open unto me—courage for my fear.
Open unto me—hope for my despair.
Open unto me—peace for my turmoil.
Open unto me—joy for my sorrow.
Open unto me—strength for my weakness.
Open unto me—wisdom for my confusion.
Open unto me—forgiveness for my sins.
Open unto me—love for my hates.
Open unto me—thy Self for my self.
Lord, Lord, open unto me! **Amen.** [24]

25

O loving God,
to turn away from you is to fall,
to turn toward you is to rise,
and to stand before you is to abide forever.
Grant us, dear God,
in all our duties your help;
in all our uncertainties your guidance;
in all our dangers your protection;
and in all our sorrows your peace;
through Jesus Christ our Lord. **Amen.** [25]

26

O God, full of compassion,
I commit and commend myself to you,
in whom I am, and live, and know.
Be the goal of my pilgrimage, and my rest by the way.
Let my soul take refuge
from the crowding turmoil of worldly thought
beneath the shadow of your wings.
Let my heart, this sea of restless waves,
find peace in you, O God. **Amen.** [26]

PREPARATION FOR Wo

Eternal Wisdom, scatter the darkness of our ignorance;
Eternal Pity, have mercy upon us,
that with all our heart and mind and strength
we may seek your face
and be brought by your infinite mercy to your holy presence;
through Jesus Christ our Lord.   **Amen.**   [30]

31   *Sarum Primer (c. 1514)*

God be in my head, and in my understanding;
God be in my eyes, and in my looking;
God be in my mouth, and in my speaking;
God be in my heart, and in my thinking;
God be at my end, and at my departing.   **Amen.**   [31]

32   *Maria Ware (1798)*

Lord, hear;
Lord, forgive;
Lord, do.
Hear what we speak not;
forgive what we speak amiss;
do what we leave undone;
that not according to our words, or our deeds,
but according to your mercy and truth,
all may work for your glory,
and the good of your kingdom,
through Jesus Christ.   **Amen.**   [32]

33   *Attributed to Francis of Assisi (1181–1226)*

Lord, make me an instrument of your peace.
Where there is hatred, let me sow love;
where there is injury, pardon;
where there is doubt, faith;
where there is despair, hope;
where there is darkness, light;
where there is sadness, joy.

O Divine Master, grant that I may not seek so much
to be consoled as to console,
to be understood as to understand,
to be loved as to love.
For it is in giving that we receive,
it is in pardoning that we are pardoned,
and it is in dying that we are born to eternal life.   **Amen.**   [33]

May the strength of God pilot us.
May the power of God preserve us.
May the wisdom of God instruct us.
May the hand of God protect us.
May the way of God direct us.
May the shield of God defend us.
May the host of God guard us against the snares of evil
and the temptations of the world.

May Christ be with us,
Christ before us,
Christ in us,
Christ over us.
May your salvation, O Lord,
be always ours this day and forevermore.   **Amen.**   [34]

35   *Clement of Rome (d.c. 99)*

O God Almighty,
Father of our Lord Jesus Christ:
Grant us, we pray,
to be grounded and settled in your truth
by the coming down of the Holy Spirit into our hearts.
That which we know not, reveal;
that which is wanting in us, fill up;
that which we know, confirm;
and keep us blameless in your service;
through the same Jesus Christ our Lord.   **Amen.**   [35]

36   *Liturgy of Malabar, 5th century*

Grant, O Lord Jesus,
that the ears which have heard the voice of your songs
may be closed to the voice of dispute;
that the eyes which have seen your great love
may also behold your blessed hope;
that the tongues which have sung your praise
may speak the truth in love;
that the feet which have walked in your courts
may walk in the region of light;
and that the bodies which have received your living body
may be restored in newness of life.
Glory to you for your inexpressible gift.   **Amen.**   [36]

I bind unto myself today
the strong name of the Trinity,
by invocation of the same,
the Three in One, and One in Three.

I bind this day to me forever,
by power of faith, Christ's incarnation;
his baptism in the Jordan river;
his death on the cross for my salvation.
His bursting from the spiced tomb;
his riding up the heavenly way;
his coming at the day of doom
I bind unto myself today.

I bind unto myself today
the virtues of the star-lit heaven,
the glorious sun's life-giving ray,
the whiteness of the moon at even,
the flashing of the lightning free,
the whirling wind's tempestuous shocks,
the stable earth, the deep salt sea
around the old eternal rocks.

I bind unto myself today
the power of God to hold and lead,
God's eye to watch, God's might to stay,
God's ear to hearken to my need,
the wisdom of my God to teach,
God's hand to guide, God's shield to ward,
the word of God to give me speech,
God's heavenly host to be my guard.

Christ be with me, Christ within me,
Christ behind me, Christ before me,
Christ beside me, Christ to win me,
Christ to comfort and restore me,
Christ beneath me, Christ above me,
Christ in quiet, Christ in danger,
Christ in hearts of all that love me,
Christ in mouth of friend and stranger.

I bind unto myself the name,
the strong name of the Trinity,
by invocation of the same,
the Three in One, the One in Three,
of whom all nature has creation,
eternal Father, Spirit, Word.
Praise to the Lord of my salvation,
salvation is of Christ the Lord.   **Amen.**   [37]

THE LAW OF GOD

38

In preparation for worship, the people may wish to meditate on the law
of God.

The Law of God *Ex. 20:1–17*

God spoke all these words, saying,
I am the Lord your God.

You shall have no other gods before me.

You shall not make for yourself an idol,
whether in the form of anything that is in heaven above
or that is on the earth beneath,
or that is in the water under the earth.
You shall not bow down to them or worship them.

You shall not make wrongful use of the name of the Lord your God.

Remember the sabbath day, and keep it holy.

Honor your father and your mother.

You shall not murder.

You shall not commit adultery.

You shall not steal.

You shall not bear false witness against your neighbor.

You shall not covet your neighbor's house;
you shall not covet your neighbor's wife,
or anything that belongs to your neighbor.

In preparation for worship, the people may wish to meditate on the summary of the law.

Summary of the Law *Matt. 22:37–40*

Our Lord Jesus said:
You shall love the Lord your God
with all your heart,
and with all your soul,
and with all your mind.
This is the greatest and first commandment.
And a second is like it:
You shall love your neighbor as yourself.
On these two commandments
hang all the law and the prophets.

PRAYERS FOR WORSHIP LEADERS

One of the following prayers (40–42) may be used with the choir:

40 *Ps. 100:1*

Worship the Lord with gladness,

and enter the Lord's presence with songs of joy.

O God,
the angels of heaven proclaim your glory without ceasing.
Help us as we serve you in your house,
that in psalms and hymns and spiritual songs
we may sing to you with our whole heart;
through Jesus Christ our Lord.   **Amen.**   [38]

41

Praise the Lord.

The Lord's name be praised.

Great God,
you have been generous
and marvelously kind.
Give us such wonder, love, and gratitude
that we may sing praises to you
and joyfully honor your name;
through Jesus Christ our Lord.   **Amen.**   [39]

O Lord, open my lips,

And my mouth shall proclaim your praise.

God of glory,
God of grace,
before whose face our vision fails,
help us to sing your praise gladly,
and to worship you in spirit and in truth;
through Jesus Christ our Lord.   **Amen.**   [40]

When elders or leaders of worship meet before worship, they may wish to
use one of the following prayers (43–45):

43

Ever-present God,
without your Word we have nothing to say;
without your Spirit we are helpless.
Give us your Holy Spirit,
that we may lead your people in prayer,
proclaim the good news,
and gratefully praise your name;
through Jesus Christ our Lord.   **Amen.**   [41]

44

Startle us, O God, with your truth,
and open our minds to your Spirit,
that we may be one with Christ our Lord,
and serve as faithful disciples,
through Jesus Christ.   **Amen.**   [42]

45

Before Holy Communion

Almighty God,
you have set a table before us,
and called us to feast with you.
Prepare us in mind and spirit
to minister in your name,
and to honor your Son, our Lord, Jesus Christ.   **Amen.**   [43]

THE SERVICE
FOR THE
LORD'S DAY

Basic Movement of the Service for the Lord's Day

With its focus upon scripture and sacrament, the main body of the service moves broadly from hearing to doing, from proclamation to thanksgiving, and from Word to table.

Gathering

The people gather in response to God's call, offering praise in words of scripture, prayer, and song. The people acknowledge their sinfulness and receive the declaration of God's forgiveness.

The Word

Scriptures are read and their message is proclaimed. Psalms, hymns, spirituals, or anthems may be sung between the readings. Responses to the proclamation of God's Word include expressions of faith and commitment, and the offering of prayers for worldwide and local needs.

The Eucharist

As hearing becomes doing, the tithes and offerings of the people are gathered, *and the table is set with bread and wine. The people are invited to the table of the Lord.* Prayer is offered in which God is praised for creation and providence, Christ's work of redemption is remembered with thanksgiving, and the Holy Spirit is invoked upon and in the church. *The bread is broken, and the bread and wine are served to the people.*

Sending

The people are sent forth with God's blessing to serve.

The Service for the Lord's Day

A Description of Its Movement and Elements[1]

From its beginning, the Christian community has gathered on the first day of the week to hear the scriptures read and proclaimed and to celebrate the Lord's Supper. This day has special significance, since it was on "the first day of the week" that Jesus' followers discovered the empty tomb and met the risen Lord.

Recognizing the importance of the resurrection, the New Testament community called the day of the week on which Christ rose "the Lord's day" (Rev. 1:10). It was the day to remember and celebrate the resurrection. The Lord's Day, the first day of the week, is therefore the very center of the church's calendar.

In the ancient story of creation, this day marked the beginning of creation. On the first day, God spoke light into being, separating light from darkness.

In Christ's resurrection, Christians saw the beginning of the "new creation" and came to regard the day of resurrection as "the eighth day of creation." The Lord's Day is therefore a sign of God's kingdom and of hope.

Gathered on the Lord's Day, Christians celebrate the age to come, which was revealed in the risen Christ, by remembering the words and deeds of Jesus and celebrating the presence of the risen Christ among them in the Word proclaimed and in the bread and cup of the Eucharist.

GATHERING

Worship begins with God. God takes the initiative and calls us into being. In the name of Christ we answer God's call and assemble as the community of faith.

As the people gather, they may informally greet one another as members of the household of faith. They may pray silently or engage in quiet meditation, or music may be offered appropriate to the season or to the scripture readings of the day. The music should help people focus their attention on God and God's kingdom. Essential announcements pertaining to the order of worship of the day may be briefly given.

CALL TO WORSHIP

The people are called to worship God. Words from scripture are spoken or sung to proclaim who God is and what God has done. We are thus reminded that our worship centers in God and not in ourselves. "Our help is in the name of the Lord, who made heaven and earth" (Ps. 124:8).

PRAYER OF THE DAY OR OPENING PRAYER

An opening prayer may be said. It may be a prayer of adoration. Adoration is the keynote of all true worship, of the creature before the Creator, of the redeemed before the Redeemer.

Or the prayer of the day may be said. This prayer typically expresses some aspect of the day, the festival, or the season, and thereby contributes to the focus of the day's worship.

The people respond with "Amen" to this and all other prayers offered by the minister or other worship leaders. In the corporate response "Amen" (*Hebrew*, meaning "so be it") the people affirm their participation in the prayer, and embrace it as their own.

Option: The prayer of the day may be used later in the service, for example, as the concluding collect to the prayers of the people.

HYMN OF PRAISE, PSALM, OR SPIRITUAL

The people sing praise to God in a hymn, psalm, or spiritual, which tells of God's greatness, majesty, love, and goodness. Praise is the joyful response to the incomparable gift of God in Jesus Christ, and so is dominant in Christian worship.

CONFESSION AND PARDON

In words of scripture the people are called to confess the reality of sin in personal and common life. Claiming the promises of God sealed in our baptism, we humbly confess our sin.

Confession is made by using a prayer, a penitential psalm, or appropriate music. Whatever the form, it will engage us in acknowledging our sinfulness and in confessing our sin to God. A period of silence may be observed before, within, or following the confession of sin. Music of a penitential character may follow the prayer.

Having confessed our sin, we remember the promises of God's redemption, and the claims God has on all human life. The assurance of God's forgiving grace is declared in the name of Jesus Christ. We accept God's forgiveness, confident that in dying to sin, God raises us to new life.

Option: The confession of sin may follow the intercessions before the Lord's Supper, instead of being included here.

THE PEACE

Having been reconciled to God in Jesus Christ, the people are invited to share signs of reconciliation and the peace of Christ. In sharing the peace, we express the reconciliation, unity, and love that come only from God, and we open ourselves to the power of God's love to heal our brokenness and make us agents of that love in the world.

Option: If the peace is not included here, it may be included at another place in the service preceding the Lord's Supper.

Option: On days when a baptism is celebrated, or there is a reaffirmation of the baptismal covenant, or another pastoral rite of the church takes place, the peace may be included in relation to those rites.

CANTICLE, PSALM, HYMN, OR SPIRITUAL

With gladness, God is praised in song, for the gift of God's grace brings joy. The response may be an appropriate psalm, hymn, canticle (i.e., a biblical song other than a psalm), spiritual, or the "Glory to God" or "Glory to the Father."

THE WORD

Worship now moves to the reading, proclaiming, and hearing of God's Word.

PRAYER FOR ILLUMINATION

A prayer for illumination may be offered before the reading and proclaiming of the scripture. This prayer seeks the illumination of the Holy Spirit and calls upon God to make us receptive to the life-giving Word, which comes to us through the scripture.

FIRST READING

PSALM

SECOND READING

ANTHEM, HYMN, PSALM, CANTICLE, OR SPIRITUAL

GOSPEL READING

There should be readings from both the Old and the New Testament to ensure that the unity and completeness of God's revelation are proclaimed. Both a reading from the epistles and a reading from the Gospels are appropriately included as the New Testament readings.

A psalm drawn from the full range of the psalms should also be included. Coming to us from the worship of ancient Judaism, the psalms have been at the heart of Christian prayer and praise across the centuries. Throughout its history the Reformed tradition has given a special place to singing the psalms in worship.

The singing of a psalm is appropriate at any place in the order of worship. However, the psalm appointed in the lectionary (pp. 1035–1048) is intended to be sung following the first reading, where it serves as a congregational meditation and response to the reading. The psalm is not intended as another reading.

The scripture readings are to be selected with care. Their selection should be guided by the seasons of the liturgical calendar, pastoral concerns, world events and conditions, and the church's mission. Attention should be given to ensure that over a period of time, worshipers will be provided all of the many and varied themes and emphases of the scripture.

The readings and the psalm may be those suggested in a lectionary. A lectionary provides consistency, and ensures that over a period of time the full witness of scripture will be read as a part of worship. A lectionary used in common with other churches, such as the one in this book, expresses a connection with the universal church. A lectionary, including a plan for reading through particular books of the Bible, may also be prepared by those who plan worship.

The readings may be read by a minister or by a member of the congregation. Or, the congregation may read the scripture responsively or antiphonally. Or, when appropriate, the congregation may read the scripture in unison.

The public reading of the scripture should be entrusted to those who have the ability to read well. Readers are to be adequately prepared and should familiarize themselves with the passages to be read. They are to give attention to their reading, so that it will be clear, audible, and sensitive to the meanings of the text.

Those hearing the reading of the scripture also have responsibility, since listening to the reading of scripture requires expectation and concentration.

In addition to the psalms, other musical forms (such as hymns, spirituals, canticles, anthems) or artistic expressions that proclaim or interpret the scripture readings or their themes may be included between the readings.

SERMON

When the Bible has been read, its message is proclaimed in a sermon or other form of exposition of God's Word. The God who speaks in scripture speaks to us now. The God who acted in biblical history acts today. Through the Holy Spirit, Christ is present in the sermon, offering grace and calling for obedience.

Preaching should present the gospel with simplicity and clarity, and be in language the people can understand. A prayer, acclamation, or ascription of praise may conclude the sermon.

The Word may also be proclaimed through music and other art forms faithful to the gospel.

The proclamation of God's Word in scripture and sermon invites a response of faith. We respond in song, affirmation of faith, prayer, and offering.

INVITATION

After the sermon, the people may be called to discipleship, giving opportunity to any who wish to make or renew personal commitment to Christ and his kingdom.

HYMN, CANTICLE, PSALM, OR SPIRITUAL

A hymn or other song is sung. It may be related to the scripture readings of the day, or it may lead to the prayers of the people or to Baptism or a pastoral rite that might follow.

AFFIRMATION OF FAITH

The people respond to the proclamation of the Word by affirming the faith.

The faith of the church both shapes our lives and expresses the hope and expectancy that are a part of the Christian life. From early in the church's life, an affirmation of faith has been central in corporate worship. Candidates for Baptism gave assent to the faith in the words of the Creed, and upon their baptism were admitted to the Eucharist. As those who are baptized, whenever we say the creed we reaffirm the profession of faith made in our baptism.

The people may affirm the faith by saying or singing a creed of the church. The Nicene Creed and the Apostles' Creed express the faith tradition of the whole church, the faith in which we were baptized. Or the people may affirm the faith in the form of an affirmation drawn from scripture, a hymn or other appropriate musical response, or one of the other confessions of the church. Or the choir may lead the congregation in affirming the faith through an anthem or other musical form.

If Baptism is to be celebrated, the congregation professes its faith using the Apostles' Creed as a part of the baptism. The Apostles' Creed is also said when baptized persons make a public profession of faith for the first time, and on other occasions of reaffirming the baptismal covenant. The Apostles' Creed is also appropriately said when new members are welcomed.

The Nicene Creed is traditionally said whenever the Lord's Supper is celebrated.

BAPTISM

As an act of the whole church, Baptism is celebrated (except for extraordinary circumstances) in the context of corporate worship. When Baptism is celebrated, it appropriately follows the reading and proclaiming of the Word.

As with the Lord's Supper, Baptism is a sign and act of God's self-giving, by which God's grace is made available to us. The sacraments give a distinctive shape to Christian worship and are the primary signs of the covenant of grace.

The meaning of Baptism is many-faceted. Baptism proclaims God's grace and love for us. In Baptism, God claims us and marks us as God's own. Baptism signifies our engrafting into Christ, and so affirms our new identity as members of the body of Christ. Through the waters of Baptism, we participate in Christ's death and resurrection by which we die to all that separates us from God and are raised to new life in Christ. In Baptism we are assured of cleansing from sin, of inclusion in God's grace and covenant, and of the gift of the Holy Spirit.

The significance of Baptism is not limited to the one being baptized. Those present who have been baptized are reminded of their place in the covenant community, of God's claim on their lives, and of their dependence upon God's grace.

The basic order of Baptism is as follows:

Presentation. Persons to be baptized are brought to the font or baptismal pool and presented for baptism. The meaning of Baptism is declared in the words of scripture. Older children, youth, and adults express their desire to be baptized. Parents promise to fulfill the responsibilities for Christian nurture. The congregation and sponsors promise to love and nurture those being baptized and to assist them to be faithful disciples.

Profession of Faith. Those coming to be baptized, parents, and sponsors make vows, renouncing the ways of evil and affirming the way of Christ. The congregation joins the candidates for Baptism (or their parents) and the sponsors in affirming the faith of the church in the words of the Apostles' Creed.

Thanksgiving Over the Water. God's saving acts are remembered with thanksgiving and the Holy Spirit is invoked, that those who are baptized may have their sins washed away, be reborn to new life, be buried and resurrected with Christ, and be incorporated into the body of Christ.

The Baptism. In the name of the triune God, the minister pours or sprinkles water visibly and generously on the head of each candidate or immerses each candidate in water.

Laying On of Hands. As a sign of the gift of the Holy Spirit in Baptism, the minister lays hands upon the head of the newly baptized (and may anoint with oil), praying for the gift of the Holy Spirit.

Welcome. The newly baptized are welcomed into the household of God, and are charged to be faithful disciples.

The Peace. The congregation may welcome the newly baptized into the household of God, sharing signs of peace.

PASTORAL RITE OF THE CHURCH

Response to the Word may include other acts of commitment and recognition.

Those previously baptized may make public their profession of faith for the first time. Baptized believers may reaffirm the covenant into which they were baptized, or transfer their church membership.

Christian marriage, ordination and installation of church officers, and commissioning for service in and to the church are other acts of commitment that may appropriately be included as responses to the Word.

The service may be an occasion to recognize and give thanks for significant events in individual or community life, for reunions and farewells, and for remembering the lives of those who died.

Witness to faith and service and interpretation of the mission and programs of the church may prepare for the people's intercessions, as well as the offering of themselves and their gifts to support the ministry of Christ and the church.

PRAYERS OF THE PEOPLE

In response to the Word, prayers are offered. In these prayers, we acknowledge God's presence in the world and in daily life.

Across the ages the church in its worship has prayed for the church universal, the world, all in authority, and those in distress or need. At no other time in its worship is the community of faith more conscious of the needs of the life of the world.

We pray for the world because God loves it. God created the world and cares for it. God sent Jesus, who died for it. God is working to lead the world toward the future God has for it. To abide in God's love is to share God's concern for the world. Our prayers should therefore be as wide as God's love and as specific as God's tender compassion for the least ones among us.

Intercession. The congregation prays for worldwide and local concerns, offering intercession for:

> the church universal, its ministry and those who minister, that the world might believe;
> the world, those in distress or special need, and all in authority, that peace and justice might prevail;
> the nation, the state, local communities, and those who govern in them, that they may know and have strength to do what is right.

Supplications. The congregation prays for its own life and ministry, offering supplications for:

> the local church, that it may have the mind of Christ in facing special issues and needs;
> those who struggle with their faith, that they be given assurance;
> those in the midst of transitions in life, that they be guided and supported;
> those who face critical decisions, that they receive wisdom;
> those who are sick, grieving, lonely, and anxious, that they be comforted and healed;
> all members, that grace conform them to God's purpose.

Option: A prayer of confession may be offered if not already included in the service.

[THE PEACE]

Option: Signs of reconciliation and peace may be exchanged here, if not included elsewhere in the service.

THE EUCHARIST

OFFERING

The Christian life is marked by the offering of one's self to God to be shaped, empowered, directed, and changed by God. In worship, God presents us with the costly self-offering of Jesus Christ. We are claimed by Christ and set free. In response to God's love in Jesus Christ we offer God our lives, our gifts, our abilities, and our material goods, for God's service.

Silence or appropriate music may accompany the gathering of the people's offerings. The tithes and offerings are gathered and received with prayer, spoken or sung.

From early centuries in Christian history, the offering has been the occasion for presenting the bread and wine to be used in the Lord's Supper. When the Lord's Supper is to be celebrated, gifts of bread and wine may therefore be brought to the table in thanksgiving for God's Word. If the elements are already in place, they are made ready for celebrating the Sacrament.

When the service does not include the Lord's Supper, the offering is followed by prayers of thanksgiving, ending with the Lord's Prayer. The service is then concluded with a hymn, spiritual, canticle, or psalm, and with the charge and blessing.

INVITATION TO THE LORD'S TABLE

From New Testament times the celebration of the Eucharist on each Lord's Day has been the norm of Christian worship. The Eucharist was given by Christ himself. Before church governments were devised, before creeds were formalized, even before the first word of the New Testament was written, the Lord's Supper was firmly fixed at the heart of Christian faith and life. From the church's inception, the Lord's Day and the Lord's Supper were joined. Along with the reading and proclamation of the scripture, the Eucharist has given witness to God's redemptive acts each Lord's Day, giving Christian worship its distinctive shape.

In this sacrament, the bread and wine, the words and actions, make the promises of God visible and concrete. The Word proclaimed in scripture and sermon is confirmed, for all that the life, death, and resurrection of Christ means is focused in the Sacrament.

It is appropriate, therefore, that the Eucharist be celebrated as often as on each Lord's Day. It shall be celebrated regularly and frequently enough so that it is clear to all that the Lord's Supper is integral to worship on the Lord's Day, and not an addition to it.

In the Eucharist the church blesses God for all that God has done, is doing, and promises to do, and offers itself in obedient service to God's reign. The church is renewed and empowered as in thanksgiving it remembers Christ's life, death, resurrection, and promised return. The people of God are sustained by the promised presence of Christ, and are assured of participation in Christ's self-offering. Christ's love is received, the covenant is renewed, and the power of Christ's reign for the renewing of the earth is proclaimed. Being made one with Christ, we are made one with all who belong to Christ, united with the church in every time and place. In this sacrament we also participate in God's future as well. It is a glad resurrection feast. Gathering around this table, the church anticipates the great banquet of the new age in God's eternal kingdom.

The Lord's Supper is therefore more than a reminder of Christ's sacrificial death and resurrection. It is a means, given us by Christ, through which the risen Lord is truly present as a continuing power and reality, until the day of his coming. While the meaning of Christ's sacrificial death is at the heart of this sacrament, it is a resurrected, living Christ whom we encounter through the bread and the wine.

The many-faceted meaning of this sacrament is seen in the names given to it. The title *Lord's Supper* recalls Jesus' institution of the sacrament with his disciples. *Eucharist* (thanksgiving) reminds us that we receive all of the benefits of God's grace with joy. *Holy Communion* reminds us that in this sacrament we are made one with Christ and with each other. *The Breaking of the Bread* describes the sacramental action by which Christ is known to his disciples.

The minister, or the one authorized to preside, invites the people to the Lord's table using suitable words from scripture. If the words of institution (1 Cor. 11:23–26, or Gospel accounts: Matt. 26:26–30; Mark 14:22–26; Luke 22:14–20) will not be spoken at the breaking of bread or included in the great thanksgiving, they are said as part of the invitation.

GREAT THANKSGIVING

The Lord's table, having been set, the one presiding then leads the people in the great thanksgiving. This prayer with its emphasis on thankful praise has been of central importance to this sacrament from very early centuries in Christian worship. Thanksgiving is so important to this sacrament that it has been given the name of Eucharist (from the New Testament Greek word *eucharistia*, meaning thanksgiving).

We praise God for all God's mighty acts in the past, present, and future.

God is praised for:
> creating all things,
> the providence of God,
> establishing the covenant,
> giving the law,
> the witness of the prophets,
> God's boundless love and mercy in spite of human failure,
> the ultimate gift of Christ,
> the immediate occasion or festival.

There may be an acclamation of praise, in which we join in one voice, with choirs of angels and with the faithful of every time and place, in adoration of the triune God: "Holy, holy, holy Lord," the song of the heavenly hosts, eternally being sung before God's majesty (Isa. 6:1–5).

Christ's work of redemption is recalled with thanks:
 his birth, life, and ministry,
 his death and resurrection,
 the promise of his coming again.
 the gift of the Sacrament [which may include the words of institution if not otherwise used].
There may be an acclamation of faith, in which we joyfully acclaim Christ who died, is risen, and will come again.

The Holy Spirit is called upon
 to draw the people into the presence of the risen Christ,
 and to make the breaking of the bread and sharing of the cup
 a communion in the body and blood of Christ,
 that the people may be
 nourished with Christ's body,
 made one with the risen Christ,
 united with all the faithful in heaven and earth,
 kept faithful as Christ's body, representing Christ in ministry in the world,
 in anticipation of the fulfillment of the kingdom Christ proclaimed.

The prayer concludes with an ascription of praise to the triune God.

LORD'S PRAYER

Following the great thanksgiving, the Lord's Prayer is said by the people.

BREAKING OF THE BREAD

The one presiding takes the bread and breaks it, and pours wine or unfermented grape juice into the cup. The action should be clearly visible to all present. If the words of institution have not previously been spoken, they are said as the bread is broken and the wine is poured. We are reminded in this action that Christ's body was broken and his blood was shed for all. The action requires a loaf of bread of sufficient size for breaking, and a chalice and a flagon or pitcher for the pouring.

COMMUNION OF THE PEOPLE

The bread and wine from the table are served to the people in a manner suitable to the occasion.

The people may gather around the table to receive the bread and cup. Or, the people may go to persons serving the elements. Or, the bread and wine may be served to the people where they are.

A portion of a loaf of bread may be broken off and placed in the people's hands. Or, the people may break off a portion of the loaf of bread. Or, the people may be offered pieces of bread prepared for distribution.

Wine may be served from a common cup. Or, several cups may be offered and shared. Or, individual cups may be prepared for distribution. Rather than drink from a common cup, communicants may dip the broken bread into the cup.

During the serving, the people may sing psalms, hymns, spirituals, or other appropriate songs. Or the choir may sing, or instrumental music may be played. Or scripture may be read. Or the people may pray in silence.

After all have been served, and the remaining elements have been returned to the table, a prayer is offered thanking God for the gift of Christ in the Sacrament, and asking for God's grace and strength to be faithful disciples.

SENDING

Acts of commitment to discipleship, declaration of intent to seek Baptism, and reaffirmation of the baptismal covenant are appropriate responses to the Word received in the Sacrament. As the service comes to a close, other acts of commitment and recognition may be observed. People may make commitments to and be commissioned to specific corporate and personal acts of evangelism, compassion, justice, reconciliation, and peacemaking in the world.

Those leaving the fellowship of a particular church to undertake these commissions, or to move to another community, may be recognized with a farewell.

Announcements pertaining to the life of the church may be included at this point. Whether included here or elsewhere, announcements in corporate worship should be restricted to those that relate directly to the ongoing mission of the congregation and have relevance for all of the members of the worshiping community.

HYMN, SPIRITUAL, CANTICLE, OR PSALM

The congregation sings a hymn, spiritual, canticle, or psalm.

CHARGE AND BLESSING

A formal dismissal concludes the service. A charge to the people to go into the world in the name of Christ may be included. The charge renews God's call to us to engage in obedient and grateful ministry as God's agents to heal life's brokenness. By the power of the Spirit, we are to be in life and ministry what Christ has redeemed us to be.

God calls the church to join the mission of Christ in service to the world. As the church engages in that mission, it bears witness to God's reign over all of life.

God sends the church in the power of the Holy Spirit to proclaim the gospel, to engage in works of compassion and reconciliation, to strive for peace and justice in its own life and in the world, to be stewards of creation and of life, caring for creation until the day when God will make all things new.

The church in both its worship and its ministry is a sign of the reign of God. God's reign is both a present reality and a promise of the future. In an age hostile to the reign of God, the church worships and serves, confident that God's rule has been established, and with hope firmly rooted in the ultimate triumph of God.

The dismissal shall include words of blessing, using a trinitarian benediction such as the apostolic benediction in 2 Cor. 13:14, or other words from scripture. Assured of God's peace and blessing, we are confident that God goes with us to our tasks. Signs of reconciliation and peace may be exchanged as the people depart.

Instrumental music may follow the blessing.

NOTE

1. The description of the Service for the Lord's Day appearing on pages 34–45 is based upon and draws much of its language from the directories for worship of the Presbyterian Church (U.S.A.) and the Cumberland Presbyterian Church:

"Directory for Worship," *Book of Order*, Presbyterian Church (U.S.A.) (Louisville, Ky.: Office of the General Assembly), W-2.2000-2.1010; 2.4000-2.4012; W-3.1000-3.1004; W-3.3000-3.3702; W-7.1000-7.6002.

"Directory for Worship," in *Confession of Faith and Government of the Cumberland Presbyterian Church and the Second Cumberland Presbyterian Church* (Memphis, Tenn.: Frontier Press), sections entitled "The Corporate Worship of God" and "The Sacraments."

This section also incorporates material appearing on pp. 12–26 of *Service for the Lord's Day*, Supplemental Liturgical Resource 1 (Philadelphia: Westminster Press, 1984), which was prepared for that trial-use resource to describe the movement of the Service for the Lord's Day and the meaning of its parts.

An Outline of the Service for the Lord's Day

GATHERING

Call to Worship
Prayer of the Day or Opening Prayer
Hymn of Praise, Psalm, or Spiritual
Confession and Pardon
The Peace
Canticle, Psalm, Hymn, or Spiritual

THE WORD

Prayer for Illumination
First Reading
Psalm
Second Reading
Anthem, Hymn, Psalm, Canticle, or Spiritual
Gospel Reading
Sermon
Invitation
Hymn, Canticle, Psalm, or Spiritual
Affirmation of Faith
[Pastoral Rite of the Church]
Prayers of the People
[The Peace]

If the Lord's Supper
is not celebrated:

THE EUCHARIST

Offering
Invitation to the Lord's Table
Great Thanksgiving
Lord's Prayer
Breaking of the Bread
Communion of the People

Offering

Prayer of Thanksgiving
Lord's Prayer

SENDING

Hymn, Spiritual, Canticle, or Psalm
Charge and Blessing

An Outline of the Service for the Lord's Day Including the Sacrament of Baptism

GATHERING

Call to Worship
Prayer of the Day or Opening Prayer
Hymn of Praise, Psalm, or Spiritual
Confession and Pardon
[The Peace]
Canticle, Psalm, Hymn, or Spiritual

THE WORD

Prayer for Illumination
First Reading
Psalm
Second Reading
Anthem, Hymn, Psalm, Canticle, or Spiritual
Gospel Reading
Sermon
Invitation
Hymn, Canticle, Psalm, or Spiritual

Baptism
   Presentation
   Profession of Faith
     with Apostles' Creed
   Thanksgiving Over the Water
   The Baptism
   Laying On of Hands
   Welcome
   The Peace
Prayers of the People

If the Lord's Supper
is not celebrated:

THE EUCHARIST

Offering
Invitation to the Lord's Table
Great Thanksgiving
Lord's Prayer
Breaking of the Bread
Communion of the People

Offering

Prayer of Thanksgiving
Lord's Prayer

SENDING

Hymn, Spiritual, Canticle, or Psalm
Charge and Blessing

The Service for the Lord's Day
Order with Liturgical Texts

GATHERING

CALL TO WORSHIP

GREETING

All may stand as the minister(s) and other worship leaders enter.

The minister greets the people, saying one of the following:

1   *2 Thess. 3:18*

The grace of the Lord Jesus Christ be with you all.

2   *2 Cor. 13:13*

The grace of our Lord Jesus Christ,
the love of God,
and the communion of the Holy Spirit
be with you all.

3   *See Ruth 2:4*

The Lord be with you.

The people answer:

And also with you.

SENTENCES OF SCRIPTURE

The minister continues:

Let us worship God.

Then one of the following, or another verse from scripture appropriate to
the day or season (pp. 165–400), is said:

1 *Ps. 124:8*

Our help is in the name of the Lord,

who made heaven and earth.

2 *Ps. 118:24*

This is the day that the Lord has made;

let us rejoice and be glad in it.

3 *Ps. 95:1, 2*

O come, let us sing to the Lord
and shout with joy to the rock of our salvation!

**Let us come into God's presence with thanksgiving,
singing joyful songs of praise.**

4 *Ps. 116:12, 13*

What shall we return to the Lord
for all the good things God has done for us?

**We will lift up the cup of salvation
and call on the name of the Lord.**

5 *Ps. 34:3*

O praise the Lord with me,

let us exalt God's name together.

6 *Ps. 96:1, 2*

O sing to the Lord a new song;

sing to the Lord, all the earth.

Sing, and give praise to God's name;

tell the glad news of salvation from day to day.

7 *Ps. 100:1, 2, 5*

Cry out with joy to the Lord, all the earth.
Worship the Lord with gladness.
Come into God's presence with singing!

**For the Lord is a gracious God,
whose mercy is everlasting;
and whose faithfulness endures to all generations.**

See Micah 6:6, 8

With what shall we come before the Holy One,
and bow ourselves before God on high?
God has shown us what is good.
What does the Holy One require of us,
but to do justice,
and to love kindness,
and to walk humbly with our God?

9 *Mal. 1:11*

From the rising of the sun to its setting
my name is great among the nations,
says the Lord of hosts.

10 *Ps. 24:1*

The earth is the Lord's and all that is in it,
the world, and those who live in it.

After the scripture verse, the minister may add:

Praise the Lord.

The Lord's name be praised.

PRAYER OF THE DAY OR OPENING PRAYER

Let us pray.

After a brief silence, the prayer of the day (pp. 165–400) or one of the following prayers may be said.

1

Almighty God,
to whom all hearts are open,
all desires, known,
and from whom no secrets are hid:
Cleanse the thoughts of our hearts
by the inspiration of your Holy Spirit,
that we may perfectly love you
and worthily magnify your holy name;
through Christ our Lord. [44]

Amen.

2

God of all glory,
on this first day
you began creation,
bringing light out of darkness.
On this first day
you began your new creation,
raising Jesus Christ out of the darkness of death.
On this Lord's Day
grant that we,
the people you create by water and the Spirit,
may be joined with all your works
in praising you for your great glory.
Through Jesus Christ,
in union with the Holy Spirit,
we praise you now and forever.   [45]

Amen.

3

O God, light of the hearts that see you,
life of the souls that love you,
strength of the thoughts that seek you:
to turn from you is to fall,
to turn to you is to rise,
to abide in you is to stand fast forever.
Although we are unworthy to approach you,
or to ask anything at all of you,
grant us your grace and blessing
for the sake of Jesus Christ our Redeemer.   [46]

Amen.

4

O God, you are infinite,
eternal and unchangeable,
glorious in holiness,
full of love and compassion,
abundant in grace and truth.
Your works everywhere praise you,
and your glory is revealed
in Jesus Christ our Savior.
Therefore we praise you,
blessed and holy Trinity,
one God, forever and ever.   [47]

Amen.

5

God of light and truth,
you are beyond our grasp or conceiving.
Before the brightness of your presence
the angels veil their faces.
With lowly reverence and adoring love
we acclaim your glory
and sing your praise,
for you have shown us your truth and love
in Jesus Christ our Savior.   [48]

Amen.

HYMN OF PRAISE, PSALM, OR SPIRITUAL

All may remain standing.

CONFESSION AND PARDON

CALL TO CONFESSION

The people are called to confess their sin using one of the following, or
other words of scripture that promise God's forgiveness.

1
                                                                1 John 1:8, 9

If we say we have no sin,
we deceive ourselves,
and the truth is not in us.
But if we confess our sins,
God who is faithful and just
will forgive us our sins
and cleanse us from all unrighteousness.

In humility and faith
let us confess our sin to God.

2
                                                          Rom. 5:8; Heb. 4:16

The proof of God's amazing love is this:
While we were sinners
Christ died for us.
Because we have faith in him,
we dare to approach God with confidence.

In faith and penitence,
let us confess our sin before God and one another.

3   *See Heb. 4:14–16*

Remember that our Lord Jesus can sympathize with us in our weaknesses,
since in every respect he was tempted as we are,
yet without sin.
Let us then with boldness approach the throne of grace,
that we may receive mercy
and find grace to help in time of need.

Let us confess our sins
against God and our neighbor.

> A pause for silent reflection follows.

CONFESSION OF SIN

> All confess their sin, using one of the following prayers or another appropriate to the occasion or season (pp. 87–89, 165–400). Silence may be kept before, during, or following the prayer.

1

**Merciful God,
we confess that we have sinned against you
in thought, word, and deed,
by what we have done,
and by what we have left undone.
We have not loved you
with our whole heart and mind and strength.
We have not loved our neighbors as ourselves.**

**In your mercy forgive what we have been,
help us amend what we are,
and direct what we shall be,
so that we may delight in your will
and walk in your ways,
to the glory of your holy name.**   [49]

2

**Holy and merciful God,
in your presence we confess
our sinfulness, our shortcomings,
and our offenses against you.
You alone know how often we have sinned
in wandering from your ways,
in wasting your gifts,
in forgetting your love.**

Have mercy on us, O Lord,
for we are ashamed and sorry
for all we have done to displease you.
Forgive our sins,
and help us to live in your light,
and walk in your ways,
for the sake of Jesus Christ our Savior.   [50]

3

Eternal God, our judge and redeemer,
we confess that we have tried to hide from you,
for we have done wrong.
We have lived for ourselves,
and apart from you.
We have turned from our neighbors,
and refused to bear the burdens of others.
We have ignored the pain of the world,
and passed by the hungry, the poor, and the oppressed.

In your great mercy forgive our sins
and free us from selfishness,
that we may choose your will
and obey your commandments;
through Jesus Christ our Savior.   [51]

4

Merciful God,
you pardon all who truly repent and turn to you.
We humbly confess our sins and ask your mercy.
We have not loved you with a pure heart,
nor have we loved our neighbor as ourselves.
We have not done justice, loved kindness,
or walked humbly with you, our God.

Have mercy on us, O God, in your loving-kindness.
In your great compassion,
cleanse us from our sin.
Create in us a clean heart, O God,
and renew a right spirit within us.
Do not cast us from your presence,
or take your Holy Spirit from us.
Restore to us the joy of your salvation
and sustain us with your bountiful Spirit.   [52]

"Lord, Have Mercy" (A), "Holy God, Holy and Mighty" (B), or "Lamb of God" (C) may be sung.

A

Lord, Have Mercy

Kyrie Eleison
PH 565, 572–574

May be sung in threefold, sixfold, or ninefold form.

Lord, have mercy.
Christ, have mercy.
Lord, have mercy.

B

Holy God, Holy and Mighty

Trisagion

Sung three times.

Holy God,
holy and mighty,
holy immortal One,
have mercy upon us.

C

Lamb of God

Agnus Dei

Jesus, Lamb of God,
have mercy on us.

Jesus, bearer of our sins,
have mercy on us.

Jesus, redeemer of the world,
grant us peace.

Or

Lamb of God, you take away the sin of the world,
have mercy on us.

Lamb of God, you take away the sin of the world,
have mercy on us.

Lamb of God, you take away the sin of the world,
grant us peace.

DECLARATION OF FORGIVENESS

The minister declares the assurance of God's forgiving grace:

1

The mercy of the Lord
is from everlasting to everlasting.
I declare to you, in the name of Jesus Christ,
you are forgiven.

May the God of mercy,
who forgives you all your sins,
strengthen you in all goodness,
and by the power of the Holy Spirit
keep you in eternal life.

Amen.

2

1 Tim. 1:15; 1 Peter 2:24

Hear the good news!

The saying is sure and worthy of full acceptance,
that Christ Jesus came into the world to save sinners.

He himself bore our sins
in his body on the cross,
that we might be dead to sin,
and alive to all that is good.

I declare to you in the name of Jesus Christ,
you are forgiven.

Amen.

3

Rom. 8:34; 2 Cor. 5:17

Hear the good news!

Who is in a position to condemn?
Only Christ,
and Christ died for us,
Christ rose for us,
Christ reigns in power for us,
Christ prays for us.

Anyone who is in Christ
is a new creation.
The old life has gone;
a new life has begun.

Know that you are forgiven
and be at peace.

Amen.

One of the following exhortations may be said, or the summary of
the law (p. 29) or the Commandments (p. 28) may be read.

1   *See Col. 3:12–14*

As God's own people,
be merciful in action,
kindly in heart, humble in mind.
Be always ready to forgive
as freely as God has forgiven you.
And, above everything else, be loving,
and never forget to be thankful
for what Christ has done for you.

2   *John 13:34*

Hear the teaching of Christ:

A new commandment I give to you,
that you love one another as I have loved you.

The Peace

The peace may be exchanged here or after the prayers of the people
(pp. 65–66). The leader says:

See John 20:19, 21, 26

Since God has forgiven us in Christ,
let us forgive one another.

The peace of our Lord Jesus Christ be with you all.

And also with you.

The people may exchange with one another, by words and gesture, signs of
peace and reconciliation.

CANTICLE, PSALM, HYMN, OR SPIRITUAL

A canticle (pp. 573–591), psalm, hymn, or spiritual may be sung.

During the seasons of Christmas and Easter, (A) "Glory to God" is especially appropriate.

When the Lord's Supper is to be celebrated, (B) "Worthy Is Christ, the Lamb" is appropriate.

On other occasions (C) "Glory to the Father" may be used.

A

Glory to God

Gloria in Excelsis
PH 566, 575, 576; PS 173

**Glory to God in the highest,
and peace to God's people on earth.**

**Lord God, heavenly King,
almighty God and Father,
we worship you, we give you thanks,
we praise you for your glory.**

**Lord Jesus Christ, only Son of the Father,
Lord God, Lamb of God,
you take away the sin of the world:
have mercy on us;
you are seated at the right hand of the Father:
receive our prayer**

**For you alone are the Holy One,
you alone are the Lord,
you alone are the Most High,
Jesus Christ,
with the Holy Spirit,
in the glory of God the Father.   Amen.**

B

Worthy Is Christ, the Lamb   *Rev. 5:12, 9, 13; 7:10, 12; 19:4, 6–9*
                                                                        PH 594

Refrain: This is the feast of victory for our God.
               Alleluia, alleluia, alleluia.

Worthy is Christ, the Lamb who was slain,
whose blood set us free to be people of God.   R

Power, riches, wisdom, and strength,
and honor, blessing, and glory are his.   R

Sing with all the people of God,
and join in the hymn of all creation.   R

Blessing, honor, glory, and might
be to God and the Lamb forever. Amen.   R

For the Lamb who was slain
has begun his reign. Alleluia.   R

C

Glory to the Father   *Gloria Patri*
                                                          PH 567, 577-579

Glory to the Father,
and to the Son,
and to the Holy Spirit:
as it was in the beginning,
is now,
and will be forever.   Amen.

The people may be seated.

THE WORD

PRAYER FOR ILLUMINATION

Let us pray.

> After a brief silence, one of the following, or another prayer for illumination (pp. 90–91), is said:

1

Lord, open our hearts and minds
by the power of your Holy Spirit,
that as the scriptures are read
and your Word is proclaimed,
we may hear with joy what you say to us today.　[53]

Amen.

2

Prepare our hearts, O God,
to accept your Word.
Silence in us any voice but your own,
that, hearing, we may also obey your will;
through Jesus Christ our Lord.　[54]

Amen.

3

O God,
by your Spirit tell us what we need to hear,
and show us what we ought to do,
to obey Jesus Christ our Savior.　[55]

Amen.

4

O Lord our God,
your Word is a lamp to our feet
and a light to our path.
Give us grace to receive your truth in faith and love,
that we may be obedient to your will
and live always for your glory;
through Jesus Christ our Savior.　[56]

Amen.

The reader may then say:

Rev. 2:7, 11, 17, 29; 3:6, 13, 22

Hear what the Spirit is saying to the church.

FIRST READING

Before the reading:

A reading from _____ .

At the conclusion of the reading:

The Word of the Lord.
Thanks be to God.

Silence may be kept.

PSALM

The psalm for the day is sung or said.

SECOND READING

Before the reading:

A reading from _____ .

At the conclusion of the reading:

The Word of the Lord.
Thanks be to God.

Silence may be kept.

ANTHEM, HYMN, PSALM, CANTICLE, OR SPIRITUAL

An anthem, hymn, psalm, canticle, or spiritual that reflects the scriptures for the day may be sung.

Gospel Reading

Before the reading of the Gospel:

A reading from _____.

Or

The Gospel of our Lord Jesus Christ according to _____.

Glory to you, O Lord.

At the conclusion of the Gospel:

The Word of the Lord.

Thanks be to God.

Or

The Gospel of the Lord.

Praise to you, O Christ.

Silence may be kept.

Sermon

After the scriptures are read, their message is proclaimed in a sermon or some other form of proclamation.

One of the following ascriptions of praise, or another (pp. 91–92), may conclude the sermon.

1   *Rev. 7:12*

Blessing and glory and wisdom
and thanksgiving and honor
and power and might
be to our God forever and ever!

Amen.

2   *1 Tim. 1:17*

Now to the Ruler of all worlds,
undying, invisible, the only God,
be honor and glory forever and ever!

Amen.

To Jesus Christ, who loves us
and freed us from our sins by his blood
and made us to be a kingdom,
priests of his God and Father,
to him be glory and dominion forever and ever.

Amen.

> Silence for reflection may follow.

INVITATION

> An invitation (pp. 92–93) may be given to any who wish to make or renew personal commitment to Christ and his kingdom.

HYMN, CANTICLE, PSALM, OR SPIRITUAL

> All may stand. If Baptism (or a pastoral rite of the church) follows, candidates may come forward during the singing.

AFFIRMATION OF FAITH

> The Nicene Creed (A), the Apostles' Creed (B), or an affirmation drawn from scripture (pp. 94–98) may be said or sung, or a portion of the *Book of Confessions*, or a portion of A Declaration of Faith may be said, the people standing.

> When Baptism is to be celebrated, or when the Public Profession of Faith or other reaffirmation of the baptismal covenant is to follow, or when new members are welcomed, the creed is not used here, since the Apostles' Creed is included in these rites.

> The Nicene Creed is ordinarily used whenever the Lord's Supper is celebrated.

A

Nicene Creed

Let us confess our faith.

We believe in one God,
the Father, the Almighty,
maker of heaven and earth,
of all that is, seen and unseen.

We believe in one Lord, Jesus Christ,
the only Son of God,
eternally begotten of the Father,
God from God, Light from Light,
true God from true God,
begotten, not made,
of one Being with the Father;
through him all things were made.
For us and for our salvation
he came down from heaven,
was incarnate of the Holy Spirit and the Virgin Mary
and became truly human.
For our sake he was crucified under Pontius Pilate;
he suffered death and was buried.
On the third day he rose again
in accordance with the Scriptures;
he ascended into heaven
and is seated at the right hand of the Father.
He will come again in glory to judge the living and the dead,
and his kingdom will have no end.

We believe in the Holy Spirit, the Lord, the giver of life,
who proceeds from the Father and the Son,
who with the Father and the Son is worshiped and glorified,
who has spoken through the prophets.
We believe in one holy catholic and apostolic church.
We acknowledge one baptism for the forgiveness of sins.
We look for the resurrection of the dead,
and the life of the world to come.   Amen.

B

Apostles' Creed

Let us confess the faith of our baptism, as we say:

I believe in God, the Father almighty,
creator of heaven and earth.

I believe in Jesus Christ, God's only Son, our Lord.
who was conceived by the Holy Spirit,
born of the Virgin Mary,
suffered under Pontius Pilate,
was crucified, died, and was buried;
he descended to the dead.
On the third day he rose again;
he ascended into heaven,
he is seated at the right hand of the Father,
and he will come again to judge the living and the dead.

I believe in the Holy Spirit,
the holy catholic church,
the communion of saints,
the forgiveness of sins,
the resurrection of the body,
and the life everlasting.   Amen.

BAPTISM

When Baptism is celebrated, it takes place here, using the baptismal liturgy on pages 403–415 or 419–429.

PASTORAL RITE OF THE CHURCH

When a pastoral rite of the church is celebrated (e.g., confirming and commissioning, or other reaffirmation of the baptismal covenant, reception of new members, ordination, installation, marriage), it takes place here.

PRAYERS OF THE PEOPLE

The minister, an elder, a deacon, or a member of the congregation leads the prayers of the people, the people standing.

Models of prayers of the people are found on pages 99–120.

Intercessions are offered for:

> the church universal
> the world and our nation
> those in authority
> the community
> persons in distressing circumstances
> those with special needs

A commemoration of those who have died may be included (pp. 121–122).

The prayers may end with a concluding collect (pp. 123–124), or the prayer of the day (pp. 165–400), if it has not already been said.

The prayer of confession may be said here if it was not included earlier in the service.

THE PEACE

> The peace may take place here if it was not included earlier in the service.

> A leader says:

See Col. 3:15 and John 20:19, 21, 26

Let the peace of Christ rule in your hearts.
To this peace we were called
as members of a single body.

The peace of Christ be with you.

And also with you.

> The people may exchange signs of peace and reconciliation with one another.

The people are seated.

IF THE LORD'S SUPPER IS NOT TO BE CELEBRATED, THE SERVICE CONTINUES ON PAGE 79.

THE EUCHARIST

OFFERING

Let us return to God the offerings of our life
and the gifts of the earth.

> One of the following, or another appropriate verse from scripture, may
> be said.

1
Ps. 24:1

The earth is the Lord's and all that is in it,
the world, and those who live in it.

2
Matt. 10:8b

Freely you have received,
freely give.

3
2 Cor. 9:6

The one who sows sparingly will also reap sparingly;
the one who sows bountifully will also reap bountifully.

4
2 Cor. 9:7

Give as you have made up your mind,
not reluctantly or under compulsion,
for God loves a cheerful giver.

5
Heb. 13:16

Do good and share what you have,
for such sacrifices are pleasing to God.

6
Acts 20:35b

Remember the words of the Lord Jesus:
It is more blessed to give than to receive.

> As the offerings are gathered, there may be an anthem, or other appropriate music.
>
> When the Lord's Supper is celebrated, the minister(s) and elders prepare the table with bread and wine during the gathering of the gifts. The bread and wine may be brought to the table, or uncovered if already in place.
>
> The offerings may be brought forward. A psalm, hymn of praise, doxology, or spiritual may be sung, the people standing. The leader may then say:

1   *See 1 Chron. 29:11*

Yours, O Lord, are grandeur and power,
majesty, splendor, and glory.

**All in the heavens and on the earth is yours,
and of your own we give you.**

Or

2

Blessed are you, God of all creation;
through your goodness we have these gifts to share.
Accept and use our offerings for your glory
and for the service of your kingdom.

Blessed be God forever.   [57]

INVITATION TO THE LORD'S TABLE

Standing at the table, the presiding minister invites the people to the
Sacrament, using one of the following or another invitation to the Lord's
table (p. 125). If B is used, the words of institution are not included in the
great thanksgiving or at the breaking of the bread.

A   *See Luke 13:29 and Luke 24:30, 31*

Friends, this is the joyful feast of the people of God!
They will come from east and west,
and from north and south,
and sit at table in the kingdom of God.

According to Luke,
when our risen Lord was at table with his disciples,
he took the bread, and blessed and broke it,
and gave it to them.
Then their eyes were opened
and they recognized him.

This is the Lord's table.
Our Savior invites those who trust him
to share the feast which he has prepared.

B   *See 1 Cor. 11:23–26; Luke 22:19–20*

Hear the words of the institution
of the Holy Supper of our Lord Jesus Christ:

The Lord Jesus, on the night of his arrest, took bread,
and after giving thanks to God,
he broke it, and gave it to his disciples, saying:

Take, eat.
This is my body, given for you.
Do this in remembrance of me.

In the same way he took the cup, saying:
This cup is the new covenant sealed in my blood,
shed for you for the forgiveness of sins.
Whenever you drink it,
do this in remembrance of me.

Every time you eat this bread and drink this cup,
you proclaim the saving death of the risen Lord,
until he comes.

With thanksgiving,
let us offer God our grateful praise.

GREAT THANKSGIVING

The people stand.

The presiding minister leads the people in the following or another great
thanksgiving appropriate to the season or occasion (pp. 126–156, 165–400):

Great Thanksgiving: *A*

The Lord be with you.

And also with you.

Lift up your hearts.

We lift them to the Lord.

Let us give thanks to the Lord our God.

It is right to give our thanks and praise.

It is truly right and our greatest joy
to give you thanks and praise,
O Lord our God, creator and ruler of the universe.
In your wisdom, you made all things
and sustain them by your power.
You formed us in your image,
setting us in this world to love and to serve you,
and to live in peace with your whole creation.
When we rebelled against you
refusing to trust and obey you,
you did not reject us,
but still claimed us as your own.
You sent prophets to call us back to your way.

Then in the fullness of time,
out of your great love for the world,
you sent your only Son to be one of us,
to redeem us and heal our brokenness.

Therefore we praise you,
joining our voices with choirs of angels,
with prophets, apostles, and martyrs,
and with all the faithful of every time and place,
who forever sing to the glory of your name:

> The people may sing or say:

**Holy, holy, holy Lord, God of power and might,
heaven and earth are full of your glory.
Hosanna in the highest.**

**Blessed is he who comes in the name of the Lord.
Hosanna in the highest.**

> The minister continues:

You are holy, O God of majesty,
and blessed is Jesus Christ, your Son, our Lord.
In Jesus, born of Mary, your Word became flesh
and dwelt among us, full of grace and truth.
He lived as one of us, knowing joy and sorrow.
He healed the sick,
fed the hungry,
opened blind eyes,
broke bread with outcasts and sinners,
and proclaimed the good news of your kingdom to the poor and needy.
Dying on the cross,
he gave himself for the life of the world.
Rising from the grave,
he won for us victory over death.
Seated at your right hand,
he leads us to eternal life.
We praise you that Christ now reigns with you in glory,
and will come again to make all things new.

> If they have not already been said, the words of institution may be
> said here, or in relation to the breaking of the bread.

> We give you thanks that the Lord Jesus,
> on the night before he died, took bread,

and after giving thanks to you,
he broke it, and gave it to his disciples, saying:
Take, eat.
This is my body, given for you.
Do this in remembrance of me.

In the same way he took the cup, saying:
This cup is the new covenant sealed in my blood,
shed for you for the forgiveness of sins.
Whenever you drink it,
do this in remembrance of me.

Remembering your gracious acts in Jesus Christ,
we take from your creation this bread and this wine
and joyfully celebrate his dying and rising,
as we await the day of his coming.
With thanksgiving, we offer our very selves to you
to be a living and holy sacrifice,
dedicated to your service.

The people may sing or say one of the following:

1

Great is the mystery of faith:

**Christ has died,
Christ is risen,
Christ will come again.**

2

Praise to you, Lord Jesus:

**Dying you destroyed our death,
rising you restored our life.
Lord Jesus, come in glory.**

3

According to his commandment:

**We remember his death,
we proclaim his resurrection,
we await his coming in glory.**

4

Christ is the bread of life:

**When we eat this bread and drink this cup,
we proclaim your death, Lord Jesus,
until you come in glory.**

The minister continues:

Gracious God,
pour out your Holy Spirit upon us
and upon these your gifts of bread and wine,
that the bread we break
and the cup we bless
may be the communion of the body and blood of Christ.
By your Spirit make us one with Christ,
that we may be one with all who share this feast,
united in ministry in every place.
As this bread is Christ's body for us,
send us out to be the body of Christ in the world.

Intercessions for the church and the world may be included here,
using these or similar prayers:

Remember your church. . . .
Unite it in the truth of your Word
and empower it in ministry to the world.

Remember the world of nations. . . .
By your Spirit renew the face of the earth;
let peace and justice prevail.

Remember our family and friends. . . .
Bless them and watch over them;
be gracious to them and give them peace.

Remember the sick and the suffering,
the aged and the dying. . . .
Encourage them and give them hope.

Rejoicing in the communion of saints,
we remember with thanksgiving
all your faithful servants, and those dear to us,
whom you have called from this life. . . .

We are grateful that for them death is no more,
nor is there sorrow, crying, or pain,
for the former things have passed away.

In union with your church in heaven and on earth,
we pray, O God, that you will fulfill your eternal purpose
in us and in all the world.

Keep us faithful in your service
until Christ comes in final victory,
and we shall feast with all your saints
in the joy of your eternal realm.

Through Christ, with Christ, in Christ,
in the unity of the Holy Spirit,
all glory and honor are yours, almighty Father,
now and forever.   [58]

Amen.

LORD'S PRAYER

The minister invites all present to sing or say the Lord's Prayer:

1

Let us pray for God's rule on earth
as Jesus taught us:

Or

2

And now, with the confidence of the children of God,
let us pray:

Or

3

As our Savior Christ has taught us, we are bold to pray:

All pray together.

Or

**Our Father in heaven,
hallowed be your name,
your kingdom come,
your will be done,
on earth as in heaven.
Give us today our daily bread.
Forgive us our sins
as we forgive those who sin against us.
Save us from the time of trial
and deliver us from evil.
For the kingdom, the power,
    and the glory are yours
now and forever.   Amen.**

**Our Father, who art in heaven,
hallowed be thy name,
thy kingdom come,
thy will be done,
on earth as it is in heaven.
Give us this day our daily bread;
and forgive us our debts,
as we forgive our debtors;
and lead us not into temptation,
but deliver us from evil.
For thine is the kingdom,
and the power, and the glory,
    forever.   Amen.**

The people may be seated.

BREAKING OF THE BREAD

If the words of institution have not previously been said, the minister breaks the bread, using A.

If the words of institution were said in the invitation to the Lord's table or were included in the great thanksgiving, the minister breaks the bread, using B. Or the bread may be broken in silence.

A   *See 1 Cor. 11:23–26; Luke 22:19–20*

The minister breaks the bread in full view of the people, saying:

The Lord Jesus, on the night of his arrest, took bread,
and after giving thanks to God,
he broke it, and gave it to his disciples, saying:
Take, eat.
This is my body, given for you.
Do this in remembrance of me.

The minister lifts the cup, saying:

In the same way he took the cup, saying:
This cup is the new covenant sealed in my blood,
shed for you for the forgiveness of sins.
Whenever you drink it,
do this in remembrance of me.

Every time you eat this bread and drink this cup,
you proclaim the saving death of the risen Lord,
until he comes.

B   *1 Cor. 10:16–17*

Because there is one loaf,
we, many as we are, are one body;
for it is one loaf of which we all partake.

The minister takes the loaf and breaks it in full view of the people, saying:

When we break the bread,
is it not a sharing in the body of Christ?

Having filled the cup, the minister lifts it in the view of the people, saying:

When we give thanks over the cup,
is it not a sharing in the blood of Christ?

COMMUNION OF THE PEOPLE

INVITATION

Then holding out both the bread and the cup to the people, the minister says one of the following:

1

The gifts of God
for the people of God.

2

Creator of all,
just as this broken bread
was first scattered upon the hills,
then was gathered and became one,

**so may your church be gathered
from the ends of the earth into your kingdom.** [59]

3 *John 6:35*

Jesus said: I am the bread of life.
Whoever comes to me will never be hungry,
and whoever believes in me will never be thirsty.

COMMUNION

The minister and those assisting receive Communion, and then serve the bread and the cup to the people.

The people may gather around the table to receive the bread and cup. Or the people may go to persons serving the elements. Or the bread and cup may be served to the people where they are.

One of the following may be used:

1

In giving the bread:

The body of Christ, given for you.   **Amen.**

In giving the cup:

The blood of Christ, shed for you.   **Amen.**

In giving the bread:

The body of Christ, the bread of heaven.   **Amen.**

In giving the cup:

The blood of Christ, the cup of salvation.   **Amen.**

During Communion, psalms, hymns, anthems, or spirituals may be sung.

PRAYER AFTER COMMUNION

After all have been served, the minister and people may sing or say Psalm 103:1, 2 (A), or one of the following prayers (B), or a similar prayer (pp. 157–158) may be prayed by the minister, or by all together.

A

Ps. 103:1, 2
PH 222, 223; PS 102

Bless the Lord, O my soul;

and all that is within me, bless God's holy name!

Bless the Lord, O my soul,

and forget not all God's benefits.

B

1

Loving God,
we thank you that you have fed us in this Sacrament,
united us with Christ,
and given us a foretaste of the heavenly banquet
in your eternal kingdom.
Send us out in the power of your Spirit
to live and work to your praise and glory,
for the sake of Jesus Christ our Lord.   [60]

Amen.

2

We thank you, O God,
that through Word and Sacrament

you have given us your Son
who is the true bread from heaven
and food of eternal life.
So strengthen us in your service
that our daily living may show our thanks;
through Jesus Christ our Lord.   [61]

Amen.

3

Gracious God,
you have made us one with all your people in heaven and on earth.
You have fed us with the bread of life,
and renewed us for your service.
Help us who have shared Christ's body and received his cup,
to be his faithful disciples
so that our daily living
may be part of the life of your kingdom,
and our love be your love
reaching out into the life of the world;
through Jesus Christ our Lord.   [62]

Amen.

4

Eternal God,
you have graciously accepted us
as living members of your Son our Savior Jesus Christ,
and you have fed us with spiritual food
in the Sacrament of his body and blood.
Send us now into the world in peace,
and grant us strength and courage
to love and serve you with gladness and singleness of heart;
through Christ our Lord.   [63]

Amen.

SENDING

HYMN, SPIRITUAL, CANTICLE, OR PSALM

The people may stand.

A hymn, a spiritual, the Canticle of Simeon (PH 603–605; PS 164–166), or
a psalm may be sung.

CHARGE AND BLESSING

CHARGE

The minister dismisses the congregation, using one of the following or a similar charge (pp. 159–160):

1   *See 1 Cor. 16:13; 2 Tim. 2:1; Eph. 6:10;*
                                                                     1 Thess. 5:13–22; and 1 Peter 2:17

Go out into the world in peace;
have courage;
hold on to what is good;
return no one evil for evil;
strengthen the fainthearted;
support the weak, and help the suffering;
honor all people;
love and serve the Lord,
rejoicing in the power of the Holy Spirit.

2

Go in peace to love and serve the Lord.

3

Go forth into the world,
rejoicing in the power of the Holy Spirit.

BLESSING

The minister gives God's blessing to the congregation, using one of the following or another scriptural benediction (p. 161). Traditionally, the **Alleluia** is omitted during Lent.

1   *2 Cor. 13:13*

The grace of the Lord Jesus Christ,
the love of God,
and the communion of the Holy Spirit
be with you all.
Alleluia!   Amen.

2   *See Num. 6:24–26*

The Lord bless you and keep you.
The Lord be kind and gracious to you.
The Lord look upon you with favor
and give you peace.
Alleluia!   Amen.

Instrumental music may follow the blessing.

IF THE LORD'S SUPPER IS NOT CELEBRATED, THE SERVICE
CONTINUES HERE FROM PAGE 66.

OFFERING

With gladness, let us present the offering of our life and labor to the Lord.

One of the following, or another appropriate verse from scripture, may
be said.

1   *Ps. 24:1*

The earth is the Lord's and all that is in it,
the world, and those who live in it.

2   *Matt. 10:8b*

Freely you have received,
freely give.

3   *2 Cor. 9:6*

The one who sows sparingly will also reap sparingly;
the one who sows bountifully will also reap bountifully.

4   *2 Cor. 9:7*

Give as you have made up your mind,
not reluctantly or under compulsion,
for God loves a cheerful giver.

5   *Heb. 13:16*

Do good and share what you have,
for such sacrifices are pleasing to God.

6   *Acts 20:35b*

Remember the words of the Lord Jesus:
It is more blessed to give than to receive.

As the offerings are gathered, there may be an anthem, or other appropriate
music.

The offerings may be brought forward. A psalm, hymn of praise, doxology,
or spiritual, may be sung, the people standing. The leader may then say:

1   *See 1 Chron. 29:10, 11*

Yours, O Lord, are grandeur and power,
majesty, splendor, and glory.

**All in the heavens and on the earth is yours,
and of your own we give you.**

Or

2

Blessed are you, God of all creation;
through your goodness we have these gifts to share.
Accept and use our offerings for your glory
and for the service of your kingdom.

Blessed be God forever.   [57]

PRAYER OF THANKSGIVING

The people may stand.

The minister leads the people in one of the following or another thanksgiving appropriate to the season or occasion (pp. 158–159, 165–400):

Let us give thanks to the Lord our God.

It is right to give our thanks and praise.

1

Eternal God,
creator of the world
and giver of all good,
we thank you for the earth, our home,
and for the gift of life.
We praise you for your love in Jesus Christ,
who came to heal this broken world,
who died rejected on the cross
and rose triumphant from the dead.
Because he lives, we live to praise you, our God forever.

Gracious God, who called us from death to life,
we give ourselves to you;
and with the church through all ages
we thank you for your saving love
in Jesus Christ our Lord.   Amen.   [64]

2

We praise you, God,
for you are gracious.
You have loved us from the beginning of time
and remember us when we are in trouble.

Your mercy endures forever.

We praise you, God,
for you came to us in Jesus Christ,
who redeemed the world
and saved us from our sins.

Your mercy endures forever.

We praise you, God,
for you send us your Holy Spirit,
to make us holy
and to lead us into all truth. [65]

Your mercy endures forever.   Amen.

3

Almighty and merciful God,
from whom comes all that is good,
we praise you for your mercies,
for your goodness that has created us,
your grace that has sustained us,
your discipline that has corrected us,
your patience that has borne with us,
and your love that has redeemed us.

Help us to love you,
and to be thankful for all your gifts
by serving you and delighting to do your will,
through Jesus Christ our Lord. [66]

Amen.

LORD'S PRAYER

The minister invites all present to pray the Lord's Prayer:

1

Let us pray for God's rule on earth
as Jesus taught us:

Or

2

And now, with the confidence of the children of God,
let us pray:

Or

3

As our Savior Christ has taught us, we are bold to pray:

> All pray together.

Or

Our Father in heaven,
hallowed be your name,
your kingdom come,
your will be done,
on earth as in heaven.
Give us today our daily bread.
Forgive us our sins
as we forgive those who sin against us.
Save us from the time of trial
and deliver us from evil.
For the kingdom, the power,
   and the glory are yours
now and forever.   Amen.

Our Father, who art in heaven,
hallowed be thy name,
thy kingdom come,
thy will be done,
on earth as it is in heaven.
Give us this day our daily bread;
and forgive us our debts,
as we forgive our debtors;
and lead us not into temptation,
but deliver us from evil.
For thine is the kingdom,
   and the power, and the glory,
      forever.   Amen.

SENDING

HYMN, SPIRITUAL, CANTICLE, OR PSALM

> A hymn, psalm, or spiritual may be sung.

CHARGE AND BLESSING

CHARGE

> The minister dismisses the congregation, using one of the following or a similar charge (pp. 159–160):

1

See 1 Cor. 16:13; 2 Tim. 2:1; Eph. 6:10;
1 Thess. 5:13–22; 1 Peter 2:17

Go out into the world in peace;
have courage;
hold on to what is good;
return no one evil for evil;
strengthen the fainthearted;
support the weak, and help the suffering;
honor all people;
love and serve the Lord,
rejoicing in the power of the Holy Spirit.

2

Go in peace to love and serve the Lord.

3

Go forth into the world,
rejoicing in the power of the Holy Spirit.

BLESSING

> The minister gives God's blessing to the congregation, using one of the
> following or another scriptural benediction (p. 161). Traditionally, the
> **Alleluia** is omitted during Lent.

1   *2 Cor. 13:13*

The grace of the Lord Jesus Christ,
the love of God,
and the communion of the Holy Spirit
be with you all.

Alleluia!   Amen.

2   *See Num. 6:24–26*

The Lord bless you and keep you.
The Lord be kind and gracious to you.
The Lord look upon you with favor
and give you peace.

Alleluia!   Amen.

> Instrumental music may follow the blessing.

ALTERNATIVES IN THE SERVICE FOR THE LORD'S DAY

Following are some alternative positions for various elements of the Service for the Lord's Day:

Procession If there is a procession of the choir, minister(s), and other leaders of worship during the first hymn, the hymn may precede the call to worship.

Confession and Pardon may take place either

1. as part of the gathering rite as in the above order;
2. following the prayers of the people, and before the peace.

The confession and pardon are used only once in the service.

The Prayer of the Day (pp. 165–400) may be used as follows:

1. following the call to worship as in the above order;
2. to conclude the prayers of the people instead of one of the concluding collects.

The Peace may take place

1. following confession and pardon as in the above order;
2. following the prayers of the people (before the offering), as is already provided for in the above order;
3. following the Lord's Prayer (before the breaking of the bread).

The peace is used only once in the service.

The Affirmation of Faith may

1. immediately follow the sermon, before the hymn, canticle, psalm, or spiritual
2. follow the hymn, canticle, psalm, or spiritual that immediately follows the sermon as in the above order.

The Prayers of the People may be included in the great thanksgiving following the invocation of the Spirit, as noted in the prayers.

Offering Instead of being collected before the celebration of the Lord's Supper, as in the above order, the tithes and offerings may be gathered after the Communion, in thanksgiving for receiving Christ in the Sacrament.

The Words of Institution are to be included in one of the following places in the order:

1. before the great thanksgiving as a warrant;
2. within the great thanksgiving in thanksgiving to God for the gift of the Sacrament;
3. as words to accompany the breaking of the bread.

The words of institution are said only once in a service.

Announcements Some congregations will choose to provide all necessary announcements in a bulletin and expect members to read them, without any mention being made as a part of worship. If announcements are made in worship, they should be brief, and appropriately placed in the order:

1. Words of welcome may be extended following the greeting at the beginning of the service and before the sentences from scripture.
2. Notices about needs or concerns for which prayer will be offered may be briefly stated immediately before the prayers of the people.
3. Notices concerning the life and ministry of the church may be briefly stated immediately before the blessing and charge at the end of the service.

Charge and Blessing

1. The charge may be said immediately before the blessing, as in the above order, the minister giving both charge and blessing.
2. The charge may follow the blessing. When the charge follows the blessing, the **Alleluia** is omitted following the blessing, and the people may respond to the charge: **Thanks be to God. Alleluia!** (**Alleluia** is traditionally omitted during Lent.) The blessing is spoken by the minister. The charge may be spoken by a deacon, an elder, or the minister.

Procession If there is a procession of the choir, minister(s) and other leaders of worship during the final hymn, the hymn may follow the charge and blessing.

Additional Texts for the Service for the Lord's Day

Prayer of Confession

Other prayers of confession may be found on pages 53–54. Prayers of confession for festivals and seasons may be found on pages 165–400.

1

Eternal God,
in whom we live and move and have our being,
whose face is hidden from us by our sins,
and whose mercy we forget in the blindness of our hearts:
Cleanse us from all our offenses,
and deliver us from proud thoughts and vain desires,
that with reverent and humble hearts
we may draw near to you,
confessing our faults,
confiding in your grace,
and finding in you our refuge and strength;
through Jesus Christ your Son. [67]

2

Almighty and merciful God,
we have erred and strayed from your ways like lost sheep.
We have followed too much
the devices and desires of our own hearts.
We have offended against your holy laws.
We have left undone those things which we ought to have done;
and we have done those things which we ought not to have done.

O Lord, have mercy upon us.
Spare those who confess their faults.
Restore those who are penitent,
according to your promises declared to the world
in Christ Jesus our Lord.
And grant, O merciful God, for his sake,
that we may live a holy, just, and humble life
to the glory of your holy name.   [68]

3

Gracious God,
our sins are too heavy to carry,
too real to hide,
and too deep to undo.
Forgive what our lips tremble to name,
what our hearts can no longer bear,
and what has become for us
a consuming fire of judgment.

Set us free from a past that we cannot change;
open to us a future in which we can be changed;
and grant us grace
to grow more and more in your likeness and image;
through Jesus Christ, the light of the world.   [69]

4

Merciful God,
in your gracious presence
we confess our sin and the sin of this world.
Although Christ is among us as our peace,
we are a people divided against ourselves
as we cling to the values of a broken world.
The profit and pleasures we pursue
lay waste the land and pollute the seas.
The fears and jealousies that we harbor
set neighbor against neighbor
and nation against nation.
We abuse your good gifts of imagination and freedom,
of intellect and reason,
and have turned them into bonds of oppression.

Lord, have mercy upon us;
heal and forgive us.
Set us free to serve you in the world
as agents of your reconciling love in Jesus Christ.   [70]

5

Almighty God,
you love us, but we have not loved you.
You call, but we have not listened.
We walk away from neighbors in need,
wrapped in our own concerns.
We condone evil, prejudice, warfare, and greed.

God of grace,
help us to admit our sin,
so that as you come to us in mercy,
we may repent, turn to you, and receive forgiveness;
through Jesus Christ our Redeemer.   [71]

6

Merciful God,
we confess that we have not loved you with our whole heart.
We have failed to be an obedient church.
We have not done your will,
we have broken your law,
we have rebelled against your love.
We have not loved our neighbors,
and we have refused to hear the cry of the needy.

Forgive us, we pray.
Free us for joyful obedience;
through Jesus Christ our Lord.   [72]

7

The pastor may offer a prayer that carefully and with pastoral sensitivity includes the confession of sins arising from pastoral care during the preceding days. The prayer must avoid any appearance of judgment, but be clearly understood as a means of engaging persons in making a confession that touches their lives. The prayer will include silence after each petition to provide for silent personal confession. The prayer closes with a strong affirmation of trust in the forgiving grace of a loving God.

PRAYER FOR ILLUMINATION

Other prayers for illumination may be found on page 60.

1

Guide us, O God,
by your Word and Spirit,
that in your light we may see light,
in your truth find freedom,
and in your will discover your peace;
through Jesus Christ our Lord.   **Amen.**   [73]

2

Gracious God,
we do not live by bread alone,
but by every word that comes from your mouth.
Make us hungry for this heavenly food,
that it may nourish us today
in the ways of eternal life;
through Jesus Christ, the bread of heaven.   **Amen.**   [74]

3

God our helper,
by your Holy Spirit, open our minds,
that as the Scriptures are read
and your Word is proclaimed,
we may be led into your truth
and taught your will,
for the sake of Jesus Christ our Lord.   **Amen.**   [75]

4

Living God,
help us so to hear your holy Word
that we may truly understand;
that, understanding, we may believe,
and, believing,
we may follow in all faithfulness and obedience,
seeking your honor and glory in all that we do;
through Christ our Lord.   **Amen.**   [76]

5

God, source of all light,
by your Word you give light to the soul.
Pour out upon us
the spirit of wisdom and understanding
that, being taught by you in Holy Scripture,
our hearts and minds may be opened to know the things
that pertain to life and holiness;
through Jesus Christ our Lord. **Amen.** [77]

6

God of mercy,
you promised never to break your covenant with us.
Amid all the changing words of our generation,
speak your eternal Word that does not change.
Then may we respond to your gracious promises
with faithful and obedient lives;
through our Lord Jesus Christ. **Amen.** [78]

7

Blessed Lord,
who caused all holy scriptures to be written for our learning:
Grant us so to hear them,
read, mark, learn, and inwardly digest them,
that we may embrace and ever hold fast
the blessed hope of everlasting life,
which you have given us in our Savior Jesus Christ. **Amen.** [79]

ASCRIPTION OF PRAISE

The following verses from scripture ascribe glory to God. One may be
used by the preacher as a prayer at the conclusion of the sermon. Other ascriptions of praise may be found on pages 62–63.

1   *Eph. 3:20, 21*

Now to the One
who by the power at work within us
is able to do far more abundantly
than all we can ask or imagine,
to God be glory in the church
and in Christ Jesus
to all generations, forever and ever. **Amen.**

2 *Rev. 5:12*

Worthy is the Lamb who was slain,
to receive power and wealth
and wisdom and might
and honor and glory and blessing!   **Amen.**

3 *1 Tim. 6:15, 16*

To the blessed and only Sovereign,
the King of kings
and Lord of lords,
who alone has immortality
and dwells in unapproachable light,
be honor and eternal dominion.   **Amen.**

4 *Rom. 11:33, 36*

O the depth of the riches and wisdom and knowledge of God!
How unsearchable are God's judgments
and how inscrutable God's ways!
For from God
and through God
and to God are all things.
To God be glory forever.   **Amen.**

5 *1 Peter 5:10, 11*

To the God of all grace,
who calls you to share God's eternal glory
in union with Christ,
be the power forever!   **Amen.**

INVITATION TO DISCIPLESHIP

1 *Acts 2:38, 39*

Peter said:
Repent, and be baptized in the name of Jesus Christ
so that your sins may be forgiven;
and you will receive the gift of the Holy Spirit.
For the promise is for you, for your children,
and for all who are far away,
everyone whom the Lord our God calls to him.

2 *Matt. 11:28, 29, 30*

Jesus said:
Come to me,
all you that are weary and are carrying heavy burdens,
and I will give you rest.
Take my yoke upon you, and learn from me;
for I am gentle and humble in heart,
and you will find rest for your souls.
For my yoke is easy,
and my burden is light.

3 *Rom. 12:1, 2*

I appeal to you therefore, brothers and sisters,
by the mercies of God,
to present your bodies as a living sacrifice,
holy and acceptable to God,
which is your spiritual worship.
Do not be conformed to this world,
but be transformed by the renewing of your minds,
so that you may discern what is the will of God,
what is good and acceptable and perfect.

4 *Rev. 3:20*

Jesus said:
Behold, I stand at the door and knock;
if you hear my voice and open the door,
I will come in to you and eat with you,
and you with me.

5 *Matt. 7:7; Luke 11:9*

Jesus said:
Ask, and you will receive;
seek, and you will find;
knock, and the door will be opened to you.

God abounds in love and mercy
and welcomes our return,
for in Christ, God came to us
that we might have abundant life.

Affirmation of Faith

The Nicene Creed (p. 64) is ordinarily said when the Eucharist is celebrated.

The Apostles' Creed (p. 65) is said when Baptism is celebrated, on the occasion of the public profession of faith by baptized persons, or other reaffirmation of the baptismal covenant. The Creed is included in each of these rites. It is also appropriately said when new members are welcomed.

On days when neither sacrament is celebrated, the people may say or sing either the Nicene Creed (p. 64) or the Apostles' Creed (p. 65). Or part of A Brief Statement of Faith (1) or another portion of the Book of Confessions may be said. Or an affirmation of faith drawn from scripture such as those which follow (2–4) may be said.

1

A Brief Statement of Faith

Care needs to be taken in extracting portions of A Brief Statement of Faith for liturgical use. In a given service, normally the opening paragraph will be used, followed by either the second, third, or fourth paragraph, ending with the concluding sentences.

In life and in death we belong to God.
  Through the grace of our Lord Jesus Christ,
    the love of God,
      and the communion of the Holy Spirit,
  we trust in the one triune God, the Holy One of Israel,
    whom alone we worship and serve.

We trust in Jesus Christ,
    fully human, fully God.
  Jesus proclaimed the reign of God:
    preaching good news to the poor
      and release to the captives,
    teaching by word and deed
      and blessing the children,
    healing the sick
      and binding up the brokenhearted,
    eating with outcasts,
    forgiving sinners,
      and calling all to repent and believe the gospel.
  Unjustly condemned for blasphemy and sedition,

Jesus was crucified,
  suffering the depths of human pain
  and giving his life for the sins of the world.
God raised this Jesus from the dead,
  vindicating his sinless life,
  breaking the power of sin and evil,
  delivering us from death to life eternal.

We trust in God,
  whom Jesus called Abba Father.
In sovereign love God created the world good
  and makes everyone equally in God's image,
    male and female, of every race and people,
  to live as one community.
But we rebel against God; we hide from our Creator.
  Ignoring God's commandments,
  we violate the image of God in others and ourselves,
  accept lies as truth,
  exploit neighbor and nature,
  and threaten death to the planet entrusted to our care.
  We deserve God's condemnation.
Yet God acts with justice and mercy to redeem creation.
  In everlasting love,
    the God of Abraham and Sarah chose a covenant people
      to bless all families of the earth.
  Hearing their cry,
    God delivered the children of Israel
      from the house of bondage.
  Loving us still,
    God makes us heirs with Christ of the covenant.
  Like a mother who will not forsake her nursing child,
  like a father who runs to welcome the prodigal home,
    God is faithful still.

We trust in God the Holy Spirit,
  everywhere the giver and renewer of life.
The Spirit justifies us by grace through faith,
  sets us free to accept ourselves and to love God and neighbor,
  and binds us together with all believers
  in the one body of Christ, the church.
The same Spirit
  who inspired the prophets and apostles
  rules our faith and life in Christ through Scripture,
  engages us through the Word proclaimed,

claims us in the waters of baptism,
feeds us with the bread of life and the cup of salvation,
and calls women and men to all ministries of the church.
In a broken and fearful world
the Spirit gives us courage
to pray without ceasing,
to witness among all peoples to Christ as Lord and Savior,
to unmask idolatries in church and culture,
to hear the voices of peoples long silenced,
and to work with others for justice, freedom, and peace.
In gratitude to God, empowered by the Spirit,
we strive to serve Christ in our daily tasks
and to live holy and joyful lives,
even as we watch for God's new heaven and new earth,
praying, "Come, Lord Jesus!"

With believers in every time and place,
we rejoice that nothing in life or in death
can separate us from the love of God in Christ Jesus our Lord.

Glory to the Father, and to the Son, and to the Holy Spirit. Amen.*

*Instead of saying this line, congregations may wish to sing a version of the
"Glory to the Father" (Gloria Patri), PH 567, 577–579.

2   *See 1 Cor. 15:1–6; Mark 16:9 (16:1–9);*
Matt. 16:16; Rev. 22:13; John 20:28

This is the good news which we have received,
in which we stand,
and by which we are saved,
if we hold it fast:
that Christ died for our sins
according to the scriptures,
that he was buried,
that he was raised on the third day,
and that he appeared
first to the women,
then to Peter, and to the Twelve,
and then to many faithful witnesses.

We believe that Jesus is the Christ,
the Son of the living God.
Jesus Christ is the first and the last,
the beginning and the end;
he is our Lord and our God.   Amen.

3   *Col. 1:15–20*

Jesus Christ is the image of the invisible God,
the firstborn of all creation;
in him all things in heaven and on earth were created,
things visible and invisible.

All things have been created through him and for him.
He himself is before all things,
and in him all things hold together.

He is head of the body, the church;
he is the beginning,
the firstborn of the dead,
so that he might come to have first place in everything.

For in him all the fullness of God was pleased to dwell,
and through him God was pleased to reconcile all things,
whether on earth or in heaven,
by making peace through the blood of his cross.   Amen.

4   *Phil. 2:5–11*

Christ Jesus,
though he was in the form of God,
did not regard equality with God
as something to be exploited,
but emptied himself,
taking the form of a slave,
being born in human likeness.
And being found in human form
he humbled himself
and became obedient to the point of death—
even death on a cross.

Therefore God also highly exalted him
and gave him the name that is above every name,
so that at the name of Jesus
every knee should bend,
in heaven and on earth and under the earth,
and every tongue should confess to the glory of God:
Jesus Christ is Lord!   Amen.

We believe there is no condemnation
for those who are in Christ Jesus;
for we know that all things work together for good
for those who love God,
who are called according to God's purpose.
We are convinced that neither death, nor life,
nor angels, nor rulers,
nor things present, nor things to come,
nor powers, nor height, nor depth,
nor anything else in all creation,
will be able to separate us from the love of God
in Christ Jesus our Lord.   Amen.

PRAYERS OF THE PEOPLE

The congregation prays for worldwide and local concerns, offering intercessions for:

> the church universal, its ministry and those who minister,
> > including ecumenical councils, churches in other places,
> > this congregation;
>
> the nations and those in authority;
> peace and justice in the world;
> the earth and a right use of its resources;
> the community and those who govern;
> the poor and the oppressed;
> the sick, the bereaved, the lonely, all who suffer in body,
> > mind, or spirit;
>
> those with special needs.
> Those who have died are remembered with thanksgiving.

The prayers are to be offered in a manner that engages the people in prayer. They may be prepared by the one leading the prayers, and offered in a free style. Or one of the forms that follow may be used. In using any of these forms, appropriate petitions and concerns may be selected, and others added. Or similar prayers may be prepared using these forms as models.

PRAYERS OF THE PEOPLE: A

Almighty God,
in Jesus Christ you taught us to pray,
and to offer our petitions to you in his name.
Guide us by your Holy Spirit,
that our prayers for others may serve your will
and show your steadfast love;
through the same Jesus Christ our Lord.   **Amen.**   [80]

Let us pray for the world.

> Silent prayer.

God our creator,
you made all things in your wisdom,
and in your love you save us.
We pray for the whole creation.
Overthrow evil powers, right what is wrong,
feed and satisfy those who thirst for justice,
so that all your children may freely enjoy the earth you have made,
and joyfully sing your praises;
through Jesus Christ our Lord.   **Amen.**   [81]

Let us pray for the church.

> Silent prayer.

Gracious God,
you have called us to be the church of Jesus Christ.
Keep us one in faith and service,
breaking bread together,
and proclaiming the good news to the world,
that all may believe you are love,
turn to your ways,
and live in the light of your truth;
through Jesus Christ our Lord.   **Amen.**   [82]

Let us pray for peace.

> Silent prayer.

Eternal God,
you sent us a Savior, Christ Jesus,
to break down the walls of hostility that divide us.
Send peace on earth,
and put down greed, pride, and anger,
which turn nation against nation and race against race.
Speed the day when wars will end
and the whole world accepts your rule;
through Jesus Christ our Lord.   **Amen.**   [83]

Let us pray for enemies.

> Silent prayer.

O God,
whom we cannot love unless we love our neighbors,
remove hate and prejudice from us and from all people,
so that your children may be reconciled
with those we fear, resent, or threaten;
and live together in your peace;
through Jesus Christ our Lord.   **Amen.**   [84]

Let us pray for those who govern us.

> Silent prayer.

Mighty God,
sovereign over the nations,
direct those who make, administer, and judge our laws;
the President of the United States
and others in authority among us (especially N., N.);
that, guided by your wisdom,
they may lead us in the way of righteousness;
through Jesus Christ our Lord.   **Amen.**   [85]

Let us pray for world leaders.

    Silent prayer.

Eternal Ruler, hope of all the earth,
give vision to those who serve the United Nations,
and to those who govern all countries;
that, with goodwill and justice,
they may take down barriers,
and draw together one new world in peace;
through Jesus Christ our Lord.   **Amen.**   [86]

Let us pray for the sick.

    Silent prayer.

Merciful God,
you bear the pain of the world.
Look with compassion on those who are sick
(especially on N., N.);
cheer them by your word,
and bring healing as a sign of your grace;
through Jesus Christ our Lord.   **Amen.**   [87]

Let us pray for those who sorrow.

    Silent prayer.

God of comfort,
stand with those who sorrow (especially N., N.);
that they may be sure that neither death nor life,
nor things present nor things to come,
shall separate them from your love;
through Jesus Christ our Lord.   **Amen.**   [88]
Let us pray for friends and families.

Silent prayer.

God of compassion,
bless us and those we love,
our friends and families;
that, drawing close to you,
we may be drawn closer to each other;
through Jesus Christ our Lord.   **Amen.**   [89]

Other petitions may be added in the same manner.

Following all of the petitions, the following commemoration of those who
have died in the faith, or a similar commemoration (pp. 121–122), may be said.

God of all generations,
we praise you for all your servants
who, having been faithful to you on earth,
now live with you in heaven.
Keep us in fellowship with them,
until we meet with all your children
in the joy of your eternal kingdom;
through Jesus Christ our Lord.   **Amen.**   [90]

The leader concludes the prayers with the following prayer, another brief
collect (pp. 123–124), or the prayer of the day (pp. 165–400).

Mighty God,
whose Word we trust,
whose Spirit enables us to pray:
Accept our requests
and further those which will bring about your purpose for the earth;
through Jesus Christ, who rules over all things.   **Amen.**   [91]

Gracious God,
because we are not strong enough
to pray as we should,
you provide Christ Jesus and the Holy Spirit
to intercede for us in power.
In this confidence we ask you
to accept our prayers.

God of mercy,

hear our prayer.

Let us pray for the church.

> Silent prayer.

Faithful God,
you formed your church from the despised of the earth
and showed them mercy,
that they might proclaim your salvation to all.
Strengthen those whom you choose today,
that they may faithfully endure all trials
by which you conform your church to the cross of Christ.

God of mercy,

hear our prayer.

Let us pray for creation.

> Silent prayer.

Creator of all,
you entrusted the earth to the human race,
yet we disrupt its peace with violence
and corrupt its purity with our greed.
Prevent your people from ravaging creation,
that coming generations
may inherit lands brimming with life.

God of mercy,

hear our prayer.

Let us pray for the world.

Silent prayer.

Sovereign God,
you hold both the history of nations
and the humble life of villages in your care.
Preserve the people of every nation from tyrants,
heal them of disease,
and protect them in time of upheaval and disaster,
that all may enter the kingdom that cannot be shaken.

God of mercy,
hear our prayer.

Let us pray for peace.

Silent prayer.

Judge of the nations,
you created humanity for salvation,
not destruction,
and sent your Son to guide us
into the way of peace.
Enable people of every race and nation
to accept each other as sisters and brothers,
your children, on whom you lavish honor and favor.

God of mercy,
hear our prayer.

Let us pray for those who govern us.

Silent prayer.

God Most High,
in Jesus of Nazareth you show us the authority that pleases you:
for he rules not by power or might,
but serves in obedience to your will.
We pray for all in authority over us:
for our President, N., for Congress,
for our Governor, N., and our state legislature, (and N., N.).
Deliver them from vain ambitions
that they may govern in wisdom and justice.

God of mercy,
hear our prayer.

Let us pray for this community.

Silent prayer.

Merciful God,
since Jesus longed to protect Jerusalem
as a hen gathers her young under her wings,
we ask you to guard and strengthen all who live and work here.
Deliver your people from jealousy and contempt
that they may show mercy to all their neighbors.

God of mercy,

hear our prayer.

Let us pray for all families
and those who live alone.

Silent prayer.

Holy God,
from whom every family on earth takes its name:
Strengthen parents to be responsible and loving
that their children may know security and joy.
Lead children to honor parents
by compassion and forgiveness.
May all people discover your parental care
by the respect and love given them by others.

God of mercy,

hear our prayer.

Let us pray for all who suffer any sorrow or trial.

Silent prayer.

Compassionate God,
your Son gives rest to those weary with heavy burdens.
Heal the sick in body, mind, and spirit.
Lift up the depressed.
Befriend those who grieve.
Comfort the anxious.
Stand with all victims of abuse and other crime.

Awaken those who damage themselves and others
through the use of any drug.
Fill all people with your Holy Spirit
that they may bear each other's burdens
and so fulfill the law of Christ.

God of mercy,

hear our prayer.

Let us give thanks for the lives of the departed
who now have rest in God.

> Silent prayer.

Eternal God,
your love is stronger than death,
and your passion more fierce than the grave.
We rejoice in the lives of those
whom you have drawn into your eternal embrace.
Keep us in joyful communion with them
until we join the saints of every people and nation,
gathered before your throne in ceaseless praise.

God of glory,
you see how all creation groans in labor
as it awaits redemption.
As we work for and await your new creation,
we trust that you will answer our prayers with grace,
and fulfill your promise
that all things work together for good
for those who love you;
through Jesus Christ our Lord. **Amen.** [92]

As God's people, called to love one another,
let us pray for the needs of the church,
the whole human family,
and all the world, saying: Hear our prayer.

That churches of all traditions,
may discover their unity in Christ
and exercise their gifts in service of all,
we pray to you, O God:

Hear our prayer.

That the earth may be freed
from war, famine, and disease,
and the air, soil, and waters cleansed of poison,
we pray to you, O God:

Hear our prayer.

That those who govern and maintain peace in every land
may exercise their powers in obedience to your commands,
we pray to you, O God:

Hear our prayer.

That you will strengthen this nation to pursue just priorities
so that the races may be reconciled;
the young, educated; and the old, cared for;
the hungry, filled; and the homeless, housed;
and the sick, comforted and healed,
we pray to you, O God:

Hear our prayer.

That you will preserve all who live and work
in this city (town, village, community)
in peace and safety,
we pray to you, O God:

Hear our prayer.

That you will comfort and empower
those who face any difficulty or trial:
the sick (especially N., N.),
the disabled, the poor, the oppressed,
those who grieve and those in prison,
we pray to you, O God:

Hear our prayer.

That_____,
we pray to you, O God:

Hear our prayer.

That you will accept our thanksgiving
for all faithful servants of Christ now at rest,
who, with us, await a new heaven and a new earth,
your everlasting kingdom,
we pray to you, O God:

Hear our prayer.

Merciful God,
as a potter fashions a vessel from humble clay,
you form us into a new creation.
Shape us, day by day,
through the cross of Christ your Son,
until we pray as continually as we breathe
and all our acts are prayer;
through Jesus Christ
and in the mystery of the Holy Spirit, we pray.   **Amen.**   [93]

Let us bring the needs of the church,
the world, and all in need,
to God's loving care, saying:
Lord, in your mercy, hear our prayer.

God of heaven and earth,
through Jesus Christ you promise to hear us
when we pray to you in his name.
Confident in your love and mercy
we offer our prayer.

Lord, in your mercy,

hear our prayer.

Empower the church throughout the world in its life and witness.
Break down the barriers that divide,
that, united in your truth and love,
the church may confess your name,
share one baptism,
sit together at one table,
and serve you in one common ministry.

Lord, in your mercy,

hear our prayer.

Guide the rulers of the nations.
Move them to set aside their fear, greed, and vain ambition,
and bow to your sovereign rule.
Inspire them to strive for peace and justice,
that all your children may dwell secure,
free of war and injustice.

Lord, in your mercy,

hear our prayer.

Hear the cries of the world's hungry and suffering.
Give us, who consume most of the earth's resources,
the will to reorder our lives,
that all may have their rightful share of the food,
medical care, and shelter,
and so have the necessities of a life of dignity.

Lord, in your mercy,
hear our prayer.

Restore among us a love of the earth you created for our home.
Help us put an end to ravishing its land, air, and waters,
and give us respect for all your creatures,
that, living in harmony with everything you have made,
your whole creation may resound in an anthem of praise
to your glorious name.

Lord, in your mercy,

hear our prayer.

Renew our nation in the ways of justice and peace.
Guide those who make and administer our laws
to build a society based on trust and respect.
Erase prejudices that oppress;
free us from crime and violence;
guard our youth from the perils of drugs and materialism.
Give all citizens a new vision of a life of harmony.

Lord, in your mercy,

hear our prayer.

Strengthen this congregation in its work and worship.
Fill our hearts with your self-giving love,
that our voices may speak your praise,
and our lives may conform to the image of your Son.
Nourish us with your Word and sacraments
that we may faithfully minister in your name,
and witness to your love and grace for all the world.

Lord, in your mercy,

hear our prayer.

Look with compassion on all who suffer.
Support with your love
those with incurable and stigmatized diseases,
those unjustly imprisoned,
those denied dignity,
those who live without hope,
those who are homeless or abandoned.

As you have moved toward us in love,
so lead us to be present with them in their suffering
in the name of Jesus Christ.

Lord, in your mercy,

hear our prayer.

Sustain those among us who need your healing touch.
Make the sick whole [especially N., N.].
Give hope to the dying [especially N., N.].
Comfort those who mourn [especially N., N.].
Uphold all who suffer in body or mind,
not only those we know and love
but also those known only to you,
that they may know the peace and joy of your supporting care.

Lord, in your mercy,

hear our prayer.

> Other petitions may be added in the same manner.

> Following all of the petitions, this commemoration of those who have died
> in the faith, or a similar commemoration (pp. 121–122), may be said.

With thanksgiving we remember before you
those saints who bore witness to the light [especially N., N.].
Grant that we may persevere in the faith
to which we have been called
and at the end behold your glory.

> The leader concludes the prayers with the following prayer, another brief
> collect (pp. 123–124), or the prayer of the day (pp. 165–400).

O God,
in your loving purpose
answer our prayers and fulfill our hopes.
In all things for which we pray,
give us the will to seek to bring them about,
for the sake of Jesus Christ.   **Amen.**   [94]

PRAYERS OF THE PEOPLE: E

This litany is based on litanies from the Eastern liturgies of St. Basil and St. John Chrysostom. It may be sung using the following musical setting.

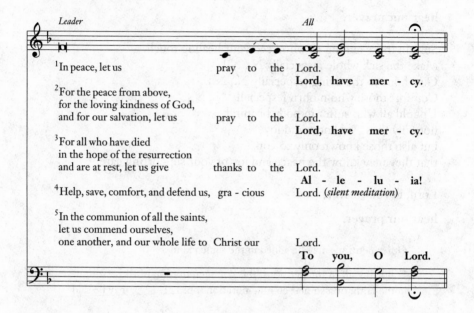

In peace, let us pray to the Lord.
Lord, have mer - cy.

For the peace from above,
for the loving kindness of God,
and for our salvation, let us pray to the Lord.
Lord, have mer - cy.

For all who have died
in the hope of the resurrection
and are at rest, let us give thanks to the Lord.
Al - le - lu - ia!

Help, save, comfort, and defend us, gra - cious Lord. (*silent meditation*)

In the communion of all the saints,
let us commend ourselves,
one another, and our whole life to Christ our Lord.
To you, O Lord.

[1]In peace, let us pray to the Lord.

Lord, have mercy.

[2]For the peace from above,
for the loving kindness of God,
and for our salvation,
let us pray to the Lord.

Lord, have mercy.

For the peace of the world,
for the unity of the church of God,
and for the well-being of all peoples,
let us pray to the Lord.

Lord, have mercy.

For this gathering of the faithful,
and for all who offer here their worship and praise,
let us pray to the Lord.

Lord, have mercy.

For all the baptized,
for all who serve in the church,
for bishops and pastors,
[for N.],
let us pray to the Lord.

Lord, have mercy.

For our president,
for the leaders of the nations,
and for all in authority,
let us pray to the Lord.

Lord, have mercy.

For this city (town, village, etc.),
for every city and community,
and for those who live in them,
let us pray to the Lord.

Lord, have mercy.

For seasonable weather,
and for abundant harvests for all to share,
let us pray to the Lord.

Lord, have mercy.

For the good earth which God has given us,
and for the wisdom and will to conserve it,
let us pray to the Lord.

Lord, have mercy.

For those who travel by land, water, or air
[or through outer space],
let us pray to the Lord.

Lord, have mercy.

For the aged and infirm,
for the widowed and orphaned,
and for the sick and the suffering,
let us pray to the Lord.

Lord, have mercy.

For the poor and the oppressed,
for those unemployed and the destitute,
for prisoners and captives,
and for all who remember and care for them,
let us pray to the Lord.

Lord, have mercy.

For deliverance in times of affliction,
strife, and need,
let us pray to the Lord.

Lord, have mercy.

> Other petitions may be added.

For_____ ,
let us pray to the Lord.

Lord, have mercy.

> Here follows commemoration of those who have died in the faith:

[3]For all who have died in the hope of the resurrection
and are at rest,
let us give thanks to the Lord.

Alleluia! (*Lent:* **To you, O Lord.**)

[4]Help, save, comfort, and defend us, gracious Lord.

> Pause for silent prayer.

[5]In the communion of all the saints,
let us commend ourselves,
one another,
and our whole life to Christ our Lord.   [95]

To you, O Lord.

> After a brief silence, the leader concludes the prayers with the following
> prayer, another brief collect (pp. 123–124), or the prayer of the day (pp. 165–
> 400). This prayer may be spoken, even though the litany itself is sung.

Almighty God,
you have given us grace at this time with one accord
to make our common supplication to you;
and you have promised through your beloved Son
that when two or three are gathered together in his name
you will be in the midst of them.
Fulfill now, O Lord, our desires and petitions
as may be best for us,
granting us in this world knowledge of your truth,
and in the age to come life everlasting.   **Amen.**   [96]

Prayers of the People: F

In peace, let us pray to the Lord, saying: "Lord, have mercy."

For the holy church of God,
that it may be filled with truth and love,
and be found without fault at the day of your coming,
we pray to you, O Lord.

Here and after every petition, the people respond:

Lord, have mercy.

For leaders of the church,
for our minister(s), and all ministers,
and for all the holy people of God,
we pray to you, O Lord.

For all who fear God and believe in you, Lord Christ,
that our divisions may cease,
and that all may be one as you and the Father are one,
we pray to you, O Lord.

For the mission of the church,
that in faithful witness
it may preach the gospel to the ends of the earth,
we pray to you, O Lord.

For those who do not yet believe,
and those who have lost their faith,
that they may receive the light of the gospel,
we pray to you, O Lord.

For the peace of the world,
that a spirit of respect and forbearance
may grow among nations and peoples,
we pray to you, O Lord.

For those in positions of public trust (especially N., N.),
that they may serve justice,
and promote the dignity and freedom of every person,
we pray to you, O Lord.

For all who live and work in this community (especially N., N.),
we pray to you, O Lord.

For a blessing upon all human labor,
and for the right use of the riches of creation,
that the world may be freed from poverty, famine, and disaster,
we pray to you, O Lord.

For the poor, the persecuted, and all who suffer;
for refugees, prisoners, and all who are in danger;
that they may be relieved and protected,
we pray to you, O Lord.

For this congregation
[for those who are present, and for those who are absent],
that we may be delivered from hardness of heart,
and show forth your glory in all that we do,
we pray to you, O Lord.

For our enemies and those who wish us harm;
and for all whom we have injured or offended,
we pray to you, O Lord.

For ourselves;
for the forgiveness of our sins,
and for the grace of the Holy Spirit to amend our lives,
we pray to you, O Lord.

For our families, friends, and neighbors;
that, being freed from anxiety,
they may live in joy, peace, and health,
we pray to you, O Lord.

For _____ , we pray to you, O Lord.

For all who have died in the communion of your church,
that, strengthened by their witness,
we may be grateful for their example,
living in justice and love
until we join them in life eternal,
we pray to you, O Lord.

Rejoicing in the fellowship of all the saints,
let us entrust ourselves, and one another,
and all of life to Christ our God.

To you, O Lord our God.

Silence.

The prayers are concluded with the following acclamation, a concluding
prayer (pp. 123–124), or the prayer of the day (pp. 165–400):

Yours is the majesty, O God, holy and eternal;
yours is the kingdom, and the power, and the glory,
now and forever. **Amen.** [97]

PRAYERS OF THE PEOPLE: G

Almighty God,
you have promised to hear
when we pray in the name of your Son.
Therefore in confidence and trust
we pray for the church.

> Particular intercessions/thanksgivings may be offered.

O God, enliven the church for its mission

that we may be salt of the earth and light to the world.

Breathe fresh life into your people.

Give us power to reveal Christ in word and action.

We pray for the world.

> Particular intercessions/thanksgivings may be offered.

Creator of all,
lead us and every people into ways of justice and peace,

that we may respect one another in freedom and truth.

Awaken in us a sense of wonder for the earth
and all that is in it.

Teach us to care creatively for its resources.

We pray for the community.

> Particular intercessions/thanksgivings may be offered.

God of truth,
inspire with your wisdom
those whose decisions affect the lives of others,

that all may act with integrity and courage.

Give grace to all whose lives are linked with ours.

**May we serve Christ in one another,
and love as he loves us.**

We pray for those in need.

Particular intercessions/thanksgivings may be offered.

God of hope,
comfort and restore all who suffer in body, mind, or spirit.

May they know the power of your healing love.

Make us willing agents of your compassion.

Strengthen us as we share in making people whole.

We remember those who have died and those who mourn.　　[98]

Particular intercessions/thanksgivings may be offered.

We remember with thanksgiving
those who have died in the faith of Christ,
and those whose faith is known to you alone.

Loving God, into your hands we commend them.

Give comfort to those who mourn.

Fill the emptiness of their loss with your never-ending peace.

We praise you for (N., N., and) all your saints
who have entered your eternal glory.

May their example inspire and encourage us.

We pray for ourselves and our ministries.

Particular intercessions/thanksgivings may be offered.

The prayers are concluded with the following prayer, a similar prayer (pp. 123–124), or the prayer of the day (pp. 165–400):

Lord, you have called us to serve you.

**Grant that we may minister in your name,
with your love in our hearts,
your truth in our minds,
your strength in our wills;
until, at the end of our journey,
we know the joy of our homecoming
and the welcome of your embrace;
through Jesus Christ our Lord.　Amen.**　　[99]

Almighty God,
who taught us to pray not only for ourselves
but for people everywhere,
hear us as we pray for others,
in the name of Jesus Christ.

Inspire the whole church with your power, unity, and peace.
Grant that all who trust you may obey your Word,
and live together in love.

Lead all nations in the way of justice and goodwill.
Direct those who govern,
that they may rule fairly, maintain order,
uphold those in need, and defend oppressed people;
that this world may claim your rule and know true peace.

Awaken all people to the danger we have inflicted upon the earth.
Implant in each a reverence for all you have made
that we may preserve the delicate balance
of creation for all coming generations.

Give grace to all who proclaim the gospel
through Word and Sacrament and deeds of mercy,
that by their teaching and example
they may reveal your love for all people.

Comfort and relieve, O Lord,
all who are in trouble . . .
sorrow . . . poverty . . . sickness . . . grief . . .
especially those known to us,
whom we name before you in silence. . . .
Heal them in body, mind, or circumstance,
working in them, by your grace,
wonders beyond all they may dream or hope.

Bring to our remembrance
all those who, having served you on earth,
now sing your praises eternally.
May their endurance give us courage
and their faithfulness give us hope;
through Jesus Christ our Savior.   **Amen.**   [100]

Commemoration of Those Who Have Died in the Faith

Other commemorations may be found on pages 102, 106, 111, and 116.

1

Eternal God,
we rejoice to know of all who, through the ages,
have placed their trust in you:
apostles, prophets, saints, and martyrs
and all the humble believers
whose names are long forgotten.
Give us the assurance
that we belong to that great company
and that we too may find the peace that passes understanding;
through Jesus Christ our Lord.   **Amen.**   [101]

2

Almighty God, we remember before you
those who have lived among us
who have directed our steps in the way,
opened our eyes to the truth,
inspired our hearts by their witness,
and strengthened our wills by their devotion.
We rejoice in their lives dedicated to your service.
We honor them in their death,
and pray that we may be united with them
in the glory of Christ's resurrection.   **Amen.**   [102]

3

We give you thanks, O God,
for all who have fought the good fight,
finished their race, and kept the faith,
and for those dear to us
who are at rest with you. . . .

Grant us grace to follow them
as they followed Christ.
Bring us, with them, to those things
which no eye has seen, nor ear heard,
which you have prepared for those who love you.
To your name,
with the church on earth and church in heaven,
we ascribe all honor and glory,
forever and ever.   **Amen.**   [103]

4

O God,
before your face the generations rise and pass away.
You are the strength of those who labor,
the rest of the blessed dead.
We rejoice in the company of your saints.
We remember all who have lived and died in faith,
and especially those dear to us who rest in you. . . .
Give us at length our portion with those who have trusted in you
and have striven to do your holy will.
To your name,
with the church on earth and the church in heaven,
we ascribe all honor and glory,
now and forever.   **Amen.**   [104]

5

Eternal God,
we remember with thanksgiving,
those who have loved and served you in your church on earth,
who now rest from their labors
[especially those most dear to us
whom we name in our hearts before you . . .].
Keep us in fellowship with all your saints,
and bring us at last
to the joy of your heavenly kingdom.   **Amen.**   [105]

6

Ever-faithful God,
you have knit together as one body in Christ
those who have been your people in all times and places.
Keep us in communion with your saints,
following their example of faith and life,
until that day when we shall dwell with them
in the joy of your eternal kingdom.   **Amen.**   [106]

PRAYERS OF THE PEOPLE: CONCLUDING COLLECTS

Other concluding collects may be found on pages 102, 106, 111, 114, 119.

1

Eternal God,
ruler of all things in heaven and earth,
accept the prayers of your people,
and strengthen us to do your will;
through Jesus Christ.   **Amen.**   [107]

2

Lord our God,
accept the fervent prayers of your people.
In your great mercy,
look with compassion on us
and all who turn to you for help,
for you are gracious, O lover of souls.
To you we give glory, O blessed Trinity,
now and forever.   **Amen.**   [108]

3

Hear our prayers, God of grace,
and help us to fulfill them,
working according to your purpose,
in peace, justice, and mercy,
in all we do;
through Jesus Christ the Lord.   **Amen.**   [109]

4

Into your hands, O God,
we commend all for whom we pray,
trusting in your mercy;
through Jesus Christ our Lord.   **Amen.**   [110]

5

O God,
who made of one blood all races and nations of earth,
and sent your Son Jesus Christ
to preach peace to those who are far off
and to those who are near:
Pour out your Spirit on the whole creation,
bring the nations of the world into your fellowship,
and hasten the coming of your kingdom;
through Jesus Christ our Lord.   **Amen.**   [111]

6

O God,
the author of peace and lover of concord,
to know you is eternal life,
to serve you is perfect freedom.
Guide us by your truth,
and order us in all our ways,
that we may always do what is right in your eyes;
through Jesus Christ our Lord.   **Amen.**   [112]

7

God of mercy,
you have promised to hear what we ask in the name of Christ.
Accept and fulfill our petitions, we pray,
not as we ask in our ignorance,
nor as we deserve in our sinfulness,
but as you know and love us in Jesus Christ our Lord.   **Amen.**   [113]

8

Eternal God,
you create us by your power
and redeem us by your love.
Guide and strengthen us by your Spirit,
that we may give ourselves in love and service
to one another and to you;
through Jesus Christ our Lord.   **Amen.**   [114]

INVITATION TO THE LORD'S TABLE

Other invitations to the Lord's table may be found on pages 68–69.

1   *Matt. 11:28, 29; John 6:35; Matt. 5:6*

Jesus said:

Come to me,
all you that are weary and are carrying heavy burdens,
and I will give you rest.
Take my yoke upon you, and learn from me;
for I am gentle and humble in heart,
and you will find rest for your souls.

I am the bread of life.
Whoever comes to me will never be hungry,
and whoever believes in me will never be thirsty.

Blessed are those who hunger and thirst for righteousness,
for they will be filled.

2   *Rev. 3:20; Ps. 34:8*

Jesus said:

Behold, I stand at the door and knock;
if those who hear my voice open the door,
I will come in to them and eat with them,
and they with me.

O taste and see that the Lord is good!
Happy are all who find refuge in God!

GREAT THANKSGIVING

Great thanksgivings for festivals and seasons may be found on pages 165–400.

Great thanksgiving A may be found on pages 69–73.

GREAT THANKSGIVING: B

The Lord be with you.

And also with you.

Lift up your hearts.

We lift them to the Lord.

Let us give thanks to the Lord our God.

It is right to give our thanks and praise.

Eternal God, holy and mighty,
it is truly right and our greatest joy
to give you thanks and praise,
and to worship you in every place where your glory abides.

> A preface appropriate to the day or season (pp. 133–137) may replace the bracketed portion that follows.

You laid the foundation of the earth,
and the heavens are the work of your hands.
They shall perish, but you shall endure.
You are always the same
and your years will never end.
You made us in your image
and called us to be your people,
but we turned from you,
leaving sin and death to reign.
Still you loved us and sought us.
In Christ your grace defeated death
and opened the way to eternal life.

Therefore we praise you,
joining our voices with the heavenly choirs
and with all the faithful of every time and place,
who forever sing to the glory of your name:

The people may sing or say:

**Holy, holy, holy Lord, God of power and might,
heaven and earth are full of your glory.
Hosanna in the highest.**

**Blessed is the One who comes in the name of the Lord.
Hosanna in the highest.**

The minister continues:

You are holy, O God of majesty,
and blessed is Jesus Christ, your Son, our Lord.
You sent your only-begotten,
in whom your fullness dwells,
to be for us the way, the truth, and the life.
Revealing your love,
Jesus taught those who would hear him,
healed those who believed in him,
received all who sought him
and lifted the burden of their sin.
We glorify you for your great power and love at work in Christ.
By the baptism of his suffering, death, and resurrection,
you gave birth to your church,
delivered us from slavery to sin and death,
and made us a new people by water and the Spirit.

> If they have not already been said, the words of institution may be
> said here, or in relation to the breaking of the bread.
>
> We give you thanks that the Lord Jesus,
> on the night before he died,
> took bread,
> and after giving thanks to you,
> he broke it, and gave it to his disciples, saying:
> Take, eat.
> This is my body, given for you.
> Do this in remembrance of me.
>
> In the same way he took the cup, saying:
> This cup is the new covenant sealed in my blood,
> shed for you for the forgiveness of sins.
> Whenever you drink it,
> do this in remembrance of me.

Remembering all your mighty and merciful acts,
we take this bread and this wine
from the gifts you have given us,
and celebrate with joy
the redemption won for us in Jesus Christ.
Accept this our sacrifice of praise and thanksgiving
as a living and holy offering of ourselves,
that our lives may proclaim the one crucified and risen.

The people may sing or say one of the following:

1

Great is the mystery of faith:

Christ has died,
Christ is risen,
Christ will come again.

2

Praise to you, Lord Jesus:

Dying you destroyed our death,
rising you restored our life.
Lord Jesus, come in glory.

3

According to his commandment:

We remember his death,
we proclaim his resurrection,
we await his coming in glory.

4

Christ is the bread of life:

When we eat this bread and drink this cup,
we proclaim your death, Lord Jesus,
until you come in glory.

The minister continues:

Gracious God,
pour out your Holy Spirit upon us
and upon these your gifts of bread and wine,
that the bread we break
and the cup we bless
may be the communion of the body and blood of Christ.
By your Spirit unite us with the living Christ
and with all who are baptized in his name,
that we may be one in ministry in every place.
As this bread is Christ's body for us,
send us out to be the body of Christ in the world.

Intercessions for the church and the world may be included here.

Help us, O God, to love as Christ loved.
Knowing our own weakness,
may we stand with all who stumble.
Sharing in his suffering,
may we remember all who suffer.
Held in his love,
may we embrace all whom the world denies.
Rejoicing in his forgiveness,
may we forgive all who sin against us.
Give us strength to serve you faithfully
until the promised day of resurrection,
when with the redeemed of all the ages
we will feast with you at your table in glory.

Through Christ, with Christ, in Christ,
in the unity of the Holy Spirit,
all glory and honor are yours, eternal God,
now and forever. **Amen.** [115]

GREAT THANKSGIVING: C

The Lord be with you.

And also with you.

Lift up your hearts.

We lift them to the Lord.

Let us give thanks to the Lord our God.

It is right to give our thanks and praise.

Holy God, Father almighty, Creator of heaven and earth,
with joy we praise you and give thanks to your name.

> A preface appropriate to the day or season (pp. 133–137) may replace the
> bracketed portion that follows.

You commanded light to shine out of darkness,
divided the sea and dry land,
created the vast universe and called it good.
You made us in your image
to live with one another in love.
You gave us the breath of life
and freedom to choose your way.
You promised yourself in covenant with Abraham and Sarah,
told us your purpose in commandments through Moses,
and called for justice in the cry of prophets.
Through long generations
you have been faithful and kind to all your children.

Great and wonderful are your works, Lord God almighty.
Your ways are just and true.

Therefore we lift our hearts in joyful praise,
joining our voices with choirs of angels,
and with all the faithful of every time and place,
who forever sing to the glory of your name:

> The people sing or say:

**Holy, holy, holy Lord, God of power and might,
heaven and earth are full of your glory.
Hosanna in the highest.**

Blessed is he who comes in the name of the Lord.
Hosanna in the highest.

We praise you, most holy God,
for sending your only Son to live among us, sharing our joy and sorrow.
He told your story, healed the sick, and was a friend of sinners.

Obeying you, he took up his cross and died that we might live.
We praise you that he overcame death and is risen to rule the world.
He is still the friend of sinners.
We trust him to overcome every power that can hurt or divide us,
and believe that when he comes in glory, we will celebrate victory with him.

> If they have not already been said, the words of institution may be
> said here, or in relation to the breaking of the bread.
>
> We give you thanks that the Lord Jesus,
> on the night before he died,
> took bread,
> and after giving thanks to you,
> he broke it, and gave it to his disciples, saying:
> Take, eat.
> This is my body, given for you.
> Do this in remembrance of me.
>
> In the same way he took the cup, saying:
> This cup is the new covenant sealed in my blood,
> shed for you for the forgiveness of sins.
> Whenever you drink it,
> do this in remembrance of me.

Remembering all your mighty and merciful acts,
we break bread and share one cup
giving thanks for your saving love in Jesus Christ.
As you raised our Lord from death
and call us with him from death to life,
we give ourselves to you
to live for him in joy and grateful praise.

The people may sing or say one of the following:

1

Great is the mystery of faith:

Christ has died,
Christ is risen,
Christ will come again.

2

Praise to you, Lord Jesus:

Dying you destroyed our death,
rising you restored our life.
Lord Jesus, come in glory.

3

According to his commandment:

We remember his death,
we proclaim his resurrection,
we await his coming in glory.

4

Christ is the bread of life:

When we eat this bread and drink this cup,
we proclaim your death, Lord Jesus,
until you come in glory.

The minister continues:

Gracious God, pour out your Holy Spirit upon us
and upon these your gifts of bread and wine.
Make them be for us the body and blood of Christ
that we may be for the world
the body of Christ, redeemed by his blood.
Send us out in the power of the Spirit
to live for others, as Christ lived for us,
announcing his death for the sins of the world,
and telling his resurrection to all people and nations.
By your Spirit draw us together into one body
and join us to Christ the Lord,
that we may remain his glad and faithful people
until we feast with him in glory.

Through Christ, with Christ, in Christ, in the unity of the Holy Spirit,
all glory and honor are yours, almighty God,
forever and ever.   **Amen.**   [116]

For use with great thanksgivings B and C.

Ordinary Time I

You commanded light to shine out of darkness,
divided the sea and dry land,
created the vast universe and called it good.
You made us in your image to live with one another in love.
You gave us the breath of life and freedom to choose your way.
You promised yourself in covenant with Abraham and Sarah,
told us your purpose in commandments through Moses,
and called for justice in the cry of prophets.
Through long generations
you have been faithful and kind to all your children.

Ordinary Time II

You laid the foundation of the earth,
and the heavens are the work of your hands.
They shall perish, but you shall endure.
You are always the same and your years will never end.
You made us in your image
and called us to be your people,
but we turned from you,
leaving sin and death to reign.
Still you loved us and sought us.
In Christ your grace defeated death
and opened the way to eternal life.   ·

Ordinary Time III (Unity or Worldwide Church; World Communion Sunday)

You formed the universe in your wisdom,
and created all things by your power.
You set us in families on the earth
to live with you in faith.
We praise you for good gifts of bread and wine,
and for the table you spread in the world
as a sign of your love for all people in Christ.

Advent

Through the words of the prophets
you promised your people the Redeemer,
and gave hope for the day
when justice shall roll down like waters,
and righteousness like an ever-flowing stream.

We rejoice that in Jesus Christ, your Son, the Savior has come
and that he will come again in power and glory
to make all things new.

Christmas

In sending us your Son, Jesus, to be born of Mary,
your Word became flesh,
and we have seen a new and radiant vision of your glory.
His name is above every name,
the Prince of peace and Savior of all.
In him we have been brought out of darkness
into your marvelous light.

Epiphany

In sending Christ the Light of the world,
you revealed your glory to the nations.
You sent a star to guide seekers of wisdom to Bethlehem,
that they might worship Christ.
Your signs and witnesses in every age
lead people from every place to worship him.
We praise you that in him we become your children,
baptized into your service.

Baptism of the Lord

In being baptized by John in Jordan's waters,
Jesus took his place with sinners
and your voice proclaimed him as your Son.
Like a dove, your Spirit descended on him,
anointing him as the Christ,
to bring good news to the poor
and proclaim release to the captives;
to restore sight to the blind
and free the oppressed.
We praise you that in our baptism
we are joined to Christ
and, with all the baptized,
are called to share his ministry.

Transfiguration of the Lord

On the holy mountain,
the divine glory of the incarnate Word was revealed.
From the heavens your voice proclaimed your beloved Son,
who is the fulfillment of the law and the prophets.
We rejoice in the divine majesty of Christ,
whose glory shone forth even when confronted with the cross.

Lent

We need not hide ourselves from you,
before whose justice no one can stand.
Your mercy was proclaimed by the apostles and the prophets,
and shown forth to us in Jesus Christ.
You give your law to guide us, and you promise new life for all,
that we may live to serve you among our neighbors
in all we do and say.

Passion/Palm Sunday

Your Son Jesus fulfilled the prophets' words
and entered the city of Jerusalem,
where he was lifted high upon the cross,
that the whole world might be drawn to him.
By his suffering and death
he defeated the power of death
becoming the source of eternal life.
The tree of defeat became the tree of victory;
where life was lost, life has been restored.

Maundy Thursday

Your Son Jesus came as a servant
to wash away our pride and feed us with the bread of life.
We praise you for inviting us
to serve one another without pride,
to forgive one another as we have been forgiven,
and to feast at his table as members of one household.

Easter

By your power you raised Jesus from death to life.
Through his victory over the grave
we are set free from the bonds of sin and the fear of death
to share the glorious freedom of the children of God.
In his rising to life
you promise eternal life to all who believe in him.
We praise you that as we break bread in faith,
we shall know the risen Christ among us.

Ascension of the Lord

You raised up Christ to rule over all creation,
giving him the name which is above all other names,
that at the name of Jesus every knee shall bow.

We praise you that, lifted in power,
he lives and reigns forever in your glory
and so fulfills his promise to be with us always
to the end of time.

Day of Pentecost

In fulfillment of Christ's promise,
you poured out the Holy Spirit upon the chosen disciples
and filled the church with power.
We thank you for sending your Spirit to us today
to kindle faith and lead us into all truth,
working in the church to make us faithful disciples,
and empowering us to proclaim the living Christ to every nation.

Trinity Sunday

You revealed your glory
as the glory also of your Son and of the Holy Spirit,
three Persons, equal in majesty, undivided in splendor,
yet one Lord, one God,
to be worshiped and adored in your eternal glory.
We praise you, Father, Son, and Holy Spirit,
great Trinity of power and love,
our God, forever and ever.

All Saints' Day (or first Sunday in November)

You have surrounded us with a great cloud of witnesses,
saints and martyrs, faithful people in every age,
that, strengthened by their witness,
and supported by their fellowship,
we may run with perseverance the race that is set before us,
and with them receive the unfading crown of glory.

Christ the King (or Reign of Christ)

You exalted the risen Christ to rule over all creation,
that he might present to you
an eternal and universal kingdom:
a kingdom of truth and life,
a kingdom of holiness and grace,
a kingdom of justice, love, and peace.

Baptism

Through the waters of baptism we are buried with Christ
so that we may rise with him to new life.

We praise you for receiving us as your sons and daughters,
for making us citizens of your kingdom,
and for giving us the Holy Spirit to guide us into all truth.

Reaffirmation of the Baptismal Covenant

By the Holy Spirit you lead us into all truth,
and give us power
to proclaim your gospel to the nations
and to serve you as your priestly people.

Ordination

You sent your Son Jesus Christ,
who came not to be served but to serve,
and to give his life a ransom for many.
We praise you that he calls his faithful servants
to lead your holy people in love;

For the ordination of a minister of Word and Sacrament, add:

to proclaim your Word
and to celebrate the sacraments of the new covenant.

Christian Marriage

You give us love
and show us its fullness
in your offering of Jesus Christ for us.
You made us in your image,
male and female you created us,
and gave us the gift of marriage,
calling a man and a woman to share their lives
and to serve each other in the bond of covenant love.
Through long generations you have been patient and kind to all.

Funeral (or Memorial Service)

You sent to us your Son Jesus Christ,
who died and rose again to save us.
By his death on the cross
you revealed that your love has no limit.
By raising him from the grave
you comfort us with the blessed hope of eternal life.
By his victory
you assure us that neither death nor life,
nor things present nor things to come,
can separate us from your love in Christ Jesus our Lord.

GREAT THANKSGIVING: D

The Lord be with you.

And also with you.

Lift up your hearts.

We lift them to the Lord.

Let us give thanks to the Lord our God.

It is right to give our thanks and praise.

It is indeed right, our duty and highest joy,
that we should at all times and in all places
give thanks to you, O holy Lord,
Father almighty, everlasting God.

You created the heavens and the earth
and all that is in them.
You made us in your own image;
and in countless ways you show us your mercy.

A proper preface may be added here:

Advent

We praise you that in the coming of your Son Jesus Christ,
your promises given by the prophets were fulfilled
and the day of our deliverance has dawned.
We rejoice in hope as we look for the triumph of his kingdom,
when he comes again.

Christmas

We praise you,
because you sent Jesus Christ, your only Son,
to be born for us of Mary,
that we might be delivered from sin,
and receive power to become your children.

Epiphany

We praise you, for in Jesus Christ,
the mystery of the Word made flesh,
you sent a light to shine upon the world,
that we might be brought out of darkness
into your marvelous light.

Lent

We praise you for Jesus Christ,
who was tempted in every way we are, yet without sin,
and who, having overcome temptation,
is able to help us in our times of trial,
and to give us strength to take up the cross and follow him.

Easter

Above all we praise you
for the glorious resurrection of your Son,
Jesus Christ our Lord.
He is the true Passover Lamb
who takes away the sin of the world.
By his death he destroyed death,
and by his rising brought us eternal life.

Day of Pentecost

We praise you
that according to the promise of Jesus Christ
the Holy Spirit came upon the whole church,
that the everlasting gospel
should be preached among all people
to bring them out of darkness
into the clear light of your truth.

The minister continues:

Therefore with angels and archangels
and the whole company of heaven,
we worship and adore your glorious name,
praising you forevermore:

The people may sing or say:

**Holy, holy, holy Lord, God of power and might,
heaven and earth are full of your glory.
Hosanna in the highest.**

**Blessed is he who comes in the name of the Lord.
Hosanna in the highest.**

The minister continues:

All glory and blessing are yours, O holy God,
for in your great mercy
you gave your only Son, Jesus Christ.
He took our human nature,
and suffered death on the cross for our redemption.
There he made a perfect sacrifice
for the sins of the whole world.

We praise you that before he suffered and died,
our Savior gave us this holy sacrament
and commanded us to continue it
as a lasting memorial of his death and sacrifice
until he comes again.

If they have not already been said, the words of institution may be
said here, or in relation to the breaking of the bread.

We give you thanks that the Lord Jesus,
on the night before he died,
took bread,
and after giving thanks to you,
he broke it, and gave it to his disciples, saying:
Take, eat.
This is my body, given for you.
Do this in remembrance of me.

In the same way he took the cup, saying:
This cup is the new covenant sealed in my blood,
shed for you for the forgiveness of sins.
Whenever you drink it,
do this in remembrance of me.

Therefore, remembering his incarnation and holy life,
his death and glorious resurrection,
his ascension and continual intercession for us,
and awaiting his coming again in power and great glory,
we claim his eternal sacrifice
and celebrate with these your holy gifts
the memorial your Son commanded us to make.

The people may sing or say one of the following:

1

Great is the mystery of faith:

Christ has died,
Christ is risen,
Christ will come again.

2

Praise to you, Lord Jesus:

Dying you destroyed our death,
rising you restored our life.
Lord Jesus, come in glory.

3

According to his commandment:

We remember his death,
we proclaim his resurrection,
we await his coming in glory.

4

Christ is the bread of life:

When we eat this bread and drink this cup,
we proclaim your death, Lord Jesus,
until you come in glory.

The minister continues:

Merciful God,
by your Holy Spirit bless and make holy
both us and these your gifts of bread and wine,
that the bread we break may be a communion in the body of Christ,
and the cup we bless may be a communion in the blood of Christ.

Here we offer ourselves to be a living sacrifice,
holy and acceptable to you.
In your mercy, accept this our sacrifice of praise and thanksgiving,
as, in communion with all the faithful in heaven and on earth,
we ask you to fulfill, in us and in all creation,
the purpose of your redeeming love.

Through Christ, with Christ, in Christ,
in the unity of the Holy Spirit,
all glory and honor are yours, almighty God,
now and forever.   **Amen.**   [117]

This great thanksgiving was prepared by the International Committee on English in the Liturgy.

Since the words of institution are included in this prayer, they are not said in the invitation to the Lord's table, or in relation to the breaking of the bread.

The Lord be with you.

And also with you.

Lift up your hearts.

We lift them to the Lord.

Let us give thanks to the Lord our God.

It is right to give our thanks and praise.

Blessed are you, strong and faithful God.
All your works, the height and the depth,
echo the silent music of your praise.

In the beginning your Word summoned light,
night withdrew, and creation dawned.
As ages passed unseen,
waters gathered on the face of the earth
and life appeared.

When the times at last had ripened
and the earth grown full in abundance,
you created in your image man and woman,
the stewards of all creation.

You gave us breath and speech,
that all the living
might find a voice to sing your praise,
and to celebrate the creation you call good.
So now, with all the powers of heaven and earth,
we sing the ageless hymn of your glory:

The people may sing or say:

**Holy, holy, holy Lord, God of power and might,
heaven and earth are full of your glory.
Hosanna in the highest.**

**Blessed is he who comes in the name of the Lord.
Hosanna in the highest.**

The minister continues:

All holy God,
how wonderful is the work of your hands!
When sin had scarred the world,
you entered into covenant to renew the whole creation.

As a mother tenderly gathers her children,
as a father joyfully welcomes his own,
you embraced a people as your own
and filled them with longing
for a peace that would last
and for a justice that would never fail.

Through countless generations
your people hungered for the bread of freedom.
From them you raised up Jesus, your Son,
the living bread, in whom ancient hungers are satisfied.
He healed the sick,
though he himself would suffer;
he offered life to sinners,
though death would hunt him down.
But with a love stronger than death,
he opened wide his arms
and surrendered his spirit.

On the night before he met with death,
Jesus came to the table with those he loved.
He took bread
and praised you, God of all creation.
He broke the bread among his disciples
and said:
Take this, all of you, and eat it.
This is my body, given for you.

When the supper was ended,
he took a cup of wine
and gave thanks to you, God of all creation.
He passed the cup among his disciples
and said:
Take this, all of you, and drink from it.
This is the cup of the new covenant sealed in my blood
for the forgiveness of sin.
Do this in remembrance of me.

Gracious God,
as we offer you our sacrifice of praise and thanksgiving,
we commemorate Jesus, your Son.
Death could not bind him,
for you raised him up in the Spirit of holiness
and exalted him as Lord of creation.

The people may sing or say one of the following:

1

Great is the mystery of faith:

**Christ has died,
Christ is risen,
Christ will come again.**

2

Praise to you, Lord Jesus:

**Dying you destroyed our death,
rising you restored our life.
Lord Jesus, come in glory.**

3

According to his commandment:

**We remember his death,
we proclaim his resurrection,
we await his coming in glory.**

4

Christ is the bread of life:

**When we eat this bread and drink this cup,
we proclaim your death, Lord Jesus,
until you come in glory.**

The minister continues:

Eternal God,
let your Holy Spirit move in power over us
and over these earthly gifts of bread and wine,
that they may be the communion of the body and blood of Christ,
and that we may become one in him.
May his coming in glory find us
ever watchful in prayer,
strong in truth and love,
and faithful in the breaking of the bread.

Then, at last, all peoples will be free,
all divisions healed,
and with your whole creation,
we will sing your praise,
through your Son, Jesus Christ.

Through Christ, with Christ, in Christ,
in the unity of the Holy Spirit,
all glory and honor are yours, almighty Father,
forever and ever.   **Amen.**   [118]

This eucharistic prayer is adapted from the Alexandrine Liturgy of St. Basil (fourth century).

Since the words of institution are included in this prayer, they are not said in the invitation to the Lord's table, or in relation to the breaking of the bread.

The Lord be with you.

And also with you.

Lift up your hearts.

We lift them to the Lord.

Let us give thanks to the Lord our God.

It is right to give our thanks and praise.

It is truly right to glorify you, Father,
and to give you thanks,
for you alone are God, living and true,
dwelling in light inaccessible from before time and forever.

Fountain of all life and source of all goodness,
you made all things and fill them with your blessing;
you created them to rejoice in the splendor of your radiance.

Countless throngs of angels stand before you
to serve you night and day,
and, beholding the glory of your presence,
they offer you unceasing praise.
Joining with them,
and giving voice to every creature under heaven,
we glorify your name
and lift our voices in joyful praise:

The people may sing or say:

**Holy, holy, holy Lord, God of power and might,
heaven and earth are full of your glory.
Hosanna in the highest.**

**Blessed is he who comes in the name of the Lord.
Hosanna in the highest.**

The minister continues:

We acclaim you, holy God, glorious in power;
your mighty works reveal your wisdom and love.
You formed us in your own image,
giving the whole world into our care,
so that, in obedience to you, our creator,
we might rule and serve all your creatures.
When our disobedience took us far from you,
you did not abandon us to the power of death.
In your mercy you came to our help,
so that in seeking you we might find you.
Again and again you called us into covenant with you,
and through the prophets you taught us to hope for salvation.

Almighty God, you loved the world so much
that in the fullness of time you sent your only Son to be our Savior.
Incarnate by the Holy Spirit, born of the Virgin Mary,
he lived as one of us, yet without sin.
To the poor he proclaimed the good news of salvation;
to prisoners, freedom;
to the sorrowful, joy.
To fulfill your purpose he gave himself up to death;
and, rising from the grave, destroyed death
and made the whole creation new.

And that we might live no longer for ourselves
but for him who died and rose for us,
God sent the Holy Spirit,
God's first gift for those who believe,
to complete God's work in the world,
and to bring to fulfillment the sanctification of all.

When the hour had come for him to be glorified
by you, his heavenly Father,
having loved his own who were in the world,
he loved them to the end:
at supper with them he took bread,
and after giving thanks to you,
he broke it, and gave it to his disciples, saying:
Take, eat.
This is my body, which is given for you.
Do this for the remembrance of me.

After supper he took the cup, saying:
This cup is the new covenant sealed in my blood,
shed for you and for all for the forgiveness of sins.
Whenever you drink it,
do it for the remembrance of me.

Holy God, we now celebrate this memorial of our redemption.
Recalling Christ's death and his descent among the dead,
proclaiming his resurrection and ascension to your right hand,
awaiting his coming in glory;
and offering to you, from the gifts you have given us,
this bread and this cup,
we praise you and we bless you.

The people may sing or say:

**We praise you, we bless you,
we give thanks to you,
and we pray to you, Lord our God.**

The minister continues:

Lord, we pray that in your goodness and mercy
your Holy Spirit may descend upon us, and upon these gifts,
sanctifying them
and showing them to be holy gifts for your holy people,
the bread of life and the cup of salvation,
the body and blood of your Son Jesus Christ.

Grant that all who share this bread and this cup
may become one body and one spirit,
a living sacrifice in Christ,
to the praise of your name.

Remember, Lord, your one holy catholic and apostolic church,
redeemed by the blood of your Christ.
Reveal its unity, guard its faith,
and preserve it in peace.

[Remember (N. and) all who minister in your church.]
[Remember all your people, and those who seek your truth.]
[Remember _____ .]
[Remember all who have died in the peace of Christ,
and those whose faith is known to you alone;
bring them into the place of eternal joy and light.]

And grant that we may find our inheritance with

> [the blessed Virgin Mary, with patriarchs, prophets, apostles,
> and martyrs, and]

all the saints who have found favor with you in ages past.
We praise you in union with them
and give you glory through your Son, Jesus Christ our Lord.

Through Christ, and with Christ, and in Christ,
all honor and glory are yours, almighty God and Father,
in the unity of the Holy Spirit,
forever and ever.   **Amen.**   [119]

> This great thanksgiving is a translation of the ancient eucharistic prayer of Hippolytus of Rome, dating from about 215. It is the earliest known text of a eucharistic prayer.
>
> Since the words of institution are included in this prayer, they are not said in the invitation to the Lord's table, or in relation to the breaking of the bread.

The Lord be with you.

And also with you.

Lift up your hearts.

We lift them to the Lord.

Let us give thanks to the Lord our God.

It is right to give our thanks and praise.

We give you thanks, O God,
through your beloved Servant, Jesus Christ,
whom you have sent in these last times
as savior and redeemer,
and messenger of your will.
He is your Word,
inseparable from you,
through whom you made all things
and in whom you take delight.

You sent him from heaven into the Virgin's womb,
where he was conceived, and took flesh.
Born of the Virgin by the power of the Holy Spirit,
he was revealed as your Son.
In fulfillment of your will
he stretched out his hands in suffering
to release from suffering those who place their trust in you,
and so won for you a holy people.

He freely accepted the death to which he was handed over,
in order to destroy death
and to shatter the chains of the evil one;
to trample underfoot the powers of hell
and to lead the righteous into light;
to fix the boundaries of death
and to manifest the resurrection.

And so he took bread, gave thanks to you, and said:
"Take, and eat;
this is my body, broken for you."
In the same way he took the cup, saying:
"This is my blood, shed for you.
When you do this, do it for the remembrance of me."

Remembering therefore his death and resurrection,
we set before you this bread and cup,
thankful that you have counted us worthy
to stand in your presence
and serve you as your priestly people.

We ask you to send your Holy Spirit
upon the offering of the holy church.
Gather into one all who share these holy mysteries,
filling them with the Holy Spirit
and confirming their faith in the truth,
that together we may praise you and give you glory,
through your Servant, Jesus Christ.

Through him all glory and honor are yours, almighty Father,
with the Holy Spirit in the holy church,
now and forever.   **Amen.**   [120]

When this prayer is used, the words of institution are said in the invitation
to the Lord's table, or in relation to the breaking of the bread.

Holy God, we praise you.
Let the heavens be joyful,
and the earth be glad.

We bless you for creating the whole world,
for your promises to your people Israel,
and for Jesus Christ in whom your fullness dwells.

Born of Mary, he shares our life.
Eating with sinners, he welcomes us.
Guiding his children, he leads us.
Visiting the sick, he heals us.
Dying on the cross, he saves us.
Risen from the dead, he gives new life.
Living with you, he prays for us.

With thanksgiving we take this bread and this cup
and proclaim the death and resurrection of our Lord.
Receive our sacrifice of praise.
Pour out your Holy Spirit upon us
that this meal may be
a communion in the body and blood of our Lord.
Make us one with Christ
and with all who share this feast.
Unite us in faith,
encourage us with hope,
inspire us to love,
that we may serve as your faithful disciples
until we feast at your table in glory.

We praise you, eternal God,
through Christ your Word made flesh,
in the holy and life-giving Spirit,
now and forever.   **Amen.**   [121]

This prayer may be used when serving Communion in the home or hospital, or in other informal situations. The dialogue may be added.

GREAT THANKSGIVING: I

The form below provides for praying the great thanksgiving in a free and spontaneous style.

The prayer may be introduced with:

The Lord be with you.

And also with you.

Lift up your hearts.

We lift them to the Lord.

Let us give thanks to the Lord our God.

It is right to give our thanks and praise.

The prayer begins with thankful praise to God:
   for God's work in creation and providence, and in covenant history;
   for the witness of the prophets;
   for God's steadfast love in spite of human failure;
   for the ultimate gift of Christ;
   and for the immediate occasion or festival.

The "Holy, Holy, Holy Lord" may be included. If included, it is introduced with these or similar words:

Therefore we praise you,
joining our voices with choirs of angels
and with all the faithful of every time and place,
who forever sing to the glory of your name:

The people may sing or say:

**Holy, holy, holy Lord, God of power and might,
heaven and earth are full of your glory.
Hosanna in the highest.**

**Blessed is he who comes in the name of the Lord.
Hosanna in the highest.**

The prayer continues with thankful recalling of the acts of salvation in
Jesus Christ:
redemption;
Christ's birth, life, and ministry;
Christ's death and resurrection;
his present intercession for us and the promise of his coming again;
the gift of the Sacrament [which may include the words of institution
if not otherwise used]:

We give you thanks
that on the night of his arrest,
Jesus took bread,
and after giving thanks to you,
he broke it, and gave it to his disciples, saying:
Take, eat.
This is my body, given for you.
Do this in remembrance of me.

In the same way he took the cup, saying:
This cup is the new covenant sealed in my blood,
shed for you for the forgiveness of sins.
Whenever you drink it,
do this in remembrance of me.

*The thankful recalling of God's saving work in Christ concludes with these
or similar words:*

Remembering your mighty acts in Jesus Christ,
we take from your creation this bread and this wine
and joyfully celebrate his dying and rising,
as we await the day of his coming.
With thanksgiving, we offer our very selves to you
to be a living and holy sacrifice
dedicated to your service.

The people may sing or say one of the following memorial acclamations:

1

Great is the mystery of faith:

**Christ has died,
Christ is risen,
Christ will come again.**

2

According to his commandment:

**We remember his death,
we proclaim his resurrection,
we await his coming in glory.**

3

Praise to you, Lord Jesus:

**Dying you destroyed our death,
rising you restored our life.
Lord Jesus, come in glory.**

4

Christ is the bread of life:

**When we eat this bread and drink this cup,
we proclaim your death, Lord Jesus,
until you come in glory.**

The Holy Spirit is called upon in these or similar words:

Gracious God,
pour out your Holy Spirit upon us
and upon these your gifts of bread and wine,
that the bread we break
and the cup we bless
may be the communion of the body and blood of Christ.

Petitions are offered that we may
be made one with the risen Christ and with all God's people;
be united with all the faithful in heaven and on earth;
be nourished with the body and blood of Christ;
receive new life and mature into the fullness of Christ;
remain faithful as Christ's body in ministry in the world;
have hope in the promise of Christ's kingdom fulfilled.

The prayer concludes with doxological praise in these or similar words:

Through Christ, with Christ, in Christ,
in the unity of the Holy Spirit,
all glory and honor are yours, almighty God,
now and forever.   **Amen.**   [122]

The outline below is provided to guide those who desire to pray the great thanksgiving in a free style.

The prayer begins with thankful praise to God
    for God's work in creation and providence, and in covenant history;
    for the witness of the prophets;
    for God's steadfast love in spite of human failure;
    for the ultimate gift of Christ;
    and for the immediate occasion or festival.

The prayer continues with thankful recalling of the acts of salvation in Jesus Christ:
    redemption;
    Christ's birth, life, and ministry;
    Christ's death and resurrection;
    his present intercession for us and the promise of his coming again;
    the gift of the Sacrament [which may include the words of institution
        if not otherwise used].

The Holy Spirit is called upon
    to lift all who share in the feast into Christ's presence;
    to make the breaking of the bread and sharing of the cup a participation
        in the body and blood of Christ;
    to make us one with the risen Christ and with all God's people;
    to unite us in communion with all the faithful in heaven and earth;
    to nourish us with the body of Christ so that we may mature into
        the fullness of Christ;
    to keep us faithful as Christ's body, representing Christ in ministry
        in the world,
    in anticipation of the fulfillment of the kingdom Christ proclaimed.

There follows an ascription of praise to the triune God.

PRAYER AFTER COMMUNION

Other prayers after Communion may be found on pages 76–77.

1

Eternal God,
we give you thanks for this holy mystery
in which you have given yourself to us.
Grant that we may go into the world
in the strength of your Spirit,
to give ourselves for others
in the name of Jesus Christ our Lord.   **Amen.**   [123]

2

Loving God,
you graciously feed us,
who have received these holy mysteries,
with the bread of life and the cup of eternal salvation.
May we who have received this sacrament,
be strengthened in your service;
we who have sung your praises
tell of your glory and truth;
we who have seen the greatness of your love
see you face to face in your kingdom.
For you have made us your own people
by the death and resurrection of your Son our Lord
and by the life-giving power of your Spirit.   **Amen.**   [124]

3

Loving God,
you have given us a share in the one bread and the one cup
and made us one with Christ.
Help us to bring your salvation and joy to all the world.
We ask this through Christ our Lord.   **Amen.**   [125]

4

O God,
you have so greatly loved us,
long sought us,
and mercifully redeemed us.
Give us grace
that in everything we may yield ourselves,
our wills and our works,
a continual thank-offering to you;
through Jesus Christ our Lord.   **Amen.**   [126]

5

God of grace,
you renew us at your table with the bread of life.
May this food strengthen us in love
and help us to serve you in each other.
We ask this in the name of Jesus the Lord.   **Amen.**   [127]

6

Almighty God,
you provide the true bread from heaven,
your Son, Jesus Christ our Lord.
Grant that we who have received the Sacrament of his body and blood
may abide in him and he in us,
that we may be filled with the power of his endless life,
now and forever.   **Amen.**   [128]

PRAYER OF THANKSGIVING

For use when the Eucharist is not celebrated

Other prayers of thanksgiving may be found on pages 80–81. Prayers of thanksgiving for festivals and seasons may be found on pages 165–400.

1

Let us give thanks to the Lord our God.

It is right to offer thanks and praise.

God of all mercies,
we give you humble thanks
for all your goodness and loving-kindness
to us and to all people.

We bless you for our creation, preservation,
and all the blessings of this life;
but above all for your boundless love
in the redemption of the world by our Lord Jesus Christ;
for the means of grace,
and for the hope of glory.

Give us such an awareness of your mercies,
that with truly thankful hearts
we may show forth your praise,
not only with our lips but in our lives,
by giving up ourselves to your service,

and by walking before you
in holiness and righteousness all our days;
through Jesus Christ our Redeemer,
to whom, with you and the Holy Spirit,
be all honor and glory now and forever.   **Amen.**   [129]

2

Let us give thanks to the Lord our God.

It is right to offer thanks and praise.

Holy God, we praise you.
Let the heavens be joyful, and the earth be glad.

We bless you for creating the whole world,
for your promise to your people Israel,
and for Jesus Christ in whom your fullness dwells.

Born of Mary, he shares our life.
Eating with sinners, he welcomes us.
Guiding his people, he leads us.
Visiting the sick, he heals us.
Dying on the cross, he saves us.
Risen from the dead, he gives new life.
Living with you, he prays for us.

Send to us your Holy Spirit
that, being made one with Christ,
we may be one with each other
and one in ministry to all the world,
until Christ comes in final victory.

We praise you, eternal God,
through Christ your Word made flesh,
in the holy and life-giving Spirit.   **Amen.**   [130]

CHARGE TO THE PEOPLE

Other charges to the people may be found on pages 78 and 82–83.

1   *Matt. 22:37–40*

Go out into the world in peace.
Love the Lord your God
with all your heart,
with all your soul,
with all your mind;
and love your neighbor as yourself.

2   *Col. 3:17*

Whatever you do, in word or deed,
do everything in the name of the Lord Jesus,
giving thanks to God through him.

3   *1 Cor. 16:13, 14*

Be watchful,
stand firm in your faith,
be courageous and strong.
Let all that you do be done in love.

4   *Micah 6:8*

God has shown you what is good.
What does the Lord require of you
but to do justice,
and to love kindness,
and to walk humbly with your God?

5   *1 John 3:23*

Go forth in the name of the Lord.
This is God's charge:
to give our allegiance to Jesus Christ
and to love one another as he commanded.

6   *See Col. 3:12–14*

As God's own,
clothe yourselves with compassion,
kindness, and patience,
forgiving each other
as the Lord has forgiven you,
and crown all these things with love,
which binds everything together in perfect harmony.

BLESSING

Other blessings may be found on page 78.

Alleluia is traditionally omitted during Lent.

1
Heb. 13:20, 21

The God of peace,
who brought back from the dead our Lord Jesus,
make you complete in everything good
so that you may do God's will,
working among us that which is pleasing in God's sight,
through Jesus Christ,
to whom be the glory forever and ever!

Alleluia! Amen.

2
Rom. 15:13

May the God of hope
fill you with all joy and peace in believing,
so that you may abound in hope
by the power of the Holy Spirit.

Alleluia! Amen.

3
See Phil. 4:7

The peace of God,
which passes all understanding,
keep your hearts and minds
in the knowledge and love of God,
and of God's Son, Jesus Christ our Lord;
and the blessing of God almighty,
the Father, the Son, and the Holy Spirit,
remain with you always.

Alleluia! Amen.

4
1 Thess. 5:23

May the God of peace
make you holy in every way
and keep your whole being—
spirit, soul, and body—
free from every fault
at the coming of our Lord Jesus Christ.

Alleluia! Amen.

RESOURCES
FOR THE
LITURGICAL YEAR

ADVENT

LIGHTING OF THE ADVENT CANDLES

At each successive lighting of the Advent candles, all texts from the preceding lightings are read in addition to the text introduced that day.

On the First Sunday of Advent and following Sundays:

We light this candle as a sign of the coming light of Christ.
Advent means coming.
We are preparing ourselves for the days

Isa. 2:4

when the nations shall beat their swords into plowshares,
and their spears into pruning hooks;
nation shall not lift up sword against nation,
neither shall they learn war any more.

And on the Second Sunday of Advent, and at successive lightings:

Isa. 11:6

The wolf shall dwell with the lamb,
the leopard shall lie down with the kid,
the calf and the lion and the fatling together,
and a little child shall lead them.

And on the Third Sunday of Advent, and at successive lightings:

Isa. 35:1

The wilderness and the dry land shall be glad,
the desert shall rejoice and blossom;
like the crocus it shall blossom abundantly,
and rejoice with joy and singing.

And on the Fourth Sunday of Advent, and at successive lightings:

Isa. 7:14b

The Lord will give you a sign.
Look, the young woman is with child
and shall bear a son,
and shall name him Immanuel (God is with us).

And on the eve of Christmas, or on Christmas Day:

Isa. 9:2

The people who walked in darkness have seen a great light;
those who lived in a land of deep darkness,
on them light has shined.

On each occasion the lighting of the candles is concluded with:

Let us walk in the light of the Lord.

LITANY FOR ADVENT
O ANTIPHONS

May be used December 17 through 23.

O Wisdom,
coming forth from the mouth of the Most High,
pervading and permeating all creation,
you order all things with strength and gentleness:
Come now and teach us the way to salvation.

Come, Lord Jesus.

O Adonai,
Ruler of the house of Israel,
you appeared in the burning bush to Moses
and gave him the law on Sinai:
Come with outstretched arm to save us.

Come, Lord Jesus.

O Root of Jesse,
rising as a sign for all the peoples,
before you earthly rulers will keep silent,
and nations give you honor:
Come quickly to deliver us.

Come, Lord Jesus.

O Key of David,
Scepter over the house of Israel,
you open and no one can close,
you close and no one can open:
Come to set free the prisoners
who live in darkness and the shadow of death.

Come, Lord Jesus.

O Radiant Dawn,
splendor of eternal light,
Sun of justice:
Come, shine on those who live in darkness
and in the shadow of death.

Come, Lord Jesus.

O Ruler of the nations,
Monarch for whom the people long,
you are the Cornerstone uniting all humanity:
Come, save us all,
whom you formed out of clay.

Come, Lord Jesus.

O Immanuel,
our Sovereign and Lawgiver,
desire of the nations and Savior of all:
Come and save us, O Lord our God.

Come, Lord Jesus.

After a brief silence, the leader concludes the litany:

God of grace,
ever faithful to your promises,
the earth rejoices in hope of our Savior's coming
and looks forward with longing
to his return at the end of time.
Prepare our hearts to receive him when he comes,
for he is Lord forever and ever.   **Amen.**   [131]

PRAYER OF CONFESSION

**God of the future,
you are coming in power to bring all nations under your rule.
We confess that we have not expected your kingdom,
for we live casual lives, ignoring your promised judgment.**

We accept lies as truth,
exploit neighbors,
abuse the earth,
and refuse your justice and peace.

In your mercy, forgive us.
Grant us wisdom to welcome your way,
and to seek things that will endure
when Christ comes to judge the world.   [132]

GREAT THANKSGIVING

The Lord be with you.

And also with you.

Lift up your hearts.

We lift them to the Lord.

Let us give thanks to the Lord our God.

It is right to give our thanks and praise.

It is truly right and our greatest joy
to give you thanks and praise,
O Lord our God, creator and ruler of the universe.
You formed us in your image
and breathed into us the breath of life.
You set us in this world to love and serve you,
and to live in peace with all that you have made.

When we turned from you,
you did not turn from us.
When we were captives in slavery,
you delivered us to freedom,
and made covenant to be our sovereign God.
When we were stubborn and stiff-necked,
you spoke to us through prophets
who looked for that day
when justice shall triumph
and peace shall reign over all the earth.

Therefore we praise you,
joining our voices with the celestial choirs
and with all the faithful of every time and place,
who forever sing to the glory of your name:

The people may sing or say:

Holy, holy, holy Lord, God of power and might,
heaven and earth are full of your glory.
Hosanna in the highest.

Blessed is he who comes in the name of the Lord.
Hosanna in the highest.

The minister continues:

You are holy, O God of majesty,
and blessed is Jesus Christ, your Son, our Lord.
You sent him into this world
to satisfy the longings of your people for a Savior,
to bring freedom to the captives of sin,
and to establish justice for the oppressed.
He came among us as one of us,
taking the lot of the poor,
sharing human suffering.
We rejoice that in his death and rising again,
you set before us the sure promise of new life,
the certain hope of a heavenly home
where we will sit at table with Christ our host.

If they have not already been said, the words of institution may be
said here, or in relation to the breaking of the bread.

We give you thanks that the Lord Jesus,
on the night before he died,
took bread,
and after giving thanks to you,
he broke it, and gave it to his disciples, saying:
Take, eat.
This is my body, given for you.
Do this in remembrance of me.

In the same way he took the cup, saying:
This cup is the new covenant sealed in my blood,
shed for you for the forgiveness of sins.
Whenever you drink it,
do this in remembrance of me.

Remembering your gracious acts in Jesus Christ,
we take from your creation this bread and this wine
and joyfully celebrate his dying and rising,
as we await the day of his coming.
With thanksgiving we offer our very selves to you
to be a living and holy sacrifice,
dedicated to your service.

The people may sing or say one of the following:

1

Great is the mystery of faith:

**Christ has died,
Christ is risen,
Christ will come again.**

2

Praise to you, Lord Jesus:

**Dying you destroyed our death,
rising you restored our life.
Lord Jesus, come in glory.**

3

According to his commandment:

**We remember his death,
we proclaim his resurrection,
we await his coming in glory.**

4

Christ is the bread of life:

**When we eat this bread and drink this cup,
we proclaim your death, Lord Jesus,
until you come in glory.**

The minister continues:

Gracious God,
pour out your Holy Spirit upon us
and upon these your gifts of bread and wine,
that the bread we break
and the cup we bless
may be the communion of the body and blood of Christ.

By your Spirit make us one with Christ,
that we may be one with all who share this feast,
united in ministry in every place.
As this bread is Christ's body for us,
send us out to be the body of Christ in the world.

Intercessions for the church and the world may be included here.

Strengthen us, O God, in the power of your Spirit
to bring good news to the poor
and lift blind eyes to sight,
to loose the chains that bind
and claim your blessing for all people.
Keep us faithful in your service
until Christ comes in final victory,
and we shall feast with all your saints
in the joy of your eternal realm.

Through Christ, with Christ, in Christ,
in the unity of the Holy Spirit,
all glory and honor are yours, almighty God,
now and forever.   **Amen.**   [133]

PRAYER OF THANKSGIVING

For use when the Eucharist is not celebrated.

Let us give thanks to the Lord our God.

It is right to give our thanks and praise.

Eternal God,
as you led your people in ages past,
you direct our journey into the future.
We give you thanks that
you came to us in Jesus Christ,
and we eagerly await his coming again
that his rule may be complete
and your righteousness reign over all the world.
Then we will feast at his royal banquet,
and sing his praises with the choirs of heaven.
By your Spirit,
open our eyes to the generosity of your hand,
and nurture our souls in all spiritual gifts.

Fill us with gratitude overflowing
that we may share life and love in praise to you,
God of all the ages,
in the gracious name of Jesus Christ, your Son,
by the power of your Holy Spirit,
now and forever.   **Amen.**   [134]

SENTENCES OF SCRIPTURE
PRAYER OF THE DAY

FIRST SUNDAY OF ADVENT

SENTENCES OF SCRIPTURE

1   *Year A B C*
                                                                 Rom. 13:11

Salvation is nearer to us now than when we first believed;
the night is far gone,
the day is near.

2   *Year A B C*
                                                                 Jer. 33:14a, 15

The days are surely coming, says the Lord,
when I will fulfill the promise:
I will cause a righteous Branch to spring up for David;
and he shall execute justice and righteousness.

3   *Year A B C*
                                                                 Isa. 2:4

They shall beat their swords into plowshares,
and their spears into pruning hooks;
nation shall not lift up sword against nation,
neither shall they learn war any more.

PRAYER OF THE DAY

1   *Year A B C*

Faithful God,
your promises stand unshaken through all generations.
Renew us in hope,
that we may be awake and alert
watching for the glorious return of Jesus Christ,
our judge and savior,
who lives and reigns with you in the unity of the Holy Spirit,
one God, forever and ever.   **Amen.**   [135]

Eternal God,
through long generations you prepared a way
for the coming of your Son,
and by your Spirit
you still bring light to illumine our paths.
Renew us in faith and hope
that we may welcome Christ to rule our thoughts
and claim our love,
as Lord of lords and King of kings,
to whom be glory always. **Amen.** [136]

3 *Year A B C*

Eternal God,
you taught us that the night is far spent
and the day is at hand.
Keep us awake and alert, watching for your kingdom,
and make us strong in faith,
so that when Christ comes in glory to judge the earth,
we may joyfully give him praise;
who lives and reigns with you and the Holy Spirit,
one God, now and forever. **Amen.** [137]

SECOND SUNDAY OF ADVENT

SENTENCES OF SCRIPTURE

1 *Year A B C*
Isa. 40:3

A voice cries:
In the wilderness prepare the way of the Lord,
make straight in the desert a highway for our God.

2 *Year A B C*
2 Peter 3:13

In accordance with God's promise
we wait for new heavens and a new earth
where righteousness is at home.

3 *Year A B C*
Isa. 11:6

The wolf shall dwell with the lamb,
the leopard shall lie down with the kid,
the calf and the lion and the fatling together,
and a little child shall lead them.

1   *Year A B C*

God of all peoples,
your servant John came baptizing
and calling for repentance.
Help us to hear his voice of judgment,
that we may also rejoice in his word of promise,
and be found pure and blameless in that glorious Day
when Christ comes to rule the earth as Prince of Peace.   **Amen.**   [138]

2   *Year A B C*

Merciful God,
you sent your messengers the prophets
to preach repentance and prepare the way for our salvation.
Give us grace to heed their warnings and forsake our sins,
that we may greet with joy
the coming of Jesus Christ our Redeemer,
who lives and reigns with you and the Holy Spirit,
one God, now and forever.   **Amen.**   [139]

3   *Year B C*

God of our salvation,
you straighten the winding ways of our hearts
and smooth the paths made rough by sin.
Keep our conduct blameless,
keep our hearts watchful in holiness,
and bring to perfection the good you have begun in us.
We ask this through him whose coming is certain,
whose day draws near;
your Son, our Lord Jesus Christ,
who lives and reigns with you in the unity of the Holy Spirit,
one God, forever and ever.   **Amen.**   [140]

THIRD SUNDAY OF ADVENT

SENTENCES OF SCRIPTURE

1   *Year A B C*
                                                                Phil. 4:4

Rejoice in the Lord always;
again, I will say, Rejoice.
Let your gentleness be known to everyone.
The Lord is near.

The Spirit of the Lord God is upon me,
because the Lord has anointed me
to bring good news to the oppressed.

The wilderness and the dry land shall be glad,
the desert shall rejoice and blossom;
like the crocus it shall blossom abundantly,
and rejoice with joy and singing.

PRAYER OF THE DAY

1

Almighty God,
you have made us and all things to serve you,
now prepare the world for your rule.
Come quickly to save us,
so that wars and violence shall end,
and your children may live in peace,
honoring one another with justice and love;
through Jesus Christ,
who lives in power with you in the unity of the Holy Spirit,
one God, now and forever.   **Amen.**   [141]

2

Eternal God,
you sent John the Baptist
to prepare the way for the coming of your Son.
Grant us the wisdom to see your purpose
and openness to hear your will,
that we too may prepare the way for Christ
who is coming in power and glory
to establish his kingdom of peace and justice;
through Jesus Christ our Judge and our Redeemer,
who lives and reigns with you and the Holy Spirit,
one God, forever.   **Amen.**   [142]

3

Almighty God,
you send your Son into a world
where the wheat must be winnowed from chaff
and wickedness clings even to what is good.

Let the fire of your Spirit purge us of greed and deceit,
so that, purified, we may find our peace in you
and you may delight in us.
We ask this through him whose coming is certain,
whose day draws near,
your Son, our Lord Jesus Christ,
who lives and reigns with you in the unity of the Holy Spirit,
one God, forever and ever.   **Amen.**   [143]

FOURTH SUNDAY OF ADVENT

SENTENCES OF SCRIPTURE

1   *Year A B C*

Isa. 45:8

Shower, O heavens, from above,
and let the skies rain down righteousness;
let the earth open, that salvation may spring up.

2   *Year A*

Isa. 7:14

Look, the young woman is with child
and shall bear a son,
and shall name him Immanuel.

3   *Year B C*

Luke 1:38

Then Mary said: Here am I,
the servant of the Lord;
let it be with me according to your word.

PRAYER OF THE DAY

1   *Year A B C*

God of grace,
you chose the Virgin Mary, full of grace,
to be the mother of our Lord and Savior.
Now fill us with your grace,
that with her, we may rejoice in your salvation,
and in all things, embrace your will;
through Jesus Christ our Lord,
who lives and reigns with you in the unity of the Holy Spirit,
one God, now and forever.   **Amen.**   [144]

God of grace,
your eternal Word took flesh among us
when Mary placed her life
at the service of your will.
Prepare our hearts for his coming again;
keep us steadfast in hope
and faithful in service,
that we may receive the coming of his kingdom,
for the sake of Jesus Christ the ruler of all,
who lives and reigns with you and the Holy Spirit,
one God, now and forever.   **Amen.**   [145]

3   *Year C*

Who are we, Lord God,
that you should come to us?
Yet you have visited your people
and redeemed us in your Son.
As we prepare to celebrate his birth,
make our hearts leap for joy at the sound of your word,
and move us by your Spirit to bless your wonderful works.
We ask this through him whose coming is certain,
whose day draws near,
your Son, our Lord Jesus Christ,
who lives and reigns with you in the unity of the Holy Spirit,
one God, forever and ever.   **Amen.**   [146]

CHRISTMAS

PRAYER OF ADORATION

Glory to you, almighty God,
for you sent your only-begotten Son,
that we might have new life.

Glory to you, Lord Jesus Christ,
for you became flesh and dwelt among us
that we might become your people.

Glory to you, Holy Spirit,
for you direct and rule our lives.

Glory to you, almighty God,
and to your Son, Jesus Christ,
and to the Holy Spirit,
now and forever.   **Amen.**   [147]

LITANY FOR CHRISTMAS: A

The Word was made flesh,

Alleluia, Alleluia!

and dwelt among us,

Alleluia, Alleluia!

Jesus, Son of the living God, splendor of the Father, Light eternal:

Glory to you, O Lord!

Jesus, King of glory, Sun of righteousness, born of the Virgin Mary:

Glory to you, O Lord!

Jesus, Wonderful Counselor, mighty God, everlasting Lord:

Glory to you, O Lord!

Jesus, Prince of Peace, Shepherd of souls, perfect in holiness:

Glory to you, O Lord!

Jesus, Friend of all, Protector of the poor, Treasure of the faithful:

Glory to you, O Lord!

Jesus, Good Shepherd, inexhaustible Wisdom, our Way, our Truth, and our Life:

Glory to you, O Lord!

Jesus, joy of the angels, and crown of all the saints:

Glory to you, O Lord!   [148]

> After a brief silence, the leader concludes the litany:

Christ is born! Give him glory!
Christ has come down from heaven! Receive him!
Christ is now on earth! Exalt him!
O earth, sing to the Lord!
O you nations, praise him in joy,
for he has been glorified!   **Amen.**   [149]

LITANY FOR CHRISTMAS: B

All the ends of the earth
have seen the salvation of our God. Alleluia!

Shout to the Lord, all the earth. Alleluia!

O Christ, splendor of God's eternal glory,
the mighty Word, sustaining the universe:
Renew our lives by your presence.

Lord, have mercy.

O Christ, born into the world in the fullness of time
for the liberation of all creation:
Release all into your promised freedom.

Lord, have mercy.

O Christ, begotten of the Father before all time,
born in a stable at Bethlehem:
May your church be a sign of hope and joy.

Lord, have mercy.

O Christ, truly God and truly human,
born to a people in fulfillment of their expectations:
Fulfill our desires in you.

Lord, have mercy.

O Christ, born of the Virgin Mary,
child of wonder and splendor,
mighty God of all ages, Prince of Peace:
May the whole world live in peace and justice.

Lord, have mercy. [150]

After a brief silence, the leader concludes the litany:

All-powerful and unseen God,
the coming of your light into our world
has brightened weary hearts with peace.
Teach us to proclaim the birth of your Son Jesus Christ,
who lives and reigns with you in the unity of the Holy Spirit,
one God, forever and ever. **Amen.** [151]

PRAYER OF CONFESSION

God of grace and truth,
in Jesus Christ you came among us
as light shining in darkness.
We confess that we have not welcomed the light,
or trusted good news to be good.
We have closed our eyes to glory in our midst,
expecting little, and hoping for less.

Forgive our doubt, and renew our hope,
so that we may receive the fullness of your grace,
and live in the truth of Christ the Lord. [152]

GREAT THANKSGIVING

The Lord be with you.

And also with you.

Lift up your hearts.

We lift them to the Lord.

Let us give thanks to the Lord our God.

It is right to give our thanks and praise.

It is truly right and our greatest joy
to give you thanks and praise,
O holy God, creator and ruler of the universe.

You created light out of darkness
and brought forth life on the earth.
You formed us in your image
and called us to love and serve you.
When we were unfaithful
and turned from your ways,
you did not forsake us,
your love remained steadfast.
You delivered us from captivity,
made covenant to be our sovereign God,
and sent prophets to call us back to your way.

In the fullness of time
you sent your only Son Jesus Christ to be our Savior.
In him, your Word, dwelling with you from all eternity,
became flesh and dwelt among us, full of grace and truth,
and we beheld your glory,
Immanuel!

Therefore we praise you,
joining our voices with the celestial choirs
and with all the faithful of every time and place,
who forever sing to the glory of your name:

The people may sing or say:

**Holy, holy, holy Lord, God of power and might,
heaven and earth are full of your glory.
Hosanna in the highest.**

**Blessed is he who comes in the name of the Lord.
Hosanna in the highest.**

The minister continues:

You are holy, O God of majesty,
and blessed is Jesus Christ, your Son, our Lord.
Born in humility,
he came to rule over all.
Helpless as an infant,
he showed the power of your love.
Poor in things of the world,
he brought the wealth of your grace.
Rejected by many,
he welcomed all who sought him.

In his dying and rising,
you gave birth to your church,
delivered us from slavery to sin and death,
and made with us a new covenant by water and the Spirit.

If they have not already been said, the words of institution may be said here, or in relation to the breaking of the bread.

We give you thanks that the Lord Jesus,
on the night before he died,
took bread,
and after giving thanks to you,
he broke it, and gave it to his disciples, saying:
Take, eat.
This is my body, given for you.
Do this in remembrance of me.

In the same way he took the cup, saying:
This cup is the new covenant sealed in my blood,
shed for you for the forgiveness of sins.
Whenever you drink it,
do this in remembrance of me.

Remembering your gracious acts in Jesus Christ,
we take from your creation this bread and this wine
and joyfully celebrate his dying and rising
as we await the day of his coming.
With thanksgiving we offer our very selves to you
to be a living and holy sacrifice,
dedicated to your service.

The people may sing or say one of the following:

1

Great is the mystery of faith:

Christ has died,
Christ is risen,
Christ will come again.

2

Praise to you, Lord Jesus:

Dying you destroyed our death,
rising you restored our life.
Lord Jesus, come in glory.

3

According to his commandment:

We remember his death,
we proclaim his resurrection,
we await his coming in glory.

4

Christ is the bread of life:

When we eat this bread and drink this cup,
we proclaim your death, Lord Jesus,
until you come in glory.

The minister continues:

Gracious God,
pour out your Holy Spirit upon us
and upon these your gifts of bread and wine,
that the bread we break
and the cup we bless
may be the communion of the body and blood of Christ.
By your Spirit make us one with Christ,
that we may be one with all who share this feast,
united in ministry in every place.
As this bread is Christ's body for us,
send us out to be the body of Christ in the world.

Intercessions for the church and the world may be included here.

Empower us by your Spirit, O God,
to be Christ's presence in the world
even as Jesus was God-with-us.
Give us courage
to speak his truth,
to seek his justice,
and to love with his love.
Keep us faithful in your service
until Christ comes in final victory
and we shall feast with all your saints
in the joy of your eternal realm.

Through Christ, with Christ, in Christ,
in the unity of the Holy Spirit,
all glory and honor are yours, almighty God,
now and forever.   **Amen.**   [153]

PRAYER OF THANKSGIVING

For use when the Eucharist is not celebrated.

1

Let us give thanks to the Lord our God.

It is right to give our thanks and praise.

God of mystery and might,
we praise and worship you,
for you came in silence, while all lay sleeping,
to enter our world as a child of humble birth.
We thank you for your Son, Jesus Christ,
born of your handmaid Mary.
In his face we behold your glory,
for in his life as in his death
is your gift of salvation.
By your Spirit,
make our hearts burn with thanksgiving,
that we may give as we have received.
Let our whole lives be gifts of praise to you,
God of love and peace,
in the gracious name of Jesus Christ, your Son,
by the power of your Holy Spirit,
now and forever.   **Amen.**   [154]

2

Let us give thanks to the Lord our God.

It is right to give our thanks and praise.

Great God of power,
we praise you for Jesus Christ,
who came to save us from our sins.
We thank you for the hope of the prophets,
the song of the angels,
and the birth of Jesus in Bethlehem.
We thank you that in Jesus you became flesh and dwelt among us,
sharing human hurts and pleasures.
Glory to you for your grace-filled love.
Glory to you, eternal God;
through Jesus Christ, Lord of lords,
and King of kings,
now and forever.   **Amen.**   [155]

CHRISTMAS EVE

SENTENCES OF SCRIPTURE

1

Year A B C
John 1:14

The Word became flesh and dwelt among us,
full of grace and truth.

We have beheld his glory. Alleluia!

2

Year A B C
Luke 2:14

Glory to God in the highest,
and peace to God's people on earth. Alleluia!

3

Year A B C
Isa. 9:2

The people who walked in darkness have seen a great light;
those who lived in a land of deep darkness—
on them light has shined.

PRAYER OF THE DAY

1

Year A B C

Good and gracious God,
on this holy night you gave us your Son,
the Lord of the universe, wrapped in swaddling clothes,
the Savior of all, lying in a manger.
On this holy night
draw us into the mystery of your love.
Join our voices with the heavenly host
that we may sing your glory on high.
Give us a place among the shepherds
that we may find the one for whom we have waited,
Jesus Christ, the Messiah and Lord,
who lives and reigns with you in the unity of the Holy Spirit,
one God, forever and ever. **Amen.** [156]

Give us, O God, such love and wonder
that with shepherds and magi,
and pilgrims unknown,
we may come to adore the holy child, the promised King;
and with our gifts worship him,
our Lord and Savior Jesus Christ,
who lives and reigns with you in the unity of the Holy Spirit,
one God, now and forever.   **Amen.**   [157]

3   *Year A B C*

Great God,
as you came at night when all was still,
so enter our lives this night.
Illumine our paths with the light of Christ's presence,
that we may clearly see the way before us,
the truth to speak,
and the life to live for him,
our Lord Jesus Christ,
who lives and reigns with you in the unity of the Holy Spirit,
one God, now and forever.   **Amen.**   [158]

CHRISTMAS DAY

SENTENCES OF SCRIPTURE

1   *Year A B C*
                                                                       Isa. 9:6

A child has been born for us,

a son given to us;

authority rests upon his shoulder,
and he is named:

Wonderful Counselor,
Mighty God,
Everlasting Father,
Prince of Peace.

2   *Year A B C*
                                                       Luke 2:10, 11

Behold I bring you good news of a great joy;
for to you is born in the city of David,
a Savior, who is Christ the Lord.

1 *Year A B C*

All glory to you, great God,
for the gift of your Son,
whom you sent to save us.
With singing angels,
let us praise your name,
and tell the earth his story,
that all may believe, rejoice, and bow down,
acknowledging your love;
through Jesus Christ our Lord,
who lives and reigns with you in the unity of the Holy Spirit,
one God, now and forever.   **Amen.**   [159]

2 *Year A B C*

God Most High,
your only Son embraced the weakness of flesh,
to give us power to become your children;
your eternal Word chose a dwelling among us,
that we might live in your presence.
Grant us a spirit of wisdom
to know how rich is the glory you have made our own,
and how great the hope to which we are called
in Jesus Christ, your Word made flesh,
who lives and reigns with you in the unity of the Holy Spirit,
in the splendor of eternal light,
God forever and ever.   **Amen.**   [160]

3 *Year A B C*

Almighty God,
you gave your only-begotten Son
to take our nature upon him,
and be born of the Virgin Mary.
Grant that we, who have been born again
and made your children by adoption and grace,
may daily be renewed by your Holy Spirit;
through our Lord Jesus Christ,
who lives and reigns with you in the unity of the Holy Spirit,
one God, now and forever.   **Amen.**   [161]

First Sunday After Christmas

Sentences of Scripture

1   *Year A B C*
                                                                  Col. 3:15, 16

Let the peace of Christ rule in your hearts;
let the word of Christ dwell in you richly.

2   *Year A B C*
                                                                  John 6:33

The bread of God is that which comes down from heaven
and gives life to the world.

3   *Year A B C*
                                                                  Titus 2:11

The grace of God has appeared,
bringing salvation to all.

Prayer of the Day

1   *Year A B C*

Almighty God,
you wonderfully created,
and yet more wonderfully restored,
the dignity of human nature.
In your mercy,
let us share the divine life of Jesus Christ
who came to share our humanity,
and who now lives and reigns with you and the Holy Spirit,
one God, now and forever.   **Amen.**   [162]

2   *Year A B C*

Almighty God,
you have shed upon us
the new light of your incarnate Word.
May this light, enkindled in our hearts,
shine forth in our lives;
through Jesus Christ our Lord,
who lives and reigns with you in the unity of the Holy Spirit,
one God, now and forever.   **Amen.**   [163]

Almighty God,
your Son Jesus Christ was presented in the temple
and acclaimed the glory of Israel
and the light of the nations.
Grant that in him we may be presented to you
and in the world may reflect his glory;
through Jesus Christ our Lord,
who lives and reigns with you in the unity of the Holy Spirit,
one God, now and forever.   **Amen.**   [164]

SECOND SUNDAY AFTER CHRISTMAS

SENTENCES OF SCRIPTURE

1   *Year A B C*
                                                                    John 1:14

The Word became flesh and dwelt among us,
full of grace and truth.

We have beheld his glory. Alleluia!

2   *Year A B C*
                                                                    See 1 Tim. 3:16

Glory to Christ
who is proclaimed among the nations,
and believed in throughout the world.

3   *Year A B C*
                                                                    Ps. 98:3

All the ends of the earth
have seen the victory of our God. Alleluia!

PRAYER OF THE DAY

1   *Year A B C*

Almighty God,
you have filled us with the light of the Word
who became flesh and lived among us.
Let the light of faith shine in all that we do;
through Jesus Christ our Lord,
who lives and reigns with you in the unity of the Holy Spirit,
one God, now and forever.   **Amen.**   [165]

Eternal God,
a thousand years in your sight
are like a watch in the night.
As you have led us in days past,
so guide us now and always,
that our hearts may learn to choose your will,
and new resolves be strengthened;
through Jesus Christ our Lord,
who lives and reigns with you in the unity of the Holy Spirit,
one God, now and forever.   **Amen.**   [166]

Also see Christmas Day, prayer of the day 2 (p. 187).

Epiphany—January 6

Or Sunday before Ephiphany

Sentences of Scripture

1

Year A B C

Isa. 60:1, 3

Arise, shine; for your light has come,

and the glory of the Lord has risen upon you.

Nations shall come to your light

and rulers to the brightness of your rising.

2

Year A B C

John 8:12

Jesus said:
I am the light of the world.
Whoever follows me will not walk in darkness
but will have the light of life.

3

Year A B C

Titus 2:11

The grace of God has dawned upon the world
with healing for all humankind.

Prayer of the Day

1

Year A B C

Lord God of the nations,
we have seen the star of your glory
rising in splendor.
The radiance of your incarnate Word
pierces the night that covers the earth
and signals the dawn of justice and peace.

May his brightness illumine our lives
and beckon all nations to walk as one in your light.
We ask this through Jesus Christ your Word made flesh,
who lives and reigns with you and the Holy Spirit,
in the splendor of eternal light,
God forever and ever.   **Amen.**   [167]

2   *Year A B C*

Eternal God,
by a star you led magi to the worship of your Son.
Guide the nations of the earth by your light,
that the whole world may see your glory;
through Jesus Christ our Lord,
who lives and reigns with you and the Holy Spirit,
one God, now and forever.   **Amen.**   [168]

3   *Year A B C*

Everlasting God,
the radiance of faithful souls,
who brought the nations to your light
and kings to the brightness of your rising:
Fill the world with your glory,
and show yourself to all the nations;
through him who is the true light
and the bright morning star,
Jesus Christ your Son, our Lord,
who lives and reigns with you and the Holy Spirit,
one God, now and forever.   **Amen.**   [169]

LITANY FOR EPIPHANY

All the ends of the earth
have seen the salvation of our God, Alleluia!

Shout to the Lord, all the earth, Alleluia!

With joy let us pray to our Savior,
the Son of God who became one of us, saying:
The grace of God be with us all.

O Christ,
let your gospel shine in every place
where the Word of life is not yet received.
Draw the whole creation to yourself
that your salvation may be known through all the earth.

The grace of God be with us all.

O Christ, Savior and Lord,
extend your church to every place.
Make it a place of welcome for people of every race and tongue.

The grace of God be with us all.

O Christ, Ruler of rulers,
direct the work and thoughts of the leaders of nations
that they may seek justice,
and further peace and freedom for all.

The grace of God be with us all.

O Christ, Master of all,
support of the weak and comfort of the afflicted,
strengthen the tempted and raise the fallen.
Watch over the lonely and those in danger.
Give hope to the despairing
and sustain the faith of the persecuted.

The grace of God be with us all.   Amen.   [170]

After a brief silence, the leader concludes the litany:

O Christ, light made manifest as the true light of God,
gladden our hearts on the joyful morning of your glory;
call us by our name on the great Day of your coming;
and give us grace to offer,
with all the hosts of heaven,
unending praise to God
in whom all things find their ending,
now and ever.   **Amen.**   [171]

PRAYER OF CONFESSION

**God of glory,
you sent Jesus among us as the light of the world,
to reveal your love for all people.
We confess that our sin and pride
hide the brightness of your light.
We turn away from the poor;
we ignore cries for justice;
we do not strive for peace.**

**In your mercy, cleanse us of our sin,
and baptize us once again with your Spirit,
that, forgiven and renewed, we may show forth your glory
shining in the face of Jesus Christ.**   [172]

GREAT THANKSGIVING

The Lord be with you.

And also with you.

Lift up your hearts.

We lift them to the Lord.

Let us give thanks to the Lord our God.

It is right to give our thanks and praise.

It is truly right and our greatest joy
to give you thanks and praise,
God of majesty and splendor.
By your power you created all that is,
making a universe out of chaos,
and ruling over all things in love.
Throughout the ages you called your people
to love and serve you,
and to be your light among the nations.
When we failed you,
you did not fail us
and sent prophets to call us back to your ways.

We praise you that in the fullness of time,
you revealed your love
by sending your Son Jesus
to be the Light of the world.
He came to heal our brokenness
and to set before us the ways of justice and peace.

Therefore we praise you,
joining our voices with angels and archangels
and with all the faithful of every time and place,
who forever sing to the glory of your name:

The people may sing or say:

**Holy, holy, holy Lord, God of power and might,
heaven and earth are full of your glory.
Hosanna in the highest.**

**Blessed is he who comes in the name of the Lord.
Hosanna in the highest.**

The minister continues:

You are holy, O God of majesty,
and blessed is Jesus Christ your Son, our Lord.
He was born to dwell among us,
full of grace and truth;
in him we have seen your glory.
Baptized by John in the Jordan,
he lived for you,
spoke your truth,
showed your love,
and gave himself for others.
In his death on the cross, he overcame death.
Rising from the tomb, he raised us to eternal life,
and made with us a new covenant
by water and the Spirit.

> If they have not already been said, the words of institution may be
> said here, or in relation to the breaking of the bread.
>
> We give you thanks that the Lord Jesus,
> on the night before he died,
> took bread,
> and after giving thanks to you,
> he broke it, and gave it to his disciples, saying:
> Take, eat.
> This is my body, given for you.
> Do this in remembrance of me.
>
> In the same way he took the cup, saying:
> This cup is the new covenant sealed in my blood,
> shed for you for the forgiveness of sins.
> Whenever you drink it,
> do this in remembrance of me.

Remembering your gracious acts in Jesus Christ,
we take from your creation this bread and this wine
and joyfully celebrate his dying and rising
as we await the day of his coming.
With thanksgiving we offer our very selves to you
to be a living and holy sacrifice,
dedicated to your service.

The people may sing or say one of the following:

1

Great is the mystery of faith:

Christ has died,
Christ is risen,
Christ will come again.

2

Praise to you, Lord Jesus:

Dying you destroyed our death,
rising you restored our life.
Lord Jesus, come in glory.

3

According to his commandment:

We remember his death,
we proclaim his resurrection,
we await his coming in glory.

4

Christ is the bread of life:

When we eat this bread and drink this cup,
we proclaim your death, Lord Jesus,
until you come in glory.

The minister continues:

Gracious God,
pour out your Holy Spirit upon us
and upon these your gifts of bread and wine,
that the bread we break
and the cup we bless
may be the communion of the body and blood of Christ.
By your Spirit make us one with Christ,
that we may be one with all who share this feast,
united in ministry in every place.
As this bread is Christ's body for us,
send us out to be the body of Christ in the world.

Intercessions for the church and the world may be included here.

Illumine our hearts, O God,
with the radiance of Christ's presence,
that our lives may show forth his love in this weary world.
Teach us to befriend the lost,
to serve the poor,
to reconcile our enemies,
and to love our neighbors.
Keep us faithful in your service
until Christ comes in final victory
and we shall feast with all your saints
in the joy of your eternal realm.

Through Christ, with Christ, in Christ,
in the unity of the Holy Spirit,
all glory and honor are yours, almighty God,
now and forever.   **Amen.**   [173]

PRAYER OF THANKSGIVING

For use when the Eucharist is not celebrated.

Let us give thanks to the Lord our God.

It is right to give our thanks and praise.

God of majesty and light,
you hold the whole world in your hand.
So we give you our great praise
that in Jesus Christ all people may see your glory.
We thank you for revealing Jesus to be your Son,
and for claiming our lives in baptism
to be his glad disciples.
By your Spirit,
may peace descend upon us
that we may follow him with grateful hearts.
Take us and all we have to be useful in your service,
God of all nations,
in the gracious name of Jesus Christ, your Son,
by the power of your Holy Spirit,
now and forever.   **Amen.**   [174]

Baptism of the Lord

Sunday between January 7 and 13

Sentences of Scripture

1

Year A B C
Luke 9:35

A voice came out of the cloud, saying:
This is my Son, my Chosen; listen to him!

2

Year A B C
Ps. 96:2–3

Sing, and bless God's name;

tell the glad news of salvation from day to day.

Proclaim God's glory to the nations,

God's marvelous deeds to all peoples.

3

Year A B C
Ps. 29:2–4

Ascribe to the Lord the glory due God's name,

worship the Lord in holy splendor.

The voice of the Lord is over the waters;

the God of glory thunders, the Lord, over mighty waters.

The voice of the Lord is powerful,

the voice of the Lord is full of majesty.

Prayer of the Day

1

Year A B C

Eternal God,
at the baptism of Jesus in the River Jordan
you proclaimed him your beloved Son,
and anointed him with the Holy Spirit.

Grant that all who are baptized into his name
may keep the covenant they have made,
and boldly confess him as Lord and Savior;
who with you and the Holy Spirit lives and reigns,
one God, in glory everlasting. **Amen.** [175]

2

Holy God,
you sent your Son to be baptized among sinners,
to seek and save the lost.
May we, who have been baptized in his name,
never turn away from the world,
but reach out in love to rescue the wayward;
by the mercy of Christ our Lord,
who lives and reigns with you and the Holy Spirit,
one God, now and forever. **Amen.** [176]

LITANY FOR BAPTISM OF THE LORD

O Christ,
by your epiphany your light shines upon us,
giving us the fullness of salvation.
Help us show your light to all we meet today.

Lord, have mercy.

O Christ of glory,
you humbled yourself to be baptized,
showing us the way of humility.
Strengthen us to serve you in humility all the days of our life.

Lord, have mercy.

O Christ,
by your baptism you cleansed us from our sin,
making us children of your Father.
Give the grace of being a child of God to all who seek you.

Lord, have mercy.

O Christ,
by your baptism you sanctified creation
and opened the door of repentance
to all who are baptized.
Make us servants of your gospel in the world.

Lord, have mercy.

O Christ,
by your baptism you revealed to us the glorious Trinity
when the voice from heaven proclaimed, "This is my beloved Son,"
and the Holy Spirit descended upon you like a dove.
Renew a heart of worship within all the baptized.

Lord, have mercy.   [177]

After a brief silence, the leader concludes the litany:

Almighty God,
you anointed Jesus at his baptism with the Holy Spirit,
and revealed him as your beloved Son.
Keep us, your children born of water and the Spirit,
faithful in your service,
that we may rejoice to be called children of God;
through the same Jesus Christ our Lord,
who lives and reigns with you and the Holy Spirit,
one God, now and forever.   **Amen.**   [178]

PRAYER OF CONFESSION

Merciful God,
in baptism you promise forgiveness and new life,
making us part of the body of Christ.
We confess that we remain preoccupied with ourselves,
separated from sisters and brothers in Christ.
We cling to destructive habits, hold grudges,
and show reluctance to welcome one another;
we allow the past to hold us hostage.

In your loving kindness, have mercy on us,
and free us from sin.
Remind us of the promises you make in baptism
so that we may rise to new life,
and live together in grace.   [179]

GREAT THANKSGIVING

The Lord be with you.

And also with you.

Lift up your hearts.

We lift them to the Lord.

Let us give thanks to the Lord our God.

It is right to give our thanks and praise.

It is truly right and our greatest joy
to give you thanks and praise,
O God of mercy and might.
In your wisdom, you made all things
and sustain them by your power.
You have called forth men and women in every age
to be your servants and speak your word.
When we rebelled against your call
and turned from your ways,
in your love you called us back to you.
You delivered us from captivity,
and made covenant to be our sovereign God.
You sent prophets to call us to justice and compassion.

Therefore we praise you,
joining our voices with the choirs of heaven
and with all the faithful of every time and place,
who forever sing to the glory of your name:

> The people may sing or say:

Holy, holy, holy Lord, God of power and might,
heaven and earth are full of your glory.
Hosanna in the highest.

Blessed is he who comes in the name of the Lord.
Hosanna in the highest.

> The minister continues:

You are holy, O God of majesty,
and blessed is Jesus Christ, your Son, our Lord,
in whom you have revealed yourself,
our light and our salvation.
Baptized in Jordan's waters,
Jesus took his place with sinners
and your voice proclaimed him your beloved.
Your Spirit anointed him
to bring good news to the poor,
to proclaim release to the captives,
to restore sight to the blind,
to free the oppressed.

He lived among us in power and grace,
touching broken lives with your healing peace.
By the baptism of his suffering, death, and resurrection
you gave birth to your church,
and made with us a new covenant
by water and the Spirit.

If they have not already been said, the words of institution may be
said here, or in relation to the breaking of the bread.

We give you thanks that the Lord Jesus,
on the night before he died,
took bread,
and after giving thanks to you,
he broke it, and gave it to his disciples, saying:
Take, eat.
This is my body, given for you.
Do this in remembrance of me.

In the same way he took the cup, saying:
This cup is the new covenant sealed in my blood,
shed for you for the forgiveness of sins.
Whenever you drink it,
do this in remembrance of me.

Remembering your gracious acts in Jesus Christ,
we take from your creation this bread and this wine
and joyfully celebrate his dying and rising,
as we await the day of his coming.
With thanksgiving we offer our very selves to you
to be a living and holy sacrifice,
dedicated to your service.

The people may sing or say one of the following:

1

Great is the mystery of faith:

Christ has died,
Christ is risen,
Christ will come again.

2

Praise to you, Lord Jesus:

Dying you destroyed our death,
rising you restored our life.
Lord Jesus, come in glory.

3

According to his commandment:

We remember his death,
we proclaim his resurrection,
we await his coming in glory.

4

Christ is the bread of life:

When we eat this bread and drink this cup,
we proclaim your death, Lord Jesus,
until you come in glory.

The minister continues:

Gracious God,
pour out your Holy Spirit upon us
and upon these your gifts of bread and wine,
that the bread we break
and the cup we bless
may be the communion of the body and blood of Christ.
By your Spirit make us one with Christ,
that we may be one with all who share this feast,
united in ministry in every place.
As this bread is Christ's body for us,
send us out to be the body of Christ in the world.

Intercessions for the church and the world may be included here.

O God, as you once claimed us in the Spirit's waters
and number us among your own beloved,
give us power to do your work,
to show your love,
and to live holy and joyful lives.
Keep us faithful in your service
until Christ comes in final victory
and we shall feast with all your saints
in the joy of your eternal realm.

Through Christ, with Christ, in Christ,
in the unity of the Holy Spirit,
all glory and honor are yours, almighty God,
now and forever.   **Amen.**   [180]

Prayer of Thanksgiving

For use when the Eucharist is not celebrated.

Let us give thanks to the Lord our God.

It is right to give our thanks and praise.

God of heaven and earth,
you call us to come in humility before you,
bringing the offering of our very selves.
As you revealed Jesus to be your Son
in his baptism at the hand of John,
so you claimed our lives in baptism,
that we might die to sin
and be raised with him to new life.
By your Spirit,
confirm in our hearts the witness
that Christ is Savior of the world
and our Lord.
Accept all we have and are, O God,
in the service of Jesus Christ,
and strengthen us with your Spirit's power,
now and forever.   **Amen.**   [181]

SUNDAYS BETWEEN BAPTISM OF THE LORD AND TRANSFIGURATION OF THE LORD

Sundays 2–8 in Ordinary Time

SECOND SUNDAY IN ORDINARY TIME

Sunday between January 14 and 20

SENTENCES OF SCRIPTURE

1
Year A B C
John 1:14, 12

The Word became flesh and lived among us,

and we have seen his glory.

To all who received him,

he gave power to become children of God.

2
Year B
See John 1:41, 16

We have found the Messiah,
Jesus Christ, who brings us truth and grace.

3
Year C
Isa. 62:4c, 5b

The Lord delights in you.
As the bridegroom rejoices over the bride,
so shall your God rejoice over you.

PRAYER OF THE DAY

1
Year A B C

Almighty God,
your Son our Savior Jesus Christ
is the light of the world.

May your people,
illumined by your Word and Sacraments,
shine with the radiance of his glory,
that he may be known, worshiped, and obeyed
to the ends of the earth;
who lives and reigns with you and the Holy Spirit,
one God, now and forever.   **Amen.**   [182]

2   *Year A B C*

Eternal God,
your Son, Jesus Christ,
now exalted as Lord of all,
pours out his gifts on the church.
Grant us that unity which your Spirit gives,
keep us in the bond of peace,
and bring all creation to worship before your throne;
through Jesus Christ our Redeemer,
who lives and reigns with you in the unity of the Holy Spirit,
one God, now and forever.   **Amen.**   [183]

3   *Year C*

Great God,
your mercy is an unexpected miracle.
Help us to believe and obey,
that we may be filled with the wine of new life,
promised in the power of Jesus Christ our Savior,
who lives and reigns with you in the unity of the Holy Spirit,
one God, now and forever.   **Amen.**   [184]

THIRD SUNDAY IN ORDINARY TIME

Sunday between January 21 and 27

SENTENCES OF SCRIPTURE

1   *Year A*
                                                                               Matt. 4:23

Jesus proclaimed the good news of the kingdom
and healed every sickness among the people.

2   *Year B*
                                                                               Mark 1:15

The time is fulfilled
and the kingdom of God is at hand;
repent, and believe the good news.

The Spirit of the Lord has anointed me
to preach good news to the poor
and release to the captives.

PRAYER OF THE DAY

1   *Year A B*

Almighty God,
by grace alone you call us
and accept us in your service.
Strengthen us by your Spirit,
and make us worthy of your call;
through Jesus Christ our Lord,
who lives and reigns with you and the Holy Spirit,
one God, now and forever.   **Amen.**   [185]

2   *Year B*

Loving God,
through your Son you have called us to repent of our sin,
to believe the good news,
and to celebrate the coming of your kingdom.
Like Christ's first apostles,
may we hear his call to discipleship,
and, forsaking old ways,
proclaim the gospel of new life to a broken world;
through our Lord and Savior Jesus Christ,
who lives and reigns with you and the Holy Spirit,
one God, now and forever.   **Amen.**   [186]

3   *Year B*

Almighty God,
you sent Jesus to proclaim your kingdom
and to teach with authority.
Anoint us with your Spirit,
that we too may bring good news to the poor,
bind up the brokenhearted,
and proclaim liberty to the captive;
through Jesus Christ our Lord,
who lives and reigns with you and the Holy Spirit,
one God, now and forever.   **Amen.**   [187]

Fourth Sunday in Ordinary Time

Sunday between January 28 and February 3

Sentences of Scripture

1   *Year A B C*
                                                               Rom. 12:1

I appeal to you, brothers and sisters,
by the mercies of God,
to present your bodies as a living sacrifice,
holy and acceptable to God.

2   *Year B*
                                                               Matt. 4:23

Jesus went throughout Galilee,
teaching, proclaiming the good news,
and healing every sickness among the people.

3   *Year C*
                                                               Luke 4:18

The Spirit of the Lord has anointed me
to preach good news to the poor
and release to the captives.

Prayer of the Day

1   *Year A B C*

Living God,
in Christ you make all things new.
Transform the poverty of our nature
by the riches of your grace,
and in the renewal of our lives
make known your glory;
through Jesus Christ our Lord,
who is alive and reigns with you and the Holy Spirit,
one God, now and forever.   **Amen.**   [188]

2   *Year A B C*

God of compassion,
you have shown us in Christ
that your love is never-ending.
Enable us to love you with all our hearts
and to love one another as Christ loved us.

Grant this through our Lord Jesus Christ,
who lives and reigns with you and the Holy Spirit,
one God, forever and ever.   **Amen.**   [189]

3   *Year A*

Holy God,
you confound the world's wisdom
in giving your kingdom to the lowly
and the pure in heart.
Give us such a hunger and thirst for justice
and perseverance in striving for peace,
that by our words and deeds
the world may see the promise of your kingdom,
revealed in Jesus Christ our Lord,
who lives and reigns with you in the unity of the Holy Spirit,
one God, forever and ever.   **Amen.**   [190]

FIFTH SUNDAY IN ORDINARY TIME

Sunday between February 4 and 10

SENTENCES OF SCRIPTURE

1   *Year A*
                                                                                     Matt. 5:14, 16

You are the light of the world.
Let your light shine before others,
so that they may see your good works
and give glory to your Father in heaven.

2   *Year B*
                                                                                         Isa. 40:31

Those who wait for the Lord
shall renew their strength,
they shall mount up with wings like eagles,
they shall run and not be weary,
they shall walk and not faint.

3   *Year 3*
                                                                                         John 8:12

Jesus said:
I am the light of the world.
Whoever follows me will not walk in darkness
but will have the light of life.

PRAYER OF THE DAY

1   *Year A B C*

Faithful God,
you have appointed us your witnesses,
to be light that shines in the world.
Let us not hide the bright hope you have given us,
but tell everyone your love,
revealed in Jesus Christ the Lord,
who lives and reigns with you in the unity of the Holy Spirit,
one God, forever and ever.   **Amen.**   [191]

2   *Year A B C*

O God,
in the folly of the cross
you reveal the great distance
between your wisdom and human understanding.
Open our minds to the simplicity of the gospel,
that, fervent in faith and tireless in love,
we may become light and salt for the world,
for the sake of Jesus Christ, your Son,
who lives and reigns with you in the unity of the Holy Spirit,
one God, forever and ever.   **Amen.**   [192]

3   *Year B C*

Most holy God,
the earth is filled with your glory,
and in your presence angels stand in awe.
Enlarge our vision,
that we may recognize your power at work in your Son
and join the apostles and prophets as heralds of your saving word.
We ask this through our Lord Jesus Christ, your Son,
who lives and reigns with you in the unity of the Holy Spirit,
God forever and ever.   **Amen.**   [193]

SIXTH SUNDAY IN ORDINARY TIME

Sunday between February 11 and 17
(Except when this Sunday is Transfiguration of the Lord)

SENTENCES OF SCRIPTURE

1   *Year A B C*
                                                                       Ps. 106:1

O give thanks, for the Lord is good.
God's love endures forever.

2

Year A
Ps. 119:1, 2

Happy are those whose way is blameless,

who walk in the law of the Lord.

Happy are those who keep the Lord's decrees,

who seek the Lord with their whole heart.

3

Year C
Luke 6:23

Rejoice and leap for joy,
for surely your reward is great in heaven.

PRAYER OF THE DAY

1

Year A

Almighty God,
you gave the law to guide our lives.
May we never shrink from your commandments,
but, as we are taught by your Son Jesus,
fulfill the law in perfect love;
through Christ our Lord and Master,
who lives and reigns with you and the Holy Spirit,
one God, now and forever.   **Amen.**   [194]

2

Year B

Almighty and ever-living God,
your Son, Jesus Christ, healed the sick
and restored them to wholeness of life.
Look with compassion on the anguish of the world,
and by your power make whole all peoples and nations;
through Jesus Christ our Lord,
who lives and reigns with you and the Holy Spirit,
one God, now and forever.   **Amen.**   [195]

3

Year C

Holy God,
you challenge the powers that rule this world
and show favor to the oppressed.
Instill in us a true sense of justice,
that we may discern the signs of your kingdom
and strive for right to prevail
for the sake of Jesus Christ our Lord,
who lives and reigns with you in the unity of the Holy Spirit,
one God, forever and ever.   **Amen.**   [196]

SEVENTH SUNDAY IN ORDINARY TIME

Sunday between February 18 and 24
(Except when this Sunday is Transfiguration of the Lord)

SENTENCES OF SCRIPTURE

1

Year A
See 1 John 2:5

The love of God is perfected
in those who obey the word of Christ.

2

Year B
Luke 4:18

The Spirit of the Lord has anointed me
to preach good news to the poor
and release to the captives.

3

Year A C
John 13:34

Jesus said:
I give you a new commandment,
that you love one another.
As I have loved you,
you also should love one another.

PRAYER OF THE DAY

1

Year A B C

Almighty God,
in signs and wonders your Son revealed
the greatness of your saving love.
Renew your people with your grace,
and sustain us by your power,
for we can do nothing without you;
through Jesus Christ our Lord,
who is alive and reigns with you and the Holy Spirit,
one God, now and forever.   **Amen.**   [197]

2

Year A C

Almighty God,
you have taught us
that all our deeds without love are worth nothing.
Send your Holy Spirit and pour into our hearts
that most excellent gift of love,

the very bond of peace and of all goodness;
through Jesus Christ our Lord,
who lives and reigns with you and the Holy Spirit,
one God, now and forever.   **Amen.**   [198]

EIGHTH SUNDAY IN ORDINARY TIME

Sunday between February 25 and 29
(Except when this Sunday is Transfiguration of the Lord)

SENTENCES OF SCRIPTURE

1   *Year A B C*

Heb. 4:12

The word of God is living and active.
It is able to judge
the thoughts and intentions of the heart.

2   *Year A B C*

Phil. 2:15, 16

Shine like stars in the world,
holding fast to the word of life.

PRAYER OF THE DAY

1   *Year A B C*

Almighty God,
renew us through the gift of your Spirit,
that we may always do and think
what is just in your sight,
that we, who can do nothing good without you,
may live according to your holy will;
through Jesus Christ our Lord,
who lives and reigns with you and the Holy Spirit,
one God, now and forever.   **Amen.**   [199]

2   *Year A B C*

Almighty God,
you have sent the Spirit of your Son into our hearts
and freed us from bondage to sin.
Give us grace to dedicate our freedom to your service,
that we and all people may be brought
to the glorious liberty of the children of God;
through Jesus Christ our Lord,
who lives and reigns with you and the Holy Spirit,
one God, forever and ever.   **Amen.**   [200]

TRANSFIGURATION OF THE LORD

SENTENCES OF SCRIPTURE
PRAYER OF THE DAY

SENTENCES OF SCRIPTURE

1

Year A B C
1 John 3:2

Beloved, we are God's children now;
what we will be has not yet been revealed.
What we do know is this:
When he is revealed,
we will be like him,
for we will see him as he is.

2

Year A B C
Matt. 17:5

A voice said:
This is my Son, the Beloved,
with whom I am well pleased.
Listen to him!

3

Year A B C
2 Cor. 4:6

God who said, "Out of darkness the light shall shine!"
is the same God who made light shine in our hearts
to bring us the knowledge of God's glory
shining in the face of Christ.

PRAYER OF THE DAY

1

Year A B C

O God,
in the transfiguration of your Son
you confirmed the mysteries of the faith
by the witness of Moses and Elijah;

and in the voice from the cloud
you foreshadowed our adoption as your children.
Make us, with Christ, heirs of your glory,
and bring us to enjoy its fullness;
through Jesus Christ our Lord,
who lives and reigns with you in the unity of the Holy Spirit,
one God, now and forever. **Amen.** [201]

2   *Year A B C*

Almighty God,
whose Son was revealed in majesty
before he suffered death upon the cross:
Give us faith to perceive his glory,
that being strengthened by his grace
we may be changed into his likeness, from glory to glory;
through Jesus Christ our Lord,
who lives and reigns with you and the Holy Spirit,
one God, now and forever. **Amen.** [202]

3   *Year A B C*

O God, glorious and faithful,
to those who seek you with a sincere heart
you reveal the beauty of your face.
Strengthen us in faith
to embrace the mystery of the cross,
and open our hearts to its transfiguring power;
that, clinging in love to your will for us,
we may walk the path of discipleship
as followers of your Son, Jesus Christ our Lord,
who lives and reigns with you and the Holy Spirit,
one God, forever and ever. **Amen.** [203]

PRAYER OF CONFESSION

**God of compassion,
in Jesus Christ you reveal the light of your glory,
but we turn away, distracted by our own plans.
We confess that we speak when we should listen,
and act when we should wait.**

**Forgive our aimless enthusiasms.
Grant us wisdom to live in your light
and to follow in the way of your beloved Son,
Jesus Christ, our Lord and Savior.** [204]

GREAT THANKSGIVING

The Lord be with you.

And also with you.

Lift up your hearts.

We lift them to the Lord.

Let us give thanks to the Lord our God.

It is right to give our thanks and praise.

It is truly right and our greatest joy
to give you thanks and praise,
eternal God our Creator.
You brought light out of darkness
and set the sun to brighten the day
and the moon and stars to illumine the night.
Your glory blinds the eyes of our sin,
while your radiance warms our needy hearts.
You lead us by the light of your truth
into the way of righteousness and peace.

Therefore we praise you,
joining our voices with the heavenly choirs
and with all the faithful of every time and place,
who forever sing to the glory of your name:

The people may sing or say:

**Holy, holy, holy Lord, God of power and might,
heaven and earth are full of your glory.
Hosanna in the highest.**

**Blessed is he who comes in the name of the Lord.
Hosanna in the highest.**

The minister continues:

You are holy, O God of majesty,
and blessed is Jesus Christ, your Son, our Lord.
On a lonely mountain
his human body was transfigured by your divine splendor.
In his face, we have glimpsed your glory.
In his life, we see your love.

For your image is untarnished in him,
and the burden of human sorrow and suffering
could not diminish his reflection of your holiness.
The world was dark at his death,
but the light of his life could not be extinguished.
From the grave he rose like the sun,
with blinding power and radiant peace.

If they have not already been said, the words of institution may be said here, or in relation to the breaking of the bread.

We give you thanks that the Lord Jesus,
on the night before he died,
took bread,
and after giving thanks to you,
he broke it, and gave it to his disciples, saying:
Take, eat.
This is my body, given for you.
Do this in remembrance of me.

In the same way he took the cup, saying:
This cup is the new covenant sealed in my blood,
shed for you for the forgiveness of sins.
Whenever you drink it,
do this in remembrance of me.

Remembering your gracious acts in Jesus Christ,
we take from your creation this bread and this wine
and joyfully celebrate his dying and rising,
as we await the day of his coming.
With thanksgiving we offer our very selves to you
to be a living and holy sacrifice,
dedicated to your service.

The people may sing or say one of the following:

1

Great is the mystery of faith:

**Christ has died,
Christ is risen,
Christ will come again.**

2

Praise to you, Lord Jesus:

**Dying you destroyed our death,
rising you restored our life.
Lord Jesus, come in glory.**

3

According to his commandment:

**We remember his death,
we proclaim his resurrection,
we await his coming in glory.**

4

Christ is the bread of life:

**When we eat this bread and drink this cup,
we proclaim your death, Lord Jesus,
until you come in glory.**

The minister continues:

Gracious God,
pour out your Holy Spirit upon us
and upon these your gifts of bread and wine,
that the bread we break
and the cup we bless
may be the communion of the body and blood of Christ.
By your Spirit make us one with Christ,
that we may be one with all who share this feast,
united in ministry in every place.
As this bread is Christ's body for us,
send us out to be the body of Christ in the world.

Intercessions for the church and the world may be included here.

Illumine our lives, O God,
with the radiance of Christ's love,
and inspire us to shine in faith and witness
as his holy disciples.
Transform us into his likeness
that we may live for you, as he lived,
and love others, as he loved them.

Give us strength to serve you faithfully
until the promised day of resurrection,
when with the redeemed of all the ages
we will feast with you at your table in glory.

Through Christ, with Christ, in Christ,
in the unity of the Holy Spirit,
all glory and honor are yours, almighty God,
now and forever. **Amen.** [205]

PRAYER OF THANKSGIVING

For use when the Eucharist is not celebrated.

Let us give thanks to the Lord our God.
It is right to give our thanks and praise.

O Lord our God,
you are great indeed,
clothed in majesty and splendor,
wrapped in light as with a robe.
In the solitude of a mountain height
you revealed your glory in Jesus Christ
even as he faced his crucifixion.
We praise you for this glimpse of the mystery of our redemption.

You loved the world so much
that you sent your beloved Son to dwell with us.
He who bears your very image,
the firstborn of all creation,
through whom all things have been created,
took our flesh and suffered death
that we may be made whole.
By his death he conquered death,
and by his rising he gives eternal life.
We praise you for your saving grace.

Transfigure us by your Spirit,
and let your love shine in all we do and say
that all the world may see the radiant light of God
guiding all creation, Jesus Christ our Lord. **Amen.** [206]

An Outline of the Service for Ash Wednesday

Gathering

Call to Worship
Prayer of the Day
Hymn, Psalm, or Canticle

The Word

Prayer for Illumination
First Reading
Second Reading
Anthem, Hymn, Psalm, Canticle, or Spiritual
Gospel Reading
Sermon
Invitation to the Observance of the Lenten Discipline
Psalm 51
Litany of Penitence
[Imposition of Ashes]
Hymn

If the Eucharist is not celebrated:

The Eucharist

Invitation to the Lord's Table
Great Thanksgiving
Lord's Prayer
Breaking of the Bread
Communion of the People

Prayer
[Offering]

Sending

Hymn, Psalm, or Spiritual
Blessing and Charge

Ash Wednesday

Gathering

All silently gather. Any procession should be in silence.

Call to Worship

All may stand as the minister(s) and other worship leaders enter.

The minister says:

Let us worship God

See John 3:17; Ps. 46:1–3

God sent Christ into the world
not to condemn the world,
but that the world might be saved through him.

God's love endures forever.

God is our refuge and strength,
a present help in trouble.
Therefore we will not fear
though the earth should change,
though the mountains shake in the heart of the sea;
though the waters roar and foam,
though the mountains tremble with its tumult.

God's love endures forever.

Prayer of the Day

Let us pray.

After a brief silence, one of the following prayers may be said:

1

Gracious God,
out of your love and mercy
you breathed into dust the breath of life,
creating us to serve you and neighbors.
Call forth our prayers and acts of tenderness,
and strengthen us to face our mortality,
that we may reach with confidence for your mercy;
in Jesus Christ our Lord,
who lives and reigns with you and the Holy Spirit,
one God, now and forever.   [207]

Amen.

2

Almighty God,
you despise nothing you have made
and you forgive the sins of all who are penitent.
Create in us new and contrite hearts,
that truly repenting of our sins,
and acknowledging our brokenness,
we may obtain from you, the God of all mercy,
full pardon and forgiveness;
through your Son, Jesus Christ our Redeemer,
who lives and reigns with you and the Holy Spirit,
one God, now and forever.   [208]

Amen.

HYMN, PSALM, OR SPIRITUAL

A hymn, psalm, or spiritual may be sung.

The people may then be seated.

THE WORD

PRAYER FOR ILLUMINATION

Let us pray.

After a brief silence, the following or another prayer for illumination
(pp. 60, 90–91) may be said:

God our helper,
by your Holy Spirit open our minds,

that as the scriptures are read and your Word is proclaimed,
we may be led into your truth
and be taught your will,
for the sake of Jesus Christ our Lord.   [75]

Amen.

FIRST READING   Joel 2:1–2, 12–17; or Isaiah 58:1–12

SECOND READING   2 Corinthians 5:20b–6:10

ANTHEM, HYMN, PSALM, CANTICLE, OR SPIRITUAL

GOSPEL READING   Matthew 6:1–6, 16–21

SERMON

INVITATION TO THE OBSERVANCE OF THE LENTEN DISCIPLINE

The following or similar words may be spoken:

Friends in Christ,
every year at the time of the Christian Passover
we celebrate our redemption
through the death and resurrection of our Lord Jesus Christ.
Lent is a time to prepare for this celebration
and to renew our life in the paschal mystery.
We begin this holy season
by acknowledging our need for repentance,
and for the mercy and forgiveness
proclaimed in the gospel of Jesus Christ.

If ashes are used, the following may be said:

We begin our journey to Easter with the sign of ashes.
This ancient sign speaks of the frailty and uncertainty of human life,
and marks the penitence of this community.

The minister continues:

I invite you, therefore, in the name of Christ,
to observe a holy Lent
by self-examination and penitence,
by prayer and fasting,
by works of love,
and by reading and meditating on the Word of God.

Let us bow before God, our Creator and Redeemer,
and confess our sin.

> The people may kneel or bow down.
> Silence is kept for reflection and self-examination.

PSALM 51

> Psalm 51:1–17 is sung or said.

Psalm 51:1–17   Tone 7; PH 195,196; PS 48

R
1 Have mercy on me, O God, according to your loving-kindness; *
    in your great compassion blot out my offenses.

2 **Wash me through and through from my wickedness** *
    and cleanse me from my sin.   R

3 For I know my transgressions, *
    and my sin is ever before me.

4 **Against you only have I sinned** *
    and done what is evil in your sight.

And so you are justified when you speak *
    and upright in your judgment.

5 **Indeed, I have been wicked from my birth,** *
    a sinner from my mother's womb.   R

6 For behold, you look for truth deep within me, *
    and will make me understand wisdom secretly.

7 **Purge me from my sin, and I shall be pure;** *
    wash me, and I shall be clean indeed.

8 Make me hear of joy and gladness, *
    that the body you have broken may rejoice.

9 **Hide your face from my sins** *
    and blot out all my iniquities.   R

10 Create in me a clean heart, O God, *
    and renew a right spirit within me.

11 **Cast me not away from your presence** *
    and take not your holy Spirit from me.

12 Give me the joy of your saving help again *
   and sustain me with your bountiful Spirit.   **R**

13 **I shall teach your ways to the wicked, ***
   and sinners shall return to you.

14 Deliver me from death, O God, *
   and my tongue shall sing of your righteousness,
   O God of my salvation.   **R**

15 **Open my lips, O Lord, ***
   and my mouth shall proclaim your praise.

16 Had you desired it, I would have offered sacrifice, *
   but you take no delight in burnt-offerings.

17 **The sacrifice of God is a troubled spirit; ***
   a broken and contrite heart, O God, you will not despise.   **R**

LITANY OF PENITENCE

> The following or another prayer of confession (pp. 53–54, 87–89, 474–475)
> may be said, the people kneeling or bowing down:

Let us pray.

Holy and merciful God,
we confess to you and to one another,
and to the whole communion of saints in heaven and on earth,
that we have sinned by our own fault
in thought, word, and deed,
by what we have done,
and by what we have left undone.

We have not loved you with our whole heart, and mind, and strength.
We have not loved our neighbors as ourselves.
We have not forgiven others as we have been forgiven.

Have mercy on us, O God.

We have not listened to your call to serve as Christ served us.
We have not been true to the mind of Christ.
We have grieved your Holy Spirit.

Have mercy on us, O God.

We confess to you, O God, all our past unfaithfulness:
The pride, hypocrisy, and impatience in our lives,

we confess to you, O God.

Our self-indulgent appetites and ways
and our exploitation of other people,

we confess to you, O God.

Our anger at our own frustration
and our envy of those more fortunate than ourselves,

we confess to you, O God.

Our intemperate love of worldly goods and comforts,
and our dishonesty in daily life and work,

we confess to you, O God.

Our negligence in prayer and worship,
and our failure to commend the faith that is in us,

we confess to you, O God.

Accept our repentance, O God,
for the wrongs we have done.
For our neglect of human need and suffering
and our indifference to injustice and cruelty,

accept our repentance, O God.

For all false judgments,
for uncharitable thoughts toward our neighbors,
and for our prejudice and contempt
toward those who differ from us,

accept our repentance, O God.

For our waste and pollution of your creation
and our lack of concern for those who come after us,

accept our repentance, O God.

Restore us, O God,
and let your anger depart from us.

**Favorably hear us, O God,
for your mercy is great.**   [209]

IMPOSITION OF ASHES

> If ashes are to be imposed, the following prayer, or a similar prayer, is said:

Almighty God,
you have created us out of the dust of the earth.
May these ashes be for us
a sign of our mortality and penitence,
and a reminder that only by your gracious gift
are we given everlasting life;
through Jesus Christ our Savior.   [210]

Amen.

> People are invited to come forward to receive the imposition of ashes.

> During the imposition, suitable hymns or psalms may be sung, or silence may be kept.

> A worship leader marks the forehead of each person with the ashes, using the following words:

Gen. 3:19

Remember that you are dust,
and to dust you shall return.

> After all who desire ashes have received them, or if ashes have not been imposed, the confession concludes with the following words, the people kneeling or bowing down:

Accomplish in us, O God, the work of your salvation,

That we may show forth your glory in the world.

By the cross and passion of our Savior,

**bring us with all your saints
to the joy of Christ's resurrection.**

HYMN

> A penitential hymn may be sung, the people seated.

> IF THE EUCHARIST IS NOT TO BE CELEBRATED, THE SERVICE CONTINUES ON PAGE 233.

The Eucharist

During the singing of the hymn, bread and wine may be brought to the table, or uncovered if already in place.

Invitation to the Lord's Table

Standing at the table, the presiding minister invites the people to the Lord's Supper, saying:

Hear the gracious words of our Savior Jesus Christ:

Matt. 11:28, 29; John 6:35, 37; Matt. 5:6

Come to me, all you that are weary
and are carrying heavy burdens,
and I will give you rest.
Take my yoke upon you,
and learn from me;
for I am gentle and lowly in heart,
and you will find rest for your souls.

I am the bread of life.
Whoever comes to me will never be hungry,
and whoever believes in me will never be thirsty.
No one who comes to me will I cast out.

Blessed are those who hunger and thirst for righteousness,
for they will be filled.

Great Thanksgiving

All may stand.

The presiding minister leads the people in the following or another great thanksgiving appropriate to the day (pp. 69–73, 126–156):

The Lord be with you.

And also with you.

Lift up your hearts.

We lift them to the Lord.

Let us give thanks to the Lord our God.

It is right to give our thanks and praise.

It is truly right and our greatest joy
to give you thanks and praise,
eternal God, creator and ruler of the universe.
You are our God,
and we are the creatures of your hand.
You made us from the dust of the earth,
breathed into us the breath of life,
and set us in your world to love and serve you.
When we rejected your love and ignored your wisdom,
you did not reject us.
You loved us still
and called us to turn again to you
in obedience and in love.

Therefore we praise you,
joining our voices with the heavenly choirs
and with all the faithful of every time and place,
who forever sing to the glory of your name:

The people may sing or say:

Holy, holy, holy Lord, God of power and might,
heaven and earth are full of your glory.
Hosanna in the highest.

Blessed is he who comes in the name of the Lord.
Hosanna in the highest.

The minister continues:

You are holy, O God of majesty,
and blessed is Jesus Christ, your Son, our Lord.
Out of your great love for the world,
you sent Jesus among us
to set us free from the tyranny of evil.
He lived as one of us,
sharing our joys and sorrows.
By his dying and rising,
he releases us from bondage to sin
and frees us from the dominion of death.

We give you thanks that the Lord Jesus,
on the night before he died, took bread,
and after giving thanks to you,
he broke it, and gave it to his disciples, saying:
Take, eat.
This is my body, given for you.
Do this in remembrance of me.

In the same way he took the cup, saying:
This cup is the new covenant sealed in my blood,
shed for you for the forgiveness of sins.
Whenever you drink it,
do this in remembrance of me.

Remembering all your mighty and merciful acts,
we take this bread and this wine from the gifts you have given us,
and celebrate with joy the redemption won for us in Jesus Christ.
Accept this our sacrifice of praise and thanksgiving
as a living and holy offering of ourselves,
that our lives may proclaim the One crucified and risen.

The people may sing or say one of the following:

1

Great is the mystery of faith:

**Christ has died,
Christ is risen,
Christ will come again.**

2

Praise to you, Lord Jesus:

**Dying you destroyed our death,
rising you restored our life.
Lord Jesus, come in glory.**

3

According to his commandment:

**We remember his death,
we proclaim his resurrection,
we await his coming in glory.**

Christ is the bread of life:

**When we eat this bread and drink this cup,
we proclaim your death, Lord Jesus,
until you come in glory.**

The minister continues:

Gracious God,
pour out your Holy Spirit upon us
and upon these your gifts of bread and wine,
that the bread we break
and the cup we bless
may be the communion of the body and blood of Christ.
By your Spirit unite us with the living Christ
and with all who are baptized in his name,
that we may be one in ministry in every place.
As this bread is Christ's body for us,
send us out to be the body of Christ in the world.

Intercessions for the church and the world may be included here.

Lead us, O God, by the power of your Spirit
to live as the Lord requires:
to do justice,
to love kindness,
and to walk humbly with you, our God.
Keep our eyes fixed on Jesus Christ
until this mortal life is ended,
and all that is earthly returns to dust.
Give us strength to serve you faithfully
until the promised day of resurrection,
when, with the redeemed of all the ages,
we will feast with you at your table in glory.

Through Christ,
all glory and honor are yours, almighty Father,
with the Holy Spirit in the holy church,
now and forever.   [211]

Amen.

LORD'S PRAYER

The minister invites all present to sing or say the Lord's Prayer.

And now, with the confidence of the children of God, let us pray:

Or

Our Father in heaven,	**Our Father, who art in heaven,**
hallowed be your name,	**hallowed be thy name,**
your kingdom come,	**thy kingdom come,**
your will be done,	**thy will be done,**
on earth as in heaven.	**on earth as it is in heaven.**
Give us today our daily bread.	**Give us this day our daily bread;**
Forgive us our sins	**and forgive us our debts,**
as we forgive those who sin against us.	**as we forgive our debtors;**
Save us from the time of trial	**and lead us not into temptation,**
and deliver us from evil.	**but deliver us from evil.**
For the kingdom, the power,	**For thine is the kingdom,**
and the glory are yours	**and the power, and the glory,**
now and forever. Amen.	**forever. Amen.**

All may be seated.

BREAKING OF THE BREAD

A. If the words of institution have previously been said, the minister breaks the bread and pours wine into the cup in silence and in full view of the people.

B. If the words of institution have not previously been said, the minister breaks the bread in full view of the people, saying:

See 1 Cor. 11:23–26; Luke 22:19–20

The Lord Jesus, on the night of his arrest, took bread,
and after giving thanks to God,
he broke it, and gave it to his disciples, saying:
Take, eat.
This is my body, given for you.
Do this in remembrance of me.

The minister pours wine into the cup, and lifts the cup, saying:

In the same way he took the cup, saying:
This cup is the new covenant sealed in my blood,
shed for you for the forgiveness of sins.
Whenever you drink it,
do this in remembrance of me.

Every time you eat this bread and drink this cup,
you proclaim the saving death of the risen Lord,
until he comes.

COMMUNION OF THE PEOPLE

Holding out both the bread and the cup to the people, the minister says:

The gifts of God
for the people of God.

The following, or another version of "Jesus, Lamb of God," may be sung or said.

Jesus, Lamb of God,

have mercy on us.

Jesus, bearer of our sins,

have mercy on us.

Jesus, redeemer of the world,

grant us peace.

The minister and those assisting receive Communion and then serve the bread and the cup to the people.

In giving the bread:

The body of Christ, given for you.   **Amen.**

In giving the cup:

The blood of Christ, shed for you.   **Amen.**

During Communion, psalms, hymns, anthems, or spirituals may be sung.

IF THE EUCHARIST IS NOT CELEBRATED, THE SERVICE CONTINUES HERE FROM PAGE 227.

PRAYER

The following prayer may be prayed by the minister, or by all together.

God of compassion,
through your Son Jesus Christ
you reconciled your people to yourself.
Following his example of prayer and fasting,
may we obey you with willing hearts
and serve one another in holy love;
through Jesus Christ our Lord.   [212]

Amen.

OFFERING

An offering may be received.

SENDING

The people may stand.

HYMN, SPIRITUAL, CANTICLE, OR PSALM

A hymn, spiritual, canticle, or psalm may be sung.

BLESSING AND CHARGE

The minister gives God's blessing to the congregation, saying:

1 Thess. 5:23

May the God of peace
make you holy in every way
and keep your whole being—
spirit, soul, and body—
free from every fault
at the coming of our Lord Jesus Christ.
Amen.

The minister, a deacon, or an elder dismisses the congregation, using the
following charge:

Go in peace to love and serve the Lord.
Thanks be to God.

All quietly depart.

LENT

LITANY FOR LENT

O Christ,
out of your fullness we have all received grace upon grace.
You are our eternal hope;
you are patient and full of mercy;
you are generous to all who call upon you.

Save us, Lord.

O Christ, fountain of life and holiness,
you have taken away our sins.
On the cross you were wounded for our transgressions
and were bruised for our iniquities.

Save us, Lord.

O Christ, obedient unto death,
source of all comfort,
our life and our resurrection,
our peace and reconciliation:

Save us, Lord.

O Christ, Savior of all who trust you,
hope of all who die for you,
and joy of all the saints:

Save us, Lord.

Jesus, Lamb of God,

have mercy on us.

Jesus, bearer of our sins,

have mercy on us.

Jesus, redeemer of the world,

grant us peace.   [213]

After a brief silence, the leader concludes the litany:

God of love,
as in Jesus Christ you gave yourself to us,
so may we give ourselves to you,
living according to your holy will.
Keep our feet firmly in the way
where Christ leads us;
make our mouths speak the truth
that Christ teaches us;
fill our bodies with the life
that is Christ within us.
In his holy name we pray.   **Amen.**   [214]

PRAYER OF CONFESSION

**God of mercy,
you sent Jesus Christ to seek and save the lost.
We confess that we have strayed from you
and turned aside from your way.
We are misled by pride,
for we see ourselves pure when we are stained,
and great when we are small.
We have failed in love,
neglected justice,
and ignored your truth.**

**Have mercy, O God, and forgive our sin.
Return us to paths of righteousness
through Jesus Christ, our Savior.**   [215]

INTERCESSION FOR LENT

Jesus, remember us when you come into your kingdom.
Hear our intercessions.

For your church around the world,

we ask new life.

For all who carry out ministries in your church,

we ask grace and wisdom.

For people who have accepted spiritual disciplines,

we ask inspired discipleship.

For Christians of every land,

we ask new unity in your name.

For Jews and Muslims and people of other faiths,

we ask your divine blessing.

For those who cannot believe,

we ask your faithful love.

For governors and rulers in every land,

we ask your guidance.

For people who suffer and sorrow,

we ask your healing peace.   [216]

After a brief silence, the leader concludes the litany:

Holy God,
your Word, Jesus Christ, spoke peace to a sinful world
and brought humanity the gift of reconciliation
by the suffering and death he endured.
Teach those who bear his name
to follow the example he gave us.
May our faith, hope, and charity
turn hatred to love, conflict to peace, and death to eternal life;
through Christ our Lord.   **Amen.**   [217]

GREAT THANKSGIVING

The Lord be with you.

And also with you.

Lift up your hearts.

We lift them to the Lord.

Let us give thanks to the Lord our God.

It is right to give our thanks and praise.

It is truly right and our greatest joy
to give you thanks and praise,
O God our creator and redeemer.
In your wisdom, you made all things
and sustain them by your power.

You formed us in your image
to love and serve you,
but we forgot your promises
and abandoned your commandments.
In your mercy, you did not reject us
but still claimed us as your own.

When we were slaves in Egypt you freed us
and led us through the waters of the sea.
You fed us with heavenly food in the wilderness,
and satisfied our thirst from desert springs.
On the holy mountain you gave us your law
to guide us in your way.
Through the waters of Jordan
you led us into the land of your promise,
and you sustained us in times of trial.
You spoke through prophets
calling us to turn from our willful ways
to new obedience and righteousness.
You sent your only Son
to be the way to eternal life.

Therefore we praise you,
joining our voices with choirs of angels
and with all the faithful of every time and place,
who forever sing to the glory of your name:

The people may sing or say:

**Holy, holy, holy Lord, God of power and might,
heaven and earth are full of your glory.
Hosanna in the highest.**

**Blessed is he who comes in the name of the Lord.
Hosanna in the highest.**

The minister continues:

You are holy, O God of majesty,
and blessed is Jesus Christ, your Son, our Lord.
He took upon himself the weight of our sin
and carried the burden of our guilt.
He shared our life in every way,
and though tempted, was sinless to the end.

Baptized as your own, he went willingly to his death
and by your power was raised to new life.
In his dying and rising,
you gave birth to your church,
delivered us from slavery to sin and death,
and made with us a new covenant by water and the Spirit.

*If they have not already been said, the words of institution may be
said here, or in relation to the breaking of the bread.*

We give you thanks that the Lord Jesus,
on the night before he died,
took bread,
and after giving thanks to you,
he broke it, and gave it to his disciples, saying:
Take, eat.
This is my body, given for you.
Do this in remembrance of me.

In the same way he took the cup, saying:
This cup is the new covenant sealed in my blood,
shed for you for the forgiveness of sins.
Whenever you drink it,
do this in remembrance of me.

Remembering all your mighty and merciful acts,
we take this bread and this wine
from the gifts you have given us,
and celebrate with joy
the redemption won for us in Jesus Christ.
Accept this our sacrifice of praise and thanksgiving
as a living and holy offering of ourselves,
that our lives may proclaim the One crucified and risen.

The people may sing or say one of the following:

1

Great is the mystery of faith:

**Christ has died,
Christ is risen,
Christ will come again.**

2

Praise to you, Lord Jesus:

Dying you destroyed our death,
rising you restored our life.
Lord Jesus, come in glory.

3

According to his commandment:

We remember his death,
we proclaim his resurrection,
we await his coming in glory.

4

Christ is the bread of life:

When we eat this bread and drink this cup,
we proclaim your death, Lord Jesus,
until you come in glory.

The minister continues:

Gracious God,
pour out your Holy Spirit upon us
and upon these your gifts of bread and wine,
that the bread we break
and the cup we bless
may be the communion of the body and blood of Christ.
By your Spirit unite us with the living Christ,
and with all who are baptized in his name,
that we may be one in ministry in every place.
As this bread is Christ's body for us,
send us out to be the body of Christ in the world.

Intercessions for the church and the world may be included here.

Help us, O God, to be obedient to your call
to love all your children,
to do justice and show mercy,
and to live in peace with your whole creation.
Guide us through the desert of life,
quench our thirst with the living waters,
satisfy our hunger with the bread of heaven.
Give us strength to serve you faithfully
until the promised day of resurrection,

when with the redeemed of all the ages
we will feast with you at your table in glory.

Through Christ,
all glory and honor are yours, almighty Father,
with the Holy Spirit in the holy church,
now and forever.   **Amen.**   [218]

Prayer of Thanksgiving

For use when the Eucharist is not celebrated.

1

Let us give thanks to the Lord our God.

It is right to give our thanks and praise.

God of mercy,
we praise you that in love
you have reached across the abyss of our sin
and brought us into your embrace.
We thank you for the sacrifice of your Son on the cross,
for the breaking of his body for our sakes,
and for the spilling of his blood
to seal us in the covenant of your love.
By your Spirit,
give us the grace of repentance,
and guide us in ways of righteousness.
Take our humble offerings
as tokens of our commitment
to follow Jesus Christ, our crucified and risen Lord.   **Amen.**   [219]

2

Let us give thanks to the Lord our God.

It is right to give our thanks and praise.

God of compassion,
we praise you that you look upon our frail lives
with love and understanding,
and that you desire for us all
new life in Jesus Christ.
We are overwhelmed by your love,
which goes to the cross for us,
endures the grave,
and leads us to new life.

By your Spirit,
strengthen our souls to be brave and bold in Christ's service.
Take our offerings,
and use them and us for your purposes,
in the name of Jesus Christ, our crucified and risen Lord.   **Amen.**   [220]

SENTENCES OF SCRIPTURE
PRAYER OF THE DAY

FIRST SUNDAY IN LENT

SENTENCES OF SCRIPTURE

1   *Year A B C*
                                                                    Matt. 4:4

One does not live by bread alone,
but by every word that comes from the mouth of God.

2   *Year A B C*
                                                                    Ps. 51:17

The sacrifice acceptable to God is a broken spirit;
a broken and contrite heart,
O God, you will not despise.

3   *Year A B C*
                                                                    Ps. 139:23, 24

Search me, O God, and know my heart;

try me and know my thoughts!

See if there is any wicked way in me,

and lead me in the way everlasting.

PRAYER OF THE DAY

1   *Year A B C*

Almighty God,
your Son fasted forty days in the wilderness,
and was tempted as we are but did not sin.
Give us grace to direct our lives
in obedience to your Spirit,

that as you know our weakness,
so we may know your power to save;
through Jesus Christ our Redeemer,
who lives and reigns with you and the Holy Spirit,
one God, now and forever.   **Amen.**   [221]

2   *Year A B C*

O Lord God,
you led your people through the wilderness
and brought them to the promised land.
So guide us,
that, following our Savior,
we may walk through the wilderness of this world
toward the glory of the world to come;
through your Son, Jesus Christ our Lord,
who lives and reigns with you and the Holy Spirit,
one God, now and forever.   **Amen.**   [222]

3   *Year A B C*

God of the covenant,
as the forty days of deluge
swept away the world's corruption
and watered new beginnings of righteousness and life,
so in the saving flood of Baptism
we are washed clean and born again.
Throughout these forty days,
unseal within us the wellspring of your grace,
cleanse our hearts of all that is not holy,
and cause your gift of new life to flourish once again.
Grant this through Jesus Christ our Redeemer,
who lives and reigns with you in the unity of the Holy Spirit,
one God, forever and ever.   **Amen.**   [223]

SECOND SUNDAY IN LENT

SENTENCES OF SCRIPTURE

1   *Year A B C*
Isa. 58:6–8

Is not this the fast I choose:
to loose the bonds of injustice;

to share your bread with the hungry;

to bring the homeless poor into your house;

when you see the naked, to clothe them?

Then your light shall break forth like the dawn,

and your healing shall spring up quickly.

2   *Year A B C*
Luke 9:23

If any want to become my followers,
let them deny themselves
and take up their cross daily
and follow me.

3   *Year A B C*
John 3:14, 15

The Son of Man must be lifted up,
that whoever believes in him may have eternal life.

PRAYER OF THE DAY

1   *Year A B C*

God of mercy,
you are full of tenderness and compassion,
slow to anger, rich in mercy,
and always ready to forgive.
Grant us grace to renounce all evil
and to cling to Christ,
that in every way we may prove to be your loving children;
through Jesus Christ our Lord,
who lives and reigns with you and the Holy Spirit,
one God, forever and ever.   **Amen.**   [224]

God of all times and places,
in Jesus Christ, lifted up on the cross,
you opened for us the path to eternal life.
Grant that we, being born again of water and the Spirit,
may joyfully serve you in newness of life
and faithfully walk in your holy ways;
through Jesus Christ our Lord,
who lives and reigns with you in the unity of the Holy Spirit,
one God, now and forever. **Amen.** [225]

3   *Year A*

God of our forebears,
as your chosen servant Abraham
was given faith to obey your call
and go out into the unknown,
so may your church be granted such faith
that we may follow you with courage
for the sake of Jesus Christ our Lord,
who lives and reigns with you and the Holy Spirit,
one God, forever and ever. **Amen.** [226]

Third Sunday in Lent

Sentences of Scripture

1   *Year A B C*
                                                       Eph. 4:32

Be kind to one another,
tenderhearted,
forgiving one another,
as God in Christ has forgiven you.

2   *Year A B C*
                                                      Ezek. 36:26

The Lord God said:
I will give you a new heart and a new mind.
I will take away your stubborn heart of stone
and give you an obedient heart.

Jesus said:
Come to me, all you that are weary
and are carrying heavy burdens,
and I will give you rest.
Take my yoke upon you,
and learn from me;
for I am gentle and lowly in heart,
and you will find rest for your souls.
For my yoke is easy,
and my burden is light.

PRAYER OF THE DAY

1   *Year A B C*

Merciful God,
in Christ you make all things new.
Transform the poverty of our nature
by the riches of your grace,
and in the renewal of our lives
make known your heavenly glory;
through Jesus Christ our Redeemer,
who lives and reigns with you and the Holy Spirit,
one God, forever and ever. **Amen.** [227]

2   *Year A B C*

Eternal God,
your kingdom has broken into our troubled world
through the life, death, and resurrection of your Son.
Help us to hear your Word and obey it,
that we may become instruments of your saving love;
through Jesus Christ our Lord,
who lives and reigns with you and the Holy Spirit,
one God, now and forever. **Amen.** [228]

3   *Year A*

O God, the fountain of life,
to a humanity parched with thirst
you offer the living water of grace
which springs up from the rock, our Savior Jesus Christ.

Grant your people the gift of your Spirit,
that we may learn to profess our faith with courage
and announce with joy the wonder of your love.
We ask this through our Lord Jesus Christ,
who lives and reigns with you in the unity of the Holy Spirit,
one God, forever and ever.   **Amen.**   [229]

FOURTH SUNDAY IN LENT

SENTENCES OF SCRIPTURE

1

Year A
John 8:12

Jesus said:
I am the light of the world.
Whoever follows me will never walk in darkness
but will have the light of life.

2

Year B
Eph. 2:8

By grace you have been saved through faith,
and this is not your own doing;
it is the gift of God.

3

Year C
Joel 2:13

Return to the Lord your God,
for God is gracious and merciful,
slow to anger, and abounding in steadfast love.

PRAYER OF THE DAY

1

Year A B C

Gracious God,
in order that the children of earth
might discern good from evil
you sent your Son to be the light of the world.
As Christ shines upon us,
may we learn what pleases you,
and live in all truth and goodness;
through Jesus Christ our Lord,
who is alive and reigns with you and the Holy Spirit,
one God, now and forever.   **Amen.**   [230]

Everlasting God,
in whom we live and move and have our being,
you have made us for yourself,
so that our hearts are restless
until they rest in you.
Give us purity of heart
and strength of purpose,
that no selfish passion may hinder us from knowing your will,
no weakness keep us from doing it;
that in your light we may see light clearly,
and in your service find perfect freedom;
through Jesus Christ our Lord,
who lives and reigns with you and the Holy Spirit,
one God, now and forever.   **Amen.**   [2]

3   *Year C*

God of compassion,
you are slow to anger, and full of mercy,
welcoming sinners who return to you with penitent hearts.
Receive in your loving embrace
all who come home to you.
Seat them at your bountiful table of grace,
that, with all your children,
they may feast with delight
on all that satisfies the hungry heart.
We ask this in the name of Jesus Christ our Savior,
who lives and reigns with you in the unity of the Holy Spirit,
one God, forever and ever.   **Amen.**   [231]

FIFTH SUNDAY IN LENT

SENTENCES OF SCRIPTURE

1   *Year A*
                                                                                      John 11:25, 26

I am the resurrection and the life, says the Lord;
Everyone who lives and believes in me will never die.

Year B
John 12:26

Whoever serves me must follow me, says the Lord,
and where I am, there will my servant be also.

Year C
Phil. 3:13, 14

Forgetting what lies behind
and straining forward to what lies ahead,
we press on toward the goal
for the prize of the heavenly call of God in Christ Jesus.

PRAYER OF THE DAY

> For Year A, also see Twentieth Sunday in Ordinary Time, prayer of the day 3 (p. 369).

Year A B C

Almighty God, our Redeemer,
in our weakness we have failed
to be your messengers of forgiveness and hope.
Renew us by your Holy Spirit,
that we may follow your commands
and proclaim your reign of love;
through Jesus Christ our Lord,
who lives and reigns with you and the Holy Spirit,
one God, now and forever.   **Amen.**   [232]

Year A B C

Almighty God,
Redeemer of all who trust you,
heed the cry of your people;
deliver us from the bondage of sin,
that we may serve you in perfect freedom
and rejoice in your unfailing love;
through Jesus Christ our Savior,
who lives and reigns with you and the Holy Spirit,
one God, forever and ever.   **Amen.**   [233]

Almighty God,
your Son came into the world
to free us all from sin and death.
Breathe upon us with the power of your Spirit,
that we may be raised to new life in Christ,
and serve you in holiness and righteousness all our days;
through the same Jesus Christ, our Lord,
who lives and reigns with you in the unity of the Holy Spirit,
one God, forever and ever.   **Amen.**   [234]

AN OUTLINE OF THE SERVICE FOR PASSION/PALM SUNDAY

GATHERING

Call to Worship
Prayer
Proclamation of the Entrance Into Jerusalem
Procession Into the Church [Hymn or Psalm]
Prayer of the Day

THE WORD

[Prayer for Illumination]
First Reading
Psalm
Second Reading
Gospel Reading
Silent Reflection and/or Sermon
Hymn
[Creed or Affirmation of Faith]
Prayers of the People
   [or Solemn Reproaches of the Cross]

If the Eucharist is not celebrated:

THE EUCHARIST

Offering	Offering
The Peace	
Invitation to the Lord's Table	
Great Thanksgiving	Prayer of Thanksgiving
Lord's Prayer	Lord's Prayer
Breaking of the Bread	
Communion of the People	
Prayer After Communion	

SENDING

Hymn, Spiritual, Canticle, or Psalm
Blessing and Charge

Passion/Palm Sunday

Gathering

If possible, the congregation gathers at a designated place outside the usual worship space, so that all may enter the church in procession.

Palm branches, or branches of other trees or shrubs, are distributed before the service.

Call to Worship

One of the following is sung or said:

1   *Ps. 118:26*

Blessed is the one who comes in the name of the Lord.

Hosanna in the highest!

2   *Zech. 9:9*

Rejoice greatly, O daughter of Zion!

Shout aloud, O daughter of Jerusalem!

Lo, your king comes to you;

triumphant and victorious is he,

humble and riding on a donkey,

on a colt, the foal of a donkey.

Prayer

The minister greets the people:

The Lord be with you.

And also with you.

Let us pray.

After a brief silence, one of the following prayers may be said.

1

We praise you, O God,
for your redemption of the world through Jesus Christ.
Today he entered the holy city of Jerusalem in triumph
and was proclaimed Messiah and king
by those who spread garments and branches along his way.
Let these branches be signs of his victory,
and grant that we who carry them
may follow him in the way of the cross,
that, dying and rising with him, we may enter into your kingdom;
through Jesus Christ, who lives and reigns
with you and the Holy Spirit, now and forever.   [235]

Amen.

2

Merciful God,
as we enter Holy Week and gather at your house of prayer,
turn our hearts again to Jerusalem,
to the life, death, and resurrection of Jesus Christ,
that united with Christ and all the faithful
we may one day enter in triumph
the city not made by human hands,
the new Jerusalem, eternal in the heavens,
where with you and the Holy Spirit,
Christ lives in glory forever.   [236]

Amen.

PROCLAMATION OF THE ENTRANCE INTO JERUSALEM

Year A: Matthew 21:1–11
Year B: Mark 11:1–10 or John 12:12–16
Year C: Luke 19:28–40

PROCESSION INTO THE CHURCH

The procession into the church begins. The hymn "All Glory, Laud, and Honor" (PH 88) or Psalm 118:1–2, 19–29 (PH 230, 232; PS 118–120) is sung.

The procession may be concluded with the singing or saying of the following:

Ps. 118:26

Blessed is he who comes in the name of the Lord.

Hosanna in the highest!

Let us pray.

PRAYER OF THE DAY

After a brief silence, one of the following prayers of the day is said, unless a prayer for illumination is to follow:

1

Everlasting God,
in your tender love for the human race
you sent your Son to take our nature, and to suffer death upon the cross.
In your mercy enable us to share in his obedience to your will
and in the glorious victory of his resurrection;
through Jesus Christ our Lord,
who lives and reigns with you and the Holy Spirit,
one God, forever and ever.   [237]

Amen.

2

God of all,
you gave your only-begotten Son to take the form of a servant,
and to be obedient even to death on a cross.
Give us the same mind that was in Christ Jesus,
that, sharing in his humility,
we may come to be with him in his glory,
who lives and reigns with you and the Holy Spirit,
one God, now and forever.   [238]

Amen.

The people may be seated.

THE WORD

PRAYER FOR ILLUMINATION

If the prayer of the day was not said, a prayer for illumination, such as the following, may be said:

Eternal God,
whose word silences the shouts of the mighty:
Quiet within us every voice but your own.
Speak to us through the suffering and death of Jesus Christ
that by the power of your Holy Spirit

we may receive grace to show Christ's love
in lives given to your service.   **Amen.**   [239]

FIRST READING   Isaiah 50:4–9a

PSALM   Psalm 31:9–16 or Psalm 118:1–2, 19–29

> Psalm 31:9–16 is sung or said (PH 182; PS 28). Or if it has not already been
> used, Psalm 118:1–2, 19–29 (PH 232; PS 118–120) may be sung or said.

SECOND READING   Philippians 2:5–11

GOSPEL READING

Year A: Matthew 26:14–27:66 or Matthew 27:11–54
Year B: Mark 14:1–15:47 or Mark 15:1–39 (40–47)
Year C: Luke 22:14–23:56 or Luke 23:1–49

SILENT REFLECTION AND/OR SERMON

> Silent reflection or a brief sermon may follow.

HYMN

> The people may stand, and sing a hymn of the passion.

CREED OR AFFIRMATION OF FAITH

> The people may stand, and may sing or say a creed of the church
> (pp. 64–65) or an affirmation drawn from scripture (pp. 94–98).

**PRAYERS OF THE PEOPLE
[OR SOLEMN REPROACHES OF THE CROSS]**

> Prayers for worldwide and local concerns are offered, or the responsive
> prayer on Christ's passion (pp. 266–267) is said. Or, if there is no Good
> Friday service, the Solemn Reproaches of the Cross may be said (see ser-
> vice for Good Friday, pp. 288–291).

> The people may be seated.

> IF THE LORD'S SUPPER IS NOT TO BE CELEBRATED, THE
> SERVICE CONTINUES ON PAGE 264.

THE EUCHARIST

OFFERING

Silence or appropriate music may accompany the gathering of the people's offerings.

Bread and wine may be brought to the table, or uncovered if already in place. The table is prepared for the celebration of the Sacrament.

All may stand as the offerings are brought forward. A psalm, hymn, doxology, or spiritual may be sung.

THE PEACE

The leader says:

The peace of Christ be with you.

Peace be with you.

The people may exchange with one another, by words and gesture, signs of peace and reconciliation.

INVITATION TO THE LORD'S TABLE

Standing at the table, the presiding minister invites the people to the Sacrament, using the following or another invitation to the Lord's table (pp. 67–68, 125).

John 6:35

Jesus said:
I am the bread of life.
Whoever comes to me will never be hungry,
and whoever believes in me will never be thirsty.

All may stand. The presiding minister leads the people in the following or another great thanksgiving appropriate for the day (pp. 69–73, 126–156).

GREAT THANKSGIVING

The Lord be with you.

And also with you.

Lift up your hearts.

We lift them to the Lord.

Let us give thanks to the Lord our God.

It is right to give our thanks and praise.

It is truly right and our greatest joy
to give you thanks and praise,
O Lord our God, creator and ruler of the universe.
In your wisdom, you made all things
and sustain them by your power.
You made us in your image,
setting us in your world to love and serve you
and to live in peace with your whole creation.
From generation to generation you have guided us,
sending prophets to turn us from wayward paths
into the way of righteousness.
Out of your great love for the world
you sent your only Son among us to redeem us
and to be the way to eternal life.

Therefore we praise you,
joining our voices with the choirs of heaven
and with all the faithful of every time and place,
who forever sing to the glory of your name:

The people may sing or say:

**Holy, holy, holy Lord, God of power and might,
heaven and earth are full of your glory.
Hosanna in the highest.**

**Blessed is he who comes in the name of the Lord.
Hosanna in the highest.**

The minister continues:

You are holy, O God of majesty,
and blessed is Jesus Christ, your Son, our Lord.
As one of us, he knew our joys and sorrows,
and our struggles with temptation.
He was like us in every way except sin.
In him we see what you created us to be.

Though blameless,
he suffered willingly for our sin.
Though innocent,
he accepted death for the guilty.
On the cross he offered himself, a perfect sacrifice,
for the life of the world.
By his suffering and death,
he freed us from sin and death.
Risen from the grave,
he leads us to the joy of new life.

The words of institution may be said here, or in relation to the breaking of the bread.

We give you thanks that the Lord Jesus,
on the night before he died,
took bread,
and after giving thanks to you,
he broke it, and gave it to his disciples, saying:
Take, eat.
This is my body, given for you.
Do this in remembrance of me.

In the same way he took the cup, saying:
This cup is the new covenant sealed in my blood,
shed for you for the forgiveness of sins.
Whenever you drink it,
do this in remembrance of me.

Remembering all your mighty and merciful acts,
we take this bread and this wine
from the gifts you have given us,
and celebrate with joy
the redemption won for us in Jesus Christ.
Accept this our sacrifice of praise and thanksgiving
as a living and holy offering of ourselves,
that our lives may proclaim the One crucified and risen.

The people may sing or say one of the following:

1

Great is the mystery of faith:

Christ has died,
Christ is risen,
Christ will come again.

2

Praise to you, Lord Jesus:

Dying you destroyed our death,
rising you restored our life.
Lord Jesus, come in glory.

3

According to his commandment:

**We remember his death,
we proclaim his resurrection,
we await his coming in glory.**

4

Christ is the bread of life:

**When we eat this bread and drink this cup,
we proclaim your death, Lord Jesus,
until you come in glory.**

The minister continues:

Gracious God,
pour out your Holy Spirit upon us
and upon these your gifts of bread and wine,
that the bread we break
and the cup we bless
may be the communion of the body and blood of Christ.
By your Spirit unite us with the living Christ
and with all who are baptized in his name,
that we may be one in ministry in every place.
As this bread is Christ's body for us,
send us out to be the body of Christ in the world.

Intercessions for the church and the world may be included here.

Lead us, O God, in the way of Christ.
Give us courage to take up our cross
and, in full reliance upon your grace, to follow him.
Help us to love you above all else
and to love our neighbor as we love ourselves,
demonstrating that love in deed and word
in the power of your Spirit.
Give us strength to serve you faithfully
until the promised day of resurrection,
when, with the redeemed of all the ages,
we will feast with you at your table in glory.

Through Christ,
all glory and honor are yours, almighty Father,
with the Holy Spirit in the holy church,
now and forever.   [240]

Amen.

LORD'S PRAYER

The minister invites all present to sing or say the Lord's Prayer.

As our Savior Christ has taught us, we are bold to pray:

All pray together.

Or

Our Father in heaven,	**Our Father, who art in heaven,**
hallowed be your name,	**hallowed be thy name,**
your kingdom come,	**thy kingdom come,**
your will be done,	**thy will be done,**
on earth as in heaven.	**on earth as it is in heaven.**
Give us today our daily bread.	**Give us this day our daily bread;**
Forgive us our sins	**and forgive us our debts,**
as we forgive those who sin against us.	**as we forgive our debtors;**
Save us from the time of trial	**and lead us not into temptation,**
and deliver us from evil.	**but deliver us from evil.**
For the kingdom, the power,	**For thine is the kingdom,**
** and the glory are yours**	**and the power, and the glory,**
now and forever. Amen.	** forever. Amen.**

The people may be seated.

BREAKING OF THE BREAD

If the words of institution have not previously been said, the minister breaks the bread, using A.

If the words of institution were included in the great thanksgiving, the minister breaks the bread, using B. Or the bread may be broken in silence.

A   *See 1 Cor. 11:23–26; Luke 22:19–20*

The minister breaks the bread in full view of the people, saying:

The Lord Jesus, on the night of his arrest, took bread,
and after giving thanks to God,
he broke it, and gave it to his disciples, saying:
Take, eat.
This is my body, given for you.
Do this in remembrance of me.

Having filled the cup, the minister lifts it in the view of the people, saying:

In the same way he took the cup, saying:
This cup is the new covenant sealed in my blood,
shed for you for the forgiveness of sins.
Whenever you drink it,
do this in remembrance of me.

Every time you eat this bread and drink this cup,
you proclaim the saving death of the risen Lord,
until he comes.

B   *1 Cor. 10:16–17*

Because there is one loaf,
we, many as we are, are one body;
for it is one loaf of which we all partake.

The minister takes the loaf and breaks it in full view of the people, saying:

When we break the bread,
is it not a sharing in the body of Christ?

Having filled the cup, the minister lifts it in the view of the people, saying:

When we give thanks over the cup,
is it not a sharing in the blood of Christ?

COMMUNION OF THE PEOPLE

INVITATION

Holding out both the bread and the cup to the people, the minister says:

The gifts of God
for the people of God.

COMMUNION

The minister and those assisting receive Communion, and they then serve
the bread and the cup to the people.

In giving the bread:

The body of Christ, given for you.   **Amen.**

In giving the cup:

The blood of Christ, shed for you.   **Amen.**

During Communion, psalms, hymns, anthems, or spirituals may be sung.

The following or another version of "Jesus, Lamb of God" may be sung or said:

Jesus, Lamb of God,

have mercy on us.

Jesus, bearer of our sins,

have mercy on us.

Jesus, redeemer of the world,

grant us peace.

PRAYER AFTER COMMUNION

After all are served, the following or a similar prayer may be prayed by the minister, or by all together.

God, our help and strength,
you have satisfied our hunger with this eucharistic food.
Strengthen our faith,
that through the death and resurrection of your Son
we may be led to salvation,
for he is Lord now and forever.   [241]

Amen.

SENDING

HYMN, SPIRITUAL, CANTICLE, OR PSALM

The people may stand.

A hymn, spiritual, canticle, or psalm may be sung.

BLESSING AND CHARGE

BLESSING

The minister gives God's blessing to the congregation, using the following or another scriptural benediction (pp. 83, 161).

The peace of God,
which passes all understanding,
keep your hearts and minds
in the knowledge and love of God,
and of God's Son, Jesus Christ our Lord;
and the blessing of God almighty,
the Father, the Son, and the Holy Spirit,
remain with you always.

Amen.

CHARGE

> The minister, a deacon, or an elder dismisses the congregation, using the
> following or a similar charge (pp. 82–83, 159–160):

Go in peace to love and serve the Lord.

Thanks be to God.

IF THE LORD'S SUPPER IS NOT CELEBRATED, THE SERVICE
CONTINUES HERE FROM PAGE 255.

OFFERING

Silence or appropriate music may accompany the gathering of the people's
offerings.

All may stand as the offerings are brought forward. A psalm, hymn, doxology, or spiritual may be sung.

PRAYER OF THANKSGIVING

The minister leads the people in the following or a similar thanksgiving:

Let us give thanks to the Lord our God.

It is right to give our thanks and praise.

Great God,
we thank you for Jesus,
who was punished for our sins,
and suffered shameful death to rescue us.
We praise you for the trust we have in him,
for mercy undeserved,
and for the love you pour out on us, and on all.
Give us gratitude, O God,
and a great desire to serve you,
by taking our cross
and following in the way of Jesus Christ,
our Lord and Savior.   [242]

Amen.

LORD'S PRAYER

The minister invites all present to sing or say the Lord's Prayer.

As our Savior Christ has taught us, we are bold to say:

All pray together.

Or

Our Father in heaven,
hallowed be your name,
your kingdom come,
your will be done,
on earth as in heaven.
Give us today our daily bread.
Forgive us our sins
as we forgive those who sin against us.
Save us from the time of trial
and deliver us from evil.
For the kingdom, the power,
   and the glory are yours
now and forever.   **Amen.**

Our Father, who art in heaven,
hallowed be thy name,
thy kingdom come,
thy will be done,
on earth as it is in heaven.
Give us this day our daily bread;
and forgive us our debts,
as we forgive our debtors;
and lead us not into temptation,
but deliver us from evil.
For thine is the kingdom,
and the power, and the glory,
   forever.   **Amen.**

SENDING

HYMN, SPIRITUAL, CANTICLE, OR PSALM

A hymn, spiritual, canticle, or psalm may be sung.

BLESSING AND CHARGE

The minister gives God's blessing to the congregation, using the following or another scriptural benediction (pp. 83, 161).

See Phil. 4:7

The peace of God,
which passes all understanding,
keep your hearts and minds
in the knowledge and love of God,
and of God's Son, Jesus Christ our Lord;
and the blessing of God almighty,
the Father, the Son, and the Holy Spirit,
remain with you always.

Amen.

The minister, a deacon, or an elder dismisses the congregation using the following or a similar charge (pp. 82–83, 159–160):

Go in peace to love and serve the Lord.

Thanks be to God.

Responsive Prayer on Christ's Passion

This litany is appropriate for use on Passion/Palm Sunday, Good Friday, or Holy Saturday.

Our Redeemer suffered death,
was buried and rose again for our sake.
With love let us adore him, aware of our needs.

Christ our teacher,
for us you were obedient, even to death:

Teach us to obey God's will in all things.

Christ our life,
by dying on the cross
you destroyed the power of evil and death:

Enable us to die with you, and to rise with you in glory.

Christ our strength,
you were despised,
and humiliated as a condemned criminal:

Teach us the humility by which you saved the world.

Christ our salvation,
you gave your life out of love for us:

Help us to love one another.

Christ our Savior,
on the cross you embraced all time
with your outstretched arms:

Gather all the scattered children of God into your realm.

Jesus, Lamb of God,

have mercy on us.

Jesus, bearer of our sins,

have mercy on us.

Jesus, redeemer of the world,

grant us peace. [243]

After a brief silence, the leader concludes the prayer:

Eternal God,
as we are baptized into the death of Jesus Christ,
so give us the grace of repentance
that we may pass through the grave with him
and be born again to eternal life.
For he is the One
who was crucified, dead, and buried,
and rose again for us,
Jesus our Savior.   **Amen.**   [244]

An Outline of the Service for Maundy Thursday

Gathering

Call to Worship
Prayer of the Day
Hymn, Psalm, or Spiritual
Confession and Pardon
The Peace
Hymn, Psalm, Canticle, or Spiritual

The Word

Prayer for Illumination
First Reading
Psalm
Second Reading
Gospel Reading
Sermon
[Creed or Affirmation of Faith]
[Footwashing]
Prayers of the People

The Eucharist

Offering
Invitation to the Lord's Table
Great Thanksgiving
Lord's Prayer
Breaking of the Bread
Communion of the People
Prayer After Communion

Or

Stripping of the Church   Psalm, Hymn, or Spiritual
                                           Charge

All depart in silence. The service continues on Good Friday.

Maundy Thursday

Gathering

Call to Worship

All may stand as the minister(s) and other worship leaders enter.

The following, or another verse from scripture appropriate for the day, is said.

John 13:34

Jesus said:
I give you a new commandment,
that you love one another.
Just as I have loved you,
you also should love one another.

The minister says:

On this day
Christ the Lamb of God
gave himself into the hands of those who would slay him.

On this day
Christ gathered with his disciples in the upper room.

On this day
Christ took a towel and washed the disciples' feet,
giving us an example that we should do to others
as he has done to us.

On this day
Christ our God gave us this holy feast,
that we who eat this bread
and drink this cup
may here proclaim his holy sacrifice
and be partakers of his resurrection,
and at the last day may reign with him in heaven.

PRAYER OF THE DAY

Let us pray.

After a brief silence, one of the following may be said:

1

Holy God, source of all love,
on the night of his betrayal
Jesus gave his disciples a new commandment,
to love one another as he loved them.
Write this commandment in our hearts;
give us the will to serve others
as he was the servant of all,
who gave his life and died for us,
yet is alive and reigns with you and the Holy Spirit,
one God, now and forever.   [245]

Amen.

2

O God, your love was embodied in Jesus Christ,
who washed disciples' feet on the night of his betrayal.
Wash us from the stain of sin,
so that, in hours of danger,
we may not fail,
but follow your Son through every trial,
and praise him always as Lord and Christ,
to whom be glory now and forever.   [246]

Amen.

HYMN, PSALM, OR SPIRITUAL

A hymn, psalm, or spiritual may be sung.

All may remain standing.

CONFESSION AND PARDON

CALL TO CONFESSION

The people are called to confess their sins, using the following or other words of scripture that promise God's forgiveness (pp. 52–53).

The proof of God's amazing love is this:
while we were sinners
Christ died for us.
Because we have faith in him,
we dare to approach God with confidence.

In faith and penitence
let us confess our sin before God and one another.

CONFESSION OF SIN

> All confess their sin, using the following or another appropriate prayer of
> confession (pp. 53–54, 87–89).

Eternal God,
whose covenant with us is never broken,
we confess that we fail to fulfill your will.
Though you have bound yourself to us,
we will not bind ourselves to you.
In Jesus Christ you serve us freely,
but we refuse your love
and withhold ourselves from others.
We do not love you fully
or love one another as you command.

In your mercy, forgive and cleanse us.
Lead us once again to your table
and unite us to Christ,
who is the bread of life
and the vine from which we grow in grace.   [247]

> The people may sing or say:

PH 565, 572–574

Lord, have mercy.
Christ, have mercy.
Lord, have mercy.

DECLARATION OF FORGIVENESS

The minister declares the assurance of God's forgiving grace:

The mercy of the Lord
is from everlasting to everlasting.
I declare to you, in the name of Jesus Christ,
you are forgiven.

May the God of mercy,
who forgives you all your sins,
strengthen you in all goodness,
and by the power of the Holy Spirit
keep you in eternal life.
Amen.

THE PEACE

John 20:19, 21, 26

Since God has forgiven us in Christ,
let us forgive one another.

The peace of the Lord Jesus Christ
be with you all.
Peace be with you.

The people may exchange with one another, by words and gesture, signs of
peace and reconciliation.

HYMN, PSALM, CANTICLE, OR SPIRITUAL

The people may be seated.

THE WORD

PRAYER FOR ILLUMINATION

Before the reading of the scripture lessons, a prayer for illumination
(pp. 60, 90–91) may be said by the reader.

FIRST READING   Exodus 12:1–14

PSALM   Psalm 116:1–2, 12–19

SECOND READING   1 Corinthians 11:23–26

GOSPEL READING   John 13:1–17, 31b–35

SERMON

CREED OR AFFIRMATION OF FAITH

> The people may stand, and may sing or say a creed of the church (pp. 64–65) or an affirmation drawn from scripture (pp. 94–98).

FOOTWASHING

> The people may be invited to wash one another's feet, pouring water over the feet and drying them.
>
> During the washing, "Where Charity and Love Prevail" (Ubi Caritas) or another appropriate psalm, hymn, or refrain may be sung. Or the washing may be done in silence.

PRAYERS OF THE PEOPLE

> Prayers are offered for worldwide and local concerns (pp. 99–120), the people standing.

THE EUCHARIST

OFFERING

> As the offerings are gathered, there may be an anthem or other appropriate music. Or there may be silence.
>
> Bread and wine may be brought to the table. The table is prepared for the celebration of the Sacrament.
>
> All may stand as the offerings are brought forward. A psalm, hymn, doxology, or spiritual may be sung.

INVITATION TO THE LORD'S TABLE

> Standing at the table, the presiding minister invites the people to the Sacrament:

See 1 Cor. 11:23–26; Luke 22:19–20

Hear the words of the institution
of the Holy Supper of our Lord Jesus Christ:

The Lord Jesus, on the night of his arrest, took bread,
and after giving thanks to God,
he broke it, and gave it to his disciples, saying:
Take, eat.
This is my body, given for you.
Do this in remembrance of me.

In the same way he took the cup, saying:
This cup is the new covenant sealed in my blood,
shed for you for the forgiveness of sins.
Whenever you drink it,
do this in remembrance of me.

Every time you eat this bread and drink this cup,
you proclaim the saving death of the risen Lord,
until he comes.

With thanksgiving,
let us offer God our grateful praise.

GREAT THANKSGIVING

> All may stand.

> The presiding minister leads the people in the following great thanksgiving, or another appropriate for the day (pp. 69–73, 125–156).

The Lord be with you.

And also with you.

Lift up your hearts.

We lift them to the Lord.

Let us give thanks to the Lord our God.

It is right to give our thanks and praise.

It is truly right and our greatest joy
to give you thanks and praise,
O Lord our God, creator and ruler of the universe.
You bring forth bread from the earth,
and create the fruit of the vine.
You made us in your image,
and freed us from the bonds of slavery.
You claimed us as your people,
and made covenant to be our God.
You fed us manna in the wilderness,
and brought us to a land flowing with milk and honey.
When we forgot you, and our faith was weak,
you spoke through prophets,
calling us to turn again to your ways.

Therefore we praise you,
joining our voices with the celestial choirs
and with all the faithful of every time and place,
who forever sing to the glory of your name:

The people may sing or say:

**Holy, holy, holy Lord, God of power and might,
heaven and earth are full of your glory.
Hosanna in the highest.**

**Blessed is he who comes in the name of the Lord.
Hosanna in the highest.**

The minister continues:

You are holy, O God of majesty,
and blessed is Jesus Christ, your Son, our Lord,
whom you sent to deliver us
from the bondage of death and slavery to sin.
In humility he descends from your heights,
to kneel in obedience to love's commands.
He who is boundless takes on the bondage of our sin.
He who is free takes our place in death's prison.

In the deserts of our wanderings, he sustains us,
giving us his body as manna for our weariness.
The cup of suffering which he drank
has become for us the cup of salvation.
In his death, he ransomed us from death's dominion;
in his resurrection, he opened the way to eternal life.

Remembering all your mighty and merciful acts,
we take this bread and this wine
from the gifts you have given us,
and celebrate with joy
the redemption won for us in Jesus Christ.
Accept this our sacrifice of praise and thanksgiving
as a living and holy offering of ourselves,
that our lives may proclaim the One crucified and risen.

The people may sing or say one of the following:

1

Great is the mystery of faith:

**Christ has died,
Christ is risen,
Christ will come again.**

2

Praise to you, Lord Jesus:

**Dying you destroyed our death,
rising you restored our life.
Lord Jesus, come in glory.**

3

According to his commandment:

**We remember his death,
we proclaim his resurrection,
we await his coming in glory.**

4

Christ is the bread of life:

**When we eat this bread and drink this cup,
we proclaim your death, Lord Jesus,
until you come in glory.**

The minister continues:

Gracious God,
pour out your Holy Spirit upon us
and upon these your gifts of bread and wine,
that the bread we break
and the cup we bless
may be the communion of the body and blood of Christ.
By your Spirit unite us with the living Christ
and with all who are baptized in his name,

that we may be one in ministry in every place.
As this bread is Christ's body for us,
send us out to be the body of Christ in the world.

Intercessions for the church and the world may be included here.

Lead us, O God, by the power of your Spirit
to live as love commands.
Bound to Christ,
set us free for joyful obedience and glad service.
As Jesus gave his life for ours,
help us to live our lives for others
with humility and persistent courage.
Give us strength to serve you faithfully
until the promised day of resurrection,
when, with the redeemed of all the ages,
we will feast with you at your table in glory.

Through Christ,
all glory and honor are yours, almighty Father,
with the Holy Spirit in the holy church,
now and forever.   [248]

Amen.

LORD'S PRAYER

The minister invites all present to sing or say the Lord's Prayer.

As our Savior Christ has taught us, we are bold to pray:

All pray together.

Or

Our Father in heaven,
hallowed be your name,
your kingdom come,
your will be done,
on earth as in heaven.
Give us today our daily bread.
Forgive us our sins
as we forgive those who sin against us.
Save us from the time of trial
and deliver us from evil.
For the kingdom, the power,
**   and the glory are yours**
now and forever.   Amen.

Our Father, who art in heaven,
hallowed be thy name,
thy kingdom come,
thy will be done,
on earth as it is in heaven.
Give us this day our daily bread;
and forgive us our debts,
as we forgive our debtors;
and lead us not into temptation,
but deliver us from evil.
For thine is the kingdom,
and the power, and the glory,
**   forever.   Amen.**

The people may be seated.

BREAKING OF THE BREAD

Because there is one bread,
we who are many are one body;
for we all partake of the one bread.

> The minister takes the loaf and breaks it in full view of the people, saying:

The bread that we break,
is it not a sharing in the body of Christ?

> Having filled the cup, the minister lifts it in the view of the people, saying:

The cup of blessing that we bless,
is it not a sharing in the blood of Christ?

COMMUNION OF THE PEOPLE

INVITATION

> Holding out both the bread and the cup to the people, the minister says:

The gifts of God
for the people of God.

COMMUNION

> The minister and those assisting receive Communion, and then serve the
> bread and cup to the people.

> In giving the bread:

The body of Christ given for you.   **Amen.**

> In giving the cup:

The blood of Christ shed for you.   **Amen.**

> During Communion, psalms, hymns, anthems, or spirituals may be sung,
> which may include the following or another version of "Jesus, Lamb of
> God." Or silence may be kept.

Jesus, Lamb of God,

have mercy on us.

Jesus, bearer of our sins,

have mercy on us.

Jesus, redeemer of the world,
grant us peace.

Prayer After Communion

> After all are served, the people may stand, and the following prayer may be offered by the minister, or by all together:

God of grace,
your Son Jesus Christ
left us this holy meal of bread and wine
in which we share his body and blood.
May we who have celebrated this sign of his great love
show in our lives the fruits of his redemption;
through Jesus Christ our Lord,
who lives and reigns with you and the Holy Spirit,
one God, now and forever.   [249]

Amen.

Or

Stripping of the Church

> The candles are extinguished, and all linens, paraments, and banners are removed from the worship space. During their removal, Psalm 22 may be read, or the congregation may bow or kneel in silent prayer.

> There is no benediction.

If the church is not stripped:

Psalm, Hymn, or Spiritual

> A psalm, hymn, or spiritual is sung.

Charge

> The people are dismissed with the following charge:

See John 13:34

Go in peace.
As Christ loved you,
love one another.

> All depart in silence.

> The service continues on Good Friday. If no Good Friday service is scheduled, then the service continues with the Easter Vigil, or on Easter.

AN OUTLINE OF THE SERVICE FOR GOOD FRIDAY

GATHERING

Call to Worship
Prayer of the Day
Hymn, Psalm, Canticle, or Spiritual

THE WORD

Prayer for Illumination
First Reading
Psalm
Second Reading
Anthem, Hymn, Psalm, Canticle, or Spiritual
Gospel Reading
Sermon
Hymn
The Solemn Intercession
Lord's Prayer
Solemn Reproaches of the Cross
Psalm, Hymn, or Spiritual

All depart in silence; service continues with the Easter Vigil.

Good Friday

Gathering

All gather in silence.

All may stand as the minister(s) and other worship leaders enter.

Call to Worship

The minister says one of the following, or another verse from scripture appropriate to the day is said.

1   *See Phil. 2:8*

Blessed be the name of the Lord our God,

who redeems us from sin and death.

For us and for our salvation,
Christ became obedient unto death,
even death on a cross.

Blessed be the name of the Lord.

2   *Isa. 53:4*

Surely he has borne our griefs

and carried our sorrows;

yet we esteemed him stricken,

smitten by God, and afflicted.

3   *1 Peter 2:24*

Christ bore our sins in his body on the cross,
that we might die to sin
and live for righteousness.

PRAYER OF THE DAY

Let us pray.

*After a brief silence, one of the following, or a similar prayer, may be said.
Or the Litany for Good Friday may be said (pp. 292–293).*

1

Merciful God,
you gave your Son to suffer the shame of the cross.
Save us from hardness of heart,
that, seeing him who died for us,
we may repent, confess our sin,
and receive your overflowing love,
in Jesus Christ our Lord.   [250]

Amen.

2

Almighty God,
look with mercy on your family
for whom our Lord Jesus Christ was willing to be betrayed
and to be given over to the hands of sinners
and to suffer death on the cross;
who now lives and reigns with you and the Holy Spirit,
one God, forever and ever.   [251]

Amen.

HYMN, PSALM, CANTICLE, OR SPIRITUAL

A hymn, psalm, canticle, or spiritual may be sung.

The people may be seated.

THE WORD

PRAYER FOR ILLUMINATION

A prayer for illumination is said (pp. 60, 90–91).

FIRST READING   Isaiah 52:13–53:12

PSALM   Psalm 22

    The psalm is sung or said.

SECOND READING   Hebrews 10:16–25 or
                                  Hebrews 4:14–16; 5:7–9

ANTHEM, HYMN, PSALM, CANTICLE, OR SPIRITUAL

    An anthem, hymn, psalm, canticle, or spiritual may be sung.

GOSPEL READING   John 18:1–19:42

    There may be silent reflection on the readings.

SERMON

    A brief sermon may follow.

HYMN

    A hymn on the passion is sung.

THE SOLEMN INTERCESSION

    Bidding prayers for the whole family of God and the afflictions of the
    world are said.

Dear people of God,
God sent Jesus into the world,
not to condemn the world,
but that the world through him might be saved,
that all who believe in him
might be delivered from the power of sin and death
and become heirs with him of eternal life.

    In the biddings that follow, the petitions may be adapted as appropriate.

    The people may be directed to stand, or to bow down.

    The silence should be of significant length.

Let us pray for the one holy catholic
and apostolic church of Christ throughout the world:

for its unity in witness and service,
for all church leaders and ministers
and the people whom they serve,
for all the people of this presbytery,
for all Christians in this community,
for those about to be baptized (particularly N., N.),

that God will confirm the church in faith,
increase it in love,
and preserve it in peace.

Silence.

Eternal God,
by your Spirit the whole body of your faithful people
is governed and sanctified.
Receive our prayers
which we offer before you
for all members of your holy church,
that in our vocation and ministry
we may truly and devoutly serve you;
through our Lord and Savior Jesus Christ.

Amen.

Let us pray for all nations and peoples of the earth,
and for those in authority among them:

for N., the President of the United States,
and the Congress and Supreme Court,
for the members and representatives of the United Nations,
for all who serve the common good,

that by God's help
they may seek justice and truth,
and live in peace and concord.

Silence.

Almighty God,
kindle, we pray, in every heart
the true love of peace,
and guide with your wisdom

those who take counsel for the nations of the earth,
that justice and peace may increase,
until the earth is filled
with the knowledge of your love;
through Jesus Christ our Lord.

Amen.

Let us pray for all who suffer
and are afflicted in body or in mind:

for the hungry and homeless,
the destitute and the oppressed,
and all who suffer persecution, doubt, and despair,
for the sorrowful and bereaved,
for prisoners and captives
and those in mortal danger,

that God will comfort and relieve them,
and grant them the knowledge of God's love,
and stir up in us the will and patience
to minister to their needs.

Silence.

Gracious God,
the comfort of all who sorrow,
the strength of all who suffer,
hear the cry of those in misery and need.
In their afflictions show them your mercy,
and give us, we pray, the strength to serve them,
for the sake of him who suffered for us,
your Son Jesus Christ our Lord.

Amen.

Let us pray for all who have not received the gospel of Christ:

for all who have not heard the words of salvation,
for all who have lost their faith,
for all whose sin has made them indifferent to Christ,
for all who actively oppose Christ by word or deed,
for all who are enemies of the cross of Christ,
and persecutors of his disciples,
for all who in the name of Christ have persecuted others,

that God will open their hearts to the truth
and lead them to faith and obedience.

Merciful God,
creator of the peoples of the earth and lover of souls,
have compassion on all who do not know you
as you are revealed in your Son Jesus Christ.
Let your gospel be preached with grace and power
to those who have not heard it.
Turn the hearts of those who resist it,
and bring home to your fold those who have gone astray;
that there may be one flock under one shepherd,
Jesus Christ our Lord.

Amen.

Let us commit ourselves to God,
and pray for the grace of a holy life,
that with all who have departed this life
and have died in the peace of Christ,
and those whose faith is known to God alone,
we may be accounted worthy
to enter into the fullness of the joy of our Lord,
and receive the crown of life in the day of resurrection.

Silence.

Eternal God of unchanging power and light,
look with mercy on your whole church.
Bring to completion your saving work,
so that the whole world may see
the fallen lifted up,
the old made new,
and all things brought to perfection
by him through whom all things were made,
our Lord Jesus Christ,
who lives and reigns with you,
in the unity of the Holy Spirit,
one God, forever and ever.   [252]

Amen.

Finally, let us pray for all those things for which our Lord would have us ask.

Lord's Prayer

All pray together:

Or

Our Father in heaven,	Our Father, who art in heaven,
hallowed be your name,	hallowed be thy name,
your kingdom come,	thy kingdom come,
your will be done,	thy will be done,
on earth as in heaven.	on earth as it is in heaven.
Give us today our daily bread.	Give us this day our daily bread;
Forgive us our sins	and forgive us our debts,
as we forgive those who sin against us.	as we forgive our debtors;
Save us from the time of trial	and lead us not into temptation,
and deliver us from evil.	but deliver us from evil.
For the kingdom, the power,	For thine is the kingdom,
and the glory are yours	and the power, and the glory,
now and forever. Amen.	forever. Amen.

A wooden, rough-hewn cross may be carried in procession into the church and placed in front of the people.

During the procession the following may be said or sung:

Behold the cross
on which was hung the salvation of the whole world.

Come, let us worship.

Behold the cross
on which was hung the salvation of the whole world.

Come, let us worship.

Behold the cross
on which was hung the salvation of the whole world.

Come, let us worship.

SOLEMN REPROACHES OF THE CROSS

The following Reproaches are sung or spoken:

O my people, O my church,
What have I done to you,
or in what have I offended you?
Answer me.
I led you forth from the land of Egypt
and delivered you by the waters of baptism,
but you have prepared a cross for your Savior.

Lord, have mercy.

Or

Holy God,
Holy and mighty,
Holy immortal One,
have mercy upon us.

I led you through the desert forty years,
and fed you with manna:
I brought you through tribulation and penitence,
and gave you my body, the bread of heaven,
but you have prepared a cross for your Savior.

Lord, have mercy.

Or

Holy God,
Holy and mighty,
Holy immortal One,
have mercy upon us.

What more could I have done for you
that I have not done?
I planted you, my chosen and fairest vineyard,
I made you the branches of my vine;
but when I was thirsty, you gave me vinegar to drink
and pierced with a spear the side of your Savior,
and you have prepared a cross for your Savior.

Lord, have mercy.

Or

**Holy God,
Holy and mighty,
Holy immortal One,
have mercy upon us.**

I went before you in a pillar of cloud,
and you have led me to the judgment hall of Pilate.
I scourged your enemies and brought you to a land of freedom,
but you have scourged, mocked, and beaten me.
I gave you the water of salvation from the rock,
but you have given me gall and left me to thirst,
and you have prepared a cross for your Savior.

Lord, have mercy.

Or

**Holy God,
Holy and mighty,
Holy immortal One,
have mercy upon us.**

I gave you a royal scepter,
and bestowed the keys to the kingdom,
but you have given me a crown of thorns.
I raised you on high with great power,
but you have prepared a cross for your Savior.

Lord, have mercy.

Or

**Holy God,
Holy and mighty,
Holy immortal One,
have mercy upon us.**

My peace I gave, which the world cannot give,
and washed your feet as a sign of my love,
but you draw the sword to strike in my name
and seek high places in my kingdom.
I offered you my body and blood,
but you scatter and deny and abandon me,
and you have prepared a cross for your Savior.

Lord, have mercy.

Or

**Holy God,
Holy and mighty,
Holy immortal One,
have mercy upon us.**

I sent the Spirit of truth to guide you,
and you close your hearts to the Counselor.
I pray that all may be one in the Father and me,
but you continue to quarrel and divide.
I call you to go and bring forth fruit,
but you cast lots for my clothing,
and you have prepared a cross for your Savior.

Lord, have mercy.

Or

**Holy God,
Holy and mighty,
Holy immortal One,
have mercy upon us.**

I grafted you into the tree of my chosen Israel,
and you turned on them with persecution and mass murder.
I made you joint heirs with them of my covenants
but you made them scapegoats for your own guilt,
and you have prepared a cross for your Savior.

Lord, have mercy.

Or

**Holy God,
Holy and mighty,
Holy immortal One,
have mercy upon us.**

I came to you as the least of your brothers and sisters;
I was hungry and you gave me no food,
I was thirsty and you gave me no drink,
I was a stranger and you did not welcome me,
naked and you did not clothe me,
sick and in prison and you did not visit me,
and you have prepared a cross for your Savior.

Lord, have mercy.

Or

Holy God,
Holy and mighty,
Holy immortal One,
have mercy upon us.

PSALM, HYMN, OR SPIRITUAL

A psalm, hymn, or spiritual may be sung.

All depart in silence.

The service continues with the Easter Vigil, or on Easter Day.

Alternative Text for Use on Good Friday

Litany for Good Friday

This may be used as an alternative to the prayer of the day.

O crucified Jesus,
Son of the Father,
conceived by the Holy Spirit,
born of the Virgin Mary,
eternal Word of God,

we worship you.

O crucified Jesus,
holy temple of God,
dwelling place of the Most High,
gate of heaven,
burning flame of love,

we worship you.

O crucified Jesus,
sanctuary of justice and love,
full of kindness,
source of all faithfulness,

we worship you.

O crucified Jesus,
ruler of every heart,
in you are all the treasures of wisdom and knowledge,
in you dwells all the fullness of the Godhead,

we worship you.

Jesus, Lamb of God,

have mercy on us.

Jesus, bearer of our sins,

have mercy on us.

Jesus, redeemer of the world,

grant us peace. [253]

After a brief silence, the leader concludes the litany:

Almighty God,
look with mercy on your family
for whom our Lord Jesus Christ was willing to be betrayed
and to be given over to the hands of sinners
and to suffer death on the cross;
who now lives and reigns with you and the Holy Spirit,
one God, forever and ever.   **Amen.**   [251]

THE GREAT VIGIL OF EASTER

First Service of Easter

The Great Vigil of Easter is the brightest jewel of Christian liturgy traced to early Christian times. It proclaims the universal significance of God's saving acts in history through four related services held on the same occasion, and consists of:

SERVICE OF LIGHT

The service begins in the darkness of night. In kindling new fire and lighting the paschal candle, we are reminded that Christ came as a light shining in darkness (John 1:5). Through the use of fire, candles, words, movement, and music, the worshiping community becomes the pilgrim people of God following the "pillar of fire" given to us in Jesus Christ, the light of the world. The paschal candle is used throughout the service as a symbol for Jesus Christ. This candle is carried, leading every procession during the vigil. Christ, the light of the world, thus provides the unifying thread to the service.

SERVICE OF READINGS

The second part of the vigil consists of a series of readings from the Old and New Testaments. These lessons provide a panoramic view of what God has done for humanity. Beginning with creation, we are reminded of our delivery from bondage in the exodus, of God's calling us to faithfulness through the cry of the prophets, of God dwelling among us in Jesus Christ, and of Christ's rising in victory from the tomb. The readings thus retell our "holy history" as God's children, summarizing the faith into which we are baptized.

SERVICE OF BAPTISM

In the earliest years of the Christian church, baptisms commonly took place at the vigil. So this vigil includes baptism and/or the renewal of the baptismal covenant. As with the natural symbol of light, water plays a critical role in the vigil. The image of water giving life—nurturing crops, sustaining life, and cleansing our bodies—cannot be missed in this part of the vigil. Nor is the ability of water to inflict death in drowning overlooked. Water brings both life and death. So also there is death and life in Baptism, for in Baptism we die to sin and are raised to life. Baptism unites believers to Christ's death and resurrection.

SERVICE OF THE EUCHARIST

The vigil climaxes in a joyous celebration of the feast of the people of God. The risen Lord invites all to participate in the new life he brings by sharing the feast which he has prepared. We thus look forward to the great Messianic feast of the kingdom of God when the redeemed from every time and place "will come from east and west, and from north and south, and sit at table in the kingdom of God" (Luke 13:29). The vigil thus celebrates what God has done, is doing, and will do.

An Outline of the Great Vigil of Easter

Service of Light

Greeting and Introduction
Opening Prayer
Lighting of the Paschal Candle
Procession Into the Church
Easter Proclamation (the Exsultet)

Service of Readings

Old Testament Readings
    Between readings:
    Psalm or canticle, silence, and prayer
Canticle or Hymn
Prayer of the Day
Epistle Reading
    Psalm
Gospel Reading
[Sermon]
Psalm, Hymn, or Anthem

Or

Service of Baptism

Presentation
Profession of Faith
Thanksgiving Over the Water
The Baptizing
Laying On of Hands
Welcome
The Peace

Service of the Eucharist

Psalm, Hymn, or Anthem
Invitation to the Lord's Table
Great Thanksgiving
Lord's Prayer
Breaking of the Bread
Communion of the People
Prayer After Communion
Psalm, Hymn, or Spiritual
Charge and Blessing

If there are no candidates for baptism:

Reaffirmation of the Baptismal Covenant

Scripture Sentences
Profession of Faith
Thanksgiving for Baptism
The Peace

THE GREAT VIGIL OF EASTER

First Service of Easter

SERVICE OF LIGHT

The vigil begins in darkness, after nightfall.

If possible, the lighting of the new fire takes place outside the church building, otherwise at the entrance to the church.

All gather in silence at the place where the new fire will be lighted.

A small candle is given to each worshiper.

GREETING AND INTRODUCTION

The minister or another leader begins with these or similar words:

Grace and peace from Jesus Christ our Lord.

And also with you.

Sisters and brothers in Christ,
on this most holy night
when our Savior Jesus Christ passed from death to life,
we gather with the church throughout the world
in vigil and prayer.
This is the Passover of Jesus Christ:
Through light and the Word,
through water and the bread and wine,
we recall Christ's death and resurrection,
we share Christ's triumph over sin and death,
and with invincible hope
we await Christ's coming again.

Hear the Word of God:
In the beginning was the Word,
and the Word was with God,
and the Word was God.
In him was life,
and the life was the light of all people.
The light shines in the darkness,
and the darkness has not overcome it.

> The new fire is lighted.

OPENING PRAYER

Let us pray.

> Pause briefly.

Eternal God, in Jesus Christ
you have given the light of life
to all the world.
Sanctify this new fire,
and inflame us with a desire to shine forth
with the brightness of Christ's rising,
until we feast at the banquet of eternal light;
through Jesus Christ, the Sun of Righteousness.   [254]

Amen.

LIGHTING OF THE PASCHAL CANDLE

> The paschal candle is lighted from the new fire, and these words are spoken:

The light of Christ rises in glory,
overcoming the darkness of sin and death.

> The candle is lifted that all may see it.

PROCESSION INTO THE CHURCH

The procession into the darkened church begins, led by the bearer of the paschal candle.

A leader and the people sing or say responsively:

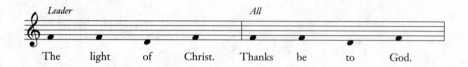

All light their candles from the paschal candle.

At the church door, the leader and people sing or say a second time:

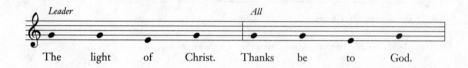

The procession continues into the church. When all have reached their places, the leader and people sing or say a third time:

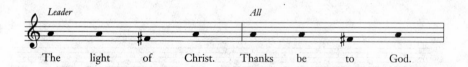

At the conclusion of the procession, the paschal candle is placed in its stand in a central location or near the pulpit or lectern.

EASTER PROCLAMATION

The ancient Easter proclamation, the Exsultet, is sung by a cantor, or choir, and the people.

Refrain for Setting I

The refrain is first sung by the choir or a cantor (soloist), then repeated by all. All sing where indicated in the text below. The complete musical setting may be found in PS 196.

Re - joice, heav-en-ly pow-ers! Sing, choirs of an - gels!

Je - sus Christ our King is ris - en!

Text and music copyright, International Committee on English in the Liturgy, Inc.

Refrain for Setting II

The refrain is first sung by the choir or a cantor (soloist), then repeated by all. All sing where indicated in the text below. The complete musical setting may be found in PS 197.

John Weaver, 1988

Re - joice, heav-en-ly powers! Sing, choirs of an - gels!

Je - sus Christ our King is ris - en!

Text copyright, International Committee on English in the Liturgy, Inc.
Music © 1988 John Weaver.

Rejoice, heavenly powers! Sing, choirs of angels!
Exult, all creation around God's throne!
Jesus Christ our King is risen!
Sound the trumpet of salvation!

Rejoice, heavenly powers!
Sing, choirs of angels!
Jesus Christ our King is risen!

Rejoice, O earth, in shining splendor,
radiant in the brightness of your King!
Christ has conquered! Glory fills you!
Darkness vanishes forever!

Rejoice, heavenly powers!
Sing, choirs of angels!
Jesus Christ our King is risen!

Rejoice, O mother church! Exult in glory!
The risen Savior shines upon you!
Let this place resound with joy,
echoing the mighty song of all God's people!

Rejoice, heavenly powers!
Sing, choirs of angels!
Jesus Christ our King is risen!

Responses for Setting I

Leader: The Lord be with you. All: And al-so with you.

Leader: Lift up your hearts. All: We lift them up to the Lord.

Leader: Let us give thanks to the Lord our God.

All: It is right to give our thanks and praise.

John Weaver, 1988

The Lord be with you. And al - so with you.

Lift up your hearts. We lift them to the Lord.

Let us give thanks to the Lord our God.

It is right to give our thanks and praise.

Text copyright, International Committee on English in the Liturgy, Inc.
Music © 1988 John Weaver.

The Lord be with you.

And also with you.

Lift up your hearts.

We lift them to the Lord.

Let us give thanks to the Lord our God.

It is right to give our thanks and praise.

It is truly right that with full hearts and minds
and voices we should praise you,
the unseen God, the all-powerful creator,
and your only Son, our Lord Jesus Christ.
For Christ has ransomed us with his blood,
and paid for us the debt of Adam's sin.

Rejoice, heavenly powers!
Sing, choirs of angels!
Jesus Christ our King is risen!

This is our passover feast,
when Christ, the true Lamb, is slain,
whose blood consecrates the homes of all believers.

This is the night when first you saved our forbears:
you freed the people of Israel from their slavery
and led them dry-shod through the sea.
This is the night when Christians everywhere,
washed clean from sin and freed from all defilement,
are restored to grace and grow together in holiness.
This is the night when Jesus Christ broke the chains of death,
and rose triumphant from the grave.

Rejoice, heavenly powers!
Sing, choirs of angels!
Jesus Christ our King is risen!

Lord God, how wonderful your care for us!
How boundless your merciful love!
To ransom a slave you gave away your Son.

Most blessed of all nights,
chosen by God to see Christ rising from the dead!

The power of this holy night
dispels all evil, washes guilt away,
restores lost innocence, brings mourners joy;
it casts out hatred, brings us peace,
and humbles earthly pride.
Night truly blessed, when heaven is wedded to earth,
and we are reconciled with God!
Therefore, gracious God, in the joy of this night,
receive our evening sacrifice of praise,
your church's solemn offering.
May this Easter candle always dispel the darkness of this night!

May the Morning Star which never sets
find this flame still burning:
Christ, that Morning Star,
who came back from the dead,
and shed his peaceful light on all creation,
your Son, who lives and reigns forever and ever. Amen.

Rejoice, heavenly powers!
Sing, choirs of angels!
Jesus Christ our King is risen!

After the singing of the Easter proclamation, the candles of the worshipers
are extinguished.

SERVICE OF READINGS

The paschal candle may be moved to the place where the scriptures will be read.

OLD TESTAMENT READINGS

Nine readings from the Old Testament are provided. At least three are to be read. The reading from Exodus 14 is always included.

Each reading is followed by:
  a. a brief period of silence
  b. the singing of a psalm or canticle [or hymn, or anthem]
  c. a prayer

In these or similar words, the leader says:

Friends in Christ,
let us listen attentively to the word of God,
recalling God's saving deeds throughout history
and how, in the fullness of time,
God's Word became flesh and dwelt among us:
Jesus Christ, our Redeemer!

First Reading: **Story of Creation**
Genesis 1:1–2:4a

Silence.

Psalm 136:1–9, 23–26 (*sung*)   PH 244; PS 139

Let us pray.

Almighty and eternal God,
you created all things in wonderful beauty and order.
Help us now to perceive
how still more wonderful is the new creation,
by which in the fullness of time
you redeemed your people
through the sacrifice of our Passover, Jesus Christ,
who lives and reigns forever and ever.   [255]

Amen.

Second Reading: **The Flood**
Genesis 7:1–5, 11–18; 8:6–18; 9:8–13

Silence.

Psalm 46 (*sung*)   PH 192, 193; PS 40, 41

Let us pray.

Faithful God,
you placed the rainbow in the skies
as the sign of your covenant with all living things.
May we who are saved through water and the Spirit,
worthily offer to you our sacrifice of thanksgiving.
We ask this in the name of Jesus Christ our Lord.   [256]

Amen.

Third Reading: **Abraham's Sacrifice of Isaac**
Genesis 22:1–18

Silence.

Psalm 16 (*sung*)   PH 165; PS 10

Let us pray.

Gracious God of all believers,
through Abraham's obedience
you made known your faithful love
to countless numbers.
By the grace of Christ's sacrifice,
fulfill in your church and in all creation
your promise of a new covenant.   [257]

Amen.

Fourth Reading: **Israel's Deliverance at the Red Sea**
Exodus 14:10–31; 15:20–21

Silence.

Exodus 15:1b–6, 11–13, 17–18 (*sung*)   Canticle of Miriam and Moses; PS 174

Let us pray.

God of steadfast love,
your wonderful deeds of old shine forth even to our own day.
Through the waters of the sea
you once delivered your chosen people from slavery,
a sign for us of the salvation of all nations
through the grace of Baptism.
Grant that all of the peoples of the earth
may be numbered among the offspring of Abraham,
and rejoice in the inheritance of Israel;
through Jesus Christ our Lord.   [258]

Amen.

Fifth Reading: **Salvation Offered Freely to All**
Isaiah 55:1–11

Silence.

Isaiah 12:2–6 (*sung*)   PS 176

Let us pray.

Eternal God,
by the power of your Word you created all things,
and by your Spirit you renew the earth.
Give now the water of life
to all who thirst for you,
and nourish with the spiritual food of bread and wine
all who hunger for you,
that our lives may bear the abundant fruit of your heavenly reign;
through Jesus Christ, the firstborn from the dead,
who, with you and the Holy Spirit,
lives and reigns forever.   [259]

Amen.

Sixth Reading: **The Wisdom of God**
  Proverbs 8:1–8, 19–21; 9:4b–6

  Silence.

  Psalm 19 (*sung*)   PH 167; PS 12, 13

  Let us pray.

  Fountain of wisdom,
  by your word you set the universe in space,
  and with your hands you molded us in your image.
  Everywhere we see signs of your loving care.
  Guide us always into your ways,
  that in your wisdom we may find life abundant,
  and live forever in the splendor of your glory;
  through Jesus Christ, the way, the truth, and the life.   [260]

  Amen.

Seventh Reading: **A New Heart and a New Spirit**
  Ezekiel 36:24–28

  Silence.

  Psalms 42 and 43 (*sung*)   PH 189, 190; PS 37, 38

  Let us pray.

  God of holiness and light,
  in the mystery of dying and rising with Christ
  you have established a new covenant of reconciliation.
  Cleanse our hearts
  and give a new spirit to all your people,
  that your saving grace may be professed
  and proclaimed to the whole world;
  through Jesus Christ our Lord.   [261]

  Amen.

Eighth Reading: **The Valley of the Dry Bones**
Ezekiel 37:1–14

Silence.

Psalm 143 (*sung*) PH 250; PS 146

Let us pray.

Living God,
by the Passover of your Son
you have brought us out of sin into righteousness,
and out of death into life.
Grant to those who are sealed by your Holy Spirit
the will and power to proclaim you to all the world;
through Jesus Christ our Lord.   [262]

Amen.

Ninth Reading: **The Gathering of God's People**
Zephaniah 3:14–20

Silence.

Psalm 98 (*sung*) PH 218, 219; PS 94, 95

Let us pray.

Eternal God of unchanging power and light,
look with mercy on your whole church.
Bring to completion your saving work,
so that the whole world may see
the fallen lifted up,
the old made new,
and all things brought to perfection
by him through whom all things were made,
your Son, Jesus Christ our Lord.   [263]

Amen.

CANTICLE OR HYMN

"Glory to God in the Highest" (p. 578; PH 566, 575, 576; PS 173), "We
Praise You, O God" (p. 577; PS 170, 171), or some other hymn is sung.

Bells may be rung.

PRAYER OF THE DAY

Let us pray.

Eternal Giver of life and light,
this holy night shines with the radiance of the risen Christ.
Renew your church with the Spirit given to us in Baptism,
that we may worship you in sincerity and truth,
and shine as a light in the world;
through Jesus Christ our Lord,
who is alive and reigns with you and the Holy Spirit,
one God, now and forever.   [264]

Amen.

EPISTLE READING

Romans 6:3–11
Psalm 114 (*sung*)   PS 114

GOSPEL READING

Year A: Matthew 28:1–10
Year B: Mark 16:1–8
Year C: Luke 24:1–12

SERMON

A brief sermon may follow.

PSALM, HYMN, OR ANTHEM

A psalm, hymn, or anthem is sung as the paschal candle is moved in procession to the baptismal font.

SERVICE OF BAPTISM

BAPTISM

Baptism may follow, using the baptismal liturgy on pages 403–415 or pages 419–429.

REAFFIRMATION OF THE BAPTISMAL COVENANT

In the event there are no candidates for Baptism, the order for the Reaffirmation of the Baptismal Covenant for a Congregation (pp. 464–471) is used.

SERVICE OF THE EUCHARIST

PSALM, HYMN, OR ANTHEM

During the singing of a psalm, hymn, or anthem, the paschal candle is moved in procession to the holy table.

INVITATION TO THE LORD'S TABLE

Standing at the table, the presiding minister invites the people to the Sacrament:

See Luke 13:29 and Luke 24:30, 31

Friends, this is the joyful feast of the people of God!
They will come from east and west
and from north and south,
and sit at table in the kingdom of God.

According to Luke,
when our risen Lord was at table with his disciples,
he took the bread, and blessed and broke it,
and gave it to them.
Then their eyes were opened
and they recognized him.

This is the Lord's table.
Our Savior invites those who trust him
to share the feast which he has prepared.

GREAT THANKSGIVING

Great thanksgiving for Easter (pp. 318–321) or great thanksgiving F (pp. 146–149).

LORD'S PRAYER

The minister invites all present to sing or say the Lord's Prayer.

Let us pray for God's rule on earth as Jesus taught us:

All pray together.

Or

Our Father in heaven,
hallowed be your name,
your kingdom come,
your will be done,
on earth as in heaven.
Give us today our daily bread.
Forgive us our sins
as we forgive those who sin against us.
Save us from the time of trial
and deliver us from evil.
For the kingdom, the power,
   and the glory are yours
now and forever.   **Amen.**

Our Father, who art in heaven,
hallowed be thy name,
thy kingdom come,
thy will be done,
on earth as it is in heaven.
Give us this day our daily bread;
and forgive us our debts,
as we forgive our debtors;
and lead us not into temptation,
but deliver us from evil.
For thine is the kingdom,
and the power, and the glory,
   forever.   **Amen.**

BREAKING OF THE BREAD

If the words of institution have not previously been said, the minister breaks the bread, using A.

If the words of institution were said in the invitation to the Lord's table, or were included in the great thanksgiving, the minister breaks the bread, using B. Or the bread may be broken in silence.

A   *See 1 Cor. 11:23–26; Luke 22:19–20*

The minister breaks the bread in full view of the people, saying:

The Lord Jesus, on the night of his arrest, took bread,
and after giving thanks to God,
he broke it, and gave it to his disciples, saying:
Take, eat.
This is my body, given for you.
Do this in remembrance of me.

The minister lifts the cup, saying:

In the same way he took the cup, saying:
This cup is the new covenant sealed in my blood,
shed for you for the forgiveness of sins.
Whenever you drink it,
do this in remembrance of me.

Every time you eat this bread and drink this cup,
you proclaim the saving death of the risen Lord,
until he comes.

B   *1 Cor. 10:16–17*

Because there is one loaf,
we, many as we are, are one body;
for it is one loaf of which we all partake.

The minister takes the loaf and breaks it in full view of the people, saying:

When we break the bread,
is it not a sharing in the body of Christ?

Having filled the cup, the minister lifts it in the view of the people, saying:

When we give thanks over the cup,
is it not a sharing in the blood of Christ?

COMMUNION OF THE PEOPLE

INVITATION

Holding out both the bread and the cup to the people, the minister says one of the following:

1

Creator of all,
just as this broken bread
was first scattered upon the hills,
then was gathered and became one,

**so may your church be gathered
from the ends of the earth into your kingdom.**   [59]

The gifts of God
for the people of God.

COMMUNION

> The minister and those assisting receive Communion and then serve the
> bread and wine to the people.

> In giving the bread:

The body of Christ, the bread of heaven.   **Amen.**

> In giving the cup:

The blood of Christ, the cup of salvation.   **Amen.**

> During Communion, psalms, hymns, anthems, or spirituals may be sung.

PRAYER AFTER COMMUNION

> After all have been served, the following, or a similar prayer, may be
> prayed by the minister or by all together, the people standing.

Let us pray.

Gracious God,
you have made us one
with all your people in heaven and on earth.
We have recalled your mighty acts in holy history.
We have seen your power
in sending light to conquer darkness,
water to give us life;
and the bread of heaven to nourish us in love.
Send us with your salvation and joy to all the world,
in the name of Jesus Christ our Lord.   [265]

Amen.

> The people may stand.

PSALM, HYMN, OR SPIRITUAL

> A psalm, hymn, or spiritual is sung.

CHARGE AND BLESSING

The minister gives God's blessing to the congregation:

Go in peace to love and serve the Lord
in the power of his resurrection. Alleluia!

2 Cor. 13:13

The grace of the Lord Jesus Christ,
the love of God,
and the communion of the Holy Spirit
be with you all.

Amen.

Christ is risen!

Christ is risen!

Christ is risen!

Christ is risen!

Christ is risen!

Christ is risen, indeed!

Alleluia, alleluia!

Easter Sunday Through Seventh Sunday of Easter

Prayer of Adoration

Glory to you, O God:
on this day you won victory over death,
raising Jesus from the grave
and giving us eternal life.

Glory to you, O Christ:
for us and for our salvation you overcame death
and opened the gate to everlasting life.

Glory to you, O Holy Spirit:
you lead us into the truth.

Glory to you, O Blessed Trinity,
now and forever.   **Amen.**   [266]

Responsive Prayer for Easter

O Christ, in your resurrection,
the heavens and the earth rejoice. Alleluia!

By your resurrection you broke open the gates of hell,
and destroyed sin and death.

Keep us victorious over sin.

By your resurrection you raised the dead,
and brought us from death to life.

Guide us in the way of eternal life.

By your resurrection you confounded your guards and executioners,
and filled the disciples with joy.

Give us joy in your service.

By your resurrection you proclaimed good news to the women and apostles,
and brought salvation to the whole world.

Direct our lives as your new creation.   [267]

After a brief silence, the leader concludes the prayer:

God of mercy,
we no longer look for Jesus among the dead,
for he is alive and has become the Lord of life.
From the waters of death you raise us with him
and renew your gift of life within us.
Increase in our minds and hearts
the risen life we share with Christ,
and help us to grow as your people
toward the fullness of eternal life with you,
through Christ our Lord,
who lives and reigns with you and the Holy Spirit,
one God, now and forever.   **Amen.**   [268]

LITANY FOR EASTER

O Christ,
after your resurrection you appeared to your disciples;
you breathed on them,
that they might receive the Holy Spirit.
You gave joy and exultation to the whole creation.
Through your victory, we pray to you:

Hear us, Lord of glory.

O Christ,
after your resurrection you sent out your disciples
to teach all nations
and to baptize them
in the name of the Father and of the Son and of the Holy Spirit;
you promised to be with them
and us until the end of the world.
Through your victory, we pray to you:

Hear us, Lord of glory.

O Christ,
through your resurrection you lifted us up,
and filled us with rejoicing.
Through your salvation you enrich us with your gifts.
Renew our lives and fill our hearts with joy.
Through your victory, we pray to you:

Hear us, Lord of glory.

O Christ,
you are glorified by angels in heaven, and worshiped on earth.
On the glorious feast of your resurrection,
we pray to you:

Hear us, Lord of glory.

Save us, O Christ our Lord, in your goodness,
extend your mercy to your people who await the resurrection,
and have mercy on us.

Hear us, Lord of glory.

O merciful God, you raised your beloved Son,
and in your love you established him as head of your church,
and ruler of the universe.
By your goodness we pray:

Hear us, Lord of glory.   [269]

After a brief silence, the leader concludes the litany:

O God,
you gave your only Son
to suffer death on the cross for our redemption,
and by his glorious resurrection
you delivered us from the power of death.
Grant us so to die daily to sin,
that we may evermore live with him in the joy of his resurrection;
through Jesus Christ our Lord,
who lives and reigns with you and the Holy Spirit,
one God, now and forever.   **Amen.**   [270]

PRAYER OF CONFESSION

Almighty God,
in raising Jesus from the grave,
you shattered the power of sin and death.
We confess that we remain captive to doubt and fear,
bound by the ways that lead to death.
We overlook the poor and the hungry,
and pass by those who mourn;
we are deaf to the cries of the oppressed,
and indifferent to calls for peace;
we despise the weak,
and abuse the earth you made.

Forgive us, God of mercy.
Help us to trust your power
to change our lives and make us new,
that we may know the joy of life abundant
given in Jesus Christ, the risen Lord. [271]

GREAT THANKSGIVING

It is suggested that invitation A (p. 68) be used as the invitation to the Lord's table when the following prayer is used.

The Lord be with you.

And also with you.

Lift up your hearts.

We lift them to the Lord.

Let us give thanks to the Lord our God.

It is right to give our thanks and praise.

It is truly right and our greatest joy
to give you thanks and praise,
eternal God, creator and ruler of the universe.
At your word the earth was made
and spun on its course among the planets.
Your hand formed us from the dust of the earth
and set us among all your creatures
to love and serve you.

When we were unfaithful to you
you kept faith with us,
your love remained steadfast.
When we were slaves in Egypt,
you broke the bonds of our oppression,
brought us through the sea to freedom,
and made covenant to be our God.
By a pillar of fire
you led us through the desert
to a land flowing with milk and honey,
and set before us the way of life.
You spoke of love and justice in the prophets,
and in the Word made flesh you lived among us,
manifesting your glory.
He died that we might live,
and is risen to raise us to new life.

Therefore we praise you,
joining our voices with angels and archangels
and with all the faithful of every time and place,
who forever sing to the glory of your name:

The people may sing or say:

**Holy, holy, holy Lord, God of power and might,
heaven and earth are full of your glory.
Hosanna in the highest.**

**Blessed is he who comes in the name of the Lord.
Hosanna in the highest.**

The minister continues:

You are holy, O God of majesty,
and blessed is Jesus Christ, your Son, our Lord,
whom you sent to save us.
He came with healing in his touch,
and was wounded for our sins.
He came with mercy in his voice,
and was mocked as one despised.
He came with peace in his heart,
and met with violence and death.

By your power he broke free from the prison of the tomb,
and at his command the gates of hell were opened.
The one who was dead now lives.
The one who humbled himself is raised to rule over all creation,
the Lamb upon the throne.
The one ascended on high is with us always, as he promised.

If they have not already been said, the words of institution may be
said here, or in relation to the breaking of the bread.

We give you thanks that the Lord Jesus,
on the night before he died,
took bread,
and after giving thanks to you,
he broke it, and gave it to his disciples, saying:
Take, eat.
This is my body, given for you.
Do this in remembrance of me.

In the same way he took the cup, saying:
This cup is the new covenant sealed in my blood,
shed for you for the forgiveness of sins.
Whenever you drink it,
do this in remembrance of me.

Remembering all your mighty and merciful acts,
we take this bread and this wine
from the gifts you have given us,
and celebrate with joy
the redemption won for us in Jesus Christ.
Accept this our sacrifice of praise and thanksgiving
as a living and holy offering of ourselves,
that our lives may proclaim the One crucified and risen.

The people may sing or say one of the following:

1

Great is the mystery of faith:

Christ has died,
Christ is risen,
Christ will come again.

2

Praise to you, Lord Jesus:

Dying you destroyed our death,
rising you restored our life.
Lord Jesus, come in glory.

3

According to his commandment:

We remember his death,
we proclaim his resurrection,
we await his coming in glory.

4

Christ is the bread of life:

When we eat this bread and drink this cup,
we proclaim your death, Lord Jesus,
until you come in glory.

The minister continues:

Gracious God,
pour out your Holy Spirit upon us
and upon these your gifts of bread and wine,
that the bread we break
and the cup we bless
may be the communion of the body and blood of Christ.
By your Spirit make us one with Christ
that we may be one with all who share this feast,
united in ministry in every place.
As this bread is Christ's body for us,
send us out to be the body of Christ in the world.

Intercessions for the church and the world may be included here.

Nourished at this table, O God,
may we know Christ's redemptive love
and live a new life in him.
Help us who recognize our Lord in the breaking of bread
to see and serve him in all whose lives are broken.
Give us who are fed at his hand,
grace to share our bread with the hungry
and with the hungry of heart.
Keep us faithful in your service
until Christ comes in final victory,
and we shall feast with all your saints
in the joy of your eternal realm.

Through Christ,
all glory and honor are yours, almighty Father,
with the Holy Spirit in the holy church,
now and forever. **Amen.**   [272]

PRAYER OF THANKSGIVING

For use when the Eucharist is not celebrated.

1

Let us give thanks to the Lord our God.

It is right to give our thanks and praise.

Eternal God,
we praise you that your glory has dawned on us,
and brought us into this Day of Resurrection.

We rejoice that the grave could not hold your Son,
and that he has conquered death,
risen to rule over all powers of this earth.
We praise you that he summons us into new life,
to follow him with joy and gladness.
By your Spirit,
lift us from doubt and despair,
and set our feet in Christ's holy way,
that our lives may be signs of his life,
and all we have may show forth his love.
Praise, glory, and thanksgiving to you, our God,
forever and ever.   **Amen.**   [273]

2

Let us give thanks to the Lord our God.

It is right to give our thanks and praise.

Eternal and ever blessed God,
Lord of heaven and earth:
we praise your glorious majesty.
Your wisdom is seen in all your works;
your grace and truth are revealed in Jesus Christ, your Son;
your power and presence are given to us through your Holy Spirit;
wherefore we adore your holy name, O blessed Trinity,
forever and ever.   **Amen.**   [274]

3

Let us give thanks to the Lord our God.

It is right to give our thanks and praise.

We give you thanks, great God,
for the hope we have in Jesus,
who died but is risen and rules over all.
We praise you for his presence with us.
Because he lives, we look for eternal life,
knowing that nothing past, present, or yet to come
can separate us from your great love
made known in Jesus Christ our Lord.   **Amen.**   [275]

SENTENCES OF SCRIPTURE
PRAYER OF THE DAY

EASTER SUNDAY

SENTENCES OF SCRIPTURE

1
Year A B C
See Luke 24:34

Alleluia! Christ is risen!

The Lord is risen indeed! Alleluia!

2
Year A B C
Matt. 28:5b–6

Do not be afraid;
I know you are looking for Jesus who was crucified.
He is not here;
for he has been raised, as he said.

Alleluia!

3
Year A B C
See 1 Cor. 5:7, 8

Alleluia! Christ our Passover is sacrificed for us;

therefore let us keep the feast. Alleluia!

PRAYER OF THE DAY

1
Year A B C

Glorious Lord of life,
by the mighty resurrection of your Son
you overcame the old order of sin and death
to make all things new in him.
Grant that we who celebrate with joy
Christ's rising from the dead
may be raised from the death of sin
to the life of righteousness;
through him who lives and reigns with you and the Holy Spirit,
one God, now and forever.   **Amen.**   [276]

Brightness of God's glory
and exact image of God's person,
whom death could not conquer
nor the tomb imprison,
as you have shared our frailty in human flesh,
help us to share your immortality in the Spirit.
Let no shadow of the grave terrify us,
and no fear of darkness turn our hearts from you.
Reveal yourself to us this day and all our days,
as the first and the last,
the Living One,
our immortal Savior and Lord.   **Amen.**   [277]

God of glory,
fill your church with the power
that flows from Christ's resurrection,
that, in the midst of the sinful world,
it may signal the beginning of a renewed humanity,
risen to new life with Christ,
who lives and reigns with you and the Holy Spirit,
one God, forever and ever.   **Amen.**   [278]

EASTER EVENING

SENTENCES OF SCRIPTURE

The disciples knew Jesus
in the breaking of the bread.
Alleluia!

PRAYER OF THE DAY

Holy God, Creator of all,
the risen Christ taught from scripture
of his death, resurrection,
and ascension into your glorious presence.
May the living Lord
breathe on us his peace,
that our eyes may be opened to recognize him in breaking bread,
and to follow wherever he leads,
who lives and reigns with you and the Holy Spirit,
one God, forever and ever.   **Amen.**   [279]

O God, worker of wonders,
you made this day for joy and gladness.
Let the risen Lord abide with us this evening,
opening the scriptures to us
and breaking bread in our midst.
Set our hearts aflame, and open our eyes,
that we may see in his sufferings
all that the prophets foretold,
and recognize him at this table
as the Christ, now entered into his glory,
who lives and reigns with you and the Holy Spirit,
one God, forever and ever.   **Amen.**   [280]

O God, whose presence is veiled from our eyes:
Grant that when we do not recognize you,
our hearts may burn within us,
and when feeling is lost,
we may cling in faith to your Word
and the power of bread broken
in the name of Jesus Christ our Lord,
who lives and reigns with you and the Holy Spirit,
one God, forever and ever.   'Amen.   [281]

Second Sunday of Easter

Sentences of Scripture

Blessed are those who have not seen
and yet have come to believe.

O give thanks to the Lord,
for the Lord is good;

God's steadfast love endures forever.

By God's great mercy
we have been born anew to a living hope
through the resurrection of Jesus Christ from the dead.

1   *Year A B C*

Almighty and eternal God,
the strength of those who believe
and the hope of those who doubt,
may we, who have not seen, have faith
and receive the fullness of Christ's blessing,
who is alive and reigns with you and the Holy Spirit,
one God, now and forever.   **Amen.**   [282]

2   *Year A B C*

Risen Christ,
whose absence leaves us paralyzed
but whose presence is overwhelming:
Breathe on us with your abundant life,
that where we cannot see
we may have courage to believe
that we may be raised with you.
To you belong honor and glory,
forever and ever.   **Amen.**   [283]

3   *Year A B C*

Living God,
for whom no door is closed,
no heart is locked,
draw us beyond our doubts,
till we see your Christ
and touch his wounds
where they bleed in others.
This we ask through Christ our Savior,
who lives and reigns with you and the Holy Spirit,
one God, now and forever.   **Amen.**   [284]

Third Sunday of Easter

Sentences of Scripture

1   *Year A B C*
                                                           Ps. 105:1–5

Call on the name of the Lord in praise;
Make known God's deeds among the nations!

**Sing to God with joyful songs;
tell of God's wonderful deeds!**

Year A B C
Rom. 6:9

Christ, being raised from the dead, will never die again;
death no longer has dominion over him.

3

Year A B C
1 Cor. 15:20

Christ has been raised from the dead,
the first fruits of those who have died.

PRAYER OF THE DAY

1

Year A B C

Lord of life,
submitting to death, you conquered the grave.
By being lifted on a cross, you draw all peoples to you.
By being raised from the dead,
you restore to humanity all that we had lost through sin.
Throughout these fifty days of Easter
we proclaim the marvelous mystery of death and resurrection.
For all praise is yours,
now and throughout eternity.   **Amen.**   [285]

2

Year A B C

Almighty God,
through your only Son you overcame death
and opened to us the gate of everlasting life.
Grant that we who celebrate our Lord's resurrection,
may, through the renewing power of your Spirit,
arise from the death of sin to the life of righteousness;
through the same Jesus Christ our Lord,
who lives and reigns with you and the Holy Spirit,
one God, now and forever.   **Amen.**   [286]

3

Year A

O God,
your Son made himself known to his disciples
in the breaking of bread.
Open the eyes of our faith,
that we may see him in his redeeming work;
who is alive and reigns with you and the Holy Spirit,
one God, now and forever.   **Amen.**   [287]

For Year A, also see Easter Evening, prayers of the day 1 and 3 (pp. 324–325).

FOURTH SUNDAY OF EASTER

SENTENCES OF SCRIPTURE

Year A B C
John 10:14

1

I am the good shepherd, says the Lord:
I know my own
and my own know me.

Year A B C
John 10:27

2

My sheep hear my voice, says the Lord.
I know them, and they follow me.

Year A B C
Ps. 95:6, 7

3

O come let us bow down and worship;
let us kneel before the Lord our maker.

For the Lord is our God;
we are the Lord's people,
the flock that God shepherds.

PRAYER OF THE DAY

Year A B C

1

God of all power,
you called from death our Lord Jesus,
the great shepherd of the sheep.
Send us as shepherds to rescue the lost,
to heal the injured,
and to feed one another
with knowledge and understanding;
through your Son, Jesus Christ our Lord,
who lives and reigns with you and the Holy Spirit,
one God, now and forever.   **Amen.**   [288]

Year A B C

2

Almighty God,
you sent Jesus, our good shepherd,
to gather us together.
May we not wander from his flock,
but follow wherever he leads us,
listening for his voice and staying near him,
until we are safely in your fold,
to live with you forever;
through Jesus Christ our Lord,
who lives and reigns with you and the Holy Spirit,
one God, now and forever.   **Amen.**   [289]

3　　　　　　　　　　　　　　　　　　　　　　　　　　　　　*Year A B C*

Jesus,
Good Shepherd of the sheep,
by whom the lost are sought
and guided into the fold:
Feed us and we shall be satisfied,
heal us and we shall be whole,
and lead us that we may be with you,
with the Father and the Holy Spirit.　　**Amen.**　　[290]

FIFTH SUNDAY OF EASTER

SENTENCES OF SCRIPTURE

1　　　　　　　　　　　　　　　　　　　　　　　　　　　　　*Year A*
　　　　　　　　　　　　　　　　　　　　　　　　　　　　　　John 14:6

I am the way, and the truth, and the life, says the Lord.
No one comes to the Father except through me.

2　　　　　　　　　　　　　　　　　　　　　　　　　　　　　*Year B*
　　　　　　　　　　　　　　　　　　　　　　　　　　　　　　John 15:5

I am the vine, you are the branches, says the Lord.
Those who abide in me and I in them bear much fruit.

3　　　　　　　　　　　　　　　　　　　　　　　　　　　　　*Year C*
　　　　　　　　　　　　　　　　　　　　　　　　　　　　　　John 13:34

Jesus said:
I give you a new commandment,
that you love one another.
Just as I have loved you,
you also should love one another.

PRAYER OF THE DAY

1　　　　　　　　　　　　　　　　　　　　　　　　　　　　　*Year A B C*

Almighty God,
your Son Jesus Christ
is the way, the truth, and the life.
Give us grace to love one another,
to follow in the way of his commandments,
and to share his risen life;
who lives and reigns with you and the Holy Spirit,
one God, now and forever.　　**Amen.**　　[291]

2   *Year A B C*

O God,
form the minds of your faithful people into a single will.
Make us love what you command
and desire what you promise,
that, amid all the changes of this world,
our hearts may be fixed where true joy is found;
through Jesus Christ our Lord,
who lives and reigns with you and the Holy Spirit,
one God, now and forever.   **Amen.**   [292]

3   *Year A B C*

We behold your glory, O God,
in the love shown by your Son,
lifted up on the cross
and exalted on high.
Be glorified anew
in the love we have for one another
as disciples of the risen Lord Jesus,
who lives and reigns with you, in the unity of the Holy Spirit,
one God, forever and ever.   **Amen.**   [293]

SIXTH SUNDAY OF EASTER

SENTENCES OF SCRIPTURE

1   *Year A*
                             John 14:15

If you love me, says the Lord,
you will keep my commandments.

2   *Year B*
                             John 15:16

Jesus said:
You did not choose me, but I chose you.
And I appointed you to go and bear fruit,
fruit that will last.

3   *Year C*
                             John 14:23

Jesus said:
Those who love me will keep my word,
and my Father will love them,
and we will come to them
and make our home with them.

1   *Year A B C*

O God,
you have prepared for those who love you
joys beyond understanding.
Pour into our hearts such love for you,
that, loving you above all else,
we may obtain your promises,
which exceed all that we can desire;
through Jesus Christ our Lord,
who is alive and reigns with you and the Holy Spirit,
one God, forever and ever.   **Amen.**   [294]

2   *Year A B C*

Risen Christ,
may we who in baptism die to sin,
rise again to new life
and find our place in your living body.
May the new covenant sealed in your blood
bring healing and reconciliation to this wounded world.
Alleluia. You are risen.
We are risen with you.
Praise and glory to the living God.   **Amen.**   [295]

3   *Year A B C*

Great and loving God,
your will for us in Jesus
is the peace which the world cannot give;
your abiding gift
is the Advocate he promised.
Calm all troubled hearts,
dispel every fear.
Keep us steadfast in love
and faithful to your word,
that we may always be your dwelling place.
Grant this through Jesus Christ, the firstborn from the dead,
who lives with you now and always in the unity of the Holy Spirit,
God forever and ever.   **Amen.**   [296]

Or Seventh Sunday of Easter

SENTENCES OF SCRIPTURE
PRAYER OF THE DAY

SENTENCES OF SCRIPTURE

1   *Year A B C*
                                                      Heb. 4:14, 16

Since we have a great high priest
who has passed through the heavens,
Jesus, the Son of God,
let us approach the throne of grace with boldness,
so that we may receive mercy
and find grace to help in time of need.

2   *Year A B C*
                                                 Matt. 28:19a, 20b

Go and make disciples of all nations, says the Lord;
I am with you always,
to the end of time.

Alleluia!

3   *Year A B C*
                                                    Acts 1:11

Why do you stand looking up toward heaven?
This Jesus will come in the same way as you saw him go into heaven.

Alleluia!

PRAYER OF THE DAY

1   *Year A B C*

God of majesty,
you led the Messiah through suffering into risen life,
and took him up to the glory of heaven.
Clothe us with the power
promised from on high,
and send us forth to the ends of the earth
as heralds of repentance
and witnesses of Jesus Christ, firstborn from the dead,
who lives with you now and always in the unity of the Holy Spirit,
God forever and ever.   **Amen.**   [297]

Almighty God,
your Son Jesus Christ ascended to the throne of heaven
that he might rule over all things as Lord.
Keep the church in the unity of the Spirit
and in the bond of peace;
bring all creation to worship at his feet,
who is alive and reigns with you and the Holy Spirit,
one God, now and forever. **Amen.** [298]

Eternal God,
by raising Jesus from the dead
you proclaimed his victory,
and by his ascension,
you declared him Lord of all.
Lift up our hearts to heaven
where he lives and reigns with you and the Holy Spirit,
one God, now and forever. **Amen.** [299]

LITANY FOR ASCENSION

Arise, O Lord, in your strength.

We will praise you for your glory!

Let us pray with joy to Christ at the right hand of God, saying:
You are the king of glory!

You have raised the weakness of our flesh.
Heal us from our sins,
and restore to us the full dignity of life.

You are the king of glory!

May our faith lead us to the Father
as we follow the road you trod.

You are the king of glory!

You have promised to draw all people to yourself;
let no one of us be separate from your body.

You are the king of glory!

Grant that by our longing we may join you in your kingdom
where your humanity and ours is glorified.

You are the king of glory!

You are true God, and you will be our judge,
so lead us to contemplate your tender mercy.

You are the king of glory!   [300]

After a brief silence, the leader concludes the litany:

O King of glory and Lord of hosts,
who ascended triumphantly above the heavens,
do not abandon us,
but send us the promised one,
the Spirit of truth.
Blessed be the holy and undivided Trinity,
now and forever.   [301]

PRAYER OF CONFESSION

**Almighty God,
you have raised Jesus from death to life,
and crowned him Lord of all.
We confess that we have not bowed before him,
or acknowledged his rule in our lives.
We have gone along with the ways of the world,
and failed to give him glory.**

**Forgive us,
and raise us from sin,
that we may be your faithful people,
obeying the commands of our Lord Jesus Christ,
who rules the world
and is head of the church, his body.**   [302]

GREAT THANKSGIVING

The great thanksgiving for Easter (pp. 318–321) should be used.

Prayer of Thanksgiving

For use when the Eucharist is not celebrated.

1

Let us give thanks to the Lord our God.

It is right to give our thanks and praise.

Great and mighty God,
we praise you that Christ has ascended
to rule at your right hand.
We rejoice before the throne of his power and peace,
for he has put down tyrannies that would destroy us,
and unmasked idols claiming our allegiance.
We thank you that he alone is Lord of our lives.
By your Spirit,
give us freedom to love with his love,
and to embrace the world with his compassion.
Accept the offering of our lives,
that we may obey your commands to serve
in the name and for the sake of Jesus Christ our Lord.   **Amen.**   [303]

2

Let us give thanks to the Lord our God.

It is right to give our thanks and praise.

Mighty God,
by your power you raised Jesus Christ to rule over us.
We praise you that he puts down tyrannies
that threaten to destroy us,
and unmasks powers that claim our allegiance.
We thank you that he alone commands our lives,
and gives us freedom to love the world.
Glory to you for the gift of his life!
Glory to you for his saving death!
Glory to you for Jesus Christ,
who lives and reigns as our risen Lord,
now and forever.   **Amen.**   [304]

See also sentences of scripture and prayers of the day for Ascension Day, pages 332–334.

SENTENCES OF SCRIPTURE

1   *Year A B C*
                                                                                             John 17:18

Jesus prayed:
As you have sent me into the world.
so I have sent them into the world.

2   *Year A B C*
                                                                                       See John 17:20–23

Jesus prayed:
I pray that they may be one, as we are one,
so that the world may know that you have sent me.

3   *Year A B C*
                                                                                             Rev. 5:13

Then I heard every creature in heaven
and on the earth and under the earth
and in the sea, and all that is in them, singing:

**To the one seated on the throne
and to the Lamb
be blessing and honor and glory and might
forever and ever!**

PRAYER OF THE DAY

1   *Year A B C*

O God,
your Son, Jesus, prayed for his disciples,
and sent them into the world
to proclaim the coming of your kingdom.
By your Holy Spirit,
hold the church in unity,
and keep it faithful to your Word,
so that, breaking bread together,
we may be one with Christ
in faith and love and service,
now and forever.   **Amen.**   [305]

Almighty God,
your blessed Son, our Savior Jesus Christ,
ascended far above all heavens that he might fill all things.
Mercifully give us faith to trust
that, as he promised,
he abides with us on earth to the end of time;
through the same Jesus Christ our Lord,
who lives and reigns with you and the Holy Spirit,
one God, now and forever.   **Amen.**   [306]

Almighty God,
your blessed Son before his passion prayed for his disciples
that they might be one, as you and he are one.
Grant that your church,
being bound together in love and obedience to you,
may be united in one body by the one Spirit,
that the world may believe in him whom you have sent,
your Son Jesus Christ our Lord;
who lives and reigns with you in the unity of the Holy Spirit,
one God, now and forever.   **Amen.**   [307]

Day of Pentecost

Sentences of Scripture

Year A B C
Joel 1:1a; 2:28–29

1

The word of the Lord to the prophet:
I will pour out my Spirit on all flesh;
your sons and your daughters shall prophesy,
your old shall dream dreams
and your young shall see visions.

Year A B C
Acts 1:8

2

You will receive power
when the Holy Spirit has come upon you,
and you shall be my witnesses
to the ends of the earth.

Year A B C
Rom. 5:5

3

The love of God has been poured into our hearts
through the Holy Spirit that has been given to us.

Prayer of Adoration

Praise and glory to you, creator Spirit of God;
you make our bread the communion of Christ's body
to heal and reconcile
and to make us the body of Christ.
You make our wine the communion of Christ's saving blood
to redeem the world.
You are truth.
You come like the wind of heaven, unseen, unbidden.
Like the dawn
you illuminate the world around us;
you grant us a new beginning every day.

You warm and comfort us.
You give us courage and fire
and strength beyond our everyday resources.
Be with us, Holy Spirit, in all we say or think,
in all we do, this and every day.   **Amen.**   [308]

PRAYER OF THE DAY

1   *Year A B C*

Almighty God,
at the feast of Pentecost
you sent your Holy Spirit to the disciples,
filling them with joy and boldness
to preach the gospel;
empower us with that same Spirit
to witness to your redeeming love
and draw all people to you;
through Jesus Christ our Lord,
who lives and reigns with you and the Holy Spirit,
one God, now and forever.   **Amen.**   [309]

2   *Year A B C*

God our creator, earth has many languages,
but your gospel proclaims your love
to all nations in one heavenly tongue.
Make us messengers of the good news
that, through the power of your Spirit,
all the world may unite in one song of praise;
through your Son, Jesus Christ our Lord,
who lives and reigns with you in the unity of the Holy Spirit,
one God, now and forever.   **Amen.**   [310]

3   *Year A B C*

O God,
who in smoke and fire upon Mount Sinai
gave the old law to Moses,
and who this day revealed the new covenant
in the fire of the Spirit:
Grant, we pray, that kindled by that same Spirit
which you wondrously poured forth upon your apostles,
we may receive with joy your commandment of love.
We ask this through Christ our Lord,
who lives and reigns with you and the Holy Spirit,
one God, now and forever.   **Amen.**   [311]

God of power,
may the boldness of your Spirit transform us,
may the gentleness of your Spirit lead us,
may the gifts of your Spirit
be our goal and our strength,
now and always.   **Amen.**   [312]

LITANY FOR PENTECOST: A

Holy Spirit, Creator,
in the beginning you moved over the waters.
From your breath all creation drew life.
Without you, life turns to dust.

Come, Holy Spirit!

Holy Spirit, Counselor,
by your inspiration, the prophets spoke and acted in faith.
You clothed them in power to be bearers of your Word.

Come, Holy Spirit!

Holy Spirit, Power,
you came as fire to Jesus' disciples;
you gave them voice before the rulers of this world.

Come, Holy Spirit!

Holy Spirit, Sanctifier,
you created us children of God;
you make us the living temple of your presence;
you intercede within us with sighs too deep for words.

Come, Holy Spirit!

Holy Spirit, Giver of life,
you guide and make holy the church you create;
you give gifts—
    the spirit of wisdom and understanding,
    the spirit of counsel and fortitude,
    the spirit of knowledge and piety,
    the spirit of the fear of the Lord,
that the whole creation may become what you want it to be.

Come, Holy Spirit!   [313]

    After a brief silence, the leader concludes the litany:

True and only Light,
from whom comes every good gift:
Send your Spirit into our lives
with the power of a mighty wind.
Open the horizons of our minds
by the flame of your wisdom.
Loosen our tongues to show your praise,
for only in your Spirit can we voice your words of peace
and acclaim Jesus as Lord.   **Amen.**   [314]

LITANY FOR PENTECOST: B

Christ has gathered the church in unity through the Spirit.
With sure hope, let us pray: Lord, hear our prayer.

Maker of all things,
in the beginning, you created heaven and earth.
In the fullness of time, you restored all things in Christ.
Renew our world, in this day, with your grace and mercy.

Lord, hear our prayer.

Life of the world,
you breathed life into the flesh you created.
Now, by your Spirit, breathe new life into the children of earth.
Turn hatred into love, sorrow into joy, and war into peace.

Lord, hear our prayer.

Lover of concord,
you desire the unity of all Christians.
Set aflame the whole church with the fire of your Spirit.
Unite us to stand in the world as a sign of your love.

Lord, hear our prayer.

God of compassion,
through your Spirit you supply every human need.
Heal the sick, and comfort the distressed.
Befriend the friendless, and help the helpless.

Lord, hear our prayer.

Source of peace,
your Spirit restores our anxious spirits.
In our labor, give us rest;
in our temptation, strength;
in our sadness, consolation.

Lord, hear our prayer.   [315]

After a brief silence, the leader concludes the litany:

God eternal,
as you sent upon the disciples
the promised gift of the Holy Spirit,
look upon your church
and open our hearts to the power of the Holy Spirit.
Kindle in us the fire of your love,
and strengthen our lives for service in your kingdom;
through your Son, Jesus Christ our Lord,
who lives and reigns with you in the unity of the Holy Spirit,
one God, now and forever. **Amen.** [316]

LITANY FOR PENTECOST: C

God's Spirit joins with our spirits, Alleluia,

to declare that we are children of God. Alleluia!

Come, Spirit of wisdom,
and teach us to value the highest gifts.

Come, Holy Spirit.

Come, Spirit of understanding,
and show us all things in the light of eternity.

Come, Holy Spirit.

Come, Spirit of counsel,
and guide us along the straight and narrow path to our heavenly home.

Come, Holy Spirit.

Come, Spirit of might,
and strengthen us against every evil spirit and interest
which would separate us from you.

Come, Holy Spirit.

Come, Spirit of knowledge,
and teach us the shortness of life and the length of eternity.

Come, Holy Spirit.

Come, Spirit of godliness,
and stir up our minds and hearts
to love and serve the Lord our God all our days.

Come, Holy Spirit.

Come, Spirit of fear of the Lord,
and make us tremble with awe and reverence
before your divine majesty.

Come, Holy Spirit.   [317]

After a brief silence, the leader concludes the litany:

Come, Holy Spirit!
Rain upon our dry and dusty lives.
Wash away our sin
and heal our wounded spirits.
Kindle within us the fire of your love
to burn away our apathy.
With your warmth bend our rigidity,
and guide our wandering feet.   **Amen.**   [318]

PRAYER OF CONFESSION

**Almighty God,
you poured your Spirit upon gathered disciples
creating bold tongues, open ears,
and a new community of faith.
We confess that we hold back the force of your Spirit among us.
We do not listen for your word of grace,
speak the good news of your love,
or live as a people made one in Christ.**

**Have mercy on us, O God.
Transform our timid lives by the power of your Spirit,
and fill us with a flaming desire to be your faithful people,
doing your will for the sake of Jesus Christ our Lord.**   [319]

GREAT THANKSGIVING

The Lord be with you.

And also with you.

Lift up your hearts.

We lift them to the Lord.

Let us give thanks to the Lord our God.

It is right to give our thanks and praise.

It is truly right and our greatest joy
to give you thanks and praise,
eternal God, creator and ruler of the universe.
With the majesty of your hand,
you shaped this world and all that is in it.
By your Holy Spirit,
you breathed life into human form,
and set us on the earth to praise and serve you.
When we wandered from your ways
and were lost in sin's wilderness,
your truth burned in the hearts of prophets
who called your people to return to the path of righteousness.
In the fullness of time
you sent your Son to be our deliverer.
In every age your Holy Spirit has led us in your ways.

Therefore we praise you,
joining our voices with choirs of angels
and with all the faithful of every time and place,
who forever sing to the glory of your name:

The people may sing or say:

**Holy, holy, holy Lord, God of power and might,
heaven and earth are full of your glory.
Hosanna in the highest.**

**Blessed is he who comes in the name of the Lord.
Hosanna in the highest.**

The minister continues:

You are holy, O God of majesty,
and blessed is Jesus Christ, your Son, our Lord.
At his baptism by John,
your Spirit came with gentle wings,
settling on him your blessing.
In the wilderness of temptation,
your Spirit stood by with power.
In his life and ministry,
your Spirit led him to serve the poor,
proclaim freedom from sin's bondage,
open eyes with faith's sight,
and befriend the friendless and the outcast.

In all he did and said,
he announced the coming of your saving might.
By his death on the cross and rising from the tomb,
he broke the power of death,
and led the way to eternal life.
Ascended to rule from on high,
Christ prays for us and promises the coming of peace and power.

> If they have not already been said, the words of institution may be
> said here, or in relation to the breaking of the bread.
>
> We give you thanks that the Lord Jesus,
> on the night before he died,
> took bread,
> and after giving thanks to you,
> he broke it, and gave it to his disciples saying:
> Take, eat.
> This is my body, given for you.
> Do this in remembrance of me.
>
> In the same way he took the cup, saying:
> This cup is the new covenant sealed in my blood,
> shed for you for the forgiveness of sins.
> Whenever you drink it,
> do this in remembrance of me.

Remembering all your mighty and merciful acts,
we take this bread and this wine
from the gifts you have given us,
and celebrate with joy
the redemption won for us in Jesus Christ.
Accept this our sacrifice of praise and thanksgiving
as a living and holy offering of ourselves,
that our lives may proclaim the One crucified and risen.

The people may sing or say one of the following:

1

Great is the mystery of faith:

**Christ has died,
Christ is risen,
Christ will come again.**

2

Praise to you, Lord Jesus:

**Dying you destroyed our death,
rising you restored our life.
Lord Jesus, come in glory.**

3

According to his commandment:

**We remember his death,
we proclaim his resurrection,
we await his coming in glory.**

4

Christ is the bread of life:

**When we eat this bread and drink this cup,
we proclaim your death, Lord Jesus,
until you come in glory.**

The minister continues:

Gracious God,
pour out your Holy Spirit upon us
and upon these your gifts of bread and wine,
that the bread we break and the cup we bless
may be the communion of the body and blood of Christ.
By your Spirit unite us with the living Christ
and with all who are baptized in his name,
that we may be one in ministry in every place.
As this bread is Christ's body for us,
send us out to be the body of Christ in the world.

Intercessions for the church and the world may be included here.

By the fire of your Spirit, O God, forge us into one church,
many and different people, together in Christ's embrace.
Set our hearts aflame with a love for the truth
and the desire to do your will,
that our witness to Christ may burn brightly
in lives of joyful discipleship.
Keep us faithful in your service
until Christ comes in final victory
and we shall feast with all your saints
in the joy of your eternal realm.

Through Christ,
all glory and honor are yours, almighty Father,
with the Holy Spirit in the holy church,
now and forever.   **Amen.**   [320]

Prayer After Communion

Gracious God,
may we who have received this sacrament
live in the unity of your Holy Spirit,
that we may show forth your gifts to all the world.
We ask this in the name of Jesus Christ.   **Amen.**   [321]

Prayer of Thanksgiving

For use when the Eucharist is not celebrated.

Let us give thanks to the Lord our God.

It is right to give our thanks and praise.

God of all might and power,
we praise you that
you forged your church in the fire of the Spirit,
and breathed life into your people
that we might be the body of Christ.
We rejoice that our Lord came to rescue us from sin
and to deliver us beyond the grave
to a rebirth and newness of life.
By your Spirit,
baptize us again with your flame of faith,
fill us with the breath of zeal,
inspire us with the witness of martyrs and saints,
and send us forth into your world
to live Christ's life in power and compassion.
Take us, O God,
and shape us according to your will,
in the service of Jesus Christ,
our Lord and Savior,
now and forever.   **Amen.**   [322]

TRINITY SUNDAY

SENTENCES OF SCRIPTURE
PRAYER OF THE DAY

SENTENCES OF SCRIPTURE

1
Year A B C
Isa. 6:3

Holy, holy, holy is the Lord of hosts;

the whole earth is full of God's glory.

2
Year A B C
Rev. 1:8

I am the Alpha and the Omega, says the Lord God,
who is and who was and who is to come, the Almighty.

3
Year A B C
Rev. 22:13

Our Lord is a great God, who says:
I am the Alpha and Omega,
the first and the last,
the beginning and the end.

PRAYER OF THE DAY

1
Year A B C

O blessed Trinity,
in whom we know the Maker of all things seen and unseen,
the Savior of all both near and far:
By your Spirit enable us so to worship your divine majesty,
that with all the company of heaven
we may magnify your glorious name, saying:
Holy, holy, holy.
Glory to you, O Lord most high.   **Amen.**   [323]

Almighty and ever-living God,
you have given us grace, by our confession of faith,
to acknowledge and worship the eternal Trinity
in the majesty of the Unity.
Keep us steadfast in this faith and worship,
and bring us at last to see you in your eternal glory,
one God, now and forever.   **Amen.**   [324]

Father, we praise you;
through your Word and Holy Spirit you created all things.
You reveal your salvation in all the world
by sending to us Jesus Christ, the Word made flesh.
Through your Holy Spirit
you give us a share in your life and love.
Fill us with the vision of your glory,
that we may always serve and praise you,
Father, Son, and Holy Spirit,
one God, forever and ever.   **Amen.**   [325]

Prayer of Confession

**God of grace, love, and communion,
we confess that we have failed to love you
with all our heart, soul, and mind;
and to love our neighbor as ourselves.
We ignore your commandments,
stray from your way, and follow other gods.**

**Have mercy on us.
Forgive our sin and raise us to new life
that we may serve you faithfully
and give honor to your holy name.**   [326]

Great Thanksgiving

The Lord be with you.

And also with you.

Lift up your hearts.

We lift them to the Lord.

Let us give thanks to the Lord our God.

It is right to give our thanks and praise.

It is truly right and our greatest joy
to give you thanks and praise,
eternal and triune God,
whom we worship as Father, Son, and Holy Spirit.
In Jesus Christ you spoke the word
that brought the world into being.
By the Holy Spirit
you brought order out of chaos
and breathed life into your creatures.
In parental love,
you stood by us in spite of our disobedience,
correcting us with gracious reproof,
and welcoming us again into your loving embrace.

Therefore we praise you,
joining our voices with choirs of angels
and with all the faithful of every time and place,
who forever sing to the glory of your name:

The people may sing or say:

**Holy, holy, holy Lord, God of power and might,
heaven and earth are full of your glory.
Hosanna in the highest.**

**Blessed is he who comes in the name of the Lord.
Hosanna in the highest.**

The minister continues:

You are holy, O God of majesty,
and blessed is Jesus Christ, your Son, our Lord.
Born of Mary, he came to dwell among us,
full of grace and truth.
To all who believed,
he gave power to become your children.
In ministry among your own
Jesus cared for all,
forgiving their failures,
healing their hurts,
and nurturing their faith,
giving himself in utter sacrifice for those he loved.
He inspired ordinary folk to Spirit-filled living
and displayed in his life, death, and rising again
the power of your Spirit.

If they have not already been said, the words of institution may be said here, or in relation to the breaking of the bread.

We give you thanks that the Lord Jesus,
on the night before he died,
took bread,
and after giving thanks to you,
he broke it, and gave it to his disciples, saying:
Take, eat.
This is my body, given for you.
Do this in remembrance of me.

In the same way he took the cup, saying:
This cup is the new covenant sealed in my blood,
shed for you for the forgiveness of sins.
Whenever you drink it,
do this in remembrance of me.

Remembering your gracious acts in Jesus Christ,
we take from your creation this bread and this wine
and joyfully celebrate his dying and rising,
as we await the day of his coming.
With thanksgiving we offer our very selves to you
to be a living and holy sacrifice,
dedicated to your service.

The people may sing or say one of the following:

1

Great is the mystery of faith:

**Christ has died,
Christ is risen,
Christ will come again.**

2

Praise to you, Lord Jesus:

**Dying you destroyed our death,
rising you restored our life.
Lord Jesus, come in glory.**

3

According to his commandment:

**We remember his death,
we proclaim his resurrection,
we await his coming in glory.**

4

Christ is the bread of life:

**When we eat this bread and drink this cup,
we proclaim your death, Lord Jesus,
until you come in glory.**

The minister continues:

Gracious God,
pour out your Holy Spirit upon us
and upon these your gifts of bread and wine,
that the bread we break
and the cup we bless
may be the communion of the body and blood of Christ.
By your Spirit make us one with Christ
that we may be one with all who share this feast,
united in ministry in every place.
As this bread is Christ's body for us,
send us out to be the body of Christ in the world.

Intercessions for the church and the world may be offered here.

Nurture us at this table, O God,
that we may grow to the stature of Jesus Christ.
Help us to love you above all else
and to love our neighbor as we love ourselves,
demonstrating that love, in deed and word,
toward all your children.
Keep us faithful in your service
until Christ comes in final victory
and we shall feast with all your saints
in the joy of your eternal realm.

Through Christ, with Christ, in Christ,
in the unity of the Holy Spirit,
all glory and honor are yours, almighty Father,
now and forever. **Amen.** [327]

Prayer of Thanksgiving

For use when the Eucharist is not celebrated.

Let us give thanks to the Lord our God.
It is right to give our thanks and praise.

Gracious Father,
giver of all good things:
For our home on earth
and for your unfailing mercy,

we give you thanks.

Christ, our Redeemer:
For your sacrifice on the cross
and rising from death that we might live,

we give you thanks and praise.

Holy Spirit, giver of life:
For your abiding presence in our lives
and for comforting and guiding us,

we give you thanks, praise, and glory.

O triune God:
To you be glory and praise
now and forever.   **Amen.**   [328]

SUNDAYS BETWEEN TRINITY SUNDAY AND CHRIST THE KING

Sundays 9–31 in Ordinary Time

SENTENCES OF SCRIPTURE
PRAYER OF THE DAY

NINTH SUNDAY IN ORDINARY TIME

Sunday between May 29 and June 4 inclusive
(If after Trinity Sunday)

SENTENCES OF SCRIPTURE

1
Year A B C
John 15:5

I am the vine, you are the branches.
Those who abide in me and I in them bear much fruit.
Apart from me you can do nothing.

2
Year A B C
John 17:17

Your word, O Lord, is truth;
sanctify us in the truth.

PRAYER OF THE DAY

1
Year A B C

Lord God of the nations,
you have revealed your will to all people
and promised us your saving help.
May we hear and do what you command,
that the darkness may be overcome
by the power of your light;
through Jesus Christ our Lord,
who lives and reigns with you and the Holy Spirit,
now and forever. **Amen.** [329]

Almighty God,
you alone can bring order to our unruly wills and affections.
Give us grace to love what you command
and desire what you promise,
that in all the changes and chances of this uncertain world,
our hearts may be surely fixed
where true joys are to be found;
through Jesus Christ our Lord,
who lives and reigns with you in the unity of the Holy Spirit,
one God, forever and ever.   **Amen.**   [330]

TENTH SUNDAY IN ORDINARY TIME

Sunday between June 5 and 11 inclusive
(If after Trinity Sunday)

SENTENCES OF SCRIPTURE

1   *Year A B C*
Luke 4:18

Jesus read from the prophet Isaiah:
The Spirit of the Lord has anointed me
to bring good news to the poor
and release to the captives.

2   *Year A B C*
John 12:31, 32

Jesus declared:
The ruler of this world will be driven out.
And I, when I am lifted up from the earth,
will draw all people to myself.

PRAYER OF THE DAY

1   *Year A B C*

O God,
you have assured the human family of eternal life
through Jesus Christ our Savior.
Deliver us from the death of sin
and raise us to new life in him,
who lives and reigns with you and the Holy Spirit,
one God, now and forever.   **Amen.**   [331]

Almighty God,
give us such a vision of your purpose
and such an assurance of your love and power,
that we may ever hold fast the hope
which is in Jesus Christ our Lord,
who lives and reigns with you in the unity of the Holy Spirit,
one God, forever and ever.   **Amen.**   [332]

ELEVENTH SUNDAY IN ORDINARY TIME

Sunday between June 12 and 18 inclusive
(If after Trinity Sunday)

SENTENCES OF SCRIPTURE

1   *Year A B C*
                                                        Mark 1:15

The kingdom of God has come near;
repent, and believe in the good news.

2   *Year A B C*
                                                     1 John 4:9, 10

In this is love,
not that we loved God
but that God loved us
and sent God's Son into the world
so that we might live through him.

3   *Year A B C*
                                                       John 3:17

God sent the Son into the world
not to condemn the world,
but that the world might be saved through him.

PRAYER OF THE DAY

1   *Year A B C*

Almighty God,
you have called us to serve you,
yet without your grace
we are unable to please you.
Mercifully grant that your Holy Spirit
may in all things direct and rule our hearts;
through Jesus Christ our Lord,
who is alive and reigns with you and the Holy Spirit,
one God, now and forever.   **Amen.**   [333]

2
Year A B C

All-powerful God,
in Jesus Christ you turned death into life,
and defeat into victory.
Increase our faith and trust in him,
that we may triumph over all evil,
in the strength of the same Jesus Christ our Lord,
who lives and reigns with you and the Holy Spirit,
one God, forever and ever.   **Amen.**   [334]

3
Year A B C

Eternal God,
your Son Jesus Christ,
now exalted as Lord of all,
pours out his gifts on the church.
Grant us that unity which your Spirit gives,
keep us in the bond of peace,
and bring all creation to worship before your throne;
for you live and reign,
one God, forever and ever.   **Amen.**   [335]

TWELFTH SUNDAY IN ORDINARY TIME

Sunday between June 19 and 25 inclusive
(If after Trinity Sunday)

SENTENCES OF SCRIPTURE

1
Year A B C
Matt. 10:39

Jesus said:
Those who find their life will lose it,
and those who lose their life for my sake will find it.

2
Year A B C
2 Cor. 5:19

In Christ God was reconciling the world to Godself,
not counting their trespasses against them,
and entrusting the message of reconciliation to us.

3

Thus says the high and exalted one
who inhabits eternity, whose name is Holy:
I dwell in a high and holy place,
but I also live with those who are broken and humble in spirit,
to revive the spirit of the humble,
to restore the courage of the broken.

PRAYER OF THE DAY

1

Teach us, good Lord,
to serve you as you deserve;
to give and not to count the cost;
to fight and not to heed the wounds;
to toil and not to seek for rest;
to labor and not to ask for any reward,
save that of knowing that we do your will;
through Jesus Christ our Lord.   **Amen.**   [336]

2

Pour out upon us, O God,
the power and wisdom of your Spirit,
that we may walk with Christ the way of the cross,
ready to offer even the gift of our lives
to show forth to the world our hope in your kingdom.
We ask this through our Lord Jesus Christ,
who lives and reigns with you in the unity of the Holy Spirit,
one God, forever and ever.   **Amen.**   [337]

3

O God our defender,
storms rage about us and cause us to be afraid.
Rescue your people from despair,
deliver your sons and daughters from fear,
and preserve us all from unbelief;
through Jesus Christ our Lord,
who lives and reigns with you and the Holy Spirit,
one God, now and forever.   **Amen.**   [338]

Thirteenth Sunday in Ordinary Time

Sunday between June 26 and July 2 inclusive

Sentences of Scripture

1

Year A B C
1 Peter 2:9

You are a chosen race, a royal priesthood,
a holy nation, God's own people,
in order that you may proclaim the mighty acts
of the One who called you
out of darkness into God's marvelous light.

2

Year A B C
2 Tim. 1:10

Our Savior, Christ Jesus, abolished death
and brought life and immortality to light
through the gospel.

3

Year A B C
1 Sam. 3:9; John 6:68

Speak, Lord, for your servant is listening;
you have the words of eternal life.

Prayer of the Day

1

Year A B C

Sovereign God, ruler of all hearts,
you call us to obey you
and favor us with true freedom.
Keep us faithful to the ways of your Son,
that, leaving behind all that hinders us,
we may fix our eyes on him
and steadfastly follow in the paths of your kingdom.
Grant this through Jesus Christ our Lord,
who lives and reigns with you in the unity of the Holy Spirit,
one God, forever and ever.   **Amen.**   [339]

2

Year A B C

Almighty God,
fount of all wisdom, crown of all knowledge,
give us eyes to see
and minds to understand your marvelous works,
that we may know you through your handiwork
and use your creation to your glory;

through Jesus Christ our Lord,
who lives and reigns with you and the Holy Spirit,
one God, now and forever. **Amen.** [340]

3 *Year A B C*

O God,
light of the minds that know you,
life of the souls that love you,
strength of the thoughts that seek you:
Help us so to know you
that we may truly love you,
so to love you
that we may fully serve you,
whose service is perfect freedom;
through Jesus Christ our Lord,
who lives and reigns with you and the Holy Spirit,
one God, now and forever. **Amen.** [8]

FOURTEENTH SUNDAY IN ORDINARY TIME

Sunday between July 3 and 9 inclusive

SENTENCES OF SCRIPTURE

1 *Year A B C*
Luke 4:18

Jesus said:
The Spirit of the Lord has anointed me
to bring good news to the poor
and release to the captives.

2 *Year A B C*
Luke 8:15

Happy are they who hear the word,
hold it fast in an honest and good heart,
and bear fruit with patient endurance.

3 *Year A B C*
Luke 10:2

The harvest is plentiful,
but the laborers are few.
Ask the Lord of the harvest
to send out laborers into the harvest.

PRAYER OF THE DAY

1   *Year A B C*

Almighty God,
your Son Jesus Christ has taught us
that what we do for the least of your children
we do also for him.
Give us the will to serve others
as he was the servant of all,
who gave up his life and died for us,
but lives and reigns with you and the Holy Spirit,
one God, now and forever.   **Amen.**   [341]

2   *Year A B C*

O Lord our God,
you are always more ready to bestow your good gifts upon us
than we are to seek them.
You are more willing to give
than we desire or deserve.
Help us so to seek that we may truly find,
so to ask that we may joyfully receive,
so to knock that the door of mercy may be opened for us;
through Jesus Christ our Lord.   **Amen.**   [5]

3   *Year B C*

God of the covenant,
in our baptism you called us
to proclaim the coming of your kingdom.
Give us courage like you gave the apostles,
that we may faithfully witness to your love and peace
in every circumstance of life,
in the name of Jesus Christ our Redeemer,
who lives and reigns with you in the unity of the Holy Spirit,
one God, forever and ever.   **Amen.**   [342]

FIFTEENTH SUNDAY IN ORDINARY TIME

Sunday between July 10 and 16 inclusive

SENTENCES OF SCRIPTURE

1   *Year A B C*
                                                                 Deut. 30:14

The word is very near to you;
it is in your mouth
and in your heart for you to observe.

The words you have spoken are spirit and life, O Lord;
you have the words of eternal life.

God is our refuge and strength,
a very present help in trouble.

PRAYER OF THE DAY

1 *Year A B C*

Eternal God,
open our eyes to see your hand at work
in the splendor of creation
and in the beauty of human life.
Touched by your hand, our world is holy.
Help us to cherish the gifts that surround us,
to share our blessings with our sisters and brothers,
and to experience the joy of life in your presence;
through Jesus Christ our Lord,
who lives and reigns with you in the unity of the Holy Spirit,
one God, forever and ever.   **Amen.**   [343]

2 *Year A*

Almighty God,
we thank you for planting in us the seed of your Word.
By your Holy Spirit, help us to receive it with joy,
and live according to it,
that we may grow in faith and hope and love;
through Jesus Christ our Lord,
who lives and reigns with you in the unity of the Holy Spirit,
one God, forever and ever.   **Amen.**   [344]

3 *Year C*

Almighty God,
you have taught us through Christ
that love fulfills the law.
May we love you with all our heart,
all our soul, all our mind, and all our strength,
and may we love our neighbor as ourselves;
through Jesus Christ our Lord,
who lives and reigns with you and the Holy Spirit,
one God, now and forever.   **Amen.**   [345]

SIXTEENTH SUNDAY IN ORDINARY TIME

Sunday between July 17 and 23 inclusive

SENTENCES OF SCRIPTURE

1 *Year A B C*
Isa. 55:11

"My word shall accomplish that which I purpose,"
says the Lord,
"and succeed in the thing for which I sent it."

2 *Year A B C*
John 10:27, 28a

My sheep hear my voice, says the Lord.
I know them and they follow me;
and I give them eternal life.

3 *Year A B C*
Col. 3:17

Whatever you do, in word or deed,
do everything in the name of the Lord Jesus.

PRAYER OF THE DAY

1 *Year A B C*

Almighty God,
in Jesus Christ you opened for us
a new and living way into your presence.
Give us pure hearts and constant wills
to worship you in spirit and in truth;
through Jesus Christ our Lord,
who lives and reigns with you and the Holy Spirit,
one God, now and forever. **Amen.** [346]

2 *Year A B C*

Eternal God,
Author of our life
and End of our pilgrimage:
Guide us by your Word and Spirit
amid all perils and temptations,
that we may not wander from your way,
nor stumble in the darkness;
but may finish our course in safety,
and come to our eternal rest in you;
through the grace and merit of Jesus Christ our Lord,
who lives and reigns with you and the Holy Spirit,
one God, now and forever. **Amen.** [347]

Eternal God,
you draw near to us in Christ
and make yourself our guest.
Amid the cares of our daily lives,
make us attentive to your voice
and alert to your presence,
that we may treasure your word above all else.
We ask this through our Lord Jesus Christ, your Son,
who lives and reigns with you in the unity of the Holy Spirit,
God forever and ever.   **Amen.**   [348]

SEVENTEENTH SUNDAY IN ORDINARY TIME

Sunday between July 24 and 30 inclusive

SENTENCES OF SCRIPTURE

1   *Year A B C*
                                                                            John 6:68

Lord, to whom can we go?
You have the words of eternal life.

2   *Year A B C*
                                                                            Rom. 8:15, 16

When we cry, "Abba! Father!"
it is that very Spirit bearing witness with our spirit
that we are children of God.

3   *Year A B C*
                                                                            Luke 11:9

Ask, and it will be given you;
seek, and you will find;
knock, and the door will be opened for you.

PRAYER OF THE DAY

1   *Year A B C*

Eternal God,
protector of all who put their trust in you,
without whom nothing is strong, nothing is holy:
Fill us with your mercy and your grace,
that, with you to rule and guide,
we may so use the good things of this present life
that we do not neglect those of eternal worth;

through Jesus Christ our Lord,
who lives and reigns with you and the Holy Spirit,
one God, now and forever. **Amen.** [349]

2 *Year B*

Gracious God,
you have placed within the hearts of all your children
a longing for your Word and a hunger for your truth.
Grant that, believing in the One whom you have sent,
we may know him to be the true bread of heaven
and food of eternal life,
Jesus Christ our Lord,
to whom with you and the Holy Spirit be glory and honor
forever and ever. **Amen.** [350]

3 *Year C*

Provident Father,
with the prayer your Son taught us always on our lips,
we ask, we seek, we knock at your door.
In our every need,
grant us the first and best of all your gifts,
the Spirit who makes us your children.
We ask this through our Lord Jesus Christ, your Son,
who lives and reigns with you in the unity of the Holy Spirit,
God forever and ever. **Amen.** [351]

EIGHTEENTH SUNDAY IN ORDINARY TIME

Sunday between July 31 and August 6 inclusive

SENTENCES OF SCRIPTURE

1 *Year A B C*
Matt. 4:4

One does not live by bread alone,
but by every word that comes from the mouth of God.

2 *Year A B C*
Col. 3:1

If you have been raised with Christ,
seek the things that are above, where Christ is,
seated at the right hand of God.

Those who wait upon the Lord
shall renew their strength.

They shall mount up with wings as eagles,

They shall run and not be weary,

They shall walk and not faint.

PRAYER OF THE DAY

O God, giver of life and health,
your Son Jesus Christ has called us
to hunger and thirst to see right prevail.
Refresh us with your grace,
that we may not be weary in well-doing;
for the sake of him who meets all our needs,
Jesus Christ our Savior,
who lives and reigns with you and the Holy Spirit,
one God, now and forever.   **Amen.**   [352]

Almighty God,
your Son Jesus Christ fed the hungry
with the bread of his life
and the Word of his kingdom.
Renew your people with your heavenly grace,
and in all our weakness
sustain us by your true and living bread,
Jesus Christ our Lord,
who lives and reigns with you and the Holy Spirit,
one God, now and forever.   **Amen.**   [353]

Almighty God,
judge of us all,
you have placed in our hands the wealth we call our own.
Through your Spirit, give us wisdom,
that our possessions may not be a curse,
but a means of blessing in our lives;
through Jesus Christ our Lord,
who lives and reigns with you in the unity of the Holy Spirit,
one God, forever and ever.   **Amen.**   [354]

NINETEENTH SUNDAY IN ORDINARY TIME

Sunday between August 7 and 13 inclusive

SENTENCES OF SCRIPTURE

1

Year A B C
Ps. 130:5

I wait for the Lord, my soul waits,
and in God's word is my hope.

2

Year A B C
John 6:51

I am the living bread that came down from heaven.
Whoever eats of this bread will live forever.

3

Year A B C
Matt. 24:42, 44

Watch and be ready,
for you do not know on what day your Lord is coming.

PRAYER OF THE DAY

1

Year A B C

Almighty God,
you sent your Holy Spirit
to be the life and light of your church.
Open our hearts to the riches of your grace,
that we may bring forth the fruit of the Spirit
in love, joy, and peace;
through Jesus Christ our Lord,
who is alive and reigns with you and the Holy Spirit,
one God, now and forever. **Amen.** [355]

2

Year A B C

Grant us, O Lord,
the grace always to do and think
what accords with your purpose;
that we, who cannot exist without you,
may be enabled to live according to your will;
through Jesus Christ our Lord,
who lives and reigns with you and the Holy Spirit,
one God, forever and ever. **Amen.** [356]

3 *Year B*

Grant, O Lord,
that we may see in you the fulfillment of all our need,
and may turn from every false satisfaction
to feed on the true and living bread
which you have given us in Jesus Christ;
who lives and reigns with you and the Holy Spirit,
one God, now and forever.   **Amen.**   [357]

TWENTIETH SUNDAY IN ORDINARY TIME

Sunday between August 14 and 20 inclusive

SENTENCES OF SCRIPTURE

1 *Year A B C*
Heb. 4:12

The word of God is living and active,
it is able to judge the thoughts and intentions of the heart.

2 *Year B*
John 6:56

Those who eat my flesh and drink my blood
abide in me, and I in them, says the Lord.

3 *Year C*
Heb. 12:1, 2b

Since we are surrounded by so great a cloud of witnesses,
let us also lay aside every weight
and the sin that clings so closely,
and let us run with perseverance the race that is set before us,
looking to Jesus, the pioneer and perfecter of our faith.

PRAYER OF THE DAY

1 *Year A B C*

Almighty God,
you have broken the tyranny of sin
and sent the Spirit of your Son into our hearts.
Give us grace to dedicate our freedom to your service,
that all people may know the glorious liberty
of the children of God;
through Jesus Christ our Lord,
who lives and reigns with you and the Holy Spirit,
one God, now and forever.   **Amen.**   [358]

Ever-loving God,
your Son, Jesus Christ, gave himself as living bread
for the life of the world.
Give us such a knowledge of his presence
that we may be strengthened
and sustained by his risen life
to serve you continually;
through Jesus Christ our Lord,
who lives and reigns with you in unity with the Holy Spirit,
one God, forever and ever.   **Amen.**   [359]

3   *Year C*

Almighty and ever-living God,
increase in us your gift of faith,
that, forsaking what lies behind
and reaching out to what is before,
we may run the way of your commandments
and win the crown of everlasting joy;
through Jesus Christ our Lord,
who lives and reigns with you and the Holy Spirit,
one God, forever and ever.   **Amen.**   [360]

TWENTY-FIRST SUNDAY IN ORDINARY TIME

Sunday between August 21 and 27 inclusive

SENTENCES OF SCRIPTURE

1   *Year A*
                                                          Matt. 16:16

Jesus is the Christ,
the Son of the living God.

2   *Year B*
                                                          John 6:68

Lord, to whom can we go?
You have the words of eternal life.
We have come to believe and know
that you are the Holy One of God.

3   *Year A B C*
                                                          John 14:6

I am the way, and the truth, and the life, says the Lord.
No one comes to the Father, except through me.

PRAYER OF THE DAY

1 *Year A B C*

Almighty and everlasting God,
by your Spirit the whole body of the church
is governed and sanctified.
Hear the prayers we offer for all your faithful people,
that in the ministry to which you have called us
we may serve you in holiness and truth;
through our Lord and Savior Jesus Christ,
who lives and reigns with you and the Holy Spirit,
one God, now and forever.   **Amen.**   [361]

2 *Year A B C*

Almighty God,
you have taught us
that all our deeds without love are worth nothing.
Send your Holy Spirit and pour into our hearts
that most excellent gift of love,
the very bond of peace and of all goodness;
through Jesus Christ our Lord,
who lives and reigns with you and the Holy Spirit,
one God, now and forever.   **Amen.**   [198]

3 *Year A*

O God, fount of all wisdom,
in the humble witness of the apostle Peter
you have shown the foundation of our faith.
Give us the light of your Spirit,
that, recognizing in Jesus of Nazareth
the Son of the living God,
we may be living stones
for the building up of your holy church;
through Jesus Christ our Lord,
who lives and reigns with you in the unity of the Holy Spirit,
one God, forever and ever.   **Amen.**   [362]

Twenty-second Sunday in Ordinary Time

Sunday between August 28 and September 3 inclusive

Sentences of Scripture

1

Year A B C
James 1:18

God gave us birth by the word of truth,
so that we would become a kind of first fruits of his creatures.

2

Year A B C
Matt. 11:29

Jesus said:
Take my yoke upon you, and learn from me;
for I am gentle and humble in heart,
and you will find rest for your souls.

3

Year A
Matt. 16:24

Jesus said:
If any want to become my followers,
let them deny themselves
and take up their cross and follow me.

Prayer of the Day

1

Year A B C

O God, author and giver of all good things,
plant in our hearts the love of your name;
increase in us true religion;
nourish us with all goodness;
and bring forth in us the fruit of good works;
through Jesus Christ our Lord,
who lives and reigns with you and the Holy Spirit,
one God, forever and ever.   **Amen.**   [363]

2

Year A B C

Almighty God,
you alone can order unruly wills and affections.
Help us to love what you command,
and desire what you promise;
that in the midst of this changing world,
our hearts may be fixed
where true joys are found;
through Jesus Christ our Lord,
who lives and reigns with you and the Holy Spirit,
one God, forever and ever.   **Amen.**   [364]

3

O God,
you invite the poor and the sinful to take their place
in the festive assembly of the new covenant.
May your church always honor the presence of the Lord
in the humble and the suffering,
and may we learn to recognize each other
as brothers and sisters,
gathered together around your table.
We ask this through our Lord Jesus Christ,
who lives and reigns with you in the unity of the Holy Spirit,
one God, forever and ever.   **Amen.**   [365]

TWENTY-THIRD SUNDAY IN ORDINARY TIME

Sunday between September 4 and 10 inclusive

SENTENCES OF SCRIPTURE

1

Year A B C
2 Cor. 5:19

In Christ God was reconciling the world to Godself,
not counting their trespasses against them,
and entrusting the message of reconciliation to us.

2

Year B
James 1:17

Every generous act of giving,
with every perfect gift,
is from above,
coming down from the Father of lights,
with whom there is no variation
or shadow due to change.

3

Year C
Ps. 119:135

Make your face shine upon your servant
and teach me your statutes.

PRAYER OF THE DAY

1   *Year A B C*

Direct and help us, O Lord, in all our deeds,
that in all our works
begun, continued, and ended in you,
we may glorify your holy name,
and finally, by your mercy,
obtain everlasting life;
through Jesus Christ our Lord,
who lives and reigns with you in the unity of the Holy Spirit,
one God, forever and ever.   **Amen.**   [366]

2   *Year A B C*

Almighty and everlasting God,
increase our faith, hope, and love;
and, that we may receive all you promise,
make us love what you have commanded;
through Jesus Christ our Lord,
who lives and reigns with you in the unity of the Holy Spirit,
one God, forever and ever.   **Amen.**   [367]

3   *Year A B C*

God of the ages,
you call the church to keep watch in the world
and to discern the signs of the times.
Grant us the wisdom which your Spirit bestows,
that with courage we may proclaim your prophetic word,
and complete the work that you have set before us;
through your Son, our Lord Jesus Christ,
who lives and reigns with you in the unity of the Holy Spirit,
one God, forever and ever.   **Amen.**   [368]

TWENTY-FOURTH SUNDAY IN ORDINARY TIME

Sunday between September 11 and 17 inclusive

SENTENCES OF SCRIPTURE

1   *Year A B C*
                                                                    John 13:34

Jesus said:
I give you a new commandment,
that you love one another
as I have loved you.

2 *Year A B C*
Gal. 6:14

May I never boast of anything
except the cross of our Lord Jesus Christ,
by which the world has been crucified to me,
and I to the world.

3 *Year C*
Luke 15:10

There is joy in the presence of the angels of God
over one sinner who repents.

PRAYER OF THE DAY

1 *Year A B C*

Almighty God,
you call your church to witness
that in Christ we are reconciled to you.
Help us so to proclaim the good news of your love,
that all who hear it may turn to you;
through Jesus Christ our Lord,
who lives and reigns with you and the Holy Spirit,
one God, now and forever. **Amen.** [369]

2 *Year A B C*

God of mercy:
Help us to forgive, as you have forgiven us.
Help us to trust you, even when hope is failing.
Help us to take up our cross daily
and follow you in your redeeming work;
through Jesus Christ our Lord,
who lives and reigns with you and the Holy Spirit,
one God, now and forever. **Amen.** [370]

3 *Year C*

Undaunted you seek the lost, O God,
exultant you bring home the found.
Touch our hearts with grateful wonder
at the tenderness of your forbearing love.
Grant us delight in the mercy that has found us,
and bring all to rejoice at the feast of forgiveness.
We ask this through our Lord Jesus Christ, your Son,
who lives and reigns with you in the unity of the Holy Spirit,
God forever and ever. **Amen.** [371]

Twenty-fifth Sunday in Ordinary Time

Sunday between September 18 and 24 inclusive

Sentences of Scripture

1

Year A B C
Phil. 1:9, 10

It is my prayer that your love may abound more and more,
so that you may approve what is excellent,
and may be pure and blameless for the day of Christ.

2

Year A B C
2 Cor. 8:9

You know the grace of our Lord Jesus Christ,
that though he was rich,
yet for your sake he became poor,
so that by his poverty you might become rich.

3

Year A B C
Ps. 100:1, 2, 5

Cry out with joy to the Lord, all the earth!

Worship the Lord with gladness!

Come into God's presence with singing!

Enter the courts of the Lord with praise!

Prayer of the Day

1

Year A B C

Almighty God,
you created the heavens and the earth,
and humankind in your image.
Teach us to discern your hand in all your works
and to serve you with reverence and thanksgiving;
through Jesus Christ our Lord,
who is alive and reigns with you and the Holy Spirit,
one God, now and forever.   **Amen.**   [372]

2

Year B

God and Father of all,
you have willed that the last shall be first,
and you have made a little child the measure of your kingdom.

Give us that wisdom which is from above,
so we may understand that, in your sight,
the one who serves is the greatest of all.
We ask this through our Lord Jesus Christ,
who lives and reigns with you in the unity of the Holy Spirit,
one God, forever and ever. **Amen.** [373]

3 *Year C*

O God,
you are rich in love for your people.
Show us the treasure that endures
and, when we are tempted by greed,
remind us of your lavish mercy.
Call us back into your service
and make us worthy to be entrusted with the wealth that never fails.
We ask this through your Son, our Lord Jesus Christ,
who lives and reigns with you in the unity of the Holy Spirit,
one God, forever and ever. **Amen.** [374]

TWENTY-SIXTH SUNDAY IN ORDINARY TIME

Sunday between September 25 and October 1 inclusive

SENTENCES OF SCRIPTURE

1 *Year A B C*
Ps. 34:8

O taste and see that the Lord is good;
happy are those who take refuge in the Lord.

2 *Year A B C*
John 17:17

Your word, O Lord, is truth;
Sanctify us in the truth.

3 *Year A B C*
2 Cor. 8:9

You know the grace of our Lord Jesus Christ,
that though he was rich,
yet for your sake he became poor,
so that by his poverty you might become rich.

PRAYER OF THE DAY

1 *Year A B C*

Grant, O merciful God,
that your church,
being gathered by your Holy Spirit into one,
may show forth your power among all peoples,
to the glory of your name;
through Jesus Christ our Lord,
who lives and reigns with you and the Holy Spirit,
one God, now and forever.   **Amen.**   [375]

2 *Year A B C*

Grant us, Lord, not to be anxious about earthly cares,
but to love that which is above,
and even now,
while we live among transient things,
to hold fast to those things that shall endure;
through Jesus Christ our Lord,
who lives and reigns with you and the Holy Spirit,
one God, forever and ever.   **Amen.**   [376]

3 *Year A B C*

O God,
by whom the meek are guided in judgment
and light rises in darkness for the godly:
Grant us, in all our doubts and uncertainties,
the grace to ask what you would have us do;
that the Spirit of wisdom may save us from all false choices,
and that in your light we may see light,
and in your straight path may not stumble;
through Jesus Christ our Lord,
who lives and reigns with you in the unity of the Holy Spirit,
one God, forever and ever.   **Amen.**   [377]

TWENTY-SEVENTH SUNDAY IN ORDINARY TIME

Sunday between October 2 and 8 inclusive

SENTENCES OF SCRIPTURE

1 *Year A B C*
John 15:16

I chose you and appointed you, says the Lord,
to go and bear fruit,
fruit that will last.

Year A B C
1 John 4:16b

God is love,
and those who abide in love abide in God,
and God abides in them.

3

Year C
2 Tim. 1:7

God did not give us a spirit of cowardice,
but rather a spirit of power and of love
and of self-discipline.

PRAYER OF THE DAY

1

Year A B C

Almighty and everlasting God,
you are always more ready to hear
than we to pray,
and to give more than we either desire or deserve.
Pour upon us the abundance of your mercy,
forgiving us those things
of which our conscience is afraid,
and giving us those good things
for which we are not worthy to ask,
except through the merits and mediation
of Jesus Christ our Savior,
who lives and reigns with you and the Holy Spirit,
one God, forever and ever. **Amen.** [378]

2

Year A B C

God of mercy, have mercy on us.
God of wisdom, illumine our minds.
God of light, shine into our hearts.
Eternal Goodness, deliver us from evil.
God of Power, be our refuge and our strength,
now and forever. **Amen.** [379]

3

Year A B C

Almighty God,
you built your church
on the foundation of the apostles and prophets,
with Jesus Christ himself as the cornerstone.
Gather your church in unity, by your Holy Spirit,
that it may manifest your power among all peoples
to the glory of your name;

through Jesus Christ our Lord,
who lives and reigns with you and the Holy Spirit,
one God, now and forever.   **Amen.**   [380]

TWENTY-EIGHTH SUNDAY IN ORDINARY TIME

Sunday between October 9 and 15 inclusive

SENTENCES OF SCRIPTURE

1

Year A B C
Eph. 1:17, 18

May God give you a spirit of wisdom and revelation
so that you may know the hope to which you are called.

2

Year A B C
Heb. 8:10

God says:
I will put my laws in their minds,
and write them on their hearts,
and I will be their God,
and they shall be my people.

3

Year A B C
1 Thess. 5:18

Give thanks in all circumstances;
for this is the will of God in Christ Jesus for you.

PRAYER OF THE DAY

1

Year A B C

Almighty God,
in our baptism you adopted us for your own.
Quicken, we pray, your Spirit within us,
that we, being renewed both in body and mind,
may worship you in sincerity and truth;
through Jesus Christ our Lord,
who lives and reigns with you and the Holy Spirit,
one God, now and forever.   **Amen.**   [381]

2

Year A B C

Merciful God,
in Jesus Christ you do not call the righteous,
but sinners to repentance.

Draw us away from the easy road
that leads to destruction,
and guide us into paths
that lead to life abundant,
that in seeking your truth,
and obeying your will,
we may know the joy of being a disciple
of Jesus Christ our Savior,
who lives and reigns with you and the Holy Spirit,
one God, now and forever.   **Amen.**   [382]

3   *Year A B C*

O God,
you have made heaven and earth
and all that is good;
and in Jesus Christ
you show us that the secret of joy
is a heart set free from selfish desires.
Help us to delight in simple things
and to rejoice always in the richness of your bounty;
through the same Jesus Christ our Lord,
who lives and reigns with you in the unity of the Holy Spirit,
one God, forever and ever.   **Amen.**   [383]

TWENTY-NINTH SUNDAY IN ORDINARY TIME

Sunday between October 16 and 22 inclusive

SENTENCES OF SCRIPTURE

1   *Year A B C*
                                                                    Phil. 2:15, 16

Shine like stars in the world,
holding fast to the word of life.

2   *Year A B C*
                                                                    Mark 10:45

The Son of Man came not to be served
but to serve,
and to give his life a ransom for many.

3   *Year A B C*
                                                                    Heb. 4:12

The word of God is living and active.
It is able to judge the thoughts and intentions of the heart.

PRAYER OF THE DAY

1   *Year A B C*

Almighty and everlasting God,
in Christ you have revealed your glory among the nations.
Preserve the works of your mercy,
that your church throughout the world
may persevere with steadfast faith
in the confession of your name;
through Jesus Christ our Lord,
who lives and reigns with you in the unity of the Holy Spirit,
one God, forever and ever.   **Amen.**   [384]

2   *Year B*

God of unchangeable power,
when you fashioned the world
the morning stars sang together
and the host of heaven shouted for joy.
Open our eyes to the wonders of creation
and teach us to use all things for good,
to the honor of your glorious name;
through Jesus Christ our Lord,
who lives and reigns with you in the unity of the Holy Spirit,
one God, forever and ever.   **Amen.**   [385]

3   *Year C*

Lord, tireless guardian of your people,
ever prepared to hear the cries of your chosen ones,
teach us to rely, day and night, on your care.
Support our prayer, lest we grow weary.
Drive us to seek your enduring justice and your ever-present help.
Grant this through your Son, our Lord Jesus Christ,
who lives and reigns with you in the unity of the Holy Spirit,
one God, forever and ever.   **Amen.**   [386]

THIRTIETH SUNDAY IN ORDINARY TIME

Sunday between October 23 and 29 inclusive

SENTENCES OF SCRIPTURE

1   *Year A B C*
                                                                     John 14:23

Jesus said:
Those who love me will keep my word,
and my Father will love them,
and we will come to them
and make our home with them.

Our Savior Christ Jesus abolished death,
and brought life and immortality to light through the gospel.

In Christ God was reconciling the world to Godself,
not counting their trespasses against them,
and entrusting the message of reconciliation to us.

PRAYER OF THE DAY

Send your Holy Spirit into our hearts, Almighty God,
to rule and direct us according to your will,
to comfort us in all our temptations and afflictions,
to defend us from all error,
and lead us into all truth;
that we, being steadfast in the faith,
may increase in love and in all good works,
and in the end obtain everlasting life;
through Jesus Christ your Son our Lord,
who lives and reigns with you and the Holy Spirit,
one God, now and forever.   **Amen.**   [387]

O God,
from whom all holy desires,
all good counsels, and all just works proceed:
Give to your servants that peace
which the world cannot give;
that our hearts may be set to obey your commandments,
and that free from the fear of our enemies
we may pass our time in trust and quietness;
through the merits of Jesus Christ our Savior,
who lives and reigns with you and the Holy Spirit,
one God, now and forever.   **Amen.**   [388]

3   *Year C*

O God,
who alone can probe the depths of the heart,
you hear the prayer of the humble
and justify the repentant sinner.
Grant us the gift of humility,
that we may see our own sins clearly
and refrain from judging our neighbor.
We make our prayer through your Son, our Lord Jesus Christ,
who lives and reigns with you in the unity of the Holy Spirit,
one God, forever and ever.   **Amen.**   [389]

THIRTY-FIRST SUNDAY IN ORDINARY TIME

Sunday between October 30 and November 5 inclusive

SENTENCES OF SCRIPTURE

1   *Year A*
                                                                                Matt. 23:9, 10

You have one Father, who is in heaven.
You have one Teacher, the Christ.

2   *Year A B C*
                                                                                   John 14:23

Jesus said:
Those who love me will keep my word,
and my Father will love them,
and we will come to them
and make our home with them.

3   *Year A B C*
                                                                                    Ps. 24:1

The earth is the Lord's and the fullness thereof,

the world and all who dwell in it.

1   *Year A B C*

Creator God,
you have filled the world with beauty.
Open our eyes to behold your gracious hand in all your works;
that, rejoicing in your whole creation,
we may learn to serve you with gladness;
for the sake of him by whom all things were made,
your Son Jesus Christ our Lord,
who lives and reigns with you and the Holy Spirit,
one God, now and forever.   **Amen.**   [390]

2   *Year A B C*

God of peace,
you taught us that in returning and rest
we shall be saved,
in quietness and in confidence
shall be our strength.
By the power of your Spirit
lift us to your presence,
where we may be still and know that you are God;
through Jesus Christ our Lord,
who lives and reigns with you in the unity of the Holy Spirit,
one God, forever and ever.   **Amen.**   [391]

3   *Year C*

Merciful God,
righteous judge of all,
you sent Jesus among us
to seek and to save those who are lost.
Grant that we,
like Zacchaeus of Jericho,
may eagerly seek the Savior,
joyfully welcome him into our homes and lives,
and gladly do what is pleasing in his sight.
We ask this through Jesus Christ our Lord,
who lives and reigns with you in unity with the Holy Spirit,
one God, now and forever.   **Amen.**   [392]

Or first Sunday in November

SENTENCES OF SCRIPTURE
PRAYER OF THE DAY

SENTENCES OF SCRIPTURE

1

Year A
Rev. 7:9–10

After this I looked,
and there was a great multitude that no one could count,
from every nation, from all tribes and peoples and languages,
standing before the throne and before the Lamb,
robed in white, with palm branches in their hands.
They cried out in a loud voice, saying:

Salvation belongs to our God
who is seated on the throne,
and to the Lamb!

2

Year B
Heb. 12:1

Since we are surrounded by so great a cloud of witnesses,
let us also lay aside every weight
and the sin that clings so closely,
and let us run with perseverance the race that is set before us.

3

Year C
Luke 13:29

People will come from east and west,
from north and south,
and will eat in the kingdom of heaven.

PRAYER OF THE DAY

1

Year A B C

Eternal God,
neither death nor life can separate us from your love.
Grant that we may serve you faithfully here on earth,
and in heaven rejoice with all your saints
who ceaselessly proclaim your glory;
through Jesus Christ our Lord,
who lives and reigns with you and the Holy Spirit,
one God, forever and ever. **Amen.** [393]

Almighty God,
you have knit together your elect
in one communion and fellowship
in the mystical body of your Son, Christ our Lord.
Give us grace so to follow your blessed saints
in all virtuous and godly living
that we may come to those ineffable joys
that you have prepared for those who truly love you;
through Jesus Christ our Savior,
who with you and the Holy Spirit lives and reigns,
one God, in glory everlasting.   **Amen.**   [394]

PRAYER OF CONFESSION

Eternal God,
in every age you have raised up men and women
to live and die in faith.
We confess that we are indifferent to your will.
You call us to proclaim your name,
but we are silent.
You call us to do what is just,
but we remain idle.
You call us to live faithfully,
but we are afraid.

In your mercy, forgive us.
Give us courage to follow in your way,
that joined with those from ages past,
who have served you with faith, hope, and love,
we may inherit the kingdom you promised in Jesus Christ.   [395]

GREAT THANKSGIVING

It is recommended that, with this prayer, invitation A (p. 68) be used.

The Lord be with you.

And also with you.

Lift up your hearts.

We lift them to the Lord.

Let us give thanks to the Lord our God.

It is right to give our thanks and praise.

It is truly right and our greatest joy
to give you thanks and praise,
O Lord our God, creator and ruler of the universe.
We praise you for saints and martyrs,
for the faithful in every age
who have followed your Son
and witnessed to his resurrection.
From every race and tongue,
from every people and nation,
you have gathered them into your kingdom.
You have shown them the path of life
and filled them with the joy of your presence.
How glorious is your heavenly realm
where the multitude of your saints rejoice with Christ!

Therefore we praise you,
joining our voices with angels and archangels,
with prophets, apostles, and martyrs,
and with all the faithful of every time and place,
who forever sing to the glory of your name:

The people may sing or say:

**Holy, holy, holy Lord, God of power and might,
heaven and earth are full of your glory.
Hosanna in the highest.**

**Blessed is he who comes in the name of the Lord.
Hosanna in the highest.**

The minister continues:

You are holy, O God of majesty,
and blessed is Jesus Christ, your Son, our Lord.
Sent to be our Savior,
he took our flesh and dwelt among us,
full of grace and truth.
His words are true.
His touch brings healing.
To all who follow him,
he gives abundant life.
When evil sought to destroy him,
and he lay in the darkness of death,
you raised him from the grave.
He is our risen Lord forever!

> If they have not already been said, the words of institution may be
> said here, or in relation to the breaking of the bread.
>
> We give you thanks that the Lord Jesus,
> on the night before he died,
> took bread,
> and after giving thanks to you,
> he broke it, and gave it to his disciples, saying:
> Take, eat.
> This is my body, given for you.
> Do this in remembrance of me.
>
> In the same way he took the cup, saying:
> This cup is the new covenant sealed in my blood,
> shed for you for the forgiveness of sins.
> Whenever you drink it,
> do this in remembrance of me.

Remembering all your mighty and merciful acts,
we take this bread and this wine
from the gifts you have given us,
and celebrate with joy
the redemption won for us in Jesus Christ.
Accept this our sacrifice of praise and thanksgiving
as a living and holy offering of ourselves,
that our lives may proclaim the One crucified and risen.

The people may sing or say one of the following:

1

Great is the mystery of faith:

Christ has died,
Christ is risen,
Christ will come again.

2

Praise to you, Lord Jesus:

Dying you destroyed our death,
rising you restored our life.
Lord Jesus, come in glory.

3

According to his commandment:

We remember his death,
we proclaim his resurrection,
we await his coming in glory.

4

Christ is the bread of life:

When we eat this bread and drink this cup,
we proclaim your death, Lord Jesus,
until you come in glory.

The minister continues:

Gracious God,
pour out your Holy Spirit upon us
and upon these your gifts of bread and wine,
that the bread we break
and the cup we bless
may be the communion of the body and blood of Christ.
By your Spirit unite us with the living Christ,
and with all who are baptized in his name,
that we may be one in ministry in every place.
As this bread is Christ's body for us,
send us out to be the body of Christ in the world.

Intercessions for the church and the world may be included here.

Number us among your saints, O God,
and join us with the faithful of every age,
that strengthened by their witness
and supported by their fellowship,
we may run with perseverance the race that is set before us,
and may with them receive the unfading crown of glory
when we stand before your throne of grace.
Give us strength to serve you faithfully
until the promised day of resurrection,
when with the redeemed of all the ages
we will feast with you at your table in glory.

Through Christ, with Christ, in Christ,
in the unity of the Holy Spirit,
all glory and honor are yours, almighty God,
now and forever.   **Amen.**   [396]

Prayer of Thanksgiving

For use when the Eucharist is not celebrated.

Let us give thanks to the Lord our God.

It is right to give our thanks and praise.

God of the ages,
we praise you for all your servants,
who have done justice, loved mercy,
and walked humbly with their God.
For apostles and martyrs and saints
of every time and place,
who in life and death have witnessed to your truth,

we praise you, O God.

For all your servants who have faithfully served you,
witnessed bravely, and died in faith,
who still are shining lights in the world,

we praise you, O God.

For those no longer remembered,
who earnestly sought you in darkness,
who held fast their faith in trial,
and served others,

we praise you, O God.

For those we have known and loved,
who by their faithful obedience and steadfast hope,
have shown the same mind that was in Christ Jesus,

we praise you, O God.

Keep us grateful for their witness,
and, like them, eager to follow in the way of Christ.
Then at the last, bring us with them
to share in the inheritance of the saints in light;
through Jesus Christ the pioneer and perfecter of our faith,
who lives and reigns with you and the Holy Spirit,
one God, forever and ever.   **Amen.**   [397]

THIRTY-SECOND SUNDAY IN ORDINARY TIME

Sunday between November 6 and 12 inclusive

SENTENCES OF SCRIPTURE

1   *Year A B C*
                                                    Matt. 24:42, 44

Watch and be ready,
for you do not know on what day your
Lord is coming.

2   *Year A B C*
                                                    Matt. 5:3

Blessed are the poor in spirit,
for theirs is the kingdom of heaven.

3   *Year A B C*
                                                    Rev. 1:5, 6

Jesus Christ, the firstborn of the dead;
to him be glory and dominion forever and ever.

PRAYER OF THE DAY

1   *Year A B C*

Lord our God,
in Jesus Christ you have taught us
that love is the fulfilling of the law.
Send your Holy Spirit upon us,
and pour into our hearts
that most excellent gift of love,
that we may love you with our whole being,
and our neighbors as ourselves;
through Jesus Christ our Lord,
who lives and reigns with you in unity with the Holy Spirit,
one God, now and forever.   **Amen.**   [398]

O God,
your blessed Son came into the world
that he might destroy the works of evil
and make us children of God and heirs of eternal life.
Grant that, having this hope,
we may purify ourselves as he is pure;
that, when he comes again with power and great glory,
we may be made like him
in his eternal and glorious kingdom;
where he lives and reigns with you and the Holy Spirit,
one God, forever and ever.   **Amen.**   [399]

3   *Year C*

God of all the living,
in the resurrection of Christ Jesus
you have given us the promise of life
which death itself cannot destroy.
In the strength of this unshakable promise
give us a new heart to live, even now, as your new creation.
We ask this through your Son, our Lord Jesus Christ,
who lives and reigns with you in the unity of the Holy Spirit,
one God, forever and ever.   **Amen.**   [400]

THIRTY-THIRD SUNDAY IN ORDINARY TIME

Sunday between November 13 and 19 inclusive

SENTENCES OF SCRIPTURE

1   *Year A B C*
                                                                    Luke 21:36

Be alert at all times,
praying that you may stand before the Son of Man.

2   *Year A B C*
                                                                    Luke 21:28

Look up and raise your heads,
because your redemption is drawing near.

3   *Year A B C*
                                                                    Isa. 12:6

Shout aloud and sing for joy,
for great in our midst is the Holy One.

Prayer of the Day

Year A B C

1

Ever-living God,
before the earth was formed
and even after it shall cease to be, you are God.
Break into our short span of life
and show us those things that are eternal,
that we may serve your purpose in all we do;
through Jesus Christ our Lord,
who lives and reigns with you in unity with the Holy Spirit,
one God, now and forever.   **Amen.**   [401]

Year A B C

2

Almighty God,
whose sovereign purpose none can make void,
give us faith to be steadfast
amid the tumults of this world,
knowing that your kingdom shall come
and your will be done,
to your eternal glory;
through Jesus Christ our Lord,
who lives and reigns with you and the Holy Spirit,
one God, now and forever.   **Amen.**   [402]

Year A B C

3

Lord God of all the ages,
the One who is, who was, and who is to come,
stir up within us a longing for your kingdom,
steady our hearts in time of trial,
and grant us patient endurance until the sun of justice dawns.
We make our prayer through your Son, our Lord Jesus Christ,
who lives and reigns with you in the unity of the Holy Spirit,
one God, forever and ever.   **Amen.**   [403]

CHRIST THE KING
(OR REIGN OF CHRIST)

Sunday between November 20 and 26 inclusive

SENTENCES OF SCRIPTURE
PRAYER OF THE DAY

SENTENCES OF SCRIPTURE

1
Year A B C
Rev. 22:13

The Lord is a great God who says:
I am the Alpha and Omega,
the first and the last,
the beginning and the end.

2
Year A B C
Mark 11:9, 10b

Blessed is the one who comes in the name of the Lord!
Hosanna in the highest!

3
Year A B C
Rev. 4:8

Day and night around the throne they never stop singing:

Holy, holy, holy is the Lord God Almighty,
who was, who is, and who is to come.

PRAYER OF THE DAY

1
Year A B C

God of power and love,
you raised Jesus from death to life,
resplendent in glory to rule over all creation.
Free the world to rejoice in his peace,

to glory in his justice,
and to live in his love.
Unite all humankind in Jesus Christ your Son,
who lives and reigns with you and the Holy Spirit,
one God, forever and ever. **Amen.** [404]

2   *Year A B C*

Almighty and everlasting God,
whose will is to restore all things
in your well-beloved Son, our Lord and King:
Grant that the people of earth,
now divided and enslaved by sin,
may be freed and brought together
under his gentle and loving rule;
who lives and reigns with you and the Holy Spirit,
one God, now and forever. **Amen.** [405]

3   *Year A B C*

Eternal God,
you set Jesus Christ to rule over all things,
and made us servants in your kingdom.
By your Spirit empower us to love the unloved,
and to minister to all in need.
Then at the last bring us to your eternal realm
where we may worship and adore you
and be welcomed into your everlasting joy;
through Jesus Christ our Lord,
who lives and reigns with you in the unity of the Holy Spirit,
one God, forever and ever. **Amen.** [406]

4   *Year A B C*

God and Father of our Lord Jesus Christ,
you gave us your Son,
the beloved one who was rejected,
the Savior who appeared defeated.
Yet the mystery of his kingship illumines our lives.
Show us in his death the victory that crowns the ages,
and in his broken body
the love that unites heaven and earth.
We ask this through your Son, our Lord Jesus Christ,
who lives and reigns with you in the unity of the Holy Spirit,
one God, forever and ever. **Amen.** [407]

PRAYER OF CONFESSION

Righteous God,
you have crowned Jesus Christ as Lord of all.
We confess that we have not bowed before him,
and are slow to acknowledge his rule.
We give allegiance to the powers of this world,
and fail to be governed by justice and love.

In your mercy, forgive us.
Raise us to acclaim him as ruler of all,
that we may be loyal ambassadors,
obeying the commands of our Lord Jesus Christ.   [408]

GREAT THANKSGIVING

The Lord be with you.

And also with you.

Lift up your hearts.

We lift them to the Lord.

Let us give thanks to the Lord our God.

It is right to give our thanks and praise.

It is truly right and our greatest joy
to give you thanks and praise,
eternal God, creator and ruler of the universe.
You fashioned this world in love,
and govern all the earth with grace and peace.
Nations and monarchs rise and fall,
but your reign is for all time,
and your mercy is without end.

In love you made us to love and serve you.
When we turned from you
and bent our knees to gods of our own making,
you spoke through prophets
to bring us back to your ways.
You gave us a vision of your holy kingdom
that we might hunger after righteousness
and thirst for justice,
and long for the day when peace will triumph
over the pride and greed of nations.
Therefore, we praise you,

joining our voices with the servants around heaven's throne
and with all the faithful of every time and place,
who forever sing to the glory of your name:

The people may sing or say:

Holy, holy, holy Lord, God of power and might,
heaven and earth are full of your glory.
Hosanna in the highest.

Blessed is he who comes in the name of the Lord.
Hosanna in the highest.

The minister continues:

You are holy, O God of majesty,
and blessed is Jesus Christ, your Son, our Lord.
Born as king in David's line,
he lived with the lowly
and cared for the least of your children.
His power was revealed in weakness,
his majesty in mercy.
His captors knelt to mock him,
giving him bruises instead of praise,
and piercing thorns for a crown.
His only earthly throne was a cross on which to die.
Even there his arms stretched out
to embrace friends and foes in love.
From the grave you raised him to your right hand
where he rules again from heaven,
and commands true loyalty from peoples and nations.

If they have not already been said, the words of institution may be
said here, or in relation to the breaking of the bread.

We give you thanks that the Lord Jesus,
on the night before he died,
took bread,
and after giving thanks to you,
he broke it, and gave it to his disciples, saying:
Take, eat.
This is my body, given for you.
Do this in remembrance of me.

In the same way he took the cup, saying:
This cup is the new covenant sealed in my blood,
shed for you for the forgiveness of sins.
Whenever you drink it,
do this in remembrance of me.

Remembering your gracious acts in Jesus Christ,
we take from your creation this bread and this wine
and joyfully celebrate his dying and rising
as we await the day of his coming.
With thanksgiving we offer our very selves to you
to be a living and holy sacrifice
dedicated to your service.

The people may sing or say one of the following:

1

Great is the mystery of faith:

Christ has died,
Christ is risen,
Christ will come again.

2

Praise to you, Lord Jesus:

Dying you destroyed our death,
rising you restored our life.
Lord Jesus, come in glory.

3

According to his commandment:

We remember his death,
we proclaim his resurrection,
we await his coming in glory.

4

Christ is the bread of life:

**When we eat this bread and drink this cup,
we proclaim your death, Lord Jesus,
until you come in glory.**

The minister continues:

Gracious God,
pour out your Holy Spirit upon us
and upon these your gifts of bread and wine
that the bread we break
and the cup we bless
may be the communion of the body and blood of Christ.
By your Spirit unite us with the living Christ
and with all who are baptized in his name,
that we may be one in ministry in every place.
As this bread is Christ's body for us,
send us out to be the body of Christ in the world.

Intercessions for the church and the world may be included here.

Lead us, O God, to conform this world
to your kingdom of love, justice, and peace.
Help us to live as the Lord requires:
to do justice,
to love kindness,
and to walk humbly with you, our God.
Keep us faithful in your service
until Christ comes in final victory
and we shall feast with all your saints
in the joy of your eternal realm.

Through Christ, with Christ, in Christ,
in the unity of the Holy Spirit,
all glory and honor are yours, almighty God,
now and forever.   **Amen.**   [409]

Prayer of Thanksgiving

For use when the Eucharist is not celebrated.

Let us give thanks to the Lord our God.

It is right to give our thanks and praise.

We praise you, great God,
for you are ruler of the universe,
and have sent your Son to be King of kings.
We rejoice that he has triumphed over all the powers of this world,
and governs the nations in justice and righteousness.
We celebrate his victory
in his life, death, resurrection, and ascension to honor and might at your side.
By your Spirit,
claim our complete loyalty,
establish Christ's rule in every land and in every heart.
Accept our homage
as we offer our lives in the service of Christ's kingdom.
He is Lord forever and ever.   **Amen.**   [410]

BAPTISM AND REAFFIRMATION OF THE BAPTISMAL COVENANT

An Outline of the Service for the Lord's Day Including the Sacrament of Baptism

Gathering

Call to Worship
Prayer of the Day or Opening Prayer
Hymn of Praise, Psalm, or Spiritual
Confession and Pardon
Canticle, Psalm, Hymn, or Spiritual

The Word

Prayer for Illumination
First Reading
Psalm
Second Reading
Anthem, Hymn, Psalm, Canticle, or Spiritual
Gospel Reading
Sermon
Hymn, Canticle, Psalm, or Spiritual
Baptism
    Presentation
    Profession of Faith
    Thanksgiving Over the Water
    The Baptism
    Laying On of Hands
    Welcome
    The Peace
Hymn, Psalm, or Spiritual
Prayers of the People

If the Eucharist is not celebrated:

The Eucharist

Offering	Offering
Invitation to the Lord's Table	
Great Thanksgiving	Prayer of Thanksgiving
Lord's Prayer	Lord's Prayer
Breaking of the Bread	
Communion of the People	

Sending

Hymn, Spiritual, Canticle, or Psalm
Charge and Blessing

THE SACRAMENT OF BAPTISM

Baptism is ordinarily celebrated as part of the worship of the congregation on the Lord's Day. It appropriately follows the reading and proclaiming of the Word.

If the liturgical practice of the congregation includes use of a paschal candle, it is lighted before the service begins.

After the sermon, an appropriate hymn, canticle, psalm, or spiritual may be sung while the candidates, sponsors, and parents assemble at the baptismal font or pool. Care should be taken to ensure that the baptism is fully visible to the congregation. An elder or a representative of the congregation may lead a procession to the place of baptism, carrying a large pitcher of water.

PRESENTATION

The minister addresses all present:

Matt. 28:18–20

Hear the words of our Lord Jesus Christ:
All authority in heaven and on earth
has been given to me.
Go therefore and make disciples of all nations,
baptizing them in the name of the Father,
and of the Son,
and of the Holy Spirit,
and teaching them to obey everything that I have commanded you.
And remember, I am with you always,
to the end of the age.

Hear also these words from Holy Scripture:

The minister then continues, using one or more of the following:

1

Eph. 4:4–6

There is one body and one Spirit,
just as you were called
to the one hope of your calling,

one Lord, one faith, one baptism,
one God and Father of all,
who is above all and through all and in all.

2   *Gal. 3:27, 28*

As many of you as were baptized into Christ
have clothed yourselves with Christ.
There is no longer Jew or Greek,
there is no longer slave or free,
there is no longer male and female;
for all of you are one in Christ Jesus.

3   *1 Peter 2:9*

You are a chosen race, a royal priesthood,
a holy nation, God's own people,
in order that you may proclaim the mighty acts
of the One who called you out of darkness
into God's marvelous light.

4   *Rom. 6:3, 4*

Do you not know
that all of us who have been baptized into Christ Jesus
were baptized into his death?
Therefore we have been buried with him by baptism into death,
so that, just as Christ was raised from the dead
by the glory of the Father,
so we too might walk in newness of life.

5   *Acts 2:39*

The promise is for you, for your children
and for all who are far away,
everyone whom the Lord our God calls.

The minister continues:

Obeying the word of our Lord Jesus,
and confident of his promises,
we baptize those whom God has called.

In baptism God claims us,
and seals us to show that we belong to God.
God frees us from sin and death,
uniting us with Jesus Christ in his death and resurrection.

By water and the Holy Spirit,
we are made members of the church, the body of Christ,
and joined to Christ's ministry of love, peace, and justice.

Let us remember with joy our own baptism,
as we celebrate this sacrament.

An elder presents each candidate for baptism, using the appropriate forms:

A

For adults and older children

On behalf of the session,
I present N. and N. to receive the sacrament of Baptism.

B

For infants and younger children

On behalf of the session,
I present N., (son, daughter) of N. and N.,
to receive the sacrament of Baptism.

The minister addresses, in turn, candidates for baptism, parents bringing
children for baptism, sponsors, and the congregation:

A

Adults and older children

The minister addresses the candidates for baptism:

N. and N., do you desire to be baptized?

The candidates respond:

I do.

B

Parent(s) of infants and younger children

The minister addresses parents presenting children for baptism:

Do you desire that N. and N. be baptized?

The parent(s) respond:

I do.

Minister:

Relying on God's grace,
do you promise to live the Christian faith,
and to teach that faith to your child?

The parent(s) respond:

I do.

C

Sponsors (if any are present)

The minister addresses the sponsors, if any are present:

Do you promise, through prayer and example,
to support and encourage N.
to be a faithful Christian?

The sponsors respond:

I do.

D

Congregation

The minister addresses the congregation:

Do you, as members of the church of Jesus Christ,
promise to guide and nurture N. and N.
by word and deed,
with love and prayer,
encouraging *them* to know and follow Christ
and to be faithful *members* of his church?

The people respond:

We do.

PROFESSION OF FAITH

Through baptism we enter the covenant God has established.
Within this covenant God gives us new life,
guards us from evil,
and nurtures us in love.

In embracing that covenant, we choose whom we will serve,
by turning from evil
and turning to Jesus Christ.

> The minister then asks the following questions of the candidates for baptism and/or the parents or guardians of children being presented for baptism.

As God embraces you within the covenant, I ask you
to reject sin,
to profess your faith in Christ Jesus,
and to confess the faith of the church,
the faith in which we baptize.

RENUNCIATIONS

> The minister continues, using one of the following:

1

Trusting in the gracious mercy of God,
do you turn from the ways of sin
and renounce evil and its power in the world?

I do.

Do you turn to Jesus Christ
and accept him as your Lord and Savior,
trusting in his grace and love?

I do.

Will you be Christ's faithful disciple,
obeying his Word and showing his love?

I will, with God's help.

2

Do you renounce all evil,
and powers in the world
which defy God's righteousness and love?

I renounce them.

Do you renounce the ways of sin
that separate you from the love of God?

I renounce them.

Do you turn to Jesus Christ
and accept him as your Lord and Savior?

I do.

Will you be Christ's faithful disciple,
obeying his Word and showing his love,
to your life's end?

I will, with God's help.

3

Trusting in the gracious mercy of God,
do you turn from the ways of sin
and renounce evil and its power in the world?

I do.

Who is your Lord and Savior?

Jesus Christ is my Lord and Savior.

Will you be Christ's faithful disciple,
obeying his Word and showing his love?

I will, with God's help.

PROFESSION

> The minister continues:

With the whole church,
let us confess our faith.

> The people may stand.

> All present profess their faith in the words of the Apostles' Creed, using
> the question and answer form (A) or reciting it directly (B).

A

Do you believe in God, the Father almighty?

**I believe in God, the Father almighty,
creator of heaven and earth.**

Do you believe in Jesus Christ?

**I believe in Jesus Christ, God's only Son, our Lord,
who was conceived by the Holy Spirit,
born of the Virgin Mary,
suffered under Pontius Pilate,
was crucified, died, and was buried;
he descended to the dead.**

On the third day he rose again;
he ascended into heaven,
he is seated at the right hand of the Father,
and he will come to judge the living and the dead.

Do you believe in the Holy Spirit?

**I believe in the Holy Spirit,
the holy catholic church,
the communion of saints,
the forgiveness of sins,
the resurrection of the body,
and the life everlasting.   Amen.**

B

**I believe in God, the Father almighty,
creator of heaven and earth.**

**I believe in Jesus Christ, God's only Son, our Lord,
who was conceived by the Holy Spirit,
born of the Virgin Mary,
suffered under Pontius Pilate,
was crucified, died, and was buried;
he descended to the dead.
On the third day he rose again;
he ascended into heaven,
he is seated at the right hand of the Father,
and he will come to judge the living and the dead.**

**I believe in the Holy Spirit,
the holy catholic church,
the communion of saints,
the forgiveness of sins,
the resurrection of the body,
and the life everlasting. Amen.**

The minister asks one of the following questions of those being baptized
on profession of their faith:

1

Will you be a faithful member of this congregation,
share in its worship and ministry
through your prayers and gifts,
your study and service,
and so fulfill your calling to be a disciple of Jesus Christ?

I will, with God's help.

Will you devote yourself to the church's teaching and fellowship,
to the breaking of bread and the prayers?

I will, with God's help.

Water is poured visibly and audibly into the font.

THANKSGIVING OVER THE WATER

One of the following prayers is said by the minister.

1

The Lord be with you.

And also with you.

Let us give thanks to the Lord our God.

It is right to give our thanks and praise.

We give you thanks, Eternal God,
for you nourish and sustain all living things
by the gift of water.
In the beginning of time,
your Spirit moved over the watery chaos,
calling forth order and life.

In the time of Noah,
you destroyed evil by the waters of the flood,
giving righteousness a new beginning.

You led Israel out of slavery,
through the waters of the sea,
into the freedom of the promised land.

In the waters of Jordan
Jesus was baptized by John
and anointed with your Spirit.
By the baptism of his own death and resurrection,
Christ set us free from sin and death,
and opened the way to eternal life.

We thank you, O God, for the water of baptism.
In it we are buried with Christ in his death.
From it we are raised to share in his resurrection,
Through it we are reborn by the power of the Holy Spirit.

The minister may touch the water.

Send your Spirit to move over this water
that it may be a fountain of deliverance and rebirth.
Wash away the sin of *all* who *are* cleansed by it.
Raise *them* to new life,
and graft *them* to the body of Christ.
Pour out your Holy Spirit upon *them*,
that they may have power to do your will,
and continue forever in the risen life of Christ.
To you, Father, Son, and Holy Spirit, one God,
be all praise, honor, and glory,
now and forever.   [411]

Amen.

2

The Lord be with you.

And also with you.

Let us give thanks to the Lord our God.

It is right to give our thanks and praise.

Eternal and gracious God, we give you thanks.
In countless ways you have revealed yourself in ages past,
and have blessed us with signs of your grace.

We praise you that through the waters of the sea,
you led your people Israel out of bondage,
into freedom in the land of your promise.

We praise you for sending Jesus your Son,
who for us was baptized in the waters of the Jordan,
and was anointed as the Christ by your Holy Spirit.
Through the baptism of his death and resurrection,
you set us free from the bondage of sin and death,
and give us cleansing and rebirth.

We praise you that in baptism
you give us your Holy Spirit,
who teaches us and leads us into all truth,
filling us with a variety of gifts,
that we might proclaim the gospel to all nations
and serve you as a royal priesthood.

The minister may touch the water.

Pour out your Spirit upon us
and upon this water,
that this font may be your womb of new birth.
May *all* who now pass through these waters
be delivered from death to life,
from bondage to freedom,
from sin to righteousness.
Bind *them* to the household of faith,
guard *them* from all evil.
Strengthen *them* to serve you with joy
until the day you make all things new.
To you be all praise, honor, and glory;
through Jesus Christ our Savior,
who, with you and the Holy Spirit,
lives and reigns forever.   [412]

Amen.

3

The minister may give thanks over the water in his or her own words:

a. praising God for God's faithfulness in the covenant;

b. thankfully remembering God's reconciling acts such as:
    the cleansing and rebirth in the flood in the time of Noah;
    the exodus through the waters of the sea;
    Jesus' baptism in the Jordan;
    the baptism of Jesus' death and his resurrection.

c. invoking the Holy Spirit
    to attend and empower the baptism;
    to make the water a water of redemption and rebirth;
    to equip the church for faithfulness.

The prayer concludes with an ascription of praise to the triune God.

THE BAPTISM

> The candidates, other than infants, who are to be baptized by pouring or sprinkling may kneel. Or if there are candidates to be immersed, they walk down into the water.

> Calling each candidate by his or her Christian (given) name or names only, the minister shall pour or sprinkle water visibly and generously on the candidate's head, or immerse the candidate in the water, while saying:

N., I baptize you
in the name of the Father,
and of the Son,
and of the Holy Spirit.

Amen.

LAYING ON OF HANDS

> The minister lays hands on the head of each person baptized, while saying one of the following:

1

O Lord, uphold N. by your Holy Spirit.
Give *him/her* the spirit of wisdom and understanding,
the spirit of counsel and might,
the spirit of knowledge and the fear of the Lord,
the spirit of joy in your presence,
both now and forever.   [413]

Amen.

2

Defend, O Lord, your servant N.
with your heavenly grace,
that *he/she* may continue yours forever,
and daily increase in your Holy Spirit more and more,
until *he/she* comes to your everlasting kingdom.   [414]

Amen.

> The minister may mark the sign of the cross on the forehead of each of the newly baptized, while saying one of the following. Oil prepared for this purpose may be used.

1

N., child of the covenant,
you have been sealed by the Holy Spirit in baptism,
and marked as Christ's own forever.

Amen.

2

N., child of God,
you have been sealed by the Holy Spirit in baptism,
and grafted into Christ forever.

Amen.

WELCOME

Candidates who have been kneeling will stand.

A representative of the session, or the minister, addresses the congregation
in these or similar words:

N. and N. *have* been received into the one holy catholic and apostolic church
   through baptism.
God has made *them members* of the household of God,
to share with us in the priesthood of Christ.
Let us welcome the newly baptized.

Welcome is extended, using (A) or (B):

A

The people respond, saying:

**With joy and thanksgiving
we welcome you into Christ's church
to share with us in his ministry,
for we are all one in Christ.**

B

Those who have been baptized are welcomed in a manner appropriate to
the particular congregation.

THE PEACE

The minister then says to all assembled at the font:

The peace of Christ be with you.

They respond:

And also with you.

The people may exchange signs of God's peace, greeting those who have been baptized.

All return to their places. An appropriate hymn, psalm, or spiritual may be sung.

The service continues with the prayers of the people, which will include petitions for the newly baptized and for those who will nurture them (pp. 416–417).

When the Lord's Supper is celebrated, it is appropriate for the newly baptized to receive Communion first.

Prayers of Intercession and Supplication
for Inclusion in the Prayers of the People

1

For the newly baptized and new members

Merciful God, you call us by name
and promise to each of us your constant love.
Watch over your *servants*, N. and N.
Deepen *their* understanding of the gospel;
strengthen *their* commitment to follow the way of Christ;
and keep *them* in the faith and communion of your church.
Increase *their* compassion for others;
send *them* into the world in witness to your love;
and bring *them* to the fullness of your peace and glory;
through Jesus Christ our Lord.   [415]

Amen.

2

For parents whose children have just been baptized

Gracious God, giver of all life,
we pray for *parents* N. and N.
Give *them* wisdom and patience
to guide *their child* in the way of Jesus Christ
and the faith of the church.

Let your peace and joy dwell in *their* home,
that *their* family life may be instructed by faith,
sustained by prayer and governed by love.
Strengthen *them* in *their* own baptism,
that *they* may rejoice as *children* of God,
and serve you faithfully,
in the name of Jesus Christ.   [416]

Amen.

3

For newly baptized infants and children

Ever-living God,
in your mercy you promised to be not only our God,
but also the God of our children.
We thank you for receiving N. and N. by baptism.

Keep *them* always in your love.
Guide *them* as *they grow* in faith.
Protect *them* in all the dangers and temptations of life.
Bring *them* to confess Jesus Christ as *their* Lord and Savior
and be his faithful *disciples* to *their* life's end;
in the name of Jesus Christ.   [417]

Amen.

4

For families

Loving God,
you nurture and guide us like a father and mother.
We pray for the families of this congregation,
and for all Christian families everywhere.
Give them strength to honor you in their homes,
and to love and serve each other.
Help all who have been baptized in your name
to live in peace and unity
as sisters and brothers in the household of faith,
and to serve others in the name of Jesus Christ.   [418]

Amen.

An Outline of the Service for the Lord's Day Including an Alternative Service for the Sacrament of Baptism

GATHERING
Call to Worship
Prayer of the Day or Opening Prayer
Hymn of Praise, Psalm, or Spiritual
Confession and Pardon
Canticle, Psalm, Hymn, or Spiritual

THE WORD
Prayer for Illumination
First Reading
Psalm
Second Reading
Anthem, Hymn, Psalm, Canticle, or Spiritual
Gospel Reading
Sermon
Hymn, Canticle, Psalm, or Spiritual
Baptism
    Introduction
    Presentation of the Candidates
    Thanksgiving Over the Water
    Profession of Faith
    The Baptism
    Laying On of Hands
    [Baptismal Garment]
    [Giving of the Light]
    Welcome
    The Peace
Hymn, Psalm, or Spiritual
Prayers of the People

If the Eucharist is not celebrated:

THE EUCHARIST
Offering
Invitation to the Lord's Table
Great Thanksgiving
Lord's Prayer
Breaking of the Bread
Communion of the People

Offering

Prayer of Thanksgiving
Lord's Prayer

SENDING
Hymn, Spiritual, Canticle, or Psalm
Charge and Blessing

AN ALTERNATIVE SERVICE FOR THE SACRAMENT OF BAPTISM

The following liturgy for the Sacrament of Baptism was prepared by the Consultation on Common Texts, an ecumenical forum for liturgical renewal among many of the major Christian denominations of North America. Its development was prompted by the growing consensus in ecumenical discussions concerning the theology and practice of Baptism. Only the rubrics have been changed to be in keeping with the style of this book.

Baptism is ordinarily celebrated as part of the worship of the congregation on the Lord's Day. It appropriately follows the reading and proclaiming of the Word.

If the liturgical practice of the congregation includes use of a paschal candle, it is lighted before the service begins.

After the sermon an appropriate hymn, canticle, psalm, or spiritual may be sung while the candidates, sponsors, and parents assemble at the baptismal font or pool. Care should be taken to ensure that the baptism be fully visible to the congregation. An elder or a representative of the congregation may lead a procession to the place of baptism, carrying a large pitcher of water.

INTRODUCTION

The minister may briefly introduce the liturgy of Baptism in these or similar words.

Brothers and sisters in Christ,
through the sacrament of Baptism
we share in the death and resurrection of Christ,
and are incorporated into Christ's holy church.
Baptism proclaims the faith of the church.
By the sign of water
God cleanses from sin, renews life,
and prefigures the reconciliation of all things promised in Christ.
In Baptism we are given the Holy Spirit
as a pledge of this reconciliation.
The same Spirit binds us to each other
and joins us to Christ's ministry of love, peace, and justice.

PRESENTATION OF THE CANDIDATES

The minster may say in these or similar words:

The candidates for Holy Baptism will now be presented.

One of the following is used, as appropriate:

A

Adults and older children

A sponsor for each candidate, in turn, presents the candidate in these or similar words:

I present N. to receive the sacrament of Baptism.

The minister addresses each candidate, using these or similar words:

Putting your whole trust
in the grace and love of Jesus Christ,
do you desire to be baptized?

The candidate responds:

I do.

The minister addresses the sponsors for each candidate:

Will you continue to walk with N.
in this new life in Christ?

The sponsors respond:

I will, with God's help.

B

Parent(s) and sponsors of infants and younger children

Candidates unable to answer for themselves are presented individually by a parent:

I present N. to receive the sacrament of Baptism.

The minister addresses the parent(s), using these or similar words:

Putting your whole trust
in the grace and love of Jesus Christ,
do you desire to have your *children* baptized?

Parents:

I do.

Minister:

Will you be responsible for nurturing the child you present
in the faith and life of the Christian community?

Parents:

I will, with God's help.

The minister addresses the sponsors:

Will you, by your prayers and witness,
help *these children* grow into the full stature of Christ?

Sponsors:

I will, with God's help.

Congregation

The minister addresses the congregation:

People of God,
will you promise to uphold and support N. and N. [*or*, these persons]
in *their* life in Christ?

All respond:

We will, with God's help.

THANKSGIVING OVER THE WATER

Water is poured visibly and audibly into the font.

The people may stand.

One of the following thanksgivings is offered by the minister:

1

The Lord be with you.

And also with you.

Let us give thanks to the Lord our God.

It is right to give our thanks and praise.

Blessed are you, gracious God,
creator of the universe, ruler of heaven and earth.
You are the source of light and life for all creation.
In your goodness you give us the sign of water.

Glory to you forever and ever.

Or

Blessed be God forever and ever.

At the beginning your Spirit was at work,
brooding over the waters of creation's birth,
bringing forth life in all its fullness.
Through the gift of water
you nourish and sustain all living things.

Glory to you forever and ever.

Or

Blessed be God forever and ever.

In the time of Noah, you destroyed the wicked
and cleansed the earth through the waters of the flood.
By the pillar of cloud and fire
you led Israel through the waters of the Red Sea
out of slavery to freedom in the promised land.

Glory to you forever and ever.

Or

Blessed be God forever and ever.

In the waters of the river Jordan
Jesus was baptized by John and
anointed by the Holy Spirit.
He is the never-failing spring
who has promised that all who thirst can come to the living water.
Glory to you forever and ever.

> Or

Blessed be God forever and ever.

By the baptism of his own death and resurrection
he set us free from bondage to sin and death
and opened to us the joy and freedom of everlasting life.
As he suffered for us,
the piercing of his side brought forth water and blood.
Glory to you forever and ever.

> Or

Blessed be God forever and ever.

That we might live no longer for ourselves,
but for him who died and rose for us,
Christ sent the Holy Spirit,
his own first gift for those who believe.
He sends us out to proclaim the gospel to all nations,
baptizing in the name of the
Father and of the Son and of the Holy Spirit.
Glory to you forever and ever.

> Or

Blessed be God forever and ever.

Therefore, saving God,
we bless you for the water with which you bless us.
We pray that N. and N. [*or*, these persons],
who come to the waters of life,
will live in your grace,
sharing in the death and resurrection of Jesus.
Send your Holy Spirit upon us
and upon this water,

> The minister may touch the water.

that all who are gathered under this sign
may be one in Christ.

Glory to you forever and ever.

Or

Blessed be God forever and ever.

We give you praise and honor and worship
through your Son, Jesus Christ our Lord,
in the unity of the Holy Spirit,
now and forever.

Glory to you forever and ever.   Amen.

Or

Blessed be God forever and ever.   Amen.   [419]

2

The Lord be with you.

And also with you.

Let us give thanks to the Lord our God.

It is right to give our thanks and praise.

We thank you, almighty God, for the gift of water.
Over water the Holy Spirit moved
in the beginning of creation.
With water you destroyed evil in the days of Noah.
Through water you led the children of Israel
out of their bondage in Egypt into the land of promise.

In water your Son Jesus received the baptism of John
and was anointed by the Holy Spirit as the Christ,
that he might lead us
through his death and resurrection,
from the bondage of sin into everlasting life.

We thank you, loving God, for the water of Baptism.
In it we are buried with Christ in his death.
By it we share in the resurrection.
Through it we are reborn by the Holy Spirit.

Therefore in joyful obedience to your Son,
we receive into the community of faith
those whom you have called and justified.

Pour out your Holy Spirit,
that as N. and N. [*or,* these persons]
are made a new creation through these baptismal waters,
they may preach good news to the poor,
proclaim release to the captives
and set at liberty those who are oppressed.
To Christ, to you, and to the Holy Spirit,
be all honor and glory,
now and forever.   [420]

Amen.

PROFESSION OF FAITH

> The minister addresses the candidates making a profession of faith, the
> parent(s), and the sponsors in these or similar words:

I ask you to reject sin,
profess your faith in Christ Jesus,
and confess the faith of the church.

RENUNCIATIONS

> The congregation may also be invited to respond as part of the reaffirma-
> tion of the baptismal covenant.

> The minister, using one of the following, says:

1

Do you renounce Satan
and all the spiritual forces of wickedness
that rebel against God?

I renounce them.

Do you renounce the evil powers of this world,
which corrupt and destroy the creatures of God?

I renounce them.

Do you renounce all sinful desires
that draw you from the love of God?

I renounce them.

Do you renounce evil and its power in the world,
which defy God's righteousness and love?

I renounce them.

Do you renounce the ways of sin
that separate you from the love of God?

I renounce them.

PROFESSION

The minister says:

Let us join with those who are to be baptized
in professing the faith of the church,
and renew our own baptismal covenant.

All present profess their faith in the words of the Apostles' Creed.

Do you believe in God, the Father almighty?

**I believe in God, the Father almighty,
creator of heaven and earth.**

Do you believe in Jesus Christ?

**I believe in Jesus Christ, God's only Son, our Lord,
who was conceived by the Holy Spirit,
born of the Virgin Mary,
suffered under Pontius Pilate,
was crucified, died, and was buried;
he descended to the dead.
On the third day he rose again;
he ascended into heaven,
he is seated at the right hand of the Father,
and he will come to judge the living and the dead.**

Do you believe in the Holy Spirit?

**I believe in the Holy Spirit,
the holy catholic church,
the communion of saints,
the forgiveness of sins,
the resurrection of the body,
and the life everlasting.   Amen.**

THE BAPTISM

Each candidate may be presented by name to the minister.

The minister immerses the candidate, or pours water three times upon the candidate, saying:

**N., I baptize you
in the name of the Father,
and of the Son,
and of the Holy Spirit.**

After each baptism the congregation may respond, saying or singing:

Amen.

Or the congregation may sing a hymn, psalm, or spiritual, or a verse such as:

**This is the fountain of life,
water made holy by the suffering of Christ,
washing all the world.**

Or

**You who are washed in this water
have hope of Christ's kingdom.**

After all have been baptized, the people may be seated.

Other actions rooted deeply in the history of Baptism may be included, such as those which follow: anointing with oil, putting on a baptismal garment, and the giving of the light. However, care shall be taken that the central act of baptizing with water is not overshadowed.

LAYING ON OF HANDS

The minister holds hands outstretched over the newly baptized, or places one or both hands on the head of each one, and says:

**All-powerful God, the Father of our Lord Jesus Christ,
we give you thanks for freeing your sons and daughters
from the power of sin
and for raising them up to a new life of grace.**

**Sustain them with your Holy Spirit:
the spirit of wisdom and understanding,
the spirit of counsel and might,
the spirit of knowledge and the fear of the Lord,
the spirit of joy in your presence.** [421]

Amen.

The minister may mark the sign of the cross on the forehead of each of the newly baptized. Oil prepared for this purpose may be used.

As the sign of the cross is being made, the minister says:

N., child of God,
I sign you with the cross:
you are marked as Christ's forever.

BAPTISMAL GARMENT

The newly baptized may be given a white garment.

As it is put on, the minister or a sponsor may say:

In Baptism you have put on Christ;
you have become a new creation.

GIVING OF THE LIGHT

Baptismal candles may be lighted from the paschal candle. These candles may be given to each of the baptized by a minister, a sponsor, or a representative of the congregation, saying:

Receive the light of Christ;
you have passed from darkness to light.

The congregation says:

You have been enlightened by Christ.
Walk always as children of the light.

WELCOME

The minister says:

With joy and thanksgiving we welcome you
into Christ's one holy catholic and apostolic church.

**We are the people of God,
members of the household of faith,
a royal priesthood.
Proclaim with us the good news of Christ
for all the world.
We are one in Christ Jesus:
share with us at the table of God's kingdom.**

THE PEACE

The minister then says to all those assembled at the font:

The peace of the Lord be always with you.

They respond:

And also with you.

The people may exchange signs of God's peace, greeting those who have been baptized.

All return to their places. An appropriate hymn, psalm, or spiritual may be sung.

The service continues with the prayers of the people, which will include petitions for the newly baptized and for those who will nurture them (pp. 416–417).

When the Lord's Supper is celebrated, it is appropriate for the newly baptized to receive Communion first.

An Outline of the Service for the Lord's Day Including Baptism and Reaffirmation of the Baptismal Covenant

Gathering

Call to Worship
Prayer of the Day or Opening Prayer
Hymn of Praise, Psalm, or Spiritual
Confession and Pardon
Canticle, Psalm, Hymn, or Spiritual

The Word

Prayer for Illumination
First Reading
Psalm
Second Reading
Anthem, Hymn, Psalm, Canticle, or Spiritual
Gospel Reading
Sermon
Hymn, Canticle, Psalm, or Spiritual
Baptism and Reaffirmation of the Baptismal Covenant
   Presentation
   Profession of Faith
   Thanksgiving Over the Water
   The Baptism
   Laying On of Hands
   Prayer for Those Reaffirming the Baptismal Covenant
   Laying On of Hands
   Welcome
   The Peace
Hymn, Psalm, or Spiritual
Prayers of the People

If the Eucharist is not celebrated:

The Eucharist

Offering	Offering
Invitation to the Lord's Table	
Great Thanksgiving	Prayer of Thanksgiving
Lord's Prayer	Lord's Prayer
Breaking of the Bread	
Communion of the People	

Sending

Hymn, Spiritual, Canticle, or Psalm
Charge and Blessing

BAPTISM AND REAFFIRMATION OF THE BAPTISMAL COVENANT

A Combined Order

The following order is provided for occasions when, for pastoral reasons, it is necessary to include with Baptism the public profession of faith of previously baptized persons, and/or the reaffirmation of faith of baptized persons.

In including such rites along with Baptism, care should be taken to ensure that Baptism is clearly recognized as the means by which persons are received into the church. While a public profession of faith for the first time, by those previously baptized, and a reaffirmation of faith are important occasions in the Christian life, neither should encroach upon the centrality of Baptism.

> This rite is ordinarily celebrated as part of the worship of the congregation on the Lord's Day. It is appropriately celebrated following the reading and proclamation of the Word.
>
> After the sermon, an appropriate hymn, canticle, psalm, or spiritual may be sung while the candidates for baptism, their sponsors and/or parents, baptized persons making a public profession of faith for the first time, and those reaffirming their faith assemble near the baptismal font or pool. Care should be taken to ensure that the baptism is fully visible to the congregation. An elder or other representative of the congregation may lead a procession to the place of baptism, carrying a large pitcher of water.

PRESENTATION

> The minister addresses those assembled at the font, and the congregation:

Matt. 28:18–20

Hear the words of our Lord Jesus Christ:
All authority in heaven and on earth
has been given to me.

Go therefore and make disciples of all nations,
baptizing them in the name of the Father,
and of the Son, and of the Holy Spirit,
and teaching them to obey everything that I have commanded you.
And remember, I am with you always, to the end of the age.

Hear also these words from Holy Scripture:

The minister then continues, using one or more of the following:

1   *Eph. 4:4–6*

There is one body and one Spirit,
just as you were called to the one hope of your calling,
one Lord, one faith, one baptism,
one God and Father of all,
who is above all and through all and in all.

2   *Gal. 3:27, 28*

As many of you as were baptized into Christ
have clothed yourselves with Christ.
There is no longer Jew or Greek,
there is no longer slave or free,
there is no longer male or female;
for all of you are one in Christ Jesus.

3   *1 Peter 2:9*

You are a chosen race, a royal priesthood,
a holy nation, God's own people,
in order that you may proclaim the mighty acts
of the One who called you out of darkness
into God's marvelous light.

4   *Rom. 6:3, 4*

Do you not know
that all of us who have been baptized into Christ Jesus
were baptized into his death?
Therefore we have been buried with him by baptism into death,
so that, just as Christ was raised from the dead by the glory of the Father,
so we too might walk in newness of life.

The minister continues:

Obeying the word of our Lord Jesus, and confident of his promises,
we baptize those whom God has called.

In baptism God claims us,
and seals us to show that we belong to God.
God frees us from sin and death,
uniting us with Jesus Christ in his death and resurrection.
By water and the Holy Spirit,
we are made members of the church, the body of Christ,
and joined to Christ's ministry of love, peace, and justice.

Let us remember with joy our own baptism,
as we celebrate this sacrament.

An elder presents each candidate, using the appropriate forms:

A

FOR BAPTISM

The elder presents the candidates for baptism:

Adults and older children

Elder:

On behalf of the session,
I present N. and N. to receive the sacrament of Baptism.

Infants and younger children

Elder:

On behalf of the session, I present N., (son, daughter) of N. and N.,
to receive the sacrament of Baptism.

The minister addresses, in turn, candidates for baptism, parents bringing
children for baptism, sponsors, and the congregation:

Adults and older children

The minister addresses the candidates for baptism:

N. and N., do you desire to be baptized?

The candidates respond:

I do.

Parent(s) of infants and younger children

The minister addresses the parents presenting children for baptism:

Do you desire that N. and N. be baptized?

The parent(s) respond:

I do.

Minister:

Relying on God's grace,
do you promise to live the Christian faith,
and to teach that faith to your child?

The parent(s) respond:

I do.

Sponsors (if any are present)

The minister addresses the sponsors, if any are present:

Do you promise, through prayer and example,
to support and encourage N.
to be a faithful Christian?

The sponsors respond:

I do.

Congregation

The minister addresses the congregation:

Do you, as members of the church of Jesus Christ,
promise to guide and nurture N. and N.,
by word and deed, with love and prayer,
encouraging *them* to know and follow Christ
and to be faithful *members* of his church?

The people respond:

We do.

B

FOR PUBLIC PROFESSION OF FAITH OF PREVIOUSLY BAPTIZED PERSONS

An elder presents the candidate(s):

N. and N. *are* presented by the session,
to make *their* public profession of faith,
reaffirming the baptismal covenant into which *they were* baptized.

The minister addresses the candidates:

We rejoice that you now desire to declare your faith,
and to share with us in our common ministry.

C

An elder presents the candidate(s):

I present N. and N., who desire to reaffirm the faith
into which *they were* baptized.

The minister addresses the candidates:

We rejoice with you as you claim again
the promises of God which are yours through your baptism.

PROFESSION OF FAITH

The minister addresses those assembled:

Through baptism we enter the covenant God has established.
In that covenant God gives us new life;
we are guarded from evil
and nurtured by the love of God and God's people.

In embracing that covenant, we choose whom we will serve,
by turning from evil
and turning to Jesus Christ.

The minister then asks the following questions of the candidates for baptism
and/or the parents or guardians of children being presented for baptism,
those making a public profession of faith, and those reaffirming their faith.

I ask you, therefore, to reject sin,
to profess your faith in Christ Jesus,
and to confess the faith of the church,
the faith in which we baptize.

RENUNCIATIONS

One of the following is used:

1

Trusting in the gracious mercy of God,
do you turn from the ways of sin
and renounce evil and its power in the world?
I do.

Do you turn to Jesus Christ
and accept him as your Lord and Savior,
trusting in his grace and love?

I do.

Will you be Christ's faithful disciple,
obeying his Word and showing his love?

I will, with God's help.

2

Do you renounce all evil,
and powers in the world
which defy God's righteousness and love?

I renounce them.

Do you renounce the ways of sin
that separate you from the love of God?

I renounce them.

Do you turn to Jesus Christ
and accept him as your Lord and Savior?

I do.

Will you be Christ's faithful disciple,
obeying his Word and showing his love,
to your life's end?

I will, with God's help.

3

Trusting in the gracious mercy of God,
do you turn from the ways of sin
and renounce evil and its power in the world?

I do.

Who is your Lord and Savior?

Jesus Christ is my Lord and Savior.

Will you be Christ's faithful disciple,
obeying his Word and showing his love?

I will, with God's help.

PROFESSION

The minister continues:

With the whole church,
let us confess our faith.

The people may then stand.

All present profess their faith in the words of the Apostles' Creed, using
the question and answer form (A) or reciting it directly (B).

A

Do you believe in God, the Father almighty?

**I believe in God, the Father almighty,
creator of heaven and earth.**

Do you believe in Jesus Christ?

**I believe in Jesus Christ, God's only Son, our Lord,
who was conceived by the Holy Spirit,
born of the Virgin Mary,
suffered under Pontius Pilate,
was crucified, died, and was buried;
he descended to the dead.
On the third day he rose again;
he ascended into heaven,
he is seated at the right hand of the Father,
and he will come to judge the living and the dead.**

Do you believe in the Holy Spirit?

**I believe in the Holy Spirit,
the holy catholic church,
the communion of saints,
the forgiveness of sins,
the resurrection of the body,
and the life everlasting.   Amen.**

B

**I believe in God, the Father almighty,
creator of heaven and earth.**

**I believe in Jesus Christ, God's only Son, our Lord,
who was conceived by the Holy Spirit,
born of the Virgin Mary,
suffered under Pontius Pilate,
was crucified, died, and was buried;
he descended to the dead.**

On the third day he rose again;
he ascended into heaven,
he is seated at the right hand of the Father,
and he will come to judge the living and the dead.

I believe in the Holy Spirit,
the holy catholic church,
the communion of saints,
the forgiveness of sins,
the resurrection of the body,
and the life everlasting.   Amen.

> The minister asks one of the following questions of those being baptized
> on profession of their faith:

1

Will you be a faithful member of this congregation,
share in its worship and ministry
through your prayers and gifts,
your study and service,
and so fulfill your calling to be a disciple of Jesus Christ?

I will, with God's help.

2   *See Acts 2:42*

Will you devote yourself to the church's teaching and fellowship,
to the breaking of bread and the prayers?

I will, with God's help.

> Those to be baptized, and those bringing infants or young children for
> baptism (and their sponsors) approach the font.

THANKSGIVING OVER THE WATER

> Water is poured visibly and audibly into the font.

> One of the following prayers is then said by the minister.

1

The Lord be with you.

And also with you.

Let us give thanks to the Lord our God.

It is right to give our thanks and praise.

We give you thanks, Eternal God,
for you nourish and sustain all living things
by the gift of water.

In the beginning of time,
your Spirit moved over the watery chaos,
calling forth order and life.

In the time of Noah,
you destroyed evil by the waters of the flood,
giving righteousness a new beginning.

You led Israel out of slavery,
through the waters of the sea,
into the freedom of the promised land.

In the waters of Jordan
Jesus was baptized by John
and anointed with your Spirit.
By the baptism of his own death and resurrection,
Christ set us free from sin and death,
and opened the way to eternal life.

We thank you, O God, for the water of Baptism.
In it we are buried with Christ in his death.
From it we are raised to share in his resurrection.
Through it we are reborn by the power of the Holy Spirit.

The minister may touch the water.

Send your Spirit to move over this water
that it may be a fountain of deliverance and rebirth.
Wash away the sin of *all* who *are* cleansed by it.
Raise *them* to new life,
and graft *them* to the body of Christ.
Pour out your Holy Spirit upon *them*,
that *they* may have power to do your will,
and continue forever in the risen life of Christ.
To you, Father, Son, and Holy Spirit, one God,
be all praise, honor, and glory,
now and forever.   [411]

Amen.

2

The Lord be with you.

And also with you.

Let us give thanks to the Lord our God.

It is right to give our thanks and praise.

Eternal and gracious God, we give you thanks.
In countless ways you have revealed yourself in ages past,
and have blessed us with signs of your grace.

We praise you that through the waters of the sea,
you led your people Israel out of bondage,
into freedom in the land of your promise.

We praise you for sending Jesus your Son,
who for us was baptized in the waters of the Jordan,
and was anointed as the Christ by your Holy Spirit.
Through the baptism of his death and resurrection,
you set us free from the bondage of sin and death,
and give us cleansing and rebirth.

We praise you that in baptism
you give us your Holy Spirit,
who teaches us and leads us into all truth,
filling us with a variety of gifts
that we might proclaim the gospel to all nations
and serve you as a royal priesthood.

> The minister may touch the water.

Pour out your Spirit upon us
and upon this water,
that this font may be your womb of new birth.
May *all* who now *pass* through these waters
be delivered from death to life,
from bondage to freedom,
from sin to righteousness.
Bind *them* to the household of faith,
guard *them* from all evil.
Strengthen *them* to serve you with joy
until the day you make all things new.
To you be all praise, honor, and glory;
through Jesus Christ our Savior,
who with you and the Holy Spirit,
lives and reigns forever.   [412]

Amen.

The minister may give thanks over the water in his or her own words:

a. praising God for God's faithfulness in the covenant;

b. thankfully remembering God's reconciling acts such as:
   the cleansing and rebirth in the flood in the time of Noah;
   the exodus through the waters of the sea;
   Jesus' baptism in the Jordan;
   the baptism of Jesus' death and his resurrection.

c. invoking the Holy Spirit
   to attend and empower the baptism;
   to make the water a water of redemption and rebirth;
   to equip the church for faithfulness.

The prayer concludes with an ascription of praise to the triune God.

THE BAPTISM

The candidates, other than infants, who are to be baptized by pouring or sprinkling may kneel, or if there are candidates to be immersed, they walk down into the water.

Calling each candidate by his or her Christian (given) name or names only, the minister shall pour or sprinkle water visibly and generously on the candidate's head, or immerse the candidate in the water, while saying:

N., I baptize you
in the name of the Father,
and of the Son,
and of the Holy Spirit.

Amen.

LAYING ON OF HANDS

The minister lays hands on the head of each person baptized while saying one of the following:

1

O Lord, uphold N. by your Holy Spirit.
Give *him/her* the spirit of wisdom and understanding,
the spirit of counsel and might,
the spirit of knowledge and the fear of the Lord,
the spirit of joy in your presence,
both now and forever.   [413]

The person responds:

Amen.

2

Defend, O Lord, your servant N.
with your heavenly grace,
that *he/she* may continue yours forever,
and daily increase in your Holy Spirit more and more,
until *he/she* comes to your everlasting kingdom.   [414]

> The person responds:

Amen.

> The minister may mark the sign of the cross on the forehead of each of the
> newly baptized, while saying one of the following. Oil prepared for this
> purpose may be used.

1

N., child of the covenant,
you have been sealed by the Holy Spirit in baptism,
and marked as Christ's own forever.

Amen.

2

N., child of God,
you have been sealed by the Holy Spirit in baptism,
and grafted into Christ forever.

Amen.   •

PRAYER FOR THOSE REAFFIRMING THE BAPTISMAL COVENANT

> Those who have been previously baptized, and who are now making a pub-
> lic profession of faith for the first time or reaffirming their faith, will step
> forward.

> The minister asks them one of the following:

1

Today you have publicly professed your faith.
Will you be a faithful member of this congregation,
share in its worship and ministry
through your prayers and gifts,
your study and service,
and so fulfill your calling to be a disciple of Jesus Christ?

I will, with God's help.

Today you have publicly professed your faith.
Will you devote yourself to the church's teaching and fellowship,
to the breaking of bread and the prayers?

I will, with God's help.

The minister offers one of the following prayers, or a similar prayer:

1

Gracious God, by water and the Spirit
you claimed us as your own,
cleansing us from sin, and giving us new life.
You made us members of your body, the church,
calling us to be your servants in the world.
Renew in N. and N. the covenant you made in *their* baptism.
Continue the good work you have begun in *them*.
Send *them* forth by the power of your Spirit
to love and serve you with joy,
and to strive for justice and peace in all the earth,
in the name of Jesus Christ our Lord.   [422]

Amen.

2

Faithful God,
in baptism you claimed us;
and by your Spirit you are at work in our lives
empowering us to live a life worthy of our calling.
We thank you for leading N. and N.
to this time and place
of reaffirming the covenant you made with *them* in *their* baptism.
Establish *them* in your truth,
and guide *them* by your Spirit,
that, together with all your people,
they may grow in faith, hope, and love,
and be faithful *disciples* of Jesus Christ,
to whom, with you and the Holy Spirit
be honor and glory, now and forever.   [423]

Amen.

Laying On of Hands

The candidates kneel.

The minister lays both hands on the head of each of the candidates in turn, while offering one of the following prayers. The sign of the cross may be marked on the forehead of candidate, using oil prepared for this purpose.

1

O Lord, uphold N. by your Holy Spirit.
Daily increase in *him/her* your gifts of grace:
the spirit of wisdom and understanding,
the spirit of counsel and might,
the spirit of knowledge and the fear of the Lord,
the spirit of joy in your presence,
both now and forever.   [413]

The candidate answers:

Amen.

2

Defend, O Lord, your servant N.
with your heavenly grace,
that *he/she* may continue yours forever,
and daily increase in your Holy Spirit more and more,
until *he/she* comes to your everlasting kingdom.   [414]

The candidate answers:

Amen.

After all of the candidates have received the laying on of hands, the candidates stand.

Welcome

A representative of the session, or the minister, addresses the congregation in these or similar words:

Through *their* baptism, N. and N. *have* been received into the one holy catholic and apostolic church. N. and N. *have* reaffirmed the covenant into which *they were* baptized.

As members of the household of God,
God has called them to serve Christ in the world.
Let us welcome them to this ministry.

Welcome is extended using (A) or (B):

A

The people respond, saying:

**With joy and thanksgiving we welcome you
to share with us in the ministry of Christ,
for we are all one in him.**

B

Those who have been baptized, or who have reaffirmed the baptismal covenant, are welcomed in a manner appropriate to the particular congregation.

THE PEACE

The minister then says to all those assembled at the font:

The peace of Christ be with you.

They respond:

And also with you.

The people may exchange signs of God's peace, greeting those who have been baptized and those who have reaffirmed the baptismal covenant.

All return to their places. An appropriate hymn, psalm, or spiritual may be sung.

The service continues with the prayers of the people, which will include petitions for the newly baptized and for those who will nurture them (pp. 416–417), and for those who have reaffirmed the baptismal covenant.

An Outline of the Service for the Lord's Day Including Reaffirmation of the Baptismal Covenant for Those Making a Public Profession of Faith

GATHERING

Call to Worship
Prayer of the Day or Opening Prayer
Hymn of Praise, Psalm, or Spiritual
Confession and Pardon
Canticle, Psalm, Hymn, or Spiritual

THE WORD

Prayer for Illumination
First Reading
Psalm
Second Reading
Anthem, Hymn, Psalm, Canticle, or Spiritual
Gospel Reading
Sermon
Hymn, Canticle, Psalm, or Spiritual
Public Profession of Faith
    Presentation
    Profession of Faith
    Laying On of Hands
    Welcome
    The Peace
Hymn, Psalm, or Spiritual
Prayers of the People

If the Eucharist is not celebrated:

THE EUCHARIST

Offering	Offering
Invitation to the Lord's Table	
Great Thanksgiving	Prayer of Thanksgiving
Lord's Prayer	Lord's Prayer
Breaking of the Bread	
Communion of the People	

SENDING

Hymn, Spiritual, Canticle, or Psalm
Charge and Blessing

REAFFIRMATION OF THE BAPTISMAL COVENANT FOR THOSE MAKING A PUBLIC PROFESSION OF FAITH

This service is for persons who were baptized as infants and nurtured in the church, and who now are making a public profession of faith.

PRESENTATION

This service takes place at the baptismal font or pool, which shall be filled with water.

After the sermon, an appropriate hymn, psalm, or spiritual or other suitable music may be sung. Baptized persons making a public profession of faith for the first time gather at the place for baptism.

An elder, representing the session, presents the candidates:

N. and N. *are* presented by the session,
for the reaffirming of the baptismal covenant
into which *they* were baptized.
They now *desire* to profess publicly *their* faith
and to assume greater responsibility
in the life of the church,
and God's mission in the world.

The minister says:

We rejoice that you now desire to declare your faith
and to share with us in our common ministry.
In baptism you were joined to Christ,
and made *members* of his church.
In the community of the people of God,
you have learned of God's purpose for you and for all creation.
You have been nurtured at the table of our Lord,
and called to witness to the gospel of Jesus Christ.

Hear these words from Holy Scripture:

The minister continues, using one or more of the following scripture texts:

1   *Eph. 2:19–22*

You are citizens with the saints
and also members of the household of God,
built upon the foundation of the apostles and prophets,
with Christ Jesus himself as the cornerstone.
In him the whole structure is joined together
and grows into a holy temple in the Lord;
in whom you also are built together spiritually
into a dwelling place for God.

2   *Eph. 2:10*

We are what God has made us,
created in Christ Jesus for good works,
which God prepared beforehand
to be our way of life.

3   *1 Peter 2:9*

You are a chosen race, a royal priesthood,
a holy nation, God's own people,
in order that you may proclaim the mighty acts
of the One who called you out of darkness
into God's marvelous light.

4   *Matt. 5:14–16*

You are the light of the world.
A city built on a hill cannot be hid.
No one after lighting a lamp puts it under the bushel basket,
but on the lampstand,
and it gives light to all in the house.
In the same way,
let your light so shine before others,
so that they may see your good works
and give glory to your Father in heaven.

PROFESSION OF FAITH

The minister, addressing those making a public profession of faith, then says:

Now, as you publicly declare your faith,
I ask you to reject sin,
to profess your faith in Christ Jesus,
and to confess the faith of the church,
the faith in which you were baptized.

RENUNCIATIONS

The minister continues, using one of the following:

1

Trusting in the gracious mercy of God,
do you turn from the ways of sin
and renounce evil and its power in the world?

I do.

Do you turn to Jesus Christ
and accept him as your Lord and Savior,
trusting in his grace and love?

I do.

Will you be Christ's faithful disciple,
obeying his Word and showing his love?

I will, with God's help.

2

Do you renounce all evil,
and powers in the world
which defy God's righteousness and love?

I renounce them.

Do you renounce the ways of sin
that separate you from the love of God?

I renounce them.

Do you turn to Jesus Christ
and accept him as your Lord and Savior?

I do.

Will you be Christ's faithful disciple,
obeying his Word and showing his love,
to your life's end?

I will, with God's help.

3

Trusting in the gracious mercy of God,
do you turn from the ways of sin
and renounce evil and its power in the world?

I do.

Who is your Lord and Savior?

Jesus Christ is my Lord and Savior.

Will you be Christ's faithful disciple,
obeying his Word and showing his love?

I will, with God's help.

PROFESSION

> The minister continues, saying:

With the whole church,
let us confess our faith.

> The congregation may stand and join the candidates in affirming the faith
> in the words of the Apostles' Creed, using the question and answer form
> (A) or reciting it directly (B).

A

Do you believe in God the Father?

**I believe in God, the Father almighty,
creator of heaven and earth.**

Do you believe in Jesus Christ, the Son of God?

**I believe in Jesus Christ, God's only Son, our Lord,
who was conceived by the Holy Spirit,
born of the Virgin Mary,
suffered under Pontius Pilate,
was crucified, died, and was buried;
he descended to the dead.
On the third day he rose again;
he ascended into heaven,
he is seated at the right hand of the Father,
and he will come to judge the living and the dead.**

Do you believe in God the Holy Spirit?

**I believe in the Holy Spirit,
the holy catholic church,
the communion of saints,
the forgiveness of sins,
the resurrection of the body,
and the life everlasting.   Amen.**

B

I believe in God, the Father almighty,
creator of heaven and earth.

I believe in Jesus Christ, God's only Son, our Lord,
who was conceived by the Holy Spirit,
born of the Virgin Mary,
suffered under Pontius Pilate,
was crucified, died, and was buried;
he descended to the dead.
On the third day he rose again;
he ascended into heaven,
he is seated at the right hand of the Father,
and he will come to judge the living and the dead.

I believe in the Holy Spirit,
the holy catholic church,
the communion of saints,
the forgiveness of sins,
the resurrection of the body,
and the life everlasting.   Amen.

> The minister asks one of the following questions of those making a profession of their faith:

1

You have publicly professed your faith.
Will you be a faithful member of this congregation,
share in its worship and ministry
through your prayers and gifts,
your study and service,
and so fulfill your calling to be a disciple of Jesus Christ?

I will, with God's help.

2   *See Acts 2:42*

You have publicly professed your faith.
Will you devote yourself to the church's teaching and fellowship,
to the breaking of bread and the prayers?

I will, with God's help.

The minister offers the following prayer, or a similar prayer may be said:

Let us pray.

Gracious God, by water and the Spirit
you claimed us as your own,
cleansing us from sin, and giving us new life.
You made us members of your body, the church,
calling us to be your servants in the world.
Renew in N. and N. the covenant you made in *their* baptism.
Continue the good work you have begun in *them*.
Send *them* forth in the power of your Spirit
to love and serve you with joy,
and to strive for justice and peace in all the earth,
in the name of Jesus Christ our Lord.   [422]

Amen.

LAYING ON OF HANDS

The candidates kneel.

The minister lays both hands on the head of each of the candidates in turn,
while offering one of the following prayers. The sign of the cross may be
marked on the forehead of the candidate. Oil prepared for this purpose
may be used.

1

O Lord, uphold N. by your Holy Spirit.
Daily increase in *him/her* your gifts of grace:
the spirit of wisdom and understanding,
the spirit of counsel and might,
the spirit of knowledge and the fear of the Lord,
the spirit of joy in your presence,
both now and forever.   [413]

The candidate answers:

Amen.

Or

2

Defend, O Lord, your servant N.
with your heavenly grace,
that *he/she* may continue yours forever,
and daily increase in your Holy Spirit more and more,
until *he/she* comes to your everlasting kingdom.   [414]

The candidate answers:

Amen.

After each candidate has received the laying on of hands, the minister prays:

Ever-living God,
guard *these* your *servants* with your protecting hand,
and let your Holy Spirit be with *them* forever.
Lead *them* to know and obey your Word,
that *they* may serve you in this life
and dwell with you forever in the life to come;
through Jesus Christ our Lord.   [424]

Amen.

WELCOME

A representative of the session, or the minister, addresses the congregation
in these or similar words:

N. and N., by publicly professing *their* faith,
have expressed *their* intention
to continue in the covenant God made with *them* in *their* baptism.
Let us welcome *them* as *they join* with us
in the worship and mission of the church.

The people respond, saying:

**With joy and thanksgiving we welcome you
to share with us in the ministry of Christ,
for we are all one in him.**

THE PEACE

The minister then says to all those assembled at the font:

The peace of God be with you.

They respond:

And also with you.

The people may exchange signs of God's peace, greeting those who have
publicly professed their faith.

AN OUTLINE OF THE SERVICE FOR THE LORD'S DAY INCLUDING REAFFIRMATION OF THE BAPTISMAL COVENANT FOR THOSE UNITING WITH A CONGREGATION

GATHERING

Call to Worship
Prayer of the Day or Opening Prayer
Hymn of Praise, Psalm, or Spiritual
Confession and Pardon
Canticle, Psalm, Hymn, or Spiritual

THE WORD

Prayer for Illumination
First Reading
Psalm
Second Reading
Anthem, Hymn, Psalm, Canticle, or Spiritual
Gospel Reading
Sermon
Hymn, Canticle, Psalm, or Spiritual
Reaffirmation of the Baptismal Covenant
   Presentation
   Profession of Faith
   [Laying On of Hands]
   Welcome
   The Peace
Hymn, Psalm, or Spiritual
Prayers of the People

If the Eucharist is not celebrated:

THE EUCHARIST

Offering	Offering
Invitation to the Lord's Table	
Great Thanksgiving	Prayer of Thanksgiving
Lord's Prayer	Lord's Prayer
Breaking of the Bread	
Communion of the People	

SENDING

Hymn, Spiritual, Canticle, or Psalm
Charge and Blessing

REAFFIRMATION OF THE BAPTISMAL COVENANT FOR THOSE UNITING WITH A CONGREGATION

Baptized persons who are transferring membership from another Christian church are received by letter of transfer.

Baptized persons who are coming from active membership in a church that does not issue certificates of transfer are received on reaffirmation of faith.

Baptized persons who have ceased to participate in the life of the church, but who now desire to participate actively in it, are restored to membership through reaffirmation of faith.

> This service takes place at the baptismal font or pool, which shall be filled with water.
>
> After the sermon, a hymn, canticle, psalm, spiritual, or other suitable music may be sung. Those who wish to reaffirm the covenant into which they were baptized, and to be received into church membership gather at the place of baptism.

PRESENTATION

> An elder, representing the session, presents those who have been received by transfer from other Christian churches, or by reaffirmation of faith, using the appropriate forms:

A

For those received by letter of transfer

> Elder:

On behalf of the session, I present N. and N.,
who *have* been received into the membership of this congregation
by transfer from N. congregation.

B

For those received by reaffirmation of faith

Elder:

On behalf of the session I present N. and N.,
who *have* been received into the membership of this congregation
by reaffirmation of faith.

Minister:

You come to us as *members* of the one holy catholic church,
into which you were baptized,
and by which you have been nurtured.
We are one with each other,
sisters and brothers in the family of God.
We rejoice in the gifts you bring to us.

As you join with us in the worship and service of this congregation,
it is fitting that together
we reaffirm the covenant into which we were baptized,
claiming again the promises of God
which are ours in our baptism.

The people may stand.

Hear these words from Holy Scripture:

The minister then continues, using one of the following:

1   *Eph. 4:4–6*

There is one body and one Spirit,
just as you were called
to the one hope of your calling,
one Lord, one faith, one baptism,
one God and Father of all,
who is above all and through all and in all.

2   *Gal. 3:27, 28*

As many of you as were baptized into Christ
have clothed yourselves with Christ.
There is no longer Jew or Greek,
there is no longer slave or free,
there is no longer male or female;
for all of you are in Christ Jesus.

You are a chosen race, a royal priesthood,
a holy nation, God's own people,
in order that you may proclaim the mighty acts
of the One who called you out of darkness
into God's marvelous light.

PROFESSION OF FAITH

> The minister, addressing those assembled at the font and the congregation,
> then says:

Sisters and brothers in Christ,
our baptism is the sign and seal of our cleansing from sin,
and of our being grafted into Christ.
Through the birth, life, death, and resurrection of Christ,
the power of sin was broken
and God's kingdom entered our world.
Through our baptism we were made citizens of God's kingdom,
and freed from the bondage of sin.
Let us celebrate that freedom and redemption
through the renewal of the promises made at our baptism.

I ask you therefore, once again to reject sin,
and to profess your faith in Christ Jesus,
and to confess the faith of the church,
in which we were baptized.

RENUNCIATIONS

> The minister continues, using one of the following:

1

Trusting in the gracious mercy of God,
do you turn from the ways of sin
and renounce evil and its power in the world?

I do.

Do you turn to Jesus Christ
and accept him as your Lord and Savior,
trusting in his grace and love?

I do.

Will you be Christ's faithful disciple,
obeying his Word and showing his love?

I will, with God's help.

Do you renounce all evil,
and powers in the world
which defy God's righteousness and love?

I renounce them.

Do you renounce the ways of sin
that separate you from the love of God?

I renounce them.

Do you turn to Jesus Christ
and accept him as your Lord and Savior?

I do.

Will you be Christ's faithful disciple,
obeying his Word and showing his love,
to your life's end?

I will, with God's help.

Trusting in the gracious mercy of God,
do you turn from the ways of sin
and renounce evil and its power in the world?

I do.

Who is your Lord and Savior?

Jesus Christ is my Lord and Savior.

Will you be Christ's faithful disciple,
obeying his Word and showing his love?

I will, with God's help.

PROFESSION

The minister continues:

With the whole church,
let us confess our faith.

All affirm the faith in the words of the Apostles' Creed, using the question
and answer form (A) or reciting it directly (B).

A

Do you believe in God the Father?

**I believe in God, the Father almighty,
creator of heaven and earth.**

Do you believe in Jesus Christ, the Son of God?

**I believe in Jesus Christ, God's only Son, our Lord,
who was conceived by the Holy Spirit,
born of the Virgin Mary,
suffered under Pontius Pilate,
was crucified, died, and was buried;
he descended to the dead.
On the third day he rose again;
he ascended into heaven,
he is seated at the right hand of the Father,
and he will come to judge the living and the dead.**

Do you believe in God the Holy Spirit?

**I believe in the Holy Spirit,
the holy catholic church,
the communion of saints,
the forgiveness of sins,
the resurrection of the body,
and the life everlasting.   Amen.**

B

**I believe in God, the Father almighty,
creator of heaven and earth.**

**I believe in Jesus Christ, God's only Son, our Lord,
who was conceived by the Holy Spirit,
born of the Virgin Mary,
suffered under Pontius Pilate,
was crucified, died, and was buried;
he descended to the dead.
On the third day he rose again;
he ascended into heaven,
he is seated at the right hand of the Father,
and he will come to judge the living and the dead.**

**I believe in the Holy Spirit,
the holy catholic church,
the communion of saints,
the forgiveness of sins,
the resurrection of the body,
and the life everlasting.   Amen.**

The minister addresses those assembled at the font, using one of the following:

1

You have publicly professed your faith.
Will you be a faithful member of this congregation,
share in its worship and ministry
through your prayers and gifts,
your study and service,
and so fulfill your calling to be a disciple of Jesus Christ?

I will, with God's help.

2   *See Acts 2:42*

You have publicly professed your faith.
Will you devote yourself to the church's teaching and fellowship,
to the breaking of bread and the prayers?

I will, with God's help.

The minister or the elder offers one of the following, or a similar prayer:

Let us pray.

1

Holy God,
we praise you for calling us to be a servant people,
and for gathering us into the body of Christ.
We thank you for choosing to add to our number
brothers and sisters in faith.
Together, may we live in your Spirit,
and so love one another,
that we may have the mind of Jesus Christ our Lord,
to whom we give honor and glory forever.   [425]

Amen.

2

For those who have not participated in the life of the church for an extended period.

Faithful God,
you work in us and for us
even when we do not know it.
When our path has led us away from you,
you guide us back to yourself.

We thank you for calling your *servants* N. and N.
to the fellowship of your people.
Renew in *them* the covenant you made in *their* baptism.
By the power of your Spirit,
strengthen *them* in faith and love,
that *they* may serve you with joy,
to the glory of Jesus Christ our Lord.   [426]

Amen.

LAYING ON OF HANDS

The laying on of hands may be included; it is especially appropriate
for those who have not participated in the life of the church for an
extended period of time.

The candidates kneel.

The minister lays both hands on the head of each of the candidates in
turn, while offering one of the following prayers. The sign of the
cross may be marked on the forehead of each candidate. Oil prepared
for this purpose may be used.

1

O Lord, uphold N. by your Holy Spirit.
Daily increase in *him/her* your gifts of grace:
the spirit of wisdom and understanding,
the spirit of counsel and might,
the spirit of knowledge and the fear of the Lord,
the spirit of joy in your presence,
both now and forever.   [413]

The candidate answers:

Amen.

2

Defend, O Lord, your servant N.,
with your heavenly grace,
that *he/she* may continue yours forever,
and daily increase in your Holy Spirit more and more,
until *he/she* comes to your everlasting kingdom.   [414]

The candidate answers:

Amen.

After each candidate has received the laying on of hands, the minister prays:

Ever-living God,
guard *these* your *servants* with your protecting hand,
and let your Holy Spirit be with *them* forever.
Lead *them* to know and obey your Word
that *they* may serve you in this life
and dwell with you forever in the life to come;
through Jesus Christ our Lord.   [424]

Amen.

WELCOME

The minister and an elder representing the session welcome the members in an appropriate manner, using these or similar words:

Welcome to this congregation and its worship and ministry.

THE PEACE

The minister then says to those assembled at the font:

The peace of Christ be with you.

They respond:

And also with you.

It is appropriate for the congregation to share signs of peace as the new members return to their places.

An Outline of the Service for the Lord's Day Including Reaffirmation of the Baptismal Covenant for a Congregation

GATHERING

Call to Worship
Prayer of the Day or Opening Prayer
Hymn of Praise, Psalm, or Spiritual
Confession and Pardon
Canticle, Psalm, Hymn, or Spiritual

THE WORD

Prayer for Illumination
First Reading
Psalm
Second Reading
Anthem, Hymn, Psalm, Canticle, or Spiritual
Gospel Reading
Sermon
Hymn, Canticle, Psalm, or Spiritual
Reaffirmation of the Baptismal Covenant
    Scripture Sentences
    Profession of Faith
    Thanksgiving for Baptism
    [Laying On of Hands]
    The Peace
Hymn, Psalm, or Spiritual
Prayers of the People

If the Eucharist is not celebrated:

THE EUCHARIST

Offering   Offering

Invitation to the Lord's Table

Great Thanksgiving   Prayer of Thanksgiving

Lord's Prayer   Lord's Prayer

Breaking of the Bread

Communion of the People

SENDING

Hymn, Spiritual, Canticle, or Psalm
Charge and Blessing

REAFFIRMATION OF THE BAPTISMAL COVENANT FOR A CONGREGATION

This liturgy is provided for occasions calling for a public reaffirmation of the baptismal covenant, and is included in the order for the Service for the Lord's Day.

It is appropriate for use on Baptism of the Lord (pp. 198–204), during Lent (pp. 235–250), on any Sunday during the Easter season (pp. 315–337), the Day of Pentecost (pp. 338–347), or All Saints' Day (pp. 385–391). This liturgy is included in the Easter Vigil (p. 310) when there is no baptism. Liturgical texts for these occasions focus on baptismal themes.

Additional liturgical texts are provided on pages 472–477 for occasions when the entire service will focus on the reaffirmation of the baptismal covenant.

> This service is led from the baptismal font or pool, which shall be filled with water.

SCRIPTURE SENTENCES

> After the sermon, the minister, standing at the baptismal font or pool, reads one of the following scripture texts.

Hear these words from Holy Scripture:

1   *1 Cor. 12:12–13, 27*

Just as the body is one
and has many members,
and all the members of the body, though many,
are one body,
so it is with Christ.

For in the one Spirit
we were all baptized into one body—
Jews or Greeks, slaves or free—
and we were all made to drink of one Spirit.

Now you are the body of Christ
and individually members of it.

2   *Deut. 7:9*

Know that the Lord your God is God,
the faithful God who keeps covenant and steadfast love
with those who love God
and keep God's commandments.

3   *Eph. 4:1–3*

Lead a life worthy of the calling to which you have been called,
with all humility and gentleness,
with patience, bearing with one another in love,
making every effort to maintain the unity of the Spirit
in the bond of peace.

4   *Micah 6:8*

God has told you what is good;
and what does the Lord require of you
but to do justice, and to love kindness,
and to walk humbly with your God?

PROFESSION OF FAITH

> The congregation may stand, as the minister continues:

Sisters and brothers in Christ,
our baptism is the sign and seal
of our cleansing from sin,
and of our being grafted into Christ.
Through the birth, life, death, and resurrection of Christ,
the power of sin was broken
and God's kingdom entered our world.
Through our baptism we were made citizens of God's kingdom,
and freed from the bondage of sin.
Let us celebrate that freedom and redemption
through the renewal of the promises made at our baptism.

I ask you, therefore,
once again to reject sin,
to profess your faith in Christ Jesus,
and to confess the faith of the church,
the faith in which we were baptized.

RENUNCIATIONS

> The minister continues, using one of the following:

1

Trusting in the gracious mercy of God,
do you turn from the ways of sin
and renounce evil and its power in the world?

I do.

Do you turn to Jesus Christ
and accept him as your Lord and Savior,
trusting in his grace and love?

I do.

Will you be Christ's faithful disciple,
obeying his Word and showing his love?

I will, with God's help.

2

Do you renounce all evil,
and powers in the world
which defy God's righteousness and love?

I renounce them.

Do you renounce the ways of sin
that separate you from the love of God?

I renounce them.

Do you turn to Jesus Christ
and accept him as your Lord and Savior?

I do.

Will you be Christ's faithful disciple,
obeying his Word and showing his love,
to your life's end?

I will, with God's help.

3

Trusting in the gracious mercy of God,
do you turn from the ways of sin
and renounce evil and its power in the world?

I do.

Who is your Lord and Savior?

Jesus Christ is my Lord and Savior.

Will you be Christ's faithful disciple,
obeying his Word and showing his love?

I will, with God's help.

PROFESSION

The minister continues:

With the whole church,
let us confess our faith.

The congregation affirms the faith in the words of the Apostles' Creed,
using the question and answer form (A) or reciting it directly (B).

A

Do you believe in God the Father?

I believe in God, the Father almighty,
creator of heaven and earth.

Do you believe in Jesus Christ, the Son of God?

I believe in Jesus Christ, God's only Son, our Lord,
who was conceived by the Holy Spirit,
born of the Virgin Mary,
suffered under Pontius Pilate,
was crucified, died, and was buried;
he descended to the dead.
On the third day he rose again;
he ascended into heaven,
he is seated at the right hand of the Father,
and he will come to judge the living and the dead.

Do you believe in God the Holy Spirit?

I believe in the Holy Spirit,
the holy catholic church,
the communion of saints,
the forgiveness of sins,
the resurrection of the body,
and the life everlasting.   Amen.

B

I believe in God, the Father almighty,
creator of heaven and earth.

I believe in Jesus Christ, God's only Son, our Lord,
who was conceived by the Holy Spirit,
born of the Virgin Mary,
suffered under Pontius Pilate,
was crucified, died, and was buried;
he descended to the dead.
On the third day he rose again;
he ascended into heaven,
he is seated at the right hand of the Father,
and he will come to judge the living and the dead.

I believe in the Holy Spirit,
the holy catholic church,
the communion of saints,
the forgiveness of sins,
the resurrection of the body,
and the life everlasting.   Amen.

THANKSGIVING FOR BAPTISM

Water is poured visibly and audibly into the font.

One of the following prayers is then said by the minister:

1

The Lord be with you.

And also with you.

Let us give thanks to the Lord our God.

It is right to give our thanks and praise.

We give you thanks, Eternal God,
for you nourish and sustain all living things
by the gift of water.
In the beginning of time,
your Spirit moved over the watery chaos,
calling forth order and life.

In the time of Noah,
you destroyed evil by the waters of the flood,
giving righteousness a new beginning.

You led Israel out of slavery,
through the waters of the sea,
into the freedom of the promised land.

In the waters of Jordan
Jesus was baptized by John
and anointed with your Spirit.

By the baptism of his own death and resurrection,
Christ set us free from sin and death,
and opened the way to eternal life.

We thank you, O God, for the water of baptism.
In it we were buried with Christ in his death.
From it we were raised to share in his resurrection,
Through it we were reborn by the power of the Holy Spirit.

Therefore in joyful obedience to your Son,
we celebrate our fellowship in him in faith.
We pray that all who have passed through the water of baptism
may continue forever in the risen life
of Jesus Christ our Savior.
To him, to you, and to the Holy Spirit,
be all honor and glory, now and forever.   [427]

Amen.

2

The Lord be with you.

And also with you.

Let us give thanks to the Lord our God.

It is right to give our thanks and praise.

Eternal and gracious God, we give you thanks.
In countless ways you have revealed yourself in ages past,
and have blessed us with signs of your grace.

We praise you that through the waters of the sea
you led your people Israel out of bondage,
into freedom in the land of your promise.

We praise you for sending Jesus your Son,
who for us was baptized in the waters of the Jordan,
and was anointed as the Christ by your Holy Spirit.
Through the baptism of his death and resurrection
you set us free from the bondage of sin and death,
and give us cleansing and rebirth.

We praise you for your Holy Spirit,
who teaches us and leads us into all truth,
filling us with a variety of gifts,
that we might proclaim the gospel to all nations
and serve you as a royal priesthood.

We rejoice that you claimed us in our baptism,
and that by your grace we are born anew.
By your Holy Spirit renew us,
that we may be empowered to do your will
and continue forever in the risen life of Christ,
to whom, with you and the Holy Spirit,
be all glory and honor,
now and forever.   [428]

Amen.

> The minister may place his or her hand into the water of the font, lift up
> some water, let it fall back into the font, and then make the sign of the
> cross over the people, while saying:

Remember your baptism and be thankful.
In the name of the Father and of the Son and of the Holy Spirit.

Amen.

Laying On of Hands

> The minister may invite persons who wish to receive the laying on
> of hands to come and kneel at the font.

> The minister lays both hands on the head of each person in turn,
> while offering one of the following prayers. The sign of the cross
> may be traced on the forehead of each person. Oil prepared for this
> purpose may be used.

1

O Lord, uphold N. by your Holy Spirit.
Daily increase in *him/her* your gifts of grace:
the spirit of wisdom and understanding,
the spirit of counsel and might,
the spirit of knowledge and the fear of the Lord,
the spirit of joy in your presence,
both now and forever.   [413]

> The candidate answers:

Amen.

2

Defend, O Lord, your servant N.
with your heavenly grace,
that *he/she* may continue yours forever,
and daily increase in your Holy Spirit more and more,
until *he/she* comes to your everlasting kingdom. [414]

The candidate answers:

Amen.

THE PEACE

The service concludes with the exchange of peace if it was not included earlier in the service.

The minister may say:

The peace of our Lord Jesus Christ be with you.

And also with you.

It is especially appropriate that the Lord's Supper follow a reaffirmation of the baptismal covenant.

Additional Liturgical Texts for the Service for the Lord's Day When Including Reaffirmation of the Baptismal Covenant for a Congregation

When the following liturgical texts are incorporated into the Service for the Lord's Day as part of the reaffirmation of the baptismal covenant, it is appropriate that the complete service be led from the baptismal font or pool, which should be uncovered and filled with water.

Sentences of Scripture

1   *1 Peter 2:9*

You are a chosen race,
a royal priesthood,
a holy nation, God's own people,
in order that you may proclaim the mighty acts
of the One who called you out of darkness
into God's marvelous light.

2   *1 Peter 2:10*

Once you were not a people
but now you are God's people;
once you had not received mercy
but now you have received mercy.

3   *1 Peter 1:3*

Blessed be God forever and ever.
By God's great mercy
we have been born anew to a living hope
through the resurrection of Jesus Christ from the dead.

Opening Prayer

1

O God Most High,
you have made the font of baptism
to be the womb from which we are reborn
in the waters of life.
Grant that all who have been born of water and the Spirit
may live in Christ as the first fruits of the new humanity,
leading others to hope in the rebirth of your whole creation,
and to serve you with joy,
now and forever.   [429]

Amen.

2

God of grace,
by the power of the Holy Spirit
you have given us new life in the waters of baptism;
strengthen us to live in righteousness and true holiness,
that we may grow into the likeness of your Son,
Jesus Christ.   [430]

Amen.

3

Open the heavens, O God,
and pour out your Spirit upon us,
that all who have been raised to new life with Christ in baptism
may, by word and deed,
show forth the risen life of Jesus Christ our Lord.   [431]

Amen.

CALL TO CONFESSION

1   *Jer. 31:33, 34*

This is the covenant
which I will make with the house of Israel,
says the Lord:
I will put my law within them,
and I will write it upon their hearts;
and I will be their God,
and they shall be my people.
I will forgive their evil deeds,
and I will remember their sin no more.

In penitence and faith,
let us confess our sins to almighty God.

2   *Heb. 10:22*

Let us draw near to God with sincerity of heart
and full assurance of faith,
our guilty hearts sprinkled clean,
our bodies washed with pure water.

Let us confess our sins
before God and one another.

CONFESSION OF SIN—A LITANY

Sovereign God,
in baptism you called us to turn from sin
and to turn to Jesus Christ;
but we stray from his ways
and do not heed your call.

> Silence.

Lord, have mercy.

Christ, have mercy.

In baptism you joined us to Christ in his death
that we might be raised with Christ in new life;
but we cherish old ways
and fail to embrace the risen life
of righteousness, justice, and love.

> Silence.

Lord, have mercy.

Christ, have mercy.

In baptism you united us with all the baptized
who confess your name;
but we foster division in the church.
We refuse to live as one people,
and so fail to witness to your reconciling love before the world.

> Silence.

Lord, have mercy.

Christ, have mercy.

In baptism you call us to ministry
in all realms of life,
but we refuse the struggle to know your will;
we do not nurture the ways of peace;
we allow enmity and hatred to grow among us,
putting neighbor against neighbor,
and nation against nation.

We abuse the earth you entrust to our care,
and live in discord with all you made.

> Silence.

Lord, have mercy.

Christ, have mercy.

In baptism you sent us to serve with compassion
all for whom Christ died;
but we ignore the suffering of the oppressed
and the plight of the poor.
We take bread from the hungry,
and will not listen to cries for justice.

> Silence.

Lord, have mercy.

Christ, have mercy.

In baptism you gave us the Holy Spirit
to teach and guide us,
but we rely on ourselves,
and refuse to trust your direction.
We spurn your eternal wisdom,
preferring the luring ways of the world.

> Silence.

Lord, have mercy.

Christ, have mercy.

Lord, have mercy on us.
Remember the promises you made to us in our baptism,
forgive our sinful ways
and heal our brokenness.
Set us free from all that enslaves us,
and raise us to new life in Jesus Christ,
that we may be your faithful servants,
showing forth your healing love to the world,
to the glory of your holy name.   [432]

Amen.

DECLARATION OF FORGIVENESS

Col. 2:12; 2 Cor. 5:17

Hear the good news!

In baptism you were buried with Christ.
In baptism also you were raised to life with him,
through faith in the power of God
who raised Christ from the dead.

Anyone who is in Christ
is a new creation.
The old life has gone;
a new life has begun.

I declare to you in the name of Jesus Christ,
you are forgiven.

Amen.

Col. 3:1

If you have been raised with Christ,
seek the things that are above,
where Christ is, seated at the right hand of God.

PRAYER FOR ILLUMINATION

Creator Spirit,
who hovered over the waters at creation's birth,
who descended in the form of a dove at Jesus' baptism,
who was poured out under the signs of fire and wind at Pentecost:
Come to us, open our hearts and minds,
so that we may hear the Word of life
and be renewed by your power,
for you live and reign with the Father and the Son,
now and forever.   [433]

Amen.

GREAT THANKSGIVING

The great thanksgiving appointed for Baptism of the Lord (pp. 200–204),
or great thanksgiving B (pp. 126–129) or C (pp. 130–132), with the preface
for the reaffirmation of the baptismal covenant (p. 137) or for Baptism of
the Lord (p. 134), may be used.

When the Lord's Supper is not celebrated, the prayer of thanksgiving for Baptism of the Lord (p. 204) may be used.

CHARGE

Eph. 4:1–2

Lead a life worthy of the calling to which you have been called,
with all humility and gentleness,
with patience, bearing with one another in love,
making every effort to maintain the unity of the Spirit
in the bond of peace.

REAFFIRMATION OF THE BAPTISMAL COVENANT MARKING OCCASIONS OF GROWTH IN FAITH

Outline
Call to Discipleship
Profession of Faith
[Laying On of Hands]
The Peace

The following service may be used in a variety of situations to mark occasions such as a significant deepening of personal commitment or answers to the call to a particular ministry in the church. When it is included in the Service for the Lord's Day, it follows the sermon.

This service takes place at the baptismal font or pool, which should be uncovered and filled with water.

Those who wish to reaffirm the baptismal covenant in marking an occasion of growth in faith gather at the baptismal font or pool.

CALL TO DISCIPLESHIP

The minister may read one or more of the following, or other appropriate scripture texts:

1   *John 8:12*

Jesus said:
I am the light of the world.
Whoever follows me will never walk in darkness,
but will have the light of life.

2   *Luke 10:2*

The harvest is plentiful,
but the laborers are few;
therefore ask the Lord of the harvest
to send out laborers into his harvest.

3   *Matt. 25:34–36*

The King will say to those on his right hand:
Come, you that are blessed by my Father,
inherit the kingdom prepared for you
from the foundation of the world;
for I was hungry and you gave me food,
I was thirsty and you gave me drink,
I was a stranger and you welcomed me,
I was naked and you clothed me,
I was sick and you took care of me,
I was in prison and you visited me.

4   *John 15:15–17*

I do not call you servants any longer,
because the servant does not know what the master is doing;
but I have called you friends,
because I have made known to you
everything that I have heard from my Father.
You did not choose me
but I chose you.
And I appointed you to go and bear fruit,
fruit that will last,
so that the Father may give to you,
whatever you ask in my name.

5   *Rom. 12:1*

I appeal to you, by the mercies of God,
to present your bodies as a living sacrifice,
holy and acceptable to God,
which is your spiritual worship.

6   *Phil. 2:13*

God is at work in you,
enabling you both to will
and to work for God's good pleasure.

The minister continues:

The call of Christ is to willing, dedicated discipleship.
Our discipleship is a manifestation of the new life
into which we enter through baptism.
It is possible because in Jesus Christ
we have been set free from the bondage of sin and death.

Discipleship is both a gift and a commitment,
an offering and a responsibility.
It is marked by change, growth, and deepened commitment.
It is lived out of a renewing sense of God's calling to us,
and of God's claim upon us made in our baptism.

On this occasion we celebrate with N. and N.,
and join with *them* in renewing *their* baptism.

> Here the minister may relate what has happened in each individual's life,
> or the persons reaffirming the baptismal covenant may share their reasons
> for making this recommitment.

PROFESSION OF FAITH

> The minister, addressing those reaffirming the baptismal covenant, then says:

The grace bestowed on you in baptism
is sufficient because it is God's grace.
By God's grace we are saved,
and enabled to grow in the faith
and to commit our lives in ways which please God.

I invite you now to claim that grace given you in baptism
by reaffirming your baptismal vows:
to renounce all that opposes God and God's kingdom
and to affirm the faith of the holy catholic church.

RENUNCIATIONS

> The minister continues, using one of the following:

1

Trusting in the gracious mercy of God,
do you turn from the ways of sin
and renounce evil and its power in the world?

I do.

Do you turn to Jesus Christ
and accept him as your Lord and Savior,
trusting in his grace and love?

I do.

Will you be Christ's faithful disciple,
obeying his Word and showing his love?

I will, with God's help.

2

Do you renounce all evil,
and powers in the world
which defy God's righteousness and love?

I renounce them.

Do you renounce the ways of sin
that separate you from the love of God?

I renounce them.

Do you turn to Jesus Christ
and accept him as your Lord and Savior?

I do.

Will you be Christ's faithful disciple,
obeying his Word and showing his love,
to your life's end?

I will, with God's help.

3

Trusting in the gracious mercy of God,
do you turn from the ways of sin
and renounce evil and its power in the world?

I do.

Who is your Lord and Savior?

Jesus Christ is my Lord and Savior.

Will you be Christ's faithful disciple,
obeying his Word and showing his love?

I will, with God's help.

PROFESSION

> The congregation may stand and join those reaffirming the baptismal
> covenant, by affirming the faith in the words of the Apostles' Creed, using
> the question and answer form (A) or reciting it directly (B).

A

Do you believe in God the Father?

**I believe in God, the Father almighty,
creator of heaven and earth.**

Do you believe in Jesus Christ, the Son of God?

I believe in Jesus Christ, God's only Son, our Lord,
who was conceived by the Holy Spirit,
born of the Virgin Mary,
suffered under Pontius Pilate,
was crucified, died, and was buried;
he descended to the dead.
On the third day he rose again;
he ascended into heaven,
he is seated at the right hand of the Father,
and he will come to judge the living and the dead.

Do you believe in God the Holy Spirit?

I believe in the Holy Spirit,
the holy catholic church,
the communion of saints,
the forgiveness of sins,
the resurrection of the body,
and the life everlasting.   Amen.

B

I believe in God, the Father almighty,
creator of heaven and earth.

I believe in Jesus Christ, God's only Son, our Lord,
who was conceived by the Holy Spirit,
born of the Virgin Mary,
suffered under Pontius Pilate,
was crucified, died, and was buried;
he descended to the dead.
On the third day he rose again;
he ascended into heaven,
he is seated at the right hand of the Father,
and he will come to judge the living and the dead.

I believe in the Holy Spirit,
the holy catholic church,
the communion of saints,
the forgiveness of sins,
the resurrection of the body,
and the life everlasting.   Amen.

If appropriate, the minister may address those reaffirming the baptismal covenant, using one of the following:

1

You have publicly professed your faith.
Will you be a faithful member of this congregation,
share in its worship and ministry
through your prayers and gifts,
your study and service,
and so fulfill your calling to be a disciple of Jesus Christ?

I will, with God's help.

2   *See Acts 2:42*

You have publicly professed your faith.
Will you devote yourself to the church's teaching and fellowship,
to the breaking of bread and the prayers?

I will, with God's help.

The minister offers the following prayer, or a similar prayer may be said.

Faithful God,
in baptism you claimed us;
and by your Spirit you are working in our lives,
empowering us to live a life worthy of our calling.
We thank you for leading N. and N.
to this time and place
of reaffirming the covenant you made with *them* in *their* baptism.
Establish *them* in your truth,
and guide *them* by your Spirit,
that, together with all your people,
they may grow in faith, hope, and love,
and be faithful disciples of Jesus Christ,
to whom, with you and the Holy Spirit
be honor and glory, now and forever.   [423]

Amen.

LAYING ON OF HANDS

The minister may lay both hands on the head of each person in turn, while saying one of the following prayers. The sign of the cross may be marked on the forehead of each person. Oil prepared for this purpose may be used.

A

O Lord, uphold N. by your Holy Spirit.
Daily increase in *him/her* your gifts of grace:
the spirit of wisdom and understanding,
the spirit of counsel and might,
the spirit of knowledge and the fear of the Lord,
the spirit of joy in your presence,
both now and forever.   [413]

The candidate answers:

Amen.

B

Defend, O Lord, your servant N.
with your heavenly grace,
that *he/she* may continue yours forever,
and daily increase in your Holy Spirit more and more,
until *he/she* comes to your everlasting kingdom.   [414]

The candidate answers:

Amen.

After all have received the laying on of hands, these or similar words
are said:

See Eph. 5:2; 1 Thess. 5:16–18

N., and N., you are *disciples* of Jesus Christ.
Live in love, as Christ loved us
and gave himself for us.
Rejoice always, pray without ceasing,
give thanks in all circumstances;
for this is the will of God in Christ Jesus for you.

THE PEACE

The minister says these or similar words:

Phil. 4:7

The peace of God, which passes all understanding,
keep your heart and your mind in Christ Jesus.

Amen.

If this rite is part of a public service, all may exchange the peace if it was
not included earlier in the service.

REAFFIRMATION OF THE BAPTISMAL COVENANT IN PASTORAL COUNSELING

Outline

Scripture Reading
Profession of Faith
Prayer
[Laying On of Hands]
The Peace

This service is for use in the context of private pastoral counseling with persons who struggle to live up to the implications of their baptism.

This service takes place at the baptismal font or pool, which should be uncovered and filled with water.

SCRIPTURE READING

One or more of the following scripture texts may be read:

Psalm 23	Psalm 91	Phil. 4:4–7
Psalm 90	2 Cor. 1:3–5	

PROFESSION OF FAITH

Using these or similar words, the minister says:

In your baptism, God acted out of grace and love for you.
You entered the covenant God established.
You were joined to Christ
and welcomed into the household of faith.
The grace of God is eternal.
Nothing can separate you from God's love.
You are still God's child,
and God cares for you.

I ask you therefore,
once again to reject sin,
to profess your faith in Christ Jesus,
and to confess the faith of the church,
the faith in which we are baptized.

The minister continues, using one of the following:

1

Trusting in the gracious mercy of God,
do you turn from the ways of sin
and renounce evil and its power in the world?

I do.

Do you turn to Jesus Christ
and accept him as your Lord and Savior,
trusting in his grace and love?

I do.

Will you be Christ's faithful disciple,
obeying his Word and showing his love?

I will, with God's help.

2

Do you renounce all evil,
and powers in the world
which defy God's righteousness and love?

I renounce them.

Do you renounce the ways of sin
that separate you from the love of God?

I renounce them.

Do you turn to Jesus Christ
and accept him as your Lord and Savior?

I do.

Will you be Christ's faithful disciple,
obeying his Word and showing his love,
to your life's end?

I will, with God's help.

3

Trusting in the gracious mercy of God,
do you turn from the ways of sin
and renounce evil and its power in the world?

I do.

Who is your Lord and Savior?

Jesus Christ is my Lord and Savior.

Will you be Christ's faithful disciple,
obeying his Word and showing his love?

I will, with God's help.

> The minister offers a prayer that is relevant to the particular concerns that have been part of the counseling situation. It may include thanksgiving, petition, intercession, confession, and forgiveness.

LAYING ON OF HANDS

> The minister continues with the laying on of hands, while offering prayer A or B:

A

O Lord, uphold N. by your Holy Spirit.
Daily increase in *him/her* your gifts of grace:
the spirit of wisdom and understanding,
the spirit of counsel and might,
the spirit of knowledge and the fear of the Lord,
the spirit of joy in your presence,
both now and forever.   [413]

> The candidate answers:

Amen.

B

Defend, O Lord, your servant N.
with your heavenly grace,
that *he/she* may continue yours forever,
and daily increase in your Holy Spirit more and more,
until *he/she* comes to your everlasting kingdom.   [414]

The candidate answers:

Amen.

THE PEACE

The minister says:

The peace of Christ be with you.

The person responds:

Amen.

DAILY
PRAYER

Opening Sentences
Morning Psalm or Morning Hymn
Psalm(s)
    Psalm
    Silent Prayer
    [Psalm Prayer]
Scripture Reading
    Silent Reflection
    [A Brief Interpretation of the Reading, or a Nonbiblical Reading]
Canticle
    Canticle of Zechariah or Other Canticle
Prayers of Thanksgiving and Intercession
    Thanksgivings and Intercessions
    Concluding Prayer
    Lord's Prayer
[Hymn or Spiritual]
Dismissal
    [Sign of Peace]

When a person is worshiping alone, or in a family group, or when circum-stances call for an abbreviated order, the following is suggested:

Psalm
Scripture Reading
    Silent Reflection
Prayers of Thanksgiving and Intercession

Morning Prayer

Opening Sentences

All may stand.

O Lord, open my lips.
And my mouth shall proclaim your praise.

And one of the following, or a seasonal alternative (pp. 524–543), is said:

1   *Lam. 3:22–23*

The Lord's unfailing love and mercy never cease,
fresh as the morning and sure as the sunrise.

2   *Ps. 74:16, 17*

You created the day and the night, O God;
you set the sun and the moon in their places;
you set the limits of the earth;
you made summer and winter.

3   *Ps. 5:2b–3*

I pray to you, O Lord;
you hear my voice in the morning;
at sunrise I offer my prayer
and wait for your answer.

4   *Rom. 11:33, 36*

O depth of wealth, wisdom, and knowledge of God!
How unsearchable are God's judgments,
how untraceable are God's ways!
The source, guide, and goal of all that is,
to God be glory forever!   Amen.

5   *Rev. 19:6, 7*

Alleluia!
For the Lord our God the Almighty reigns.
Let us rejoice and exult and give God the glory.

6   *Heb. 13:15*

Through Jesus let us continually offer up a sacrifice of praise to God,
the fruit of lips that acknowledge God's name.

7   *Rev. 4:11*

You are worthy, our Lord and God,
to receive glory and honor and power
for you created all things,
and by your will they existed
and were created.

MORNING PSALM OR MORNING HYMN

One of the morning psalms (95:1–7; 100; 63:1–8; 51:1–12) or a morning
hymn is sung.

Psalm 95:1–7   Tone 2; PH 215; PS 89, 90

Refrain: **Let us shout for joy ***
            to the Rock of our salvation.

R

1   Come, let us sing to the LORD; *
     let us shout for joy to the Rock of our salvation.

2   **Let us come before God's presence with thanksgiving ***
     and raise a loud shout to the LORD with psalms.   R

3   For the LORD is a great God, *
     and a great Sovereign above all gods.

4   **The LORD holds the caverns of the earth, ***
     and sustains the heights of the hills.

5   The sea belongs to God, who made it, *
     whose hands have molded the dry land.   **R**

6   **Come, let us bow down, and bend the knee, ***
     and kneel before the LORD our Maker.

     [Unison]

7   **For the LORD is our God,**
     and we are the people of God's pasture and the sheep of
         God's hand. *
     Oh, that today you would hearken to God's voice!   R

492 / MORNING PRAYER

Psalm 100   Tone 3; PH 220; PS 97–101

Refrain: **Shout for joy to God, all the earth,** *
            Alleluia! Praise the Lord!

R

1 Be joyful in the LORD, all you lands; *
   2 serve the LORD with gladness
      and come before God's presence with a song.

3 **Know this: The LORD alone is God;** *
      we belong to the LORD, who made us,
      we are God's people and the sheep of God's pasture.   **R**

4 Enter God's gates with thanksgiving;
   go into the holy courts with praise; *
      give thanks and call upon the name of the LORD.

5 **For good is the LORD,**
   whose mercy is everlasting; *
      and whose faithfulness endures from age to age.   **R**

Psalm 63:1–8   Tone 6 or 8; PH 198, 199; PS 53, 54

Refrain: **O God, you are my God;** *
            earnestly will I seek you.

R

1 O God, you are my God; eagerly I seek you; *
      my soul thirsts for you, my flesh faints for you,
      as in a barren and dry land where there is no water.

2 **Therefore I have gazed upon you in your holy place,** *
      that I might behold your power and your glory.

3 For your loving-kindness is better than life itself; *
      my lips shall give you praise.

4 **So will I bless you as long as I live** *
      and lift up my hands in your name.   **R**

5 My soul is content, as with marrow and fatness, *
      and my mouth praises you with joyful lips,

6 **when I remember you upon my bed,** *
      and meditate on you in the night watches.

7 For you have been my helper, *
      and under the shadow of your wings I will rejoice.

8 **My soul clings to you;** *
   your right hand holds me fast.   R

Psalm 51:1–12   Tone 7; PH 195, 196; PS 47

Refrain: **Create in me a clean heart, O God,** *
           and renew a right spirit within me.

R

1 Have mercy on me, O God, according to your loving-kindness; *
   in your great compassion blot out my offenses.

2 **Wash me through and through from my wickedness** *
   and cleanse me from my sin.   R

3 For I know my transgressions, *
   and my sin is ever before me.

4 **Against you only have I sinned** *
   and done what is evil in your sight.

   And so you are justified when you speak *
   and upright in your judgment.

5 **Indeed, I have been wicked from my birth,** *
   a sinner from my mother's womb.   R

6 For behold, you look for truth deep within me, *
   and will make me understand wisdom secretly.

7 **Purge me from my sin, and I shall be pure;** *
   wash me, and I shall be clean indeed.

8 Make me hear of joy and gladness, *
   that the body you have broken may rejoice.

9 **Hide your face from my sins** *
   and blot out all my iniquities.   R

10 Create in me a clean heart, O God, *
   and renew a right spirit within me.

11 **Cast me not away from your presence** *
   and take not your holy Spirit from me.

   [Unison]

12 **Give me the joy of your saving help again** *
   and sustain me with your bountiful Spirit.   R

All may be seated.

PSALM(S)

One or more additional psalms (pp. 611–783, 1050–1095) are sung or said.

Silence for reflection follows each psalm.

A psalm prayer may follow the silence.

SCRIPTURE READING

At the conclusion of the reading of scripture (pp. 1050–1095), the reader may say:

The Word of the Lord.

Thanks be to God.

Silence follows for reflection on the meaning of the scripture.

The scripture may be briefly interpreted, or a nonbiblical reading may be read.

CANTICLE

The Canticle of Zechariah or another canticle (pp. 573–591; PS 158–191) may be sung or said.

All may stand.

Canticle of Zechariah   *Benedictus; Luke 1:68–79*
                                                             PH 601, 602; PS 158–160

Refrain: **You have come to your people ***
          and set them free.

Or

          In the tender compassion of our God *
          the dawn from on high shall break upon us.

R
Blessed are you, Lord, the God of Israel; *
   you have come to your people and set them free.
You have raised up for us a mighty Savior, *
   born of the house of your servant David.   **R**

Through your holy prophets, you promised of old
to save us from our enemies, *
   from the hands of all who hate us,
to show mercy to our forebears, *
   and to remember your holy covenant.   R

This was the oath you swore to our father Abraham: *
   to set us free from the hands of our enemies,
free to worship you without fear, *
   holy and righteous before you,
   all the days of our life.   R

And you, child, shall be called the prophet of the Most High, *
   for you will go before the Lord to prepare the way,
to give God's people knowledge of salvation *
   by the forgiveness of their sins.   R

In the tender compassion of our God *
   the dawn from on high shall break upon us,
to shine on those who dwell in darkness and the shadow of death,*
   and to guide our feet into the way of peace.   R

PRAYERS OF THANKSGIVING AND INTERCESSION

Satisfy us with your love in the morning,

and we will live this day in joy and praise.

> One of the following, or other prayers of thanksgiving and intercession,
> may be said:

1

Sunday

Mighty God of mercy, we thank you for the resurrection dawn bringing the
glory of our risen Lord who makes every day new. Especially we thank you for
   the beauty of your creation . . .
      the new creation in Christ and all gifts of healing and forgiveness . . .
      the sustaining love of family and friends . . .
      the fellowship of faith in your church. . . .
Merciful God of might, renew this weary world, heal the hurts of all your children, and bring about your peace for all in Christ Jesus, the living Lord. Especially we pray for
      those who govern nations of the world . . .
      the people in countries ravaged by strife or warfare . . .
      all who work for peace and international harmony . . .
      all who strive to save the earth from destruction . . .
      the church of Jesus Christ in every land. . . .   [434]

Monday

We praise you, God our creator, for your handiwork in shaping and sustaining your wondrous creation. Especially we thank you for

the miracle of life and the wonder of living . . .

particular blessings coming to us in this day . . .

the resources of the earth . . .

gifts of creative vision and skillful craft . . .

the treasure stored in every human life. . . .

We dare to pray for others, God our Savior, claiming your love in Jesus Christ for the whole world, committing ourselves to care for those around us in his name. Especially we pray for

those who work for the benefit of others . . .

those who cannot work today . . .

those who teach and those who learn . . .

people who are poor . . .

the church in Europe. . . .   [435]

3

Tuesday

Eternal God, we rejoice this morning in the gift of life, which we have received by your grace, and the new life you give in Jesus Christ. Especially we thank you for

the love of our families . . .

the affection of our friends . . .

strength and abilities to serve your purpose today . . .

this community in which we live . . .

opportunities to give as we have received. . . .

God of grace, we offer our prayers for the needs of others and commit ourselves to serve them even as we have been served in Jesus Christ. Especially we pray for

those closest to us, families, friends, neighbors . . .

refugees and homeless men, women and children . . .

the outcast and persecuted . . .

those from whom we are estranged . . .

the church in Africa. . . .   [436]

4

Wednesday

God of all mercies, we praise you that you have brought us to this new day, brightening our lives with the dawn of promise and hope in Jesus Christ. Especially we thank you for
>the warmth of sunlight, the wetness of rain and snow, and all that nourishes the earth . . .
>the presence and power of your Spirit . . .
>the support and encouragement we receive from others . . .
>those who provide for public safety and well-being . . .
>the mission of the church around the world. . . .

Merciful God, strengthen us in prayer that we may lift up the brokenness of this world for your healing, and share in the saving love of Jesus Christ. Especially we pray for
>those in positions of authority over others . . .
>the lonely and forgotten . . .
>children without families or homes . . .
>agents of caring and relief . . .
>the church in Asia and the Middle East. . . .   [437]

5

Thursday

Loving God, as the rising sun chases away the night, so you have scattered the power of death in the rising of Jesus Christ, and you bring us all blessings in him. Especially we thank you for
>the community of faith in our church . . .
>those with whom we work or share common concerns . . .
>the diversity of your children . . .
>indications of your love at work in the world . . .
>those who work for reconciliation. . . .

Mighty God, with the dawn of your love you reveal your victory over all that would destroy or harm, and you brighten the lives of all who need you. Especially we pray for
>families suffering separation . . .
>people different from ourselves . . .
>those isolated by sickness or sorrow . . .
>the victims of violence or warfare . . .
>the church in the Pacific region. . . .   [438]

6

Friday

Eternal God, we praise you for your mighty love given in Christ's sacrifice on the cross, and the new life we have received by his resurrection. Especially we thank you for

the presence of Christ in our weakness and suffering . . .

the ministry of Word and Sacrament . . .

all who work to help and heal . . .

sacrifices made for our benefit . . .

opportunities for our generous giving. . . .

God of grace, let our concern for others reflect Christ's self-giving love, not only in our prayers, but also in our practice. Especially we pray for

those subjected to tyranny and oppression . . .

wounded and injured people . . .

those who face death . . .

those who may be our enemies . . .

the church in Latin America. . . .   [439]

Saturday

Great and wonderful God, we praise and thank you for the gift of renewal in Jesus Christ. Especially we thank you for

opportunities for rest and recreation . . .

the regenerating gifts of the Holy Spirit . . .

activities shared by young and old . . .

fun and laughter . . .

every service that proclaims your love. . . .

You make all things new, O God, and we offer our prayers for the renewal of the world and the healing of its wounds. Especially we pray for

those who have no leisure . . .

people enslaved by addictions . . .

those who entertain and enlighten . . .

those confronted with temptation . . .

the church in North America. . . .   [440]

Individual prayers of thanksgiving and intercession may be offered.

There may be silent prayer.

The leader then says one of the following prayers, or a similar prayer. For seasonal alternatives see pages 524–543.

1

Eternal God,
our beginning and our end,
be our starting point and our haven,
and accompany us in this day's journey.
Use our hands
to do the work of your creation,
and use our lives
to bring others the new life you give this world
in Jesus Christ, Redeemer of all.   [441]

Amen.

2

As you cause the sun to rise, O God,
bring the light of Christ to dawn in our souls
and dispel all darkness.
Give us grace to reflect Christ's glory;
and let his love show in our deeds,
his peace shine in our words,
and his healing in our touch,
that all may give him praise, now and forever.   [442]

Amen.

3

Eternal God,
your touch makes this world holy.
Open our eyes to see your hand at work
in the splendor of creation,
and in the beauty of human life.
Help us to cherish the gifts that surround us,
to share your blessings with our sisters and brothers,
and to experience the joy of life in your presence.
We ask this through Christ our Lord.   [443]

Amen.

4

Eternal God,
you never fail to give us each day all that we ever need,
and even more.
Give us such joy in living
and such peace in serving Christ,
that we may gratefully make use of all your blessings,
and joyfully seek our risen Lord
in everyone we meet.
In Jesus Christ we pray.   [444]

Amen.

5

O God,
you are the well-spring of life.
Pour into our hearts the living water of your grace,
that we may be refreshed to live this day in joy,
confident of your presence
and empowered by your peace,
in Jesus Christ our Lord.   [445]

Amen.

6

Eternal God,
you call us to ventures
of which we cannot see the ending,
by paths as yet untrodden,
through perils unknown.
Give us faith to go out with courage,
not knowing where we go,
but only that your hand is leading us
and your love supporting us;
through Jesus Christ our Lord.   [446]

Amen.

7

God our creator,
yours is the morning and yours is the evening.
Let Christ the sun of righteousness
shine forever in our hearts
and draw us to that light
where you live in radiant glory.
We ask this for the sake of Jesus Christ our Redeemer.   [447]

Amen.

All sing (musical settings: PH 571, 589, 590; PS 192–195) or say:

Or

Our Father in heaven,
hallowed be your name,
your kingdom come,
your will be done,
on earth as in heaven.
Give us today our daily bread.
Forgive us our sins
as we forgive those who sin against us.
Save us from the time of trial
and deliver us from evil.
For the kingdom, the power,
  and the glory are yours
now and forever.   Amen.

Our Father, who art in heaven,
hallowed be thy name,
thy kingdom come,
thy will be done,
on earth as it is in heaven.
Give us this day our daily bread;
and forgive us our debts,
as we forgive our debtors;
and lead us not into temptation,
but deliver us from evil.
For thine is the kingdom,
  and the power, and the glory,
  forever.   Amen.

[Hymn or Spiritual]

Dismissal

The leader dismisses the people using one of the following:

1   *1 Tim. 6:21*

The grace of God be with us all, now and always.

Amen.

Bless the Lord.

The Lord's name be praised.

2   *Rom. 15:13*

May the God of hope fill us with all joy and peace
through the power of the Holy Spirit.

Amen.

Bless the Lord.

The Lord's name be praised.

3
1 Tim. 1:17

To God be honor and glory forever and ever.

Amen.

Bless the Lord.

The Lord's name be praised.

4
2 Peter 3:18

May we continue to grow in the grace and knowledge of Jesus Christ, our Lord and Savior.

Amen.

Bless the Lord.

The Lord's name be praised.

A sign of peace may be exchanged by all.

AN OUTLINE OF EVENING PRAYER

Service of Light   Or   Opening Sentences
    Opening Sentences   Evening Hymn
    Evening Hymn: Hymn to
        Christ the Light
    Thanksgiving for Light
    Evening Psalm
        Psalm 141
        Silent Prayer
        Psalm Prayer

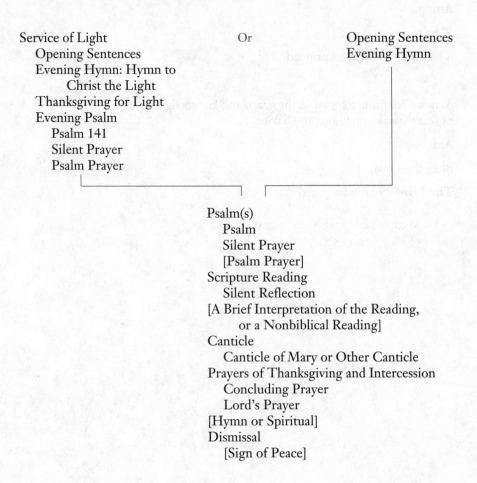

           Psalm(s)
             Psalm
             Silent Prayer
             [Psalm Prayer]
           Scripture Reading
             Silent Reflection
           [A Brief Interpretation of the Reading,
             or a Nonbiblical Reading]
           Canticle
             Canticle of Mary or Other Canticle
           Prayers of Thanksgiving and Intercession
             Concluding Prayer
             Lord's Prayer
           [Hymn or Spiritual]
           Dismissal
             [Sign of Peace]

When a person is worshiping alone, or in a family group, or when circumstances call for an abbreviated order, the following is suggested:

Psalm
Scripture Reading
    Silent Reflection
Prayers of Thanksgiving and Intercession

EVENING PRAYER

Evening prayer may begin with the service of light.

If evening prayer is not to include the service of light, the service begins on page 513.

SERVICE OF LIGHT

The room should be dimly lit. A large lighted candle may be carried in procession to a prominent place as the opening sentences are sung or said. Or a lamp or candle already in place may be lighted as the people gather.

OPENING SENTENCES

One of the following is sung or said.

All may stand.

1   *See John 1:5; 8:12; Luke 24:29*

Jesus Christ is the light of the world,

the light no darkness can overcome.

Stay with us, Lord, for it is evening

and the day is almost over.

Let your light scatter the darkness

and illumine your church.

2

Light and peace in Jesus Christ our Lord.

Thanks be to God.

3

See Rev. 22:20

Advent

The Spirit and the church cry out:

Come, Lord Jesus.

All those who await his appearance pray:

Come, Lord Jesus.

The whole creation pleads:

Come, Lord Jesus.

4

See Isa. 9:2, 6; John 1:4–5, 14

Christmas–Epiphany

The people who walked in darkness
have seen a great light.

**The light shines in the darkness,
and the darkness has not overcome it.**

Those who dwell in the land of deep darkness,
on them has the light shined.

**We have beheld Christ's glory,
glory as of the only Son of the Father.**

For to us a child is born, to us a Son is given.

**In him was life,
and the life was the light of all people.**

5

See 2 Cor. 6:2; Ps. 85:4; 80:3

Lent

Behold, now is the acceptable time;

now is the day of salvation.

Turn us again, O God of our salvation,

that the light of your face may shine on us.

May your justice shine like the sun;

and may the poor be lifted up.

6

Easter–Pentecost

Jesus Christ is risen from the dead.

Alleluia, Alleluia, Alleluia!

We are illumined by the brightness of his rising.

Alleluia, Alleluia, Alleluia!

Death has no more dominion over us.

Alleluia, Alleluia, Alleluia!

EVENING HYMN

Hymn to Christ the Light   *Phos Hilaron*
PH 548, 549; PS 167–169

> As the hymn is sung, additional candles may be lighted from the
> flame of the large candle and the lights turned up.

O radiant Light, O Sun divine,
of God the Father's deathless face,
O image of the Light sublime,
that fills the heavenly dwelling place.

O Son of God, the source of life,
praise is your due by night and day.
Our happy lips must raise the strain
of your esteemed and splendid name.

Lord Jesus Christ, as daylight fades,
as shine the lights of eventide,
we praise the Father with the Son,
the Spirit blest and with them one.

THANKSGIVING FOR LIGHT

> The thanksgiving for light may be sung or spoken.

The Lord be with you.

And also with you.

Let us give thanks to the Lord our God.

It is right to give our thanks and praise.

The leader continues, using one of the following prayers:

1

We give you thanks and praise, O God,
for you are without beginning and without end.
Through your Son, Jesus Christ,
you have created and preserved the world;
Father of Christ and the giver of the Spirit,
you rule over all creation.
The day you have made for the works of light
and the night for our refreshment and strength.

O Lord of love and source of all good,
receive our evening sacrifice of praise.

You have guided us through this day
to the beginning of night;
grant us, in Christ, an evening filled with peace
and a night free from sin;
and when at last we come to our own end,
bring us into the everlasting life of your kingdom,
where you live and reign with Jesus Christ, your Son,
in the unity of the Holy Spirit,
God, forever and ever.   [448]

Amen.

2

We praise you, O Lord our God, Ruler of the universe,
by whose word the shadows of evening fall.
Your wisdom opens the gates of morning;
your understanding orders the changes of time and seasons;
your will controls the stars as they travel through the skies.
You are the Creator of both night and day,
making light recede before darkness,
and darkness before light.
You cause day to pass,
and bring on the night,
setting day and night apart.
You are the Lord of hosts.

Living and eternal God, rule over us always,
to the end of time.
Blessed are you, O Lord,
whose word makes evening fall.   [449]

Amen.

3

Blessed are you, Lord God of all creation.
In the beginning you separated light from darkness
and placed all your works in our hands.
You have given us the light of day
that we might see your wonders
in all we say and do;
you give us the gentle darkness of the night
that we might rest from our burdens
and be refreshed in body and spirit.

Break through the darkness of our sins
with the splendor of your mercy and love.
Send your light to dispel our fears and anxieties
and fill us with hope and joy.

Glory, praise, and honor are yours, O God,
through Jesus Christ our Lord,
in the power of the Holy Spirit,
now and forever.   [450]

Amen.

4

We give you thanks and praise, O God of endless light,
through our Lord Jesus Christ.

In him your light shines in our hearts
and reveals the light that never fades.
As daylight comes to an end
and darkness begins to fall,
we thank you for the light of day,
created for our work and pleasure,
and bless you for the gift of this evening light.

All praise to you, O God,
through Jesus Christ, your Son:
through him all glory and honor is yours,
with the Holy Spirit,
in the holy church
now and forever.   [451]

Amen.

5

Advent

Blessed are you, O Lord our God, Ruler of the universe,
creator of light and darkness.
In this holy season,
when the sun's light is swallowed up
by the growing darkness of the night,
you renew your promise to reveal among us
the splendor of your glory,
made flesh and visible to us in Jesus Christ, your Son.
Through the prophets
you teach us to hope for his reign of peace.

Through the outpouring of your Spirit
you give sight to our souls,
that we may see your glory
in the presence of Christ.
Strengthen us where we are weak,
support us in our efforts to do your will,
and free our tongues to sing your praise,
for to you all honor and blessing are due,
now and forever.   [452]

Amen.

6

Christmas–Epiphany

Blessed are you, O Lord our God,
for you have made our gladness greater and increased our joy
by sending to dwell among us
the Wonderful Counselor, the Prince of Peace.
Born of Mary,
proclaimed to the shepherds
and acknowledged to the ends of the earth,
your unconquered Sun of righteousness
gives light in darkness and establishes us in freedom.

All glory in the highest be to you,
through Christ, the Son of your favor,
in the abiding presence of your Spirit,
this night and forever and ever.   [453]

Amen.

7

Lent

Blessed are you, O Lord our God,
the Shepherd of Israel,
their pillar of cloud by day,
their pillar of fire by night.
In these forty days
you lead us into the desert of repentance
that in this pilgrimage of prayer
we might learn to be your people once more.
In fasting and service
you bring us back to your heart.
You open our eyes to your presence in the world
and you free our hands
to lead others to the wonders of your grace.

Be with us in these journey days,
for without you we are lost and will perish.
To you alone be dominion and glory,
forever and ever.   [454]

Amen.

8

Easter–Pentecost

Blessed are you,
O Lord, Redeemer God.
You destroyed the bonds of death
and from the darkness of the tomb
drew forth the light of the world.
You led us through the waters of death,
and made us children of light
singing Alleluias
and dancing to the music of new life.

Pour out your Spirit upon us
that dreams and visions
bring us ever closer to the kingdom of Jesus Christ,
our risen Savior.
Through him and in the Holy Spirit
all glory be to you, almighty God,
this night and forever and ever.   [455]

Amen.

While Psalm 141 is being sung, incense may be burned.

Refrain: Let my prayer rise before you as incense,*
the lifting of my hands as the evening sacrifice.

R

1   O LORD, I call to you; come to me quickly; *
    hear my voice when I cry to you.

2   **Let my prayer be set forth in your sight as incense, ***
    the lifting up of my hands as the evening sacrifice.

3   Set a watch before my mouth, O LORD,
    and guard the door of my lips; *
        4 let not my heart incline to any evil thing.

    Let me not be occupied in wickedness with evildoers, *
    nor eat of their choice foods.   R

5   Let the righteous smite me in friendly rebuke;
    let not the oil of the unrighteous anoint my head; *
        for my prayer is continually against their wicked deeds.

8   But my eyes are turned to you, Lord GOD; *
    in you I take refuge;
    do not strip me of my life.   R

9   Protect me from the snare which they have laid for me *
    and from the traps of the evildoers.

10 **Let the wicked fall into their own nets, ***
    while I myself escape.   R

After the psalm, the leader says:

Let us pray.

Pause for silent prayer.

Holy God,
let the incense of our prayer ascend before you,
and let your loving-kindness descend upon us,
that with devoted hearts we may sing your praises
with the church on earth and the whole heavenly host,
and glorify you forever and ever.   [456]

Amen.

The service may continue with evening prayer, beginning with the psalm(s) on page 515.

Or, when an evening meal or other evening activity follows, the service may be concluded with:
   a brief lesson from scripture
   the Lord's Prayer
   an additional hymn (optional)
   a grace or blessing

EVENING PRAYER

When evening prayer begins with the service of light (pp. 505–513), the opening sentences and the evening hymn are omitted. The service proceeds with the psalm(s) on page 515.

OPENING SENTENCES

All may stand.

1

Ps. 24:34

Our help is in the name of the Lord,

who made heaven and earth.

Or

2

See Ps. 70:1

O God, come to our assistance.

O Lord, hasten to help us.

Or

3

Light and peace in Jesus Christ our Lord.

Thanks be to God.

And one of the following, or a seasonal alternative (pp. 524–543), is said:

1   *Dan. 2:22–23*

God reveals deep and mysterious things,
and knows what is hidden in darkness.
God is surrounded by light.
To you, O God, we give thanks and praise.

2   *Ps. 139:11–12*

I could ask the darkness to hide me
or the light around me to become night,
but even darkness is not dark for you,
and the night is as bright as the day;
for darkness is as light with you.

3   *Rev. 21:23–24*

The city of God has no need of sun or moon,
for the glory of God is its light,
and its lamp is the Lamb.
By its light shall the nations walk,
and the rulers of earth shall bring their treasures into it.

4   *Rev. 22:5*

In the city of God, night shall be no more;
they need no light of lamp or sun,
for the Lord God will be their light,
and they will reign forever and ever.

5   *Zech. 14:5c, 7, and 1 John 1:5*

God will come, and there shall be continuous day,
for at evening time there shall be light.
God is light;
in God there is no darkness at all.

6   *2 Cor. 4:6*

God who said, "Out of darkness the light shall shine!"
is the same God who made light shine in our hearts
to bring us the knowledge of God's glory
shining in the face of Christ.

7   *2 Sam. 22:29, 33*
You are my lamp, O Lord.
My God lightens my darkness.
This God is my strong refuge
and has made my way safe.

EVENING HYMN

> An evening hymn is sung.
>
> IF THE SERVICE OF LIGHT IS USED, THE SERVICE CONTINUES
> HERE FROM PAGE 513.
>
> All may be seated.

PSALM(S)

> One or more psalms (pp. 611–783) are sung or said.
>
> Silence for reflection follows each psalm.
>
> A psalm prayer may follow the silence.

SCRIPTURE READING

> At the conclusion of the reading of scripture (pp. 1050–1095), the reader
> may say:

The Word of the Lord.

Thanks be to God.

> Silence follows for reflection on the meaning of the scripture.
>
> The scripture may be briefly interpreted, or a nonbiblical reading may be
> read.

CANTICLE

The Canticle of Mary (Magnificat) or another canticle may be sung or said.

All may stand.

The Canticle of Mary

The Magnificat; Luke 1:46–55
PH 600; PS 161–163

Refrain: **My soul proclaims the greatness of the Lord, ***
my spirit rejoices in God my Savior.

R

My soul proclaims the greatness of the Lord,
my spirit rejoices in God my Savior, *
    for you, Lord, have looked with favor on your lowly servant.
From this day all generations will call me blessed: *
    you, the Almighty, have done great things for me
    and holy is your name.
You have mercy on those who fear you, *
    from generation to generation.   **R**

You have shown strength with your arm, *
    and scattered the proud in their conceit,
casting down the mighty from their thrones *
    and lifting up the lowly.
You have filled the hungry with good things, *
    and sent the rich away empty.   **R**

You have come to the aid of your servant Israel, *
    to remember the promise of mercy,
the promise made to our forebears, *
    to Abraham and his children for ever.   **R**

PRAYERS OF THANKSGIVING AND INTERCESSION

The prayers of thanksgiving and intercession may take the form of a litany (A) or of the prayers appointed for each day of the week (B).

A

The litany on pages 112–114 may be sung.

B

The following prayers may be used:

Ps. 141:2

Let my prayer rise before you as incense,

the lifting of my hands as an evening sacrifice.

If Psalm 141 has been previously sung, the following verses are used:

Ps. 25:1–2

To you, O Lord, I lift my soul.

O God, in you I trust.

One of the following, or other prayers of thanksgiving and intercession, are said:

1

Sunday

We lift our voices in prayers of praise, holy God, for you have lifted us to new life in Jesus Christ, and your blessings come in generous measure. Especially we thank you for

the privilege of worship and service in this congregation . . .

the good news of the gospel of Jesus Christ for us . . .

food and drink to share in the Lord's name . . .

our calling to discipleship. . . .

We hold up before you human needs, God of compassion, for you have come to us in Jesus Christ and shared our life so we may share his resurrection. Especially we pray for

the healing of those who are sick . . .

the comfort of the dying . . .

the renewal of those who despair . . .

the Spirit's power in the church. . . .   [457]

2

Monday

We rejoice in your generous goodness, O God, and celebrate your lavish gifts to us this day, for you have shown your love in giving Jesus Christ for the salvation of the world. Especially we give thanks for

the labors of those who have served us today . . .

friends with whom we have shared . . .

those whom we love and have loved us . . .

opportunities for our work to help others . . .

all beauty that delights us. . . .

Gracious God, we know you are close to all in need, and by our prayers for others we come closer to you. We are bold to claim for others your promises of new life in Jesus Christ, as we claim them for ourselves. Especially we pray for

> those in dangerous occupations . . .
> physicians and nurses . . .
> those who are ill or confined to nursing homes . . .
> those who mourn . . .
> the Roman Catholic Church. . . .   [458]

3

Tuesday

Eternal God, we thank you for being with us today, and for every sign of your truth and love in Jesus Christ. Especially we thank you for

> the gift of peace in Christ . . .
> reconciliation in our relationships . . .
> each new insight into your love . . .
> energy and courage to share your love . . .
> the ministries of the church. . . .

Gracious God, we remember in our own hearts the needs of others, that we may reach up to claim your love for them, and reach out to give your love in the name of Christ. Especially we pray for

> racial harmony and justice . . .
> those imprisoned . . .
> strangers we have met today . . .
> friends who are bereaved . . .
> Orthodox and Coptic churches. . . .   [459]

4

Wednesday

Give us your peace, O God, that we may rejoice in your goodness to us and to all your children, and be thankful for your love revealed in Jesus Christ. Especially we thank you for

> people who reveal your truth and righteousness . . .
> courage to be bold disciples . . .
> those who show hospitality . . .
> surprises that have blessed us . . .
> the unity of the church of Jesus Christ. . . .

Give us your peace, O God, that we may be confident of your care for us and all your children, as we remember the needs of others. Especially we pray for

> friends and relatives who are far away . . .
> neighbors in special need . . .
> those who suffer hunger and thirst . . .
> those who work at night while others sleep . . .
> Episcopal and Methodist churches. . . .   [460]

5

Thursday

We give you our praise and thanks, O God, for all gifts of love we have received from you, and for your persistent mercy in Jesus Christ. Especially we thank you for

    work we have accomplished pleasing to you . . .

    the faithful witness of Christian people . . .

    the example of righteousness we see in parents and teachers . . .

    the innocence and openness we see in children . . .

    all works of Christian compassion. . . .

We give you our cares and concerns, O God, because we know you are kind and care for your children in every circumstance. Especially we pray for

    those who struggle with doubt and despair . . .

    people afflicted with disease . . .

    those called to special ministries . . .

    people neglected or abused . . .

    Baptist, Disciples of Christ, and other free churches. . . .   [461]

6

Friday

Merciful God, we praise you that you give strength for every weakness, forgiveness for our failures, and new beginnings in Jesus Christ. Especially we thank you for

    the guidance of your spirit through this day . . .

    signs of new life and hope . . .

    people who have helped us . . .

    those who struggle for justice . . .

    expressions of love unexpected or undeserved. . . .

Almighty God, you know all needs before we speak our prayers, yet you welcome our concerns for others in Jesus Christ. Especially we pray for

    those who keep watch over the sick and dying . . .

    those who weep with the grieving . . .

    those who are without faith and cannot accept your love . . .

    the aged who are lonely, distressed or weak . . .

    Reformed, Presbyterian, and Lutheran churches. . . .   [462]

7

Saturday

God of glory, we praise you for your presence in our lives, and for all goodness that you shower upon your children in Jesus Christ. Especially we thank you for
 promises kept and hope for tomorrow . . .
 the enjoyment of friends . . .
 the wonders of your creation . . .
 love from our parents, our sisters and brothers, our spouses and children . . .
 pleasures of living. . . .
God of grace, we are one with all your children, for we are sisters and brothers of Jesus Christ, and we offer our prayers for all whom we love. Especially we pray for
 those we too often forget . . .
 people who have lost hope . . .
 victims of tragedy and disaster . . .
 those who suffer mental anguish . . .
 ecumenical councils and church agencies. . . .   [463]

> Individual prayers of thanksgiving and intercession may be offered.
>
> There may be silent prayer.
>
> The leader then says one of the following prayers, or a similar prayer. For seasonal alternatives see pages 524–543.

1

As you have made this day, O God,
you also make the night.
Give light for our comfort.
Come upon us with quietness and still our souls,
that we may listen for the whisper of your Spirit
and be attentive to your nearness in our dreams.
Empower us to rise again in new life
to proclaim your praise,
and show Christ to the world,
for he reigns forever and ever.   [464]

Amen.

2

Great God, you are one God,
and you bring together what is scattered
and mend what is broken.
Unite us with the scattered peoples of the earth
that we may be one family of your children.
Bind up all our wounds,
and heal us in spirit,
that we may be renewed as disciples
of Jesus Christ, our Master and Savior. [465]

Amen.

3

God of all who fear you,
make us one with all your saints
and with any who are in need.
Teach us to befriend the weak,
and welcome the outcast,
that we may serve the Lord Jesus Christ
and live to offer him glory.
In his holy name we pray. [466]

Amen.

4

God our shepherd,
you have brought us through this day
to a time of reflection and rest.
Calm our souls,
and refresh us with your peace.
Keep us close to Christ
and draw us closer to one another
in the bonds of his wondrous love.
We pray through Christ our Lord. [467]

Amen.

5

To you, O God
we give up the burdens of this day,
trusting your love and mercy.
To you, O God,
we surrender ourselves,
trusting our risen Lord to lead us always
in the way of peace,
today, tomorrow, and forever. [468]

Amen.

6

Protect your people, O God,
and keep us safe
until the coming of your new dawn
and the establishment of your righteous rule.
By your Holy Spirit,
stir up within us a longing
for the light of your new day,
and guide us by the radiance of Jesus Christ
your Son, our risen Lord.   [469]

Amen.

7

Abide with us, O Lord,
for evening comes and the day is almost over.
Abide with us,
for the days are hastening on
and we hasten with them.
Abide with us and with all your faithful people,
until the daystar rises and the morning light appears,
and we shall abide with you forever.   [470]

Amen.

All sing (musical settings: PH 571, 589, 590; PS 192–195) or say:

Or

Our Father in heaven,
hallowed be your name,
your kingdom come,
your will be done,
on earth as in heaven.
Give us today our daily bread.
Forgive us our sins
as we forgive those who sin against us.
Save us from the time of trial
and deliver us from evil.
For the kingdom, the power,
  and the glory are yours
now and forever.   Amen.

Our Father, who art in heaven,
hallowed be thy name,
thy kingdom come,
thy will be done,
on earth as it is in heaven.
Give us this day our daily bread;
and forgive us our debts,
as we forgive our debtors;
and lead us not into temptation,
but deliver us from evil.
For thine is the kingdom,
and the power, and the glory,
  forever.   Amen.

[HYMN OR SPIRITUAL]

DISMISSAL

The leader dismisses the people using one of the following:

1   *Phil. 4:23*

May the grace of the Lord Jesus Christ be with us all.

Amen.

Bless the Lord.

The Lord's name be praised.

2   *2 Thess. 3:16*

May the Lord, who is our peace,
give us peace at all times and in every way.

Amen.

Bless the Lord.

The Lord's name be praised.

3   *Phil. 4:7*

May the peace of God, which surpasses all understanding,
guard our hearts and minds in Christ Jesus.

Amen.

Bless the Lord.

The Lord's name be praised.

A sign of peace may be exchanged by all.

ALTERNATIVE TEXTS FOR SEASONS AND FESTIVALS: MORNING AND EVENING PRAYER

ADVENT

MORNING PRAYER

OPENING SENTENCES

1   *See Isa. 55:12*

The mountains and the hills shall break forth into singing,
and all the trees of the forest shall clap their hands.
For behold, our Lord and Ruler is coming to reign forever.
Alleluia!

2   *Ps. 85:10–11*

Love and faithfulness will meet;
justice and peace will embrace.
Faithfulness will spring from the earth
and justice will look down from heaven.

3

The Lord shall come when morning dawns,
and earth's dark night is past.
As the sentry waits for daybreak,
so my soul hopes for the Lord.

4

Like the sun in the morning sky,
the Savior of the world will come.
Like rain on the meadow,
he will descend.

Morning Hymn

Seasonal hymn (alternative to the morning psalm):

"Sleepers, Wake!" A Voice Astounds Us   PH 17

Canticle

While traditionally sung in morning prayer throughout the year,

Canticle of Zechariah (pp. 573–574) PH 601, 602; PS 158–160

is particularly appropriate when sung during Advent. Other canticles include:

Canticle of Thanksgiving (p. 580)	PS 175
Seek the Lord (pp. 580–581)	PS 176
The New Jerusalem (p. 581)	PS 177
A Canticle of Creation (pp. 584–585)	PS 180, 181
A Canticle of Praise	PS 182
The Desert Shall Blossom (pp. 579–580)	PH 18

Prayers of Thanksgiving and Intercession

The Litany for Advent—O Antiphons (pp. 166–167) is appropriate to use from December 17 through 22.

Prayer concluding thanksgiving and intercession

1

God of all wisdom,
our hearts yearn for the warmth of your love,
and our minds search for the light of your Word.
Increase our longing for Christ our Savior,
and strengthen us to grow in love,
that at the dawn of his coming
we may rejoice in his presence
and welcome the light of his truth.
This we ask in the name of Jesus Christ. [471]

Amen.

2

O Christ, splendor of the glory of God,
and perfect image of the Eternal One who begot you,
we praise you for the infinite love which sent you among us;
we confess you as the light and life of the world;
and we adore you as our Lord and our God,
now and forever. [472]

Amen.

3

Holy God,
the mystery of your eternal Word
took flesh among us
when Mary, without reserve, entrusted her life to you.
Strengthen us by the example of her humility,
that we may always be ready to do your will
and welcome Christ into our lives,
who lives and reigns forever and ever. [473]

Amen.

EVENING PRAYER

OPENING SENTENCES

1   *Isa. 40:5*

The glory of the Lord shall be revealed,
and all people shall see it together.

2   *See Isa. 45:8*

Drop down the dew from above, O heavens,
and let the clouds rain justice.
Let the earth's womb be opened,
and bring forth a Savior.

3   *Ps. 96:11, 13*

Let the heavens be glad and let the earth rejoice,
for the Lord comes to judge the earth,
to judge the world with justice
and the nations with truth.

4   *Matt. 3:2*

Repent, for the kingdom of heaven is at hand.

EVENING HYMN

Seasonal alternative to "Hymn to Christ the Light" (Phos Hilaron):

O Come, O Come, Emmanuel   PH 9

CANTICLE

While traditionally sung in evening prayer throughout the year,

Canticle of Mary (p. 575)   PH 600; PS 161–163

is particularly appropriate when sung during Advent. Other canticles include:

Christ, the Head of All Creation (p. 589)   PS 186
Jesus Christ Is Lord (p. 589)   PS 187

PRAYERS OF THANKSGIVING AND INTERCESSION

The Litany for Advent—O Antiphons (pp. 166–167) is appropriate to use from December 17 through 22.

Prayer concluding thanksgiving and intercession

1

God of the prophets,
you sent your messenger into the wilderness of Jordan
to prepare human hearts for the coming of your Son.
Help us to prepare for Christ's coming,
and to hear the good news and repent,
that we may be ready to welcome the Lord,
our Savior, Jesus Christ.   [474]

Amen.

2

God of hope and joy,
the day draws near when the glory of your Son
will brighten the night of the waiting world.
Let no sorrow hinder the joy
of those who seek him.
Let no sin obscure the vision of wisdom
seen by those who find him.
We ask this through Christ our Lord.   [475]

Amen.

3

God of grace,
ever faithful to your promises,
the earth rejoices in hope of the Savior's coming
and looks forward with longing
to his return at the end of time.
Prepare our hearts to receive him when he comes,
for he is Lord forever and ever.   [476]

Amen.

CHRISTMAS

MORNING PRAYER

OPENING SENTENCES

1   *Luke 2:14*

Glory to God in the highest,
and peace to God's people on earth.   Alleluia!

2   *Luke 2:10, 11*

Behold I bring you good news of a great joy;
for to you is born in the city of David
a Savior, who is Christ the Lord.

3   *John 1:14*

The Word became flesh and dwelt among us,
and we beheld his glory.   Alleluia!

MORNING HYMN

Seasonal hymn (alternative to the morning psalm):

O Morning Star, How Fair and Bright   PH 69
Break Forth, O Beauteous Heavenly Light   PH 26

CANTICLE

While traditionally sung in morning prayer throughout the year,

Canticle of Zechariah (pp. 573–574)   PH 601, 602; PS 158–160

is particularly appropriate when sung during Christmas. Other canticles include:

PRAYERS OF THANKSGIVING AND INTERCESSION

One of the litanies appointed for use during Christmas (pp. 178–180) may be used.

Prayer concluding thanksgiving and intercession

All-powerful and unseen God,
the coming of your light into the world
has brightened weary hearts with peace.
Teach us to proclaim the birth of your Son Jesus Christ,
who lives and reigns with you in the unity of the Holy Spirit,
one God, forever and ever.   [151]

Amen.

EVENING PRAYER

OPENING SENTENCES

1

Today Christ is born;
today salvation has appeared;
today angels are singing and archangels rejoicing;
today the just exult and say:
Glory to God in the highest.   Alleluia!

2   *1 John 4:9*

In this, O God, your love was revealed among us,
that you sent your only Son into the world
so that we might live through him.

EVENING HYMN

Seasonal alternatives to "Hymn to Christ the Light" (Phos Hilaron):

Of the Father's Love Begotten	PH 309
Lo, How a Rose E'er Blooming	PH 48

CANTICLE

While traditionally sung in evening prayer or prayer at the close of day throughout the year,

Canticle of Mary (p. 575)	PH 600; PS 161–163
Canticle of Simeon (p. 576)	PH 603–605; PS 164–166

are particularly appropriate when sung in evening prayer during Christmas. Other canticles include:

Christ, the Head of All Creation (p. 589)	PS 185
Jesus Christ Is Lord (p. 589)	PS 186

PRAYERS OF THANKSGIVING AND INTERCESSION

One of the litanies appointed for use during Christmas (pp. 178–180) may be used.

Prayer concluding thanksgiving and intercession

1

Eternal God,
in Jesus Christ your light shines in our darkness,
giving joy in sorrow
and comfort in loneliness.
Fill us with the mystery of your Word made flesh,
until our hearts overflow with praise and joy,
for he is the beginning and the end of all that exists,
living forevermore.   [478]

Amen.

2

O God,
you loved the world so much
that you gave your only Son for us.
Increase and strengthen our faith
and fix it firmly on the mystery of your Word made flesh,
that we may triumph over all evil
through Christ who reigns now and forever.   [479]

Amen.

Epiphany

Morning Prayer

Opening Sentences

1 *Isa. 60:1, 3, 6*

Arise, shine, for your light is come!
The glory of the Lord is risen upon you!
Nations shall come to your light,
and rulers to the brightness of your dawn.
They shall come from Sheba, bearing gold and incense,
singing the praise of God.

2

For Baptism of the Lord

Sealed with the sign of the Spirit,
Jesus rises from the waters.
The Baptizer knows him and foretells:
This is the Lamb of God
who takes away the sin of the world.

Morning Hymn

Seasonal hymn, alternative to the morning psalm:

Brightest and Best of the Stars of the Morning   PH 67

Canticle

Alternatives to Canticle of Zechariah:

We Praise You, O God (p. 577)	PH 460; PS 170, 171
Glory to God (p. 578)	PH 566, 575, 576; PS 173
The New Jerusalem (p. 581)	PS 177

PRAYERS OF THANKSGIVING AND INTERCESSION

The litany appointed for use on Epiphany (pp. 192–193) may be used.

Prayer concluding thanksgiving and intercession

Lord Jesus, unconquered light,
your power has dawned upon the world with transforming love.
Grant that we, who greet you on this joyful morning,
may be found faithful at the day's end,
and in that final day be gathered with all your children,
to that city whose light is the radiance of your face,
for you reign in splendor now and forever.   [480]

Amen.

EVENING PRAYER

OPENING SENTENCES

1

This is a holy day adorned with three mysteries:
Today a star leads the magi to the manger;
today water is made wine at the wedding;
today Christ is baptized by John in the Jordan to save us.
Alleluia!

2   *Mal. 1:11*

From the rising of the sun to its setting
my name is great among the nations,
and in every place incense is offered to my name,
and a pure offering;
for my name is great among the nations,
says the Lord of hosts.

EVENING HYMN

Seasonal alternatives to "Hymn to Christ the Light" (Phos Hilaron):

Let All Mortal Flesh Keep Silence	PH 5
What Star Is This, with Beams So Bright	PH 68

CANTICLE

Alternatives to Canticle of Mary:

Christ, the Head of All Creation (p. 589)   PS 185
Jesus Christ Is Lord (p. 589)   PS 186
The Mystery of Our Religion (p. 590)

PRAYERS OF THANKSGIVING AND INTERCESSION

The litany appointed for use on Baptism of the Lord (pp. 199–200) may be used.

Prayer concluding thanksgiving and intercession

1

Eternal Light,
you have shown us your glory in Christ, the Word made flesh.
Your light is strong,
your love is near.
Draw us beyond the limits which this world imposes,
to the life where the Spirit makes all life complete,
through Jesus Christ our Lord. [481]

Amen.

2

Almighty God,
who anointed Jesus at his baptism with the Holy Spirit,
and revealed him as your beloved Son:
Keep us, your children born of water and the Spirit,
faithful in your service,
that we may rejoice to be called children of God,
through the same Jesus Christ our Lord. [482]

Amen.

LENT

In daily prayer there is a tradition of using the Great Litany (pp. 787–791) as an alternative service on all Wednesdays and Fridays of Lent, beginning the Friday after Ash Wednesday and continuing until the Friday before Passion/Palm Sunday.

MORNING PRAYER

OPENING SENTENCES

1
Ps. 86:5–6

O Lord, you are kind and forgiving,
full of love to all who call on you.
Listen to my prayer, O Lord;
hear the cries of my pleading.

2
Ps. 86:11–12

Show me your way, O Lord,
that I may follow in your truth.
Teach me to revere your name,
and my whole heart will praise you.

3
Matt. 16:24

Jesus told his disciples:
If any want to become my followers,
let them deny themselves
and take up their cross and follow me.

4
Ps. 51:10

Create in me a clean heart, O God,
and renew a right spirit within me.

5

For Holy Week
1 Peter 2:24

Christ himself bore our sins in his body on the cross,
so that, free from sins, we might live to righteousness;
by his wounds we have been healed.

MORNING HYMN

Seasonal hymn, alternative to the morning psalm:

There's a Wideness in God's Mercy	PH 298
Holy Week: Ah, Holy Jesus	PH 93

CANTICLE

Alternatives to Canticle of Zechariah:

Seek the Lord (pp. 580–581)	PS 176
A Canticle of Penitence (pp. 585–586)	PS 183
We Praise You, O God (p. 577)	PH 460; PS 170, 171
Glory to God (p. 578)	PH 566, 575, 576; PS 173
The New Jerusalem (p. 581)	PS 177

PRAYERS OF THANKSGIVING AND INTERCESSION

The litany appointed for use during Lent (pp. 235–236) or the Intercession for Lent (pp. 236–237) may be used.

Prayer concluding thanksgiving and intercession

1

God of all joy,
fill our souls to overflowing
with the fullness of your grace.
In this season,
remind us of your triumph over the tragedy of the cross,
and your victory for us over the powers of sin and death,
so that we may reflect your glory
as disciples of Jesus Christ,
our risen Lord.   [483]

Amen.

2

God of love,
as you have given your life to us,
so may we live according to your holy will
revealed in Jesus Christ.
Make us bold to share your life,
and show your love,
in the power of your Holy Spirit.
Grant this through Jesus Christ our Redeemer and Lord.   [484]

Amen.

3

Take all our doubts and uncertainties, O God,
and fill us with such faith
that we may be confident of your love
and loyal in the service of him
who died and yet lives for us,
Jesus Christ the Lord.   [485]

Amen.

EVENING PRAYER

OPENING SENTENCES

1   *Ps. 51:17*

The sacrifice acceptable to God is a humble spirit;
a broken and contrite heart, O God,
you will not despise.

2   *Ps. 143:10*

Teach me to do your will,
for you are my God.

3   *Ps. 103:8*

You, O Lord, are full of compassion and mercy,
slow to anger, and rich in kindness.

4   *Rom. 5:8*

God shows such love for us
in that while we still were sinners
Christ died for us.

EVENING HYMN

Seasonal alternatives to "Hymn to Christ the Light" (Phos Hilaron):

Jesus, Thou Joy of Loving Hearts	PH 510, 511
O Sacred Head, Now Wounded	PH 98

CANTICLE

Alternatives to Canticle of Mary:

A Canticle of the Redeemed (p. 587)	PS 184
Jesus Christ Is Lord (p. 589)	PS 186
The Beatitudes (p. 590)	PS 188
Christ the Servant (p. 591)	PS 189

Maundy Thursday: A Canticle of Love (p. 588)   PS 187

PRAYERS OF THANKSGIVING AND INTERCESSION

The litany appointed for use during Lent (pp. 235–236) or the Intercession
for Lent (pp. 236–237) may be used.

Prayer concluding thanksgiving and intercession

1

Eternal God,
as we are baptized into the death of Jesus Christ,
so give us the grace of repentance
that we may pass through the grave with him
and be born again to eternal life,
for he is the One who was crucified, dead, and buried,
and rose again for us,
Jesus our Savior.   [486]

Amen.

2

Eternal God,
source and goal of all life,
lead us to life eternal
by the mighty love of Jesus Christ,
who suffered on the cross,
was raised from the dead,
and lifted into glory
where with outstretched arms
he welcomes the world in his strong and loving embrace.
In his holy name we pray,
now and forever.   [487]

Amen.

3

Lord Jesus Christ,
who stretched out your arms of love on the hard wood of the cross
that everyone might come within the reach of your saving embrace:
So clothe us in your Spirit
that we, reaching forth our hands in love,
may bring those who do not know you
to the knowledge and love of you;
for the honor of your name.   [488]

Amen.

EASTER

MORNING PRAYER

OPENING SENTENCES

1

Alleluia! Christ is risen!

Christ is risen indeed, Alleluia!

2   *1 Cor. 15:20*

Christ has been raised from the dead,
the first fruits of those who have fallen asleep.

3

Ascension   *Heb. 2:9*

We see Jesus,
who for a little while was made lower than the angels.
He is crowned with glory and honor. Alleluia!

MORNING HYMN

Seasonal hymn, alternative to the morning psalm:

Come, Ye Faithful, Raise the Strain	PH 114, 115
Ascension: At the Name of Jesus	PH 148

CANTICLE

Alternatives to Canticle of Zechariah:

We Praise You, O God (p. 577)	PH 460; PS 170, 171
Glory to God (p. 578)	PS 173
Canticle of Miriam and Moses (pp. 578–579)	PS 174
Canticle of David (p. 583)	
A Canticle of Creation (pp. 584–585)	PS 180, 181
A Canticle of Praise	PS 182

PRAYERS OF THANKSGIVING AND INTERCESSION

The Responsive Prayer for Easter (pp. 315–316) or the Litany for Easter
(pp. 316–317) may be used. The Litany for Ascension (pp. 333–334) may
be used on Ascension of the Lord.

Prayer concluding thanksgiving and intercession

1

God of mercy,
we no longer look for Jesus among the dead,
for he is alive and has become the Lord of life.
From the waters of death you raise us with him
and renew your gift of life within us.
Increase in our hearts and minds
the risen life we share with Christ,
and help us to grow as your people
toward the fullness of eternal life with you,
through Christ our Lord. [268]

Amen.

2

God of grace,
you cause the sun to rise
and chase away the shadows of death.
Each day you promise resurrection,
that we may be born again to new life
and overcome all that would hurt or destroy.
Fill us with the Holy Spirit,
that we may be alive again
with the power and the peace of Jesus Christ,
our risen Lord. [490]

Amen.

EVENING PRAYER

OPENING SENTENCES

1   *See Rom. 6:4–11*

In baptism, we were buried with Christ;
in baptism we were also raised with Christ.
Once we were spiritually dead;
now God has brought us life with Christ. Alleluia!

2   *1 Peter 1:3*

By God's great mercy
we have been born anew to a living hope
through the resurrection of Jesus Christ from the dead.
Blessed be God the Father of our Lord Jesus Christ.

Ascension

We have a great high priest who has passed through the heavens,
Jesus, the Son of God.
Let us with boldness approach the throne of grace.

EVENING HYMN

Seasonal alternatives to "Hymn to Christ the Light" (Phos Hilaron):

The Strife Is O'er	PH 119
Ascension: The Head That Once Was Crowned	PH 149

CANTICLE

Alternatives to Canticle of Mary:

A Canticle to the Lamb (p. 586)	PS 191
Canticle of the Redeemed (p. 587)	PS 184
Christ, the Head of All Creation (p. 589)	PS 185
Jesus Christ Is Lord (p. 589)	PS 186
Christ Our Passover (p. 591)	PS 190

PRAYERS OF THANKSGIVING AND INTERCESSION

The Responsive Prayer for Easter (pp. 315–316) or the Litany for Easter
(pp. 316–317) may be used. The Litany for Ascension (pp. 333–334) may
be used on Ascension of the Lord.

Prayer concluding thanksgiving and intercession

1

Stay with us, Lord Jesus,
for evening draws near.
Be our companion on the way
to set our hearts on fire with new hope.
Help us to recognize your presence among us
in the scriptures we read
and in the breaking of bread,
that our lives may worship you now and forever.   [491]

Amen.

Sovereign God,
the whole universe is within your reach,
and all things are ordered by your hand.
You have claimed us to be your people
and appointed us disciples of Jesus Christ, our risen Lord.
As you have protected our lives,
so preserve our souls
and keep before us always
the vision of our Redeemer
that we may see and follow
and give him glory forever and ever.   [492]

Amen.

3

You have shown your glory, O God,
in raising Jesus from the dead.
Raise us to new life in him,
and empower us to serve you.
May your words be in our mouths,
your strength in our arms,
and your love in our hearts,
that we may be worthy disciples
of Jesus Christ the living Lord.   [493]

Amen.

PENTECOST

MORNING PRAYER

OPENING SENTENCES

Acts 1:8

You shall receive power
when the Holy Spirit has come upon you,
and you shall be my witnesses.

MORNING HYMN

Seasonal hymn, alternative to the morning psalm:

Pentecost: Come, Holy Spirit, Heavenly Dove   PH 126

CANTICLE

Alternatives to Canticle of Zechariah:

We Praise You, O God (p. 577)   PH 460; PS 170, 171
Glory to God (p. 578)   PS 173
Canticle of Miriam and Moses (pp. 578–579)   PS 174
God's Chosen One (p. 579)
The Spirit of the Lord (p. 582)

PRAYERS OF THANKSGIVING AND INTERCESSION

One of the litanies appointed for Pentecost (pp. 340–343) may be used.

Prayer concluding thanksgiving and intercession

1

True and only Light,
from whom comes every good gift,
send your Spirit into our lives
with the power of a mighty wind.
Open the horizons of our minds
by the flame of your wisdom.
Loosen our tongues to sing your praise,
for only in your Spirit
can we tell of your glory
and acclaim Jesus as Lord.   [314]

Amen.

2

God, our creator,
as in the beginning you formed us out of the dust of the earth
and breathed us into life,
so now, by your Spirit, breathe into us new life.
As at Pentecost your Spirit fell upon waiting disciples,
and empowered them as your faithful witnesses,
now, by your Spirit, fill us with joy and boldness.
May the power of your Spirit transform us,
the prompting of your Spirit lead us,
and the gifts of your Spirit mark our lives,
now and forever.   [494]

Amen.

EVENING PRAYER

OPENING SENTENCES

Rom. 5:5

God's love has been poured into our hearts
through the Holy Spirit that has been given to us.

EVENING HYMN

Seasonal alternative to "Hymn to Christ the Light" (Phos Hilaron):

Pentecost: Come, Holy Spirit, Our Souls Inspire   PH 125

CANTICLE

Alternative to Canticle of Mary:

Canticle of the Redeemed (p. 587)   PS 184
A Canticle for Pentecost (pp. 587–588)

PRAYERS OF THANKSGIVING AND INTERCESSION

One of the litanies appointed for Pentecost (pp. 340–343) may be used.

Prayer concluding thanksgiving and intercession

Holy God,
who suddenly appeared upon your children like the flaring of fire
and illumined a multitude with a common mind:
so fill us, and all your faithful,
with the Holy Spirit,
that in a blaze of truth
we may know that we are your sons and daughters,
one family of faith,
one body given life through Christ our Head,
who reigns with you and the Holy Spirit
forever and ever.   [495]

Amen.

Opening Sentences
[Hymn]
Psalm
   Psalm
   Silent Prayer
   Psalm Prayer
Scripture Reading
   Silent Reflection
Prayers of the People
   Individual Prayers
   Concluding Prayer
   Lord's Prayer
[Hymn or Canticle]
Dismissal
   [Sign of Peace]

When a person is worshiping alone, or in a family group, or when circumstances call for an abbreviated order, the following is suggested:

Psalm
Scripture Reading
   Silent Reflection
Prayers of Thanksgiving and Intercession

MIDDAY PRAYER

> All may stand.

Our help is in the name of the Lord,
who made heaven and earth.   *Ps. 124:8*

> And one of the following:

1   *Mal. 1:11*

From the rising of the sun to its setting
my name is great among the nations,
says the Lord of hosts.

Praise the Lord.
The name of the Lord be praised.

2   *Deut. 32:11*

Like an eagle teaching her young to fly,
catching them safely on her spreading wings,
the Lord kept Israel from falling.

Praise the Lord.
The Lord's name be praised.

3   *Isa. 40:31*

Those who trust in the Lord for help
will find their strength renewed.
They will rise on wings like eagles;
they will run and not get weary;
they will walk and not grow weak.

Praise the Lord.
The Lord's name be praised.

[HYMN]

> Following the hymn, all may sit.

PSALM

One of the following, or another psalm, is sung or said:

Psalm 19:1–6	PH 166	PS 12
Psalm 67	PH 202	PS 59, 60
Psalm 113	PH 225, 226	PS 113
Psalm 119:97–104		PS 123
Psalm 119:129–136		PS 124
Psalm 121	PH 234	PS 125
Psalm 122	PH 235	PS 126
Psalm 124	PH 236	PS 128
Psalm 126	PH 237	PS 130, 131
Psalm 127	PH 238	PS 132
Psalm 128	PH 239	PS 133
Psalm 130	PH 240	PS 134

Silence for reflection follows each psalm. A psalm prayer may follow the silence.

SCRIPTURE READING

At the conclusion of the reading from scripture (pp. 1050–1095), the reader may say:

The Word of the Lord.

Thanks be to God

Silence may follow for reflection on the meaning of the scripture.

PRAYERS OF THE PEOPLE

All may stand.

INDIVIDUAL PRAYERS

There may be a brief time of prayer, spoken and silent, in which the promises of God are claimed for individual and corporate needs and concerns.

CONCLUDING PRAYER

The leader concludes with one of the following or a similar prayer:

1

Eternal God,
send your Holy Spirit into our hearts,
to direct and rule us according to your will,

to comfort us in all our afflictions,
to defend us from all error,
and to lead us into all truth;
through Jesus Christ our Lord. [496]

Amen.

2

God, our creator,
you have given us work to do
and call us to use our talents for the good of all.
Guide us as we work,
and teach us to live
in the Spirit who made us your sons and daughters,
in the love that made us sisters and brothers,
through Jesus Christ our Lord. [497]

Amen.

3

Enable us, O God,
to do all things as unto you;
that small things may be filled with greatness,
and great things may be crowned with humility;
through Jesus Christ our Lord. [498]

Amen.

4

Eternal God,
your hand shaped our lives by grace
and your hand rescued us from sin by love.
May your hand guide us through this day,
shielding us from all evil,
strengthening us to do justice and love,
in Jesus Christ our Lord. [499]

Amen.

5

New every morning is your love,
great God of light,
and all day long you are working for good in the world.
Stir up in us the desire to serve you,
to live peacefully with our neighbors,
and to devote each day to your Son,
our Savior, Jesus Christ the Lord. [500]

Amen.

6

Noon

Blessed Savior,
at this hour you hung upon the cross,
stretching out your loving arms.
Grant that all the peoples of the earth
may be drawn to your redeeming love;
for your kingdom's sake.   [501]

Amen.

7

Noon

God of mercy,
this midday moment of rest is your welcome gift.
Bless the work we have begun,
make good its defects,
and let us finish it in a way that pleases you.
Grant this through Christ our Lord.   [502]

Amen.

LORD'S PRAYER

All sing (musical settings: PH 571, 589, 590; PS 192–195) or say:

Or

Our Father in heaven,	**Our Father, who art in heaven,**
hallowed be your name,	**hallowed be thy name,**
your kingdom come,	**thy kingdom come,**
your will be done,	**thy will be done,**
on earth as in heaven.	**on earth as it is in heaven.**
Give us today our daily bread.	**Give us this day our daily bread;**
Forgive us our sins	**and forgive us our debts,**
as we forgive those who sin against us.	**as we forgive our debtors;**
Save us from the time of trial	**and lead us not into temptation,**
and deliver us from evil.	**but deliver us from evil.**
For the kingdom, the power,	**For thine is the kingdom,**
and the glory are yours	**and the power, and the glory,**
now and forever. Amen.	**forever. Amen.**

[HYMN OR CANTICLE]

DISMISSAL

> The leader concludes:

Phil. 4:9

The God of peace be with us.

Amen.

Bless the Lord.

The Lord's name be praised.

> A sign of peace may be exchanged by all.

AN OUTLINE OF PRAYER AT THE CLOSE OF DAY

Opening Sentences
Hymn
Prayer of Confession
Psalm
    Psalm
    Silent Prayer
    [Psalm Prayer]
Scripture Reading
    Silent Reflection
Prayer
    Prayers
    Lord's Prayer
Canticle of Simeon
Dismissal
    [Sign of Peace]

Prayer at the Close of Day

Opening Sentences

All may stand.

See Ps. 70:11

O God, come to our assistance.

O Lord, hasten to help us.

The Lord grant us a restful night and peace at the last.

Amen.

Hymn

A hymn appropriate to the end of the day may be sung.

Prayer of Confession

Almighty God, Maker of all things,

have mercy on us.

Jesus Christ, Redeemer of the world,

have mercy on us.

Holy Spirit, Giver of life,

have mercy on us.

After a brief silence for self-examination, one of the following prayers is said:

1

Merciful God,
we confess that we have sinned against you
in thought, word, and deed,
by what we have done,
and by what we have left undone.
We have not loved you
with our whole heart and mind and strength;
we have not loved our neighbors as ourselves.

In your mercy forgive what we have been,
help us amend what we are,
and direct what we shall be,
so that we may delight in your will
and walk in your ways
to the glory of your holy name.   [49]

2

Eternal God,
in whom we live and move and have our being,
your face is hidden from us by our sins,
and we forget your mercy in the blindness of our hearts.
Cleanse us from all our offenses,
and deliver us from proud thoughts and vain desires.
With lowliness and meekness
may we draw near to you,
confessing our faults,
confiding in your grace,
and finding in you our refuge and strength;
through Jesus Christ your Son.   [67]

3

Leader:
I confess to God Almighty,
before the whole company of heaven,
and to you, my brothers and sisters,
that I have sinned by my own fault,
in thought, word, and deed;
wherefore I pray God Almighty to have mercy on me,
forgive me all my sins,
and bring me to everlasting life.   [503]

All:
May Almighty God have mercy on you,
pardon and deliver you from all your sins
and give you time to amend your life.

Leader:
Amen.

All:

I confess to God Almighty,
before the whole company of heaven,
and to you, my brothers and sisters,
that I have sinned by my own fault,
in thought, word, and deed;
wherefore I pray God Almighty to have mercy on me,
forgive me all my sins,
and bring me to everlasting life.   [503]

Leader:

May Almighty God have mercy on you,
pardon and deliver you from all your sins
and give you time to amend your life.

All:

Amen.

All may sit.

PSALM

One of the following psalms is sung or said:

Psalm 4	PH 160	PS 3
Psalm 23	PH 170–175	PS 18–20
Psalm 33:1–12 or 33:13–22	PH 185	PS 30, 31
Psalm 34:1–10 or 34:11–22		PS 32, 33
Psalm 91:1–2, 4, 9–16	PH 212	PS 85
Psalm 121	PH 234	PS 125
Psalm 134	PH 242	PS 138
Psalm 136:1–9, 23–26	PH 243	PS 139
Psalm 139:1–12	PH 248	PS 142, 143

Silence for reflection follows each psalm.

A psalm prayer may follow the silence.

SCRIPTURE READING

One of the following is read:

1   *Matt. 11:28–30*

[Jesus said:] Come to me, all you that are weary and are carrying heavy burdens, and I will give you rest. Take my yoke upon you, and learn from me; for I am gentle and humble in heart, and you will find rest for your souls. For my yoke is easy, and my burden is light.

2   *1 Thess. 5:23*

May the God of peace . . . sanctify you entirely; and may your spirit and soul and body be kept sound and blameless at the coming of our Lord Jesus Christ.

3   *Matt. 6:31–34*

Do not worry, saying, "What will we eat?" or "What will we drink?" or "What will we wear?" For it is the Gentiles who strive for all these things. But strive first for the kingdom of God and his righteousness, and all these things will be given to you as well.

4   *2 Cor. 4:6–10*

It is the God who said, "Let light shine out of darkness," who has shone in our hearts to give the light of the knowledge of the glory of God in the face of Jesus Christ.

5   *1 John 4:18–20*

There is no fear in love, but perfect love casts out fear; for fear has to do with punishment, and whoever fears has not reached perfection in love. We love because he first loved us. Those who say, "I love God," and hate their brothers or sisters, are liars; for those who do not love a brother or sister whom they have seen, cannot love God whom they have not seen.

6   *Rev. 22:3c–5*

[The servants of the Lamb] will worship him; they will see his face, and his name will be on their foreheads. And there will be no more night; they need no light of lamp or sun, for the Lord God shall be their light, and they will reign forever and ever.

7 *John 14:27*

[Jesus said:] Peace I leave with you; my peace I give to you. I do not give to you as the world gives. Do not let your hearts be troubled, and do not let them be afraid.

8 *Rom. 8:38–39*

I am convinced that neither death, nor life, nor angels, nor rulers, nor things present, nor things to come, nor powers, nor height, nor depth, nor anything else in all creation, will be able to separate us from the love of God in Christ Jesus our Lord.

9 *Deut. 6:4–7*

Hear, O Israel: The Lord is our God, the Lord alone. You shall love the Lord your God with all your heart, and with all your soul, and with all your might. Keep these words that I am commanding you today in your heart. Recite them to your children and talk about them when you are at home and when you are away, when you lie down and when you rise.

At the conclusion of the reading the leader may add:

The Word of the Lord.

Thanks be to God.

Silent reflection.

PRAYER

All may stand. A or B is sung or said:

A *See Ps. 31:5; 17:8, 15*

Into your hands, O Lord, I commend my spirit;

for you have redeemed me, O Lord, O God of truth.

Keep us, O Lord, as the apple of your eye;

hide us under the shadow of your wings.

In righteousness I shall see you;

when I awake your presence shall give me joy.

Or

I will lie down in peace and take my rest,

for in God alone I dwell unafraid.

One of the following prayers is then said:

1

O Lord, support us all the day long
until the shadows lengthen
and the evening comes,
and the busy world is hushed,
and the fever of life is over,
and our work is done.
Then, in your mercy,
grant us a safe lodging,
and a holy rest,
and peace at the last;
through Jesus Christ our Lord.   [504]

Amen.

2

O God,
you have designed this wonderful world,
and know all things good for us.
Give us such faith
that, by day and by night,
at all times and in all places,
we may without fear
entrust those who are dear to us
to your never-failing love,
in this life
and in the life to come;
through Jesus Christ our Lord.   [505]

Amen.

3

Keep watch, dear Lord,
with those who work or watch
or weep this night,
and give your angels charge over those who sleep.

Tend the sick, Lord Christ;
give rest to the weary,
bless the dying,
soothe the suffering,
pity the afflicted,
shield the joyous;
and all for your love's sake.   [506]

Amen.

4

O God,
who appointed the day for labor
and the night for rest:
Grant that we may rest in peace and quietness
during the coming night
so that tomorrow
we may go forth to our appointed labors.
Take us into your holy keeping,
that no evil may befall us
nor any ill come near our home.
When at last our days are ended
and our work is finished,
grant that we may depart in your peace,
in the sure hope of that glorious kingdom
where there is day without night,
light without darkness,
and life without shadow of death forever;
through Jesus Christ,
the Light of the world.   [507]

Amen.

5

Visit this place, O Lord,
and drive from it all snares of the enemy;
let your holy angels dwell with us
to preserve us in peace;
and let your blessing be upon us always,
through Jesus Christ our Lord.   [508]

Amen.

6

Eternal God,
the hours of both day and night are yours,
and to you the darkness is no threat.
Be present, we pray,
with those who labor in these hours of night,
especially those who watch and work on behalf of others.
Grant them diligence in their watching,
faithfulness in their service,
courage in danger,
and competence in emergencies.
Help them to meet the needs of others
with confidence and compassion;
through Jesus Christ our Lord.   [509]

Amen.

7

O God our Creator,
by whose mercy and might
the world turns safely into darkness
and returns again to light:
We give into your hands our unfinished tasks,
our unsolved problems,
and our unfulfilled hopes,
knowing that only those things which you bless will prosper.
To your great love and protection
we commit each other
and all for whom we have prayed,
knowing that you alone are our sure defender,
through Jesus Christ our Lord.   [510]

Amen.

8

Send your peace into our hearts, O Lord,
at the evening hour,
that we may be contented with your mercies of this day,
and confident of your protection for this night;
and now, having forgiven others,
even as you forgive us,
may we have a pure comfort
and a healthful rest
within the shelter of this home;
through Jesus Christ our Savior.   [511]

Amen.

9

Be our light in the darkness, O Lord,
and in your great mercy
defend us from all perils and dangers of this night;
for the love of your only Son,
our Savior Jesus Christ.   [512]

Amen.

10

Be present, merciful God,
and protect us through the silent hours of this night,
so that we who are wearied
by the changes and chances of this fleeting world
may rest in your eternal changelessness;
through Jesus Christ our Lord.   [513]

Amen.

11

Merciful God,
give our bodies restful sleep
and let the work we have done today
bear fruit in eternal life.
We ask this through Christ our Lord.   [514]

Amen.

12

Eternal and everlasting God,
in the growing quietness of the evening
and the deepening shadows of the night,
grant us sleep and rest.
With the stilling of the day's doings,
and the end of coming and going about us,
make us to be sleepy with heavy eyes and tired limbs.
As your creatures are lying down in the wood,
as the bird is quiet in its nest
and the wild thing in its hole,
as the stream is still in its bed
reflecting the great expanse of stars above,
may we in our sleep reflect our confidence in you,
and our assurance in your constant peace.
In our sleep give us that deeper communion of our souls
with you who restores unto health.
For your name's sake.   [515]

Amen.

All sing (musical settings: PH 571, 589, 590; PS 192–195) or say:

Or

Our Father in heaven,	**Our Father, who art in heaven,**
hallowed be your name,	**hallowed be thy name,**
your kingdom come,	**thy kingdom come,**
your will be done,	**thy will be done,**
on earth as in heaven.	**on earth as it is in heaven.**
Give us today our daily bread.	**Give us this day our daily bread;**
Forgive us our sins	**and forgive us our debts,**
as we forgive those who sin against us.	**as we forgive our debtors;**
Save us from the time of trial	**and lead us not into temptation,**
and deliver us from evil.	**but deliver us from evil.**
For the kingdom, the power,	**For thine is the kingdom,**
and the glory are yours	**and the power, and the glory,**
now and forever. Amen.	**forever. Amen.**

CANTICLE

The Canticle of Simeon (Nunc Dimittis) may be sung or said.

Canticle of Simeon   *Nunc Dimittis; Luke 2:29–32*
                               PH 603–605; PS 164–166

Refrain: **Guide us waking, O Lord,**
           and guard us sleeping; *
           that awake we may watch with Christ,
           and asleep rest in his peace.

R

Now, Lord, you let your servant go in peace: *
    your word has been fulfilled.
My own eyes have seen the salvation *
    which you have prepared in the sight of every people:
a light to reveal you to the nations *
    and the glory of your people Israel.   **R**

DISMISSAL

May Almighty God bless, preserve, and keep us,
this night and forevermore.

Amen.

Bless the Lord.

The Lord's name be praised.

A sign of peace may be exchanged.

An Outline of Vigil of the Resurrection

For Saturday evening, the Eve of the Lord's Day

Opening Sentences
Evening Hymn: Hymn to Christ the Light (Phos Hilaron)
Thanksgiving for Light
Psalm 118
   Silent Prayer
   Psalm Prayer
The Resurrection Gospel
   Psalm 150
   Reading of a Gospel account of the resurrection
Thanksgiving for Our Baptism
Canticle
   Canticle of Miriam and Moses
      or
   We Praise You, O God
Prayer
Dismissal
   [Sign of Peace]

VIGIL OF THE RESURRECTION

For Saturday evening, the Eve of the Lord's Day

This service is for use late Saturday evening, as an alternative to Evening Prayer.

It takes place at the font, which should be filled with water, or around a container of water.

The room should be dimly lit. The paschal candle or another suitable candle or lamp may be lit.

Since the service is brief, all may stand throughout the service.

OPENING SENTENCES

One of the following is sung or said:

1   *See John 8:12; 1:5*

Jesus Christ is the light of the world

the light no darkness can overcome.

Or

2

Light and peace in Jesus Christ our Lord.

Thanks be to God.

EVENING HYMN

Hymn to Christ the Light

Phos Hilaron
PH 548, 549; PS 167–169

As the hymn is sung, additional candles may be lighted from the flame of
the paschal candle.

O radiant Light, O Sun divine,
of God the Father's deathless face,
O image of the Light sublime,
that fills the heavenly dwelling place.

O Son of God, the source of life,
praise is your due by night and day.
Our happy lips must raise the strain
of your esteemed and splendid name.

Lord Jesus Christ, as daylight fades,
as shine the lights of eventide,
we praise the Father with the Son,
the Spirit blest and with them one.

THANKSGIVING FOR LIGHT

The Lord be with you.

And also with you.

Let us give thanks to the Lord our God.

It is right to give our thanks and praise.

The leader continues:

We praise and thank you, O God,
through your Son, Jesus Christ our Lord.
Through him you have enlightened us
by revealing the Light that never fades,
for death has been destroyed
and radiant life is everywhere restored.
What was promised is fulfilled;
we have been joined to God
through renewed life in the Spirit of the risen Lord.

Glory and praise to you, through Jesus your Son,
who lives and reigns with you and the Holy Spirit,
in the kingdom of light eternal,
forever and ever.   [516]

Amen.

Or

We praise and glorify you, Lord God,
for Christ, our life, is risen
and has conquered sin and death.
He has broken the chains that bind us
and freed us to live in his kingdom of light.

May Christ enlighten the hearts of all who believe.
May Christ transform this world that longs to see him,
enlightening the hearts of all who believe,
and restore all creation to its rightful place.

Glory, praise, thanksgiving, and blessing to you, O God,
victor over sin and death,
now and forever.   [517]

Amen.

Psalm 118

Psalm 118:1–4, 14–21; or Psalm 118:22–29 is sung or said:

Psalm 118:1–4, 14–21   Tone 3; PH 231; PS 118–120

Refrain: Give thanks to God, *
whose love endures forever.

R

¹ Give thanks to the LORD, who is good, *
   whose mercy endures forever.

² **Let Israel now proclaim, ***
   "The mercy of the LORD endures forever."

³ Let the house of Aaron now proclaim, *
   "The mercy of the LORD endures forever."

⁴ **Let those who fear the LORD now proclaim, ***
   "The mercy of the LORD endures forever."   R

14 The LORD is my strength and my song *
   and has become my salvation.

15 **There is a sound of exultation and victory ***
   in the tents of the righteous:

16 "The right hand of the LORD has triumphed! *
   the right hand of the LORD is exalted!
   the right hand of the LORD has triumphed!"

17 **I shall not die, but live, ***
   and declare the works of the LORD.

18 The LORD has punished me sorely *
   but did not hand me over to death.   **R**

19 **Open for me the gates of righteousness; ***
   I will enter them;
   I will offer thanks to the LORD.

20 "This is the gate of the LORD; *
   those who are righteous may enter."

21 **I will give thanks to you, for you answered me ***
   and have become my salvation.   R

Or

Psalm 118:22–29   Tone 3; PH 232; PS 120

Refrain: **This is the day the Lord has made. ***
            Alleluia! Alleluia!

22 The same stone which the builders rejected *
   has become the chief cornerstone.

23 **This is the LORD's doing, ***
   and it is marvelous in our eyes.

24 On this day the LORD has acted; *
   we will rejoice and be glad in it.   **R**

25 **Hosanna, LORD, hosanna! ***
   LORD, send us now success.

26 Blessed is the one who comes in the name of the LORD; *
   we bless you from the house of the LORD.

27 **God is the LORD, who has shined upon us; ***
   form a procession with branches up to the horns of the altar.

²⁸ "You are my God, and I will thank you; *
you are my God, and I will exalt you."

²⁹ **Give thanks to the L**ORD**, who is good; ***
whose mercy endures forever.   R

> After the psalm, the leader says:

Let us pray.

> Pause for silent prayer.

Almighty God,
by raising Christ your Son,
you conquered the power of death
and opened for us the way to eternal life.
Let our celebration this night
raise us up and renew our lives
by the Spirit who lives within us.
Grant this through our Lord Jesus Christ, your Son,
who lives and reigns with you and the Holy Spirit,
one God, forever and ever.   [518]
Amen.

THE RESURRECTION GOSPEL

Psalm 150   Tone 1 or 3; PH 258; PS 157

Refrain: Praise the Lord. Praise the Lord.*
Praise the name of the Lord.

R

¹ Hallelujah!
Praise God in the holy temple; *
give praise in the firmament of heaven.

² **Praise God who is mighty in deed; ***
give praise for God's excellent greatness.   R

³ Praise God with the blast of the ram's-horn; *
give praise with lyre and harp.

4 **Praise God with timbrel and dance; ***
give praise with strings and pipe.

5 Praise God with resounding cymbals; *
give praise with loud-clanging cymbals.

6 **Let everything that has breath ***
praise the LORD.
Hallelujah!   R

One of the following accounts of the resurrection is then read:

Matt. 28:1–10, 16–20	Luke 24:13–35	John 20:19–31
Mark 16:1–7	Luke 24:36–53	John 21:1–14
Mark 16:9–20	John 20:1–10	
Luke 23:55–24:9	John 20:11–18	

At the conclusion of the reading of scripture, the reader may say:

The gospel of the Lord.

Praise to you, O Christ.

Silence follows for reflection on the meaning of the scripture.

The scripture may be briefly interpreted.

THANKSGIVING FOR OUR BAPTISM

The congregation may gather at the font or around a container of water
where thanks may be offered in these or similar words.

The Lord be with you.

And also with you.

Let us give thanks to the Lord our God.

It is right to give our thanks and praise.

We give you thanks, Eternal God,
for you nourish and sustain all living things
by the gift of water.

In the beginning of time,
your Spirit moved over the watery chaos,
calling forth order and life.

In the time of Noah,
you destroyed evil by the waters of the flood,
giving righteousness a new beginning.

You led Israel out of slavery,
through the waters of the sea,
into the freedom of the promised land.

In the waters of Jordan
Jesus was baptized by John
and anointed with your Spirit.
By the baptism of his own death and resurrection,
Christ set us free from sin and death,
and opened the way to eternal life.

We thank you, O God, for the water of baptism.
In it we were buried with Christ in his death.
From it we were raised to share in his resurrection.
Through it we were reborn by the power of the Holy Spirit.

Therefore in joyful obedience to your Son,
we celebrate our fellowship in him in faith.
We pray that all who have passed through the water of baptism
may continue forever in the risen life
of Jesus Christ our Savior.
To him, to you, and to the Holy Spirit,
be all honor and glory, now and forever.   [426]
Amen.

      One of the following may be used:

1

      The leader may place his or her hand into the water, lift up some water, let
      it fall back into the font (or container of water), and then make the sign of
      the cross over the people, while saying:

Remember your baptism and be thankful.
In the name of the Father and of the Son and of the Holy Spirit.
Amen.

All approach the water. Each person dips a hand into the water and may make the sign of the cross, remembering his or her baptism.

During the ritual the Canticle of Miriam and Moses or "We Praise You, O God" (Te Deum Laudamus) is sung.

CANTICLE

Canticle of Miriam and Moses   *Ex. 15:1, 2, 11, 13, 17–18*

PS 174

Refrain: **Strong and unfailing is your love.** *
Alleluia! Alleluia!

R

I will sing to the LORD, for the LORD has triumphed gloriously; *
the horse and its rider have been thrown into the sea.
The LORD is my strength and my song; *
and has become my salvation.   R

You are my God, I will praise you, *
the God of my people, I exalt you.
Who among the gods, O LORD, is like you; *
who is like you, majestic in holiness,
Who among the gods, O LORD, is like you; *
awesome in splendor, doing wonders?   R

With unfailing love you led the people you redeemed; *
in your strength, you guided them to your holy dwelling.
You brought them in and planted them on your mountain, *
the place, O LORD, you chose for your dwelling,
the sanctuary, O LORD, your hands established. *
You, LORD, will reign forever and ever.   R

Or

We Praise You, O God   *Te Deum Laudamus*

PH 460; PS 170, 171

We praise you, O God,
we acclaim you as Lord,
all creation worships you,
Father everlasting.

To you, all angels, all the powers of heaven,
the cherubim and seraphim, sing in endless praise:
Holy, holy, holy Lord, God of power and might,
heaven and earth are full of your glory.

The glorious company of apostles praise you.
The noble fellowship of prophets praise you.
The white-robed army of martyrs praise you.

Throughout the world the holy church acclaims you;
Father, of majesty unbounded,
your true and only Son, worthy of all praise,
the Holy Spirit, advocate and guide.

You, Christ, are the king of glory,
the eternal Son of the Father.
When you took our flesh to set us free
you humbly chose the Virgin's womb.

You overcame the sting of death
and opened the kingdom of heaven to all believers.

You are seated at God's right hand in glory.
We believe that you will come, and be our judge.

Come then, Lord, and help your people,
bought with the price of your own blood,
and bring us with your saints
to glory everlasting.

PRAYER

To our God belong victory, glory, and power,

for right and justice are God's judgments.

Praise our God, all you who serve God.

You who revere God, great and small.

Let us rejoice and triumph and give God praise.

The time has come for the wedding feast of the Lamb!

O God who brought your people out of slavery with a mighty hand,
strengthen us to take our stand with you
beside the oppressed of the world,
that in the victory of Christ
every fetter of body, mind, and spirit may be broken,
and the whole human family, restored to your image,
may sing your praise in joy, freedom and peace;
through the same Jesus Christ our Lord.   [519]

Amen. Alleluia!

DISMISSAL

May God the Father, who raised Christ Jesus from the dead,
continually show us loving kindness.

Amen.

May God the Son, victor over sin and death,
grant us a share in the joy of his resurrection.

Amen.

May God the Spirit, giver of light and peace,
renew our hearts in love.

Amen.

May almighty God, the Father, the Son, and the Holy Spirit,
continue to bless us.

Amen. Alleluia!

A sign of peace may be exchanged.

Canticles and Ancient Hymns: Texts

The texts of the canticles which are pointed may be sung to psalm tone B on pages 601–608. The refrains displayed with the canticles may also be sung to the tone selected. See page 600 for a description of singing with pointed texts.

1

Canticle of Zechariah   *Benedictus; Luke 1:68–79*

PH 601, 602; PS 158–160

Refrain: **You have come to your people ***
          and set them free.

          Or

          In the tender compassion of our God *
          the dawn from on high shall break upon us.

R

Blessed are you, Lord, the God of Israel; *
   you have come to your people and set them free.
You have raised up for us a mighty Savior, *
   born of the house of your servant David.   **R**

Through your holy prophets, you promised of old
to save us from our enemies, *
   from the hands of all who hate us,
to show mercy to our forebears, *
   and to remember your holy covenant.   **R**

This was the oath you swore to our father Abraham: *
   to set us free from the hands of our enemies,
free to worship you without fear, *
   holy and righteous before you,
   all the days of our life.   **R**

And you, child, shall be called the prophet of the Most High, *
    for you will go before the Lord to prepare the way,
to give God's people knowledge of salvation *
    by the forgiveness of their sins.   **R**

In the tender compassion of our God *
    the dawn from on high shall break upon us,
to shine on those who dwell in darkness and the shadow of death, *
    and to guide our feet into the way of peace.   **R**

Alternative seasonal refrains:

1

For Advent

The Lord proclaims: Repent, *
the kingdom of God is upon you. Alleluia!

2

For Christmas–Epiphany

You have raised up for us a mighty Savior, *
born of the house of David. Alleluia!

3

For Lent

God has given us knowledge of salvation *
by the forgiveness of our sins.

4

For Easter

The Lord, the God of Israel, has set us free. *
Alleluia! Alleluia!

Canticle of Mary   *Magnificat; Luke 1:46–55*

PH 600; PS 161–163

Refrain: **My soul proclaims the greatness of the Lord;***
my spirit rejoices in God my Savior.

R

My soul proclaims the greatness of the Lord,
my spirit rejoices in God my Savior, *
for you, Lord, have looked with favor on your lowly servant.
From this day all generations will call me blessed: *
you, the Almighty, have done great things for me
and holy is your name.
You have mercy on those who fear you, *
from generation to generation.   **R**

You have shown strength with your arm, *
and scattered the proud in their conceit,
casting down the mighty from their thrones *
and lifting up the lowly.
You have filled the hungry with good things, *
and sent the rich away empty.   **R**

You have come to the aid of your servant Israel, *
to remember the promise of mercy,
the promise made to our forebears, *
to Abraham and his children for ever.   **R**

Alternative seasonal refrains:

1   *Luke 1:30, 31*

For Advent

Fear not, Mary, you have found favor with the Lord;*
Behold, you shall conceive and bear a Son. Alleluia!

2   *John 1:14*

For Christmas–Epiphany

The Word was made flesh and dwelt among us,*
and we beheld his glory. Alleluia!

For Lent

Let justice roll down like waters,*
and righteousness like an everflowing stream.

For Easter

This is the day the Lord has made. Alleluia! *
Let us rejoice and be glad in it.

3

Canticle of Simeon   *Nunc Dimittis; Luke 2:29–32*
                                                PH 603–605; PS 164–166

Refrain for Prayer at the Close of Day

> **Guide us waking, O Lord,**
> **and guard us sleeping; ***
> **that awake we may watch with Christ,**
> **and asleep rest in his peace.**

R

Now, Lord, you let your servant go in peace: *
    your word has been fulfilled.
My own eyes have seen the salvation *
    which you have prepared in the sight of every people:
a light to reveal you to the nations *
    and the glory of your people Israel.   R

4

Hymn to Christ the Light   *Phos Hilaron*
                                                PH 548, 549; PS 167–169

O radiant Light, O Sun divine,
of God the Father's deathless face,
O image of the Light sublime,
that fills the heavenly dwelling place.

O Son of God, the source of life,
praise is your due by night and day.
Our happy lips must raise the strain
of your esteemed and splendid name.

Lord Jesus Christ, as daylight fades,
as shine the lights of eventide,
we praise the Father with the Son,
the Spirit blest and with them one.

5

We Praise You, O God

Te Deum Laudamus
PH 460; PS 170–171

We praise you, O God,
we acclaim you as Lord,
all creation worships you,
Father everlasting.

To you, all angels, all the powers of heaven,
the cherubim and seraphim, sing in endless praise:
Holy, holy, holy Lord, God of power and might,
heaven and earth are full of your glory.

The glorious company of apostles praise you.
The noble fellowship of prophets praise you.
The white-robed army of martyrs praise you.

Throughout the world the holy church acclaims you;
Father, of majesty unbounded,
your true and only Son, worthy of all praise,
the Holy Spirit, advocate and guide.

You, Christ, are the king of glory,
the eternal Son of the Father.
When you took our flesh to set us free
you humbly chose the Virgin's womb.

You overcame the sting of death
and opened the kingdom of heaven to all believers.

You are seated at God's right hand in glory.
We believe that you will come, and be our judge.

Come then, Lord, and help your people,
bought with the price of your own blood,
and bring us with your saints
to glory everlasting.

6

Glory to God

Gloria in Excelsis
PH 566, 575, 576; PS 173

Glory to God in the highest,
and peace to God's people on earth.

Lord God, heavenly King,
almighty God and Father,
we worship you, we give you thanks,
we praise you for your glory.

Lord Jesus Christ, only Son of the Father,
Lord God, Lamb of God,
you take away the sin of the world:
have mercy on us;
you are seated at the right hand of the Father:
receive our prayer.

For you alone are the Holy One,
you alone are the Lord,
you alone are the Most High,
Jesus Christ,
with the Holy Spirit,
in the glory of God the Father. Amen.

7

Canticle of Miriam and Moses

Ex. 15:1, 2, 11, 13, 17–18
PS 174

Refrain: **Strong and unfailing is your love, ***
Alleluia! Alleluia!

R

I will sing to the LORD, for the LORD has triumphed gloriously; *
the horse and its rider have been thrown into the sea.
The LORD is my strength and my song; *
and has become my salvation. **R**

You are my God, I will praise you, *
the God of my people, I exalt you.
Who among the gods, O LORD, is like you; *
who is like you, majestic in holiness,
Who among the gods, O LORD, is like you; *
awesome in splendor, doing wonders? **R**

With unfailing love you led the people you redeemed; *
  in your strength, you guided them to your holy dwelling.
You brought them in and planted them on your mountain, *
  the place, O LORD, you chose for your dwelling,
the sanctuary, O LORD, your hands established. *
  You, LORD, will reign forever and ever.   R

8

God's Chosen One

Isa. 11:1–4, 6, 9

A shoot shall come out from the stump of Jesse, *
  and a branch shall grow out of its roots,
The Spirit of the LORD shall rest on him, *
  the spirit of wisdom and understanding,
the spirit of counsel and might, *
  the spirit of knowledge and the fear of the LORD.

He shall not judge by what his eyes see, *
  or decide by what his ears hear,
but with righteousness he shall judge the poor, *
  and decide with equity for the meek of the earth.

The wolf shall live with the lamb, *
  the leopard shall lie down with the kid,
the calf and the lion cub together, *
  and a little child shall lead them.
They shall not hurt or destroy on all my holy mountain, *
  for the earth shall be full of the knowledge of the LORD
  as the waters cover the sea.

9

The Desert Shall Blossom

Isa. 35:1, 2, 5, 6, 10
PH 18

The desert shall rejoice and blossom, *
  it shall rejoice with gladness and singing.
The glory of the LORD shall be revealed, *
  and the majesty of our God.

Then shall the eyes of the blind be opened, *
  and the ears of the deaf unstopped,
then shall the lame leap like the deer, *
  and the tongue of the speechless shall sing for joy.

For waters shall break forth in the wilderness, *
  and streams in the desert.
The ransomed of the LORD shall return, *
  and come with singing, with everlasting joy upon their heads.
They shall obtain joy and gladness, *
  and sorrow and sighing shall flee away.

10

Canticle of Thanksgiving   *First Song of Isaiah; Isa. 12:2–6*

PS 175

Refrain: Sing praises, for the Lord has done great things. *
Let this be known in all the earth.

R

Surely God is my salvation; *
  I will trust, and will not be afraid,
for the LORD GOD is my stronghold and my song, *
  and has become my Savior.   **R**

With joy you will draw water from the wells of salvation. *
  And in that day you will say:
Give thanks and call upon the name of the LORD. *
  Make known among the nations what the LORD has done;
  proclaim that the name of the LORD is exalted.   **R**

Sing praises, for the LORD has done great things; *
  let this be known in all the earth.
Shout, and sing for joy, O people of God, *
  for great in your midst is the Holy One.   **R**

11

Seek the Lord   *Second Song of Isaiah; Isa. 55:6–11*

PS 176

Refrain: You are full of mercy, O Lord, *
for you will abundantly pardon.

R

Seek the LORD who is still to be found; *
  call upon God who is yet at hand.
Let the wicked forsake their way, *
  and the unrighteous their thoughts;
let them return to the LORD, who will have mercy, *
  to our God, who will abundantly pardon.   **R**

For my thoughts are not your thoughts; *
    nor are your ways my ways, says the LORD.
For as the heavens are higher than the earth; *
    so are my ways higher than your ways
    and my thoughts than your thoughts.   **R**

For as the rain and snow fall from the heavens; *
    and return not again but water the earth,
bringing forth life and giving growth; *
    giving seed to the sower and bread to the hungry;
so is my word that goes forth from my mouth; *
    it shall not return to me empty,
but it shall accomplish that which I desire; *
    and achieve the purpose for which I sent it.   **R**

12

The New Jerusalem   *Third Song of Isaiah; Isa. 60:1–3, 18, 19*

PS 177

Refrain: The Lord will be our everlasting light; *
           and God will be our glory.

R

Arise, shine, for your light has come; *
    and the glory of the LORD has risen upon you,
though darkness covers the earth *
    and dark night is over the nations.   **R**

But upon you the LORD will rise, *
    and the glory of the LORD will appear over you.
Nations shall come to your light; *
    and rulers to the brightness of your dawn.   **R**

No longer will violence be heard in your land, *
    nor ruin or destruction within your borders.
You will name your walls Salvation, *
    and all your gates Praise.   **R**

No more will the sun be your light by day, *
    nor by night will you need the brightness of the moon,
for the LORD will be your everlasting light, *
    and your God will be your glory.   **R**

13

The Spirit of the Lord   *Isa. 61:1–3, 10, 11*

The Spirit of the Lord GOD is upon me, *
   because the LORD has anointed me
   to bring good news to the oppressed.

The LORD has sent me to bind up the broken-hearted, *
   to proclaim liberty to the captives,
   and release for those in prison,
to comfort all who mourn, *
   to give them a garland instead of ashes,
the oil of gladness instead of mourning, *
   a garment of splendor for the heavy heart.
They shall be called trees of righteousness, *
   planted for the glory of the LORD.

Therefore I will greatly rejoice in the Lord, *
   my whole being shall exult in my God,
for God has robed me with salvation as a garment, *
   and clothed me with integrity as a cloak.
For the Lord GOD will cause righteousness and praise, *
   to spring up before all the nations.

14

Canticle of Hannah   *1 Sam. 2:1–4, 7, 8*

My heart exults in the LORD; *
   my strength is exalted in my God.
There is none holy like the LORD; *
   there is none beside you, no rock like our God.
For you, O LORD, are a God of knowledge; *
   and by you our actions are weighed.
The bows of the mighty are broken; *
   but the feeble gird on strength.

You, LORD, make poor and make rich; *
   you bring low and you also exalt.
You raise up the poor from the dust, *
   and lift the needy from the ash-heap.
You make them sit with princes, *
   and inherit a seat of honor.
For yours, O LORD, are the pillars of the earth; *
   and on them you have set the world.

15

Canticle of David   *1 Chron. 29:10–13*

Blessed are you, O LORD, *
    God of our ancestor Israel, forever and ever.
Yours, O LORD, are grandeur and power, *
    majesty, splendor, and glory.
For all in the heavens and on the earth is yours; *
    yours, O LORD, is the kingdom;
    you are exalted as head above all.

Riches and honor come from you, *
    and you rule over all.
In your hand are power and might; *
    it is yours to make great and to give strength to all.
And now we thank you, our God, *
    and praise your glorious name.

16

The Steadfast Love of the Lord   *Lam. 3:22–26*
                                                    PS 179

The steadfast love of the LORD never ceases, *
    God's mercies never come to an end;
they are new every morning *
    your faithfulness, O LORD, is great.
You are all that I have, *
    and therefore I will wait for you.
You, O LORD, are good to those who wait for you, *
    to all those who seek you.
It is good to wait in patience *
    for the salvation of the LORD.

Canticle of Judith   *Judith 16:13–15*

I will sing a new song to my God: *
    Lord, you are great and glorious,
    wonderful in strength, invincible.
Let the whole creation serve you, *
    for you spoke, and all things came into being.
You sent out your breath and it formed them; *
    no one is able to resist your voice.
Mountains and seas are stirred to their depths; *
    rocks melt like wax at your presence.
But to those who revere you, *
    you will continue to show mercy.

A Canticle of Creation   *Song of the Three Young Men 35–65, 34*
                                                         PS 180, 181

Invocation
Let the whole creation bless the Lord.*

Praise and exalt our God forever.

I. *The Cosmic Order*
O let the heavens bless the Lord.
Bless the Lord, you angels of the Lord; *
  bless the Lord, all the heavenly hosts.

Praise and exalt our God forever.

Bless the Lord, you waters above the heavens; *
  bless the Lord, sun and moon and stars of the sky.

Praise and exalt our God forever.

Bless the Lord, every shower of rain and fall of dew; *
  bless the Lord, every breeze and gusty wind.

Praise and exalt our God forever.

Bless the Lord, fire and heat; *
  bless the Lord, scorching wind and bitter cold.

Praise and exalt our God forever.

Bless the Lord, each drop of dew and flake of snow; *
  bless the Lord, nights and days, light and darkness.

Praise and exalt our God forever.

Bless the Lord, frost and cold, ice and sleet; *
  bless the Lord, thunderclouds and lightning flashes.

Praise and exalt our God forever.

II. *The Earth and Its Creatures*
O let the earth bless the Lord.
Bless the Lord, mountains and hills; *
  bless the Lord, all that grows from the earth.

Praise and exalt our God forever.

Bless the Lord, O springs of water; *
  bless the Lord, seas and rivers.

Praise and exalt our God forever.

Bless the Lord, you whales; *
    bless the Lord, all that swim in the depths of the seas.

Praise and exalt our God forever.

Bless the Lord, all birds of the air; *
    bless the Lord, beasts of the wild, flocks and herds.

Praise and exalt our God forever.

III. *The People of God*
O let all who dwell on the earth, bless the Lord.
Bless the Lord, men and women, children and youth; *
    bless the Lord, all people everywhere.

Praise and exalt our God forever.

Bless the Lord, you people of God; *
    bless the Lord, priests and all who serve the Lord.

Praise and exalt our God forever.

Bless the Lord, all who are upright in spirit; *
    bless the Lord, all who are holy and humble in heart.

Praise and exalt our God forever.

Doxology
Let us bless the Lord: Father, Son and Holy Spirit. *
    Blessed are you, O Lord, in the vast expanse of heaven.
    Praise and exalt our God forever.

19

A Canticle of Penitence   *Prayer of Manasseh*
                                    Prayer of Manasseh 1–2, 4, 6–7a, 11, 13c–15
                                                              PS 183

Refrain: **O Lord, you are full of compassion,***
            long-suffering, and abounding in mercy.

R
O Lord almighty and God of our ancestors, *
    you made the heavens and the earth, in their glorious array.
All things quake with fear at your presence; *
    they tremble because of your power.
But your merciful promise is beyond all measure; *
    it surpasses all that our minds can fathom.   **R**

Lord, you are full of compassion, *
    long-suffering, and abounding in mercy.
And now, O Lord, I humble my heart, *
    and make my appeal, sure of your gracious goodness.
For you, O Lord, are the God of the penitent, *
    and in me you will show forth your goodness.   R

Unworthy as I am, you will save me, *
    and so I will praise you continually, all the days of my life.
For all the host of heaven sing your praises, *
    and your glory is forever and ever.   R

20

A Canticle to the Lamb   *Rev. 4:11; 5:9–10, 12, 13*
                                            PS 191

Refrain: **Worthy is the Lamb that was slain ***
            to receive glory and honor.

R
    You are worthy, O Lord our God, *
        to receive glory and honor and power,
    for you created all things, *
        and by your will they were created and have their being.   R

    You are worthy, O Christ, for you were slain, *
        and by your blood have ransomed us for God,
    from every tribe and people and nation, *
        a royal house of priests to our God.   R

    Worthy is the Lamb who was slain, *
        to receive power and wealth, wisdom and might,
        honor and glory and blessing.
    To the one seated upon the throne, and to Christ the Lamb, *
        be blessing and honor, glory and might, forever and ever.   R

21

Canticle of the Redeemed *Rev. 15:3–4*

PS 184

Refrain: Your ways are just and true,*
O Sovereign of all the ages.

R

O Ruler of the universe, Lord God,
great and wonderful are your deeds, *
   surpassing human understanding.
Your ways are just and true, *
   O Sovereign of all the ages.   R

Who can fail to do you homage, Lord,
and sing the praises of your name, *
   for you alone are holy.
All nations will come and worship in your presence, *
   for your just and holy works have been revealed.   R

22

A Canticle for Pentecost *John 14:16; 16:13a; 14:26*
Acts 2:2, 4a; Rom. 8:26;

Joel 2:28

Refrain: I will pour out my Spirit on all flesh.*
Your sons and your daughters shall prophesy,
your old shall dream dreams*
and your young shall see visions.

R

I will ask the Father,
who will give you another Advocate, *
   to be with you for ever.
The Spirit of truth, having come, *
   will guide you into all truth.   R

The Advocate, the Holy Spirit *
   whom the Father will send in my name,
will teach you all things, *
   and remind you of all that I have said to you.   R

And suddenly from heaven there came a sound *
   like the rush of a violent wind,
and it filled the entire house where they were sitting. *
   All were filled with the Holy Spirit.   R

The Spirit helps us in our weakness; *
    for we do not know how we ought to pray,
but the Spirit pleads for us *
    with sighs too deep for words.   **R**

23

A Canticle of Love   *1 John 4:7, 8; 1 Cor. 13:4–10, 12–13*

PS 187

Refrain: **Faith, hope and love abide,** *
              and the greatest of these is love.

R

Beloved, let us love one another, *
    for love is of God.
All who love are born of God and know God; *
    all who do not love do not know God.   **R**

Love does not insist on its own way, *
    is not quick to take offense;
it does not rejoice at wrong, *
    but rejoices in the right.   **R**

Love is patient and kind; *
    love is not envious or boastful;
it is not arrogant or rude. *
    Love bears all things and believes all things,
Love hopes all things and endures all things. *
    Love will never come to an end.   **R**

Prophecies will vanish; tongues will cease; *
    and knowledge will pass away.
For our knowledge and our prophecy are imperfect, *
    but when the perfect comes, the imperfect will pass away.   **R**

Now I know in part, *
    then I will know fully,
    even as I have been fully known.
Now abide faith, hope, and love, these three; *
    and the greatest of these is love.   **R**

24

Christ, the Head of All Creation *Col. 1:15–20*

PS 185

Refrain: **Glory to you,***
the firstborn of all creation!

R

Christ is the image of the invisible God, *
  the firstborn of all creation.
In him all things in heaven and on earth were created, *
  all that is seen and all that is unseen,
thrones and dominions, rulers and powers, *
  through him and for him all things were created.   **R**

Christ is before all things, *
  the one in whom all things hold together.
Christ is head of the body, the church; *
  he is its beginning, the firstborn from the dead,
  to be in all things alone supreme.   **R**

For in Christ, O God, you were pleased to have all your fullness dwell, *
  and through him to reconcile all things to yourself.
You made peace by the blood of his cross, *
  and brought back to yourself all things in heaven and on earth.   **R**

Jesus Christ Is Lord *Phil. 2:5c–11*

PS 186

Christ Jesus, though he was in the form of God, *
  did not regard equality with God a thing to be grasped,
but emptied himself, taking the form of a slave, *
  being born in human likeness.
And being found in human form, he humbled himself, *
  and became obedient unto death, even death on a cross.

Therefore God has highly exalted him *
  and bestowed on him the name above every name,
that at the name of Jesus every knee should bend, *
  in heaven and on earth and under the earth,
and every tongue confess to the glory of God: *
  Jesus Christ is Lord!

The Mystery of Our Religion

1 Tim. 3:16; 6:15, 16

Christ Jesus our Lord was revealed in flesh, *
    and was vindicated in the Spirit,
he was seen by angels, *
    and proclaimed among the nations;
he was believed in throughout the world, *
    and was taken up in glory.

He will be revealed in due time by God, *
    the blessed and only ruler, the sovereign Lord of all,
who alone has immortality, *
    and dwells in unapproachable light,
whom no one has ever seen or can see, *
    to whom alone be honor and might forever and ever.

The Beatitudes

Matt. 5:3–12
PS 188

Blessed are the poor in spirit, *
    for the kingdom of heaven is theirs.
Blessed are the sorrowful, *
    for they will be comforted.
Blessed are those of a gentle spirit, *
    for they will inherit the earth.
Blessed are those who hunger and thirst to see right prevail, *
    for they will be filled.
Blessed are those who show mercy, *
    for mercy will be shown to them.
Blessed are those whose hearts are pure, *
    for they will see God.
Blessed are the peacemakers, *
    for they will be called children of God.
Blessed are those who are persecuted for the cause of right, *
    for theirs is the kingdom of heaven.
Blessed are you when you are reviled, and persecuted *
    and all kinds of evil are uttered against you on my account.
Rejoice and be glad, *
    for your reward is great in heaven.

Christ the Servant   *1 Peter 2:21–25*
                                                              PS 189

Refrain: Christ bore our sins on the cross;*
            by his wounds we are healed.

R

Jesus Christ suffered for you, leaving you an example: *
   that you should follow in his steps.
Christ committed no sin, no deceit was found on his lips. *
   When he was abused, he did not return abuse;
when suffering, he did not threaten; *
   but he trusted the one who judges justly.   **R**

Christ bore our sins in his body on the cross, *
   so that, free from sins, we might live for righteousness.
By his wounds you have been healed. *
   For you were straying like sheep,
but have now returned *
   to the shepherd and guardian of your souls.*   **R**

Christ Our Passover   *1 Cor. 5:7–8; Rom. 6:9–11;*
                                                   1 Cor. 15:20–22
                                                        PS 190

Alleluia! Christ our paschal lamb has been sacrificed. *
   Therefore, let us keep the feast,
not with the old leaven, the leaven of malice and evil, *
   but with the unleavened bread of sincerity and truth.
   Alleluia!

Christ, being raised from the dead, will never die again; *
   death no longer has dominion over him.
The death that he died, he died to sin, once for all; *
   but the life he lives, he lives to God.
So also consider yourselves dead to sin *
   and alive to God in Christ Jesus. Alleluia!

Christ has been raised from the dead, *
   the first fruits of those who have died.
For since by one human being came death, *
   by one human being has also come the resurrection of the dead.
For as in Adam all die, *
   so also in Christ will all be made alive. Alleluia!

PRAYERS AT MEALTIME

As a sign of reverence, some fold hands for prayer before the meal. Others, standing about the table, lift hands as a sign of praise. Others join hands around the table as a sign of peace and unity. Still others make the sign of the cross after the prayer.

1

Blessed are you, O Lord our God,
ruler of the universe,
for you give us food to sustain our lives
and make our hearts glad.   [520]

Amen.

2

Blessed are you, Lord.
You have fed us from our earliest days;
you give food to every living creature.
Fill our hearts with joy and delight.
Give us what we need
and enough to spare for works of mercy
in honor of Christ Jesus, our Lord.
Through him may glory, honor and power be yours for ever.   [521]

Amen.

3

Blessed are you, Lord, God of all creation,
for you feed the whole world with your goodness,
with grace, with loving kindness and tender mercy.
You give food to all creatures,
and your loving kindness endures forever.
Because of your great goodness, food has never failed us;
O may it not fail us forever and ever
for the sake of your great name.
You nourish and sustain all creatures
and do good to all.
Blessed are you, O Lord, for you give food to all.   [522]

Amen.

4

Creator of the universe,
you give us this gift of food to nourish us and give us life.
Bless this food that you have made
and human hands have prepared.
May it satisfy our hunger,
and in sharing it together
may we come closer to one another.   [523]

Amen.

5

Bless us, O Lord, and these your gifts
which we are about to receive from your goodness,
through Christ our Lord.   [524]

Amen.

6

Come, Lord Jesus, be our guest,
and let these gifts to us be blessed.   [525]

Amen.

7

All good gifts around us
are sent from heaven above,
then thank the Lord, O thank the Lord,
for all God's love.   [526]

Amen.

8

For health and strength and daily food,
we praise your name, O Lord.   [527]

Amen.

9

The eyes of all wait upon you, O Lord,
and you give them their food in due season.
You open wide your hand,
and satisfy the needs of every living thing.
Thanks be to you.   [528]

Amen.

10

God of grace,
sustain our bodies with this food,
our hearts with true friendship,
and our souls with your truth,
for Christ's sake.   [529]

Amen.

11

Lord Jesus, be our holy guest,
our morning joy, our evening rest;
and with our daily bread impart
your love and peace to every heart.   [530]

Amen.

12

Give us grateful hearts, O God, for all your mercies,
and make us mindful of the needs of others;
through Jesus Christ our Lord.   [531]

Amen.

The following (13–17) are taken from psalms and may be said in unison by
all at the table. They may be used before the meal or after all have eaten.

13   *See Ps. 19:1, 2*

**The heavens are telling the glory of God;
and the firmament proclaims God's handiwork.
In the day we give glory to God,
and at night we remember God's love.**

14   *Ps. 24:1*

**The earth is the Lord's and all that is in it,
the world, and those who live in it.**

15   *Ps. 100:1, 2, 4b*

**Make a joyful noise to the Lord, all the earth.
Worship the Lord with gladness;
come into God's presence with singing.
Give thanks, and bless God's name.**

16   *Ps. 103:1, 2*

Bless the Lord, O my soul,
and all that is within me, bless God's holy name.
Bless the Lord, O my soul,
and do not forget all God's benefits.

17   *Ps. 121:1, 2*

I lift up my eyes to the hills—
from where will my help come?
My help comes from the Lord
who made heaven and earth.

18

The following grace is based upon Jewish and Christian table blessings.
The actions are signs of gratitude to God for the joy of food and drink and
for the presence of those about the table. If circumstances do not allow for
blessings over both wine and bread, a blessing may be said over either.

A person at the table takes a glass of wine, or appropriate beverage, lifts it,
and says:

Blessed are you, O Lord our God,
Ruler of all creation,
for you give us the fruit of the vine.   [532]
Amen.

The glass is passed and each person at the table drinks from it.

The same person, or another, takes bread, holds it up for all to see, and
says:

Blessed are you, O Lord our God,
Ruler of all creation,
for you bring forth bread from the earth.   [533]
Amen.

The bread is broken and passed to those about the table for each one to eat
of it.

THE PSALMS

THE PSALMS

PSALMS IN CORPORATE WORSHIP

THE PSALMS THAT FOLLOW ARE for use in corporate worship. One hundred twenty-seven psalms are represented, including all the psalms displayed in the Lectionary for Sundays and Festivals (pp. 1035–1048) and in the list of Psalms for Daily Prayer (pp. 1049–1095), as well as those suggested in the services contained in this book. They are presented in a form that invites a variety of uses.

SINGING THE PSALMS

It is preferable that the psalms be sung. *The Psalter—Psalms and Canticles for Singing* provides a rich and varied collection of responsorial settings for singing the psalms. *The Presbyterian Hymnal* contains a large collection of metrical psalms and a few responsorial settings.

The psalm texts that follow are pointed to enable the psalms to be sung to simple psalm tones such as those provided in *The Psalter—Psalms and Canticles for Singing*, and on pages 601–610 of this book.

Eight refrains with a choice of tones are provided in this book. The pointing system displayed in the psalm texts and tones is the system most commonly used. This enables these psalm texts to be sung to many tones found in other resources.

The most common practice in singing the psalms to psalm tones is to sing them responsorially. In singing the psalms responsorially, a choir or cantor (soloist) sings the psalm to a tone, with the congregation singing a metrical refrain. The refrains, used together with either of the tones (A and B) that follow, provide for responsorial psalmody.

Some groups, however (for example, groups meeting regularly for daily prayer), may choose to sing the psalm in a responsive pattern. The group is divided into two sections. The singing of the psalm alternates between the two sections, one section singing one verse, the other section singing the next verse. Or the entire psalm may be sung in unison. In either instance, the refrain is not ordinarily used. Or the refrain may be used only at the beginning and at the end of the psalm. Tone B is then used, since it may be used with or without the refrain.

Tone B may also be used in singing the canticles on pages 573–591, and therefore provides additional resources for use with the canticle settings in *The Psalter—Psalms and Canticles for Singing*.

READING THE PSALMS

Some congregations will choose to read the psalms. The psalms that follow are presented in a form that will assist in reading the psalms responsively, antiphonally, or in unison.

In reading the psalms responsively, a leader reads the lightface type, the congregation reads the boldface type.

In reading the psalms antiphonally, the group is divided into two parts, such as the right and left sections of a congregation. One part of the group reads the lightface type, the other reads the boldface type.

PSALM PRAYERS

Psalm prayers are provided for each of the psalms in this book. These prayers are used in daily prayer, where praying the psalms is central. Each psalm prayer captures some theme or image from the psalm and often adds Christian implications drawn from the psalm. The prayer helps us to pray the psalm and to see Christ in the psalm as we pray. Psalm prayers may also be composed that capture images in the psalms that address the immediate needs of the worshipers. The psalm prayer is spoken by the leader after the psalm is sung or read. Ordinarily, the leader upon completion of the singing or reading of the psalm will say, "Let us pray." Silence follows for silent prayer and reflection on the psalm. After the silence, the leader offers the prayer.

INSTRUCTIONS FOR SINGING PSALM TONES

1. A suggested psalm tone is noted with each psalm. The suggested tones match the spirit and theme of the psalm.

2. In presenting the psalm, the refrain is first played by the organist, pianist, or other instrumentalist, then is sung by the cantor or choir, and then is sung by all. The cantor sings the verses of the psalm, with the congregation singing the refrain wherever noted in the psalm text (**R**).

3. In singing the text of the psalm, each measure of the psalm tone is sung to a psalm half-verse, noted by an asterisk (*). Begin singing on the first note of the measure, then move to the second note on the syllable with a dot (·) above it. The third and fourth notes of the tone accommodate the remainder of each phrase of the text. When there are more than three syllables in a half-verse ending, the additional syllables are sung on the last note. When two syllables are joined by a tie (___) they are sung on the one note.

Congregations are free to reproduce the melody line of the refrains and tones in a church bulletin. See pages 609–610 for refrains that may be reproduced.

THE PSALM REFRAINS AND TONES

Two tones appear with each refrain. Either tone A or tone B may be used when the refrain is sung. When the whole group sings the text of the psalm (instead of a cantor or choir) the refrain is not used, or is used only at the beginning and end of the psalm. Tone B is then used.

1: ALLELUIA

REFRAIN

TONE 1 (A)

TONE 1 (B)

Text: Hal H. Hopson
Music: Hal H. Hopson

2: PRAISE

REFRAIN

Let the peo-ple praise you, O God;____ let   all the peo-ple praise you.

TONE 2 (A) ✱

TONE 2 (B) ✱

Text: Hal H. Hopson
Music: Hal H. Hopson

3: LORDSHIP

Psalm 135:1

REFRAIN

TONE 3 (A)

TONE 3 (B)

Text: Hal H. Hopson
Music: Hal H. Hopson

4: SALVATION HISTORY

Psalm 78:4

REFRAIN

TONE 4 (A)

TONE 4 (B)

Text: Hal H. Hopson
Music: Hal H. Hopson

5: GOD'S LAW

Psalm 119:174

REFRAIN

TONE 5 (A)

TONE 5 (B)

Text: Hal H. Hopson
Music: Hal H. Hopson

6: TRUST

Psalm 46:1

Text: Hal H. Hopson
Music: Hal H. Hopson

7: PENITENTIAL

Psalm 130:1–2

REFRAIN

TONE 7 (A)

TONE 7 (B)

Text: Hal H. Hopson
Music: Hal H. Hopson

8: LAMENT

Psalm 22:19

REFRAIN

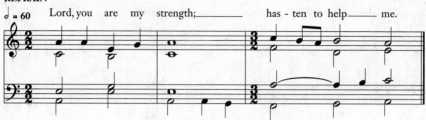

TONE 8 (A)

TONE 8 (B)

Text: Hal H. Hopson
Music: Hal H. Hopson

Free permission is granted by the publisher to reproduce the refrains that follow in church bulletins for congregational participation.

Hal H. Hopson

1

Al - le - lu - ia! Al - le - lu - ia! Al - le - lu - ia!

Hal H. Hopson

2

Let the peo-ple praise you, O God; ___ Let all the peo-ple praise you.

Hal H. Hopson

3

Praise the Lord. Praise the Lord. Praise the name of the Lord.

Hal H. Hopson

4

Tell out the deeds of the Lord; ___ Tell out the won-ders God has wrought.

Hal H. Hopson

O Lord, my de-light,_____ my de - light is in your law.

Hal H. Hopson

God is our ref - uge; God is our strength.

Hal H. Hopson

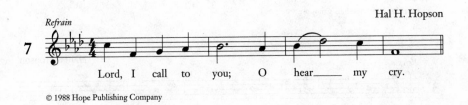

Lord, I call to you; O hear_____ my cry.

Hal H. Hopson

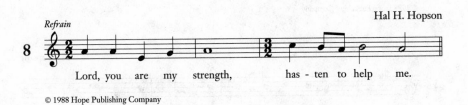

Lord, you are my strength, has - ten to help me.

THE PSALMS

PSALM 1 Tone 5 or 6; PH 158; PS 1

R

1 Happy are they who have not walked in the counsel of the wicked, *
   nor lingered in the way of sinners,
   nor sat in the seats of the scornful!

2 **Their delight is in the law of the LORD, ***
   and on this law they meditate day and night. R

3 They are like trees planted by streams of water,
   bearing fruit in due season, with leaves that do not wither; *
   everything they do shall prosper.

4 **It is not so with the wicked; ***
   they are like chaff which the wind blows away. R

5 Therefore the wicked shall not stand upright when judgment comes, *
   nor the sinner in the council of the righteous.

6 **For the LORD knows the way of the righteous, ***
   but the way of the wicked is doomed. R

Eternal God,
in your loving wisdom you set us beside the fountain of life,
like a tree planted by running streams.
Fill us with a love of your wisdom,
that we may bear fruit in the beauty of holiness;
through Christ, the way, the truth, and the life. **Amen.** [534]

PSALM 2 Tone 6; PH 159; PS 2

R

1 Why are the nations in an uproar? *
   Why do the peoples mutter empty threats?

2 **Why do the kings of the earth rise up in revolt,**
   and the rulers plot together, *
   against the LORD and against the LORD's anointed?

3 "Let us break their yoke," they say; *
   "let us cast off their bonds from us."   R

4 **The One enthroned in heaven is laughing; ***
   the LORD has them in derision.

5 Then in wrath the LORD speaks to them, *
   and divine rage fills them with terror.

6 **"I myself have set my king ***
   upon my holy hill of Zion."   R

7 Let me announce the decree of the LORD: *
   the LORD said to me, "You are my Son;
   this day have I begotten you.

8 **Ask of me, and I will give you the nations for your inheritance ***
   and the ends of the earth for your possession.

9 You shall crush them with an iron rod *
   and shatter them like a piece of pottery."   R

10 **And now, you kings, be wise; ***
   be warned, you rulers of the earth.

11 Submit to the LORD with fear, *
   and with trembling bow down in worship;

12 **lest the LORD be angry and you perish; ***
   for divine wrath is quickly kindled.

   [Unison]

13 **Happy are they all ***
   who take refuge in the LORD!   R

   Sovereign God,
   you gave us your only begotten to be the Savior of the world,
   and you crowned him with grace to rule over all.
   Give us humility
   that we may faithfully serve him,
   and so know the joy
   given to all who take refuge in Christ our Lord.   **Amen.**   [535]

R

1　Answer me when I call, O God, defender of my cause; *
　　you set me free when I am hard-pressed;
　　have mercy on me and hear my prayer.

2　**"You mortals, how long will you dishonor my glory; ***
　　how long will you worship dumb idols
　　and run after false gods?"

3　Know that the LORD does wonders for the faithful; *
　　when I cry out, the LORD will hear me.　　**R**

4　**Tremble, then, and do not sin; ***
　　speak to your heart in silence upon your bed.

5　Offer the appointed sacrifices *
　　and put your trust in the LORD.　　**R**

6　**Many are saying, "Oh, that we might see better times!" ***
　　Lift up the light of your countenance upon us, O LORD.

7　You have put gladness in my heart, *
　　more than when grain and wine and oil increase.

8　**I lie down in peace; at once I fall asleep; ***
　　for only you, LORD, make me dwell in safety.　　**R**

O God, source of deliverance and help,
do not let our hearts be troubled,
but fill us with such confidence and joy
that we may sleep in your peace and rise in your light;
through Jesus Christ our Lord.　**Amen.**　　[536]

R

1　Give ear to my words, O LORD; *
　　consider my meditation.

2　**Hearken to my cry for help, my Sovereign and my God, ***
　　for I make my prayer to you.

3　In the morning, LORD, you hear my voice; *
　　early in the morning I make my appeal and watch for you.　　**R**

4 **For you are not a God who takes pleasure in wickedness, ***
      and evil cannot dwell with you.

5 Braggarts cannot stand in your sight; *
      you hate all those who work wickedness.

6 **You destroy those who speak lies; ***
      the bloodthirsty and deceitful, O LORD, you abhor.   **R**

7 But as for me, through the greatness of your mercy I will go into your house; *
      I will bow down toward your holy temple in awe of you.

8 **Lead me, O LORD, in your righteousness,**
   because of those who lie in wait for me; *
      make your way straight before me.   **R**

9 For there is no truth in their mouth; *
      there is destruction in their heart;

   their throat is an open grave; *
      they flatter with their tongue.

10 Declare them guilty, O God; *
      let them fall, because of their schemes.

   Because of their many transgressions cast them out, *
      for they have rebelled against you.   **R**

11 But all who take refuge in you will be glad; *
      they will sing out their joy forever.

   You will shelter them, *
      so that those who love your name may exult in you.

   [Unison]

12 **For you, O LORD, will bless the righteous; ***
      you will defend them with your favor as with a shield.   **R**

   You alone, O God, are holy and righteous,
   and we praise you for protecting us in times of trial.
   Keep us safe from all evil
   and lead us in paths of justice
   that we may know the joy of trusting Jesus Christ
   our shield and defender.   **Amen.**   [537]

R

1 LORD, do not rebuke me in your anger; *
     do not punish me in your wrath.

2 **Have pity on me, LORD, for I am weak; ***
     heal me, LORD, for my bones are racked.

3 My spirit shakes with terror; *
     how long, O LORD, how long?   **R**

4 **Turn, O LORD, and deliver me; ***
     save me for your mercy's sake.

5 For in death no one remembers you; *
     and who will give you thanks in the grave?   **R**

6 **I grow weary because of my groaning; ***
     every night I drench my bed
     and flood my couch with tears.

7 My eyes are wasted with grief *
     and worn away because of all my enemies.   **R**

8 **Depart from me, all evildoers, ***
     for the LORD has heard the sound of my weeping.

9 The LORD has heard my supplication; *
     the LORD accepts my prayer.

10 **All my enemies shall be confounded and quake with fear; ***
     they shall turn back and suddenly be put to shame.   **R**

Merciful God,
     you know our anguish, not from afar,
     but in the suffering of Jesus Christ.
     Take all our grieving and sorrow,
     all our pain and tears,
     and heal us according to your promises
     in Jesus Christ our Lord.   **Amen.**   [538]

R

1 O LORD my God, I take refuge in you; *
     save and deliver me from all who pursue me;

2 **lest like a lion they tear me in pieces ***
     and snatch me away with none to deliver me.

3 O LORD my God, if I have done these things: *
     if there is any wickedness in my hands,

4 **if I have repaid my friend with evil, ***
     or plundered anyone who without cause is my enemy;

5 then let my enemy pursue and overtake me, *
     trample my life into the ground,
     and lay my honor in the dust.   **R**

6 **Stand up, O LORD, in your wrath; ***
     rise up against the fury of my enemies.

   Awake, O my God, decree justice; *
     7 let the assembly of the peoples gather round you.

   Be seated on your lofty throne, O Most High; *
     8 **O LORD, judge the nations.**

   Give judgment for me according to my righteousness, O LORD, *
     and according to my innocence, O Most High.   **R**

9 **Let the malice of the wicked come to an end,**
   but establish the righteous; *
     for you test the mind and heart, O righteous God.

10 God is my shield and defense, *
     the savior of the true in heart.

11 **God is a righteous judge; ***
     God sits in judgment every day.   R

12 If they will not repent, God will whet a sword, *
     bending a bow and making it ready.

13 **God has prepared weapons of death, ***
     making arrows into shafts of fire.

14 Look at those who are in labor with wickedness, *
     who conceive evil, and give birth to a lie.

¹⁵ They dig a pit and make it deep *
   and fall into the hole that they have made.

¹⁶ Their malice turns back upon their own head; *
   their violence falls on their own scalp.   **R**

¹⁷ **I will bear witness that the L**ORD **is righteous;** *
   I will praise the name of the LORD **Most High.**   **R**

O God, our judge and redeemer,
by the light of your truth
let the righteous know your goodness
and sinners know your mercy,
that together they may give you grateful praise;
through Jesus Christ our Lord.   **Amen.**   [539]

PSALM 8   Tone 3; PH 162, 163; PS 5

R

¹ O L̇ORD our Lord, *
   how exalted is your name in all the world!

² **Out of the mouths of infants and children** *
   your majesty is praised above the heavens.

   You have set up a stronghold against your adversaries, *
      to quell the enemy and the avenger.   **R**

³ **When I consider your heavens, the work of your fingers,** *
   the moon and the stars you have set in their courses,

⁴ what are human beings that you should be mindful of them? *
   mortals that you should seek them out?   **R**

⁵ **You have made them but little lower than the angels;** *
   you adorn them with glory and honor;

⁶ you give them mastery over the works of your hands; *
   you put all things under their feet: **R**

⁷ **All sheep and oxen,** *
   even the wild beasts of the field,

⁸ the birds of the air, the fish of the sea, *
   and whatsoever walks in the paths of the sea.

⁹ **O L**ORD **our Lord,** *
   how exalted is your name in all the world!   **R**

God of glory,
despite the majesty of your creation
you sought us out,
and through Christ
you crowned us with dignity and honor,
giving us dominion over your works.
Enable us so to care for the earth
that all creation may radiate the splendor
of Jesus Christ our Lord.   **Amen.**   [540]

PSALM 9   Tone 8; PS 6

R

1 I will give thanks to you, O LORD, with my whole heart; *
    I will tell of all your marvelous works.

2 **I will be glad and rejoice in you; ***
    I will sing to your name, O Most High.   R

3 When my enemies are driven back, *
    they will stumble and perish at your presence.

4 **For you have maintained my right and my cause; ***
    you sit upon your throne judging right.   R

5 You have rebuked the ungodly and destroyed the wicked; *
    you have blotted out their name forever and ever.

6 **As for the enemy, they are finished, in perpetual ruin, ***
    their cities ploughed under, the memory of them perished;   R

7 but you, O LORD, are enthroned forever; *
    you have set up your throne for judgment.

8 **It is you who rule the world with righteousness; ***
    you judge the peoples with equity.

9 The LORD will be a refuge for the oppressed, *
    a refuge in time of trouble.

10 **Those who know your name will put their trust in you, ***
    for you never forsake those who seek you, O LORD.   R

11 Sing praise to the LORD who dwells in Zion; *
    proclaim to the peoples the things the LORD has done.

12 **The Avenger of blood will remember them, ***
    and will not forget the cry of the afflicted.

13 Have pity on me, O LORD; *
    see the misery I suffer from those who hate me,
    O you who lift me up from the gate of death;

14 so that I may tell of all your praises
    and rejoice in your salvation *
        in the gates of the city of Zion.   R

15 The ungodly have fallen into the pit they dug, *
    and in the snare they set is their own foot caught.

16 The LORD is known by divine acts of justice; *
    the wicked are trapped in the works of their own hands.   R

17 The wicked shall be given over to the grave, *
    and also all the peoples that forget God.

18 For the needy shall not always be forgotten, *
    and the hope of the poor shall not perish forever.

19 Rise up, O LORD, let not the ungodly have the upper hand; *
    let them be judged before you.

20 Put fear upon them, O LORD; *
    let the ungodly know they are but mortal.   R

God Most High,
in Jesus Christ you rule the world with righteousness
and judge the nations with equity.
Cast down the haughty and lift up the lowly.
Make us compassionate to the needy
that we may be close to Jesus Christ,
our servant Lord.   **Amen.**   [541]

PSALM 10   Tone 8

R

1 Why do you stand so far off, O LORD, *
    and hide yourself in time of trouble?

2 The wicked arrogantly persecute the poor, *
    but they are trapped in the schemes they have devised.

3 The wicked boast of their heart's desire; *
    the covetous curse and revile the LORD.

4 The wicked are so proud that they care not for God; *
    their only thought is, "God does not matter."   R

5 Their ways are devious at all times;
　　your judgments are far above out of their sight; *
　　　they defy all their enemies.

6 **They say in their heart, "I shall not be shaken; ***
　　no harm shall happen to me ever."

7 Their mouth is full of cursing, deceit, and oppression; *
　　under their tongue are mischief and wrong.

8 **They lurk in ambush in public squares**
　　and in secret places they murder the innocent; *
　　　they spy out the helpless.　　R

9 They lie in wait, like a lion in a covert;
　　they lie in wait to seize upon the lowly; *
　　　they seize the lowly and drag them away in their net.

10 **The innocent are broken and humbled before them; ***
　　the helpless fall before their power.

11 They say in their heart, "God has forgotten; *
　　God's face is hidden; God will never notice."　　R

12 **Rise up, O LORD;**
　　lift up your hand, O God; *
　　　do not forget the afflicted.

13 Why should the wicked revile God? *
　　why should they say in their heart that you do not care?

14 **Surely, you behold trouble and misery; ***
　　you see it and take it into your own hand.

　　The helpless commit themselves to you, *
　　　for you are the helper of orphans.　　R

15 **Break the power of the wicked and evil; ***
　　search out their wickedness until you find none.

16 The LORD is Sovereign forever and ever; *
　　the ungodly shall perish from your land.

17 **The LORD will hear the desire of the humble; ***
　　you will strengthen their heart and your ears shall hear;

　　[Unison]

18 **to give justice to the orphan and oppressed, ***
　　so that mere mortals may strike terror no more.　　R

O Lord,
you are the hope of the weak,
the orphaned, and the oppressed.
You subvert the wicked and their plans
and strengthen the hearts of the helpless.
Blessed are you, Lord God,
Sovereign of the universe. **Amen.** [542]

PSALM 12   Tone 8

R

1 Help me, LORD, for there is no godly one left; *
   the faithful have vanished from among us.

2 **All speak falsely with their neighbor; ***
   with a smooth tongue they speak from a double heart.

3 Oh, that the LORD would cut off all smooth tongues, *
   and close the lips that utter proud boasts!

4 **Those who say, "With our tongue will we prevail; ***
   our lips are our own; who is lord over us?" R

5 "Because the needy are oppressed,
and the poor cry out in misery, *
   I will rise up," says the LORD,
   "and give them the help they long for."

6 **The words of the LORD are pure words, ***
   like silver refined from ore
   and purified seven times in the fire. R

7 O LORD, watch over us *
   and save us from this generation forever.

8 **The wicked prowl on every side, ***
   and that which is worthless is highly prized by everyone. R

God of justice,
in Jesus Christ you championed the weak
and befriended outcasts.
Through the shining light of his goodness
you expose hypocrisy.
Give us courage to follow his example,
that we may be faithful disciples
of our Lord, Jesus Christ. **Amen.** [543]

R

1 How long, O LORD?
Will you forget me forever? *
　how long will you hide your face from me?

2 **How long shall I have perplexity in my mind,**
and grief in my heart, day after day? *
　how long shall my enemy triumph over me?   R

3 Look upon me and answer me, O LORD my God; *
　give light to my eyes, lest I sleep in death;

4 **lest my enemy say, "I have prevailed," ***
　and my foes rejoice that I have fallen.   R

5 But I put my trust in your mercy; *
　my heart is joyful because of your saving help.

6 **I will sing to you, O LORD,**
for you have dealt with me richly; *
　I will praise the name of the Lord Most High.   R

Loving and merciful God,
hear the prayers of those who cry to you,
and shine with the light of your presence
on those who live in the shadow of death.
May we rejoice in your saving help
and sing you songs of praise
in the name of our risen Savior, Jesus Christ.   **Amen.**   [544]

PSALM 14   Tone 8; PS 8

R

1 Fools say in their heart, "There is no God." *
　All are corrupt and commit abominable acts;
　there is none who does any good.

2 **The LORD looks down from heaven upon us all,** *
　to see if there is any who is wise,
　if there is one who seeks after God.

3 Every one has proved faithless;
all alike have turned bad; *
　there is none who does good; no, not one.   R

4 **Have they no knowledge, all those evildoers** *
     who eat up my people like bread
     and do not call upon the LORD?

5 See how they tremble with fear, *
     because God is in the company of the righteous.

6 **Their aim is to confound the plans of the afflicted,** *
     but the LORD is their refuge.

[Unison]

7 **Oh, that Israel's deliverance would come out of Zion!** *
     when the LORD restores the fortunes of the chosen people,
     Jacob will rejoice and Israel be glad.   R

God of wisdom and justice,
deliver us from the foolishness of ignoring you.
Teach us your wisdom through Jesus Christ,
that we may seek your goodness
and embody your love to all your people,
for the sake of Jesus Christ our Lord.   **Amen.**   [545]

PSALM 15   Tone 6; PH 164; PS 9

R

1 LORD, who may dwell in your tabernacle? *
     who may abide upon your holy hill?

2 **Those who lead a blameless life and do what is right,** *
     who speak the truth from their heart.   R

3 There is no guile upon their tongue;
   they do no evil to their friend; *
     they do not heap contempt upon their neighbor.

4 **In their sight the wicked are rejected,** *
     but they honor those who fear the LORD.   R

They have sworn to do no wrong *
   and do not take back their word.

5 **They do not give their money in hope of gain,** *
     nor do they take a bribe against the innocent.

[Unison]

Those who do these things *
     shall never be overthrown.   R

God of love,
you adopted us as your children.
Grant that we may pass through this world with such integrity
that no one will have just complaint against us.
At the end,
may we inherit what has been prepared for us in heaven;
through our Savior, Jesus Christ. **Amen.** [546]

PSALM 16   Tone 6; PH 165; PS 10

R

1   Protect me, O God, for I take refuge in you; *
      I have said to the LORD, "You are my Lord,
         my good above all other."

2   **All my delight is upon the godly that are in the land, ***
      upon those who are noble among the people.   R

3   But those who run after other gods *
      shall have their troubles multiplied.

4   **Their libations of blood I will not offer, ***
      nor take the names of their gods upon my lips.   R

5   O LORD, you are my portion and my cup; *
      it is you who uphold my lot.

6   **My boundaries enclose a pleasant land; ***
      indeed, I have a goodly heritage.   R

7   I will bless the LORD who gives me counsel; *
      my heart teaches me, night after night.

8   **I have set the LORD always before me; ***
      because you are at my right hand I shall not fall.   R

9   My heart, therefore, is glad, and my spirit rejoices; *
      my body also shall rest in hope.

10 **For you will not abandon me to the grave, ***
      nor let your holy one see the pit.   R

[Unison]

11 **You will show me the path of life; ***
      in your presence there is fullness of joy,
         and in your right hand are pleasures forevermore.   R

Gracious God,
in whom all hearts are glad
and all souls rejoice:
Show us the path of your presence,
that we may follow it in hope
and be filled with resurrection joy;
through Jesus Christ, our risen Savior. **Amen.** [547]

Psalm 17

Tone 8 or 7; PS 11

R

1 Hear my plea of innocence, O LORD;
give heed to my cry; *
　listen to my prayer, which does not come from lying lips.

2 **Let my vindication come forth from your presence; ***
let your eyes be fixed on justice. R

3 Weigh my heart, summon me by night, *
　melt me down; you will find no impurity in me.

4 **I give no offense with my mouth as others do; ***
I have heeded the words of your lips.

5 My footsteps hold fast to the ways of your law; *
　in your paths my feet shall not stumble. R

6 **I call upon you, O God, for you will answer me; ***
incline your ear to me and hear my words.

7 Show me your marvelous loving-kindness, *
　O Savior of those who take refuge at your right hand
　from those who rise up against them. R

8 **Keep me as the apple of your eye; ***
hide me under the shadow of your wings,

9 from the wicked who assault me, *
　from my deadly enemies who surround me.

10 **They have closed their heart to pity, ***
and their mouth speaks proud things.

11 They press me hard,
now they surround me, *
　watching how they may cast me to the ground,

12 **like a lion, greedy for its prey, ***
and like a young lion lurking in secret places. R

13 Arise, O LORD; confront them and bring them down; *
    deliver me from the wicked by your sword.

14 **Deliver me, O LORD, by your hand** *
    from those whose portion in life is this world;

    whose bellies you fill with your treasure, *
        who are well supplied with children
        and leave their wealth to their little ones.

15 **But at my vindication I shall see your face;** *
    when I awake, I shall be satisfied, beholding your likeness.   **R**

    Good Lord, you are the searcher of human hearts.
    When we are surrounded by dangers,
    show us your favor,
    without which we would perish.
    Let not our hearts be earthbound,
    but may we follow your commandments
    and aspire to heaven's joy,
    which is won for us in Jesus Christ our Savior. **Amen.**   [548]

PSALM 18   Tone 3

R

1 I love you, O LORD my strength, *
    O LORD my stronghold, my crag, and my haven.

2 **My God, my rock in whom I put my trust,** *
    my shield, the horn of my salvation, and my refuge;
    you are worthy of praise.

3 I will call upon the LORD, *
    and so shall I be saved from my enemies.   **R**

4 **The breakers of death rolled over me,** *
    and the torrents of oblivion made me afraid.

5 The cords of hell entangled me, *
    and the snares of death were set for me.

6 **I called upon the LORD in my distress** *
    and cried out to my God for help.   **R**

    You heard my voice from your heavenly dwelling; *
    my cry of anguish came to your ears.

7　The earth reeled and rocked; *
　　the roots of the mountains shook;
　　they reeled because of your anger.

8　Smoke rose from your nostrils
　　and a consuming fire out of your mouth; *
　　hot burning coals blazed forth from you.

9　**You parted the heavens and came down** *
　　with a storm cloud under your feet.

10　You mounted on cherubim and flew; *
　　you swooped on the wings of the wind.　　R

11　**You wrapped darkness about you;** *
　　you made dark waters and thick clouds your pavilion.

12　From the brightness of your presence, through the clouds, *
　　burst hailstones and coals of fire.

13　**O LORD, you thundered out of heaven;** *
　　O Most High, you uttered your voice.

14　You loosed your arrows and scattered them; *
　　you hurled thunderbolts and routed them.

15　**The beds of the seas were uncovered,**
　　and the foundations of the world laid bare, *
　　at your battle cry, O LORD,
　　at the blast of the breath of your nostrils.　　R

16　You reached down from on high and grasped me; *
　　you drew me out of great waters.

17　**You delivered me from my strong enemies**
　　and from those who hated me; *
　　for they were too mighty for me.

18　They confronted me in the day of my disaster; *
　　but the LORD was my support.

19　**You brought me out into an open place;** *
　　you rescued me because you delighted in me.　　R

20　The LORD rewarded me because of my righteous dealing; *
　　because my hands were clean God rewarded me;

21　**for I have kept the ways of the LORD** *
　　and have not offended against my God;

22 for all God's judgments are before my eyes, *
  and the decrees of the LORD I have not put away from me;

23 **for I have been blameless with the LORD ***
  and have kept myself from iniquity;

24 Therefore the LORD rewarded me according to my righteous dealing, *
  seeing the cleanness of my hands.   R

25 **With the faithful you show yourself faithful, O God; ***
  with the forthright you show yourself forthright.

26 With the pure you show yourself pure, *
  but with the crooked you are wily.

27 **You will save a lowly people, ***
  but you will humble the haughty eyes.

28 You, O LORD, are my lamp; *
  my God, you make my darkness bright.

29 **With you I will break down an enclosure; ***
  with the help of my God I will scale any wall.   R

30 As for you, O God, your ways are perfect;
  the words of the LORD are tried in the fire; *
  you are a shield to all who trust in you.

31 **For who is God, but the LORD? ***
  who is the Rock, except our God?

32 It is God who girds me about with strength *
  and makes my way secure.   R

33 **You make me sure-footed like a deer ***
  and let me stand firm on the heights.

34 You train my hands for battle *
  and my arms for bending even a bow of bronze.

35 **You have given me your shield of victory; ***
  your right hand also sustains me;
  your loving care makes me great.

36 You lengthen my stride beneath me, *
  and my ankles do not give way.   R

37 **I pursue my enemies and overtake them; ***
  I will not turn back till I have destroyed them.

³⁸ I strike them down, and they cannot rise; *
  they fall defeated at my feet.

³⁹ You have girded me with strength for the battle; *
  you have cast down my adversaries beneath me;
 ⁴⁰ you have put my enemies to flight.

I destroy those who hate me;
⁴¹ they cry out, but there is none to help them; *
  they cry to the LORD, who does not answer.

⁴² I beat them small like dust before the wind; *
  I trample them like mud in the streets.   R

⁴³ You deliver me from the strife of the peoples; *
  you put me at the head of the nations.

⁴⁴ A people I have not known shall serve me;
no sooner shall they hear than they shall obey me; *
  strangers will cringe before me.

⁴⁵ The foreign peoples will lose heart; *
  they shall come trembling out of their strongholds.   R

⁴⁶ The LORD lives! Blessed is my Rock! *
  Exalted is the God of my salvation!

⁴⁷ The LORD is the God who gave me victory *
  and cast down the peoples beneath me.

⁴⁸ You rescued me from the fury of my enemies;
  you exalted me above those who rose against me; *
  you saved me from my deadly foe.   R

⁴⁹ Therefore will I extol you among the nations, O LORD, *
  and sing praises to your name.

⁵⁰ You multiply the victories of your king; *
  you show loving-kindness to your anointed,
  to David and his descendants forever.   R

Praise to you, God of our salvation.
You come to our help and set us free.
May your strength be our shield
and your word, our lamp,
that we may serve you with pure hearts
and find deliverance in Jesus Christ, our Savior.   **Amen.**   [549]

R

1 The heavens declare the glory of God, *
and the firmament shows forth the work of God's hands.

2 **One day tells its tale to another, ***
and one night imparts knowledge to another.

3 Although they have no words or language, *
and their voices are not heard,

4 **their sound has gone out into all lands, ***
and their message to the ends of the world.   R

In the deep has God set a pavilion for the sun; *
5 it comes forth like a bridegroom out of his chamber;
it rejoices like a champion to run its course.

6 **It goes forth from the uttermost edge of the heavens**
and runs about to the end of it again; *
nothing is hidden from its burning heat.   R

7 The law of the LORD is perfect and revives the soul; *
the testimony of the LORD is sure and gives wisdom to the innocent.

8 **The statutes of the LORD are just and rejoice the heart; ***
the commandment of the LORD is clear and gives light to the eyes.   R

9 The fear of the LORD is clean and endures forever; *
the judgments of the LORD are true and righteous altogether.

10 **More to be desired are they than gold, more than much fine gold, ***
sweeter far than honey, than honey in the comb.   R

11 By them also is your servant enlightened, *
and in keeping them there is great reward.

12 **Can people tell how often they offend? ***
cleanse me from my secret faults.

13 Above all, keep your servant from presumptuous sins;
let them not get dominion over me; *
then shall I be whole and sound,
and innocent of a great offense.   R

14 **Let the words of my mouth and the meditation of my heart**
 be acceptable in your sight, *
 O LORD, my strength and my redeemer.   R

Faithful God,
you sent us your Word as the sun of truth and justice
to shine upon all the world.
Open our eyes to see your glory in all your works,
that, rejoicing in your whole creation,
we may learn to serve you with gladness,
for the sake of him through whom all things were made,
Jesus Christ our Lord.   **Amen.**   [550]

PSALM 20   Tone 6; PH 169; PS 14

R

1 May the LORD answer you in the day of trouble, *
     the name of the God of Jacob defend you.

2 **From God's holy place may you receive help; ***
     may God strengthen you out of Zion.

3 May God remember all your offerings *
     and accept your burnt sacrifice;   R

4 **grant you your heart's desire ***
     and prosper all your plans.

5 We will shout for joy at your victory

   and triumph in the name of our God; *
     may the LORD grant all your requests.   R

6 **Now I know that the LORD gives victory to the anointed one; ***
     out of God's holy heaven will come an answer;
     the right hand of the LORD works victorious strength.

7 Some put their trust in chariots and some in horses, *
     but we will call upon the name of the LORD our God.

8 **They collapse and fall down, ***
     but we will arise and stand upright.

   [Unison]

9 **O LORD, give victory to the king ***
     and answer us when we call.   R

Almighty God,
you have given victory to Christ, your anointed one.
Keep us from stumbling into lesser loyalties,
and give us strength to stand firm,
trusting in the grace and peace
of Jesus Christ our Lord. **Amen.** [551]

PSALM 22

Tone 8; PH 168; PS 15–17

R

1 My God, my God, why have you forsaken me? *
       and are so far from my cry
       and from the words of my distress?

2 **O my God, I cry in the daytime, but you do not answer; ***
       by night as well, but I find no rest.   R

3 Yet you are the Holy One, *
       enthroned upon the praises of Israel.

4 **Our ancestors put their trust in you; ***
       they trusted, and you delivered them.

5 They cried out to you and were delivered; *
       they trusted in you and were not put to shame.   R

6 **But as for me, I am a worm and not a man, ***
       scorned by all and despised by the people.

7 All who see me laugh me to scorn; *
       they curl their lips and wag their heads, saying,

8 **"He trusted in the LORD; let the LORD deliver him; ***
       let God rescue him, if God delights in him."   R

9 Yet you are the one who took me out of the womb, *
       and kept me safe upon my mother's breast.

10 **I have been entrusted to you ever since I was born; ***
        you were my God when I was still in my mother's womb.

11 Be not far from me, for trouble is near, *
        and there is none to help.   R

12 **Many young bulls encircle me; ***
        strong bulls of Bashan surround me.

13 They open wide their jaws at me, *
    like a ravening and a roaring lion.

14 I am poured out like water;
    all my bones are out of joint; *
    my heart within my breast is melting wax.

15 My mouth is dried out like a pot-sherd;
    my tongue sticks to the roof of my mouth; *
    and you have laid me in the dust of the grave.   R

16 Packs of dogs close me in,
    and gangs of evildoers circle around me; *
    17 they pierce my hands and my feet;
    I can count all my bones.

    They stare and gloat over me; *
    18 they divide my garments among them;
    they cast lots for my clothing.   R

19 Be not far away, O LORD; *
    you are my strength; hasten to help me.

20 Save me from the sword, *
    my life from the power of the dog.

21 Save me from the lion's mouth, *
    my wretched body from the horns of wild bulls.   R

22 I will declare your name to the community; *
    in the midst of the congregation I will praise you.

23 Praise the LORD, you that are God-fearing; *
    stand in awe of the LORD, O offspring of Israel;
    all you of Jacob's line, give glory.

24 For the LORD does not despise nor abhor the poor in their poverty;
    neither is the LORD's face hidden from them; *
    but when they cry out, the LORD hears them.   R

25 My praise is of God in the great assembly; *
    I will perform my vows in the presence of those who
        worship the LORD.

26 The poor shall eat and be satisfied,
    and those who seek the LORD shall give praise: *
    "May your heart live forever!"

27 **All the ends of the earth shall remember and turn to God, ***
  and all the families of the nations shall bow before the LORD.

28 For sovereignty belongs to the LORD, *
  who rules over the nations.   R

29 **To the L**ORD **alone all who sleep in the earth bow down in worship; ***
  all who go down to the dust fall before the LORD.

30 My soul shall live for God;
  my descendants shall serve the LORD; *
    they shall be known as the LORD's forever.

31 **They shall come and make known to a people yet unborn ***
  the saving deeds that God has done.   R

Eternal God,
your tortured Son felt abandoned,
and cried out in anguish from the cross,
yet you delivered him.
He overcame the bonds of death
and rose in triumph from the grave.
Do not hide your face from those who cry out to you.
Feed the hungry, strengthen the weak,
and break the chains of the oppressed,
that your people may rejoice in your saving deeds.
This we ask in the name of Jesus Christ our Savior.   **Amen.**   [552]

PSALM 23   Tone 6; PH 170–175; PS 18–20

R

1 The LORD is my shepherd; *
    I shall not be in want.

2 **You make me lie down in green pastures ***
    and lead me beside still waters.   R

3 You revive my soul *
    and guide me along right pathways for your name's sake.

4 **Though I walk through the valley of the shadow of death,**
  I shall fear no evil; *
      for you are with me;
      your rod and your staff, they comfort me.   R

5 You spread a table before me in the presence of those who trouble me; *
    you have anointed my head with oil,
    and my cup is running over.

6 **Surely your goodness and mercy shall follow me all the days of my life, ***
    and I will dwell in the house of the LORD forever.   R

    Lord Jesus Christ, our good shepherd,
    in the waters of Baptism you give us birth,
    and at your table you nourish us with heavenly food.
    In your goodness and mercy,
    lead us along safe paths,
    beyond the terrors of evil and death,
    to the house of the Lord
    where we may rest securely in you forever. **Amen.**   [553]

PSALM 24   Tone 3; PH 176, 177; PS 21, 22

R

1 The earth is the LORD's and all that is in it, *
    the world and all who dwell therein.

2 **For it is the LORD who founded it upon the seas ***
    and made it firm upon the rivers of the deep.   R

3 "Who can ascend the hill of the LORD? *
    and who can stand in God's holy place?"

4 **"Those who have clean hands and a pure heart, ***
    who have not pledged themselves to falsehood,
    nor sworn by what is a fraud.

5 They shall receive a blessing from the LORD *
    and a just reward from the God of their salvation."

6 **Such is the generation of those who seek the LORD, ***
    of those who seek your face, O God of Jacob.   R

7 Lift up your heads, O gates;
    lift them high, O everlasting doors; *
    and the glorious Sovereign shall come in.

8 **"Who is this glorious Sovereign?" ***
    "The LORD, strong and mighty,
    the LORD, mighty in battle."

9 Lift up your heads, O gates;
     lift them high, O everlasting doors; *
         and the glorious Sovereign shall come in.

10 **"And who is this glorious Sovereign?"** *
     "The Lord,
         the Lord of hosts is the glorious Sovereign."   **R**

God of all creation,
open our hearts
that Christ, the King of glory, may enter and rule our lives.
Give us clean hands and pure hearts,
that we may stand in your presence and receive your blessing
through the same, Jesus Christ our Lord.   **Amen.**   [554]

PSALM 25   Tone 8 or 7; PH 178; PS 23

R

1 To you, O Lord, I lift up my soul;
    2my God, I put my trust in you; *
        let me not be humiliated,
        nor let my enemies triumph over me.

3 **Let none who look to you be put to shame;** *
     let the treacherous be disappointed in their schemes.   **R**

4 Show me your ways, O Lord, *
     and teach me your paths.

5 **Lead me in your truth and teach me,** *
     for you are the God of my salvation;
     in you have I trusted all the day long.   **R**

6 Remember, O Lord, your compassion and love, *
     for they are from everlasting.

7 **Remember not the sins of my youth and my transgressions;** *
     remember me according to your love
     and for the sake of your goodness, O Lord.   **R**

8 Gracious and upright are you, O Lord; *
     therefore you teach sinners in your way.

9 **You guide the humble in doing right** *
     and teach your way to the lowly.

10 All your paths, O LORD, are love and faithfulness *
    to those who keep your covenant and your testimonies.   **R**

11 **For your name's sake, O LORD, ***
    forgive my sin, for it is great.

12 Who are they who fear the LORD? *
    the LORD will teach them the way that they should choose.   **R**

13 **They shall dwell in prosperity, ***
    and their offspring shall inherit the land.

14 The LORD is a friend to the God-fearing *
    and will show them the holy covenant.

15 **My eyes are ever looking to the LORD, ***
    who shall pluck my feet out of the net.   **R**

16 Turn to me and have pity on me, *
    for I am left alone and in misery.

17 **The sorrows of my heart have increased; ***
    bring me out of my troubles.

18 Look upon my adversity and misery *
    and forgive me all my sin.   **R**

19 **Look upon my enemies, for they are many, ***
    and they bear a violent hatred against me.

20 Protect my life and deliver me; *
    let me not be put to shame, for I have trusted in you.

21 **Let integrity and uprightness preserve me, ***
    for my hope has been in you.

[Unison]

22 **Deliver Israel, O God, ***
    out of all their troubles.   **R**

Covenant Friend,
remember not our sins,
but recall your compassion to your children.
We turn to you for guidance and life,
turn also to us and be gracious,
that we may always follow in the way
of Jesus Christ our Redeemer. **Amen.** [555]

R

1 Give judgment for me, O LORD,
   for I have lived with integrity; *
      I have trusted in the LORD and have not faltered.

2 **Test me, O LORD, and try me; ***
      examine my heart and my mind.

3 For your love is before my eyes; *
      I have walked faithfully with you.   **R**

4 **I have not sat with the worthless, ***
      nor do I consort with the deceitful.

5 I have hated the company of evildoers; *
      I will not sit down with the wicked.

6 **I will wash my hands in innocence, O LORD, ***
      that I may go in procession round your altar,

7 singing aloud a song of thanksgiving *
      and recounting all your wonderful deeds.   **R**

8 **LORD, I love the house in which you dwell ***
      and the place where your glory abides.

9 Do not sweep me away with sinners, *
      nor my life with those who thirst for blood,

10 **whose hands are full of evil plots, ***
      and their right hand full of bribes.   **R**

11 As for me, I will live with integrity; *
      redeem me, O LORD, and have pity on me.

12 **My foot stands on level ground; ***
      in the full assembly I will bless the LORD.   **R**

Eternal God,
   you know what is in our hearts and minds;
   you test us to strengthen our faith.
   Keep your love always before us,
   and direct our steps,
   that we may be steadfast in your way
   and join with all your saints
   to give you praise, now and forever. **Amen.** [556]

R

1 The LORD is my light and my salvation;
whom then shall I fear? *
   the LORD is the strength of my life;
   of whom then shall I be afraid?

2 **When evildoers came upon me to eat up my flesh, ***
   it was they, my foes and my adversaries, who stumbled and fell.

3 Though an army should encamp against me, *
   yet my heart shall not be afraid;

and though war should rise up against me, *
   yet will I put my trust in the LORD.

4 One thing have I asked of the LORD;
one thing I seek; *
   that I may dwell in the house of the LORD all the days of my life;

to behold the fair beauty of the LORD, *
   to seek God in the temple.   R

5 For on the day of trouble the LORD shall shelter me in safety; *
   the LORD shall hide me in the secrecy of the holy place
   and set me high upon a rock.

6 **Even now the LORD lifts up my head ***
   above my enemies round about me.

Therefore I will offer in the holy place an oblation
with sounds of great gladness; *
   I will sing and make music to the LORD.   R

7 **Hearken to my voice, O LORD, when I call; ***
   have mercy on me and answer me.

8 You speak in my heart and say, "Seek my face." *
   Your face, LORD, will I seek.

9 **Hide not your face from me, ***
   nor turn away your servant in displeasure.

You have been my helper;
cast me not away; *
   do not forsake me, O God of my salvation.

10 **Though my father and my mother forsake me,** *
   the LORD will sustain me.   **R**

11 Show me your way, O LORD; *
   lead me on a level path, because of my enemies.

12 **Deliver me not into the hand of my adversaries,** *
   for false witnesses have risen up against me,
   and also those who speak malice.

13 What if I had not believed
   that I should see the goodness of the LORD *
   in the land of the living!

14 **O tarry and await the LORD's pleasure;**
   be strong, and the LORD shall comfort your heart; *
   wait patiently for the LORD.   **R**

O God, guardian and guide of all your people,
protect and lead us through times of trouble,
establishing our faith on the rock of Jesus Christ,
who is the way, the truth, and the life.   **Amen.**   [557]

PSALM 28   Tone 8

R

1 O LORD, I call to you;
   my Rock, do not be deaf to my cry; *
      lest, if you do not hear me,
      I become like those who go down to the pit.

2 **Hear the voice of my prayer when I cry out to you,** *
   when I lift up my hands to your holy of holies.   **R**

3 Do not snatch me away with the wicked or with the evildoers, *
   who speak peaceably with their neighbors,
   while strife is in their hearts.

4 **Repay them according to their deeds,** *
   and according to the wickedness of their actions.

According to the work of their hands repay them, *
   and give them their just deserts.

5 **O LORD, they have no understanding of your doings,**
   nor of the works of your hands; *
      therefore you will break them down and not build them up.   **R**

6 Blessed is the LORD! *
      for you have heard the voice of my prayer.

7 **The LORD is my strength and my shield; ***
      my heart trusts in you, and I have been helped;

   therefore my heart dances for joy, *
      and in my song will I praise you.   **R**

8 **You, O LORD, are the strength of your people, ***
      a safe refuge for your anointed.

   [Unison]

9 **Save your people and bless your inheritance; ***
      shepherd them and carry them forever.   R

   Strong Shepherd of your people,
   you hear us when we lift our hands in prayer to you.
   Strengthen us to offer you thanks
   for the mighty works that you have done,
   and make our hearts leap for joy;
   through Jesus Christ our Lord.   **Amen.**   [558]

PSALM 29   Tone 3; PH 180; PS 26

R

1 Ascribe to the LORD, you gods, *
      ascribe to the LORD glory and strength.

2 **Ascribe to the LORD the glory that is due the holy name; ***
      worship the LORD in the beauty of holiness.   R

3 The voice of the LORD is upon the waters;
   the God of glory thunders; *
      the LORD is upon the mighty waters.

4 **The voice of the LORD is a powerful voice; ***
      the voice of the LORD is a voice of splendor.   R

5 The voice of the LORD breaks the cedar trees; *
      the LORD breaks the cedars of Lebanon;

6 **the LORD makes Lebanon skip like a calf, ***
      and Mount Hermon like a young wild ox.   R

7 The voice of the LORD splits the flames of fire;
the voice of the LORD shakes the wilderness; *
the LORD shakes the wilderness of Kadesh.

8 **The voice of the LORD makes the oak trees writhe ***
and strips the forests bare.

9 And in the temple of the LORD *
all are crying, "Glory!"   **R**

10 **The LORD sits enthroned above the flood; ***
the LORD sits enthroned as Sovereign forevermore.

[Unison]

11 **The LORD shall give strength to the chosen people; ***
the LORD shall give the people the blessing of peace.   R

God of mystery and power,
open our eyes to the fire of your love,
and open our ears to the thunder of your justice,
that we may receive your gifts of blessing and peace,
to the glory of your name;
through Jesus Christ our Lord.   **Amen.**   [559]

PSALM 30   Tone 3; PH 181; PS 27

R

1 I will exalt you, O LORD,
because you have lifted me up *
and have not let my enemies triumph over me.

2 **O LORD my God, I cried out to you, ***
and you restored me to health.

3 You brought me up, O LORD, from the dead; *
you restored my life as I was going down to the grave.   **R**

4 **Sing to the LORD, you faithful servants; ***
give thanks for the remembrance of God's holiness.

5 For God's wrath lasts but the twinkling of an eye, *
God's favor endures for a lifetime.

Weeping may spend the night, *
but joy comes in the morning.

6 While I felt secure, I said,
  "I shall never be disturbed. *
     7You, LORD, with your favor, made me as strong as the mountains."

  Then you hid your face, *
    and I was filled with fear.   R

8 I cried to you, O LORD; *
    I pleaded with the Lord, saying,

9 **"What profit is there in my blood, if I go down to the pit? ***
    will the dust praise you or declare your faithfulness?

10 Hear, O LORD, and have mercy upon me; *
    O LORD, be my helper."   R

11 **You have turned my wailing into dancing; ***
    you have put off my sack-cloth and clothed me with joy.

   [Unison]

12 **Therefore my heart sings to you without ceasing; ***
    O LORD my God, I will give you thanks forever.   R

   Loving God,
   glorious in giving and restoring life,
   do not hide your face from your people overcome with loneliness and fear.
   Turn our weeping into dancing,
   our despair into joy,
   and raise us up with Christ,
   that we may rejoice in your presence forever. **Amen.**   [560]

PSALM 31   Tone 6 or 8; PH 182, 183; PS 28

R
1 In you, O LORD, have I taken refuge;
    let me never be put to shame; *
      deliver me in your righteousness.

2 **Incline your ear to me; ***
    make haste to deliver me.   R

3 Be my strong rock, a castle to keep me safe,
    for you are my crag and my stronghold; *
      for the sake of your name, lead me and guide me.

4 **Take me out of the net that they have secretly set for me, ***
    for you are my tower of strength.

5 Into your hands I commend my spirit, *
        for you have redeemed me,
           O LORD, O God of truth.   **R**

6 **I hate those who cling to worthless idols,** *
        and I put my trust in the LORD.

7 I will rejoice and be glad because of your mercy; *
        for you have seen my affliction;
           you know my distress.

8 **You have not shut me up in the power of the enemy;** *
        you have set my feet in an open place.   R

9 Have mercy on me, O LORD, for I am in trouble; *
        my eye is consumed with sorrow,
           and also my throat and my belly.

10 **For my life is wasted with grief,**
        and my years with sighing; *
           my strength fails me because of affliction,
              and my bones are consumed.   R

11 I have become a reproach to all my enemies and even to my neighbors,
        a dismay to those of my acquaintance; *
           when they see me in the street they avoid me.

12 **I am forgotten, out of mind, as if I were dead;** *
        I am as useless as a broken pot.

13 For I have heard the whispering of the crowd;
        fear is all around; *
           they put their heads together against me;
              they plot to take my life.   **R**

14 **But as for me, I have trusted in you, O LORD.** *
        I have said, "You are my God.

15 My times are in your hand; *
        rescue me from the hand of my enemies,
           and from those who persecute me.

16 **Make your face to shine upon your servant,** *
        and in your loving-kindness save me."   R

17 LORD, let me not be ashamed for having called upon you; *
        rather, let the wicked be put to shame;
           let them be silent in the grave.

¹⁸ **Let the lying lips be silenced which speak against the righteous,** *
     haughtily, disdainfully, and with contempt.   R

¹⁹ How great is your goodness, O LORD!
     which you have laid up for those who fear you; *
          which you have done in the sight of all
          for those who put their trust in you.

²⁰ **You hide them in the covert of your presence from those**
               who slander them; *
     you keep them in your shelter from the strife of tongues.   R

²¹ Blessed be the LORD! *
     for you have shown me the wonders of your love in a besieged city.

²² **Yet I said in my alarm,**
     "I have been cut off from the sight of your eyes." *
     Nevertheless, you heard the sound of my entreaty
     when I cried out to you.   R

²³ Love the LORD, all you who are faithful; *
     the LORD protects the pious,
     but repays to the full those who act haughtily.

²⁴ **Be strong and let your heart take courage,** *
     all you who wait for the LORD.   R

Helper of the helpless,
comforter of the afflicted,
may your servants who stand in the midst of evil
find strength in the knowledge of your presence,
and praise you for the wonders of your love;
through Jesus Christ our Redeemer.   **Amen.**   [561]

PSALM 32   Tone 6; PH 184; PS 29

R

¹ Happy are they whose transgressions are forgiven, *
     and whose sin is put away!

² **Happy are they to whom the LORD imputes no guilt,** *
     and in whose spirit there is no guile!   R

³ While I held my tongue, my bones withered away, *
     because of my groaning all day long.

4 **For your hand was heavy upon me day and night; ***
   my moisture was dried up as in the heat of summer.

5 Then I acknowledged my sin to you, *
   and did not conceal my guilt.   **R**

I said, "I will confess my transgressions to the LORD." *
   Then you forgave me the guilt of my sin.

6 Therefore all the faithful will make their prayers to you in time of trouble; *
   when the great waters overflow, they shall not reach them.

7 **You are my hiding-place;**
you preserve me from trouble; *
   you surround me with shouts of deliverance.   **R**

8 "I will instruct you and teach you in the way that you should go; *
   I will guide you with my eye.

9 **Do not be like horse or mule, which have no understanding; ***
   who must be fitted with bit and bridle,
   or else they will not stay near you."

10 Great are the tribulations of the wicked; *
   but mercy embraces those who trust in the LORD.

11 **Be glad, you righteous, and rejoice in the LORD; ***
   shout for joy, all who are true of heart.   **R**

Merciful God,
we confess that we have squandered your blessings
and turned our backs on your love.
Help us to repent and return to you,
confident that you will welcome us as your sons and daughters
in Jesus Christ. **Amen.**   [562]

PSALM 33   Tone 6; PH 185; PS 30, 31

R

1 Rejoice in the LORD, you righteous; *
   it is good for the just to sing praises.

2 **Praise the LORD with the harp; ***
   play upon the psaltery and lyre.

3 Sing for the LORD a new song; *
   sound a fanfare with all your skill upon the trumpet.   **R**

4 **For your word, O LORD, is right, ***
    and all your works are sure.

5 You love righteousness and justice; *
    your loving-kindness, O LORD, fills the whole earth.

6 **By your word, O LORD, were the heavens made, ***
    by the breath of your mouth all the heavenly hosts.

7 You gather up the waters of the ocean as in a water-skin *
    and store up the depths of the sea.   **R**

8 **Let all the earth fear the LORD; ***
    let all who dwell in the world stand in reverence.

9 For the LORD spoke, and it came to pass; *
    the LORD commanded, and it stood fast.   **R**

10 **The LORD brings the will of the nations to naught ***
    and thwarts the designs of the peoples.

11 But the LORD's will stands fast forever, *
    and the designs of the LORD's heart from age to age.

12 **Happy is the nation whose God is the LORD! ***
    happy the people you have chosen to be your own!   R

13 O LORD, you look down from heaven *
    and behold all the people in the world.

14 **From where you sit enthroned you turn your gaze ***
    on all who dwell on the earth.

15 You fashion all the hearts of them *
    and understand all their works.

16 **There is no ruler that can be saved by a mighty army; ***
    a warrior is not delivered by great strength.

17 The horse is a vain hope for deliverance; *
    for all its strength it cannot save.   **R**

18 **Behold, your eye, O LORD, is upon those who fear you, ***
    on those who wait upon your love,

19 to pluck their lives from death, *
    and to feed them in time of famine.   **R**

20 **Our soul waits for you, O LORD; ***
    you are our help and our shield.

21 Indeed, our heart rejoices in you, *
    for in your holy name we put our trust.

22 **Let your loving-kindness, O LORD, be upon us, ***
    as we have put our trust in you.   **R**

Lord God,
with your Son you made heaven and earth,
and through him you continue to accomplish your purpose for creation.
Make us witnesses to your truth and instruments of your peace,
that all may know you are the God of justice,
and trust your holy name;
through Jesus Christ our Savior. **Amen.**   [563]

PSALM 34   Tone 6; PH 187; PS 32, 33

R

1 At all times I will bless the LORD, *
    whose praise shall ever be in my mouth.

2 **I will glory in the LORD; ***
    let the humble hear and rejoice.

3 Proclaim with me the greatness of the LORD; *
    let us exalt the name of the LORD together.   **R**

4 **I sought the LORD, who answered me ***
    and delivered me out of all my terror.

5 Look upon the LORD and be radiant, *
    and let not your faces be ashamed.   **R**

6 **I called in my affliction and the LORD heard me ***
    and saved me from all my troubles.

7 The angel of the LORD encompasses the God-fearing, *
    and the LORD will deliver them.

8 **Taste and see that the LORD is good; ***
    happy are they who trust in the LORD!   **R**

9 Fear the LORD, you holy ones, *
    for those who are God-fearing lack nothing.

10 **The young lions lack and suffer hunger, ***
    but those who seek the LORD lack nothing that is good.   **R**

11 Come, children, and listen to me; *
    I will teach you the fear of the LORD.

12 Who among you loves life *
    and desires long life to enjoy prosperity?

13 Keep your tongue from evil-speaking *
    and your lips from lying words.

14 Turn from evil and do good; *
    seek peace and pursue it.   R

15 The eyes of the LORD are upon the righteous, *
    and the ears of the LORD are open to their cry.

16 The face of the LORD is against those who do evil, *
    to root out the remembrance of them from the earth.

17 The righteous cry, and the LORD hears them *
    and delivers them from all their troubles.

18 The LORD is near to the brokenhearted *
    and will save those whose spirits are crushed.   R

19 Many are the troubles of the righteous, *
    but the LORD will deliver the just out of them all.

20 The LORD will keep safe the bones of the righteous; *
    not one of them shall be broken.

21 Evil shall slay the wicked, *
    and those who hate the righteous will be punished.

22 The LORD ransoms the life of those chosen to serve, *
    and none will be punished who trust in the LORD.   R

Graciously hear us, Lord, for you alone we seek.
Quiet us with the peace which passes understanding,
and make us radiant with the knowledge of your goodness;
through Jesus Christ our Lord.   **Amen.**   [564]

PSALM 35   Tone 8

R

1 Fight those who fight me, O LORD; *
    attack those who are attacking me.

2 Take up shield and armor *
    and rise up to help me.

3 Draw the sword and bar the way against those who pursue me; *
    say to my soul, "I am your salvation."   **R**

4 **Let those who seek after my life be shamed and humbled, ***
    let those who plot my ruin fall back and be dismayed.

5 Let them be like chaff before the wind, *
    and let the angel of the LORD drive them away.

6 **Let their way be dark and slippery, ***
    and let the angel of the LORD pursue them.   R

7 For they have secretly spread a net for me without a cause; *
    without a cause they have dug a pit to take me alive.

8 **Let ruin come upon them unawares; ***
    let them be caught in the net they hid;
    let them fall into the pit they dug.

9 Then I will be joyful in you, O LORD; *
    I will glory in your victory.

10 **My very bones will say, "LORD, who is like you? ***
    You deliver the poor from those who are too strong for them,
    the poor and needy from those who rob them."   R

11 Malicious witnesses rise up against me; *
    they charge me with matters I know nothing about.

12 **They pay me evil in exchange for good; ***
    my soul is full of despair.

13 But when they were sick I dressed in sack-cloth *
    and humbled myself by fasting;

14 **I prayed with my whole heart,**
    as one would for a friend or a brother; *
    I behaved like one who mourns for a mother,
    bowed down and grieving.   R

15 But when I stumbled, they were glad and gathered together;
    they gathered against me; *
    strangers whom I did not know tore me to pieces and would not stop.

16 **They put me to the test and mocked me; ***
    they gnashed at me with their teeth.   R

17 O Lord, how long will you look on? *
     rescue me from the roaring beasts,
     and my life from the young lions.

18 **I will give you thanks in the great congregation; ***
     I will praise you in the mighty throng.   R

19 Do not let my treacherous foes rejoice over me, *
     nor let those who hate me without a cause wink at each other.

20 **For they do not plan for peace, ***
     but invent deceitful schemes against the quiet in the land.

21 They opened their mouths at me and said, *
     "Aha! we saw it with our own eyes."   **R**

22 **You saw it, O LORD; do not be silent; ***
     O Lord, be not far from me.

23 Awake, arise, to my cause! *
     to my defense, my God and my Lord!

24 **Give me justice, O LORD my God,**
     according to your righteousness; *
     do not let them triumph over me.

25 Do not let them say in their hearts,
     "Aha! just what we want!" *
     Do not let them say, "We have swallowed you up."   **R**

26 **Let all who rejoice at my ruin be ashamed and disgraced; ***
     let those who boast against me be clothed with dismay and shame.

27 Let those who favor my cause sing out with joy and be glad; *
     let them say always, "Great are you, O LORD;
     you desire the prosperity of your servant."

28 **And my tongue shall be talking of your righteousness ***
     and of your praise all the day long.   R

God of our salvation,
come quickly to free the poor from their oppressors,
and establish your reign of justice on earth,
that your people may sing out with joy;
through Jesus Christ our Lord.   **Amen.**   [565]

R

1 There is a voice of rebellion deep in the heart of the wicked; *
 there is no fear of God before their eyes.

2 **They flatter themselves in their own eyes ***
 that their hateful sin will not be found out.

3 The words of their mouth are wicked and deceitful; *
 they have left off acting wisely and doing good.

4 **They think up wickedness upon their beds**
and have set themselves in no good way; *
 they do not abhor that which is evil.   R

5 Your love, O LORD, reaches to the heavens, *
 and your faithfulness to the clouds.

6 **Your righteousness is like the strong mountains,**
your justice like the great deep; *
 you save humans and beasts alike, O LORD.   R

7 How priceless is your love, O God! *
 your people take refuge under the shadow of your wings.

8 **They feast upon the abundance of your house; ***
 you give them drink from the river of your delights.

9 For with you is the well of life, *
 and in your light we see light.   R

10 **Continue your loving-kindness to those who know you, ***
 and your favor to those who are true of heart.

11 Let not the foot of the proud come near me, *
 nor the hand of the wicked push me aside.

12 **See how they are fallen, those who work wickedness! ***
 they are cast down and shall not be able to rise.   R

Eternal God,
you satisfy our hunger
by feeding us with the bread of life,
and you quench our thirst for righteousness
by your mighty acts.
Nourish us always by your Spirit,
that we may grow into the stature of Jesus Christ.   **Amen.**   [566]

R

1 Do not fret yourself because of evildoers; *
       do not be jealous of those who do wrong.

2 **For they shall soon wither like the grass, ***
       and like the green grass fade away.   R

3 Put your trust in the LORD and do good; *
       dwell in the land and feed on its riches.

4 **Take delight in the LORD, ***
       who shall give you your heart's desire.   R

5 Commit your way to the LORD; put your trust in the LORD, *
       who will bring it to pass.

6 **The LORD will make your righteousness as clear as the light ***
       and your just dealing as the noonday.

7 Be still before the LORD; *
       wait patiently for the LORD.

   Do not fret yourself over the one who prospers, *
       the one who succeeds in evil schemes.   R

8 Refrain from anger, leave rage alone; *
       do not fret yourself; it leads only to evil.

9 **For evildoers shall be cut off, ***
       but those who wait upon the LORD shall possess the land.   R

10 In a little while the wicked shall be no more; *
       you shall search out their place, but they will not be there.

11 **But the lowly shall possess the land; ***
       they will delight in abundance of peace.   R

       *   *   *

39 But the deliverance of the righteous comes from the LORD, *
       who is their stronghold in time of trouble.

40 **The LORD will help them and rescue them; ***
       the LORD will rescue them from the wicked and deliver them,
       because in the LORD they seek refuge.   R

God our strength,
give us the humility to trust in your loving care,
and the patience to be faithful in seeking your kingdom,
that we may come to share in the inheritance of your saints;
through Jesus Christ our Savior.   **Amen.**   [567]

PSALM 38   Tone 7

R

1 O LORD, do not rebuke me in your anger; *
    do not punish me in your wrath.

2 **For your arrows have already pierced me, ***
    and your hand presses hard upon me.   R

3 There is no health in my flesh,
  because of your indignation; *
      there is no soundness in my body, because of my sin.

4 **For my iniquities overwhelm me; ***
    like a heavy burden they are too much for me to bear.   R

5 My wounds stink and fester *
    by reason of my foolishness.

6 **I am utterly bowed down and prostrate; ***
    I go about in mourning all the day long.

7 Searing pain fills my innards; *
    there is no health in my body.

8 **I am utterly numb and crushed; ***
    I wail, because of the groaning of my heart.   R

9 O Lord, you know all my desires, *
    and my sighing is not hidden from you.

10 **My heart is pounding, my strength has failed me, ***
    and the brightness of my eyes is gone from me.

11 My friends and companions draw back from my affliction; *
    my neighbors stand afar off.   **R**

12 **Those who seek after my life lay snares for me; ***
    those who strive to hurt me speak of my ruin
    and plot treachery all the day long.

13 But I am like the deaf who do not hear, *
    like those who are mute and do not open their mouth.

14 **I have become like one who does not hear ***
     and from whose mouth comes no defense.   R

15 For in you, O LORD, have I fixed my hope; *
     you will answer me, O Lord my God.

16 **For I said, "Do not let them rejoice at my expense, ***
     those who gloat over me when my foot slips."   R

17 Truly, I am on the verge of falling, *
     and my pain is always with me.

18 **I will confess my iniquity ***
     and be sorry for my sin.

19 Those who are my enemies without cause are mighty, *
     and many in number are those who wrongfully hate me.

20 **Those who repay evil for good slander me, ***
     because I follow the course that is right.   R

21 O LORD, do not forsake me; *
     be not far from me, O my God.

22 **Make haste to help me, ***
     O Lord of my salvation.   R

God of compassion,
when we are weighed down by the burden of our sins,
help us to remember that you do not forsake us,
but show mercy through Jesus Christ our Savior.   **Amen.**   [568]

PSALM 39   Tone 8

R

1 I said, "I will keep watch upon my ways, *
     so that I do not offend with my tongue.

   I will put a muzzle on my mouth *
   while the wicked are in my presence."

2 So I held my tongue and said nothing; *
     I refrained from rash words;
     but my pain became unbearable.

3 **My heart was hot within me;**
   while I pondered, the fire burst into flame; *
   I spoke out with my tongue: R

4 LORD, let me know my end and the number of my days, *
    so that I may know how short my life is.

5 **You have given me a mere handful of days,**
    and my lifetime is as nothing in your sight; *
        truly, even those who stand erect are but a puff of wind.

6 We walk about like a shadow,
    and in vain we are in turmoil; *
        we heap up riches and cannot tell who will gather them.   **R**

7 **And now, what is my hope? ***
        O Lord, my hope is in you.

8 Deliver me from all my transgressions *
    and do not make me the taunt of the fool.

9 **I fell silent and did not open my mouth, ***
    for surely it was you that did it.

10 Take your affliction from me; *
    I am worn down by the blows of your hand.   **R**

11 **With rebukes for sin you punish us;**
    like a moth you eat away all that is dear to us; *
        truly, everyone is but a puff of wind.   R

12 Hear my prayer, O LORD,
    and give ear to my cry; *
        hold not your peace at my tears.

    For I am but a sojourner with you, *
        a wayfarer, as all my ancestors were.

    [Unison]

13 **Turn your gaze from me, that I may be glad again, ***
        before I go my way and am no more.   R

    God of hope,
    when we are troubled by fear and uncertainty,
    teach us to commit our lives to your care,
    and to trust in the knowledge of your love and forgiveness,
    that we may find peace in Jesus Christ our Redeemer.   **Amen.**   [569]

R

1 I waited patiently upon you, O LORD; *
  you stooped to me and heard my cry.

2 **You lifted me out of the desolate pit, out of the mire and clay; ***
  you set my feet upon a high cliff and made my footing sure.

3 You put a new song in my mouth,
  a song of praise to our God; *
    many shall see, and stand in awe,
    and put their trust in the LORD.   **R**

4 **Happy are they who trust in the LORD! ***
  they do not resort to evil spirits or turn to false gods.

5 Great things are they that you have done, O LORD my God!
  how great your wonders and your plans for us! *
    there is none who can be compared with you.

  Oh, that I could make them known and tell them! *
  but they are more than I can count.   R

6 In sacrifice and offering you take no pleasure *
  (you have given me ears to hear you);

  burnt-offering and sin-offering you have not required, *
  ⁷ and so I said, "Behold, I come.

  In the roll of the book it is written concerning me: *
    ⁸ 'I love to do your will, O my God;
    your law is deep in my heart.' "   **R**

9 **I proclaimed righteousness in the great congregation; ***
  behold, I did not restrain my lips;
  and that, O LORD, you know.

10 Your righteousness have I not hidden in my heart;
  I have spoken of your faithfulness and your deliverance; *
    I have not concealed your love and faithfulness from the great congregation.

11 **You are the LORD;**
  do not withhold your compassion from me; *
    let your love and your faithfulness keep me safe forever,   R

12 for innumerable troubles have crowded upon me;
   my sins have overtaken me, and I cannot see; *
      they are more in number than the hairs of my head,
      and my heart fails me.   **R**

13 **Be pleased, O LORD, to deliver me; ***
   O LORD, make haste to help me.

14 Let them be ashamed and altogether dismayed
   who seek after my life to destroy it; *
      let them draw back and be disgraced
      who take pleasure in my misfortune.

15 **Let those who say "Aha!" and gloat over me be confounded, ***
   because they are ashamed.   R

16 Let all who seek you rejoice in you and be glad; *
      let those who love your salvation continually say,
      "Great is the LORD!"

17 **Though I am poor and afflicted, ***
   the Lord will have regard for me.

   [Unison]

   You are my helper and my deliverer; *
      do not tarry, O my God.   R

   O God,
   none can compare with you,
   for your wondrous deeds for our salvation are without number.
   Make us bold witnesses to your faithfulness
   that all the earth may rejoice in your love toward us
   in Jesus Christ our Redeemer.   **Amen.**   [570]

PSALM 41   Tone 8

R

1 Happy are they who consider the poor and needy! *
   the LORD will deliver them in the time of trouble.

2 **The LORD preserves them and keeps them alive,**
   so that they may be happy in the land; *
      the LORD does not hand them over to the will of their enemies.

3 The LORD sustains them on their sickbed *
   and ministers to them in their illness.   R

4 I said, "LORD, be merciful to me; *
   heal me, for I have sinned against you."

5 My enemies are saying wicked things about me, *
   asking when I will die, and when my name will perish.

6 Even if they come to see me, they speak empty words; *
   their heart collects false rumors;
   they go outside and spread them.

7 All my enemies whisper together about me *
   and devise evil against me.   R

8 They say that a deadly thing has fastened on me, *
   that I have taken to my bed and will never get up again.

9 Even my best friend, whom I trusted,
   who broke bread with me, *
      has scorned me and turned against me.

10 But you, O LORD, be merciful to me and raise me up, *
   and I shall repay them.   R

11 By this I know you are pleased with me, *
   that my enemy does not triumph over me.

12 In my integrity you hold me fast, *
   and shall set me before your face forever.

   [Unison]

13 Blessed be the LORD God of Israel, *
   from age to age. Amen. Amen.   R

   Remember us, gracious God,
   when we are lonely and depressed,
   and support us in the night of grief and despair,
   for you are faithful
   and you do not abandon your broken ones.
   We ask this in the name of Jesus Christ our Lord.   **Amen.**   [571]

R

1 As the deer longs for the water-brooks, *
     so longs my soul for you, O God.

2 **My soul is athirst for God, athirst for the living God; ***
     when shall I come to appear before the presence of God?

3 My tears have been my food day and night, *
     while all day long they say to me,
     "Where now is your God?"   **R**

4 **I pour out my soul when I think on these things: ***
     how I went with the multitude and led them into the house of God,

   with the voice of praise and thanksgiving, *
     among those who keep holy-day.

5 **Why are you so full of heaviness, O my soul? ***
     and why are you so disquieted within me?   **R**

   Put your trust in God; *
     for I will yet give thanks to the One
     who is the help of my countenance, 6 and my God.

   My soul is heavy within me; *
     therefore I will remember you from the land of Jordan,
     and from the peak of Mizar among the heights of Hermon.

7 One deep calls to another in the noise of your cataracts; *
     all your rapids and floods have gone over me.

8 **The LORD grants loving-kindness in the daytime; ***
     in the night season the song of the LORD is with me,
     a prayer to the God of my life.   R

9 I will say to the God of my strength,
     "Why have you forgotten me? *
     and why do I go so heavily while the enemy oppresses me?"

10 **While my bones are being broken, ***
     my enemies mock me to my face;

   all day long they mock me *
     and say to me, "Where now is your God?"   **R**

11 **Why are you so full of heaviness, O my soul? ***
     and why are you so disquieted within me?

[Unison]

Put your trust in God; *
    for I will yet give thanks to the One
    who is the help of my countenance, and my God.   **R**

Gracious God,
in the night of distress we forget the days of sun and joy.
When we do not know your presence,
preserve us from the deep torrent of despair.
We ask this in the name of Jesus Christ our Lord.   **Amen.**   [572]

PSALM 43   Tone 8; PS 38

R

1 Give judgment for me, O God,
    and defend my cause against an ungodly people; *
      deliver me from the deceitful and the wicked.

2 **For you are the God of my strength;**
    why have you put me from you? *
      and why do I go so heavily while the enemy oppresses me?   **R**

3 Send out your light and your truth, that they may lead me, *
    and bring me to your holy hill
    and to your dwelling;

4 **that I may go to the altar of God,**
    to the God of my joy and gladness; *
      and on the harp I will give thanks to you, O God my God.   **R**

5 Why are you so full of heaviness, O my soul? *
    and why are you so disquieted within me?

Put your trust in God; *
    for I will yet give thanks to the One
    who is the help of my countenance, and my God.   **R**

Eternal God, source of everlasting light,
send forth your truth into our hearts,
and bring us into your presence with joy and gladness
in the name of Jesus Christ the Lord.   **Amen.**   [573]

R

1 My heart is stirring with a noble song;
  let me recite what I have fashioned for the king; *
    my tongue shall be the pen of a skilled writer.

2 **You are the fairest of men; ***
    grace flows from your lips,
    because God has blessed you forever.

3 Strap your sword upon your thigh, O mighty warrior, *
    in your pride and in your majesty.   R

4 **Ride out and conquer in the cause of truth ***
    and for the sake of justice.

5 Your right hand will show you marvelous things; *
    your arrows are very sharp, O mighty warrior.

  The peoples are falling at your feet, *
    and the king's enemies are losing heart.   R

6 Your throne, O God, endures forever and ever, *
    a scepter of righteousness is the scepter of your reign;
    7 you love righteousness and hate iniquity.

  Therefore God, your God, has anointed you *
    with the oil of gladness above your fellows.

8 All your garments are fragrant with myrrh, aloes, and cassia, *
    and the music of strings from ivory palaces makes you glad.

9 **Kings' daughters stand among the noble women of the court; ***
    on your right hand is the queen,
    adorned with the gold of Ophir.   R

10 "Hear, O daughter; consider and listen closely; *
    forget your people and your father's house.

11 **The king will have pleasure in your beauty; ***
    he is your master; therefore do him honor.

12 The people of Tyre are here with a gift; *
    the rich among the people seek your favor."   R

13 **All glorious is the princess as she enters; ***
    her gown is cloth-of-gold.

¹⁴ In embroidered apparel she is brought to the king; *
 after her the bridesmaids follow in procession.

¹⁵ With joy and gladness they are brought, *
 and enter into the palace of the king.   R

¹⁶ "In place of fathers, O king, you shall have sons; *
 you shall make them princes over all the earth.

¹⁷ I will make your name to be remembered
 from one generation to another; *
 therefore nations will praise you forever and ever."   R

God of majesty,
you exalted Jesus, the Anointed One,
that every knee on earth might bow before him.
Strengthen us to confess him as our Sovereign,
and to serve him with joy,
that we might be led even to the marriage supper of the Lamb,
Christ Jesus our Lord.   **Amen.**   [574]

PSALM 46   Tone 6; PH 191–193; PS 40, 41

R

¹ God is our refuge and strength, *
 a very present help in trouble.

² Therefore we will not fear, though the earth be moved, *
 and though the mountains be toppled into the depths of the sea;

³ though its waters rage and foam, *
 and though the mountains tremble at its tumult.

The LORD of hosts is with us; *
 the God of Jacob is our stronghold.   R

⁴ There is a river whose streams make glad the city of God, *
 the holy habitation of the Most High.

⁵ God is in the midst of the city;
 it shall not be overthrown; *
 God shall help it at the break of day.

⁶ The nations make much ado, and the realms are shaken; *
 God has spoken, and the earth shall melt away.

⁷ The LORD of hosts is with us; *
 the God of Jacob is our stronghold.   R

8 Come now and look upon the works of the LORD, *
    what awesome things God has done on earth.

9 **It is the LORD who makes war to cease in all the world,** *
    who breaks the bow, and shatters the spear,
    and burns the shields with fire.

10 "Be still, then, and know that I am God; *
    I will be exalted among the nations;
    I will be exalted in the earth."

11 **The LORD of hosts is with us;** *
    the God of Jacob is our stronghold.   **R**

God our strength,
you are the only refuge of all who trust you.
Fortify us with your goodness to live in quietness of spirit,
that we may serve you all our days;
through Jesus Christ, your Son. **Amen.**   [575]

PSALM 47   Tone 2; PH 194; PS 42

R

1 Clap your hands, all you peoples; *
    shout to God with a cry of joy.

2 **For the LORD Most High is to be feared,** *
    the great Sovereign over all the earth.

3 The LORD subdues the peoples under us, *
    and the nations under our feet.

4 **The LORD chooses our inheritance for us,** *
    the pride of the beloved Jacob.   **R**

5 God has gone up with a shout, *
    the LORD with the sound of the ram's-horn.

6 **Sing praises to God, sing praises;** *
    sing praises to our Sovereign, sing praises.

7 For God is Sovereign of all the earth; *
    sing praises with all your skill.   **R**

8 **God reigns over the nations;** *
    God sits upon heaven's holy throne.

9 The nobles of the peoples have gathered together *
    with the people of the God of Abraham.

¹⁰ **The rulers of the earth belong to God,** *
    and God is highly exalted. **R**

God of power and righteousness,
you stand in power over all authorities,
and you rule over all governments.
Let the peoples of the earth rejoice
and the leaders of nations follow the way of Jesus Christ,
the Prince of Peace. **Amen.** ^[576]

PSALM 48   Tone 3; PS 43

R

¹ Great is the LORD, and highly to be praised; *
    in the city of our God is the LORD's holy hill.

² **Beautiful and lofty, the joy of all the earth, is the hill of Zion,** *
    the city of the great Sovereign and the very center of the world.

³ God is in the citadels of Zion; *
    God is known to be its sure refuge.   **R**

⁴ **Behold, the rulers of the earth assembled** *
    and marched forward together.

⁵ They looked and were astounded; *
    they retreated and fled in terror.

⁶ **Trembling seized them there;** *
    ⁷**they writhed like a woman in childbirth,**
    like ships of the sea when the east wind shatters them.

⁸ As we have heard, so have we seen,
    in the city of the LORD of hosts, in the city of our God; *
    God has established it forever.   **R**

⁹ **We have waited in silence on your loving-kindness, O God,** *
    in the midst of your temple.

¹⁰ Your praise, like your name, O God, reaches to the world's end; *
    your right hand is full of justice.

¹¹ **Let Mount Zion be glad**
    and the cities of Judah rejoice, *
        because of your judgments.   **R**

12 Make the circuit of Zion;
walk round about it; *
   count the number of its towers.

13 **Consider well its bulwarks;**
examine its strongholds; *
   that you may tell those who come after.

[Unison]

This God is our God forever and ever; *
   God shall be our guide forevermore.   **R**

Gracious God,
you have made us fellow citizens
with the saints in the city of your eternal light.
In the time of upheaval, when the foundations shake,
teach us to wait in silence on your steadfast and transforming love,
made known to us in Jesus Christ our Lord. **Amen.**   [577]

PSALM 49   Tone 6; PS 44

R

1 Hear this, all you peoples;
hearken, all you who dwell in the world, *
   2 you of high degree and low, rich and poor together.

3 **My mouth shall speak of wisdom, ***
   and my heart shall meditate on understanding.

4 I will incline my ear to a proverb *
   and set forth my riddle upon the harp.   **R**

5 **Why should I be afraid in evil days, ***
   when the wickedness of those at my heels surrounds me,

6 the wickedness of those who put their trust in their goods, *
   and boast of their great riches?

7 **We can never ransom ourselves, ***
   or deliver to God the price of our life;

8 for the ransom of our life is so great, *
   that we should never have enough to pay it,

9 **in order to live forever and ever, ***
   and never see the grave.   **R**

10 For we see that the wise die also;
  like the dull and stupid they perish *
    and leave their wealth to those who come after them.

11 **Their graves shall be their homes forever,**
  their dwelling places from generation to generation, *
    though they call the lands after their own names.

12 Even though honored, they cannot live forever; *
    they are like the beasts that perish.   **R**

13 **Such is the way of those who foolishly trust in themselves,** *
    and the end of those who delight in their own words.

14 Like a flock of sheep they are destined to die;
  death is their shepherd; *
    they go down straightway to the grave.

  Their form shall waste away, *
    and the land of the dead shall be their home.

15 But God will ransom my life *
    and snatch me from the grasp of death.   **R**

16 **Do not be envious when some become rich,** *
    or when the grandeur of their house increases;

17 for they will carry nothing away at their death, *
    nor will their grandeur follow them.

18 **Though they thought highly of themselves while they lived,** *
    and were praised for their success,

19 they shall join the company of their ancestors, *
    who will never see the light again.

20 **Those who are honored, but have no understanding,** *
    are like the beasts that perish.   R

  Giver of all wisdom,
  deliver us from the folly of betraying our eternal birthright
  for temporal gain.
  Teach us to hold firmly to you
  so that we may not treasure things,
  but show the imperishable riches of your love
  in Jesus Christ. **Amen.**   [578]

R

1 The LORD, the God of gods, has spoken *
   and has called the earth from the rising of the sun to its setting.

2 **Out of Zion, perfect in its beauty, ***
   God shines forth in glory.   R

3 Our God will come and will not keep silence; *
   before God there is a consuming flame,
   and round about a raging storm.

4 **God calls the heavens and the earth from above ***
   to witness the judgment of the chosen people.

5 "Gather before me my loyal followers, *
   those who have made a covenant with me
   and sealed it with sacrifice."

6 **Let the heavens declare the rightness of God's cause; ***
   for it is God who is judge.   R

7 Hear, O my people, and I will speak:
   "O Israel, I will bear witness against you; *
   for I am God, your God.

8 **I do not accuse you because of your sacrifices; ***
   your offerings are always before me.

9 I will take no bull-calf from your stalls, *
   nor he-goats out of your pens;

10 **for all the beasts of the forest are mine, ***
   the herds in their thousands upon the hills.

11 I know every bird in the sky, *
   and the creatures of the fields are in my sight.   R

12 **If I were hungry, I would not tell you, ***
   for the whole world is mine and all that is in it.

13 Do you think I eat the flesh of bulls, *
   or drink the blood of goats?

14 **Offer to God a sacrifice of thanksgiving ***
   and make good your vows to the Most High.

15 Call upon me in the day of trouble; *
   I will deliver you, and you shall honor me."   R

¹⁶ **But to the wicked God says: ***
   "Why do you recite my statutes,
   and take my covenant upon your lips;

¹⁷ since you refuse discipline, *
   and toss my words behind your back?

¹⁸ **When you see thieves, you make them your friends, ***
   and you cast in your lot with adulterers.   R

¹⁹ You have loosed your lips for evil, *
   and harnessed your tongue to a lie.

²⁰ **You are always speaking evil of your kin ***
   and slandering your own flesh and blood.

²¹ These things you have done, and I kept still, *
   and you thought that I am like you.   R

   I have made my accusation; *
   I have put my case in order before your eyes.

²² Consider this well, you who forget God, *
   lest I rend you and there be none to deliver you.

²³ **Whoever offers me the sacrifice of thanksgiving honors me; ***
   but to those who keep in my way will I show the salvation of God."   R

   Almighty God,
   because Jesus your servant became obedient to death,
   his sacrifice was greater than all the sacrifices of old.
   Accept our offering of praise,
   and help us to do your will,
   until our whole life becomes worship in spirit and truth;
   through Jesus Christ our Lord. **Amen.**   [579]

PSALM 51   Tone 7; PH 195, 196; PS 47–49

R

¹ Have mercy on me, O God, according to your loving-kindness; *
   in your great compassion blot out my offenses.

² **Wash me through and through from my wickedness ***
   and cleanse me from my sin.   R

³ For I know my transgressions, *
   and my sin is ever before me.

4 **Against you only have I sinned ***
   and done what is evil in your sight.

And so you are justified when you speak *
and upright in your judgment.

5 **Indeed, I have been wicked from my birth, ***
   a sinner from my mother's womb.   R

6 For behold, you look for truth deep within me, *
   and will make me understand wisdom secretly.

7 **Purge me from my sin, and I shall be pure; ***
   wash me, and I shall be clean indeed.

8 Make me hear of joy and gladness, *
   that the body you have broken may rejoice.

9 **Hide your face from my sins ***
   and blot out all my iniquities.   R

10 Create in me a clean heart, O God, *
   and renew a right spirit within me.

11 **Cast me not away from your presence ***
   and take not your holy Spirit from me.

12 Give me the joy of your saving help again *
   and sustain me with your bountiful Spirit.   **R**

13 **I shall teach your ways to the wicked, ***
   and sinners shall return to you.

14 Deliver me from death, O God, *
   and my tongue shall sing of your righteousness,
   O God of my salvation.   **R**

15 **Open my lips, O Lord, ***
   and my mouth shall proclaim your praise.

16 Had you desired it, I would have offered sacrifice, *
   but you take no delight in burnt-offerings.

17 **The sacrifice of God is a troubled spirit; ***
   a broken and contrite heart, O God, you will not despise.   R

18 Be favorable and gracious to Zion, *
   and rebuild the walls of Jerusalem.

19 **Then you will be pleased with the appointed sacrifices,**
   with burnt-offerings and oblations; *
      then shall they offer young bullocks upon your altar. **R**

God of mercy,
you know us better than we know ourselves,
and still you love us.
Wash us from all our sins,
create in us clean hearts,
and strengthen us by your Holy Spirit
that we may give you praise;
through Jesus Christ our Savior. **Amen.** [580]

PSALM 52 Tone 8; PS 50

R

1 You tyrant, why do you boast of wickedness *
   against the godly all day long?

2 **You plot ruin;**
   your tongue is like a sharpened razor, *
      O worker of deception.

3 You love evil more than good *
   and lying more than speaking the truth.

4 **You love all words that hurt, ***
   O you deceitful tongue. **R**

5 Oh, that God would demolish you utterly, *
   topple you, and snatch you from your dwelling,
   and root you out of the land of the living!

6 **The righteous shall see and tremble, ***
   and they shall laugh at you, saying,

7 "This is the one who did not take God for a refuge, *
   but trusted in great wealth
   and relied upon wickedness." **R**

8 **But I am like a green olive tree in the house of God; ***
   I trust in the mercy of God forever and ever.

[Unison]

9 **I will give you thanks for what you have done ***
   and declare the goodness of your name in the presence of the godly. **R**

Sovereign God,
you cut down trees that bear no fruit,
and prune fruitful trees that they may bear more.
Make us grow like rich olive trees in your kingdom,
firmly rooted in the power and mercy
of Jesus Christ our Lord. **Amen.** [581]

PSALM 53

Tone 8

R

1 Fools say in their heart, "There is no God."*
All are corrupt and commit abominable acts;
there is none who does any good.

2 **God looks down from heaven upon us all,***
to see if there is any who is wise,
if there is one who seeks after God.

3 Every one has proved faithless;
all alike have turned bad;*
there is none who does good; no, not one. **R**

4 **Have they no knowledge, those evildoers***
who eat up my people like bread
and do not call upon God?

5 See how greatly they tremble,
such trembling as never was;*
for God has scattered the bones of the enemy;
they are put to shame, because God has rejected them.

6 **Oh, that Israel's deliverance would come out of Zion!***
when God restores the fortunes of the chosen people
Jacob will rejoice and Israel be glad. R

Holy God,
apart from you nothing is true, nothing is holy.
Deliver us from evil
and strengthen us when we are weak,
so that all who believe in Christ
may rejoice in his glory now and forever. **Amen.** [582]

PSALM 54

R

1 Save me, O God, by your name;*
   in your might, defend my cause.

2 **Hear my prayer, O God;***
   give ear to the words of my mouth.

3 For the arrogant have risen up against me,
   and the ruthless have sought my life,*
      those who have no regard for God.   R

4 **Behold, God is my helper;***
   it is the Lord who sustains my life.

5 Render evil to those who spy on me;*
   in your faithfulness, destroy them.

6 **I will offer you a freewill sacrifice***
   and praise your name, O LORD, for it is good.

[Unison]

7 **For you have rescued me from every trouble,***
   and my eye has seen the ruin of my foes.   R

God our helper, hear our prayer
and uphold your church in times of testing.
Deliver us from evil,
so that from the rising of the sun to its setting
we may offer you our sacrifice of praise;
through Jesus Christ our Lord.   **Amen.**   [583]

PSALM 55

R

1 Hear my prayer, O God;*
   do not hide yourself from my petition.

2 **Listen to me and answer me;***
   I have no peace, because of my cares.

I am shaken by the 3 noise of the enemy*
   and by the pressure of the wicked;

for they have cast an evil spell upon me*
   and are set against me in fury.   R

4 My heart quakes within me, *
      and the terrors of death have fallen upon me.

5 **Fear and trembling have come over me, ***
      and horror overwhelms me.

6 And I said, "Oh, that I had wings like a dove! *
      I would fly away and be at rest.

7 **I would flee to a far-off place ***
      and make my lodging in the wilderness.

8 I would hasten to escape *
      from the stormy wind and tempest."   **R**

9 **Swallow them up, O Lord;**
   confound their speech; *
      for I have seen violence and strife in the city.

10 Day and night the sentries make their rounds upon its walls, *
      but trouble and misery are in the midst of it.

11 **There is corruption at its heart; ***
      its streets are never free of oppression and deceit.   R

12 For had it been an adversary who taunted me,
   then I could have borne it; *
      or had it been enemies who vaunted themselves against me,
      then I could have hidden from them.

13 **But it was you, my companion, ***
      my own familiar friend, dear to my own heart.

14 We took sweet counsel together, *
      and walked with the throng in the house of God.

15 **Let death come upon them suddenly;**
   let them go down alive into the grave; *
      for wickedness is in their dwellings, in their very midst.   R

16 But I will call upon God, *
      and the LORD will deliver me.

17 **In the evening, in the morning, and at noonday,**
   I will complain and lament, *
      and the LORD will hear my voice.

18 God will bring me safely back from the battle waged against me; *
      for there are many who fight me.

19 **God, who is enthroned of old, will hear me and bring them down; ***
they never change; they do not fear God.   R

20 My companion stretched forth a hand against a comrade *
and broke a covenant.

21 **The speech of my companion is softer than butter, ***
but with war at heart.

The words of my comrade are smoother than oil, *
but they are drawn swords.   **R**

22 **Cast your burden upon the LORD,**
who will sustain you; *
the LORD will never let the righteous stumble.

23 For you will bring the bloodthirsty and deceitful *
down to the pit of destruction, O God.

They shall not live out half their days, *
but I will put my trust in you.   R

God of grace,
when we are frightened and alone,
help us to trust you and cast our burdens upon you,
that we may be upheld by your saving strength.
We ask this in the name of Jesus Christ.   **Amen.**   [584]

PSALM 56   Tone 8

R

1 Have mercy on me, O God,
for my enemies are hounding me; *
all day long they assault and oppress me.

2 **They hound me all the day long; ***
truly there are many who fight against me, O Most High.

3 Whenever I am afraid, *
I will put my trust in you.

4 **In God, whose word I praise,**
in God I trust and will not be afraid, *
for what can flesh do to me?   R

5 All day long they damage my cause; *
their only thought is to do me evil.

6 **They band together; they lie in wait;***
   they spy upon my footsteps;
   because they seek my life.

7 Shall they escape despite their wickedness?*
   O God, in your anger, cast down the peoples.   **R**

8 **You have noted my lamentation;**
   put my tears into your bottle;*
   are they not recorded in your book?

9 Whenever I call upon you, my enemies will be put to flight;*
   this I know, for God is on my side.

10 **In God the LORD, whose word I praise,**
   in God I trust and will not be afraid,*
   11 **for what can mortals do to me?   R**

12 I am bound by the vow I made to you, O God;*
   I will present to you thank-offerings;

13 **for you have rescued my soul from death and my feet from stumbling,***
   that I may walk before God in the light of the living.   R

O God,
   when our path is hard and dangerous,
   give us the grace of quiet confidence.
   Remind us that we belong to you in baptism,
   for you have claimed us in Jesus Christ,
   the way, the truth, and the life.   **Amen.**

PSALM 57   Tone 8

R

1 Be merciful to me, O God, be merciful,
   for I have taken refuge in you;*
      in the shadow of your wings will I take refuge
      until this time of trouble has gone by.

2 **I will call upon you, O Most High God,***
   the God who maintains my cause.

3 You will send from heaven and save me;
   you will confound those who trample upon me;*
      O God, you will send forth your love and your faithfulness.   **R**

4 **I lie in the midst of lions that devour the people;** *
 their teeth are spears and arrows,
 their tongue a sharp sword.

6 They have laid a net for my feet,
 and I am bowed low; *
 they have dug a pit before me,
 but have fallen into it themselves.

5 **Exalt yourself above the heavens, O God,** *
 and your glory over all the earth.

7 My heart is firmly fixed, O God, my heart is fixed; *
 I will sing and make melody. **R**

8 **Wake up, my spirit;**
 awake, lute and harp; *
 I myself will waken the dawn.

9 I will confess you among the peoples, O LORD; *
 I will sing praise to you among the nations.

10 **For your loving-kindness is greater than the heavens,** *
 and your faithfulness reaches to the clouds.

 [Unison]

11 **Exalt yourself above the heavens, O God,** *
 and your glory over all the earth. **R**

 Merciful God,
 refuge in times of trouble,
 our only hope in living,
 and our only salvation in dying,
 keep us in your care
 that we may always praise you
 and faithfully proclaim your name before the nations;
 in Jesus Christ our Lord. **Amen.** [586]

PSALM 59   Tone 8

R

1 Rescue me from my enemies, O God; *
 protect me from those who rise up against me.

2 **Rescue me from evildoers** *
 and save me from those who thirst for my blood. **R**

3 See how they lie in wait for my life,
how the mighty gather together against me; *
not for any offense or fault of mine, O LORD.

4 **Not because of any guilt of mine** *
they run and prepare themselves for battle.   R

Rouse yourself, come to my side, and see; *
5 for you, LORD God of hosts, are Israel's God.

Awake, and punish all the ungodly; *
show no mercy to those who are faithless and evil.

6 They go to and fro in the evening; *
they snarl like dogs and run about the city.

7 **Behold, they boast with their mouths,**
and taunts are on their lips; *
"For who," they say, "will hear us?"   R

8 But you, O LORD, you laugh at them; *
you laugh all the ungodly to scorn.

9 **My eyes are fixed on you, O my Strength; ***
for you, O God, are my stronghold.

10 My merciful God comes to meet me; *
God will let me look in triumph on my enemies.   **R**

11 **Slay them, O God, lest my people forget; ***
send them reeling by your might
and put them down, O Lord our shield.

12 For the sins of their mouths, for the words of their lips,
for the cursing and lies that they utter, *
let them be caught in their pride.

13 **Make an end of them in your wrath; ***
make an end of them, and they shall be no more.

Let everyone know that God rules in Jacob, *
and to the ends of the earth.   **R**

14 **They go to and fro in the evening; ***
they snarl like dogs and run about the city.

15 They forage for food, *
and if they are not filled, they howl.

16 **For my part, I will sing of your strength;** *
   I will celebrate your love in the morning;

   for you have become my stronghold, *
   a refuge in the day of my trouble.

17 **To you, O my Strength, will I sing;** *
   for you, O God, are my stronghold and my merciful God.   **R**

God of power,
deliver us from evil
and confirm our trust in you,
that at dusk we may sing of your justice
and at dawn exult in your mercy;
through Jesus Christ our Lord.   **Amen.**   [587]

PSALM 62   Tone 6; PH 197; PS 52

R

1   For God alone my soul in silence waits; *
    from God comes my salvation.

2   **God alone is my rock and my salvation,** *
    my stronghold, so that I shall not be greatly shaken.   **R**

3   How long will you assail me to crush me,
    all of you together, *
        as if you were a leaning fence, a toppling wall?

4   **They seek only to bring me down from my place of honor;** *
    lies are their chief delight.

    They bless with their lips, *
    but in their hearts they curse.   **R**

5   **For God alone my soul in silence waits;** *
    truly, my hope is in God.

6   God alone is my rock and my salvation, *
    my stronghold, so that I shall not be shaken.

7   **In God is my safety and my honor;** *
    God is my strong rock and my refuge.   **R**

8   Put your trust in God always, O people, *
    pour out your hearts before God, who is our refuge.

9 **Those of high degree are but a fleeting breath,** *
　　even those of low estate cannot be trusted.

On the scales they are lighter than a breath, *
　　all of them together.

10 **Put no trust in extortion;**
　　in robbery take no empty pride; *
　　though wealth increase, set not your heart upon it.　　**R**

11 God has spoken once, twice have I heard it, *
　　that power belongs to God.

12 **Steadfast love is yours, O Lord,** *
　　for you repay all people according to their deeds.　　**R**

Lord God,
in a threatening world we look to you as our rock of hope.
Hear us as we pour out our hearts to you,
and give us your grace and protection;
through Jesus Christ our Lord.　**Amen.**　[588]

PSALM 63　　　　　　　　　　　　Tone 6 or 8; PH 198, 199; PS 53, 54

R

1 O God, you are my God; eagerly I seek you; *
　　my soul thirsts for you, my flesh faints for you,
　　as in a barren and dry land where there is no water.

2 **Therefore I have gazed upon you in your holy place,** *
　　that I might behold your power and your glory.

3 For your loving-kindness is better than life itself; *
　　my lips shall give you praise.

4 **So will I bless you as long as I live** *
　　and lift up my hands in your name.　　**R**

5 My soul is content, as with marrow and fatness, *
　　and my mouth praises you with joyful lips,

6 **when I remember you upon my bed,** *
　　and meditate on you in the night watches.

7 For you have been my helper, *
　　and under the shadow of your wings I will rejoice.

8 **My soul clings to you;***
   your right hand holds me fast.   R

9 May those who seek my life to destroy it*
   go down into the depths of the earth;

10 **let them fall upon the edge of the sword,***
   and let them be food for jackals.

[Unison]

11 **But I will rejoice in God;**
   all those who swear by God will be glad;*
   for the mouth of those who speak lies shall be stopped.   R

Creating God,
deep within our hearts we yearn for your presence,
and hunger and thirst for your righteousness.
Satisfy us by the power of your Spirit,
yet keep us restless to seek your will
as we follow where Christ may lead.   **Amen.**   [589]

PSALM 65
Tone 6; PH 200, 201; PS 55, 56

R

1 You are to be praised, O God, in Zion;*
   to you shall vows be performed in Jerusalem.

2 **To you that hear prayer shall all flesh come,***
   because of their transgressions.   R

3 Our sins are stronger than we are,*
   but you will blot them out.

4 **Happy are they whom you choose**
   and draw to your courts to dwell there!*
   they will be satisfied by the beauty of your house,
   by the holiness of your temple.   R

5 Awesome things will you show us in your righteousness,
   O God of our salvation,*
   O Hope of all the ends of the earth
   and of the seas that are far away.

6 **You make fast the mountains by your power;***
   they are girded about with might.   R

PSALM 65 / 681

7 You still the roaring of the seas, *
   the roaring of their waves,
   and the clamor of the peoples.

8 **Those who dwell at the ends of the earth will tremble**
     at your marvelous signs; *
   you make the dawn and the dusk to sing for joy.   **R**

9 You visit the earth and water it abundantly;
   you make it very plenteous; *
   the river of God is full of water.

   You prepare the grain, *
   for so you provide for the earth.   **R**

10 You drench the furrows and smooth out the ridges; *
   with heavy rain you soften the ground and bless its increase.

11 **You crown the year with your goodness, ***
   and your paths overflow with plenty.   **R**

12 May the fields of the wilderness be rich for grazing, *
   and the hills be clothed with joy.

13 **May the meadows cover themselves with flocks,**
   and the valleys cloak themselves with grain; *
   let them shout for joy and sing.   **R**

   Lord God, joy is your gift;
   beauty, abundance, and peace
   are tokens of your work in all creation.
   Work also in our lives,
   that by these signs we may see the splendor of your love
   and praise you through Jesus Christ our Lord.   **Amen.**   [590]

Psalm 66

Tone 6; PS 57, 58

R

1 Be joyful in God, all you lands; *
   2 sing the glory of God's name;
   sing the glory of God's praise.

3 **Say to God, "How awesome are your deeds! ***
   because of your great strength your enemies cringe before you.

4 All the earth bows down before you, *
   sings to you, sings out your name."   **R**

5 **Come now and see the works of God,** *
   how wonderful God's actions toward all people.

6 God turned the sea into dry land,
   so that they went through the water on foot, *
   and there we rejoiced in God.

7 **In might God rules forever**
   and keeps watch over the nations; *
   let no rebel rise up against God.   R

8 Bless our God, you peoples; *
   make the voice of praise to be heard.

9 **God holds our souls in life,** *
   and will not allow our feet to slip.

10 For you, O God, have proved us; *
   you have tried us just as silver is tried.

11 **You brought us into the snare;** *
   you laid heavy burdens upon our backs.

12 You let enemies ride over our heads;
   we went through fire and water; *
   but you brought us out into a place of refreshment.   R

13 **I will enter your house with burnt-offerings**
   and will pay you my vows, *
   ¹⁴which I promised with my lips
   and spoke with my mouth when I was in trouble.

15 I will offer you sacrifices of fat beasts
   with the smoke of rams; *
   I will give you oxen and goats.   R

16 **Come and listen, all you who fear God,** *
   and I will tell you what God has done for me.

17 I cried out with my mouth, *
   and God's praise was on my tongue.

18 **If I had found evil in my heart,** *
   the Lord would not have heard me;

19 but in truth God has heard me *
   and attended to the voice of my prayer.   R

²⁰ **Blessed be God, who has not rejected my prayer,*
nor withheld steadfast love from me. R**

God of power and might,
you bring your people out of darkness and slavery
into light and freedom
through the waters of salvation.
Receive our sacrifice of praise and thanksgiving,
and keep us always in your steadfast love;
through Jesus Christ our Lord. **Amen.** [591]

PSALM 67

Tone 2; PH 202, 203; PS 59, 60

R

¹ O God, be merciful to us and bless us;*
show us the light of your countenance and come to us.

² **Let your ways be known upon earth,*
your saving health among all nations.**

³ Let the peoples praise you, O God;*
let all the peoples praise you. **R**

⁴ **Let the nations be glad and sing for joy,*
for you judge the peoples with equity
and guide all the nations upon earth.**

⁵ Let the peoples praise you, O God;*
let all the peoples praise you. **R**

⁶ **The earth has brought forth its increase;*
may God, our own God, bless us.**

[Unison]

⁷ **O God, give us your blessing;*
may all the ends of the earth stand in awe of you. R**

Light of the world,
you have come into the world's darkness
and the darkness cannot overwhelm the light.
Let your holy name be known through all the earth,
that all people and nations may praise you
and walk in your ways;
through Jesus Christ our Lord. **Amen.** [592]

R

1 O God, arise, and let your enemies be scattered;*
   let those who hate you flee before you.

2 **Let them vanish like smoke when the wind drives it away;***
   as the wax melts at the fire,
   so let the wicked perish at the presence of God.

3 But let the righteous be glad and rejoice before God;*
   let them also be merry and joyful.   **R**

4 **Sing to God, sing praises to God's name;**
   exalt the One who rides upon the heavens;*
   the name of our God is the LORD; rejoice before the LORD!

5 Defender of widows, father of orphans,*
   God in heaven's holy habitation!

6 **God gives the solitary a home and brings forth prisoners into freedom;***
   but the rebels shall live in dry places.   R

7 O God, when you went forth before your people,*
   when you marched through the wilderness,

8 **the earth shook, and the skies poured down rain,**
   at the presence of God, the God of Sinai,*
   at the presence of God, the God of Israel.

9 You sent a gracious rain, O God, upon your inheritance;*
   you refreshed the land when it was weary.

10 **Your people found their home in it;***
   in your goodness, O God, you have made provision for the poor.   R

11 The Lord gave the word;*
   great was the company of women who bore the tidings:

12 **"Kings with their armies are fleeing away;***
   the women at home are dividing the spoils."

13 Though you lingered among the sheepfolds,*
   you shall be like a dove whose wings are covered with silver,
   whose feathers are like green gold.

14 **When the Almighty scattered kings,***
   it was like snow falling in Zalmon.   R

15 O mighty mountain, O hill of Bashan! *
   O rugged mountain, O hill of Bashan!

16 **Why do you look with envy, O rugged mountain,**
   at the hill on which God chose to rest? *
   truly, the LORD will dwell there forever.   R

17 The chariots of God are twenty thousand,
   even thousands of thousands; *
   the Lord comes in holiness from Sinai.

18 **You have gone up on high and led captivity captive;**
   you have received gifts even from your enemies, *
   that the LORD God might dwell among them.

19 Blessed be the Lord day by day, *
   the God of our salvation, who bears our burdens.

20 **You are our God, the God of our salvation; ***
   God is the LORD, by whom we escape death.   R

21 You, O God, shall crush the heads of your enemies, *
   and the hairy scalp of those who go on still in their wickedness.

22 **The Lord has said, "I will bring them back from Bashan; ***
   I will bring them back from the depths of the sea;

23 that your foot may be dipped in blood, *
   the tongues of your dogs in the blood of your enemies."   R

24 **They see your procession, O God, ***
   your procession into the sanctuary, my Sovereign and my God.

25 The singers go before, musicians follow after, *
   in the midst of young women playing upon the hand-drums.

26 **Bless God in the congregation; ***
   bless the LORD, you that are of the fountain of Israel.

27 There is Benjamin, least of the tribes, at the head;
   the princes of Judah in a company; *
   and the princes of Zebulon and Naphtali.   R

28 **Send forth your strength, O God; ***
   establish, O God, what you have wrought for us.

29 Rulers shall bring gifts to you, *
   for your temple's sake at Jerusalem.

³⁰ **Rebuke the wild beast of the reeds,** *
and the peoples, a herd of wild bulls with its calves.

Trample down those who lust after silver; *
scatter the peoples that delight in war.

³¹ **Let tribute be brought out of Egypt;** *
let Ethiopia stretch out its hands to God. **R**

³² Sing to God, O realms of the earth; *
sing praises to the Lord.

³³ **God rides in the heavens, the ancient heavens;** *
God's voice thunders forth, a mighty voice.

³⁴ Ascribe power to God, *
whose majesty is over Israel,
whose strength is in the skies.

³⁵ **How wonderful is God in the holy places!** *
the God of Israel giving strength and power to the chosen people!
Blessed be God! **R**

Lord Jesus,
you came to us in our bondage,
and led us to freedom by the cross and resurrection.
May our lives praise you,
and our lips proclaim your mighty power to all people
that they may find their hope in you,
and live to your honor and glory,
now and forever. **Amen.** [593]

PSALM 69

Tone 8

R

¹ Save me, O God, *
for the waters have risen up to my neck.

² **I am sinking in deep mire,** *
and there is no firm ground for my feet.

I have come into deep waters, *
and the torrent washes over me. **R**

³ **I have grown weary with my crying;**
my throat is inflamed; *
my eyes have failed from looking for my God.

4 Those who hate me without a cause are more than the hairs of my head;
my lying foes who would destroy me are mighty. *
    Must I then give back what I never stole?

5 **O God, you know my foolishness, ***
    and my faults are not hidden from you.

6 Let not those who hope in you be put to shame through me,
        Lord GOD of hosts; *
    let not those who seek you be disgraced because of me,
        O God of Israel.   **R**

7 **Surely, for your sake have I suffered reproach, ***
    and shame has covered my face.

8 I have become a stranger to my own kindred, *
    an alien to my mother's children.

9 **Zeal for your house has eaten me up; ***
    the scorn of those who scorn you has fallen upon me.

10 I humbled myself with fasting, *
    but that was turned to my reproach.   **R**

11 **I put on sack-cloth also, ***
    and became a byword among them.

12 Those who sit at the gate murmur against me, *
    and the drunkards make songs about me.   **R**

13 **But as for me, this is my prayer to you, ***
    at the time you have set, O LORD:

    "In your great mercy, O God, *
    answer me with your unfailing help.

14 **Save me from the mire; do not let me sink; ***
    let me be rescued from those who hate me
    and out of the deep waters.

15 Let not the torrent of waters wash over me,
    neither let the deep swallow me up; *
        do not let the pit shut its mouth upon me.   **R**

16 **Answer me, O LORD, for your love is kind; ***
    in your great compassion, turn to me.

17 Hide not your face from your servant; *
    be swift and answer me, for I am in distress.

¹⁸ **Draw near to me and redeem me;** *
     because of my enemies deliver me.   **R**

¹⁹ You know my reproach, my shame, and my dishonor; *
     my adversaries are all in your sight."

²⁰ **Reproach has broken my heart, and it cannot be healed;** *
     I looked for sympathy, but there was none,
     for comforters, but I could find no one.

²¹ They gave me gall to eat, *
     and when I was thirsty, they gave me vinegar to drink.   **R**

²² **Let the table before them be a trap** *
     and their sacred feasts a snare.

²³ Let their eyes be darkened, that they may not see, *
     and give them continual trembling in their inner parts.

²⁴ **Pour out your indignation upon them,** *
     and let the fierceness of your anger overtake them.

²⁵ Let their camp be desolate, *
     and let there be none to dwell in their tents.

²⁶ **For they persecute the one whom you have stricken** *
     and add to the pain of those whom you have pierced.

²⁷ Lay to their charge guilt upon guilt, *
     and let them not receive your vindication.

²⁸ **Let them be wiped out of the book of the living** *
     and not be written among the righteous.   **R**

²⁹ As for me, I am afflicted and in pain; *
     your help, O God, will lift me up on high.

³⁰ **I will praise the name of God in song;** *
     I will proclaim the greatness of the LORD with thanksgiving.

³¹ This will please the LORD more than an offering of oxen, *
     more than bullocks with horns and hoofs.

³² **The afflicted shall see and be glad;** *
     you who seek God, your heart shall live.

³³ For the Lord listens to the needy *
     and does not despise those who are in prison.   **R**

34 **Let the heavens and the earth give praise,** *
   the seas and all that moves in them;

35 for God will save Zion and rebuild the cities of Judah; *
   they shall live there and have it in possession.

36 **The servants of the LORD will inherit it,** *
   and those who love the name of God will dwell therein.   **R**

Blessed are you, God of hope;
you restore the fallen
and rebuild the broken walls.
Teach us the song of thanksgiving,
for you are the strength of your people;
through Jesus Christ our Lord.   **Amen.**   [594]

PSALM 70   Tone 8; PS 62

R

1 Be pleased, O God, to deliver me; *
   O LORD, make haste to help me.

2 **Let those who seek my life be ashamed**
   and altogether dismayed; *
   let those who take pleasure in my misfortune
   draw back and be disgraced.

3 Let those who say to me "Aha!" and gloat over me turn back, *
   because they are ashamed.   **R**

4 **Let all who seek you rejoice and be glad in you;** *
   let those who love your salvation say forever,
   "Great is the LORD!"

5 But as for me, I am poor and needy; *
   come to me speedily, O God.

   You are my helper and my deliverer; *
   O LORD, do not tarry.   **R**

God, our help and deliverer,
do not abandon us
among the many temptations of life,
but deliver us from evil
and turn our tears and struggles into joy;
through Jesus Christ our Lord.   **Amen.**   [595]

R

1 In you, O LORD, have I taken refuge; *
    let me never be ashamed.

2 **In your righteousness, deliver me and set me free; ***
    incline your ear to me and save me.

3 Be my strong rock, a castle to keep me safe; *
    you are my crag and my stronghold.   **R**

4 **Deliver me, my God, from the hand of the wicked, ***
    from the clutches of the evildoer and the oppressor.

5 For you are my hope, O Lord GOD, *
    my confidence since I was young.

6 **I have been sustained by you ever since I was born;**
    from my mother's womb you have been my strength; *
    my praise shall be always of you.   R

7 I have become a portent to many; *
    but you are my refuge and my strength.

8 **Let my mouth be full of your praise ***
    and your glory all the day long.

9 Do not cast me off in my old age; *
    forsake me not when my strength fails.

10 **For my enemies are talking against me, ***
    and those who lie in wait for my life take counsel together.

11 They say that God has forsaken me,
    that they will come after me and seize me; *
    because there is none who will save.   **R**

12 **O God, be not far from me; ***
    come quickly to help me, O my God.

13 Let those who set themselves against me be put to shame and be disgraced; *
    let those who seek to do me evil be covered with scorn and reproach.

14 **But I shall always wait in patience, ***
    and shall praise you more and more.   R

15 My mouth shall recount your mighty acts
    and saving deeds all day long; *
    though I cannot know the number of them.

16 **I will begin with the mighty works of the Lord GOD;** *
 I will recall your righteousness, yours alone. R

17 O God, you have taught me since I was young, *
 and to this day I tell of your wonderful works.

18 **And now that I am old and gray-headed, O God, do not forsake me,** *
 till I make known your strength to this generation
 and your power to all who are to come.

19 Your righteousness, O God, reaches to the heavens; *
 you have done great things;
 who is like you, O God?

20 **You have showed me great troubles and adversities,** *
 but you will restore my life
 and bring me up again from the deep places of the earth.

21 You strengthen me more and more; *
 you enfold and comfort me, R

22 **therefore I will praise you upon the lyre for your faithfulness, O my God;** *
 I will sing to you with the harp, O Holy One of Israel.

23 My lips will sing with joy when I play to you, *
 and so will my soul, which you have redeemed.

24 **My tongue will proclaim your righteousness all day long,** *
 for they are ashamed and disgraced who sought to do me harm. R

God our strong fortress,
do not desert us in old age.
Help us to follow your will
through all our years
and under all circumstances,
that forever we may praise your faithfulness;
through your Son, Jesus Christ our Lord. **Amen.** [596]

PSALM 72   Tone 3; PH 204, 205; PS 64, 65

R

1 Give the king your justice, O God, *
 and your righteousness to the king's son;

2 **that he may rule your people righteously** *
 and the poor with justice;

3 that the mountains may bring prosperity to the people, *
 and the little hills bring righteousness.

4 **He shall defend the needy among the people ***
 and shall rescue the poor and crush the oppressor. R

5 He shall live as long as the sun and moon endure, *
 from one generation to another.

6 **He shall come down like rain upon the mown field, ***
 like showers that water the earth.

7 In his time shall the righteous flourish; *
 there shall be abundance of peace till the moon shall be no more. R

8 **He shall rule from sea to sea, ***
 and from the river to the ends of the earth.

9 His foes shall bow down before him, *
 and his enemies lick the dust.

10 **The kings of Tarshish and of the isles shall pay tribute, ***
 and the rulers of Arabia and Saba offer gifts.

11 All kings shall bow down before him, *
 and all the nations do him service.

12 **For he shall deliver the poor who cries out in distress, ***
 and the oppressed who has no helper.

13 He shall have pity on the lowly and poor *
 and shall preserve the lives of the needy.

14 **He shall redeem their lives from oppression and violence, ***
 and dear shall their blood be in his sight. R

15 Long may he live!
 and may there be given to him gold from Arabia; *
 may prayer be made for him always,
 and may they bless him all the day long.

16 **May there be abundance of grain on the earth,**
 growing thick even on the hilltops; *
 may its fruit flourish like Lebanon,
 and its grain like grass upon the earth.

17 May his name remain forever
 and be established as long as the sun endures; *
 may all the nations bless themselves in him and call him blessed. R

¹⁸ **Blessed be the Lord God, the God of Israel, ***
   who alone does wondrous deeds!

[Unison]

¹⁹ **And blessed be God's glorious name forever! ***
   and may all the earth be filled with the glory of the Lord.
   Amen. Amen.   R

O God, bring our nation and all nations
to uphold justice and equity,
that poverty, oppression, and violence may vanish
and all may know peace and plenty;
in the name of Jesus Christ, the ruler of all.   **Amen.**   [597]

Psalm 73   Tone 6

R

¹ Truly, God is good to Israel, *
   to those who are pure in heart.

² **But as for me, my feet had nearly slipped; ***
   I had almost tripped and fallen;

³ because I envied the proud *
   and saw the prosperity of the wicked: **R**

⁴ **For they suffer no pain, ***
   and their bodies are sleek and sound;

⁵ in the misfortunes of others they have no share; *
   they are not afflicted as others are;

⁶ **therefore they wear their pride like a necklace ***
   and wrap their violence about them like a cloak.

⁷ Their iniquity comes from gross minds, *
   and their hearts overflow with wicked thoughts.

⁸ **They scoff and speak maliciously; ***
   out of their haughtiness they plan oppression.

⁹ They set their mouths against the heavens, *
   and their evil speech runs through the world.   **R**

¹⁰ **And so the people turn to them ***
   and find in them no fault.

11 They say, "How should God know? *
  is there knowledge in the Most High?"

12 **So then, these are the wicked; ***
  always at ease, they increase their wealth.

13 In vain have I kept my heart clean, *
  and washed my hands in innocence.

14 **I have been afflicted all day long, ***
  and punished every morning.   R

15 Had I gone on speaking this way, *
  I should have betrayed the generation of your children.

16 **When I tried to understand these things, ***
  it was too hard for me;

17 until I entered the sanctuary of God *
  and discerned the end of the wicked.

18 **Surely, you set them in slippery places; ***
  you cast them down in ruin.

19 Oh, how suddenly do they come to destruction, *
  come to an end, and perish from terror!

20 **Like a dream when one awakens, O Lord, ***
  when you arise you will make their image vanish.   R

21 When my mind became embittered, *
  I was sorely wounded in my heart.

22 **I was stupid and had no understanding; ***
  I was like a brute beast in your presence.

23 Yet I am always with you; *
  you hold me by my right hand.

24 **You will guide me by your counsel, ***
  and afterwards receive me with glory.

25 Whom have I in heaven but you? *
  and having you I desire nothing upon earth.

26 **Though my flesh and my heart should waste away, ***
  God is the strength of my heart and my portion forever.   R

27 Truly, those who forsake you will perish; *
    you destroy all who are unfaithful.

28 **But it is good for me to be near God; ***
    I have made the Lord GOD my refuge.

[Unison]

I will speak of all your works *
    in the gates of the city of Zion.   **R**

God our strength,
you give honor to the pure in heart
and uphold all who trust in you.
Deliver us from chasing after this world's illusions
that we may follow instead
the imperishable truth of your Word
in Jesus Christ our Lord. **Amen.** [598]

PSALM 77   Tone 8; PS 66

R

1 I will cry aloud to God; *
    I will cry aloud, and God will hear me.

2 **In the day of my trouble I sought the Lord; ***
    my hands were stretched out by night and did not tire;
    I refused to be comforted.

3 I think of God, I am restless, *
    I ponder, and my spirit faints.   **R**

4 **You will not let my eyelids close; ***
    I am troubled and I cannot speak.

5 I consider the days of old; *
    I remember the years long past;

6 **I commune with my heart in the night; ***
    I ponder and search my mind.   **R**

7 Will the Lord cast me off forever *
    and show favor to me no more?

8 **Has the loving-kindness of the LORD come to an end? ***
    has God's promise failed forevermore?

9 Has God forgotten to be gracious, *
    and in anger withheld compassion?

10 **And I said, "My grief is this: ***
    the right hand of the Most High has lost its power."   R

11 I will remember the works of the LORD, *
    and call to mind your wonders of old time.

12 **I will meditate on all your acts ***
    and ponder your mighty deeds.

13 Your way, O God, is holy; *
    who is so great a god as our God?

14 **You are the God who works wonders ***
    and have declared your power among the peoples.

15 By your strength you have redeemed your people, *
    the children of Jacob and Joseph.   R

16 **The waters saw you, O God;**
    the waters saw you and trembled; *
    the very depths were shaken.

17 The clouds poured out water;
    the skies thundered; *
    your arrows flashed to and fro;

18 **the sound of your thunder was in the whirlwind;**
    your lightnings lit up the world; *
    the earth trembled and shook.

19 Your way was in the sea,
    and your paths in the great waters, *
    yet your footsteps were not seen.

20 **You led your people like a flock ***
    by the hand of Moses and Aaron.   R

God of the ages,
by signs and wonders you established your ancient covenant,
and through the sacrifice of your Son
you confirmed the new covenant yet more wondrously.
Guide your church to the land of promise,
that there we may celebrate your name with lasting praise
through Jesus Christ our Lord. **Amen.** [599]

R

1 Hear my teaching, O my people; *
   incline your ears to the words of my mouth.

2 **I will open my mouth in a parable; ***
   I will declare the mysteries of ancient times.

3 That which we have heard and known,
   and what our ancestors have told us, *
      we will not hide from their children.   R

4 **We will recount to generations to come**
   the praiseworthy deeds and the power of the LORD, *
      and the wonderful works God has done.

5 God set up decrees for Jacob
   and established a law for Israel, *
      commanding them to teach it to their children;

6 **that the generations to come might know,**
   and the children yet unborn; *
      that they in their turn might tell it to their children;

7 so that they might put their trust in God, *
   and not forget the deeds of God,
      but keep God's commandments;

8 **and not be like their ancestors,**
   a stubborn and rebellious generation, *
      a generation whose heart was not steadfast,
      and whose spirit was not faithful to God.   R

         *   *   *

12 God worked marvels in the sight of their ancestors, *
    in the land of Egypt, in the field of Zoan.

13 **God split open the sea and let them pass through, ***
    making the waters stand up like walls.

14 God led them with a cloud by day, *
    and all the night through with a glow of fire.

15 **God split the hard rocks in the wilderness ***
    and gave them drink as from the great deep.

16 God brought streams out of the cliff, *
   and the waters gushed out like rivers.   R

   *   *   *

34 **Whenever God slew them, they would repent, ***
   and they would diligently search for God.

35 They would remember that God was their rock, *
   and the Most High God their redeemer.

36 **But they flattered God with their mouths ***
   and lied to God with their tongues.

37 Their heart was not steadfast toward God, *
   and they were not faithful to the covenant.

38 **But being so merciful, God forgave their sins**
   and did not destroy them; *
      many times God held back anger
      and did not permit divine wrath to be roused.   R

   *   *   *

God of pilgrims,
strengthen our faith, we pray.
Guide us through the uncertainties of our journey,
and hold before us the vision of your eternal kingdom,
made known to us in Jesus Christ our Lord.   **Amen.**   [600]

PSALM 79   Tone 8; PS 69

R

1 O God, the heathen have come into your inheritance;
   they have profaned your holy temple; *
      they have made Jerusalem a heap of rubble.

2 **They have given the bodies of your servants as food**
         for the birds of the air, *
      and the flesh of your faithful ones to the beasts of the field.

3 They have shed their blood like water on every side of Jerusalem, *
   and there was no one to bury them.

4 **We have become a reproach to our neighbors, ***
      an object of scorn and derision to those around us.   R

5 How long will you be angry, O LORD? *
   will your fury blaze like fire forever?

6 **Pour out your wrath upon the heathen who have not known you** *
   and upon the realms that have not called upon your name.

7 For they have devoured the people of Jacob *
   and made their dwelling a ruin.   **R**

8 **Remember not our past sins;**
   let your compassion be swift to meet us; *
   for we have been brought very low.

   [Unison]

9 **Help us, O God our Savior, for the glory of your name;** *
   deliver us and forgive us our sins, for your name's sake.   **R**

Gracious God,
in times of sorrow and depression,
when hope itself seems lost,
help us to remember the transforming power of your steadfast love
and to give thanks for that new life we cannot now imagine.
We ask this in the name of Jesus Christ our Savior.   **Amen.**   [601]

PSALM 80   Tone 8; PH 206; PS 70, 71

R

1 Hear, O Shepherd of Israel, leading Joseph like a flock; *
   shine forth, you that are enthroned upon the cherubim.

2 **In the presence of Ephraim, Benjamin, and Manasseh,** *
   stir up your strength and come to help us.

3 Restore us, O God of hosts; *
   show the light of your countenance, and we shall be saved.   **R**

4 **O LORD God of hosts,** *
   how long will you be angered
   despite the prayers of your people?

5 You have fed them with the bread of tears; *
   you have given them bowls of tears to drink.

6 **You have made us the derision of our neighbors,** *
   and our enemies laugh us to scorn.

7 Restore us, O God of hosts; *
      show the light of your countenance, and we shall be saved. **R**

8 **You have brought a vine out of Egypt; ***
      you cast out the nations and planted it.

9 You prepared the ground for it; *
      it took root and filled the land.

10 **The mountains were covered by its shadow ***
      and the towering cedar trees by its boughs.

11 You stretched out its tendrils to the sea *
      and its branches to the river.

12 **Why have you broken down its wall, ***
      so that all who pass by pluck off its grapes?

13 The wild boar of the forest has ravaged it, *
      and the beasts of the field have grazed upon it. **R**

14 **Turn now, O God of hosts, look down from heaven;**
      behold and tend this vine; *
      15preserve what your right hand has planted.

16 They burn it with fire like rubbish; *
      at the rebuke of your countenance let them perish.

17 **Let your hand be upon the one at your right hand, ***
      the one you have made so strong for yourself.

18 And so will we never turn away from you; *
      give us life, that we may call upon your name.

19 **Restore us, O Lord God of hosts; ***
      show the light of your countenance, and we shall be saved. **R**

Lord God,
   you so tend the vine you planted
   that now it extends its branches throughout the world.
   Keep us in Christ as branches on the vine,
   that grafted firmly in your love,
   we may show the whole world your great power
   and bear the fruit of righteousness;
   through Jesus Christ our Lord. **Amen.**   [602]

R

1 Sing with joy to God our strength *
   and raise a loud shout to the God of Jacob.

2 **Raise a song and sound the timbrel, ***
   the merry harp, and the lyre.

3 Blow the ram's-horn at the new moon, *
   and at the full moon, the day of our feast.

4 **For this is a statute for Israel, ***
   a law of the God of Jacob.

5 God laid it as a solemn charge upon Joseph, *
   when the people came out of the land of Egypt.   R

   I heard an unfamiliar voice saying, *
   ⁶"I eased their shoulder from the burden;
   their hands were set free from bearing the load.

7 You called on me in trouble, and I saved you; *
   I answered you from the secret place of thunder
   and tested you at the waters of Meribah.

8 **Hear, O my people, and I will admonish you: ***
   O Israel, if you would but listen to me!

9 There shall be no strange god among you; *
   you shall not worship a foreign god.

10 **I am the LORD your God,**
   who brought you out of the land of Egypt and said, *
   'Open your mouth wide, and I will fill it.'   R

11 And yet my people did not hear my voice, *
   and Israel would not obey me.

12 **So I gave them over to the stubbornness of their hearts, ***
   to follow their own devices.

13 Oh, that my people would listen to me! *
   that Israel would walk in my ways!

14 **I should soon subdue their enemies ***
   and turn my hand against their foes.

15 Those who hate the LORD would cringe before me, *
   and their punishment would last forever.

16 **But Israel would I feed with the finest wheat** *
    and satisfy them with honey from the rock."   **R**

God our strength,
you rescue us in times of trouble
and set us in places of safety.
Help us to listen always to your voice
and feed us always with that living bread
given for the life of the world,
your Son, Jesus Christ our Lord. **Amen.** [603]

PSALM 82

Tone 8; PS 73

R

1 God arises in the council of heaven *
    and gives judgment in the midst of the gods:

2 **"How long will you judge unjustly,** *
    and show favor to the wicked?

3 Save the weak and the orphan; *
    defend the humble and needy;

4 **rescue the weak and the poor;** *
    deliver them from the power of the wicked.   **R**

5 They do not know, neither do they understand;
they go about in darkness; *
    all the foundations of the earth are shaken.

6 **Now I say to you, "You are gods,** *
    and all of you children of the Most High;

7 nevertheless, you shall die like mortals, *
    and fall like any leader' "

8 **Arise, O God, and rule the earth,** *
    for you shall take all nations for your own.   **R**

Strength of the weak,
defender of the needy,
rescuer of the poor,
deliver us from the power of wickedness,
that we may rejoice in your justice now and forever;
through Jesus Christ our Lord. **Amen.** [604]

R

¹ How dear to me is your dwelling, O LORD of hosts! *
  ²My soul has a desire and longing for the courts of the LORD;
  my heart and my flesh rejoice in the living God.

³ The sparrow has found her a house
  and the swallow a nest where she may lay her young; *
  by the side of your altars, O LORD of hosts,
  my Sovereign and my God.

⁴ Happy are they who dwell in your house! *
  they will always be praising you.   **R**

⁵ Happy are the people whose strength is in you! *
  whose hearts are set on the pilgrims' way.

⁶ Those who go through the desolate valley will find it a place of springs, *
  for the early rains have covered it with pools of water.

⁷ They will climb from height to height, *
  and the God of gods will appear in Zion.   R

⁸ LORD God of hosts, hear my prayer; *
  hearken, O God of Jacob.

⁹ Behold our defender, O God; *
  and look upon the face of your anointed.   R

¹⁰ For one day in your courts is better than a thousand in my own room, *
  and to stand at the threshold of the house of my God
  than to dwell in the tents of the wicked.

¹¹ For the LORD God is both sun and shield; *
  the LORD will give grace and glory;

  no good thing will the LORD withhold *
  from those who walk with integrity.

¹² O LORD of hosts, *
  happy are they who put their trust in you!   R

  Lord, your presence is better than life itself.
  You are strength to all in need,
  and hope to those who travel through sorrow.

As the sparrow and the swallow entrust their young to you,
so we place our lives before you.
Receive them in the name and for the sake of
Jesus Christ our Lord. **Amen.** [605]

PSALM 85
Tone 8; PS 76–78

R

1 You have been gracious to your land, O LORD, *
  you have restored the good fortune of Jacob.

2 **You have forgiven the iniquity of your people ***
  and blotted out all their sins.

3 You have withdrawn all your fury *
  and turned yourself from your wrathful indignation.   R

4 **Restore us then, O God our Savior; ***
  let your anger depart from us.

5 Will you be displeased with us forever? *
  will you prolong your anger from age to age?

6 **Will you not give us life again, ***
  that your people may rejoice in you?

7 Show us your mercy, O LORD, *
  and grant us your salvation.   R

8 **I will listen, O LORD God, to what you are saying, ***
  for you are speaking peace to your faithful people
  and to those who turn their hearts to you.

9 Truly, your salvation is very near to those who fear you, *
  that your glory may dwell in our land.   R

10 **Mercy and truth have met together; ***
   righteousness and peace have kissed each other.

11 Truth shall spring up from the earth, *
   and righteousness shall look down from heaven.

12 **O LORD, you will indeed grant prosperity, ***
   and our land will yield its increase.

[Unison]

13 **Righteousness shall go before you, ***
   and peace shall be a pathway for your feet.   R

God of grace,
you loved the world so much
that you gave your only Son to be our Savior.
Help us to rejoice in your redeeming grace
by showing mercy,
and by walking in the way of justice and peace,
for the sake of Jesus Christ, redeemer of the world. **Amen.** [606]

PSALM 86

Tone 8; PS 79

R

1 Bow down your ear, O LORD, and answer me, *
 for I am poor and in misery.

2 **Keep watch over my life, for I am faithful; ***
 save your servant, for I put my trust in you.

3 Be merciful to me, O LORD, for you are my God; *
 I call upon you all the day long. R

4 **Gladden the soul of your servant, ***
 for to you, O LORD, I lift up my soul.

5 For you, O LORD, are good and forgiving, *
 and great is your love toward all who call upon you.

6 **Give ear, O LORD, to my prayer, ***
 and attend to the voice of my supplications.

7 In the time of my trouble I will call upon you, *
 for you will answer me. R

8 **Among the gods there is none like you, O LORD, ***
 nor anything like your works.

9 All nations you have made will come and worship you, O LORD, *
 and glorify your name.

10 **For you are great;**
 you do wondrous things; *
 and you alone are God. R

11 Teach me your way, O LORD,
 and I will walk in your truth; *
 knit my heart to you that I may fear your name.

12 **I will thank you, O LORD my God, with all my heart, ***
 and glorify your name forevermore.

13 For great is your love toward me; *
   you have delivered me from the nethermost pit.   R

14 **The arrogant rise up against me, O God,**
   and a violent mob seeks my life; *
      they have not set you before their eyes.

15 But you, O LORD, are gracious and full of compassion, *
   slow to anger, and full of kindness and truth.

16 **Turn to me and have mercy upon me; ***
      give your strength to your servant;
      and save the child of your handmaid.

   [Unison]

17 **Show me a sign of your favor,**
   so that those who hate me may see it and be ashamed; *
      because you, O LORD, have helped me and comforted me.   R

   Eternal God,
   in every time and place and circumstance your people call on you,
   rejoicing in your love and cherishing your truth.
   Hear the prayers of our hearts
   that we may be protected from sin
   and delivered from evil;
   through Jesus Christ our Lord.   **Amen.**   [607]

PSALM 88   Tone 8

R

1 O LORD, my God, my Savior, *
      by day and night I cry to you.

2 **Let my prayer enter into your presence; ***
      incline your ear to my lamentation.   R

3 For I am full of trouble; *
      my life is at the brink of the grave.

4 **I am counted among those who go down to the pit; ***
      I have become like one who has no strength;

5 lost among the dead, *
      like the slain who lie in the grave,

   Whom you remember no more, *
      for they are cut off from your hand.

6 You have laid me in the depths of the pit, *
    in dark places, and in the abyss.

7 **Your anger weighs upon me heavily, ***
    and all your great waves overwhelm me.   **R**

8 You have put my friends far from me;
  you have made me to be abhorred by them; *
    I am in prison and cannot get free.

9 **My sight has failed me because of trouble; ***
    LORD, I have called upon you daily;
    I have stretched out my hands to you.

10 Do you work wonders for the dead? *
    will those who have died stand up and give you thanks?

11 **Will your loving-kindness be declared in the grave? ***
    your faithfulness in the land of destruction?

12 Will your wonders be known in the dark? *
    or your righteousness in the country where all is forgotten?   **R**

13 **But as for me, O LORD, I cry to you for help; ***
    in the morning my prayer comes before you.

14 LORD, why have you rejected me? *
    why have you hidden your face from me?

15 **Ever since my youth, I have been wretched and at the point of death; ***
    I have borne your terrors with a troubled mind.

16 Your blazing anger has swept over me; *
    your terrors have destroyed me;

17 **they surround me all day long like a flood; ***
    they encompass me on every side.

    [Unison]

18 **My friend and my neighbor you have put away from me, ***
    and darkness is my only companion.   **R**

O Lord,
where we are plunged into the darkness of despair,
make known to us the wonders of your grace,
for you alone are God
and from you comes all our help and strength.
We ask this in the name of Jesus Christ. **Amen.**   [608]

R

1   Your love, O LORD, forever will I sing; *
      from age to age my mouth will proclaim your faithfulness.

2   **For I am persuaded that your love is established forever; ***
      you have set your faithfulness firmly in the heavens.

3   "I have made a covenant with my chosen one; *
      I have sworn an oath to David my servant:

4   'I will establish your line forever, *
      and preserve your throne for all generations.'"   **R**

5   The heavens bear witness to your wonders, O LORD, *
      and to your faithfulness in the assembly of the holy ones;

6   **for who in the skies can be compared to the LORD? ***
      who is like the LORD among the gods?

7   God is much to be feared in the council of the holy ones, *
      great and terrible to all those circled around.   **R**

8   **Who is like you, LORD God of hosts? ***
      O mighty LORD, your faithfulness is all around you.

9   You rule the raging of the sea *
      and still the surging of its waves.

10 **You have crushed Rahab of the deep with a deadly wound; ***
      you have scattered your enemies with your mighty arm.   **R**

11 Yours are the heavens; the earth also is yours; *
      you laid the foundations of the world and all that is in it.

12 **You have made the north and the south; ***
      Tabor and Hermon rejoice in your name.

13 You have a mighty arm; *
      strong is your hand and high is your right hand.

14 **Righteousness and justice are the foundations of your throne; ***
      love and truth go before your face.   **R**

15 Happy are the people who know the festal shout! *
      they walk, O LORD, in the light of your presence.

¹⁶ **They rejoice daily in your name;** *
   they are jubilant in your righteousness.

¹⁷ For you are the glory of their strength, *
   and by your favor our might is exalted.

¹⁸ **Truly, the LORD is our ruler;** *
   the Holy One of Israel is our Sovereign.   R

¹⁹ You spoke once in a vision and said to your faithful people: *
   "I have set the crown upon a warrior
   and have exalted one chosen out of the people.

²⁰ **I have found David my servant;** *
   with my holy oil have I anointed him.

²¹ My hand will hold him fast *
   and my arm will make him strong.

²² **No enemy shall deceive him,** *
   nor any wicked man bring him down.

²³ I will crush his foes before him *
   and strike down those who hate him.   R

²⁴ **My faithfulness and love shall be with him,** *
   and he shall be victorious through my name.

²⁵ I shall make his dominion extend *
   from the great sea to the river.

²⁶ **He will say to me, 'You are my father,** *
   my God, and the rock of my salvation.'

²⁷ I will make him my firstborn *
   and higher than the rulers of the earth.

²⁸ **I will keep my love for him forever,** *
   and my covenant will stand firm for him.

²⁹ I will establish his line forever *
   and his throne as the days of heaven.   R

³⁰ **If his children forsake my law** *
   and do not walk according to my judgments;

³¹ if they break my statutes *
   and do not keep my commandments;

³² **I will punish their transgressions with a rod** *
   and their iniquities with the lash;

33 But I will not take my love from him, *
      nor let my faithfulness prove false.

34 I will not break my covenant, *
      nor change what has gone out of my lips.   R

35 Once for all I have sworn by my holiness: *
      'I will not lie to David.

36 His line shall endure forever *
      and his throne as the sun before me;

37 it shall stand fast forevermore like the moon, *
      the abiding witness in the sky.'"   **R**

38 But you have cast off and rejected your anointed; *
      you have become enraged at him.

39 You have broken your covenant with your servant, *
      defiled his crown, and hurled it to the ground.

40 You have breached all his walls *
      and laid his strongholds in ruins.

41 All who pass by despoil him; *
      he has become the scorn of his neighbors.

42 You have exalted the right hand of his foes *
      and made all his enemies rejoice.

43 You have turned back the edge of his sword *
      and have not sustained him in battle.

44 You have put an end to his splendor *
      and cast his throne to the ground.

45 You have cut short the days of his youth *
      and have covered him with shame.   **R**

46 How long will you hide yourself, O LORD?
will you hide yourself forever? *
      how long will your anger burn like fire?

47 Remember, LORD, how short life is, *
      how frail you have made all flesh.

48 Who can live and not see death? *
      who can escape from the power of the grave?   R

49 Where, Lord, are your loving-kindnesses of old, *
    which you promised David in your faithfulness?

50 **Remember, Lord, how your servant is mocked, ***
    how I carry in my bosom the taunts of many peoples,

51 the taunts your enemies have hurled, O LORD, *
    which they hurled at the heels of your anointed.

52 **Blessed be the LORD forevermore! ***
    Amen, I say, Amen.   R

Remember us, gracious God,
when we cannot see your way and purpose,
and renew in us the joy of your kingdom of light and life.
We ask this in the name of Jesus Christ the Lord.   **Amen.**   [609]

PSALM 90   Tone 8; PH 210, 211; PS 83, 84

R

1 Lord, you have been our refuge *
    from one generation to another.

2 **Before the mountains were brought forth,**
    or the land and the earth were born, *
    from age to age you are God.   R

3 You turn us back to the dust and say, *
    "Go back, O child of earth."

4 **For a thousand years in your sight are like yesterday when it is past ***
    and like a watch in the night.   R

5 You sweep us away like a dream; *
    we fade away suddenly like the grass.

6 **In the morning it is green and flourishes; ***
    in the evening it is dried up and withered.   R

7 For we consume away in your displeasure; *
    we are afraid because of your wrathful indignation.

8 **Our iniquities you have set before you, ***
    and our secret sins in the light of your countenance.   R

9 When you are angry, all our days are gone; *
    we bring our years to an end like a sigh.

¹⁰ **The span of our life is seventy years,**
    perhaps in strength even eighty; *
      yet the sum of them is but labor and sorrow,
      for they pass away quickly and we are gone. **R**

¹¹ Who regards the power of your wrath? *
    who rightly fears your indignation?

¹² **So teach us to number our days** *
    that we may apply our hearts to wisdom. **R**

¹³ Return, O L<small>ORD</small>; how long will you tarry? *
    be gracious to your servants.

¹⁴ **Satisfy us by your loving-kindness in the morning;** *
    so shall we rejoice and be glad all the days of our life. **R**

¹⁵ Make us glad by the measure of the days that you afflicted us *
    and the years in which we suffered adversity.

¹⁶ **Show your servants your works** *
    and your splendor to their children.

    [Unison]

¹⁷ **May the graciousness of the L<small>ORD</small> our God be upon us;** *
    prosper the work of our hands;
    prosper our handiwork. **R**

Eternal God,
you alone are constant in this changing world.
Grant us true wisdom of heart
and guide us in serving you all the days of our life;
through Jesus Christ our Lord. **Amen.** [610]

P<small>SALM</small> 91   Tone 6; PH 212; PS 85

R

¹ You who dwell in the shelter of the Most High, *
    abide under the shadow of the Almighty.

² **You shall say to the L<small>ORD</small>,**
    "You are my refuge and my stronghold, *
    my God in whom I put my trust."

³ God shall deliver you from the snare of the hunter *
    and from the deadly pestilence.

4 **God's pinions will cover you,**
   and you shall find refuge under the wings of the LORD, *
      whose faithfulness shall be a shield and buckler.   R

5 You shall not be afraid of any terror by night, *
      nor of the arrow that flies by day;

6 **Of the plague that stalks in the darkness, ***
      nor of the sickness that lays waste at mid-day.

7 A thousand shall fall at your side
   and ten thousand at your right hand, *
      but it shall not come near you.

8 **Your eyes have only to behold ***
      to see the reward of the wicked.   R

9 Because you have made the LORD your refuge, *
      and the Most High your habitation,

10 **there shall no evil happen to you, ***
      neither shall any plague come near your dwelling.   R

11 For God shall give the holy angels charge over you, *
      to keep you in all your ways.

12 **They shall bear you in their hands, ***
      lest you dash your foot against a stone.

13 You shall tread upon the lion and adder; *
      you shall trample the young lion and the serpent under your feet.   R

14 **Because they are bound to me in love,**
   therefore will I deliver them; *
      I will protect them, because they know my name.

15 They shall call upon me, and I will answer them; *
      I am with them in trouble;
      I will rescue them and bring them to honor.

16 **With long life will I satisfy them, ***
      and show them my salvation.   R

O God,
to know you is to live,
to serve you is to reign.
Defend us from every enemy,
that, trusting in your protective care,
we may have no fear;
through the power of Jesus Christ our Lord.   **Amen.**   [611]

R

1 It is a good thing to give thanks to the LORD, *
   and to sing praises to your name, O Most High;

2 **to tell of your loving-kindness early in the morning ***
   and of your faithfulness in the night season;

3 on the psaltery, and on the lyre, *
   and to the melody of the harp.

4 **For you have made me glad by your acts, O LORD; ***
   and I shout for joy because of the works of your hands.   R

5 LORD, how great are your works! *
   your thoughts are very deep.

6 **The dullard does not know,**
   nor does the fool understand, *
      7 **that though the wicked grow like weeds,**
      and all the workers of iniquity flourish,

   they flourish only to be destroyed forever; *
      8 but you, O LORD, are exalted forevermore.

9 **For lo, your enemies, O LORD,**
   lo, your enemies shall perish, *
   and all the workers of iniquity shall be scattered.   R

10 But my horn you have exalted like the horns of wild bulls; *
   I am anointed with fresh oil.

11 **My eyes also gloat over my enemies, ***
   and my ears rejoice to hear the doom of the wicked
          who rise up against me.   R

12 The righteous shall flourish like a palm tree, *
   and shall spread abroad like a cedar of Lebanon.

13 **Those who are planted in the house of the LORD ***
   shall flourish in the courts of our God;

14 they shall still bear fruit in old age; *
   they shall be green and succulent;

15 **that they may show how upright the LORD is, ***
   my Rock, in whom there is no fault.   R

Creator God,
you have planted your Word in our hearts
that you might harvest forth justice.
So root us in your love,
that we may always flourish,
yielding all the fruits of the Spirit
from youth to old age;
through Christ our Lord.   **Amen.**   [612]

PSALM 93

Tone 2; PH 213; PS 87

R

1   You, O LORD, are Sovereign;
you have put on splendid apparel; *
       you, O LORD, have put on your apparel
       and girded yourself with strength.

   You have made the whole world so sure *
   that it cannot be moved;

2   ever since the world began, your throne has been established; *
       you are from everlasting.   **R**

3   **The waters have lifted up, O LORD,**
   the waters have lifted up their voice; *
       the waters have lifted up their pounding waves.

4   Mightier than the sound of many waters,
   mightier than the breakers of the sea, *
       mightier is the LORD who dwells on high.

5   **Your testimonies are very sure, ***
       and holiness adorns your house, O LORD,
       forever and forevermore.   R

Omnipotent God,
your glory is incomprehensible,
your majesty infinite,
and your power incomparable.
Found us on the certainty of your promises,
that no matter what happens,
we may be firm in faith
and live uprightly in your church,
bought by the blood of Jesus Christ.   **Amen.**   [613]

R

1 O LORD God of vengeance, *
   O God of vengeance, show yourself.

2 **Rise up, O Judge of the world; ***
   give the arrogant their just deserts.

3 How long shall the wicked, O LORD, *
   how long shall the wicked triumph?   **R**

4 **They bluster in their insolence; ***
   all evildoers are full of boasting.

5 They crush your people, O LORD, *
   and afflict your chosen nation.

6 **They murder the widow and the stranger ***
   and put the orphans to death.

7 Yet they say, "The LORD does not see, *
   the God of Jacob takes no notice."   **R**

8 **Consider well, you dullards among the people; ***
   when will you fools understand?

9 Does the One who planted the ear not hear? *
   does the One who formed the eye not see?

10 **Does the One who admonishes the nations not punish? ***
    does the One who teaches all the world have no knowledge?

11 The LORD knows our human thoughts; *
    how like a puff of wind they are.   **R**

12 **Happy are they whom you instruct, O LORD! ***
    whom you teach out of your law;

13 to give them rest in evil days, *
    until a pit is dug for the wicked.

14 **For you, O LORD, will not abandon your people, ***
    nor will you forsake your own.

15 For judgment will again be just, *
    and all the true of heart will follow it.   **R**

16 Who rose up for me against the wicked? *
    who took my part against the evildoers?

17 If the LORD had not come to my help, *
    I should soon have dwelt in the land of silence.

18 As often as I said, "My foot has slipped," *
    your love, O LORD, upheld me.

19 When many cares fill my mind, *
    your consolations cheer my soul.   R

20 Can a corrupt tribunal have any part with you, *
    one which frames evil into law?

21 They conspire against the life of the just *
    and condemn the innocent to death.

22 But the LORD has become my stronghold, *
    and my God the rock of my trust.

[Unison]

23 The LORD will turn their wickedness back upon them
    and destroy them in their own malice; *
    the LORD our God will destroy them.   R

Faithful God,
you do not abandon your people to the power of evil.
Grant that those who suffer for the sake of justice
may find strength in the cross of Jesus
and be filled with your peace now and forever.   **Amen.**   [614]

PSALM 95   Tone 2; PH 214, 215; PS 88–90

R

1 Come, let us sing to the LORD; *
    let us shout for joy to the Rock of our salvation.

2 Let us come before God's presence with thanksgiving *
    and raise a loud shout to the LORD with psalms.   R

3 For the LORD is a great God, *
    and a great Sovereign above all gods.

4 The LORD holds the caverns of the earth, *
    and sustains the heights of the hills.

5 The sea belongs to God, who made it, *
    whose hands have molded the dry land.   **R**

6 **Come, let us bow down, and bend the knee, ***
    and kneel before the LORD our Maker.

7 For the LORD is our God,
    and we are the people of God's pasture and the sheep of God's hand. *
    Oh, that today you would hearken to God's voice!   **R**

8 **Harden not your hearts,**
    as your ancestors did in the wilderness, *
    at Meribah, and on that day at Massah,
    when they tempted me.

9 They put me to the test, *
    though they had seen my works.

10 **Forty years long I detested that generation and said, ***
    "This people are wayward in their hearts;
    they do not know my ways."

[Unison]

11 **So I swore in my wrath, ***
    "They shall not enter into my rest."   **R**

O Lord, our protector and our strength,
you guide us as the sheep of your fold.
In your goodness sustain us,
that our hearts may never be hardened
through unbelief of your holy Word,
but that we may serve you in true and living faith
and so enter into your heavenly rest;
through Jesus Christ our Lord.   **Amen.**   [615]

PSALM 96   Tone 3; PH 216, 217; PS 91, 92

R

1 Sing to the LORD a new song; *
    sing to the LORD, all the whole earth.

2 **Sing to the LORD and bless the LORD's name; ***
    proclaim the good news of salvation from day to day.

3 Declare the glory of the LORD among the nations *
    and the wonders of the LORD among all peoples.   **R**

4 **For great is the LORD and greatly to be praised, ***
   more to be feared than all gods.

5 As for all the gods of the nations, they are but idols; *
   but it is the LORD who made the heavens.

6 **Oh, the majesty and magnificence of the presence of the LORD! ***
   Oh, the power and the splendor of the sanctuary of our God!   R

7 Ascribe to the LORD, you families of the peoples; *
   ascribe to the LORD honor and power.

8 **Ascribe to the LORD the honor due the divine name; ***
   come to the holy courts with your offerings.

9 Worship the LORD in the beauty of holiness; *
   let the whole earth tremble in awe.   **R**

10 **Tell it out among the nations: "The LORD is Sovereign! ***
   the LORD has made the world so firm that it cannot be moved
   and will judge the peoples with equity."

11 Let the heavens rejoice, and let the earth be glad;
   let the sea thunder and all that is in it; *
   12 let the field be joyful and all that is therein.

   Then shall all the trees of the wood shout for joy
13 **before the LORD who is coming, ***
   who is coming to judge the earth.

   [Unison]

   The LORD will judge the world with righteousness *
   and the peoples with truth.   R

   Ever-living God,
   the heavens were glad and the earth rejoiced
   when you sent your Son, the incarnate Word,
   to dwell with us.
   Help us to proclaim your glory to those who do not know you,
   until the whole earth sings a new song to you
   now and forever. **Amen.**   [616]

R

1 The LORD is Sovereign;
   let the earth rejoice; *
     let the multitude of the isles be glad.

2 **Clouds and darkness are round about you, ***
   righteousness and justice are the foundations of your throne.

3 A fire goes before you *
   and burns up your enemies on every side.

4 **Your lightnings light up the world; ***
   the earth sees it and is afraid.

5 The mountains melt like wax at the presence of the LORD, *
   at the presence of the Lord of the whole earth.   **R**

6 **The heavens declare your righteousness, O LORD, ***
   and all the peoples see your glory.

7 Confounded be all who worship carved images
   and delight in false gods! *
     Bow down before the LORD, all you gods.

8 **Zion hears and is glad, and the cities of Judah rejoice, ***
   because of your judgments, O LORD.

9 For you are the LORD,
   most high over all the earth; *
     you are exalted far above all gods.   **R**

10 **The LORD loves those who hate evil; ***
   the LORD preserves the lives of the faithful
   and delivers them from the hand of the wicked.

11 Light has sprung up for the righteous, *
   and joyful gladness for those who are truehearted.

12 **Rejoice in the LORD, you righteous, ***
   and to the holy name of the LORD give your praise.   R

   O God,
   you clothe the sky with light, and ocean depths with darkness.
   You work your mighty wonders among us.
   Claim us for your purposes,
   that we may be among those who see your glory and give you praise,
   for you live and reign, now and forever. **Amen.** [617]

PSALM 98 Tone 2; PH 218, 219; PS 94, 95

R

1 Sing to the LORD a new song, *
   for the LORD has done marvelous things.

   The right hand and the holy arm of the LORD *
   have secured the victory.

2 The LORD has made known this victory *
   and has openly showed righteousness in the sight of the nations.

3 **The LORD remembers mercy and faithfulness to the house of Israel, ***
   and all the ends of the earth have seen the victory of our God.   R

4 Shout with joy to the LORD, all you lands; *
   lift up your voice, rejoice, and sing.

5 **Sing to the LORD with the harp, ***
   with the harp and the voice of song.

6 With trumpets and the sound of the horn *
   shout with joy before the Sovereign, the LORD.   R

7 **Let the sea make a noise and all that is in it, ***
   the lands and those who dwell therein.

8 Let the rivers clap their hands, *
   and let the hills ring out with joy before the LORD,
   who is coming to judge the earth.

9 **In righteousness shall the LORD judge the world ***
   and the peoples with equity.   R

   Eternal God,
   you redeemed humanity by sending your only Son
   in fulfillment of your promises of old.
   Let the truth and power of your salvation
   be known in all places of the earth,
   that all nations may give you praise, honor, and glory;
   through Jesus Christ your Son. **Amen.**   [618]

R

1　The LORD is Sovereign;
　　let the people tremble; *
　　　　the LORD is enthroned upon the cherubim;
　　　　let the earth shake.

2　**The LORD is great in Zion ***
　　and is high above all peoples.　　R

3　Let them confess the name of the LORD,
　　which is great and awesome; *
　　　　the LORD is the Holy One.

4　**"O mighty Sovereign, lover of justice,**
　　you have established equity; *
　　　　you have executed justice and righteousness in Jacob."

5　Proclaim the greatness of the LORD our God, *
　　　　and fall down before the footstool of the Holy One.　　R

6　**Moses and Aaron among your priests,**
　　and Samuel among those who call upon your name, *
　　　　they called upon you, O LORD, and you answered them.

7　You spoke to them out of the pillar of cloud; *
　　　　they kept your testimonies and the decree that you gave them.　　R

8　**O LORD our God, you answered them indeed; ***
　　you were a God who forgave them,
　　　　yet punished them for their evil deeds.

[Unison]

9　**Proclaim the greatness of the LORD our God**
　　and worship upon God's holy hill; *
　　　　for the LORD our God is the Holy One.　　R

　Holy God,
　　you are exalted over all the nations,
　　and just in all your ways.
　　Strengthen us to worship you with our deeds
　　and to proclaim your greatness with our lips,
　　for the glory of Jesus Christ our Lord.　**Amen.**　[619]

PSALM 100

R

1 Be joyful in the LORD, all you lands; *
  2 serve the LORD with gladness
  and come before God's presence with a song.

3 **Know this: The LORD alone is God; ***
  we belong to the LORD, who made us,
  we are God's people and the sheep of God's pasture.   R

4 Enter God's gates with thanksgiving;
  go into the holy courts with praise; *
  give thanks and call upon the name of the LORD.

5 **For good is the LORD,**
  whose mercy is everlasting; *
  and whose faithfulness endures from age to age.   R

Mighty God,
by your power you created us,
and by your goodness you call us to be your people.
Accept the offering of our worship
that every race and nation may enter your courts,
praising you in song;
through Jesus Christ our Lord.   **Amen.**   [620]

PSALM 102

R

1 LORD, hear my prayer, and let my cry come before you; *
  2 hide not your face from me in the day of my trouble.

Incline your ear to me; *
  when I call, make haste to answer me,   R

3 for my days drift away like smoke, *
  and my bones are hot as burning coals.

4 **My heart is smitten like grass and withered, ***
  so that I forget to eat my bread.

5 Because of the voice of my groaning *
  I am but skin and bones.

6 **I have become like a vulture in the wilderness, ***
  like an owl among the ruins.

7 I lie awake and groan; *
  I am like a sparrow, lonely on a house-top.

8 **My enemies revile me all day long, ***
  and those who scoff at me have taken an oath against me.

9 For I have eaten ashes for bread *
  and mingled my drink with weeping.

10 **Because of your indignation and wrath ***
   you have lifted me up and thrown me away.

11 My days pass away like a shadow, *
   and I wither like the grass.   **R**

12 **But you, O LORD, endure forever, ***
   and your name from age to age.

13 You will arise and have compassion on Zion,
   for it is time to have mercy upon it; *
   indeed, the appointed time has come.

14 **For your servants love its very rubble, ***
   and are moved to pity even for its dust.

15 The nations shall fear your name, O LORD, *
   and all the rulers of the earth your glory.

16 **For you, O LORD, will build up Zion, ***
   and your glory will appear.

17 You will look with favor on the prayer of the homeless; *
   you will not despise their plea.   **R**

18 **Let this be written for a future generation, ***
   so that a people yet unborn may praise the LORD.

19 For the LORD looked down from the holy place on high *
   and from the heavens beheld the earth;

20 **to hear the groan of the captive ***
   and to set free those condemned to die;

21 that they may declare in Zion the name of the LORD, *
   and the praise of our God in Jerusalem;

22 **when the peoples are gathered together, ***
   and the realms also, to serve the LORD.   R

23 The LORD has brought down my strength before my time *
   and shortened the number of my days;

24 and I said, "O my God,
  do not take me away in the midst of my days; *
    your years endure throughout all generations.

25 In the beginning, O LORD, you laid the foundations of the earth, *
    and the heavens are the work of your hands;

26 they shall perish, but you will endure;
  they all shall wear out like a garment; *
    as clothing you will change them,
    and they shall be changed;

27 but you are always the same, *
    and your years will never end.

28 The children of your servants shall continue, *
    and their offspring shall stand fast in your sight."   R

Lord, while our days vanish like shadows
and our lives wear out like a garment,
you are eternal.
Although our earthly lives come to an end,
help us to live in Christ's endless life
and at length attain our home,
the heavenly Jerusalem,
where he lives and reigns with you and the Holy Spirit,
now and forever. **Amen.** [621]

PSALM 103   Tone 4; PH 222, 223; PS 102, 103

R

1 Bless the LORD, O my soul, *
    and all that is within me, bless God's holy name.

2 **Bless the LORD, O my soul, ***
    and forget not all the benefits of the LORD,

3 who forgives all your sins *
    and heals all your infirmities;

4 **who redeems your life from the grave ***
    and crowns you with mercy and loving-kindness;

5 who satisfies you with good things, *
    and your youth is renewed like an eagle's.   R

6 **The LORD executes righteousness ***
    and judgment for all who are oppressed.

7 To Moses were made known God's ways *
      and to the children of Israel the works of the LORD.

8 **The LORD is full of compassion and mercy, ***
      slow to anger and of great kindness.

9 The LORD will not always accuse us *
      nor remain angry forever.

10 **The LORD has not dealt with us according to our sins, ***
      nor rewarded us according to our wickedness.   R

11 For as the heavens are high above the earth, *
      so is the LORD's mercy great upon the God-fearing.

12 **As far as the east is from the west, ***
      so far has the LORD removed our sins from us.

13 As a father cares for his children, *
      so does the LORD care for the God-fearing.

14 **For the LORD knows whereof we are made ***
      and remembers that we are but dust.   R

15 Our days are like the grass; *
      we flourish like a flower of the field;

16 **when the wind goes over it, it is gone, ***
      and its place shall know it no more.

17 But the merciful goodness of the LORD endures forever on the God-fearing, *
      and the righteousness of the LORD on children's children;

18 **on those who keep the holy covenant ***
      and remember the commandments and do them.   R

19 The LORD has set up a throne in heaven, *
      and the sovereignty of the LORD has dominion over all.

20 **Bless the LORD, you holy angels,**
      you mighty ones who do God's bidding, *
      and hearken to the voice of God's word.

21 Bless the LORD, all you holy hosts, *
      you holy ministers who do God's will.

22 **Bless the LORD, all you works of God,**
      in all places of God's dominion; *
      bless the LORD, O my soul.   R

God of might and mercy,
you bring us to new life each day,
and nurture us in your tender love.
Keep us far from all sinfulness,
that our lives may be a blessing to you;
in Jesus Christ our Lord.   **Amen.**   [622]

PSALM 104   Tone 1 or 3; PH 224; PS 104, 105

R

1 Bless the LORD, O my soul; *
      O LORD my God, how excellent is your greatness!
      you are clothed with majesty and splendor.

2 **You wrap yourself with light as with a cloak ***
      and spread out the heavens like a curtain.

3 You lay the beams of your chambers in the waters above; *
      you make the clouds your chariot;
      you ride on the wings of the wind.

4 **You make the winds your messengers ***
      and flames of fire your servants.   R

5 You have set the earth upon its foundations, *
      so that it never shall move at any time.

6 **You covered it with the deep as with a mantle; ***
      the waters stood higher than the mountains.

7 At your rebuke they fled; *
      at the voice of your thunder they hastened away.

8 **They went up into the hills and down to the valleys beneath, ***
      to the places you had appointed for them.

9 You set the limits that they should not pass; *
      they shall not again cover the earth.   R

10 **You send the springs into the valleys; ***
      they flow between the mountains.

11 All the beasts of the field drink their fill from them, *
      and the wild asses quench their thirst.

12 **Beside them the birds of the air make their nests ***
      and sing among the branches.

13 You water the mountains from your dwelling on high; *
      the earth is fully satisfied by the fruit of your works.   R

14 **You make grass grow for flocks and herds** *
   and plants to serve humankind;

that they may bring forth food from the earth, *
   15and wine to gladden our hearts,

oil to make a cheerful countenance, *
   and bread to strengthen the heart.

16 The trees of the LORD are full of sap, *
   the cedars of Lebanon which the LORD planted,

17 **in which the birds build their nests,** *
   and in whose tops the stork makes its dwelling.   **R**

18 The high hills are a refuge for the mountain goats, *
   and the stony cliffs for the rock badgers.

19 **You appointed the moon to mark the seasons,** *
   and the sun knows the time of its setting.

20 You make darkness that it may be night, *
   in which all the beasts of the forest prowl.

21 **The lions roar after their prey** *
   and seek their food from God.

22 The sun rises, and they slip away *
   and lay themselves down in their dens.

23 **Mortals go forth to their work** *
   and to their labor until the evening.   **R**

24 O LORD, how manifold are your works! *
   in wisdom you have made them all;
   the earth is full of your creatures.

25 **Yonder is the great and wide sea**
   with its living things too many to number, *
   creatures both small and great.

26 There move the ships,
   and there is that Leviathan, *
   which you have made for the sport of it.   **R**

27 **All of them look to you** *
   to give them their food in due season.

28 You give it to them; they gather it; *
   you open your hand, and they are filled with good things.

²⁹ **You hide your face, and they are terrified;** *
   you take away their breath,
   and they die and return to their dust.

³⁰ You send forth your Spirit, and they are created; *
   and so you renew the face of the earth.   R

³¹ **May your glory, O Lord, endure forever;** *
   may you rejoice in all your works.

³² You look at the earth and it trembles; *
   you touch the mountains and they smoke.

³³ **I will sing to the LORD as long as I live;** *
   I will praise my God while I have my being.

³⁴ May these words of mine please you; *
   I will rejoice in the LORD.

³⁵ **Let sinners be consumed out of the earth,** *
   and the wicked be no more.

[Unison]

Bless the LORD, O my soul. *
Hallelujah!   R

God of majesty,
we are constantly surrounded by your gifts
and touched by your grace;
our words of praise do not approach the wonders of your love.
Send forth your Spirit,
that our lives may be refreshed
and the whole world may be renewed,
in Jesus Christ our Lord.   **Amen.**   [623]

PSALM 105   Tone 4; PS 106, 107

R

¹ Give thanks to the LORD and call upon God's name; *
   make known the deeds of the LORD among the peoples.

² **Sing to the LORD, sing praises,** *
   and speak of all God's marvelous works.

³ Glory in God's holy name; *
   let the hearts of those who seek the LORD rejoice.

⁴ **Search for the LORD and the strength of the LORD;** *
   continually seek the face of God.

5   Remember the marvels God has done, *
    the wonders and the judgments of God's mouth,

6   **O offspring of Abraham, God's servant, ***
    O children of Jacob, God's chosen.   R

7   The LORD is our God, *
    whose judgments prevail in all the world.

8   **The LORD has always been mindful of the covenant, ***
    the promise made for a thousand generations:

9   The covenant made with Abraham, *
    the oath sworn to Isaac,

10 **which God established as a statute for Jacob, ***
    an everlasting covenant for Israel,

11 Saying, "To you will I give the land of Canaan *
    to be your allotted inheritance."   R

12 **When they were few in number, ***
    of little account, and sojourners in the land,

13 wandering from nation to nation *
    and from one realm to another,

14 **God let no one oppress them ***
    and rebuked rulers for their sake,

15 saying, "Do not touch my anointed *
    and do my prophets no harm."   R

16 **Then the LORD called for a famine in the land ***
    and destroyed the supply of bread.

17 The LORD sent a man before them, *
    Joseph, who was sold as a slave.

18 **They bruised his feet in fetters; ***
    his neck they put in an iron collar.

19 Until his prediction came to pass, *
    the word of the LORD tested him.

20 **The king sent and released him; ***
    the ruler of the peoples set him free.

21 He set him as a master over his household, *
    as a ruler over all his possessions,

22 **to instruct his officials according to his will** *
   and to teach his elders wisdom.   R

23 Israel came into Egypt, *
   and Jacob became a sojourner in the land of Ham.

24 **The LORD made the chosen people exceedingly fruitful;** *
   the LORD made them stronger than their enemies;

25 whose heart God turned, so that they hated the chosen people, *
   and dealt unjustly with the servants of the LORD.   R

26 **There came Moses, the servant of the LORD,** *
   and Aaron whom God had chosen.

27 They worked signs from the LORD among them, *
   and portents in the land of Ham.

28 **God sent darkness, and it grew dark;** *
   but the Egyptians rebelled against the words of the LORD.

29 God turned their waters into blood *
   and caused their fish to die.

30 **Their land was overrun by frogs,** *
   in the very chambers of their rulers.

31 God spoke, and there came swarms of insects *
   and gnats within all their borders.

32 **God gave them hailstones instead of rain,** *
   and flames of fire throughout their land.

33 God blasted their vines and their fig trees *
   and shattered every tree in their country.

34 **God spoke, and the locust came,** *
   and young locusts without number,

35 which ate up all the green plants in their land *
   and devoured the fruit of their soil.

36 **God struck down the firstborn of their land,** *
   the first fruits of all their strength.   R

37 God led out the chosen people with silver and gold; *
   in all their tribes there was not one that stumbled.

38 **Egypt was glad of their going,** *
   because they were afraid of them.

39 God spread out a cloud for a covering *
    and a fire to give light in the night season.

40 **They asked, and quails appeared, ***
    and God satisfied them with bread from heaven.

41 God opened the rock, and water flowed, *
    so the river ran in the dry places.

42 **For God remembered the holy promise ***
    and Abraham, chosen to serve.   R

43 So God led forth the people with gladness, *
    the chosen ones with shouts of joy.

44 **God gave the chosen people the lands of the nations, ***
    and they took the fruit of others' toil,

[Unison]

45 **that they might keep God's statutes ***
    and observe the laws of the LORD.
    Hallelujah!   R

God of our salvation,
through the death and resurrection of Jesus Christ,
you have fulfilled your promise to our ancestors in the faith
to redeem the world from slavery
and to lead us into the promised land.
Grant us living water from the rock
and bread from heaven,
that we may survive our desert pilgrimage
and praise you forever;
through Jesus Christ our Redeemer. **Amen.** [624]

PSALM 106
Tone 4; PS 108

R

1 Hallelujah!
Give thanks to the LORD, who is good, *
    whose mercy endures forever.

2 **Can anyone declare the mighty acts of the LORD ***
    or show forth all God's praise?

3 Happy are those who act with justice *
    and always do what is right!   R

4 **Remember me, O LORD, with the favor you have for your people, ***
    and visit me with your saving help;

5 that I may see the prosperity of your elect
  and be glad with the gladness of your people, *
    that I may glory with your inheritance.   **R**

6 **We have sinned as our ancestors did; ***
    we have done wrong and dealt wickedly.

7 In Egypt they did not consider your marvelous works,
  nor remember the abundance of your love; *
    they defied the Most High at the Red Sea.

8 **But you saved them for your name's sake, ***
    to make your power known.

9 The LORD rebuked the Red Sea, and it dried up; *
    God led them through the deep as through a desert.

10 **The LORD saved them from the hand of those who hated them ***
    and redeemed them from the hand of the enemy.

11 The waters covered their oppressors; *
    not one of them was left.

12 **Then they believed the words of the LORD ***
    and sang out songs of praise.   R

13 But they soon forgot the deeds of the LORD *
    and did not await divine counsel.

14 **A craving seized them in the wilderness, ***
    and they put God to the test in the desert.

15 God gave them what they asked, *
    but sent leanness into their soul.

16 **They envied Moses in the camp, ***
    and Aaron, the holy one of the LORD.

17 The earth opened and swallowed Dathan *
    and covered the company of Abiram.

18 **Fire blazed up against their company, ***
    and flames devoured the wicked.   R

19 Israel made a bull-calf at Horeb *
    and worshiped a molten image;

20 **and so they exchanged their glory** *
   for the image of an ox that feeds on grass.

21 They forgot God their Savior, *
   who had done great things in Egypt,

22 **wonderful deeds in the land of Ham,** *
   and fearful things at the Red Sea.

23 So God would have destroyed them,
   had not Moses, the chosen one, stood before God in the breach, *
   to turn away divine wrath from consuming them.   R

24 **They refused the pleasant land** *
   and would not believe God's promise.

25 They grumbled in their tents *
   and would not listen to the voice of the LORD.

26 **So God's hand was lifted against them,** *
   to overthrow them in the wilderness,

27 to cast out their seed among the nations, *
   and to scatter them throughout the lands.   R

28 **They joined themselves to Baal-Peor** *
   and ate sacrifices offered to the dead.

29 They provoked the LORD to anger with their actions, *
   and a plague broke out among them.

30 **Then Phinehas stood up and interceded,** *
   and the plague came to an end.

31 This was reckoned to Phinehas as righteousness *
   throughout all generations forever.

32 **Again they provoked God's anger at the waters of Meribah,** *
   and the LORD punished Moses because of them;

33 for they so embittered his spirit *
   that he spoke rash words with his lips.   R

34 **They did not destroy the peoples** *
   as the LORD had commanded them.

35 They intermingled with the heathen *
   and learned their pagan ways,

36 **so that they worshiped their idols,** *
   which became a snare to them.

³⁷ They sacrificed their sons *
    and their daughters to evil spirits.

**³⁸ They shed innocent blood,
    the blood of their sons and daughters, *
    which they offered to the idols of Canaan,
    and the land was defiled with blood.**

³⁹ Thus they were polluted by their actions *
    and went whoring in their evil deeds.   **R**

**⁴⁰ Therefore the wrath of the Lord was kindled against the people *
    and God abhorred the chosen inheritance.**

⁴¹ God gave them over to the hand of the heathen, *
    and those who hated them ruled over them.

**⁴² Their enemies oppressed them, *
    and they were humbled under their hand.**

⁴³ Many a time did God deliver them,
    but they rebelled through their own devices, *
    and were brought down in their iniquity.

**⁴⁴ Nevertheless, the Lord saw their distress *
    and heard their lamentation.**

⁴⁵ God remembered the covenant with them *
    and out of abundant mercy relented.   **R**

**⁴⁶ God caused them to be pitied *
    by those who held them captive.**

⁴⁷ Save us, O Lord our God,
    and gather us from among the nations, *
    that we may give thanks to your holy name
    and glory in your praise.

**⁴⁸ Blessed be the Lord, the God of Israel,
    from everlasting and to everlasting; *
    and let all the people say, "Amen!"
    Hallelujah!   R**

Merciful God,
remembering your covenant,
you graciously pardoned those who rebelled against you.
Grant that, where sin abounds,
grace may abound more;
through Jesus Christ our Lord.   **Amen.**   [625]

R

¹ Give thanks to the LORD, who is good, *
 whose mercy endures forever.

² Let all those whom the LORD has redeemed proclaim *
 that the LORD redeemed them from the hand of the foe.

³ God gathered them out of the lands; *
 from the east and from the west,
 from the north and from the south.   R

⁴ Some wandered in desert wastes; *
 they found no way to a city where they might dwell.

⁵ They were hungry and thirsty; *
 their spirits languished within them.

⁶ Then in their trouble they cried to the LORD, *
 who delivered them from their distress.

⁷ The LORD put their feet on a straight path *
 to go to a city where they might dwell.

⁸ Let them give thanks for the mercy of God, *
 for the wonders the LORD does for all people.

⁹ For God satisfies the thirsty *
 and fills the hungry with good things.   R

¹⁰ Some sat in darkness and deep gloom, *
 bound fast in misery and iron;

¹¹ because they rebelled against the words of God *
 and despised the counsel of the Most High.

¹² So God humbled their spirits with hard labor; *
 they stumbled, and there was none to help.

¹³ Then in their trouble they cried to the LORD, *
 who delivered them from their distress.

¹⁴ The LORD led them out of darkness and deep gloom *
 and broke their bonds asunder.

¹⁵ Let them give thanks for the mercy of God, *
 for the wonders the LORD does for all people.

16 **For God shatters the doors of bronze** *
   and breaks in two the iron bars.   R

17 Some were fools and took to rebellious ways; *
   they were afflicted because of their sins.

18 **They abhorred all manner of food** *
   and drew near to death's door.

19 Then in their trouble they cried to the LORD, *
   who delivered them from their distress.

20 **God sent forth a word to heal them** *
   and saved them from the grave.

21 Let them give thanks for the mercy of God, *
   for the wonders the LORD does for all people.

22 **Let them offer a sacrifice of thanksgiving** *
   and recount the deeds of God with shouts of joy.   R

23 Some went down to the sea in ships *
   and plied their trade in deep waters;

24 **they beheld the works of the LORD,** *
   whose wonders are in the deep.

25 Then the LORD spoke, and a stormy wind arose, *
   which tossed high the waves of the sea.

26 **They mounted up to the heavens and fell back to the depths;** *
   their hearts melted because of their peril.

27 They reeled and staggered like drunkards *
   and were at their wits' end.

28 **Then in their trouble they cried to the LORD,** *
   who delivered them from their distress.

29 God stilled the storm to a whisper *
   and quieted the waves of the sea.

30 **Then were they glad because of the calm,** *
   and God brought them to the harbor they were bound for.

31 Let them give thanks for the mercy of God, *
   for the wonders the LORD does for all people.

32 **Let them exalt the LORD in the congregation of the people** *
   and praise God in the council of the elders.   R

33 The LORD changed rivers into deserts, *
   and water-springs into thirsty ground,

34 **a fruitful land into salt flats,** *
   because of the wickedness of those who dwell there.

35 God changed deserts into pools of water *
   and dry land into water-springs.

36 **God settled the hungry there,** *
   and they founded a city to dwell in.

37 They sowed fields, and planted vineyards, *
   and brought in a fruitful harvest.   **R**

38 **God blessed them, so that they increased greatly;** *
   God did not let their herds decrease.

39 Yet when they were diminished and brought low, *
   through stress of adversity and sorrow,

40 **(God pours contempt on nobles** *
   and makes them wander in trackless wastes)

41 God lifted up the poor out of misery *
   and multiplied their families like flocks of sheep.

42 **The upright will see this and rejoice,** *
   but all wickedness will shut its mouth.

[Unison]

Whoever is wise will ponder these things, *
and consider well the mercies of the LORD.   R

O God,
you are light to the lost,
bread to the hungry,
deliverance to the captive,
healing to the sick,
eternal vision to the dying,
and harbor to every soul in peril.
Gather the wanderers from every corner of the world
into the community of your mercy and grace,
that we may eternally praise you
for our salvation in Jesus Christ our Lord. **Amen.** [626]

R

1 My heart is firmly fixed, O God, my heart is fixed; *
   I will sing and make melody.

2 **Wake up, my spirit;**
   awake, lute and harp; *
   I myself will waken the dawn.

3 I will confess you among the peoples, O LORD; *
   I will sing praises to you among the nations.

4 **For your loving-kindness is greater than the heavens, ***
   and your faithfulness reaches to the clouds.   R

5 Exalt yourself above the heavens, O God, *
   and your glory over all the earth.

6 **So that those who are dear to you may be delivered, ***
   save with your right hand and answer me.   R

7 From God's holy place came a voice; *
   God said, "I will exult and parcel out Shechem;
   I will divide the valley of Succoth.

8 **Gilead is mine and Manasseh is mine; ***
   Ephraim is my helmet and Judah my scepter.

9 Moab is my washbasin,
   on Edom I throw down my sandal to claim it, *
   and over Philistia will I shout in triumph."   R

10 **Who will lead me into the strong city? ***
   who will bring me into Edom?

11 Have you not cast us off, O God? *
   you no longer go out, O God, with our armies.

12 **Grant us your help against the enemy, ***
   for vain is the help of mortals.

   [Unison]

13 **With God we will do valiant deeds, ***
   and God shall tread our enemies under foot.   R

O God,
your love is wider than all the universe
and your mercy greater than the heights of heaven.
When we are tempted to break faith with you,
put a new song of love on our lips,
that we may sing your praises to all nations on earth,
through your Son, our only hope and defense.   **Amen.**   [627]

PSALM 110   Tone 6

R

1 The LORD said to my lord, "Sit at my right hand, *
   until I make your enemies your footstool."   **R**

2 **The LORD will send the scepter of your power out of Zion, ***
   saying, "Rule over your enemies round about you.

3 Nobility has been yours from the day of your birth; *
   in the beauty of holiness have I begotten you,
   like dew from the womb of the morning."

4 **The LORD has sworn and will not recant: ***
   "You are a priest forever after the order of Melchizedek."   **R**

5 The lord who is at God's right hand
   will smite rulers in the day of his wrath; *
   he will rule over the nations.

6 **He will heap high the corpses ***
   and will smash heads over the wide earth.

[Unison]

He will drink from the brook beside the road *
and therefore will lift high his head.   **R**

Jesus Christ,
King of kings and Lord of lords,
born as one of us,
exalted now on high,
priest of the new covenant,
judge who will come at the end of time,
glory to you forever and ever.   **Amen.**   [628]

R

1 Hallelujah!
I will give thanks to the LORD with my whole heart, *
   in the assembly of the upright, in the congregation.

2 **Great are the deeds of the LORD! ***
   they are studied by all who delight in them.

3 Full of majesty and splendor is the work of the LORD, *
   whose righteousness endures forever.

4 **Gracious and full of compassion is the LORD, ***
   whose marvelous works are to be remembered.

5 The LORD gives food to the God-fearing, *
   ever mindful of the covenant.   R

6 **The LORD has shown the chosen people works of power ***
   in giving them the lands of the nations.

7 The hands of the LORD work faithfulness and justice; *
   all the commandments of the LORD are sure.

8 **They stand fast forever and ever, ***
   because they are done in truth and equity.

9 The LORD sent redemption to the chosen people,
commanding the covenant forever; *
   holy and awesome is the name of the LORD.

10 **The fear of the LORD is the beginning of wisdom; ***
   those who act accordingly have a good understanding;
   the praise of the LORD endures forever.   R

Faithful God,
you have nourished us in your holy covenant
with the food and drink of Christ's love.
Keep us firm in our faith
and loyal in our love,
that we may obediently serve as disciples of Jesus Christ,
our Lord and Savior.   **Amen.**   [629]

R

1 Hallelujah!
   Happy are they who fear the LORD *
      and have great delight in the LORD's commandments!

2 **Their descendants will be mighty in the land; ***
      the generation of the upright will be blessed.

3 Wealth and riches will be in their house, *
      and their righteousness will last forever.   R

4 **Light shines in the darkness for the upright; ***
      the righteous are merciful and full of compassion.

5 It is good for them to be generous in lending *
      and to manage their affairs with justice.

6 **For they will never be shaken; ***
      the righteous will be kept in everlasting remembrance.   R

7 They will not be afraid of any evil rumors; *
      their heart is right;
      they put their trust in the LORD.

8 **Their heart is established and will not shrink, ***
      until they see their desire upon their enemies.

9 They have given freely to the poor, *
      and their righteousness stands fast forever;
      they will hold up their head with honor.

10 **The wicked will see it and be angry;**
   they will gnash their teeth and pine away; *
      the desires of the wicked will perish.   R

   Eternal God,
   in the order of your creation
   you have given righteousness, justice, peace, and love
   for the enlightenment of all people.
   Keep us always in that light
   so that throughout our lives,
   we may show forth the glory of Jesus Christ,
   the light of the world.   **Amen.**   [630]

R

1 Hallelujah!
Give praise, you servants of the LORD; *
    praise the name of the LORD.

2 **Let the name of the LORD be blessed, ***
    from this time forth forevermore.

3 From the rising of the sun to its going down *
    let the name of the LORD be praised.

4 **High above all nations is the LORD, ***
    whose glory is above the heavens.   R

5 Who is like the LORD our God, who sits enthroned on high *
    but stoops to behold the heavens and the earth?

6 **The LORD takes up the weak out of the dust ***
    and lifts up the poor from the ashes.

7 The LORD sets them with the nobles, *
    with the nobles of the chosen people.

8 **The LORD makes the woman of a childless house ***
    to be a joyful mother of children.   R

Sovereign God,
you subdue the arrogant
and raise the humble;
you feed the hungry
and reveal the poverty of wealth.
Help us to praise your name in all times and places,
that we may be faithful servants
of Jesus Christ our Lord.   **Amen.**   [631]

PSALM 114   Tone 4; PS 114

R

1 Hallelujah!
When Israel came out of Egypt, *
    the house of Jacob from a people of strange speech,

2 **Judah became God's sanctuary ***
    and Israel God's dominion.

3 The sea beheld it and fled; *
   Jordan turned and went back.

4 **The mountains skipped like rams,** *
   and the little hills like young sheep.   **R**

5 What ailed you, O sea, that you fled? *
   O Jordan, that you turned back?

6 **You mountains, that you skipped like rams?** *
   you little hills like young sheep?

7 Tremble, O earth, at the presence of the Lord, *
   at the presence of the God of Jacob,

8 **who turned the hard rock into a pool of water** *
   and flint-stone into a flowing spring.   **R**

Mighty God,
by your power you led your people out of slavery in Egypt,
and raised the dead Christ to life.
Deliver us continually by your power
from slavery to freedom
and from death to life,
for the glory of Jesus Christ our Savior. **Amen.**   [632]

PSALM 115

Tone 6; PH 227

R

1 Not to us, O LORD, not to us,
   but to your name give glory; *
      because of your love and because of your faithfulness.

2 **Why should the heathen say,** *
   "Where then is their God?"   **R**

3 Our God is in heaven; *
   whatever God wills to do, God does.

4 **Their idols are silver and gold,** *
   the work of human hands.

5 They have mouths, but they cannot speak; *
   eyes have they, but they cannot see;

6 **they have ears, but they cannot hear;** *
   noses, but they cannot smell;

7 they have hands, but they cannot feel;
   feet, but they cannot walk; *
      they make no sound with their throat.

8 **Those who make them are like them,** *
   and so are all who put their trust in them.   **R**

9 O Israel, trust in the LORD, *
   who is your help and your shield.

10 **O house of Aaron, trust in the LORD,** *
    who is your help and your shield.

11 You who fear the LORD, trust in the LORD, *
    who is your help and your shield.   **R**

12 **The LORD has been mindful of us and will bless us;** *
    the LORD will bless the house of Israel
    and will bless the house of Aaron;

13 the LORD will bless the God-fearing, *
    both small and great together.   **R**

14 **May the LORD increase you more and more,** *
    you and your children after you.

15 May you be blessed by the LORD, *
    the maker of heaven and earth.   **R**

16 **The heaven of heavens is the LORD's,** *
    but the LORD entrusted the earth to its peoples.

17 The dead do not praise the LORD, *
    nor all those who go down into silence;

18 **but we will bless the LORD,** *
    from this time forth forevermore.
    Hallelujah!   R

God, you delivered Israel from the worship of false gods.
Redeem your people in every age
from the pursuit of all that is worthless and untrue;
through Jesus our Savior,
who came to bring us life in all its fullness. **Amen.** [633]

R

1 I love the LORD, because the LORD has heard the voice of my supplication *
　　² and inclined an ear to me whenever I cried out.

3 **The cords of death entangled me;**
　　the grip of the grave took hold of me; *
　　　I came to grief and sorrow.

4 Then I called upon the name of the LORD: *
　　"O LORD, I pray you, save my life."　　R

5 **Gracious is the LORD and righteous; ***
　　our God is full of compassion.

6 The LORD watches over the innocent; *
　　I was brought very low, and the LORD helped me.

7 **Turn again to your rest, O my soul, ***
　　for the LORD has treated you well.　　R

8 For you have rescued my life from death, *
　　my eyes from tears, and my feet from stumbling.

9 **I will walk in the presence of the LORD ***
　　in the land of the living.

10 I believed, even when I said,
　　"I have been brought very low." *
　　¹¹In my distress I said, "No one can be trusted."　　R

12 **How shall I repay you, O LORD, ***
　　for all the good things you have done for me?

13 I will lift up the cup of salvation *
　　and call upon the name of the LORD.

14 **I will fulfill my vows to the LORD ***
　　in the presence of all the chosen people.

15 Precious in your sight, O LORD, *
　　is the death of your servants.　　R

16 **O LORD, I am your servant; ***
　　I am your servant and the child of your handmaid;
　　you have freed me from my bonds.

17 I will offer you the sacrifice of thanksgiving *
    and call upon the name of the LORD.

18 **I will fulfill my vows to the LORD ***
    in the presence of all the people,

[Unison]

19 **in the courts of the LORD's house, ***
    in the midst of you, O Jerusalem.
    Hallelujah!   **R**

God our Redeemer,
you have delivered us from death in the resurrection of Jesus Christ
and brought us to new life by the power of your Spirit.
Give us grace to keep our promises
to praise and serve you all our days;
through Jesus Christ our Lord. **Amen.**   [634]

PSALM 117   Tone 3; PH 229; PS 117

R

1 Praise the LORD, all you nations; *
    give praise, all you peoples.

2 **For the loving-kindness of the LORD toward us is great, ***
    and the faithfulness of the LORD endures forever.
    Hallelujah!   **R**

Lord God,
you have revealed your kindness to all peoples.
Gather all nations to yourself,
that in all the various tongues of the earth
one hymn of praise may rise to you;
through Jesus Christ our Lord. **Amen.**   [635]

PSALM 118   Tone 3; PH 230–232; PS 118–120

R

1 Give thanks to the LORD, who is good, *
    whose mercy endures forever.

2 **Let Israel now proclaim, ***
    "The mercy of the LORD endures forever."

3 Let the house of Aaron now proclaim, *
   "The mercy of the LORD endures forever."

4 Let those who fear the LORD now proclaim, *
   "The mercy of the LORD endures forever." R

5 I called to the LORD in my distress; *
   the LORD answered by setting me free.

6 The LORD is at my side, therefore I will not fear; *
   what can anyone do to me?

7 The LORD is at my side to help me; *
   I will triumph over those who hate me.

8 It is better to rely on the LORD *
   than to put any trust in flesh.

9 It is better to rely on the LORD *
   than to put any trust in rulers.   **R**

10 All the ungodly encompass me; *
   in the name of the LORD I will repel them.

11 They hem me in, they hem me in on every side; *
   in the name of the LORD I will repel them.

12 They swarm about me like bees;
   they blaze like a fire of thorns; *
   in the name of the LORD I will repel them.

13 I was pressed so hard that I almost fell, *
   but the LORD came to my help.   **R**

14 The LORD is my strength and my song *
   and has become my salvation.

15 There is a sound of exultation and victory *
   in the tents of the righteous:

16 "The right hand of the LORD has triumphed! *
   the right hand of the LORD is exalted!
   the right hand of the LORD has triumphed!"

17 I shall not die, but live, *
   and declare the works of the LORD.

18 The LORD has punished me sorely *
   but did not hand me over to death.   R

19 Open for me the gates of righteousness; *
   I will enter them;
   I will offer thanks to the LORD.

20 "This is the gate of the LORD; *
   those who are righteous may enter."   R

21 I will give thanks to you, for you answered me *
   and have become my salvation.

22 The same stone which the builders rejected *
   has become the chief cornerstone.

23 This is the LORD's doing, *
   and it is marvelous in our eyes.

24 On this day the LORD has acted; *
   we will rejoice and be glad in it.   R

25 Hosanna, LORD, hosanna! *
   LORD, send us now success.

26 Blessed is the one who comes in the name of the LORD; *
   we bless you from the house of the LORD.

27 God is the LORD, who has shined upon us; *
   form a procession with branches up to the horns of the altar.

28 "You are my God, and I will thank you; *
   you are my God, and I will exalt you."

[Unison]

29 Give thanks to the LORD, who is good; *
   whose mercy endures forever.   R

Holy and mighty God,
your Son's triumph over sin and death
has opened to us the gate of eternal life.
Purify our hearts
that we may follow him
and share in the radiance of his glory.
We ask this for the sake of our risen Lord.   **Amen.**   [636]

R

1 Happy are they whose way is blameless, *
   who walk in the law of the LORD!

2 **Happy are they who observe your decrees ***
   and seek you with all their hearts!

3 Who never do any wrong, *
   but always walk in your ways.

4 **You laid down your commandments, ***
   that we should fully keep them.

5 Oh, that my ways were made so direct *
   that I might keep your statutes!

6 **Then I should not be put to shame, ***
   when I regard all your commandments.

7 I will thank you with an unfeigned heart, *
   when I have learned your righteous judgments.

8 **I will keep your statutes; ***
   do not utterly forsake me.   R

9 How shall the young cleanse their way? *
   By keeping to your words.

10 **With my whole heart I seek you; ***
   let me not stray from your commandments.

11 I treasure your promise in my heart, *
   that I may not sin against you.

12 **Blessed are you, O LORD; ***
   instruct me in your statutes.

13 With my lips will I recite *
   all the judgments of your mouth.

14 **I have taken greater delight in the way of your decrees ***
   than in all manner of riches.

15 I will meditate on your commandments *
   and give attention to your ways.

16 **My delight is in your statutes; ***
   I will not forget your word.   R

17 Deal bountifully with your servant, *
    that I may live and keep your word.

18 **Open my eyes, that I may see ***
    the wonders of your law.

19 I am a stranger here on earth; *
    do not hide your commandments from me.

20 **My soul is consumed at all times ***
    with longing for your judgments.

21 You have rebuked the insolent; *
    cursed are they who stray from your commandments!

22 **Turn from me shame and rebuke, ***
    for I have kept your decrees.

23 Even though rulers sit and plot against me, *
    I will meditate on your statutes.

24 **For your decrees are my delight, ***
    and they are my counselors.   R

    *   *   *

33 Teach me, O LORD, the way of your statutes, *
    and I shall keep it to the end.

34 **Give me understanding, and I shall keep your law; ***
    I shall keep it with all my heart.

35 Make me go in the path of your commandments, *
    for that is my desire.

36 **Incline my heart to your decrees ***
    and not to unjust gain.

37 Turn my eyes from watching what is worthless; *
    give me life in your ways.

38 **Fulfill your promise to your servant, ***
    which you make to those who fear you.

39 Turn away the reproach which I dread, *
    because your judgments are good.

40 **Behold, I long for your commandments; ***
    in your righteousness preserve my life.   R

    *   *   *

73 Your hands have made me and fashioned me; *
      give me understanding, that I may learn your commandments.

74 **Those who fear you will be glad when they see me, ***
      because I trust in your word.

75 I know, O LORD, that your judgments are right *
      and that in faithfulness you have afflicted me.

76 **Let your loving-kindness be my comfort, ***
      as you have promised to your servant.

77 Let your compassion come to me, that I may live, *
      for your law is my delight.

78 **Let the arrogant be put to shame, for they wrong me with lies; ***
      but I will meditate on your commandments.

79 Let those who fear you turn to me, *
      and also those who know your decrees.

80 **Let my heart be sound in your statutes, ***
      that I may not be put to shame.   R

      *   *   *

97 Oh, how I love your law! *
      all the day long it is in my mind.

98 **Your commandment has made me wiser than my enemies, ***
      and it is always with me.

99 I have more understanding than all my teachers, *
      for your decrees are my study.

100 **I am wiser than the elders, ***
      because I observe your commandments.

101 I restrain my feet from every evil way, *
      that I may keep your word.

102 **I do not shrink from your judgments, ***
      because you yourself have taught me.

103 How sweet are your words to my taste! *
      they are sweeter than honey to my mouth.

104 **Through your commandments I gain understanding; ***
      therefore I hate every lying way.   R

105 Your word is a lantern to my feet *
    and a light upon my path.

106 **I have sworn and am determined ***
    to keep your righteous judgments.

107 I am deeply troubled; *
    preserve my life, O LORD, according to your word.

108 **Accept, O LORD, the willing tribute of my lips, ***
    and teach me your judgments.

109 My life is always in my hand, *
    yet I do not forget your law.

110 **The wicked have set a trap for me, ***
    but I have not strayed from your commandments.

111 Your decrees are my inheritance forever; *
    truly, they are the joy of my heart.

112 **I have applied my heart to fulfill your statutes ***
    forever and to the end.   **R**

       *   *   *

129 Your decrees are wonderful; *
    therefore I obey them with all my heart.

130 **When your word goes forth it gives light; ***
    it gives understanding to the simple.

131 I open my mouth and pant; *
    I long for your commandments.

132 **Turn to me in mercy, ***
    as you always do to those who love your name.

133 Steady my footsteps in your word; *
    let no iniquity have dominion over me.

134 **Rescue me from those who oppress me, ***
    and I will keep your commandments.

135 Let your countenance shine upon your servant *
    and teach me your statutes.

136 **My eyes shed streams of tears, ***
    because people do not keep your law.   **R**

137 You are righteous, O LORD, *
    and upright are your judgments.

138 **You have issued your decrees ***
   with justice and in perfect faithfulness.

139 My indignation has consumed me, *
   because my enemies forget your words.

140 **Your word has been tested to the uttermost, ***
   and your servant holds it dear.

141 I am small and of little account, *
   yet I do not forget your commandments.

142 **Your justice is an everlasting justice ***
   and your law is the truth.

143 Trouble and distress have come upon me, *
   yet your commandments are my delight.

144 **The righteousness of your decrees is everlasting; ***
   grant me understanding, that I may live.   R

   Holy God,
   you are just in all your ways
   and your commandments are the greatest of treasures.
   Give us understanding of your law
   and direct us according to your will
   that we may be faithful in serving you
   for the sake of Jesus our Lord.   **Amen.**   [637]

PSALM 121   Tone 6; PH 234; PS 125

R

1 I lift up my eyes to the hills; *
   from where is my help to come?

2 **My help comes from the LORD, ***
   the maker of heaven and earth.   R

3 The LORD will not let your foot be moved, *
   and the One who watches over you will not fall asleep.

4 **Behold, the One who keeps watch over Israel ***
   shall neither slumber nor sleep;   R

5 it is the LORD who watches over you; *
   the LORD is your shade at your right hand,

6 **so that the sun shall not strike you by day,** *
  nor the moon by night.   R

7 The L<small>ORD</small> shall preserve you from all evil; *
  the L<small>ORD</small> shall keep you safe.

8 **The L<small>ORD</small> shall watch over your going out and your coming in,** *
  from this time forth forevermore.   R

God, our helper,
you are strength greater than the mountains;
you look to our needs and watch over us day and night.
Teach us to hold confidently to your grace
that in times of fear and danger
we may know you are near and depend on you,
our sure deliverer.   **Amen.**   [638]

PSALM 122   Tone 2; PH 235; PS 126

R

1 I was glad when they said to me, *
  "Let us go to the house of the L<small>ORD</small>."

2 **Now our feet are standing** *
  within your gates, O Jerusalem.   R

3 Jerusalem is built as a city *
  that is at unity with itself;

4 **to which the tribes go up,**
  the tribes of the L<small>ORD</small>, *
      the assembly of Israel,
      to praise the name of the L<small>ORD</small>.

5 For there are the thrones of judgment, *
  the thrones of the house of David.   R

6 **Pray for the peace of Jerusalem:** *
  "May they prosper who love you.

7 Peace be within your walls *
  and quietness within your towers.

8 **For the sake of my kindred and companions,** *
  I pray for your prosperity.

9 **Because of the house of the LORD our God, ***
  I will seek to do you good."   R

Lord Jesus,
because there was no peace in Jerusalem,
you wept hard tears.
Bring all nations under your rule
that they make peace
and, with thanksgiving
enter together the heavenly Jerusalem
where you live and reign with the Father
and the Holy Spirit, now and forever.   **Amen.**   [639]

PSALM 123   Tone 8; PS 127

R

1   To you I lift up my eyes, *
      to you enthroned in the heavens.

2   **As the eyes of servants look to the hand of their masters, ***
      and the eyes of a maid to the hand of her mistress,

    so our eyes look to you, O LORD our God, *
      until you show us your mercy.   R

3   **Have mercy upon us, O LORD, have mercy, ***
      for we have had more than enough of contempt,

[Unison]

4   **too much of the scorn of the indolent rich, ***
      and of the derision of the proud.   R

Lord, our creator and redeemer,
we look to you for all that we need.
Look with favor on us, your servants,
and give us your grace;
for the sake of your Son, Jesus Christ our Lord.   **Amen.**   [640]

PSALM 124   Tone 3; PH 236; PS 128

R

1 If the LORD had not been on our side, *
    let Israel now say;

2 **if the LORD had not been on our side, ***
    when enemies rose up against us;

3 then would they have swallowed us up alive *
    in their fierce anger toward us;

4 **then would the waters have overwhelmed us ***
    and the torrent gone over us;

5 then would the raging waters *
    have gone right over us.   R

6 **Blessed be the LORD, ***
    who has not given us over to be a prey for their teeth.

7 We have escaped like a bird from the snare of the fowler; *
    the snare is broken, and we have escaped.

8 **Our help is in the name of the LORD, ***
    the maker of heaven and earth.   R

Helper and defender of Israel,
rescue the peoples of the world from destructive anger,
and set us free to love and serve each other
in the peace of Christ our Lord.   **Amen.**   [641]

PSALM 125   Tone 6; PS 129

R

1 Those who trust in the LORD are like Mount Zion, *
    which cannot be moved, but stands fast forever.

2 **The hills stand about Jerusalem; ***
    so does the LORD stand round about the chosen people,
    from this time forth forevermore.

3 The scepter of the wicked shall not hold sway over the land
            allotted to the just, *
    so that the just shall not put their hands to evil.

4 **Show your goodness, O LORD, to those who are good ***
    and to those who are true of heart.

[Unison]

5 **As for those who turn aside to crooked ways,**
   the LORD will lead them away with the evildoers; *
       but peace be upon Israel.   **R**

Almighty God,
surround us with your power
and defend us from the forces of evil.
Keep us standing on the solid rock of your Word,
that we may not fall,
but remain upright in your presence;
through the Lord Jesus Christ.   **Amen.**   [642]

PSALM 126   Tone 8; PH 237; PS 130, 131

R

1 When the LORD restored the fortunes of Zion, *
       then were we like those who dream.

2 **Then was our mouth filled with laughter, ***
       and our tongue with shouts of joy.

Then they said among the nations, *
       "The LORD has done great things for them."

3 **The LORD has done great things for us, ***
       and we are glad indeed.   **R**

4 Restore our fortunes, O LORD, *
       like the watercourses of the Negev.

5 **Those who sowed with tears ***
       will reap with songs of joy.

[Unison]

6 **Those who go out weeping, carrying the seed, ***
       will come again with joy, shouldering their sheaves.   **R**

Faithful God,
let the seeds of justice,
which we have sown in tears,
grow and increase in your sight.
May we reap in joy the harvest for which we patiently hope;
in Jesus Christ our Lord.   **Amen.**   [643]

R

1 Unless the LORD builds the house, *
    their labor is in vain who build it.

   Unless the LORD watches over the city, *
   in vain the sentries keep vigil.

2 It is in vain that you rise so early and go to bed so late; *
    vain, too, to eat the bread of toil,
    for to the beloved the LORD gives sleep.   R

3 **Children are a heritage from the LORD, ***
   and the fruit of the womb is a gift.

4 Like arrows in the hand of a warrior *
    are the children of one's youth.

5 **Happy are the warriors with a quiver full of them! ***
   they shall not be put to shame
   when they contend with their enemies in the gate.   R

   Lord God,
   the land is brought to flower
   not with human tears
   but with the tears of your Son.
   Grant that those who labor for you
   may not trust in their own work
   but in your help;
   through Jesus Christ our Lord.   **Amen.**   [644]

R

1 Happy are they all who fear the LORD, *
    and who follow in the ways of the LORD!

2 **You, O man, shall eat the fruit of your labor; ***
   happiness and prosperity shall be yours.   R

3 Your wife shall be like a fruitful vine within your house, *
    your children like olive shoots round about your table.

4 **The husband who fears the LORD ***
   shall thus indeed be blessed.   R

⁵ The LORD bless you from Zion, *
and may you see the prosperity of Jerusalem all the days of your life.

⁶ May you live to see your children's children; *
may peace be upon Israel.   R

Gracious God,
giver of life in its fullness,
you take no pleasure in human want
but intend your bounty to be shared among your children.
Lead us in the ways of justice and peace,
for Jesus Christ's sake.   **Amen.**   ^[645]

PSALM 130   Tone 7; PH 240; PS 134

R

¹ Out of the depths have I called to you, O LORD;
    ² LORD, hear my voice; *
        let your ears consider well the voice of my supplication.   **R**

³ If you, LORD, were to note what is done amiss, *
    O Lord, who could stand?

⁴ For there is forgiveness with you; *
    therefore you shall be feared.   R

⁵ I wait for you, O LORD; my soul waits for you; *
    in your word is my hope.

⁶ My soul waits for the LORD,
    more than sentries for the morning, *
        more than sentries for the morning.   R

⁷ O Israel, wait for the LORD, *
    for with the LORD there is mercy;

[Unison]

⁸ there is plenteous redemption with the LORD, *
    who shall redeem Israel from all their sins.   R

O God,
you come to us in the depths of our darkest despair,
in the suffering of Jesus Christ.
By the rising of your Son,
give us new light to guide us,

that we may always praise your holy name;
through Jesus Christ our Lord.   **Amen.**   [646]

PSALM 131

R

1 O LORD, I am not proud; *
    I have no haughty looks.

  I do not occupy myself with great matters, *
    or with things that are too hard for me.

2 But I still my soul and make it quiet,
    like a child upon its mother's breast; *
      my soul is quieted within me.

3 **O Israel, wait upon the LORD, ***
    from this time forth forevermore.   **R**

Lord Jesus, gentle and humble of heart,
you promised your kingdom to those who are like children.
Never let pride reign in our hearts.
In compassion embrace all who willingly bear your gentle yoke
now and forever.   **Amen.**   [647]

PSALM 132

R

1 LORD, remember David, *
    and all the hardships he endured;

2 **how he swore an oath to the LORD ***
    and vowed a vow to the Mighty One of Jacob:

3 "I will not come under the roof of my house,*
    nor climb up into my bed;

4 **I will not allow my eyes to sleep, ***
    nor let my eyelids slumber;

5 until I find a place for the LORD, *
    a dwelling for the Mighty One of Jacob."   **R**

6 **"The ark! We heard it was in Ephrathah; ***
    we found it in the fields of Jearim.

7 Let us go to God's dwelling place; *
   let us fall upon our knees before God's footstool."

8 **Arise, O LORD, into your resting-place, ***
   you and the ark of your strength.

9 Let your priests be clothed with righteousness; *
   let your faithful people sing with joy.

10 **For your servant David's sake, ***
   do not turn away the face of your anointed.   R

11 The LORD has sworn an oath to David, *
   and in truth will not break it:

"A son, the fruit of your body *
will I set upon your throne.

12 If your children keep my covenant
   and my testimonies that I shall teach them, *
      their children will sit upon your throne forevermore."   R

13 **For the LORD has chosen Zion ***
   and desired it for the holy habitation:

14 "This shall be my resting-place forever; *
   here will I dwell, for in Zion I delight.

15 **I will surely bless the provisions of Zion, ***
   and satisfy its poor with bread.

16 I will clothe its priests with salvation, *
   and its faithful people will rejoice and sing.

17 **There will I make the horn of David flourish; ***
   I have prepared a lamp for my anointed.

[Unison]

18 **As for his enemies, I will clothe them with shame; ***
   but as for him, his crown will shine."   R

Faithful God,
we remember your promises to David,
and how you kept them in Jesus Christ.
Come to dwell among us in Christ,
that we at last may come to dwell with you forever. **Amen.**   [648]

R

1 Oh, how good and pleasant it is, *
      when the community lives together in unity!

2 **It is like fine oil upon the head ***
      that runs down upon the beard,

   upon the beard of Aaron, *
      and runs down upon the collar of his robe.

3 **It is like the dew of Hermon ***
      that falls upon the hills of Zion.

[Unison]

For there the LORD has ordained the blessing: *
   life forevermore.   R

Creator of the universe,
from whom all things come,
to whom all things return,
give your people such unity of heart and mind,
that all the world may grow in the life of your eternal kingdom;
through Jesus Christ our Lord.   **Amen.**   [649]

R

1 Behold now, bless the LORD, all you servants of the LORD, *
      you that stand by night in the house of the LORD.

2 **Lift up your hands in the holy place and bless the LORD; ***
      3 **the LORD who made heaven and earth bless you out of Zion.   R**

Lord, where two or three gather in your name,
you promise to be with them.
Look upon your family gathered in your name,
and graciously pour out your blessing upon us;
for the sake of Jesus Christ our Lord.   **Amen.**   [650]

R

1 Hallelujah!
  Praise the name of the LORD; *
    give praise, you servants of the LORD,

2 **you who stand in the house of the LORD, ***
  in the courts of the house of our God.

3 Praise the LORD, for the LORD is good; *
    sing praises to the name of God, for it is lovely.

4 **For the LORD has chosen Jacob ***
  and taken Israel as a possession.   R

5 For I know that the LORD is great, *
    and that our Lord is above all gods.

6 **The LORD does whatever the LORD wills, in heaven and on earth, ***
  in the seas and all the deeps.

7 The LORD brings up rain clouds from the ends of the earth, *
    sends out lightning with the rain,
    and brings the winds out of heaven's storehouse.   R

8 **It was the LORD who struck down the firstborn of Egypt, ***
  the firstborn both of humans and beasts.

9 The LORD sent signs and wonders into the midst of you, O Egypt, *
    against Pharaoh and all his servants.

10 **The LORD overthrew many nations ***
   and put mighty rulers to death:

11 Sihon, king of the Amorites,
     and Og, the king of Bashan, *
     and all the realms of Canaan.

12 **The LORD gave their land to be an inheritance, ***
   an inheritance for Israel, the chosen people.   R

13 O LORD, your name is everlasting; *
     your renown, O LORD, endures from age to age.

14 **For you, O LORD, give your people justice ***
   and show compassion to your servants.   R

¹⁵ The idols of the heathen are silver and gold, *
　　the work of human hands.

¹⁶ They have mouths, but they cannot speak; *
　　eyes have they, but they cannot see.

¹⁷ They have ears, but they cannot hear; *
　　neither is there any breath in their mouth.

¹⁸ Those who make them are like them, *
　　and so are all who put their trust in them.　　R

¹⁹ Bless the LORD, O house of Israel; *
　　O house of Aaron, bless the LORD.

²⁰ Bless the LORD, O house of Levi; *
　　you who fear the LORD, bless the LORD.

　　[Unison]

²¹ Blessed be the LORD out of Zion, *
　　who dwells in Jerusalem.
　　Hallelujah!　　R

Deliver us, O God,
from the tyranny of idols;
they cannot give happiness or life;
they bind us to the ways of death.
Claim us as your own
and lead us in the way, the truth, and the life,
Jesus Christ our Lord.　**Amen.**　[651]

PSALM 136　　　　　　　　　　　　Tone 4; PH 243, 244; PS 139

R

¹ Give thanks to the LORD, who is good, *
　　for the mercy of God endures forever.

² Give thanks to the God of gods, *
　　for the mercy of God endures forever.

³ Give thanks to the Lord of lords, *
　　for the mercy of God endures forever.　　R

⁴ Who only does great wonders, *
　　for the mercy of God endures forever;

5 who by wisdom made the heavens, *
    for the mercy of God endures forever;

6 **who spread out the earth upon the waters,** *
    for the mercy of God endures forever;

7 who created great lights, *
    for the mercy of God endures forever;

8 **the sun to rule the day,** *
    for the mercy of God endures forever;

9 the moon and the stars to govern the night, *
    for the mercy of God endures forever.   **R**

10 **Who struck down the firstborn of Egypt,** *
    for the mercy of God endures forever;

11 and brought out Israel from among them, *
    for the mercy of God endures forever;

12 **with a mighty hand and a stretched-out arm,** *
    for the mercy of God endures forever;

13 who divided the Red Sea in two, *
    for the mercy of God endures forever;

14 **and made Israel to pass through the midst of it,** *
    for the mercy of God endures forever;

15 but swept Pharaoh and his army into the Red Sea, *
    for the mercy of God endures forever;

16 **who led the chosen people through the wilderness,** *
    for the mercy of God endures forever.   R

17 Who struck down great rulers, *
    for the mercy of God endures forever;

18 **and slew mighty kings,** *
    for the mercy of God endures forever;

19 Sihon, king of the Amorites, *
    for the mercy of God endures forever;

20 **and Og, the king of Bashan,** *
    for the mercy of God endures forever;

21 and gave away their lands for an inheritance, *
    for the mercy of God endures forever;

²² an inheritance for Israel, the chosen servant, *
   for the mercy of God endures forever.   **R**

²³ Who remembered us in our low estate, *
   for the mercy of God endures forever;

²⁴ **and delivered us from our enemies, ***
   for the mercy of God endures forever;

²⁵ who gives food to all creatures, *
   for the mercy of God endures forever.

²⁶ **Give thanks to the God of heaven, ***
   for the mercy of God endures forever.   R

God of everlasting love,
through your Word you made all things
in heaven and on earth;
you have opened to us the path from death to life.
Listen to the song of the universe,
the hymn of resurrection sung by your church,
and give us your blessing;
through Jesus Christ our Lord.   **Amen.**   [652]

PSALM 137   Tone 8; PH 245, 246; PS 140

R

¹ By the waters of Babylon we sat down and wept, *
   when we remembered you, O Zion.

² **As for our harps, we hung them up ***
   on the trees in the midst of that land.

³ For those who led us away captive asked us for a song,
   and our oppressors called for mirth: *
      "Sing us one of the songs of Zion."   **R**

⁴ **How shall we sing the LORD's song ***
   upon an alien soil.

⁵ If I forget you, O Jerusalem, *
   let my right hand forget its skill.

⁶ **Let my tongue cleave to the roof of my mouth**
   if I do not remember you, *
      if I do not set Jerusalem above my highest joy.   R

7   Remember the day of Jerusalem, O LORD,
    against the people of Edom, *
        who said, "Down with it! down with it!
        even to the ground!"

8   **O city of Babylon, doomed to destruction, ***
        happy the one who pays you back
        for what you have done to us!

    [Unison]

9   **Happy shall they be who take your little ones, ***
        and dash them against the rock!   R

    God of courage and compassion,
    comfort the exiled and oppressed,
    strengthen the faith of your people,
    and bring us all to our true home,
    the kingdom of our Lord and Savior Jesus Christ.   **Amen.**   [653]

PSALM 138   Tone 3; PH 247; PS 141

R

1   I will give thanks to you, O LORD, with my whole heart; *
        before the gods I will sing your praise.

2   **I will bow down toward your holy temple**
    and praise your name, *
        because of your love and faithfulness;

    for you have glorified your name *
        and your word above all things.

3   **When I called, you answered me; ***
        you increased my strength within me.   R

4   All the rulers of the earth will praise you, O LORD, *
        when they have heard the words of your mouth.

5   **They will sing of the ways of the LORD, ***
        that great is the glory of the LORD.

6   The LORD is high, yet the LORD cares for the lowly *
        and perceives the haughty from afar.   **R**

7   **Though I walk in the midst of trouble, you keep me safe; ***
        you stretch forth your hand against the fury of my enemies;
        your right hand shall save me.

8 O LORD, you will make good your purpose for me; *
   O LORD, your love endures forever;
   do not abandon the works of your hands.   R

God of creation and fulfillment,
help us to seek and discover your purposes,
that we may become willing instruments of your grace,
and that all the world may come to love and praise your name,
in the kingdom of your Son, Jesus Christ our Lord.   **Amen.**   [654]

PSALM 139   Tone 6; PH 248; PS 142, 143

R

1 LORD, you have searched me out and known me; *
   2 you know my sitting down and my rising up;
   you discern my thoughts from afar.

3 **You trace my journeys and my resting-places ***
   and are acquainted with all my ways.

4 Indeed, there is not a word on my lips, *
   but you, O LORD, know it altogether.

5 **You press upon me behind and before ***
   and lay your hand upon me.

6 Such knowledge is too wonderful for me; *
   it is so high that I cannot attain to it.   R

7 **Where can I go then from your Spirit? ***
   where can I flee from your presence?

8 If I climb up to heaven, you are there; *
   if I make the grave my bed, you are there also.

9 **If I take the wings of the morning ***
   and dwell in the uttermost parts of the sea,

10 even there your hand will lead me *
   and your right hand hold me fast.

11 **If I say, "Surely the darkness will cover me, ***
   and the light around me turn to night,"

12 darkness is not dark to you;
   the night is as bright as the day; *
   darkness and light to you are both alike.   R

¹³ **For you yourself created my inmost parts; ***
   you knit me together in my mother's womb.

¹⁴ I will thank you because I am marvelously made; *
   your works are wonderful, and I know it well.

¹⁵ **My body was not hidden from you, ***
   while I was being made in secret
   and woven in the depths of the earth.

¹⁶ Your eyes beheld my limbs, yet unfinished in the womb;
   all of them were written in your book; *
      they were fashioned day by day,
      when as yet there was none of them.

¹⁷ **How deep I find your thoughts, O God! ***
   how great is the sum of them!

¹⁸ If I were to count them, they would be more in number than the sand; *
   to count them all, my life span would need to be like yours.   **R**

¹⁹ **Oh, that you would slay the wicked, O God! ***
   You that thirst for blood, depart from me.

²⁰ They speak despitefully against you; *
   your enemies take your name in vain.

²¹ **Do I not hate those, O Lord, who hate you? ***
   and do I not loathe those who rise up against you?

²² I hate them with a perfect hatred; *
   they have become my own enemies.

²³ **Search me out, O God, and know my heart; ***
   try me and know my restless thoughts.

[Unison]

²⁴ **Look well whether there be any wickedness in me ***
   and lead me in the way that is everlasting.   **R**

Almighty God, creator of the universe,
we are awed by your wondrous works
and overwhelmed by your infinite wisdom.
For all your majesty we praise you;
yet even more
we rejoice that you do not forget us,
that you want to know us,
that you come to care for us,
sisters and brothers of Jesus Christ, your Son.   **Amen.**   [655]

R

1 O LORD, I call to you; come to me quickly; *
      hear my voice when I cry to you.

2 **Let my prayer be set forth in your sight as incense, ***
      the lifting up of my hands as the evening sacrifice.

3 Set a watch before my mouth, O LORD,
      and guard the door of my lips; *
        4 let not my heart incline to any evil thing.

   Let me not be occupied in wickedness with evildoers, *
      nor eat of their choice foods.   R

5 Let the righteous smite me in friendly rebuke;
      let not the oil of the unrighteous anoint my head; *
        for my prayer is continually against their wicked deeds.

6 **Let their rulers be overthrown in stony places, ***
      that they may know my words are true.

7 As when a plower turns over the earth in furrows, *
      let their bones be scattered at the mouth of the grave.

8 **But my eyes are turned to you, Lord GOD; ***
      in you I take refuge;
      do not strip me of my life.

9 Protect me from the snare which they have laid for me *
      and from the traps of the evildoers.

10 **Let the wicked fall into their own nets, ***
      while I myself escape.   R

   Holy God,
      let the incense of our prayer ascend before you,
      and let your loving-kindness descend upon us,
      that with devoted hearts we may sing your praises
      with the church on earth and the whole heavenly host,
      and glorify you forever and ever. **Amen.**   [456]

PSALM 142   Tone 8

R

1 I cry to the LORD with my voice; *
      to the LORD I make loud supplication.

2 **I pour out my complaint before you, O LORD,** *
   and tell you all my trouble.

3 When my spirit languishes within me, you know my path; *
   in the way wherein I walk they have hidden a trap for me.

4 **I look to my right hand and find no one who knows me;** *
   I have no place to flee to, and no one cares for me.   R

5 I cry out to you, O LORD; *
   I say, "You are my refuge,
   my portion in the land of the living."

6 **Listen to my cry for help, for I have been brought very low;** *
   save me from those who pursue me,
   for they are too strong for me.

[Unison]

7 **Bring me out of prison, that I may give thanks to your name;** *
   when you have dealt bountifully with me,
   the righteous will gather around me.   R

God our refuge,
when all friends have forsaken us
and enemies line all our paths,
come quickly to our aid.
Lead us out from captivity
into the light of your freedom,
secured for us in the sacrifice
of Jesus Christ our Lord. **Amen.** [656]

PSALM 143   Tone 7; PH 250; PS 146

R

1 LORD, hear my prayer,
   and in your faithfulness heed my supplications; *
   answer me in your righteousness.

2 **Enter not into judgment with your servant,** *
   for in your sight shall no one living be justified.

3 For my enemy has sought my life,
   crushed me to the ground, *
   and made me live in dark places like those who are long dead.

4 **My spirit faints within me;** *
   my heart within me is desolate.   R

5 I remember the time past;
   I muse upon all your deeds; *
      I consider the works of your hands.

6 **I spread out my hands to you; ***
      my soul gasps to you like a thirsty land.

7 O LORD, make haste to answer me; my spirit fails me; *
      do not hide your face from me
      or I shall be like those who go down to the pit.

8 **Let me hear of your loving-kindness in the morning,**
   for I put my trust in you; *
      show me the road that I must walk,
      for I lift up my soul to you.   R

9 Deliver me from my enemies, O LORD, *
      for I flee to you for refuge.

10 **Teach me to do what pleases you, for you are my God; ***
      let your good Spirit lead me on level ground.

11 Revive me, O LORD, for your name's sake; *
      for your righteousness' sake, bring me out of trouble.

12 **Of your goodness, destroy my enemies**
   and bring all my foes to naught, *
      for truly I am your servant.   R

God of our hope,
when we are distracted by care and sickness,
help us to recognize your image in ourselves and others,
that we may be made whole
and the world become the kingdom of our Lord and Savior Jesus Christ.
Amen.   [657]

PSALM 144   Tone 6

R

1 Blessed be the LORD my rock! *
      who trains my hands to fight and my fingers to battle;

2 **my help and my fortress, my stronghold and my deliverer, ***
      my shield in whom I trust,
      who subdues the peoples under me.   R

3 O LORD, what are we that you should care for us? *
      mere mortals that you should think of us?

4 **We are like a puff of wind; ***
   our days are like a passing shadow.   R

5 Bow your heavens, O LORD, and come down; *
   touch the mountains, and they shall smoke.

6 **Hurl the lightning and scatter them; ***
   shoot out your arrows and rout them.

7 Stretch out your hand from on high; *
   rescue me and deliver me from the great waters,
   from the hand of foreign peoples,

8 **whose mouths speak deceitfully ***
   and whose right hand is raised in falsehood.   R

9 O God, I will sing to you a new song; *
   I will play to you on a ten-stringed lyre.

10 **You give victory to rulers ***
   and have rescued David your servant.

11 Rescue me from the hurtful sword *
   and deliver me from the hand of foreign peoples,

   whose mouths speak deceitfully *
   and whose right hand is raised in falsehood.   R

12 May our sons be like plants well nurtured from their youth, *
   and our daughters like sculptured corners of a palace.

13 **May our barns be filled to overflowing with all manner of crops; ***
   may the flocks in our pastures increase by thousands
        and tens of thousands;
   14**may our cattle be fat and sleek.**

   May there be no breaching of the walls, no going into exile, *
   no wailing in the public squares.

15 **Happy are the people of whom this is so! ***
   happy are the people whose God is the LORD!   R

   Generous and bountiful God,
   give compassion to the prosperous
   and comfort to the needy,
   that all people may come to love and praise you;
   through Jesus Christ our Lord.   **Amen.**   [658]

R

1 I will exalt you, O God my Sovereign, *
     and bless your name forever and ever.

2 **Every day will I bless you ***
     and praise your name forever and ever.

3 Great is the LORD and greatly to be praised; *
     there is no end to your greatness.   **R**

4 **One generation shall praise your works to another ***
     and shall declare your power.

5 I will ponder the glorious splendor of your majesty *
     and all your marvelous works.

6 **They shall speak of the might of your wondrous acts, ***
     and I will tell of your greatness.

7 They shall publish the remembrance of your great goodness; *
     they shall sing of your righteous deeds.

8 **The LORD is gracious and full of compassion, ***
     slow to anger and of great kindness.

9 O LORD, you are loving to everyone, *
     and your compassion is over all your works.   **R**

10 **All your works praise you, O LORD, ***
     and your faithful servants bless you.

11 They make known the glory of your reign *
     and speak of your power;

12 **that the peoples may know of your power ***
     and the glorious splendor of your reign.

13 Your reign is an everlasting reign; *
     your dominion endures throughout all ages.

   O LORD, you are faithful in all your words *
   and merciful in all your deeds.   R

14 The LORD upholds all those who fall *
     and lifts up those who are bowed down.

15 **The eyes of all wait upon you, O LORD, ***
     and you give them their food in due season.

16 You open wide your hand *
 and satisfy the needs of every living creature. **R**

17 **O Lord, you are righteous in all your ways ***
 and loving in all your works.

18 O Lord, you are near to those who call upon you, *
 to all who call upon you faithfully.

19 **You fulfill the desire of those who fear you; ***
 you hear their cry and help them.

20 O Lord, you preserve all those who love you, *
 but you destroy all the wicked.

21 **My mouth shall speak the praise of the Lord; ***
 let all flesh bless your holy name forever and ever. **R**

Merciful Lord,
you are faithful in all your promises,
and just in all your ways.
Govern us, for we are weak;
strengthen us, for we are failing;
refresh us, for we are famished;
abundantly bestow your gifts upon us.
Defend us from evil,
that we be not tempted from your way,
but may praise your name forever. **Amen.** [659]

Psalm 146   Tone 3; PH 253, 254; PS 150–152

R

1 Hallelujah!
 Praise the Lord, O my soul! *
   2 I will praise the Lord as long as I live;
     I will sing praises to my God while I have my being. **R**

3 **Put not your trust in rulers, nor in any child of earth, ***
 for there is no help in them.

4 When they breathe their last, they return to earth, *
 and in that day their thoughts perish. **R**

5 **Happy are they who have the God of Jacob for their help! ***
 whose hope is in the Lord their God;

6 who made heaven and earth, the seas, and all that is in them; *
  who keeps faith forever;

7 **who gives justice to those who are oppressed, ***
  and food to those who hunger.   R

  The LORD sets the prisoners free;
   8the LORD opens the eyes of the blind; *
  the LORD lifts up those who are bowed down;

  the LORD loves the righteous
   9and cares for the stranger; *
  the LORD sustains the orphan and widow,
  but frustrates the way of the wicked.   R

[Unison]

10 **The LORD shall reign forever, ***
  your God, O Zion, throughout all generations.
  Hallelujah!   R

  Blessed are those who put their trust in you, O God,
  our sure rock and refuge.
  Guard us from giving to any other
  the allegiance which belongs only to you.
  Shine upon us with the brightness of your light,
  that we may love you with a pure heart
  and praise you forever;
  through Jesus Christ our Lord. **Amen.**   [660]

PSALM 147   Tone 1 or 3; PH 255; PS 153–154

R

1 Hallelujah!
  How good it is to sing praises to our God! *
  how pleasant it is to honor the LORD with praise!

2 **The LORD rebuilds Jerusalem ***
  and gathers the exiles of Israel.

3 The LORD heals the brokenhearted *
  and binds up their wounds.

4 **The LORD counts the number of the stars ***
  and calls them all by their names.

5 Great is our Lord and mighty in power, *
  whose wisdom is beyond limit.

6 **The LORD lifts up the lowly, ***
    but casts the wicked to the ground.   R

7 Sing to the LORD with thanksgiving; *
    make music to our God upon the harp.

8 **God covers the heavens with clouds ***
    and prepares rain for the earth;

    God makes grass to grow upon the mountains *
    and green plants to serve humankind.

9 **God provides food for flocks and herds ***
    and for the young ravens when they cry.

10 The LORD is not impressed by the might of a horse *
    and has no pleasure in the strength of a man;

11 **but the LORD has pleasure in the God-fearing, ***
    in those who await God's gracious favor.   R

12 Worship the LORD, O Jerusalem; *
    praise your God, O Zion;

13 **for God has strengthened the bars of your gates ***
    and blessed your children within you.

14 God has established peace on your borders *
    and satisfies you with the finest wheat.   R

15 **God's command is sent out to the earth, ***
    and the word of the LORD runs very swiftly.

16 God gives snow like wool *
    and scatters hoarfrost like ashes.

17 **God scatters hail like bread crumbs; ***
    who can stand against the cold of the LORD?

18 God's word is sent forth and melts them; *
    God's stormwinds blow, and the waters flow.

19 **God's word is declared to Jacob, ***
    God's statutes and judgments to Israel.

    [Unison]

20 **The LORD has not done so to any other nation; ***
    to them God's judgments have not been revealed.
    Hallelujah!   R

Psalm 147:1–11

Loving God,
great builder of the heavenly Jerusalem,
you know the number of the stars
and call them by name.
Heal hearts that are broken,
gather those who have been scattered,
and enrich us all from the fullness of your eternal wisdom,
Jesus Christ our Lord.   **Amen.**   [661]

Psalm 147:12–20

O Lord,
marvelous is your might
by which you cast down the proud
and lift up the humble.
Restore and rebuild your church.
Gather your scattered sheep
and nourish us by your holy Word,
that we may follow your will
and come at last to the heritage
prepared for us in Christ Jesus.   **Amen.**   [662]

PSALM 148   Tone 1 or 3; PH 256; PS 155

R

1 Hallelujah!
Praise the LORD from the heavens; *
praise the LORD in the heights.

2 **Praise the LORD, all you holy angels; ***
praise the LORD, all heavenly host.   R

3 Praise the LORD, sun and moon; *
praise the LORD, all you shining stars.

4 **Praise the LORD, heaven of heavens, ***
and you waters above the heavens.

5 Let them praise the name of the LORD, *
who commanded, and they were created.

6 **The LORD made them stand fast forever and ever ***
and gave them a law which shall not pass away.   R

7 Praise the LORD from the earth, *
you sea-monsters and all deeps;

8 **fire and hail, snow and fog, ***
   tempestuous wind, obeying God's will;

9 mountains and all hills, *
   fruit trees and all cedars;

10 **wild beasts and all cattle, ***
   creeping things and winged birds;

11 kings of the earth and all peoples, *
   rulers and all judges of the world;

12 **young men and women, ***
   old and young together.   R

13 Let them praise the name of the LORD, *
   for the name of the LORD only is exalted,
   and the splendor of the LORD is over earth and heaven.

14 **The LORD has raised up strength for the chosen people**
   and praise for all loyal servants, *
   the children of Israel, a people who are near to the LORD.
   Hallelujah!   R

God Most High,
by your Word you created a wondrous universe,
and through your Spirit
you breathed into it the breath of life.
Accept creation's hymn of praise from our lips,
and let the praise that is sung in heaven
resound in the heart of every creature on earth,
to the glory of the Father, and the Son, and the Holy Spirit,
now and forever. **Amen.**   [663]

PSALM 149   Tone 1 or 3; PH 257; PS 156

R

1 Hallelujah!
   Sing to the LORD a new song; *
   sing praise to God in the congregation of the faithful.

2 **Let Israel rejoice in their Maker; ***
   let the children of Zion be joyful in their Sovereign.

3 Let them praise God's name in the dance; *
   let them sing praise to the LORD with timbrel and harp.

4 **For the LORD takes pleasure in the chosen people ***
   and adorns the poor with victory.

5 Let the faithful rejoice in triumph; *
   let them be joyful on their beds.

6 **Let the praises of God be in their throat ***
   and a two-edged sword in their hand;   **R**

7 to wreak vengeance on the nations *
   and punishment on the peoples;

8 **to bind their rulers in chains ***
   and their nobles with links of iron;

[Unison]

9 **to inflict on them the judgment decreed; ***
   this is glory for all God's faithful people.
   Hallelujah!   **R**

God our Maker,
you crown the humble with honor
and exalt the faithful who gather in your name.
Because you have favored us with life,
we dance before you in our joy
and praise you with unending song
for Jesus Christ our Lord.   **Amen.**   [664]

PSALM 150   Tone 1 or 3; PH 258; PS 157

R

1 Hallelujah!
   Praise God in the holy temple; *
   give praise in the firmament of heaven.

2 **Praise God who is mighty in deed; ***
   give praise for God's excellent greatness.   **R**

3 Praise God with the blast of the ram's-horn; *
   give praise with lyre and harp.

4 **Praise God with timbrel and dance; ***
   give praise with strings and pipe.

5 Praise God with resounding cymbals; *
   give praise with loud-clanging cymbals.

6 **Let everything that has breath ***
   praise the Lord.
   Hallelujah! R

Great and glorious God,
in your wisdom you created us,
in Jesus Christ you came to redeem us,
and through your Holy Spirit you guide and sanctify us.
Give us breath to sing of your majesty,
and with all creation,
praise you as the true life of all;
through Jesus Christ,
who reigns with you and the Holy Spirit;
one God forever. **Amen.** [665]

PRAYERS
FOR VARIOUS
OCCASIONS

THE GREAT LITANY

The Great Litany is appropriate for times of special petition or supplication. It may be sung or said. In daily prayer, there is a tradition that it is to be used as a separate service on all Wednesdays and Fridays of Lent beginning the Friday after Ash Wednesday until Palm Sunday. There is a long tradition of singing the Great Litany in procession on Sundays of Advent and Lent, and at penitential times. If the entire litany is not used, the Prayer of Approach to God and the Concluding Prayers are used, but a selection of appropriate petitions may be made from the remaining sections.

PRAYER OF APPROACH TO GOD

O God the Father, creator of heaven and earth,

Have mercy on us.

O God the Son, redeemer of the world,

Have mercy on us.

O God the Holy Spirit, advocate and guide,

Have mercy on us.

Holy, blessed, and glorious Trinity,
three persons and one God,

Have mercy on us.

PRAYERS FOR DELIVERANCE

Remember not, Lord Christ, our offenses,
nor the offenses of our forebears.
Spare us, good Lord,
spare your people whom you have redeemed with your precious blood.

Spare us, good Lord.

From all spiritual blindness;
from pride, vainglory, and hypocrisy;
from envy, hatred, and malice;
and from all want of charity,

Good Lord, deliver us.

From all deadly sin;
and from the deceits of the world,
the flesh, and the devil,

Good Lord, deliver us.

From all false doctrine, heresy, and schism;
from hardness of heart,
and contempt for your Word and commandments,

Good Lord, deliver us.

From earthquake and tempest;
from drought, fire, and flood;
from civil strife and violence;
from war and murder;
and from dying suddenly and unprepared,

Good Lord, deliver us.

Prayer Recalling Christ's Saving Work

By the mystery of your holy incarnation,
by your baptism, fasting, and temptation;
and by your proclamation of the kingdom,

Good Lord, deliver us.

By your bloody sweat and bitter grief;
by your cross and suffering;
and by your precious death and burial,

Good Lord, deliver us.

By your mighty resurrection;
by your glorious ascension;
and by the coming of the Holy Spirit,

Good Lord, deliver us.

In our times of trouble;
in our times of prosperity;
in the hour of death,
and on the day of judgment,

Good Lord, deliver us.

PRAYERS OF INTERCESSION

Receive our prayers, O Lord our God.

Hear us, good Lord.

For the church

Govern and direct your holy church;
fill it with love and truth;
and grant it that unity which is your will.

Hear us, good Lord.

Enlighten all ministers
with true knowledge and understanding of your Word,
that by their preaching and living
they may declare it clearly
and show its truth.

Hear us, good Lord.

Encourage and prosper your servants
who spread the gospel in all the world,
and send out laborers into the harvest.

Hear us, good Lord.

Bless and keep your people,
that all may find and follow their true vocation and ministry.

Hear us, good Lord.

Give us a heart to love and reverence you,
that we may diligently live according to your commandments.

Hear us, good Lord.

To all your people
give grace to hear and receive your Word,
and to bring forth the fruit of the Spirit.

Hear us, good Lord.

Strengthen those who stand firm in the faith,
encourage the fainthearted,
raise up those who fall,
and finally give us the victory.

Hear us, good Lord.

For our country

Rule the hearts of your servants,
the President of the United States (*or* of this nation),
and all others in authority,
that they may do justice, and love mercy,
and walk in the ways of truth.

Hear us, good Lord.

Bless and defend all who strive for our safety and protection,
and shield them in all dangers and adversities.

Hear us, good Lord.

Grant wisdom and insight to those who govern us,
and to judges and magistrates the grace to execute justice with mercy.

Hear us, good Lord.

For all people

To all nations grant unity, peace, and concord,
and to all people give dignity, food, and shelter.

Hear us, good Lord.

Grant us abundant harvests,
strength and skill to conserve the resources of the earth,
and wisdom to use them well.

Hear us, good Lord.

Enlighten with your Spirit all who teach
and all who learn.

Hear us, good Lord.

Come to the help of all who are in danger, necessity, and trouble;
protect all who travel by land, air, or water;
and show your pity on all prisoners and captives.

Hear us, good Lord.

Strengthen and preserve all women who are in childbirth,
and all young children,
and comfort the aged, the bereaved, and the lonely.

Hear us, good Lord.

Defend and provide for the widowed and the orphaned,
the refugees and the homeless,
the unemployed,
and all who are desolate and oppressed.

Hear us, good Lord.

Heal those who are sick in body or mind,
and give skill and compassion to all who care for them.

Hear us, good Lord.

Grant us true repentance,
forgive our sins,
and strengthen us by your Holy Spirit
to amend our lives according to your Holy Word.

Hear us, good Lord.

CONCLUDING PRAYERS

Son of God, we ask you to hear us.

Son of God, we ask you to hear us.

Lamb of God, you take away the sin of the world,

have mercy on us.

Lamb of God, you take away the sin of the world,

have mercy on us.

Lamb of God, you take away the sin of the world,

grant us peace.

Lord, have mercy on us.

Christ, have mercy on us.

Lord, have mercy on us.   [666]

> The Lord's Prayer is said, unless the Lord's Supper is to follow.
>
> The Litany concludes with the following or some other collect.

Let us pray.

Almighty God,
you have given us grace at this time with one accord
to make our common supplication to you;
and you have promised through your beloved Son
that when two or three are gathered together in his name
you will be in the midst of them.
Fulfill now, O Lord, our desires and petitions
as may be best for us;
granting us in this world knowledge of your truth,
and in the age to come life everlasting.   **Amen.**   [96]

LITANIES AND PRAYERS FOR VARIOUS OCCASIONS

A LITANY OF THANKSGIVING

Give thanks to the Lord who is good.

God's love is everlasting.

Come, let us praise God joyfully.

Let us come to God with thanksgiving.

For the good world;
for things great and small, beautiful and awesome;
for seen and unseen splendors;

Thank you, God.

For human life;
for talking and moving and thinking together;
for common hopes and hardships shared from birth until our dying;

Thank you, God.

For work to do and strength to work;
for the comradeship of labor;
for exchanges of good humor and encouragement;

Thank you, God.

For marriage;
for the mystery and joy of flesh made one;
for mutual forgiveness and burdens shared;
for secrets kept in love;

Thank you, God.

For family;
for living together and eating together;
for family amusements and family pleasures;

Thank you, God.

For children;
for their energy and curiosity;
for their brave play and startling frankness;
for their sudden sympathies;

Thank you, God.

For the young;
for their high hopes;
for their irreverence toward worn-out values;
for their search for freedom;
for their solemn vows;

Thank you, God.

For growing up and growing old;
for wisdom deepened by experience;
for rest in leisure;
and for time made precious by its passing;

Thank you, God.

For your help in times of doubt and sorrow;
for healing our diseases;
for preserving us in temptation and danger;

Thank you, God.

For the church into which we have been called;
for the good news we receive by Word and Sacrament;
for our life together in the Lord;

We praise you, God.

For your Holy Spirit,
who guides our steps and brings us gifts of faith and love;
who prays in us and prompts our grateful worship;

We praise you, God.

Above all, O God, for your Son Jesus Christ,
who lived and died and lives again for our salvation;
for our hope in him;
and for the joy of serving him;

**We thank and praise you, Eternal God,
for all your goodness to us.**

Give thanks to the Lord, who is good.

God's love is everlasting. [667]

A Litany of Confession

Almighty God: you alone are good and holy.
Purify our lives and make us brave disciples.
We do not ask you to keep us safe,
but to keep us loyal,
so we may serve Jesus Christ,
who, tempted in every way as we are,
was faithful to you.

Amen.

From lack of reverence for truth and beauty;
from a calculating or sentimental mind;
from going along with mean and ugly things;

O God, deliver us.

From cowardice that dares not face truth;
laziness content with half-truth;
or arrogance that thinks we know it all;

O God, deliver us.

From artificial life and worship;
from all that is hollow or insincere;

O God, deliver us.

From trite ideals and cheap pleasures;
from mistaking hard vulgarity for humor;

O God, deliver us.

From being dull, pompous, or rude;
from putting down our neighbors;

O God, deliver us.

From cynicism about others;
from intolerance or cruel indifference;

O God, deliver us.

From being satisfied with things as they are,
in the church or in the world;
from failing to share your indignation about injustice;

O God, deliver us.

From selfishness, self-indulgence, or self-pity;

O God, deliver us.

From token concern for the poor,
for lonely or loveless people;
from confusing faith with good feeling,
or love with wanting to be loved;

O God, deliver us.

For everything in us that may hide your light;

O God, light of life, forgive us. [668]

PRAYERS FOR THE WORLD

1

For Peace

Eternal God,
in your perfect realm no sword is drawn
but the sword of righteousness,
and there is no strength but the strength of love.
So mightily spread abroad your Spirit,
that all peoples may be gathered
under the banner of the Prince of Peace,
as your children;
to you be dominion and glory,
now and forever. **Amen.** [669]

2

For Peace   *Brother Roger of Taizé*

Lord Christ,
at times we are like strangers on this earth,
taken aback by all the violence, the harsh oppositions.
Like a gentle breeze, you breathe upon us the Spirit of peace.
Transfigure the deserts of our doubts,
and so prepare us to be bearers of reconciliation
wherever you place us,
until the day when a hope of peace
dawns in our world. **Amen.** [670]

3

For Racial Peace

Great God over us all,
destroy prejudice that turns us against one another.
Teach us that we are all children of your love,
whether we are black or red or white or yellow.

Encourage us to live together,
loving one another in peace,
so that someday a golden race of people
may have the world,
giving praise to Jesus Christ our Lord.   **Amen.**   [671]

4

For Racial and Cultural Diversity

O God,
you created all people in your image.
We thank you for the astonishing variety
of races and cultures in this world.
Enrich our lives by ever-widening circles of friendship,
and show us your presence in those who differ most from us,
until our knowledge of your love is made perfect
in our love for all your children;
through your Son, Jesus Christ our Lord.   **Amen.**   [672]

5

For Peace Among Nations

Almighty God,
guide the nations of the world into ways of justice and truth,
and establish among them that peace
which is the fruit of righteousness,
that they may become the kingdom
of our Lord and Savior Jesus Christ.   **Amen.**   [673]

6

For Hope ·   *A prayer of the Chippewa*

We pray that someday an arrow will be broken,
not in something or someone,
but by each of humankind,
to indicate peace, not violence.
Someday, oneness with creation,
rather than domination over creation,
will be the goal to be respected.
Someday fearlessness to love and make a difference
will be experienced by all people.
Then the eagle will carry our prayer for peace and love,
and the people of the red, white, yellow, brown,
and black communities
can sit in the same circle together to communicate in love
and experience the presence of the Great Mystery in their midst.
Someday can be today for you and me.   **Amen.**   [674]

7

For the Human Family

O God, you made us in your own image
and redeemed us through Jesus your Son.
Look with compassion on the whole human family,
take away the arrogance and hatred that infect our hearts,
break down the walls that separate us,
unite us in bonds of love,
and, through our struggle and confusion,
work to accomplish your purposes on earth;
that, in your good time,
all nations and races may serve you in harmony
around your heavenly throne;
through Jesus Christ our Lord.   **Amen.**   [675]

8

For World Community

Almighty God,
in Jesus Christ you have ordered us
to live as loving neighbors.
Though we are scattered in different places,
speak different words,
or descend from different races,
give us common concern,
so that we may be one people,
who share the governing of the world
under your guiding purpose.
May greed, war, and lust for power be curbed,
and all people enter the community of love
promised in Jesus Christ our Lord.   **Amen.**   [676]

9

For World Unity   *A prayer from Zaire*

O God,
you love justice and you establish peace on earth.
We bring before you the disunity of today's world:
the absurd violence, and the many wars,
which are breaking the courage of the peoples of the world;
militarism and the armaments race,
which are threatening life on the planet;
human greed and injustice,
which breed hatred and strife.

Send your Spirit and renew the face of the earth;
teach us to be compassionate toward the whole human family;
strengthen the will of all those who fight for justice and for peace;
lead all nations into the path of peace,
and give us that peace which the world cannot give. **Amen.**   [677]

10

For World Religions

We thank you, God of the universe,
that you call all people to worship you
and to serve your purpose in this world.
We praise you for the gift of faith
we have received in Jesus Christ.
We praise you also for diverse faith
among the peoples of the earth.
For you have bestowed your grace
that Christians, Jews, Muslims,
Buddhists, and others
may celebrate your goodness,
act upon your truth,
and demonstrate your righteousness.
In wonder and awe
we praise you great God. **Amen.**   [678]

11

For International Organizations   *From the Mainau Prayerbook*

O God,
we pray for all international organizations of goodwill,
that their efforts may lead to a strengthening
of those influences which make for peace.
Great sacrifices have been made for war;
awaken in us and in all people, O God,
the willingness to make great sacrifices for peace,
so that the day may be hastened
when no nation shall draw the sword against another,
and people no longer shall learn to fight.
We ask in the name of him who is the Prince of Peace. **Amen.**   [679]

12

For Governments of the World

High God, holy God:
you rule the ways of peoples,
and govern every earthly government.
Work with those who work for peace.
Make every person in authority an agent of your reconciliation,
and every diplomat an ambassador of hope.
Bring peace and goodwill among all people,
fulfilling among us the promise made
in Jesus Christ, who was born to save the world.　**Amen.**　[680]

13

In a Time of International Crisis

Eternal God, our only hope,
our help in times of trouble:
show nations ways to work out differences.
Do not let threats multiply
or power be used without compassion.
May your will overrule human willfulness,
so that people may agree and settle claims peacefully.
Hold back those who are impulsive,
lest desire for vengeance overwhelm our common welfare.
Bring peace to earth, through Jesus Christ,
the Prince of Peace and Savior of us all.　**Amen.**　[681]

PRAYERS FOR THE NATURAL ORDER

14

For Creation
A prayer from Samoa

Almighty God, your word of creation
caused the water to be filled
with many kinds of living beings
and the air to be filled with birds.
We rejoice in the richness of your creation,
and we pray for your wisdom
for all who live on this earth,
that we may wisely manage and not destroy what you have made
for us and for our descendants.
In Jesus' name we pray.　**Amen.**　[682]

15

For Creation   *"Canticle of the Sun"—Francis of Assisi*

O Most High, Almighty, good Lord God,
to you belong praise, glory, honor, and blessing!

Praised be my Lord God for all creatures,
and especially for our brother the sun,
who brings us the day and who brings us the light;
fair is he and shines with a very great splendor;
O Lord, he signifies you to us.

Praised be my Lord for our sister the moon,
and for the stars,
which you have set clear and lovely in heaven.

Praised be my Lord for our brother the wind,
and for air and cloud, calms and all weather,
by which you uphold life in all creatures.

Praised be my Lord for our sister water,
who is very useful to us and humble
and precious and clean.

Praised be my Lord for our brother fire,
through whom you give us light in the darkness
and he is very bright and pleasant
and very mighty and strong.

Praised be my Lord for our mother the earth,
which sustains and keeps us
and brings forth many diverse fruits
and flowers of many colors, and grass.

Praised be my Lord for all those
who pardon one another for love's sake,
and who endure weakness and tribulation;
blessed are those who endure peaceably,
for you, O Most High, will give them a crown.

Praised be my Lord for our sister,
the death of the body, from which no one can escape.
Woe to those who die in mortal sin!

Blessed are those who are found to be in your most holy will,
for the second death shall have no power to do them harm.

Praise and bless the Lord, and give thanks.
Serve the Lord with humility.   **Amen.**   [683]

16

For Fruits of the Earth

Almighty God,
we thank you for making the fruitful earth produce
what is needed for life.
Bless those who work in the fields;
give us favorable weather;
and grant that we may all share the fruits of the earth,
rejoicing in your goodness;
through your Son, Jesus Christ our Lord. **Amen.** [684]

17

For the Harvest

Most gracious God,
according to your wisdom
deep waters are opened up
and clouds drop gentle moisture.
We praise you for the return of planting and harvest seasons,
for the fertility of the soil,
for the harvesting of crops,
and for all other blessings
which you in your generosity pour on this nation and people.
Give us a full understanding of your mercy,
and lives which will be respectful,
holy, and obedient to you throughout all our days;
through Jesus Christ our Lord. **Amen.** [685]

18

When There Is a Natural Disaster

God of earthquake, wind, and fire,
tame natural forces that defy control,
or shock us by their fury.
Keep us from calling disaster your justice;
and help us, in good times or in calamity,
to trust your mercy which never ends,
and your power,
which in Jesus Christ stilled storms,
raised the dead,
and put down demonic powers. **Amen.** [686]

19

For Natural Resources

Almighty God,
in giving us dominion over things on earth,
you made us co-workers in your creation.
Give us wisdom and reverence
to use the resources of nature,
so that no one may suffer from our abuse of them,
and that generations yet to come
may continue to praise you for your bounty;
through your Son, Jesus Christ our Lord.   **Amen.**   [687]

20

For Nature

We give you thanks, most gracious God,
for the beauty of earth and sky and sea;
for the richness of mountains, plains, and rivers;
for the songs of birds
and the loveliness of flowers.
We praise you for these good gifts,
and pray that we may safeguard them for our posterity.
Grant that we may continue to grow
in our grateful enjoyment of your abundant creation,
to the honor and glory of your name,
now and forever.   **Amen.**   [688]

21

For Nature   *Fyodor Mikhailovich Dostoevsky (1821–1881)*

Lord, may we love all your creation,
all the earth and every grain of sand in it.
May we love every leaf, every ray of your light.

May we love the animals;
you have given them the rudiments of thought and joy untroubled.
Let us not trouble it;
let us not harass them,
let us not deprive them of their happiness,
let us not work against your intent.

For we acknowledge unto you that all is like an ocean,
all is flowing and blending,
and that to withhold any measure of love from anything in your universe
is to withhold that same measure from you.   **Amen.**   [689]

22

For a Right Use of Nature's Power

Mighty God,
your power fills heaven and earth,
is hidden in atoms
and flung from the sun.
Control us
so that we may never turn natural forces to destruction,
or arm nations with cosmic energy;
but guide us with wisdom and love,
so that we may tame power to good purpose,
for the building of human community
and the betterment of our common lives;
through Jesus Christ our Lord.   **Amen.**   [690]

PRAYERS FOR THE CHURCH
AND OTHER PEOPLE OF FAITH

23

For the Church

Almighty and ever-living God,
ruler of all things in heaven and earth,
hear our prayers for this congregation.
Strengthen the faithful,
arouse the careless,
and restore the penitent.
Grant us all things necessary for our common life,
and bring us all to be of one heart and mind
within your holy church;
through Jesus Christ our Lord.   **Amen.**   [691]

24

For the Proclamation of the Gospel

By your word, O God, your creation sprang forth,
and we were given the breath of life.
By your word, eternal God,
death is overcome,
Christ is raised from the tomb,
and we are given a new life in the power of your Spirit.
May we boldly proclaim this good news,
by the words of our mouths
and the deeds of our lives,
rejoicing always in your powerful presence;
through Jesus Christ our risen Lord.   **Amen.**   [692]

25

For a New Church Building

Eternal God, high and holy,
no building can contain your glory
or display the wonders of your love.
May this space be used as
a gathering place for people of goodwill.
When we worship, let us worship gladly;
when we study, let us learn your truth.
May every meeting held here
meet with your approval,
so that this building may stand
as a sign of your Spirit at work in the world,
and as a witness to our Lord and Savior,
Jesus Christ. **Amen.** [693]

26

For Founders and Previous Leaders of a Congregation

We thank you, Lord God,
for brave and believing people
who brought your message to this place.
Let us not forget them,
especially N., N.
By their energies this church was gathered,
given order, and continued.
Remembering all those Christians who have gone before us,
may we follow as they followed,
in the way, truth, and life of Jesus Christ,
the head of the church. **Amen.** [694]

27

For an Inclusive Church

How great is your love, Lord God,
how wide is your mercy!
Never let us board up the narrow gate that leads to life
with rules or doctrines that you dismiss;
but give us a Spirit to welcome all people with affection,
so that your church may never exclude secret friends of yours,
who are included in the love of Jesus Christ,
who came to save us all. **Amen.** [695]

28

For a Meeting of the General Assembly, Synod, or Presbytery

Almighty God,
in Jesus Christ you called disciples
and, by the Holy Spirit, made them one church to serve you.
Be with members of our *General Assembly/synod/presbytery.*
Help them to welcome new things you are doing in the world,
and to respect old things you keep and use.
Save them from empty slogans or senseless controversy.
In their deciding,
determine what is good for us and for all people.
As this *General Assembly/synod/presbytery* meets,
let your Spirit rule,
so that our church may be joined in love and service to Jesus Christ,
who, having gone before us,
is coming to meet us in the promise of your kingdom.   **Amen.**   [696]

29

For a Church Meeting

Eternal God, you called us to be a special people,
to preach the gospel and show mercy.
Keep your Spirit with us as we meet together,
so that in everything we may do your will.
Guide us lest we stumble
or be misguided by our own desires.
May all we do be done
for the reconciling of the world,
for the upbuilding of the church,
and for the greater glory of Jesus Christ our Lord.   **Amen.**   [697]

30

For New Church Members

Almighty God, by the love of Jesus Christ you draw people to faith,
and welcome them into the church family.
May we show your joy by embracing new brothers and sisters,
who with us believe
and with us will work to serve you.
Keep us close together in your Spirit,
breaking bread in faith and love,
one with Jesus Christ our Lord and Master.   **Amen.**   [698]

31

For the Mission of the Church

By your will, O God,
we go out into the world
with good news of your undying love,
and minister in the midst of human need
to show wonders of your grace.
We pray for men and women
who minister for you in_____.
May they be strengthened by our concern,
and supported by our gifts.
Do not let them be discouraged,
but make them brave and glad and hopeful in your word;
through Jesus Christ the Lord.   **Amen.**   [699]

32

For the Mission of the Church

Almighty God, you sent your Son Jesus Christ
to reconcile the world to yourself.
We praise and bless you
for those whom you have sent in the power of the Spirit
to preach the gospel to all nations.
We thank you that in all parts of the earth
a community of love has been gathered together
by their prayers and labors,
and that in every place your servants call upon your name;
for the kingdom and the power and the glory
are yours forever.   **Amen.**   [700]

33

For Trust

Loving God,
you want us to give thanks for all things,
to fear nothing except losing you,
and to lay all our cares on you,
knowing that you care for us.
Protect us from faithless fears and worldly anxieties,
and grant that no clouds in this mortal life
may hide from us the light of your immortal love
shown to us in your Son, Jesus Christ our Lord.   **Amen.**   [701]

34

For Courage in Christ's Mission

Toyohiko Kagawa (1888–1960)

O God, show us clearly the heart of the kingdom of God.
We do not protest
even if our life is destined to lead to the cross,
or if the way leads to our losing our lives.
We will march in the face of distress and contrary winds.
Teach us how to dispense with unnecessary things.
Let us go forward without fear of death
in order to fulfill our mission simply, surely, and steadily.
Reveal to us our station clearly,
and strengthen us to teach and guide, by our example, all persons,
even those who are ruled by evil.
We pray that you may find us worthy to work through us.   **Amen.**   [702]

35

For a Moderator

Almighty God,
you called us into the church,
and from among us chose leaders to direct us in your way.
We thank you for N., our Moderator.
Enlarge *his/her* gifts
and help *him/her* to obey you,
so that we may enjoy good work under *his/her* guidance,
loyally serving Jesus Christ the Lord.   **Amen.**   [703]

36

For Church Musicians and Artists

God of majesty,
whom saints and angels delight to worship in heaven:
Be with your servants who make art and music for your people,
that with joy we on earth may glimpse your beauty,
and bring us to the fulfillment of that hope of perfection
which will be ours as we stand before your unveiled glory.
We pray in the name of Jesus Christ our Lord.   **Amen.**   [704]

37

For Church Musicians and Artists

God of life,
you filled the world with beauty.
Thank you for artists who see clearly,
who with trained skill
can paint, shape, or sing your truth to us.

Keep them attentive
and ready to applaud the wonder of your works,
finding in the world signs of the love
revealed in Jesus Christ our Lord.   **Amen.**   [705]

38

For Deacons in the Church

God of love and compassion,
you poured out your life in service
in your Son, Jesus Christ.
By word and example he taught us
to find fulfillment in giving ourselves,
and greatness in serving others.
Bless those called to be deacons,
who lead us in service and caring.
Empower them by the grace of your Spirit,
that your whole church may give its life for the sake of the world,
in the name of Jesus Christ
who came not to be served, but to serve.   **Amen.**   [706]

39

For Ministers of the Word and Sacrament

Almighty God,
through your Son Jesus Christ
you gave the holy apostles many gifts
and commanded them to feed your flock.
Inspire all pastors to preach your Word diligently
and your people to receive it willingly,
that finally we may receive the crown of eternal glory;
through Jesus Christ our Lord.   **Amen.**   [707]

40

For Elders in the Church

God of righteousness and truth,
you brought us into your church
to show in our life together
something of the orderliness of your creation,
and the love of Jesus Christ.
Bless those called to be elders,
that they may govern wisely and fairly.

Give them full measure of your Spirit,
that they may refresh your people
along the journey of faith,
discerning, teaching, and sharing the Word of life,
Jesus Christ our Lord.   **Amen.**   [708]

41

At an Ordination   *Philip Melanchthon (1497–1560)*

Merciful God,
through the mouth of your beloved Son, our Lord Jesus Christ,
you said to us,
"The harvest is plentiful but the laborers are few;
pray therefore the Lord of the harvest
to send out laborers into his harvest."
We respond to your divine command, O Lord,
and sincerely beseech you
to richly bestow the Holy Spirit on these your servants
and on all of us who are called to your ministry
that we, with a great multitude,
may be your evangelists, true and steadfast against evil.
So may your name be hallowed,
your kingdom come,
and your will be done.
Hear this our prayer
through your beloved Son, Jesus Christ our Lord,
who, with you and the Holy Spirit,
lives and reigns throughout eternity.   **Amen.**   [709]

42

For Peace in the Church

God of our lives,
by the power of your Holy Spirit
we have been drawn together by one baptism into one faith,
serving one Lord and Savior.
Do not let us tear away from one another
through division or hard argument.
May your peace embrace our differences,
preserving us in unity,
as one body of Jesus Christ our Lord.   **Amen.**   [710]

43

For Church Secretaries

God of creation,
you bring order out of chaos
and set us in this world to do your will.
Bless those who serve your cause
as secretaries in church offices.
Confirm their dedication,
that their love for you may show in diligence.
Strengthen their compassion
that they may represent your love
to church members and strangers they encounter.
May their work be appreciated by all
as important to the ministry of Christ Jesus,
our Lord and Savior.   **Amen.**   [711]

44

For Stewardship in the Church

Righteous God,
you have taught us that the poor shall have your kingdom,
and that the gentle-minded shall inherit the earth.
Keep the church poor enough to preach to poor people,
and humble enough to walk with the despised.
Never weigh us down with property or accumulated funds.
Save your church from vain display or lavish comforts,
so that we may travel light
and move through the world
showing your generous love
made known in Jesus Christ our Lord.   **Amen.**   [712]

45

For Teachers in the Church

Almighty God,
you have given your law to guide us in a life of love,
and you have appointed teachers to interpret your will.
Create in those who instruct your people
a mind to study your Word,
and good understanding,
so that we may all learn your truth
and do it gladly;
for the sake of Jesus Christ our Master.   **Amen.**   [713]

46

For Seminaries

Almighty God,
in Jesus Christ you called ordinary people to be disciples
and sent them out to teach and preach your truth.
Bring to seminaries men and women
who are honest and eager to serve you.
Give them tender hearts to care for others,
and tough minds to wrestle with your Word,
so that, as they speak and act for you,
people may repent and return to love,
believing in Jesus Christ,
who is our Lord and Master.   **Amen.**   [714]

47

At the Time of a Minister's Retirement

God of grace,
we thank you for the gifts of Christian ministry
given in your servant, N.
We celebrate the years of *his/her* labor
in the fields of the Lord,
and rejoice in the blessings so many have received.
Give your servant a sense of fulfillment and completion,
a time of refreshment and rest, and new opportunities
for living the good news of your love in Jesus Christ.   **Amen.**   [715]

48

For Church Unity   *A prayer from Zaire*

O God,
you are the giver of life.
We pray for the church in the whole world.
Sanctify her life, renew her worship,
give power to her witnessing,
restore her unity.
Give strength to those who are searching together
for that kind of obedience which creates unity.
Heal the divisions separating your children one from another,
so that they will make fast, with bonds of peace,
the unity which the Spirit gives.   **Amen.**   [716]

49

For Church Unity

Holy God, giver of peace, author of truth,
we confess that we are divided and at odds with one another,
that a bad spirit has risen among us
and set us against your Holy Spirit of peace and love.
Take from us the mistrust, party spirit, contention,
and all evil that now divides us.
Work in us a desire for reconciliation,
so that, putting aside personal grievances,
we may go about your business with a single mind,
devoted to our Lord and Savior, Jesus Christ. **Amen.** [717]

50

For Church Unity   *Dionysius of Alexandria (d. 264)*

God,
good beyond all that is good,
fair beyond all that is fair,
in you is calmness, peace, and concord.
Heal the dissensions that divide us from one another
and bring us back to a unity of love
bearing some likeness to your divine nature.
Through the embrace of love
and the bonds of godly affection,
make us one in the Spirit
by your peace which makes all things peaceful.
We ask this through the grace, mercy, and tenderness
of your Son, Jesus Christ our Lord. **Amen.** [718]

51

For Other Churches

Almighty God,
in Jesus Christ you called disciples
and prayed for them to be joined in faith.
We pray for Christian churches from which we are separated.
Let us never be so sure of ourselves
that we condemn the faith of others
or refuse reunion with them,
but make us ever ready to reach out for more truth,
so that your church may be one in the Spirit;
through Jesus Christ our Lord. **Amen.** [719]

52

For Candidates for Church Service

God of prophets and apostles,
you have chosen leaders to train your people
in the way of Jesus Christ.
We thank you that in our day
you are still claiming men and women
for special work within the church.
As N. has dedicated *himself/herself* to you,
let us pledge ourselves to *him/her*,
so that, surrounded by affection and hope,
he/she may grow in wisdom,
mature in love,
and become a faithful worker,
approved by Jesus Christ our Lord.   **Amen.**   [720]

53

For Enemies of the Church

Strong God of love:
your Son Jesus told us
that his church would be persecuted
as he was persecuted.
If we should suffer for righteousness' sake,
save us from self-righteousness.
Give us grace to pray for enemies,
and to forgive them,
even as you have forgiven us;
through Jesus Christ,
who was crucified but is risen,
whom we praise forever.   **Amen.**   [721]

54

Thanksgiving for Heroes and Heroines of the Faith

We give thanks to you, O Lord our God,
for all your servants and witnesses of time past:
for Abraham, the father of believers,
and for Sarah, his wife,
for Moses the lawgiver, and Aaron the priest,
for Miriam and Joshua,
Deborah and Gideon,
Samuel and Hannah, his mother;
for Isaiah and all the prophets;
for Mary, the mother of our Lord;
for Peter and Paul and all the apostles;

for Mary, Martha, and Mary Magdalene;
for Stephen, the first martyr,
and all the saints and martyrs
in every time and in every land.
In your mercy, give us, as you gave them,
the hope of salvation
and the promise of eternal life;
through the firstborn from the dead,
Jesus Christ our Lord.   **Amen.**   [722]

55

Thanksgiving for Heroes and Heroines of the Faith

Eternal and Almighty God,
we give you thanks for all your faithful people
who have followed your will in a grand procession of praise
throughout the world and down through the centuries,
into our own time and place.
We hear their stories in the pages of scripture,
in the records of history,
in the recollections of our families
and in our own childhood memories.
As we remember these people,
inspire us by your Spirit to join their ranks
and follow our Lord through life,
to be bold as they were, and brave as well,
witnessing to your righteous truth and generous love.
Give us grace, O God,
that we will leave a legacy of faithfulness
to encourage and challenge those who follow us
along the way of discipleship;
through Jesus Christ our Lord.   **Amen.**   [723]

56

Remembrance of Those Who Have Died

> See also prayers commemorating those who have died in the faith, pages
> 102, 106, 111, 116, 121–122.

With reverence and affection
we remember before you, O everlasting God,
all our departed friends and relatives.
Keep us in union with them
here, through faith and love toward you,

that hereafter we may enter into your presence
and be numbered with those who serve you
and look upon your face in glory everlasting;
through your Son, Jesus Christ our Lord.   **Amen.**   [724]

57

For Jews

Almighty God, you are the one true God,
and have called forth people of faith
in every time and place.
Your promises are sure and true.
We bless you for your covenant given to Abraham and Sarah,
that you keep even now with the Jews.
We rejoice that you have brought us into covenant with you
by the coming of your Son, Jesus Christ,
himself a Jew, nurtured in the faith of Israel.
We praise you that you are faithful to covenants made
with us and Jewish brothers and sisters,
that together we may serve your will,
and come at last to your promised peace.   **Amen.**   [725]

58

For Muslims

Eternal God,
you are the one God to be worshiped by all,
the one called Allah by your Muslim children,
descendants of Abraham as we are.
Give us grace to hear your truth
in the teachings of Mohammed, the prophet,
and to show your love as disciples of Jesus Christ,
that Christians and Muslims together
may serve you in faith and friendship.   **Amen.**   [726]

59

For Our Nation   *Woodrow Wilson (1856–1924)*

Almighty God, ruler of all the peoples of the earth,
forgive, we pray, our shortcomings as a nation;
purify our hearts to see and love truth;
give wisdom to our counselors
and steadfastness to our people;
and bring us at last to the fair city of peace,
whose foundations are mercy, justice, and goodwill,
and whose builder and maker you are;
through your Son, Jesus Christ our Lord.   **Amen.**   [727]

60

For Our Country

Almighty God,
you have given us this good land as our heritage.
Make us always remember your generosity
and constantly do your will.
Bless our land with honest industry,
sound learning,
and an honorable way of life.
Save us from violence, discord, and confusion;
from pride and arrogance,
and from every evil way.
Make us who come from many nations
with many different languages
a united people.
Defend our liberties
and give those whom we have entrusted with the authority of government
the spirit of wisdom,
that there might be justice and peace in our land.
When times are prosperous, let our hearts be thankful;
and, in troubled times, do not let our trust in you fail.
We ask all this through Jesus Christ our Lord.   **Amen.**   [728]

61

For Government Leaders

O Lord, our governor,
your glory shines throughout the world.
We commend our nation to your merciful care,

that we may live securely in peace
and may be guided by your providence.
Give all in authority the wisdom and strength
to know your will and to do it.
Help them remember that they are called to serve the people
as lovers of truth and justice;
through Jesus Christ our Lord. **Amen.** [729]

62

For the Courts of Justice

Almighty God,
you sit in judgment to declare what is just and right.
Bless the courts and the magistrates in our land.
Give them the spirit of wisdom and understanding,
that they may perceive the truth
and administer the law impartially
as instruments of your divine will.
We pray in the name of him who will come to be our judge,
your Son, Jesus Christ our Lord. **Amen.** [730]

63

For State and Local Governments

Almighty God,
bless those who hold office in the government of this *state/city/town*,
that they may do their work
in a spirit of wisdom, kindness, and justice.
Help them use their authority to serve faithfully
and to promote the general welfare;
through your Son, Jesus Christ our Lord. **Amen.** [731]

64

At the Time of an Election

Under your law we live, great God,
and by your will we govern ourselves.
Help us as good citizens
to respect neighbors whose views differ from ours,
so that without partisan anger,
we may work out issues that divide us,
and elect candidates to serve the common welfare;
through Jesus Christ the Lord. **Amen.** [732]

65

For Those in the Military

Righteous God, you rule the nations.
Guard brave men and women
who risk themselves in battle for their country.
Give them compassion for enemies
who also fight for patriotic causes.
Keep our sons and daughters from hate that hardens,
or from scorekeeping with human lives.
Though they must be at war,
let them live for peace,
as eager for agreement as for victory.
Encourage them as they encourage one another,
and never let hard duty separate them
from loyalty to your Son, our Lord, Jesus Christ.   **Amen.**   [733]

66

During a National Crisis

God of ages,
in your sight nations rise and fall,
and pass through times of peril.
Now when our land is troubled,
be near to judge and save.
May leaders be led by your wisdom;
may they search your will and see it clearly.
If we have turned from your way,
help us to reverse our ways and repent.
Give us your light and your truth to guide us;
through Jesus Christ,
who is Lord of this world, and our Savior.   **Amen.**   [734]

PRAYERS FOR THE SOCIAL ORDER

67

For Social Justice

Grant, O God,
that your holy and life-giving Spirit
may so move every human heart,
that the barriers which divide us may crumble,
suspicions disappear,
and hatreds cease,
and that, with our divisions healed,
we might live in justice and peace;
through your Son, Jesus Christ our Lord.   **Amen.**   [735]

68

For Social Justice

You give us prophets, holy God,
to cry out for justice and mercy.
Open our ears to hear them,
and to follow the truth they speak,
lest we support injustice to secure our own well-being.
Give prophets the fire of your Word,
but love as well.
Though they speak for you,
may they know that they stand with us before you,
and have no Messiah other than your Son,
Jesus Christ, the Lord of all.   **Amen.**   [736]

69

For Social Justice   *Martin Luther King, Jr. (1929–1968)*

Yes, Jesus,
I want to be on your right side
or your left side,
not for any selfish reason.
I want to be on your right or your best side,
not in terms of some political kingdom or ambition,
but I just want to be there
in love and in justice and in truth
and in commitment to others,
so we can make of this old world a new world.   **Amen.**   [737]

70

For Those Suffering from Addictions

O blessed Jesus,
you ministered to all who came to you.
Look with compassion upon all who through addiction
have lost their health and freedom.
Restore to them the assurance
of your unfailing mercy;
remove the fears that attack them;
strengthen them in the work of their recovery;
and to those who care for them,
give patient understanding and persevering love;
for your mercy's sake.   **Amen.**   [738]

71

For Those in Business

God of the covenant:
you give love without return,
and lavish gifts without looking for gain.
Watch over the ways of business,
so that those who buy or sell, get or lend,
may live justly and show mercy
and walk in your ways.
May profits be fair and contracts kept.
In our dealings with each other
may we display true charity;
through Jesus Christ,
who has loved us with mercy.   **Amen.**   [739]

72

For Those in Commerce and Industry

Almighty God,
your Son Jesus Christ dignified our labor
by sharing our toil.
Be with your people where they work;
make those who carry on the industries and commerce of this land
responsive to your will;
and to all of us,
give pride in what we do
and a just return for our labor;
through your Son, Jesus Christ our Lord.   **Amen.**   [740]

73

For Cities

God of heaven and earth,
in your Word you have given us a vision of that holy city
to which the nations of the world bring their glory.
Look upon and visit the cities of the earth.
Renew the ties of mutual regard that form our civic life.
Send us honest and able leaders.
Help us to eliminate poverty, prejudice, and oppression,
that peace may prevail with righteousness,
and justice with order,
and that men and women from various cultures
and with differing talents

may find with one another
the fulfillment of their humanity;
through Jesus Christ our Lord.   **Amen.**   [741]

74

For the Neighborhood

O Lord, our creator,
by your holy prophet you taught your ancient people
to seek the welfare of the cities in which they lived.
We commend our neighborhood to your care,
that it might be kept free from social strife and decay.
Give us strength of purpose and concern for others,
that we may create here a community of justice and peace
where your will may be done;
through your Son, Jesus Christ our Lord.   **Amen.**   [742]

75

For Students

Eternal God,
your wisdom is greater than our small minds can attain,
and your truth shows up our little learning.
To those who study,
give curiosity, imagination,
and patience enough to wait and work for insight.
Help them to doubt with courage,
but to hold all their doubts
in the larger faith of Jesus Christ our Lord.   **Amen.**   [743]

76

For Graduates

Eternal God,
in your will our lives are lived,
and by your wisdom truth is found.
We pray for graduates who finish a course of study,
and move on to something new.
Take away anxiety or confusion of purpose,
and give them confidence in the future you plan,
where energies may be gathered up
and given to neighbors in love;
for the sake of Jesus Christ our Lord.   **Amen.**   [744]

77

For Responsible Citizenship

Lord, keep this nation under your care.
Bless the leaders of our land,
that we may be a people at peace among ourselves
and a blessing to other nations of the earth.
Help us elect trustworthy leaders,
contribute to wise decisions for the general welfare,
and thus serve you faithfully in our generation,
to the honor of your holy name;
through Jesus Christ the Lord. **Amen.** [745]

78

For Those Who Suffer for the Sake of Conscience

God of love and strength,
your Son forgave his enemies
while he was suffering shame and death.
Strengthen those who suffer for the sake of conscience.
When they are accused, save them from speaking in hate;
when they are rejected, save them from bitterness;
when they are imprisoned, save them from despair.
To us, your servants,
give grace to respect their witness
and to discern the truth,
that our society may be cleansed and strengthened.
This we ask for the sake of our merciful and righteous judge,
Jesus Christ our Lord. **Amen.** [746]

PRAYERS FOR THE FAMILY
AND PERSONAL LIFE

79

For Those Engaged to Marry

Almighty God,
in the beginning you made man and woman
to join themselves in shared affection.
May those who engage to marry be filled with joy.
Let them be so sure of each other
that no fear or disrespect may shake their vows.

Though their eyes may be bright with love for each other,
keep in sight a wider world,
where neighbors want and strangers beg,
and where service is a joyful duty;
through Jesus Christ the Lord.   **Amen.**   [747]

80

For the Newly Married

God of grace,
in your wisdom you made man and woman
to be one flesh in love.
As in Jesus Christ you came to serve us,
let newlyweds serve each other,
putting aside selfishness and separate rights.
May they build homes where there is free welcome.
At work or in leisure,
let them enjoy each other,
forgive each other,
and embrace each other faithfully,
serving the Lord of love, Jesus Christ.   **Amen.**   [748]

81

For Families

Eternal God, our creator,
you set us to live in families.
We commend to your care
all the homes where your people live.
Keep them, we pray, free from bitterness,
from the thirst for personal victory,
and from pride in self.
Fill them with faith, virtue, knowledge,
moderation, patience, and godliness.
Knit together in enduring affection
those who have become one in marriage.
Let children and parents have full respect for one another;
and light the fire of kindliness among us all,
that we may show affection for each other;
through Jesus Christ our Lord.   **Amen.**   [749]

82

For a Family

Robert Louis Stevenson (1850–1894)

Lord, behold our family here assembled.
We thank you for this place in which we dwell,
for the love that unites us,
for the peace given us this day,
for the hope with which we expect the morrow;
for the health, the work, the food, and the bright skies
that make our lives delightful;
for our friends in all parts of the earth.

Give us courage and gaiety and the quiet mind.
Spare to us our friends, soften to us our enemies.
Bless us, if it may be, in all our innocent endeavors;
if it may not, give us the strength to endure that which is to come;
that we may be brave in peril,
constant in tribulation,
temperate in wrath and in all changes of fortune
and down to the gates of death,
loyal and loving to one another.

As the clay to the potter,
as the windmill to the wind,
as children of their parent,
we beseech of you this help and mercy
for Christ's sake. **Amen.** [750]

83

For Single People

Almighty God,
grant that those who live alone
may not be lonely in their solitude,
but may find fulfillment
in loving you and their neighbors
as they follow in the footsteps of Jesus Christ our Lord. **Amen.** [751]

84

For Parents

Almighty God, from whom we receive our life,
you have blessed us with the joy and care of children.
As we bring them up,
give us calm strength and patient wisdom,
that we may teach them to love
whatever is just and true and good,
following the example of our Savior Jesus Christ. **Amen.** [752]

85

For Children

Great God,
guard the laughter of children.
Bring them safely through injury and illness,
so they may live the promises you give.
Do not let us be so preoccupied with our purposes
that we fail to hear their voices,
or pay attention to their special vision of the truth;
but keep us with them,
ready to listen and to love,
even as in Jesus Christ you have loved us,
your grown-up, wayward children. **Amen.** [753]

86

For Young People

Almighty God,
you see your children growing up
in an uncertain and confusing world.
Show them that your ways give more life
than the ways of the world,
and that following you
is better than chasing after selfish goals.
Help them to take failure,
not as a measure of their worth,
but as an opportunity for a new start.
Give them strength to hold their faith in you
and to keep alive their joy in your creation;
through Jesus Christ our Lord. **Amen.** [754]

87

For Young People

Almighty God,
again and again you have called upon young people
to force change or fire human hopes.
Never let older people be so set in their ways
that they refuse to hear young voices,
or so firm in their grip on power
that they reject youth's contributions.
Let the young be candid, but not cruel.
Keep them dreaming dreams that you approve,
and living in the Spirit of the young man Jesus,
the crucified one who now rules the world. **Amen.** [755]

88

At the Birth of a Child

Mighty God,
by your love we are given children
through the miracle of birth.
May we greet each new son and daughter with joy,
and surround them all with faith,
so they may know who you are
and want to be your disciples.
Never let us neglect children,
but help us enjoy them,
showing them the welcome you have shown us all;
through Jesus Christ the Lord.   **Amen.**   [756]

89

At a Birthday

O God, our times are in your hand:
Look with favor, we pray, on your servant N.,
as *he/she* begins another year.
Grant that *he/she* may grow in wisdom and grace,
and strengthen *his/her* trust in your goodness
all the days of *his/her* life;
through Jesus Christ our Lord.   **Amen.**   [757]

90

For Parents

Almighty God, giver of life and love,
bless N. and N.
Grant them wisdom and devotion
in the ordering of their common life,
that each may be to the other
a strength in need,
a counselor in perplexity,
a comfort in sorrow,
and a companion in joy.
And so knit their wills together in your will
and their spirits in your Spirit,
that they may live together in love and peace
all the days of their life;
through Jesus Christ our Lord.   **Amen.**   [758]

91

For Families with One Parent

Gracious God,
we are never away from your care,
and what we lack you give in love.
Watch over families where, by death or separation,
a parent is left alone with children.
Lift bitterness and the burden of lonely obligation.
Show them that they live under your protection,
so they have not less love, but more;
through Jesus Christ,
your Son and our eternal brother.   **Amen.**   [759]

92

For Those Having Marital Difficulty

Lord God, you set us in families,
where we learn to live together in charity and truth.
Strengthen weak bonds of love.
Where separation threatens,
move in with forgiving power.
Melt hard hearts,
free fixed minds,
break the hold of stubborn pride.
Lay claim on us,
so that our separate claims may be set aside in love;
through Jesus Christ our Lord.   **Amen.**   [760]

93

For the Divorced or Separated

God of grace,
you are always working to hold us together,
to heal division,
and make love strong.
Help men and women whose marriages fail
to know that you are faithful.
Restore confidence,
bring understanding,
and ease the hurt of separation.
If they marry others,
instruct them in better love,
so that vows may be said and kept with new resolve;
through Jesus Christ our Lord.   **Amen.**   [761]

94

For Orphans

Gracious God,
you remember all your children,
especially those who are left alone,
innocent victims of the acts of others.
Remind us of the orphans of this world,
that we may show special care
and embrace them with your love.
Give them confidence in your parental guidance,
so they will find a home in your family of faith,
with brothers and sisters who follow Jesus Christ,
your Son, our Lord.   **Amen.**   [762]

95

In a Personal Crisis   *Attributed to Augustine of Hippo (354–430)*

God of life,
there are days when the burdens we carry
are heavy on our shoulders and weigh us down,
when the road seems dreary and endless,
the skies gray and threatening,
when our lives have no music in them,
and our hearts are lonely,
and our souls have lost their courage.
Flood the path with light,
turn our eyes to where the skies are full of promise;
tune our hearts to brave music;
give us the sense of comradeship
with heroes and saints of every age;
and so quicken our spirits
that we may be able to encourage
the souls of all who journey with us on the road of life,
to your honor and glory.   **Amen.**   [763]

96

In a Personal Crisis   *Teresa of Lisieux (1873–1897)*

Just for today,
what does it matter, O Lord, if the future is dark?
To pray now for tomorrow I am not able.
Keep my heart only for today,
grant me your light—
just for today.   **Amen.**   [764]

97

In a Personal Crisis
Thomas à Kempis (c. 1380–1471)

Write your blessed name, O Lord,
upon my heart,
there to remain so indelibly engraven,
that no prosperity,
no adversity,
shall ever move me from your love.
Be to me a strong tower of defense,
a comforter in tribulation,
a deliverer in distress,
a very present help in trouble,
and a guide to heaven
through the many temptations and dangers of this life.   **Amen.**   [765]

98

Self-Dedication

Almighty God,
so draw our hearts to you,
so guide our minds,
so fill our imaginations,
so control our wills,
that we may be wholly yours,
utterly dedicated to you.
Use us as you will,
always to your glory and the welfare of your people;
through our Lord and Savior Jesus Christ.   **Amen.**   [766]

99

For Faithfulness
Thomas Aquinas (c. 1225–1274)

Give me, O Lord, a steadfast heart,
which no unworthy affection may drag downward;
give me an unconquered heart,
which no tribulation can wear out;
give me an upright heart,
which no unworthy purpose may tempt aside.
Bestow on me also, O Lord my God,
understanding to know you,
diligence to seek you,
wisdom to find you,
and a faithfulness that may finally embrace you;
through Jesus Christ our Lord.   **Amen.**   [767]

100

For Guidance

Direct us, O Lord, in all our doings
with your most gracious favor
and further us with your continual help,
that in all our works,
begun, continued, and ended in you,
we may glorify your holy name,
and finally, by your mercy, obtain everlasting life;
through Jesus Christ our Lord.   **Amen.**   [768]

101

For Appreciation of Truth and Beauty

Give us, O Lord, a reverence for the truth,
the desire both to think and to speak truly.
Save us from all fear of truth.
Grant us all an appreciation of beauty
and things that are lovely.
Increase our reverence for them;
help us to see in them a part of your revelation of yourself,
that beauty becomes you no less than truth and righteousness;
through Jesus Christ our Lord,
who lives and reigns with you and the Holy Spirit,
one God, now and forever.   **Amen.**   [769]

102

For the Sick

O God,
the strength of the weak and the comfort of sufferers,
mercifully hear our prayers
and grant to your servant N.,
the help of your power,
that *his/her* sickness may be turned into health
and our sorrow into joy;
through Jesus Christ.   **Amen.**   [770]

103

During an Illness   *Ambrose of Milan (340–397)*

You are medicine for me when I am sick.
You are my strength when I need help.
You are life itself when I fear death.

You are the way when I long for heaven.
You are light when all is dark.
You are my food when I need nourishment!   **Amen.**   [771]

104

For Healing

Mighty and merciful God,
you sent Jesus Christ to heal broken lives.
We praise you that today
you send healing in doctors and nurses,
and bless us with technology in medicine.
We claim your promises of wholeness
as we pray for those who are ill in body or mind,
who long for your healing touch.
Make the weak strong,
the sick healthy,
the broken whole,
and confirm those who serve them
as agents of your love.
Then all shall be renewed in vigor
to point to the risen Christ,
who conquered death that we might live eternally.   **Amen.**   [772]

105

For Health Restored

Almighty God,
we rejoice that, by the power of your Spirit,
you have given the gift of health and wholeness
to your servant N.
In thanksgiving we renew our commitment to you,
so that health regained
may provide opportunities for service
in the helping and healing work of Jesus Christ,
our Lord and Savior.   **Amen.**   [773]

106

For Leisure

O God,
give us times of refreshment and peace
in the course of this busy life.
Grant that we may so use our leisure
to rebuild our bodies and renew our minds,
that our spirits may be opened to the goodness of your creation;
through Jesus Christ our Lord.   **Amen.**   [774]

107

For Those Who Are Absent *Henry van Dyke (1852–1933)*

Almighty God, we commend to your goodness
all who are near and dear to us,
wherever they may be today.
Watch over them;
provide for them;
bless them in body and soul;
at last bring them and us
into the perfect and eternal joy of heaven;
through Jesus Christ our Lord. **Amen.** [775]

Prayers for the Human Condition

108

For the Afflicted

Almighty and everlasting God,
you are the comfort of the sad
and strength to those who suffer.
Let the prayers of your children who are in any trouble
rise to you.
To everyone in distress
grant mercy,
grant relief,
grant refreshment;
through Jesus Christ our Lord. **Amen.** [776]

109

For the Mentally Distressed

Mighty God,
in Jesus Christ you dealt with spirits that darken minds
or set people against themselves.
Give peace to those who are torn by conflict,
are cast down,
or dream deceiving dreams.
By your power,
drive from our minds
demons that shake confidence and wreck love.
Tame unruly forces in us,
and bring us to your truth,
so that we may accept ourselves
as good, glad children of your love,
known in Jesus Christ. **Amen.** [777]

110

For the Middle-Aged

Eternal God,
you have led us through our days and years,
made wisdom ripe and faith mature.
Show men and women your purpose for them,
so that, when youth is spent,
they may not find life empty or labor stale,
but may devote themselves to dear loves and worthy tasks,
with undiminished strength;
for the sake of Jesus Christ the Lord.   **Amen.**   [778]

111

For the Aged

O Lord God,
look with mercy on all whose increasing years bring them
isolation, distress, or weakness.
Provide for them homes of dignity and peace;
give them understanding helpers
and the willingness to accept help;
and, as their strength diminishes,
increase their faith
and their assurance of your love.
We pray in the name of Jesus Christ our Lord.   **Amen.**   [779]

112

For the Bereaved

O merciful God,
you teach us in your Holy Word
that you do not willingly afflict or grieve your children.
Look with pity on the sorrows of N., your servant,
for whom we pray.
Remember *him/her*, O Lord, in mercy.
Strengthen *him/her* in patience,
comfort *him/her* with the memory of your goodness,
let your presence shine on *him/her*,
and give *him/her* peace;
through Jesus Christ our Lord.   **Amen.**   [780]

113

For the Lonely

God of comfort, companion of the lonely:
be with those who by neglect or willful separation are left alone.
Fill empty places with present love,
and long times of solitude with lively thoughts of you.
Encourage us to visit lonely men and women,
so they may be cheered by the Spirit of Jesus Christ,
who walked among us as a friend,
and is our Lord forever.   **Amen.**   [781]

114

For the Oppressed

Look with compassion, O God,
upon the people in this land
who live with injustice, terror, disease, and death
as their constant companions.
Have mercy upon us.
Help us to eliminate cruelty to these our neighbors.
Strengthen those who spend their lives
establishing equal protection of the law
and equal opportunities for all.
And grant that every one of us may enjoy
a fair portion of the abundance of this land;
through your Son, Jesus Christ our Lord.   **Amen.**   [782]

115

For the Outcast

God of grace,
no one is beyond the reach of your love,
or outside your limitless mercy.
Move us toward those the world despises and people reject,
so we may venture to follow Christ,
and risk showing his love.
Stand with those who are outcast;
strengthen them in peace;
encourage them by your presence;
and use them to build on the cornerstone of Christ,
until differences are honored and respected,
and all people together give you glory.   **Amen.**   [783]

116

For the Poor and Neglected   *Mother Teresa of Calcutta*

Make us worthy, Lord,
to serve our fellow human beings throughout the world
who live and die in poverty and hunger.
Give them through our hands this day their daily bread,
and by our understanding love,
give peace and joy.   **Amen.**   [784]

117

For the Retired

Your love for us never ends, eternal God,
even when by age or weakness we can no longer work.
When we retire,
keep us awake to your will for us.
Give us energy to enjoy the world,
to attend to neighbors busy people neglect,
and to contribute wisely to the life of the church.
If we can offer nothing but our prayers,
remind us that our prayers are a useful work you want,
so that we may live always serving Jesus Christ,
our hope and our true joy.   **Amen.**   [785]

118

For the Sexually Confused

God of creation,
you made men and women to find in love
fulfillment as your creatures.
We pray for those who deny physical love,
who are repelled by flesh,
or frightened by their daydreams.
Straighten us all out, O Lord,
and show us who we are,
so that we may affirm each other bodily in covenants of love,
approved by Jesus Christ our Lord.   **Amen.**   [786]

119

For Those in Distress *The Liturgy of St. Mark*

Almighty and everlasting God,
the comfort of the sad,
the strength of those who suffer,
let the prayers of your children who cry out of any tribulation
come to you.
To every soul that is distressed,
grant mercy, grant relief, grant refreshment;
through Jesus Christ our Lord.   **Amen.**   [787]

120

At a Time of Tragedy

God of compassion,
you watch our ways,
and weave out of terrible happenings
wonders of goodness and grace.
Surround those who have been shaken by tragedy
with a sense of your present love,
and hold them in faith.
Though they are lost in grief,
may they find you and be comforted;
through Jesus Christ who was dead, but lives
and rules this world with you.   **Amen.**   [788]

121

For Travelers

The world is yours, mighty God,
and all people live by your faithfulness.
Watch over those who are traveling,
who drive or fly,
or speed through space.
May they be careful, but not afraid,
and safely reach their destinations.
Wherever we wander in your spacious world,
teach us that we never journey beyond your loving care,
revealed in Jesus Christ the Lord.   **Amen.**   [789]

122

For the Unemployed

Gracious God,
we remember before you
those who suffer want and anxiety from lack of work.
Guide the people of this land
so to use our wealth and resources
that all persons may find suitable and fulfilling employment
and receive just payment for their labor;
through your Son, Jesus Christ our Lord.   **Amen.**   [790]

CHRISTIAN
MARRIAGE

OUTLINE OF CHRISTIAN MARRIAGE: RITE I

A Service for General Use

Entrance
Sentences of Scripture
Statement on the Gift of Marriage
Prayer
Declarations of Intent
Affirmations of the Families
Affirmations of the Congregation
   [Psalm, Hymn, or Spiritual]
Readings from Scripture
Sermon
   [Psalm, Hymn, or Spiritual]
Vows
Exchange of Rings (or Other Symbols)
Prayer
Lord's Prayer
Announcement of Marriage
Charge and Blessing
   [Psalm, Hymn, Spiritual, or Anthem]

CHRISTIAN MARRIAGE: RITE I

A Service for General Use

The following marriage rite is brief and may be used in a variety of settings, although a Christian marriage service should be held in the place where the community of faith gathers for worship.

As a service of Christian worship, the marriage service is under the direction of the minister and the supervision of the session.

ENTRANCE

As the people gather, music appropriate to the praise of God may be offered. At the appointed time the bride, groom, and other members of the wedding party enter and come and stand before the minister. The families of the bride and groom may stand with the couple.

During the entrance of the wedding party, the people may stand and sing a psalm, hymn, or spiritual. Or an anthem may be sung, or instrumental music played.

SENTENCES OF SCRIPTURE

The minister calls the people to worship, either before or after the entrance, using one of the following, or another appropriate verse from scripture.

1   *1 John 4:16*

God is love,
and those who abide in love,
abide in God,
and God abides in them.

2   *Ps. 118:24*

This is the day that the Lord has made;
let us rejoice and be glad in it.

3   *Ps. 106:1*

O give thanks, for the Lord is good.
God's love endures forever.

STATEMENT ON THE GIFT OF MARRIAGE

The minister says:

We gather in the presence of God
to give thanks for the gift of marriage,
to witness the joining together of N. and N.,
to surround them with our prayers,
and to ask God's blessing upon them,
so that they may be strengthened for their life together
and nurtured in their love for God.

God created us male and female,
and gave us marriage
so that husband and wife may help and comfort each other,
living faithfully together in plenty and in want,
in joy and in sorrow,
in sickness and in health,
throughout all their days.

God gave us marriage
for the full expression of the love between a man and a woman.
In marriage a woman and a man belong to each other,
and with affection and tenderness
freely give themselves to each other.

God gave us marriage
for the well-being of human society,
for the ordering of family life,
and for the birth and nurture of children.

God gave us marriage as a holy mystery
in which a man and a woman are joined together,
and become one,
just as Christ is one with the church.

In marriage, husband and wife are called to a new way of life,
created, ordered, and blessed by God.
This way of life must not be entered into carelessly,
or from selfish motives,
but responsibly, and prayerfully.

We rejoice that marriage is given by God,
blessed by our Lord Jesus Christ,
and sustained by the Holy Spirit.
Therefore, let marriage be held in honor by all.

PRAYER

The minister says:

Let us pray:

Gracious God,
you are always faithful in your love for us.
Look mercifully upon N. and N.,
who have come seeking your blessing.
Let your Holy Spirit rest upon them
so that with steadfast love
they may honor the promises they make this day,
through Jesus Christ our Savior.   [791]

Amen.

The congregation may be seated.

DECLARATIONS OF INTENT

The minister addresses the bride and groom individually, using either
A or B:

A

N., understanding that God has created, ordered, and blessed the covenant
of marriage,
do you affirm your desire and intention to enter this covenant?

Answer:

I do.

B

If both are baptized, the following may be used:

N., in your baptism
you have been called to union with Christ and the church.
Do you intend to honor this calling
through the covenant of marriage?

Answer:

I do.

AFFIRMATIONS OF THE FAMILIES

The minister may address the families of the bride and groom:

N., N. [*Names of family members*],
do you give your blessing to N. and N.,
and promise to do everything in your power to uphold them in their marriage?

The families of the bride and groom answer:

1

**We (*I*) give our (*my*) blessing
and promise our (*my*) loving support.**

Or

2

We (*I*) do.

The families of the bride and groom may be seated.

AFFIRMATION OF THE CONGREGATION

The minister may address the congregation, saying:

Will all of you witnessing these vows
do everything in your power
to uphold N. and N. in their marriage?

Answer:

We will.

A psalm, hymn, spiritual, or anthem may be sung.

READING FROM SCRIPTURE

The following, or a similar prayer for illumination (pp. 90–91), may
be said.

God of mercy,
your faithfulness to your covenant
frees us to live together
in the security of your powerful love.

Amid all the changing words of our generation,
speak your eternal Word that does not change.
Then may we respond to your gracious promises
by living in faith and obedience;
through our Lord Jesus Christ.   [792]

Amen.

> One or more scripture passages are read (pp. 893–902).

SERMON

> After the scriptures are read, a brief sermon may be given.
>
> A psalm, hymn, spiritual, or other music may follow.

VOWS

> The people may stand.
>
> The minister addresses the couple:

N. and N.,
since it is your intention to marry,
join your right hands,
and with your promises
bind yourselves to each other as husband and wife.

> The bride and groom face each other and join right hands. They in turn
> then make their vows to each other, using A or B.

A

> The man says:

**I, N., take you, N., to be my wife;
and I promise,
before God and these witnesses,
to be your loving and faithful husband;
in plenty and in want;
in joy and in sorrow;
in sickness and in health;
as long as we both shall live.**

The woman says:

**I, N., take you, N., to be my husband;
and I promise,
before God and these witnesses,
to be your loving and faithful wife;
in plenty and in want;
in joy and in sorrow;
in sickness and in health;
as long as we both shall live.**

B

The man says:

**Before God and these witnesses,
I, N., take you, N., to be my wife,
and I promise to love you,
and to be faithful to you,
as long as we both shall live.**

The woman says:

**Before God and these witnesses
I, N., take you, N., to be my husband,
and I promise to love you,
and to be faithful to you,
as long as we both shall live.**

EXCHANGE OF RINGS (OR OTHER SYMBOLS)

If rings are to be exchanged, the minister may say to the couple:

What do you bring as the sign of your promise?

When the rings are presented, the minister may say the following prayer.

By your blessing, O God,
may these rings be to N. and N.
symbols of unending love and faithfulness,
reminding them of the covenant they have made this day,
through Jesus Christ our Lord.   [793]

Amen.

The bride and groom exchange rings using A or B or other appropriate words. The traditional trinitarian formula should be omitted for both the bride and groom if one of the marriage partners is not a professing Christian.

A

The one giving the ring says:

N., I give you this ring as a sign of our covenant,
in the name of the Father,
and of the Son,
and of the Holy Spirit.

The one receiving the ring says:

I receive this ring as a sign of our covenant,
in the name of the Father,
and of the Son,
and of the Holy Spirit.

B

As each ring is given, the one giving the ring says:

This ring I give you,
as a sign of our constant faith
and abiding love,
in the name of the Father,
and of the Son,
and of the Holy Spirit.

PRAYER

The couple may kneel.

One of the following prayers, or a similar prayer, is said:

Let us pray:

1

Eternal God,
Creator and preserver of all life,
author of salvation, and giver of all grace:
look with favor upon the world you have made and redeemed,
and especially upon N. and N.

Give them wisdom and devotion
in their common life,
that each may be to the other
a strength in need,
a counselor in perplexity,
a comfort in sorrow,
and a companion in joy.

Grant that their wills
may be so knit together in your will,
and their spirits in your Spirit,
that they may grow in love and peace
with you and each other
all the days of their life.

Give them the grace,
when they hurt each other,
to recognize and confess their fault,
and to seek each other's forgiveness
and yours.

Make their life together
a sign of Christ's love
to this sinful and broken world,
that unity may overcome estrangement,
forgiveness heal guilt,
and joy conquer despair.

Give them such fulfillment of their mutual love
that they may reach out in concern for others.

[Give to them, if it is your will,
the gift of children,
and the wisdom to bring them up
to know you,
to love you,
and to serve you.]

Grant that all who have witnessed these vows today
may find their lives strengthened,
and that all who are married
may depart with their own promises renewed.

Enrich with your grace
all husbands and wives, parents and children,
that, loving and supporting one another,
they may serve those in need
and be a sign of your kingdom.

Grant that the bonds by which all your children
are united to one another
may be so transformed by your Spirit
that your peace and justice may fill the earth,
through Jesus Christ our Lord.   [794]

Amen.

2

Eternal God,
without your grace no promise is sure.
Strengthen N. and N.
with patience, kindness, gentleness,
and all other gifts of your Spirit,
so that they may fulfill the vows they have made.
Keep them faithful to each other and to you.
Fill them with such love and joy
that they may build a home of peace and welcome.
Guide them by your Word
to serve you all their days.

Help us all, O God,
to do your will in each of our homes and lives.
Enrich us with your grace
so that, supporting one another,
we may serve those in need
and hasten the coming of peace, love, and justice on earth,
through Jesus Christ our Lord.   [795]

Amen.

LORD'S PRAYER

The minister invites all present to sing or say the Lord's Prayer.

As our Savior Christ has taught us, we are bold to say:

All pray together.

Or

Our Father in heaven,
hallowed be your name,
your kingdom come,
your will be done,
on earth as in heaven.
Give us today our daily bread.
Forgive us our sins
as we forgive those who sin against us.
Save us from the time of trial
and deliver us from evil.
For the kingdom, the power,
   and the glory are yours
now and forever.   Amen.

Our Father, who art in heaven,
hallowed be thy name,
thy kingdom come,
thy will be done,
on earth as it is in heaven.
Give us this day our daily bread;
and forgive us our debts,
as we forgive our debtors;
and lead us not into temptation,
but deliver us from evil.
For thine is the kingdom,
and the power, and the glory,
   forever.   Amen.

ANNOUNCEMENT OF MARRIAGE

The minister addresses the congregation:

Before God
and in the presence of this congregation,
N. and N. have made their solemn vows to each other.
They have confirmed their promises by the joining of hands
[and by the giving and receiving of rings].
Therefore, I proclaim that they are now husband and wife.

Blessed be the Father and the Son and the Holy Spirit now and forever.

The minister joins the couple's right hands.

The congregation may join the minister saying:

**Those whom God has joined together
let no one separate.**

CHARGE AND BLESSING

CHARGE TO THE COUPLE

The minister addresses the couple, using one of the following:

1   *See Col. 3:12–14*

As God's own,
clothe yourselves with compassion,
kindness, and patience,
forgiving each other
as the Lord has forgiven you,
and crown all these things with love,
which binds everything together in perfect harmony.

2   *Col. 3:17*

Whatever you do, in word or deed,
do everything in the name of the Lord Jesus,
giving thanks to God through him.

BLESSING

The minister gives God's blessing to the couple and the congregation,
using one of the following:

1   *See Num. 6:24–26*

The Lord bless you and keep you.
The Lord be kind and gracious to you.
The Lord look upon you with favor
and give you peace.

Amen.

2

The grace of Christ attend you,
the love of God surrounding you,
the Holy Spirit keep you,
that you may live in faith,
abound in hope,
and grow in love,
both now and forevermore.

Amen.

A psalm, hymn, spiritual, or anthem may be sung, or instrumental music
may be played, as the wedding party leaves.

AN OUTLINE OF CHRISTIAN MARRIAGE: RITE II

A Service Based on the Service for the Lord's Day

GATHERING

Call to Worship
Psalm, Hymn of Praise, or Spiritual
Confession and Pardon
The Peace
Canticle, Psalm, Hymn, or Spiritual

THE WORD

Readings from Scripture
Sermon
Creed
Psalm, Hymn, or Spiritual
Christian Marriage
   Statement on the Gift of Marriage
   Prayer
   Declarations of Intent
   Affirmations of the Families
   Affirmation of the Congregation
     [Psalm, Hymn, Spiritual, or Anthem]
   Vows
   Exchange of Rings (or Other Symbols)
   Prayer
     [Lord's Prayer]
   Announcement of Marriage
   Charge to the Couple
   Blessing of the Couple
Psalm, Hymn, Spiritual, or Anthem
Prayers of the People

If the Eucharist is not celebrated:

THE EUCHARIST

Offering   Offering
Invitation to the Lord's Table
Great Thanksgiving   Prayer of Thanksgiving
Lord's Prayer   Lord's Prayer
Breaking of the Bread
Communion of the People

SENDING

Hymn, Spiritual, Canticle, or Psalm
Charge and Blessing

CHRISTIAN MARRIAGE: RITE II

A Service Based on the Service for the Lord's Day

This rite follows the order of the Service for the Lord's Day and is designed for use when the marriage is to be included as a part of the Lord's Day worship or on any other occasion when the full order of Christian worship is appropriate. The rite is arranged to allow for the inclusion of the Lord's Supper, if desired. As a service of Christian worship, the marriage service is under the direction of the minister and the supervision of the session.

GATHERING

The bride, groom, their families, and other members of the wedding party may gather for worship with other members of the congregation, or they may enter together before the call to worship. Music appropriate to the season, to the scriptural texts of the day, or to the celebration of marriage may be offered.

All may stand as the minister(s), other worship leaders, and the wedding party enter.

CALL TO WORSHIP

GREETING

The minister greets the people:

See Ruth 2:4

The Lord be with you.

And also with you.

SENTENCES OF SCRIPTURE

The minister continues:

Let us worship God.

Then one of the following is said:

1 *Ps.118:24*

This is the day that the Lord has made;

Let us rejoice and be glad in it.

2 *1 John 4:16*

God is love,
and those who abide in love
abide in God,

and God abides in them.

3 *1 John 4:7–8*

Beloved, let us love one another, for love is of God.
All who love are born of God and know God.
All who do not love do not know God,
for God is love.

4 *Ps. 106:1*

O give thanks, for the Lord is good.

God's love endures forever.

PSALM, HYMN OF PRAISE, OR SPIRITUAL

CONFESSION AND PARDON

CALL TO CONFESSION

The people are called to confess their sin, using the following or other
words of scripture that promise God's forgiveness (pp. 52–53).

Jer. 31:33–34

This is the covenant
that I will make with the house of Israel,
says the Lord:
I will put my law within them,
and I will write it on their hearts;
and I will be their God,
and they shall be my people.
I will forgive their evil deeds,
and remember their sin no more.

In penitence and faith,
let us confess our sins to almighty God.

CONFESSION OF SIN

All confess their sin, using one of the following or another prayer of confession (pp. 53–54, 87–89). Silence may be kept before, during, or following the prayer.

1

Merciful God,
we confess that we have sinned against you
in thought, word, and deed,
by what we have done,
and by what we have left undone.
We have not loved you
with our whole heart and mind and strength.
We have not loved our neighbors as ourselves.

In your mercy forgive what we have been,
help us amend what we are,
and direct what we shall be,
so that we may delight in your will
and walk in your ways,
to the glory of your holy name.   [49]

2

Almighty God,
you created us for life together,
but we have turned from your will.
We have not loved as you commanded.
We have broken the promises we have made to you
and to one another.
We have taken much and given little.

Forgive our disobedience, O God,
and strengthen us in love,
so that we may serve you as a faithful people,
and live together in your joy;
through Jesus Christ our Lord.   [796]

DECLARATION OF FORGIVENESS

The following may be sung in threefold, sixfold, or ninefold form.

Lord, have mercy.
Christ, have mercy.
Lord, have mercy.

The minister declares the assurance of God's forgiving grace, using the following or another declaration of forgiveness (pp. 56–57):

Rom. 8:34; 2 Cor. 5:17

Hear the good news!

Who is in a position to condemn?
Only Christ,
and Christ died for us,
Christ rose for us,
Christ reigns in power for us,
Christ prays for us.

Anyone who is in Christ
is a new creation.
The old life has gone;
a new life has begun.

Know that you are forgiven
and be at peace.

Amen.

THE PEACE

The minister says:

See John 20:19, 21, 26

Since God has forgiven us in Christ,
let us forgive one another.

The peace of our Lord Jesus Christ be with you all.

And also with you.

The people may exchange with one another, by words and gestures, and by signs of peace and reconciliation.

CANTICLE, PSALM, HYMN, OR SPIRITUAL

A canticle (pp. 573–591), psalm, hymn, or spiritual may be sung.

The people may be seated.

THE WORD

READINGS FROM SCRIPTURE

The following or another prayer for illumination (pp. 60, 90–91) is said:

God of mercy,
your faithfulness to your covenant
frees us to live together
in the security of your powerful love.
Amid all the changing words of our generation,
speak your eternal Word that does not change.
Then may we respond to your gracious promises
by living in faith and obedience;
through our Lord Jesus Christ.   [792]
Amen.

Readings suggested in a lectionary, or other appropriate readings from both Testaments, are read. Between the readings the psalm for the day, hymns, spirituals, or anthems related to the lessons may be sung.

SERMON

After the scriptures are read, their message is proclaimed in a sermon. An ascription of praise (pp. 62–63, 91–92) may conclude the sermon.

CREED

The people may stand and say or sing a creed of the church or an affirmation of faith drawn from scripture (pp. 64–65, 94–98).

PSALM, HYMN, OR SPIRITUAL

A psalm, hymn, or spiritual may be sung.

The bride, groom, and other members of the wedding party come and stand before the minister. The families of the bride and groom may stand with the couple.

CHRISTIAN MARRIAGE

STATEMENT ON THE GIFT OF MARRIAGE

The minister says:

N. and N. have come to make their marriage vows
in the presence of God
and of this congregation.
Let us now witness their promises to each other
and surround them with our prayers,
giving thanks to God for the gift of marriage
and asking God's blessing upon them,
so that they may be strengthened for their life together
and nurtured in their love for God.

God created us male and female,
and gave us marriage
so that husband and wife may help and comfort each other,
living faithfully together in plenty and in want,
in joy and in sorrow,
in sickness and in health,
throughout all their days.

God gave us marriage
for the full expression of the love between a man and a woman.
In marriage a woman and a man belong to each other,
and with affection and tenderness
freely give themselves to each other.

God gave us marriage
for the well-being of human society,
for the ordering of family life,
and for the birth and nurture of children.

God gave us marriage as a holy mystery
in which a man and a woman are joined together,
and become one,
just as Christ is one with the church.

In marriage, husband and wife are called to a new way of life,
created, ordered, and blessed by God.
This way of life must not be entered into carelessly,
or from selfish motives,
but responsibly, and prayerfully.

We rejoice that marriage is given by God,
blessed by our Lord Jesus Christ,
and sustained by the Holy Spirit.
Therefore, let marriage be held in honor by all.

PRAYER

The minister says:

Let us pray:

Gracious God,
you are always faithful in your love for us.
Look mercifully upon N. and N.,
who have come seeking your blessing.
Let your Holy Spirit rest upon them
so that with steadfast love
they may honor the promises they make this day,
through Jesus Christ our Savior.   [791]

Amen.

The congregation may be seated.

DECLARATIONS OF INTENT

The minister addresses the bride and groom individually, using either A or B:

A

N., understanding that God has created, ordered, and blessed the covenant
   of marriage,
do you affirm your desire and intention to enter this covenant?

Answer:

I do.

B

If both are baptized, the following may be used:

N., in your baptism
you have been called to union with Christ and the church.
Do you intend to honor this calling
through the covenant of marriage?

Answer:

I do.

Affirmations of the Families

The minister may address the families of the bride and groom:

N., N. [*Names of family members*],
do you give your blessing to N. and N.,
and promise to do everything in your power to uphold them in their marriage?

The families of the bride and groom answer:

1

**We (*I*) give our (*my*) blessing
and promise our (*my*) loving support.**

Or

2

We (*I*) do.

The families of the bride and groom may be seated.

Affirmation of the Congregation

The congregation may stand and the minister may address it, saying:

Will all of you witnessing these vows
do everything in your power
to uphold N. and N. in their marriage?

Answer:

We will.

A psalm, hymn, spiritual, or anthem may be sung.

Vows

The people remain standing.

The minister addresses the couple:

N. and N.,
since it is your intention to marry,
join your right hands,
and with your promises
bind yourselves to each other as husband and wife.

The bride and groom face each other and join right hands. They in turn then make their vows to each other, using A or B.

A

The man says:

I, N., take you, N., to be my wife;
and I promise,
before God and these witnesses,
to be your loving and faithful husband;
in plenty and in want;
in joy and in sorrow;
in sickness and in health;
as long as we both shall live.

The woman says:

I, N., take you, N., to be my husband;
and I promise,
before God and these witnesses,
to be your loving and faithful wife;
in plenty and in want;
in joy and in sorrow;
in sickness and in health;
as long as we both shall live.

B

The man says:

Before God and these witnesses,
I, N., take you, N., to be my wife,
and I promise to love you,
and to be faithful to you
as long as we both shall live.

The woman says:

Before God and these witnesses
I, N., take you, N., to be my husband,
and I promise to love you,
and to be faithful to you,
as long as we both shall live.

EXCHANGE OF RINGS (OR OTHER SYMBOLS)

If rings are to be exchanged, the minister may say to the couple:

What do you bring as the sign of your promise?

When the rings are presented, the minister may say the following prayer.

By your blessing, O God,
may these rings be to N. and N.
symbols of unending love and faithfulness,
reminding them of the covenant they have made this day,
through Jesus Christ our Lord.   [793]

Amen.

The bride and groom exchange rings using A or B or other appropriate
words. The traditional trinitarian formula should be omitted for both the
bride and groom if one of the marriage partners is not a professing Christian.

A

The one giving the ring says:

**N., I give you this ring as a sign of our covenant,
in the name of the Father,
and of the Son,
and of the Holy Spirit.**

The one receiving the ring says:

**I receive this ring as a sign of our covenant,
in the name of the Father,
and of the Son,
and of the Holy Spirit.**

B

As each ring is given, the one giving the ring says:

**This ring I give you,
as a sign of our constant faith
and abiding love,
in the name of the Father,
and of the Son,
and of the Holy Spirit.**

The couple may kneel.

One of the following prayers, or a similar prayer, is said:

Let us pray:

1

Eternal God,
Creator and preserver of all life,
author of salvation,
and giver of all grace:
look with favor upon the world you have made and redeemed,
and especially upon N. and N.

Give them wisdom and devotion in their common life,
that each may be to the other
a strength in need,
a counselor in perplexity,
a comfort in sorrow,
and a companion in joy.

Grant that their wills may be so knit together in your will,
and their spirits in your Spirit,
that they may grow in love and peace
with you and each other
all the days of their life.

Give them the grace,
when they hurt each other,
to recognize and confess their fault,
and to seek each other's forgiveness
and yours.

Make their life together
a sign of Christ's love to this sinful and broken world,
that unity may overcome estrangement,
forgiveness heal guilt,
and joy conquer despair.

Give them such fulfillment of their mutual love
that they may reach out in concern for others.

[Give to them, if it is your will,
the gift of children,
and the wisdom to bring them up
to know you, to love you,
and to serve you.]

Grant that all who have witnessed these vows today
may find their lives strengthened,
and that all who are married
may depart with their own promises renewed.

Enrich with your grace
all husbands and wives, parents and children,
that, loving and supporting one another,
they may serve those in need
and be a sign of your kingdom.

Grant that the bonds by which all your children
are united to one another
may be so transformed by your Spirit
that your peace and justice may fill the earth,
through Jesus Christ our Lord.   [794]

Amen.

2

Eternal God,
without your grace no promise is sure.
Strengthen N. and N.
with patience, kindness, gentleness,
and all other gifts of your Spirit,
so that they may fulfill the vows they have made.
Keep them faithful
to each other and to you.
Fill them with such love and joy
that they may build a home of peace and welcome.
Guide them by your Word
to serve you all their days.

Help us all, O God,
to do your will in each of our homes and lives.
Enrich us with your grace
so that, supporting one another,
we may serve those in need
and hasten the coming of peace, love, and justice on earth,
through Jesus Christ our Lord.   [795]

Amen.

LORD'S PRAYER

If the Lord's Supper is not celebrated, the Lord's Prayer is said or sung here or after the prayer of thanksgiving.

If the Lord's Supper is celebrated, the Lord's Prayer follows the great thanksgiving.

Or

Our Father in heaven,
hallowed be your name,
your kingdom come,
your will be done,
on earth as in heaven.
Give us today our daily bread.
Forgive us our sins
as we forgive those
    who sin against us.
Save us from the time of trial
and deliver us from evil.
For the kingdom, the power,
    and the glory are yours
now and forever.   Amen.
	Our Father, who art in heaven,
	hallowed be thy name,
	thy kingdom come,
	thy will be done,
	on earth as it is in heaven.
	Give us this day our daily bread;
	and forgive us our debts,
	as we forgive our debtors;
	and lead us not into temptation,
	but deliver us from evil.
	For thine is the kingdom,
	and the power, and the glory,
	forever. Amen.

ANNOUNCEMENT OF MARRIAGE

The minister addresses the congregation:

Before God
and in the presence of this congregation,
N. and N. have made their solemn vows to each other.
They have confirmed their promises by the joining of hands
[and by the giving and receiving of rings].
Therefore, I proclaim that they are now husband and wife.

Blessed be the Father and the Son and the Holy Spirit now and forever.

The minister joins the couple's right hands.

The congregation may join the minister saying:

Those whom God has joined together
let no one separate.

CHARGE TO THE COUPLE

The minister addresses the couple, using one of the following:

1

See Col. 3:12–14

As God's own,
clothe yourselves with compassion,
kindness, and patience,
forgiving each other
as the Lord has forgiven you,
and crown all these things with love,
which binds everything together in perfect harmony.

2

Col. 3:17

Whatever you do, in word or deed,
do everything in the name of the Lord Jesus,
giving thanks to God through him.

BLESSING OF THE COUPLE

The minister addresses the couple, using one of the following blessings:

1

The grace of Christ attend you,
the love of God surrounding you,
the Holy Spirit keep you,
that you may live in faith,
abound in hope,
and grow in love,
both now and forevermore.

Amen.

2

Gracious God,
we give you thanks for your tender love
in sending Jesus Christ
to dwell among us, full of grace and truth,
and to make the way of the cross
to be the way of life.
We thank you also
for making holy the marriage of man and woman in his name.

By the power of your Holy Spirit,
pour out your blessing in abundance
upon this man and this woman.
Defend them from every enemy.
Lead them into all peace.
Let their love for each other
be a seal upon their hearts,
a mantle about their shoulders,
and a crown upon their foreheads.
Bless them in their work and in their companionship;
in their sleeping and in their waking;
in their joys and in their sorrows;
in their life and in their death.
Finally, in your mercy,
bring them to that table
where your saints feast forever in your presence;
through Jesus Christ our Lord,
who with you and the Holy Spirit lives and reigns,
one God, forever and ever.   [797]

Amen.

Psalm, Hymn, Spiritual, or Anthem

A psalm, hymn, spiritual, anthem, or other appropriate music may be sung here.

> If the service is neither a Lord's Day service nor a service including the Lord's Supper, it may conclude immediately with the charge and blessing of the people (pp. 880–881), and the wedding party may recess. Or the service may continue as indicated below.

Prayers of the People

Prayers for worldwide and local concerns are offered (pp. 99–120).

IF THE LORD'S SUPPER IS NOT TO BE CELEBRATED, THE SERVICE CONTINUES ON PAGE 877.

THE EUCHARIST

OFFERING

If there is an offering, an anthem or other appropriate music may accompany the gathering of the people's offerings.

When the Lord's Supper is celebrated, the minister(s) and elders prepare the table with bread and wine during the gathering of the gifts. The bread and wine may be brought to the table, or uncovered if already in place.

The offerings may be brought forward. A psalm, hymn of praise, doxology, or spiritual may be sung, the people standing.

INVITATION TO THE LORD'S TABLE

Standing at the table, the presiding minister invites the people to the Sacrament, using one of the following or another invitation to the Lord's table (p. 125). If B is used, the words of institution are not included in the great thanksgiving or at the breaking of the bread.

A   *See Luke 13:29; 24:30, 31*

Friends, this is the joyful feast of the people of God!
They will come from east and west,
and from north and south,
and sit at table in the kingdom of God.

According to Luke,
when our risen Lord was at table with his disciples,
he took the bread, and blessed and broke it,
and gave it to them.
Then their eyes were opened
and they recognized him.

This is the Lord's table.
Our Savior invites those who trust him
to share the feast which he has prepared.

B   *See 1 Cor. 11:23–26; Luke 22:19–20*

Hear the words of the institution
of the Holy Supper of our Lord Jesus Christ:

The Lord Jesus, on the night of his arrest, took bread,
and after giving thanks to God,
he broke it, and gave it to his disciples, saying:
Take, eat.

This is my body, given for you.
Do this in remembrance of me.

In the same way he took the cup, saying:
This cup is the new covenant sealed in my blood,
shed for you for the forgiveness of sins.
Whenever you drink it,
do this in remembrance of me.

Every time you eat this bread and drink this cup,
you proclaim the saving death of the risen Lord,
until he comes.

With thanksgiving,
let us offer God our grateful praise.

GREAT THANKSGIVING

> All may stand.
>
> The presiding minister leads the people in the great thanksgiving, using
> the following prayer, or great thanksgiving B or C (pp. 126–129, 130–132)
> with the proper preface for Christian Marriage (p. 137).

The Lord be with you.

And also with you.

Lift up your hearts.

We lift them to the Lord.

Let us give thanks to the Lord our God.

It is right to give our thanks and praise.

It is truly right and our greatest joy
to give you thanks and praise,
O holy Father, creator of all things,
and source of every blessing.
By your power and wisdom
you brought the universe into being,
and created us in your image.
You made us male and female
and gave us the freedom to be joined as husband and wife,
united in body and heart.
In your providence you gave us this earth
to care for it and to delight in it.
With its bounty you preserve our life.

You called us to love and serve you,
but we turned against you
to follow our own ways.
Yet you did not forsake us,
for your love is unfailing in every age.
You bound yourself to us with a covenant,
claiming us as your people,
and promising faithfulness as our God.
You made the union of husband and wife
a sign of your covenant with your people.

Therefore we praise you,
joining our voices with choirs of angels
and with all the faithful of every time and place,
who forever sing to the glory of your name:

The people may sing or say:

**Holy, holy, holy Lord, God of power and might,
heaven and earth are full of your glory.
Hosanna in the highest.**

**Blessed is he who comes in the name of the Lord.
Hosanna in the highest.**

The minister continues:

You are holy, O God of majesty,
and blessed is Jesus Christ, your Son, our Lord,
whom you sent, out of love for the world,
to be our Savior.
By the power of the Holy Spirit,
Christ was born as one of us,
shared our joys and sorrows,
and offered his life in perfect obedience and trust.
By his death,
Christ delivered us from our sins,
reconciling us to you.
Risen from the tomb,
he gives us new and abundant life,
and offers healing for every human relationship.
By his sacrificial love,
Christ sanctified the church to be his holy bride.
Even now he prepares the wedding banquet.

If they have not already been said, the words of institution may be said here or in relation to the breaking of the bread.

We give you thanks that the Lord Jesus,
on the night before he died,
took bread,
and after giving thanks to you,
he broke it, and gave it to his disciples, saying:
Take, eat.
This is my body, given for you.
Do this in remembrance of me.

In the same way he took the cup, saying:
This cup is the new covenant sealed in my blood,
shed for you for the forgiveness of sins.
Whenever you drink it,
do this in remembrance of me.

Remembering all your mighty and merciful acts,
we take this bread and this wine
from the gifts you have given us,
and celebrate with joy
the redemption won for us in Jesus Christ.
Accept this our sacrifice of praise and thanksgiving,
as a living and holy offering of ourselves,
that our lives may proclaim the One crucified and risen.

The people may sing or say one of the following:

1

Great is the mystery of faith:

Christ has died,
Christ is risen,
Christ will come again.

2

Praise to you, Lord Jesus:

Dying you destroyed our death,
rising you restored our life.
Lord Jesus, come in glory.

3

According to his commandment:

**We remember his death,
we proclaim his resurrection,
we await his coming in glory.**

4

Christ is the bread of life:

**When we eat this bread and drink this cup,
we proclaim your death, Lord Jesus,
until you come in glory.**

The minister continues:

Gracious God,
pour out your Holy Spirit upon us
and upon these your gifts of bread and wine,
that the bread we break
and the cup we bless
may be the communion of the body and blood of Christ.
By your Spirit make us one with Christ,
that we may be one with all who share this feast,
united in ministry in every place.

Give N. and N. the spirit of peace,
that they may become one in heart and mind,
and rejoice together in your gift of marriage.
Let their love for each other
witness to your divine love in the world.
Strengthen the church
to proclaim your justice, joy, and peace
and to live for your kingdom in the world.
Keep us faithful in your service
until Christ comes in final victory
and we shall feast with all your saints
in the joy of your eternal realm
at the marriage supper of the Lamb,
Jesus Christ our Lord.

Through Christ, with Christ, in Christ,
in the unity of the Holy Spirit,
all glory and honor are yours, almighty God,
now and forever.   [798]

Amen.

LORD'S PRAYER

The minister invites all present to sing or say the Lord's Prayer.

As our Savior Christ has taught us, we are bold to say:

All pray together.

Or

Our Father in heaven,
hallowed be your name,
your kingdom come,
your will be done,
on earth as in heaven.
Give us today our daily bread.
Forgive us our sins
as we forgive those who sin against us.
Save us from the time of trial
and deliver us from evil.
For the kingdom, the power,
   and the glory are yours
now and forever.   Amen.
	Our Father, who art in heaven,
	hallowed be thy name,
	thy kingdom come,
	thy will be done,
	on earth as it is in heaven.
	Give us this day our daily bread;
	and forgive us our debts,
	as we forgive our debtors;
	and lead us not into temptation,
	but deliver us from evil.
	For thine is the kingdom,
	and the power, and the glory,
	   forever. Amen.

BREAKING OF THE BREAD

If the words of institution have not previously been said, the minister breaks the bread, using A.

If the words of institution were said in the invitation to the Lord's table, or were included in the great thanksgiving, the minister breaks the bread, using B. Or the bread may be broken in silence.

A   *1 Cor. 11:23–26; Luke 22:19–20*

The minister breaks the bread in full view of the people, saying:

The Lord Jesus, on the night of his arrest, took bread,
and after giving thanks to God,
he broke it, and gave it to his disciples, saying:
Take, eat.
This is my body, given for you.
Do this in remembrance of me.

The minister lifts the cup, saying:

In the same way he took the cup, saying:
This cup is the new covenant sealed in my blood,
shed for you for the forgiveness of sins.
Whenever you drink it,
do this in remembrance of me.

Every time you eat this bread and drink this cup,
you proclaim the saving death of the risen Lord,
until he comes.

B   *1 Cor. 10:16–17*

Because there is one loaf,
we, many as we are, are one body;
for it is one loaf of which we all partake.

The minister takes the loaf and breaks it in full view of the congregation.

When we break the bread,
is it not a sharing in the body of Christ?

Having filled the cup, the minister lifts it in the view of the people.

When we give thanks over the cup,
is it not a sharing in the blood of Christ?

COMMUNION OF THE PEOPLE

INVITATION

Then holding out both the bread and the cup to the people, the minister says:

The gifts of God
for the people of God.

COMMUNION

The minister and those assisting receive Communion and then serve the bread and the cup to the people.

In giving the bread:

The body of Christ, the bread of heaven.   **Amen.**

In giving the cup:

The blood of Christ, the cup of salvation.   **Amen.**

During Communion, psalms, hymns, anthems, or spirituals may be sung.

PRAYER AFTER COMMUNION

After all have been served, the following, or a similar prayer (pp. 76–77, 157–158), may be prayed by the minister, or by all together, the people standing.

Loving God,
we thank you that you have fed us in this holy meal,
united us with Christ,
and given us a foretaste of the marriage feast of the Lamb.
So strengthen us in your service
that our daily living may show our thanks,
through Jesus Christ our Lord.   [799]

Amen.

SENDING

HYMN, SPIRITUAL, CANTICLE, OR PSALM

A hymn, spiritual, canticle, or psalm may be sung.

CHARGE AND BLESSING

CHARGE

The minister, a deacon, or an elder dismisses the congregation, using one of the following or a similar charge (pp. 78, 82–83, 159–160):

1   *1 Cor. 16:13; 2 Tim. 2:1; Eph. 6:10;*
                                                         1 Thess. 5:13–22; 1 Peter 2:17

Go out into the world in peace;
have courage;
hold on to what is good;
return no one evil for evil;
strengthen the fainthearted;
support the weak, and help the suffering;
honor all people;
love and serve the Lord,
rejoicing in the power of the Holy Spirit.

2

Go in peace to love and serve the Lord.

BLESSING

The minister gives God's blessing to the congregation, using one of the following or another scriptural benediction (pp. 78, 83, 161). Traditionally, the **Alleluia** is omitted during Lent.

1
2 Cor. 13:14

The grace of the Lord Jesus Christ,
the love of God,
and the communion of the Holy Spirit
be with you all.

Alleluia!   Amen.

2
See Num. 6:24–26

The Lord bless you and keep you.
The Lord be kind and gracious to you.
The Lord look upon you with favor
and give you peace.

Alleluia!   Amen.

Instrumental music is appropriate.

IF THE LORD'S SUPPER IS NOT CELEBRATED, THE SERVICE
CONTINUES HERE FROM PAGE 867.

OFFERING

If there is an offering, an anthem or other appropriate music may accompany the gathering of the people's offerings.

The offerings may be brought forward. A psalm, hymn of praise, doxology, or spiritual may be sung, the people standing.

PRAYER OF THANKSGIVING

The minister leads the people in one of the following or a similar prayer of thanksgiving:

Let us give thanks to the Lord our God.
It is right to give our thanks and praise.

The minister continues, using one of the following, or a similar prayer.

1

O holy Father, creator of all things
and source of every blessing,
by your power and wisdom
you brought the universe into being
and created us in your image.
You made us male and female,
and gave us the freedom to be joined as husband and wife,
united in body and heart.
In your providence you gave us this earth,
to care for it and delight in it,
and with its bounty you preserve our life.

You called us to love and serve you,
but we turned against you
to follow our own ways.
Yet you did not forsake us,
for your love is unfailing in every age.
You bound yourself to us with a covenant,
claiming us as your people,
and promising faithfulness as our God.
You made the union of husband and wife
a sign of your covenant with your people.

We praise you, O Lord our God,
for out of your great love for the world
you gave your only Son to be our Savior.
By the power of the Holy Spirit,
Christ was born as one of us,
shared our joys and sorrows,
and offered his life in perfect obedience and trust.
By his death
Christ delivered us from our sins,
reconciling us to you.
Rising from the tomb,
he gives us new and abundant life,
and offers healing for every human relationship.
By his sacrificial love
Christ sanctified the church to be his holy bride.
Even now he prepares the wedding banquet.

Give N. and N. the spirit of love and peace,
that they may become one in heart and mind,
and rejoice together in your gift of marriage.
Let their love for each other
witness to your divine love in the world.
Strengthen the church in every place
to proclaim your justice, joy, and peace,
and to live for your kingdom in the world.
Keep us faithful in your service
until Christ comes in final victory
and we shall feast with all your saints
in the joy of your eternal realm
at the marriage supper of the Lamb,
Jesus Christ our Lord.

Through Christ, with Christ, in Christ,
in the unity of the Holy Spirit,
all glory and honor,
now and forever.   [800]

Amen.

2

Almighty and merciful God,
from whom comes every good,
we praise you for your mercies,
for your goodness that has created us,
your grace that has sustained us,
your discipline that has corrected us,
your patience that has borne with us,
and your love that has redeemed us.

Help us to love you,
and to be thankful for all your gifts
by serving you and delighting to do your will,
through Jesus Christ our Lord.   [66]

Amen.

LORD'S PRAYER

The minister invites all present to sing or say the Lord's Prayer.

As our Savior Christ has taught us, we are bold to say:

All pray together.

Or

Our Father in heaven,
hallowed be your name,
your kingdom come,
your will be done,
on earth as in heaven.
Give us today our daily bread.
Forgive us our sins
as we forgive those who sin against us.
Save us from the time of trial
and deliver us from evil.
For the kingdom, the power,
    and the glory are yours
now and forever.   Amen.

Our Father, who art in heaven,
hallowed be thy name,
thy kingdom come,
thy will be done,
on earth as it is in heaven.
Give us this day our daily bread;
and forgive us our debts,
as we forgive our debtors;
and lead us not into temptation,
but deliver us from evil.
For thine is the kingdom,
and the power, and the glory,
    forever.   Amen.

SENDING

HYMN, SPIRITUAL, CANTICLE, OR PSALM

A hymn, spiritual, canticle, or psalm may be sung.

CHARGE AND BLESSING

CHARGE

The minister, a deacon, or an elder dismisses the congregation, using one of the following or a similar charge (pp. 78, 82–83, 159–160):

1

See 1 Cor. 16:13; 2 Tim. 2:1; Eph. 6:10;
1 Thess. 5:13–22; 1 Peter 2:17

Go out into the world in peace;
have courage;
hold on to what is good;
return no one evil for evil;
strengthen the fainthearted;
support the weak, and help the suffering;
honor all people;
love and serve the Lord,
rejoicing in the power of the Holy Spirit.

2

Go in peace to love and serve the Lord.

BLESSING

The minister gives God's blessing to the congregation, using one of the following or another scriptural benediction (pp. 78, 83, 161). Traditionally, the **Alleluia** is omitted during Lent.

1

2 Cor. 13:14

The grace of the Lord Jesus Christ,
the love of God,
and the communion of the Holy Spirit
be with you all.

Alleluia!   Amen.

The Lord bless you and keep you.
The Lord be kind and gracious to you.
The Lord look upon you with favor
and give you peace.

Alleluia! Amen.

Instrumental music may follow the blessing.

AN OUTLINE OF CHRISTIAN MARRIAGE: RITE III

A Service for Those
Previously Married in a Civil Ceremony

Entrance
Sentences of Scripture
Statement on the Gift of Marriage
Prayer
Declarations of Intent
    [Affirmation of the Families]
Affirmation of the Congregation
    [Psalm, Hymn, Spiritual, or Anthem]
Readings from Scripture
Sermon
    [Psalm, Hymn, or Spiritual]
Vows
Prayer
Lord's Prayer
Charge and Blessing
    [Psalm, Hymn, Spiritual, or Anthem]

CHRISTIAN MARRIAGE: RITE III

A Service for Those
Previously Married in a Civil Ceremony

This rite is designed to allow those who have been previously married in a civil ceremony to make the promises of Christian marriage before the witness of the church and in the context of Christian worship. The service may be used independently or, with the necessary alterations, it may be incorporated into the Service for the Lord's Day.

ENTRANCE

At the appointed time, the couple come and stand before the minister. The families of the bride and groom may stand with the couple.

During the entrance of the couple, the people may stand and sing a psalm, hymn, or spiritual. Or an anthem may be sung, or instrumental music may be played.

SENTENCES OF SCRIPTURE

The minister calls the people to worship either before or after the entrance, using one of the following, or another appropriate verse from scripture.

1   *1 John 4:16*

God is love,
and those who abide in love
abide in God,
and God abides in them.

2   *Ps. 118:24*

This is the day that the Lord has made;
let us rejoice and be glad in it.

3   *Ps. 106:1 and elsewhere*

O give thanks, for the Lord is good.
God's love endures forever.

Statement on the Gift of Marriage

The minister says:

N. and N. have been married according to the law of the state,
and have spoken vows pledging loyalty and love.
Now, in the presence of God and the church,
they come to reaffirm those vows
and in faith to confess their common purpose in the Lord.
We gather to witness their promises to each other,
to surround them with our prayers,
to give thanks to God for the gift of marriage,
and to ask God's blessing upon them,
so that they may be strengthened for their life together
and nurtured in their love for God.

God created us male and female,
and gave us marriage
so that husband and wife may help and comfort each other,
living faithfully together in plenty and in want,
in joy and in sorrow,
in sickness and in health,
throughout all their days.

God gave us marriage
for the full expression of the love between a man and a woman.
In marriage a woman and a man belong to each other,
and with affection and tenderness
freely give themselves to each other.

God gave us marriage
for the well-being of human society,
for the ordering of family life,
and for the birth and nurture of children.

God gave us marriage as a holy mystery
in which a man and a woman are joined together,
and become one,
just as Christ is one with the church.

In marriage, husband and wife are called to a new way of life,
created, ordered, and blessed by God.
It is to be lived prayerfully, and in joyful obedience to Christ.

We rejoice that marriage is given by God,
blessed by our Lord Jesus Christ,
and sustained by the Holy Spirit.
Therefore, let marriage be held in honor by all.

PRAYER

The minister says:

Let us pray:

Gracious God,
you are always faithful in your love for us.
Look mercifully upon N. and N.,
who have come seeking your blessing.
Let your Holy Spirit rest upon them
so that with steadfast love
they may honor the promises they make this day,
through Jesus Christ our Savior.   [791]

Amen.

The congregation may be seated.

DECLARATIONS OF INTENT

The minister addresses the man and woman individually:

N., you have heard how God has created, ordered, and blessed the covenant
of marriage.
Now in the presence of God and the church,
do you wish to affirm the vows of Christian marriage?

Answer:

I do.

AFFIRMATIONS OF THE FAMILIES

If appropriate, the minister may address the families of the bride and
groom:

N., N. [*Names of family members*],
do you give your blessing to N. and N.,
and promise to do everything in your power to uphold them in
their marriage?

The families of the bride and groom answer:

1

**We (*I*) give our (*my*) blessing
and promise our (*my*) loving support.**

Or

2

We (*I*) do.

The families of the bride and groom may be seated.

AFFIRMATION OF THE CONGREGATION

The minister may address the congregation, saying:

Will all of you witnessing these vows
do everything in your power
to uphold N. and N. in their marriage?

Answer:

We will.

A psalm, hymn, spiritual, or anthem may be sung.

READINGS FROM SCRIPTURE

The following or a similar prayer for illumination (pp. 60, 90–91) may be
said.

God of mercy,
your faithfulness to your covenant
frees us to live together
in the security of your powerful love.
Amid all the changing words of our generation,
speak your eternal Word that does not change.
Then may we respond to your gracious promises
by living in faith and obedience;
through our Lord Jesus Christ.   [792]

Amen.

One or more scripture passages are read (pp. 893–902).

SERMON

After the scriptures are read, a brief sermon may be given.

A psalm, hymn, spiritual, or other music may follow.

VOWS

The people may stand.

The minister addresses the couple:

N. and N.,
join your right hands,
and in faith make your promises to each other
as husband and wife.

The couple face each other and join their right hands. They, in turn, then make their vows to each other, using A or B.

A

The man says:

**N., you are my wife,
and I promise,
before God and these witnesses,
to be your loving and faithful husband;
in plenty and in want;
in joy and in sorrow;
in sickness and in health;
as long as we both shall live.**

The woman says:

**N., you are my husband,
and I promise,
before God and these witnesses,
to be your loving and faithful wife;
in plenty and in want;
in joy and in sorrow;
in sickness and in health;
as long as we both shall live.**

B

The man says:

**N., you are my wife.
Before God and these witnesses,
I promise to love you,
and to be faithful to you,
as long as we both shall live.**

The woman says:

**N., you are my husband.
Before God and these witnesses,
I promise to love you,
and to be faithful to you
as long as we both shall live.**

PRAYER

The couple may kneel.

One of the following prayers, or a similar prayer, is said:

Let us pray:

1

Eternal God,
Creator and preserver of all life,
author of salvation
and giver of all grace:
look with favor upon the world you have made and redeemed,
and especially upon N. and N.

Give them wisdom and devotion in their common life,
that each may be to the other
a strength in need,
a counselor in perplexity,
a comfort in sorrow,
and a companion in joy.

Grant that their wills may be so knit together in your will,
and their spirits in your Spirit,
that they may grow in love and peace
with you and each other
all the days of their life.

Give them the grace,
when they hurt each other,
to recognize and confess their fault,
and to seek each other's forgiveness
and yours.

Make their life together
a sign of Christ's love
to this sinful and broken world,
that unity may overcome estrangement,
forgiveness heal guilt,
and joy conquer despair.

Give them such fulfillment of their mutual love
that they may reach out in concern for others.

[Give to them, if it is your will,
the gift of children,
and the wisdom to bring them up
to know you, to love you,
and to serve you.]

Grant that all who have witnessed these vows today
may find their lives strengthened,
and that all who are married
may depart with their own promises renewed.

Enrich with your grace
all husbands and wives, parents and children,
that, loving and supporting one another,
they may serve those in need
and be a sign of your kingdom.

Grant that the bonds by which all your children
are united to one another
may be so transformed by your Spirit
that your peace and justice may fill the earth,
through Jesus Christ our Lord. [794]

Amen.

2

Eternal God,
without your grace no promise is sure.
Strengthen N. and N. with patience, kindness, gentleness,
and all other gifts of your Spirit,
so that they may fulfill the vows they have made.
Keep them faithful to each other and to you.
Fill them with such love and joy
that they may build a home of peace and welcome.
Guide them by your Word
to serve you all their days.

Help us all, O God,
to do your will in each of our homes and lives.
Enrich us with your grace
so that, supporting one another,
we may serve those in need
and hasten the coming of peace, love, and justice on earth,
through Jesus Christ our Lord.   [795]

Amen.

LORD'S PRAYER

The minister invites all present to sing or say the Lord's Prayer.

As our Savior Christ has taught us, we are bold to say:

All pray together.

Or

Our Father in heaven,
hallowed be your name,
your kingdom come,
your will be done,
on earth as in heaven.
Give us today our daily bread.
Forgive us our sins
as we forgive those who sin against us.
Save us from the time of trial
and deliver us from evil.
For the kingdom, the power,
  and the glory are yours
now and forever.   Amen.

Our Father, who art in heaven,
hallowed be thy name,
thy kingdom come,
thy will be done,
on earth as it is in heaven.
Give us this day our daily bread;
and forgive us our debts,
as we forgive our debtors;
and lead us not into temptation,
but deliver us from evil.
For thine is the kingdom,
and the power, and the glory,
  forever.   Amen.

The minister joins the couple's right hands.

The congregation may join the minister, saying:

**Those whom God has joined together
let no one separate.**

CHARGE AND BLESSING

CHARGE TO THE COUPLE

The minister addresses the couple, using one of the following:

1   *See Col. 3:12–14*

As God's own,
clothe yourselves with compassion,
kindness, and patience,
forgiving each other
as the Lord has forgiven you,
and crown all these things with love,
which binds everything together in perfect harmony.

2   *Col. 3:17*

Whatever you do, in word or deed,
do everything in the name of the Lord Jesus,
giving thanks to God through him.

BLESSING

The minister gives God's blessing to the couple and the congregation,
using one of the following:

1   *See Num. 6:24–26*

The Lord bless you and keep you.
The Lord be kind and gracious to you.
The Lord look upon you with favor
and give you peace.

Amen.

2

The grace of Christ attend you,
the love of God surrounding you,
the Holy Spirit keep you,
that you may live in faith,
abound in hope,
and grow in love,
both now and forevermore.

Amen.

> A psalm, hymn, spiritual, or anthem may be sung, or instrumental music
> may be played, as the wedding party leaves.

SCRIPTURE READINGS
FOR CHRISTIAN MARRIAGE

The following readings are particularly appropriate for use in the service of Christian marriage. An asterisk * indicates that the text of that particular reading is included in this resource (pp. 895–902).

LIST OF SUGGESTED READINGS

OLD TESTAMENT

Gen. 1:26–31	Humankind created in the image of God
* Gen. 2:18–24	Bone of my bones and flesh of my flesh
* Song of Sol. 8:6–7	Set me as a seal upon your heart
* Prov. 3:3–6	Trust the Lord with all your heart
* Isa. 54:5–8	Your Maker is your husband
Jer. 31:31–34	The Lord will make a new covenant

PSALMS

The following psalms are appropriate for singing or reading in the service. For another translation of the psalms see pages 611–783.

Ps. 8	Mortals crowned with glory and honor
* Ps. 67	May God be gracious to us
* Ps. 95:1–7	O come, let us sing to the Lord
* Ps. 100	Make a joyful noise to the Lord
* Ps. 103:1–5, 15–18	Bless the Lord, O my soul
Ps. 117	Great is God's steadfast love
Ps. 121	Lift up my eyes to the hills

Ps. 128	Happy is everyone who fears the Lord
* Ps. 136:1–9, 26	O give thanks, for God is good
* Ps. 145	I will exalt you, O God my King
Ps. 148	Praise the Lord
Ps. 150	Everything that breathes praise the Lord

EPISTLES

* Rom. 12:1–2, 9–18	A living sacrifice . . . let love be genuine
* 1 Cor. 13:1–13	Faith, hope, love . . . greatest is love
Col. 3:12–17	Clothe yourselves with love
1 John 4:7–12	Let us love one another . . . God is love
Rev. 19:1, 5–9	Rejoicing at the marriage of the Lamb

GOSPELS

* Matt. 5:1–10	The Beatitudes
* Matt. 5:13–16	Salt of the earth . . . light of the world
Matt. 19:3–6	No longer two, but one flesh
* Matt. 22:35–40	Love the Lord with all your heart, soul, mind
* Mark 10:6–9	What God has joined, let no one separate
John 2:1–11	The wedding at Cana
* John 15:1–17	Jesus, the true vine

Scripture Readings

All readings are from the New Revised Standard Version of the Bible.

Old Testament

1   *Genesis 2:18–24*

The LORD God said, "It is not good that the man should be alone; I will make him a helper as his partner." So out of the ground the LORD God formed every animal of the field and every bird of the air, and brought them to the man to see what he would call them; and whatever the man called every living creature, that was its name. The man gave names to all cattle, and to the birds of the air, and to every animal of the field; but for the man there was not found a helper as his partner. So the LORD God caused a deep sleep to fall upon the man, and he slept; then he took one of his ribs and closed up its place with flesh. And the rib that the LORD God had taken from the man he made into a woman and brought her to the man. Then the man said,

"This at last is bone of my bones and flesh of my flesh;
    this one shall be called Woman, for out of Man this one was taken."

Therefore a man leaves his father and his mother and clings to his wife, and they become one flesh.

2   *Song of Solomon 8:6–7*

Set me as a seal upon your heart,
    as a seal upon your arm;
for love is strong as death,
    passion fierce as the grave.
Its flashes are flashes of fire,
    a raging flame.
Many waters cannot quench love,
    neither can floods drown it.
If one offered for love
    all the wealth of his house,
    it would be utterly scorned.

3   *Proverbs 3:3–6*

Do not let loyalty and faithfulness forsake you;
    bind them around your neck,
    write them on the tablet of your heart.
So you will find favor and good repute
    in the sight of God and of people.

Trust in the LORD with all your heart,
   and do not rely on your own insight.
In all your ways acknowledge him,
   and he will make straight your paths.

4   *Isaiah 54:5–8*

For your Maker is your husband,
   the LORD of hosts is his name;
the Holy One of Israel is your Redeemer,
   the God of the whole earth he is called.
For the LORD has called you
   like a wife forsaken and grieved in spirit,
like the wife of a man's youth when she is cast off,
   says your God.
For a brief moment I abandoned you,
   but with great compassion I will gather you.
In overflowing wrath for a moment
   I hid my face from you,
but with everlasting love I will have compassion on you,
   says the LORD, your Redeemer.

PSALMS

For another translation of the psalms see pages 611–783.

5   *Psalm 67*

May God be gracious to us and bless us
   and make his face to shine upon us,
that your way may be known upon earth,
   your saving power among all nations.
Let the peoples praise you, O God;
   let all the peoples praise you.

Let the nations be glad and sing for joy,
   for you judge the peoples with equity
   and guide the nations upon earth.
Let the peoples praise you, O God;
   let all the peoples praise you.

The earth has yielded its increase;
   God, our God, has blessed us.
May God continue to bless us;
   let all the ends of the earth revere him.

6   *Psalm 95:1–7*

O come, let us sing to the LORD;
    let us make a joyful noise to the rock of our salvation!
Let us come into his presence with thanksgiving;
    let us make a joyful noise to him with songs of praise!
For the LORD is a great God,
    and a great King above all gods.
In his hand are the depths of the earth;
    the heights of the mountains are his also.
The sea is his, for he made it,
    and the dry land, which his hands have formed.

O come, let us worship and bow down,
    let us kneel before the LORD, our Maker!
For he is our God,
    and we are the people of his pasture,
    and the sheep of his hand.

O that today you would listen to his voice!

7   *Psalm 100*

Make a joyful noise to the LORD, all the earth.
Worship the LORD with gladness;
    come into his presence with singing.

Know that the LORD is God.
    It is he that made us, and we are his;
    we are his people, and the sheep of his pasture.

Enter his gates with thanksgiving,
    and his courts with praise.
    Give thanks to him, bless his name.

For the LORD is good;
    his steadfast love endures forever,
    and his faithfulness to all generations.

8   *Psalm 103:1–5, 15–18*

Bless the LORD, O my soul,
    and all that is within me,
    bless his holy name.
Bless the LORD, O my soul,
    and do not forget all his benefits—
who forgives all your iniquity,
    who heals all your diseases,

who redeems your life from the Pit,
    who crowns you with steadfast love and mercy,
who satisfies you with good as long as you live
    so that your youth is renewed like the eagle's.

As for mortals, their days are like grass;
    they flourish like a flower of the field;
for the wind passes over it, and it is gone,
    and its place knows it no more.
But the steadfast love of the LORD is from everlasting to everlasting
    on those who fear him,
    and his righteousness to children's children,
to those who keep his covenant
    and remember to do his commandments.

9   *Psalm 136:1–9, 26*

O give thanks to the LORD, for he is good,
    for his steadfast love endures forever.
O give thanks to the God of gods,
    for his steadfast love endures forever.
O give thanks to the LORD of lords,
    for his steadfast love endures forever;

who alone does great wonders,
    for his steadfast love endures forever;
who by understanding made the heavens,
    for his steadfast love endures forever;
who spread out the earth on the waters,
    for his steadfast love endures forever;
who made the great lights,
    for his steadfast love endures forever;
the sun to rule over the day,
    for his steadfast love endures forever;
the moon and stars to rule over the night,
    for his steadfast love endures forever;

O give thanks to the God of heaven,
    for his steadfast love endures forever.

10   *Psalm 145*

I will extol you, my God and King,
    and bless your name forever and ever.
Every day I will bless you,
    and praise your name forever and ever.
Great is the LORD, and greatly to be praised;
    his greatness is unsearchable.

One generation shall laud your works to another,
and shall declare your mighty acts.
On the glorious splendor of your majesty,
and on your wondrous works, I will meditate.
The might of your awesome deeds shall be proclaimed,
and I will declare your greatness.
They shall celebrate the fame of your abundant goodness,
and shall sing aloud of your righteousness.

The LORD is gracious and merciful,
slow to anger and abounding in steadfast love.
The LORD is good to all,
and his compassion is over all that he has made.

All your works shall give thanks to you, O LORD,
and all your faithful shall bless you.
They shall speak of the glory of your kingdom,
and tell of your power,
to make known to all people your mighty deeds,
and the glorious splendor of your kingdom.
Your kingdom is an everlasting kingdom,
and your dominion endures throughout all generations.

The LORD is faithful in all his words,
and gracious in all his deeds.
The LORD upholds all who are falling,
and raises up all who are bowed down.
The eyes of all look to you,
and you give them their food in due season.
You open your hand,
satisfying the desire of every living thing.
The LORD is just in all his ways,
and kind in all his doings.
The LORD is near to all who call on him,
to all who call on him in truth.
He fulfills the desire of all who fear him;
he also hears their cry, and saves them.
The LORD watches over all who love him,
but all the wicked he will destroy.

My mouth will speak the praise of the LORD,
and all flesh will bless his holy name forever and ever.

11   *Romans 12:1–2, 9–18*

I appeal to you therefore, brothers and sisters, by the mercies of God, to present your bodies as a living sacrifice, holy and acceptable to God, which is your spiritual worship. Do not be conformed to this world, but be transformed by the renewing of your minds, so that you may discern what is the will of God—what is good and acceptable and perfect.

Let love be genuine; hate what is evil, hold fast to what is good; love one another with mutual affection; outdo one another in showing honor. Do not lag in zeal, be ardent in spirit, serve the Lord. Rejoice in hope, be patient in suffering, persevere in prayer. Contribute to the needs of the saints; extend hospitality to strangers.

Bless those who persecute you; bless and do not curse them. Rejoice with those who rejoice, weep with those who weep. Live in harmony with one another; do not be haughty, but associate with the lowly; do not claim to be wiser than you are. Do not repay anyone evil for evil, but take thought for what is noble in the sight of all. If it is possible, so far as it depends on you, live peaceably with all.

12   *1 Corinthians 13:1–13*

If I speak in the tongues of mortals and of angels, but do not have love, I am a noisy gong or a clanging cymbal. And if I have prophetic powers, and understand all mysteries and all knowledge, and if I have all faith, so as to remove mountains, but do not have love, I am nothing. If I give away all my possessions, and if I hand over my body so that I may boast, but do not have love, I gain nothing.

Love is patient; love is kind; love is not envious or boastful or arrogant or rude. It does not insist on its own way; it is not irritable or resentful; it does not rejoice in wrongdoing, but rejoices in the truth. It bears all things, believes all things, hopes all things, endures all things.

Love never ends. But as for prophecies, they will come to an end; as for tongues, they will cease; as for knowledge, it will come to an end. For we know only in part, and we prophesy only in part; but when the complete comes, the partial will come to an end. When I was a child, I spoke like a child, I thought like a child, I reasoned like a child; when I became an adult, I put an end to childish ways. For now we see in a mirror, dimly, but then we will see face to face. Now I know only in part; then I will know fully, even as I have been fully known. And now faith, hope, and love abide, these three; and the greatest of these is love.

13 *Matthew 5:1–10*

When Jesus saw the crowds, he went up the mountain; and after he sat down, his disciples came to him. Then he began to speak, and taught them, saying:

"Blessed are the poor in spirit, for theirs is the kingdom of heaven.

"Blessed are those who mourn, for they will be comforted.

"Blessed are the meek, for they will inherit the earth.

"Blessed are those who hunger and thirst for righteousness, for they will be filled.

"Blessed are the merciful, for they will receive mercy.

"Blessed are the pure in heart, for they will see God.

"Blessed are the peacemakers, for they will be called children of God.

"Blessed are those who are persecuted for righteousness' sake, for theirs is the kingdom of heaven."

14 *Matthew 5:13–16*

You are the salt of the earth; but if salt has lost its taste, how can its saltiness be restored? It is no longer good for anything, but is thrown out and trampled under foot.

You are the light of the world. A city built on a hill cannot be hid. No one after lighting a lamp puts it under the bushel basket, but on the lampstand, and it gives light to all in the house. In the same way, let your light shine before others, so that they may see your good works and give glory to your Father in heaven.

15 *Matthew 22:35–40*

A lawyer asked him a question to test him. "Teacher, which commandment in the law is the greatest?" He said to him, " 'You shall love the Lord your God with all your heart, and with all your soul, and with all your mind.' This is the greatest and first commandment. And a second is like it: 'You shall love your neighbor as yourself.' On these two commandments hang all the law and the prophets."

16 *Mark 10:6–9*

From the beginning of creation, "God made them male and female." "For this reason a man shall leave his father and mother and be joined to his wife, and the two shall become one flesh." So they are no longer two, but one flesh." Therefore what God has joined together, let no one separate.

I am the true vine, and my Father is the vinegrower. He removes every branch in me that bears no fruit. Every branch that bears fruit he prunes to make it bear more fruit. You have already been cleansed by the word that I have spoken to you. Abide in me as I abide in you. Just as the branch cannot bear fruit by itself unless it abides in the vine, neither can you unless you abide in me. I am the vine, you are the branches. Those who abide in me and I in them bear much fruit, because apart from me you can do nothing. Whoever does not abide in me is thrown away like a branch and withers; such branches are gathered, thrown into the fire, and burned. If you abide in me, and my words abide in you, ask for whatever you wish, and it will be done for you. My Father is glorified by this, that you bear much fruit and become my disciples. As the Father has loved me, so I have loved you; abide in my love. If you keep my commandments, you will abide in my love, just as I have kept my Father's commandments and abide in his love. I have said these things to you so that my joy may be in you, and that your joy may be complete.

This is my commandment, that you love one another as I have loved you. No one has greater love than this, to lay down one's life for one's friends. You are my friends if you do what I command you. I do not call you servants any longer, because the servant does not know what the master is doing; but I have called you friends, because I have made known to you everything that I have heard from my Father. You did not choose me but I chose you. And I appointed you to go and bear fruit, fruit that will last, so that the Father will give you whatever you ask him in my name. I am giving you these commands so that you may love one another.

THE FUNERAL:
A SERVICE OF
WITNESS TO THE
RESURRECTION

COMFORTING THE BEREAVED

Outline

Scripture Sentences
Prayer
Hymn
Psalm
Reading(s) from Scripture
Prayer
Lord's Prayer
Blessing

It is appropriate for family and friends to gather for prayer, in the home or funeral establishment, on the day or night before the funeral. This brief service may be used for such occasions. Psalms and scripture readings suggested in the funeral rite may also be included. Prayers from the funeral rite, comparable to those in this service, may be substituted. The service may be led by the minister or another representative of the church.

SENTENCES OF SCRIPTURE

Scripture sentences, such as the following, are said:

1   *Rom. 15:13*

May the God of hope
fill you with all joy and peace in believing,
so that you may abound in hope
by the power of the Holy Spirit.

2   *Ps. 46:1*

God is our refuge and strength,
a very present help in trouble.

3   *Deut. 33:27*

The eternal God is your dwelling place,
and underneath are the everlasting arms.

4   *Matt. 5:4*

Blessed are those who mourn,
for they will be comforted.

5   *2 Cor. 1:3–4*

Praise be to the God and Father of our Lord Jesus Christ,
the Father of mercies and God of all comfort,
who comforts us in all our sorrows,
so that we can comfort others in their sorrow,
with the consolation we have received from God.

PRAYER

One of the following, or a similar prayer, is said:

1

Eternal God,
our help in every time of trouble,
send your Holy Spirit to comfort and strengthen us,
that we may have hope of life eternal
and trust in your goodness and mercy,
through Jesus Christ our Lord.   [801]

Amen.

2

Jesus said, "Come to me, all who labor
and are heavily burdened,
and I will give you rest."

Let us pray for our *brother/sister* N.,
that *he/she* may rest from *his/her* labors,
and enter into the light of God's eternal rest.

Receive, O Lord, your servant,
for *he/she* returns to you.
May *he/she* hear your words of welcome,
"Come, you blessed of my Father,"
and receive the unfading crown of glory.
May the angels surround *him/her*
and the saints welcome *him/her* in peace.

**Into your hands, O Lord,
we commend our brother/sister N.**

Gracious God,
in whose presence live all who die in the Lord,
receive our *brother/sister* N.,
into your merciful arms,
and the joys of your heavenly home.
May *he/she* and all the departed rest in your peace.   [802]

Amen.

HYMN

A hymn may be sung.

PSALM

A psalm may be read or sung (pp. 948, 954–958, 611–783).

READINGS FROM SCRIPTURE

One or more readings from scripture may be read (pp. 947–963).

An interpretation of the readings, and reflections on the life of the deceased,
may follow. Informal conversations with the family may be appropriate.

PRAYER

One or more of the following, or a similar prayer (pp. 921–924) may be said:

1

Holy God,
Lord of life and death,
you made us in your image
and hold us in your care.
We thank you for your servant N.,
for the gift of *his/her* life,
and for the love and mercy *he/she* received from you and gave to us.
Especially we praise you for your love in Jesus Christ,
who died and rose from the grave
to free us from evil,
and give us life eternal.
Grant that when our time on earth is ended,
we may be united with all the saints
in the joys of your eternal home,
through Jesus Christ our Lord.   [803]

Amen.

2

Almighty God, source of all mercy and giver of comfort:
Deal graciously with those who mourn,
that, casting all their sorrow on you,
they may know the consolation of your love;
through your Son, Jesus Christ our Lord. [804]

Amen.

3

God our creator,
your Holy Spirit prays for us
even when we do not know how to pray.
Send your Spirit to comfort us in our need and loss,
and help us to commend N. to your merciful care;
through Jesus Christ our Lord. [805]

Amen.

4

At the death of a child:

Loving God,
your beloved Son took children into his arms and blessed them.
Give us grace,
that we may entrust N. to your never-failing care and love,
and bring us all to your heavenly kingdom;
through Jesus Christ our Lord. [806]

Amen.

5

At the death of a child:

Holy God,
yours is the beauty of childhood
and yours is the fullness of years.
Comfort us in our sorrow,
strengthen us with hope,
and breathe peace into our troubled hearts.
Assure us that the love in which we rejoiced for a time is not lost,
and that N. is with you,
safe in your eternal love and care.
We ask this in the name of Jesus Christ,
who took little children into his arms and blessed them. [807]

Amen.

Lord's Prayer

All pray together:

Or

Our Father in heaven,
hallowed be your name,
your kingdom come,
your will be done,
on earth as in heaven.
Give us today our daily bread.
Forgive us our sins
as we forgive those who sin against us.
Save us from the time of trial
and deliver us from evil.
For the kingdom, the power,
   and the glory are yours
now and forever.   Amen.

Our Father, who art in heaven,
hallowed be thy name,
thy kingdom come,
thy will be done,
on earth as it is in heaven.
Give us this day our daily bread;
and forgive us our debts,
as we forgive our debtors;
and lead us not into temptation,
but deliver us from evil.
For thine is the kingdom,
and the power, and the glory,
   forever.   Amen.

Blessing

The leader says this blessing:

The Lord bless us,
defend us from all evil,
and bring us to everlasting life.

Amen.

An Outline of the Funeral:
A Service of Witness to the Resurrection

[Placing of the Pall]
Sentences of Scripture
Psalm, Hymn, or Spiritual
Prayer
[Confession and Pardon]
Readings from Scripture
Sermon
Affirmation of Faith
[Hymn]
Prayers of Thanksgiving, Supplication, and Intercession

———————— Or ————————

Psalm, Hymn, or Spiritual
Invitation to the Table
Great Thanksgiving
Lord's Prayer
Breaking of the Bread
Communion of the People

Lord's Prayer

Commendation
Blessing
Procession (Psalm, Hymn, or Biblical Song)

THE FUNERAL: A SERVICE OF WITNESS TO THE RESURRECTION

When death occurs, the pastor and other officers of the congregation should be informed as soon as possible, in order that they might provide appropriate consolation and support to the family and friends, and assist them in making arrangements for the funeral.

Except for compelling reasons, the service for a believing Christian is normally held in the church, at a time when the congregation can be present. When the deceased was not known to be a believer or had no connection with a church, then it is appropriate to hold the service elsewhere and to omit or adapt portions of it as seems fitting. The ceremonies and rites of fraternal, civic, or military organizations, if any, should occur at some other time and place.

Family members, friends, or members of the congregation may be invited by the minister to share in the service.

This order is intended for use with the body or ashes of the deceased present, but it may be adapted for use as a memorial service. The committal may follow or precede this service, as preferred.

When the body is present, the coffin should be closed before the service begins. It may be covered with a white funeral pall.

PLACING OF THE PALL

A pall may be placed over the coffin at the time the body is received at the entrance to the church, or, if there is to be a procession, immediately before the procession.

As the pall is placed over the coffin by the pallbearers, the minister says one of the following:

1   *Gal. 3:27*

For as many of you as were baptized into Christ
have clothed yourselves with Christ.

In *his/her* baptism N. was clothed with Christ;
in the day of Christ's coming,
he/she shall be clothed with glory.

2   *Rom. 6:3–5*

When we were baptized in Christ Jesus,
we were baptized into his death.
We were buried therefore with him by baptism into death,
so that, as Christ was raised from the dead by the glory of the Father,
we too might live a new life.
For if we have been united with Christ in a death like his,
we will certainly be united with him in a resurrection like his.

Appropriate music may be offered as the people gather.

All may stand as the minister(s) and other worship leaders enter.

If there is a procession into the place of worship, the minister leads it as the
congregation sings a psalm or a hymn. Or, the minister may say or sing one
or more of the sentences of scripture below, while leading the procession.

If the coffin or urn of ashes has already been brought in, the minister begins the service with one or more of the following, or similar sentences.

SENTENCES OF SCRIPTURE

1   *Ps. 124:8*

Our help is in the name of the Lord,
who made heaven and earth.

2   *Rom. 6:3–5*

When we were baptized in Christ Jesus,
we were baptized into his death.
We were buried therefore with him by baptism into death,
so that, as Christ was raised from the dead by the glory of the Father,
we too might live a new life.
For if we have been united with Christ in a death like his,
we will certainly be united with him in a resurrection like his.

3   *John 11:25–26*

I am the resurrection and the life, says the Lord.
Those who believe in me, even though they die,
 shall live,
and everyone who lives and believes in me will never die.

4   *Rev. 21:6; 22:13; 1:17–18; John 14:19*

I am the Alpha and the Omega,
the beginning and the end,
the first and the last.
I was dead and behold I am alive forever and ever;
and I have the keys of Death and Hades.
Because I live, you also will live.

5   *Matt. 11:28*

Come to me, all you that are weary
and are carrying heavy burdens,
 and I will give you rest.

6   *1 Peter 1:3–4*

Praise be to the God and Father of our Lord Jesus Christ,
whose great mercy gave us new birth into a living hope
by the resurrection of Jesus Christ from the dead!
The inheritance to which we are born
is one that nothing can destroy or spoil or wither.

7   *Ps. 46:1*

God is our refuge and strength,
a very present help in trouble.
Therefore we will not fear.

8   *John 14:27*

Peace I leave with you;
my peace I give to you.
I do not give to you as the world gives.
Do not let your hearts be troubled,
and do not let them be afraid.

9   *Ps. 103:13; Isa. 66:13*

As a father has compassion for his children,
so the Lord has compassion for those who fear God.
As a mother comforts her child,
so I will comfort you, says the Lord.

10　　　　　　　　　　　　　　　　　　　　　　　　　*Deut. 33:27*

The eternal God is your dwelling place,
and underneath are the everlasting arms.

11　　　　　　　　　　　　　　　　　　　　　　　*Rom. 8:38–39*

I am convinced that neither death, nor life,
nor angels, nor rulers,
nor things present, nor things to come,
nor powers, nor height, nor depth,
nor anything else in all creation,
will be able to separate us from the love of God
in Christ Jesus our Lord.

12　　　　　　　　　　　　　　　　　　　　　　　*Rev. 1:17–18*

Do not be afraid,
I am the first and the last,
and the living one;
I was dead, and behold, I am alive forever and ever.

13　　　　　　　　　　　　　　　　　　　　　　　　*Isa. 41:10*

Do not fear, for I am with you,
do not be afraid, for I am your God;
I will strengthen you, I will help you,
I will uphold you with my victorious right hand.

14　　　　　　　　　　　　　　　　　　　　　　　　*Matt. 5:4*

Blessed are those who mourn,
for they will be comforted.

15　　　　　　　　　　　　　　　　　　　　　　　*2 Cor. 1:3–4*

Praise be to the God and Father of our Lord Jesus Christ,
the Father of mercies and God of all comfort,
who comforts us in all our sorrows,
so that we can comfort others in their sorrow,
with the consolation we have received from God.

16　　　　　　　　　　　　　　　　　　*1 Thess. 4:14, 17–18*

We believe that Jesus died and rose again;
and so it will be for those who have died in Christ.
God will raise them to be with the Lord for ever.
Comfort one another with these words.

17   *Rom. 14:8*

   If we live, we live to the Lord;
   and if we die, we die to the Lord;
   so then, whether we live or whether we die,
   we are the Lord's.

18   *Rev. 14:13*

   Blessed are the dead who die in the Lord, says the Spirit.
   They will rest from their labors,
   and their deeds follow them.

19   *John 10:14; Isa. 40:11*

   Jesus said:
   I am the good shepherd.
   I know my own and my own know me.
   He will feed his flock like a shepherd;
   he will gather the lambs in his arms,
   and carry them in his bosom.

PSALM, HYMN, OR SPIRITUAL

   The congregation may sing a psalm, hymn of praise, or spiritual.

PRAYER

   The Lord be with you.

   And also with you.

   Let us pray.

   After a brief silence, one of the following, or a similar prayer, is said.

1

   Eternal God,
   maker of heaven and earth:
   You formed us from the dust of the earth,
   and by your breath you gave us life.
   We glorify you.

   Jesus Christ,
   the resurrection and the life:
   You tasted death for all humanity,
   and by rising from the grave
   you opened the way to eternal life.
   We praise you.

Holy Spirit,
author and giver of life:
You are the comforter of all who sorrow,
our sure confidence
and everlasting hope.
We worship you.

To you, O blessed Trinity,
be glory and honor, forever and ever.   [808]

Amen.

2

O God, who gave us birth,
you are ever more ready to hear than we are to pray.
You know our needs before we ask,
and our ignorance in asking.
Show us now your grace,
that as we face the mystery of death
we may see the light of eternity.

Speak to us once more your solemn message of life and of death.
Help us to live as those who are prepared to die.
And when our days here are ended,
enable us to die as those who go forth to live,
so that living or dying,
our life may be in Jesus Christ our risen Lord.   [809]

Amen.

3

Eternal God, we bless you for the great company
of all those who have kept the faith,
finished their race,
and who now rest from their labor.
We praise you for those dear to us
whom we name in our hearts before you. . . .
Especially we thank you for N.,
whom you have now received into your presence.

Help us to believe where we have not seen,
trusting you to lead us through our years.
Bring us at last with all your saints
into the joy of your home,
through Jesus Christ our Lord.   [810]

Amen.

4

Eternal God,
we acknowledge the uncertainty of our life on earth.
We are given a mere handful of days,
and our span of life seems nothing in your sight.
All flesh is as grass;
and all its beauty is like the flower of the field.
The grass withers, the flower fades;
but your word will stand forever.
In this is our hope,
for you are our God.
Even in the valley of the shadow of death,
you are with us.

O Lord, let us know our end
and the number of our days,
that we may learn how fleeting life is.
Turn your ear to our cry, and hear our prayer.
Do not be silent at our tears,
for we live as strangers before you,
wandering pilgrims as all our ancestors were.
But you are the same
and your years shall have no end.   [811]

Amen.

CONFESSION AND PARDON

A prayer of confession may also be said.

CALL TO CONFESSION

The minister says:

Let us now ask God to cleanse our hearts,
to redeem our memories,
and to renew our confidence in the goodness of God.

All confess their sin, using the following prayer:

**Holy God, you see us as we are,
and know our inmost thoughts.
We confess that we are unworthy of your gracious care.
We forget that all life comes from you
and that to you all life returns.
We have not always sought or done your will.**

We have not lived as your grateful children,
nor loved as Christ loved us.
Apart from you, we are nothing.
Only your grace can sustain us.

Lord, in your mercy, forgive us,
heal us and make us whole.
Set us free from our sin,
and restore to us the joy of your salvation
now and forever.   [812]

Silent prayer may follow.

DECLARATION OF FORGIVENESS

The minister declares the assurance of God's forgiving grace:

1   *Rom. 8:34; 2 Cor. 5:17*

Hear the good news!
Who is in a position to condemn?
Only Christ,
and Christ died for us,
Christ rose for us,
Christ reigns in power for us,
Christ prays for us.

Anyone who is in Christ
is a new creation.
The old life has gone;
a new life has begun.

Know that you are forgiven
and be at peace.

Amen.

2

The mercy of the Lord
is from everlasting to everlasting.
I declare to you, in the name of Jesus Christ,
you are forgiven.

May the God of mercy,
who forgives you all your sins,
strengthen you in all goodness,
and by the power of the Holy Spirit
keep you in eternal life.

Amen.

Before the readings, the people may sing a thankful response to the
mercy of God.

The people may be seated.

READINGS FROM SCRIPTURE

Before the readings, one of the following, or another prayer for illumination (pp. 60, 90–91), may be said by the reader:

1

Source of all true wisdom,
calm the troubled waters of our hearts,
and still all other voices but your own,
that we may hear and obey
what you tell us in your Word,
through the power of your Spirit.   [813]

Amen.

2

Eternal God,
Your love for us is everlasting;
you alone can turn the shadow of death
into the brightness of the morning light.
Help us to turn to you with believing hearts.
In the stillness of this hour,
speak to us of eternal things,
so that, hearing the promises in scripture,
we may have hope and be lifted above our distress
into the peace of your presence;
through Jesus Christ our Lord.   [814]

Amen.

One or more selections from scripture are read.

It is appropriate that there be readings from both the Old and New Testaments (pp. 947–963) and that they include a reading from the Gospels. A psalm (pp. 948, 954–958, 611–783) or a canticle (pp. 573–591) may be sung or read between the readings.

SERMON

After the scriptures are read, their message may be proclaimed in a brief sermon. Expressions of gratitude to God for the life of the deceased may follow.

AFFIRMATION OF FAITH

The congregation may stand and say or sing the Apostles' Creed (which follows). Or the congregation may sing "We Praise You, O God" (p. 577; PH 460; PS 170, 171) instead of or following the creed. Or another affirmation of faith (number 2 on page 96, or number 5 on page 98) may be said:

Let us confess the faith of our baptism, as we say:

**I believe in God, the Father almighty,
creator of heaven and earth.**

**I believe in Jesus Christ, God's only Son, our Lord,
who was conceived by the Holy Spirit,
born of the Virgin Mary,
suffered under Pontius Pilate,
was crucified, died, and was buried;
he descended to the dead.
On the third day he rose again;
he ascended into heaven,
he is seated at the right hand of the Father,
and he will come again to judge the living and the dead.**

**I believe in the Holy Spirit,
the holy catholic church,
the communion of saints,
the forgiveness of sins,
the resurrection of the body,
and the life everlasting.   Amen.**

[HYMN]

A hymn of confident faith may be sung by the congregation.

Prayers of Thanksgiving, Supplication, and Intercession

> One of the following, or a similar prayer, is offered. Additional prayers
> may be found on pages 907–908.

1

O God of grace,
you have given us new and living hope in Jesus Christ.
We thank you that by dying
Christ destroyed the power of death,
and by rising from the grave
opened the way to eternal life.

Help us to know that because he lives,
we shall live also;
and that neither death nor life,
nor things present nor things to come
shall be able to separate us from your love
in Christ Jesus our Lord.   [815]

Amen.

2

O God,
before whom generations rise and pass away,
we praise you for all your servants
who, having lived this life in faith,
now live eternally with you.

Especially we thank you for your servant N.,
whose baptism is now complete in death.
We praise you for the gift of *his/her* life,
for all in *him/her* that was good and kind and faithful,
for the grace you gave *him/her*,
that kindled in *him/her* the love of your dear name,
and enabled *him/her* to serve you faithfully.

> Here mention may be made of the person's characteristics or service.

We thank you that for *him/her* death is past and pain ended,
and that *he/she* has now entered the joy you have prepared;
through Jesus Christ our Lord.   [816]

Amen.

3

Almighty God,
in Jesus Christ you promised many rooms within your house.
Give us faith to see, beyond touch and sight,
some sure sign of your kingdom,
and, where vision fails,
to trust your love which never fails.
Lift heavy sorrow
and give us good hope in Jesus,
so we may bravely walk our earthly way,
and look forward to glad reunion in the life to come,
through Jesus Christ our Lord.   [817]

Amen.

4

For our *brother/sister* N.,
let us pray to our Lord Jesus Christ
who said, "I am the resurrection and the life."
Lord, you consoled Martha and Mary in their distress;
draw near to us who mourn for N.,
and dry the tears of those who weep.

Hear us, Lord.

You wept at the grave of Lazarus, your friend;
comfort us in our sorrow.

Hear us, Lord.

You raised the dead to life;
give to our *brother/sister* eternal life.

Hear us, Lord.

You promised paradise to the repentant thief;
bring N. to the joys of heaven.

Hear us, Lord.

Our *brother/sister* was washed in baptism
and anointed with the Holy Spirit;
give *him/her* fellowship with all your saints.

Hear us, Lord.

He/she was nourished at your table on earth;
welcome *him/her* at your table in the heavenly kingdom.

Hear us, Lord.

Comfort us in our sorrows at the death of N.;
let our faith be our consolation,
and eternal life our hope.   [818]

Amen.

5

At the death of a child:

Loving God,
you are nearest to us when we need you most.
In this hour of sorrow we turn to you,
trusting in your loving mercy.

We bless you for the gift of this child
for *his/her* baptism into your church,
for the joy *he/she* gave all who knew *him/her*
for the precious memories that will abide with us,
and for the assurance that *he/she* lives forever
in the joy and peace of your presence.   [819]

Amen.

6

At the death of a child:

O God,
your love cares for us in life
and watches over us in death.
We bless you for our Savior's joy in little children
and for the assurance that of such is the kingdom of heaven.
In our sorrow,
make us strong to commit ourselves, and those we love,
to your unfailing care.
In our perplexity,
help us to trust where we cannot understand.
In our loneliness,
may we remember N. in love,
trusting *her/him* to your keeping
until the eternal morning breaks;
through Jesus Christ our Lord.   [820]

Amen.

After a sudden death:

God of compassion,
comfort us with the great power of your love
as we mourn the sudden death of N.
In our grief and confusion,
help us find peace
in the knowledge of your loving mercy to all your children,
and give us light to guide us
into the assurance of your love;
through Jesus Christ our Lord.   [821]

Amen.

Silence may be observed for reflection and prayer.

WHEN THE LORD'S SUPPER IS CELEBRATED, THE SERVICE
CONTINUES ON PAGE 928.

LORD'S PRAYER

If the Lord's Supper is not celebrated, the prayers conclude with the
Lord's Prayer.

The minister invites all present to sing or say the Lord's Prayer.

And now, with the confidence of the children of God,
let us pray:

All pray together.

Or

Our Father in heaven,	**Our Father, who art in heaven,**
hallowed be your name,	**hallowed be thy name,**
your kingdom come,	**thy kingdom come,**
your will be done,	**thy will be done,**
on earth as in heaven.	**on earth as it is in heaven.**
Give us today our daily bread.	**Give us this day our daily bread;**
Forgive us our sins	**and forgive us our debts,**
as we forgive those who sin against us.	**as we forgive our debtors;**
Save us from the time of trial	**and lead us not into temptation,**
and deliver us from evil.	**but deliver us from evil.**
For the kingdom, the power,	**For thine is the kingdom,**
and the glory are yours	**and the power, and the glory,**
now and forever. Amen.	**forever. Amen.**

COMMENDATION

The people may sing a hymn, or the following may be sung:

You only are immortal, the creator and maker of all.
We are mortal, formed of the earth,
and to earth shall we return.
This you ordained when you created us, saying,
"You are dust,
and to dust you shall return."
All of us go down to the dust;
yet even at the grave we make our song:
Alleluia, alleluia, alleluia.

Give rest, O Christ, to your servant with all your saints,
where there is neither pain nor sorrow nor sighing,
but life everlasting.

The people may stand.

The minister, facing the body, says one of the following:

1

Into your hands, O merciful Savior,
we commend your servant N.
Acknowledge, we humbly pray,
a sheep of your own fold,
a lamb of your own flock,
a sinner of your own redeeming.
Receive *him/her* into the arms of your mercy,
into the blessed rest of everlasting peace,
and into the glorious company of the saints in light. [822]

Amen.

2

Holy God,
by your creative power you gave us life,
and in your redeeming love you have given us new life in Christ.
We commend N. to your merciful care
in the faith of Christ our Lord
who died and rose again to save us,
and who now lives and reigns with you and the Holy Spirit,
one God, now and forever. [823]

Amen.

BLESSING

The minister may then pronounce God's blessing on the people, using one of the following:

1   *Heb. 13:20, 21*

The God of peace,
who brought back from the dead our Lord Jesus,
make you complete in everything good
so that you may do God's will,
working among us that which is pleasing in God's sight,
through Jesus Christ,
to whom be the glory forever and ever!

2   *See Phil. 4:7*

The peace of God,
which passes all understanding,
keep your hearts and minds
in the knowledge and love of God,
and of God's Son, Jesus Christ our Lord;
and the blessing of God almighty,
the Father, the Son, and the Holy Spirit,
remain with you always.

Amen.

3

May God in endless mercy
bring the whole church,
the living and departed,
to a joyful resurrection
in the fulfillment of the eternal kingdom.

Amen.

PROCESSION

The procession forms and leaves the church, the minister preceding the coffin. As the procession leaves the church, a psalm, a hymn, or this canticle may be sung or said. The pall may be removed before the coffin leaves the church and is taken to the place of interment.

Luke 2:29–32
PH 603–605; PS 164–166

Now, Lord, you let your servant go in peace:
your word has been fulfilled.
My own eyes have seen the salvation
which you have prepared in the sight of every people:
a light to reveal you to the nations
and the glory of your people Israel.

Glory to the Father, and to the Son,
and to the Holy Spirit,
as it was in the beginning,
is now, and will be forever.   **Amen.**

WHEN THE LORD'S SUPPER IS CELEBRATED, THE SERVICE
CONTINUES HERE FROM PAGE 924.

PSALM, HYMN, OR SPIRITUAL

A psalm, hymn, or spiritual may be sung as the table is prepared.

The bread and wine may be brought to the table or uncovered if already in
place.

INVITATION TO THE LORD'S TABLE

Standing at the table, the presiding minister invites the people to the
Sacrament, using one of the following or another invitation to the Lord's
table (pp. 68, 125). If B is used, the words of institution are not included in
the great thanksgiving, or at the breaking of the bread.

A   *Matt. 11:28, 29; John 6:35; Matt. 5:6*

Jesus said:
Come to me,
all you that are weary and are carrying heavy burdens,
and I will give you rest.
Take my yoke upon you, and learn from me;
for I am gentle and humble in heart,
and you will find rest for your souls.

I am the bread of life.
Whoever comes to me will never be hungry,
and whoever believes in me will never be thirsty.

Blessed are those who hunger and thirst for righteousness,
for they will be filled.

B   *See 1 Cor. 11:23–26; Luke 22:19–20*

Hear the words of the institution
of the Holy Supper of our Lord Jesus Christ:

The Lord Jesus, on the night of his arrest, took bread,
and after giving thanks to God,
he broke it, and gave it to his disciples, saying:
Take, eat.
This is my body, given for you.
Do this in remembrance of me.

In the same way he took the cup, saying:
This cup is the new covenant sealed in my blood,
shed for you for the forgiveness of sins.
Whenever you drink it,
do this in remembrance of me.

Every time you eat this bread and drink this cup,
you proclaim the saving death of the risen Lord,
until he comes.

With thanksgiving,
let us offer God our grateful praise.

GREAT THANKSGIVING

All may stand.

The minister leads the people in the following or another great thanksgiving (pp. 69–73, 126–156, 387–390):

The Lord be with you.

And also with you.

Lift up your hearts.

We lift them to the Lord.

Let us give thanks to the Lord our God.

It is right to give our thanks and praise.

It is truly right and our greatest joy
to give you thanks and praise,
O holy Father, God of all the ages.
You are the source of life,
creating all things in your wisdom,
and sustaining them by your power.
You made us in your image,
forming us from the dust of the earth,
and breathing into us the breath of life.
You made us to know you,
to love and serve you;
but we rebelled against you,
seeking to be our own god.
In your mercy, you did not forsake us.
You made a covenant with us,
claiming us as your people,
and promising faithfulness as our God.
Through the prophets you called us to return to your ways.

Out of your great love for the world,
you gave your only Son to redeem us,
and opened the way to eternal life.
He formed for himself a new people
born of water and the Spirit.
In ways beyond number you have shown us your mercy.

Therefore we praise you,
joining our voices with the heavenly choirs
and with all the faithful of every time and place,
who forever sing to the glory of your name:

> The people may sing or say:

**Holy, holy, holy Lord, God of power and might,
heaven and earth are full of your glory.
Hosanna in the highest.**

**Blessed is he who comes in the name of the Lord.
Hosanna in the highest.**

> The minister continues:

You are holy, O God of majesty,
and blessed is Jesus Christ, your Son, our Lord.
He lived as one of us,
knew our joy, our pain and sorrow,
and died our death.
By his death on the cross
you revealed that your love has no limit.
By raising him from death
you conquered the last enemy,
crushed all evil powers,
and gave new life to the world.
In his victory
you comfort us with the hope of eternal life,
and assure us that neither death nor life,
nor things present nor things to come,
can separate us from your love in Christ Jesus our Lord.

Risen and ascended, Christ is alive forevermore,
and by the power of the Holy Spirit is with us always.
Reigning with you in glory,
Christ intercedes for us,
our high priest and our advocate.

If they have not already been said, the words of institution may be said here, or in relation to the breaking of the bread.

We give you thanks that the Lord Jesus,
on the night before he died,
took bread,
and after giving thanks to you,
he broke it, and gave it to his disciples, saying:
Take, eat.
This is my body, given for you.
Do this in remembrance of me.

In the same way he took the cup, saying:
This cup is the new covenant sealed in my blood,
shed for you for the forgiveness of sins.
Whenever you drink it,
do this in remembrance of me.

Remembering your gracious acts in Jesus Christ,
we take from your creation this bread and this wine
and joyfully celebrate his death and resurrection,
as we await the day of his coming.
With thanksgiving, we offer our very selves to you
to be a living and holy sacrifice,
dedicated to your service.

The people may sing or say one of the following:

1

Great is the mystery of faith:

**Christ has died,
Christ is risen,
Christ will come again.**

2

Praise to you, Lord Jesus:

**Dying you destroyed our death,
rising, you restored our life.
Lord Jesus, come in glory.**

3

According to his commandment:

**We remember his death,
we proclaim his resurrection,
we await his coming in glory.**

4

Christ is the bread of life:

**When we eat this bread and drink this cup,
we proclaim your death, Lord Jesus,
until you come in glory.**

The minister continues:

Gracious God,
pour out your Holy Spirit upon us,
and upon these your gifts of bread and wine,
that the bread we break and the cup we bless
may be the communion of the body and blood of Christ.
By your Spirit unite us with the living Christ
and with all who are baptized in his name,
that we may be one in ministry in every place.

Remember our *brother/sister* N.,
whose baptism is now complete in death.
Bring *him/her*, and all who have died in the peace of Christ,
into your eternal joy and light.

Strengthen us to run with determination
the race that lies before us,
our eyes fixed on Jesus
on whom our faith depends,
so that when this mortal life is ended,
we may receive, with all your saints,
the unfading crown of glory.
Give us strength to serve you faithfully
until the promised day of resurrection,
when with the redeemed of all the ages
we will feast with you at your table in glory.

Through Christ, with Christ, in Christ,
in the unity of the Holy Spirit,
all glory and honor are yours, almighty God,
now and forever.   [824]

Amen.

LORD'S PRAYER

The minister invites all present to sing or say the Lord's Prayer.

And now, with the confidence of the children of God,
let us pray:

All pray together.

Or

Our Father in heaven,	**Our Father, who art in heaven,**
hallowed be your name,	**hallowed be thy name,**
your kingdom come,	**thy kingdom come,**
your will be done,	**thy will be done,**
on earth as in heaven.	**on earth as it is in heaven.**
Give us today our daily bread.	**Give us this day our daily bread;**
Forgive us our sins	**and forgive us our debts,**
as we forgive those who sin against us.	**as we forgive our debtors;**
Save us from the time of trial	**and lead us not into temptation,**
and deliver us from evil.	**but deliver us from evil.**
For the kingdom, the power,	**For thine is the kingdom,**
** and the glory are yours**	**and the power, and the glory,**
now and forever. Amen.	**forever. Amen.**

The people may be seated.

BREAKING OF THE BREAD

If the words of institution have not previously been said, the minister
breaks the bread, using A.

If the words of institution were said in the invitation to the Lord's table, or
were included in the great thanksgiving, the minister breaks the bread,
using B. Or the bread may be broken in silence.

A   *1 Cor. 11:23–26; Luke 22:19–20*

The minister breaks the bread in full view of the people, saying:

The Lord Jesus, on the night of his arrest, took bread,
and after giving thanks to God,
he broke it, and gave it to his disciples, saying:
Take, eat.
This is my body, given for you.
Do this in remembrance of me.

The minister lifts the cup, saying:

In the same way he took the cup, saying:
This cup is the new covenant sealed in my blood,
shed for you for the forgiveness of sins.
Whenever you drink it,
do this in remembrance of me.

Every time you eat this bread and drink this cup,
you proclaim the saving death of the risen Lord,
until he comes.

B   *1 Cor. 10:16–17*

Because there is one loaf,
we, many as we are, are one body;
for it is one loaf of which we all partake.

The minister takes the loaf and breaks it in full view of the congregation.

When we break the bread,
is it not a sharing in the body of Christ?

Having filled the cup, the minister lifts it in the view of the people.

When we give thanks over the cup,
is it not a sharing in the blood of Christ?

COMMUNION OF THE PEOPLE

INVITATION

Then, holding out both the bread and the cup to the people, the minister
says:

The gifts of God
for the people of God.

COMMUNION

The minister and those assisting receive Communion, and then serve the
bread and the cup to the people.

In giving the bread:

The body of Christ, given for you.   **Amen.**

In giving the cup:

The blood of Christ, shed for you.   **Amen.**

During Communion, the Agnus Dei ("Jesus, Lamb of God"), which follows, or psalms, hymns, or spirituals may be sung, or silence kept.

**Jesus, Lamb of God,
have mercy on us.**

**Jesus, bearer of our sins,
have mercy on us.**

**Jesus, redeemer of the world,
grant us peace.**

Or

**Lamb of God, you take away the sin of the world,
have mercy on us.**

**Lamb of God, you take away the sin of the world,
have mercy on us.**

**Lamb of God, you take away the sin of the world,
grant us peace.**

After all have been served, the following prayer may be said by the minister, or by all together.

Almighty God,
we thank you that in your great love
you have fed us with the spiritual food and drink
of the body and blood of your Son Jesus Christ,
and have given us a foretaste of the heavenly banquet.
Grant that this Sacrament may be to us
a comfort in affliction,
and a pledge of our inheritance
in that kingdom where there is no death,
neither sorrow nor crying,
but the fullness of joy with all your saints;
through Jesus Christ our Savior.   [825]

Amen.

COMMENDATION

The people may sing a hymn, or the following may be sung:

You only are immortal, the creator and maker of all.
We are mortal, formed of the earth,
and to earth shall we return.
This you ordained when you created us, saying,
"You are dust,
and to dust you shall return."
All of us go down to the dust;
yet even at the grave we make our song:
Alleluia, alleluia, alleluia.
Give rest, O Christ, to your servant with all your saints,
where there is neither pain nor sorrow nor sighing,
but life everlasting.

The people may stand.

The minister, facing the body, says one of the following:

1

Into your hands, O merciful Savior,
we commend your servant N.
Acknowledge, we humbly pray,
a sheep of your own fold,
a lamb of your own flock,
a sinner of your own redeeming.
Receive *him/her* into the arms of your mercy,
into the blessed rest of everlasting peace,
and into the glorious company of the saints in light.   [822]

Amen.

2

Holy God,
by your creative power you gave us life,
and in your redeeming love you have given us new life in Christ.
We commend N. to your merciful care
in the faith of Christ our Lord
who died and rose again to save us,
and who now lives and reigns with you and the Holy Spirit,
one God, now and forever.   [823]

Amen.

BLESSING

The minister may then pronounce God's blessing upon the people, using one of the following:

1   *Heb. 13:20, 21*

The God of peace,
who brought back from the dead our Lord Jesus,
make you complete in everything good
so that you may do God's will,
working among us that which is pleasing in God's sight,
through Jesus Christ,
to whom be the glory forever and ever!

2   *See Phil. 4:7*

The peace of God,
which passes all understanding,
keep your hearts and minds
in the knowledge and love of God,
and of God's Son, Jesus Christ our Lord;
and the blessing of God almighty,
the Father, the Son, and the Holy Spirit,
remain with you always.

Amen.

3

May God in endless mercy
bring the whole church,
the living and departed,
to a joyful resurrection
in the fulfillment of the eternal kingdom.

Amen.

PROCESSION

The procession forms and leaves the church, the minister preceding the coffin. As the procession leaves the church, a psalm, a hymn, or this canticle may be sung or said. The pall may be removed before the coffin leaves the church and is taken to the place of interment.

Now, Lord, you let your servant go in peace:
your word has been fulfilled.
My own eyes have seen the salvation
which you have prepared in the sight of every people:
a light to reveal you to the nations
and the glory of your people Israel.

Glory to the Father, and to the Son,
and to the Holy Spirit,
as it was in the beginning,
is now, and will be forever.   Amen.

The Committal

If preferred, the committal service may take place before the general service. In either case, the minister precedes the body (or ashes) to the appointed place, saying one or more of the following sentences:

SCRIPTURE SENTENCES

1   *Job 19:25*

I know that my Redeemer lives,
and that at the last he will stand upon the earth.

2   *John 11:25–26*

I am the resurrection and the life, says the Lord.
Those who believe in me, even though they die,
shall live,
and everyone who lives and believes in me will never die.

3   *2 Cor. 5:1*

We know that if the earthly tent we live in is destroyed,
we have a building from God,
a house not made with hands,
eternal in the heavens.

4   *Rev. 1:17–18; John 14:19*

Do not be afraid,
I am the first and the last,
and the living one.
I was dead, and behold,
I am alive for forever and ever.
Because I live, you also will live.

5

    If we live, we live to the Lord,
    and if we die, we die to the Lord;
    so then, whether we live or whether we die,
    we are the Lord's.

6
                                                   Ps. 16:11

    You show me the path of life;
    in your presence there is fullness of joy;
    in your right hand are pleasures forevermore.

7
                                                 John 6:68

    Lord, to whom shall we go?
    You have the words of eternal life.

8

    Christ is risen from the dead,
    trampling down death by death,
    and giving life to those in the tomb.

> When there is no other service than the committal service, a prayer (such as those on pp. 915–917, 921–924) may be said after the people have gathered.

COMMITTAL

Earth burial

> The coffin is lowered into the grave or placed in its resting place. While earth is cast on the coffin, the minister says:

In sure and certain hope of the resurrection to eternal life,
through our Lord Jesus Christ,
we commend to almighty God our *brother/sister* N.,
and we commit *his/her* body to the ground,
earth to earth, ashes to ashes, dust to dust.

Rev. 14:13

Blessed are the dead who die in the Lord, says the Spirit.
They rest from their labors,
and their works follow them.

Burial at sea

> As the body is lowered into the water, the minister says:

In sure and certain hope of the resurrection to eternal life,
through our Lord Jesus Christ,

we commend to almighty God our *brother/sister* N.,
and we commit *his/her* body to the deep.

Rev. 14:13

Blessed are the dead who die in the Lord, says the Spirit.
They rest from their labors,
and their works follow them.

At a cremation service

> As the body is placed in the crematory, the minister says:

In sure and certain hope of the resurrection to eternal life,
through our Lord Jesus Christ,
we commend to almighty God our *brother/sister* N.,
and we commit *his/her* body to be returned to its elements,
ashes to ashes, dust to dust.

Rev. 14:13

Blessed are the dead who die in the Lord, says the Spirit.
They rest from their labors,
and their works follow them.

At a columbarium

> As the ashes are placed in their resting place, the minister says:

In sure and certain hope of the resurrection to eternal life,
through our Lord Jesus Christ,
we commend to almighty God our *brother/sister* N.,
and we commit *his/her* ashes to their final resting place.

Rev. 14:13

Blessed are the dead who die in the Lord, says the Spirit.
They rest from their labors,
and their works follow them.

LORD'S PRAYER

> The Lord's Prayer may be said.

> The minister says:

And now, with the confidence of the children of God,
let us pray:

All pray together:

Or

Our Father in heaven,	Our Father, who art in heaven,

Our Father in heaven,
hallowed be your name,
your kingdom come,
your will be done,
on earth as in heaven.
Give us today our daily bread.
Forgive us our sins
as we forgive those who sin against us.
Save us from the time of trial
and deliver us from evil.
For the kingdom, the power,
  and the glory are yours
now and forever.   Amen.

Our Father, who art in heaven,
hallowed be thy name,
thy kingdom come,
thy will be done,
on earth as it is in heaven.
Give us this day our daily bread;
and forgive us our debts,
as we forgive our debtors;
and lead us not into temptation,
but deliver us from evil.
For thine is the kingdom,
and the power, and the glory,
  forever.   Amen.

PRAYERS

The minister says one or more of the following, or other appropriate prayers:

1

O Lord, support us all the day long
until the shadows lengthen
and the evening comes
and the busy world is hushed,
and the fever of life is over,
and our work is done.
Then, in your mercy,
grant us a safe lodging,
and a holy rest,
and peace at the last;
through Jesus Christ our Lord.   [504]

Amen.

2

O God,
you have designed this world,
and know all things good for us.
Give us such faith
that, by day and by night,

in all times and in all places,
we may without fear
entrust those who are dear to us
to your never-failing love,
in this life and in the life to come;
through Jesus Christ our Lord. [826]

Amen.

3

God of all mercies
and giver of all comfort:
Look graciously, we pray, on those who mourn,
that, casting all their care on you,
they may know the consolation of your love;
through Jesus Christ our Lord. [827]

Amen.

4

Almighty God,
Father of the whole family in heaven and on earth:
Stand by those who sorrow,
that, as they lean on your strength,
they may be upheld,
and believe the good news of life beyond life;
through Jesus Christ our Lord. [828]

Amen.

5

God of boundless compassion,
our only sure comfort in distress:
Look tenderly upon your children
overwhelmed by loss and sorrow.
Lighten our darkness with your presence
and assure us of your love.
Enable us to see beyond this place and time
to your eternal kingdom,
promised to all who love you in Christ the Lord. [829]

Amen.

6

Merciful God,
you heal the broken in heart
and bind up the wounds of the afflicted.
Strengthen us in our weakness,
calm our troubled spirits,
and dispel our doubts and fears.
In Christ's rising from the dead
you conquered death and opened the gates to everlasting life.
Renew our trust in you
that by the power of your love
we shall one day be brought together again
with our *brother/sister*.
Grant this, we pray, through Jesus Christ our Lord.   [830]

Amen.

7

God of all consolation,
our refuge and strength in sorrow,
by dying, our Lord Jesus Christ conquered death;
by rising from the grave he restored us to life.
Enable us to go forward in faith to meet him,
that, when our life on earth is ended,
we may be united with all who love him
in your heavenly kingdom,
where every tear will be wiped away;
through Jesus Christ our Lord.   [831]

Amen.

8

Gracious God,
your mercies are beyond number.
Lead us, by your Spirit,
in holiness and righteousness,
in confidence of a living faith,
and in the strength of a sure hope,
that we may live in favor with you,
and in perfect love with all;
through Jesus Christ our Lord.   [832]

Amen.

9

God, whose days are without end:
Help us always to remember how brief life is,
and that the hour of our death is known only to you.
Lead us, by your Holy Spirit,
to live in holiness and justice all our days.
Then after serving you in the fellowship of your church,
in faith, hope, and love,
may we enter with joy into the fullness of your kingdom,
through Jesus Christ our Lord.   [833]

Amen.

10

Rest eternal grant *him/her*, O Lord;
and let light perpetual shine upon *him/her*.   [834]

11

At the committal of a child

Loving God,
your beloved Son took children into his arms and blessed them.
Give us grace
that we may entrust N. to your never-failing care and love,
and bring us all to your heavenly kingdom;
through Jesus Christ our Lord.   [806]

Amen.

12

At the committal of a child

Loving God,
give us faith to believe,
though this child has died,
that you welcome *him/her*
and will care for *him/her*,
until, by your mercy,
we are together again in the joy of your promised kingdom;
through Jesus Christ our Lord.   [835]

Amen.

Blessing

The minister dismisses the people with one of the following blessings.

1   *2 Cor. 13:14*

The grace of the Lord Jesus Christ,
the love of God,
and the communion of the Holy Spirit
be with you all.

Amen.

2   *See Num 6:24–26*

The Lord bless you and keep you.
The Lord be kind and gracious to you.
The Lord look upon you with favor
and give you peace.

Amen.

3   *See Phil. 4:7*

The peace of God,
which passes all understanding,
keep your hearts and minds
in the knowledge and love of God,
and of God's Son, Jesus Christ our Lord;
and the blessing of God almighty,
the Father, the Son, and the Holy Spirit,
remain with you always.

Amen.

4   *Heb. 13:20, 21*

Go in peace,
and may the God of peace,
who brought back from the dead our Lord Jesus,
make you complete in everything good
so that you may do God's will,
working among us that which is pleasing in God's sight,
through Jesus Christ,
to whom be the glory forever and ever!

Amen.

Scripture Readings for Services on Occasions of Death

The following readings are particularly appropriate for use in the funeral service, and in ministry with the dying and bereaved. An asterisk * indicates that the text of that particular reading is included in this resource (pp. 951–963).

List of Suggested Readings

OLD TESTAMENT

* Job 19:23–27	I know that my redeemer lives
Isa. 25:6–9	God will swallow up death forever
Isa. 26:1–4, 19	God will keep them in peace
* Isa. 40:1–11, 28–31	Comfort my people
* Isa. 40:28–31	Those who wait for the Lord shall renew their strength
Isa. 43:1–3a, 18–19, 25	When you pass through the waters, I will be with you
Isa. 44:6–8	I am the first and the last
Isa. 55:1–3, 6–13	Ho, everyone who thirsts
Isa. 61:1–4, 10–11	The spirit of the Lord is upon me
* Isa. 65:17–25	I create new heavens and a new earth
Lam. 3:19–26, 31b–32	The Lord's steadfast love
Dan. 12:1–3	Many of those who sleep in the dust shall awake
Joel 2:12–13, 23–24, 26–29	Return to the Lord with all your heart

Some have found this passage from an Apocryphal book useful in certain circumstances:

Wisdom of Solomon
   3:1–7, 9; 5:15–16   The souls of the righteous are in the hand of God

   At the loss of a child:

Zech. 8:1–8   Children playing in the streets of the city
* Isa. 65:17–25   I create new heavens and a new earth

   For those whose faith is unknown:

* Eccl. 3:1–15   For everything there is a season
Lam. 3:1–9, 19–23   The Lord's steadfast love

PSALMS

The following psalms are appropriate for singing or reading in the service. For another translation of the psalms see pages 611–783.

Ps. 16:5–11	The Lord is my chosen portion
* Ps. 23	The Lord is my shepherd
Ps. 27:1, 4–9a, 13–14	The Lord is my light and my salvation
Ps. 39: 4–5, 12	Lord, let me know my end
Ps. 42:1–6a	As a deer longs for flowing streams
Ps. 43	Give judgment for me, O God
* Ps. 46:1–5, 10–11	A very present help in trouble
* Ps. 90:1–10, 12	Teach us to number our days
Ps. 91	The one who dwells in the shelter of the Most High
* Ps. 103	Bless the Lord, O my soul
Ps. 106:1–5	O give thanks to the Lord
Ps. 116:1–9, 15	The Lord has heard my voice
Ps. 118	Open the gates of righteousness
* Ps. 121	I lift up my eyes to the hills
* Ps. 130	Out of the depths I cry to the Lord
* Ps. 139:1–12	Where shall I go from your spirit?
Ps. 145	I will extol you, O God my King
Ps. 146	Hallelujah! praise the Lord, O my soul

EPISTLES

Rom. 5:1–11	Hope does not disappoint
Rom. 6:3–9	Baptized into Christ's death, raised to live with him
* Rom. 8:14–23, 31–39	Nothing can separate us from the love of God
* Rom. 14:7–9, 10b–12	Whether we live or die, we are the Lord's
1 Cor. 15:3–8, 12–20a	Christ raised from the dead
1 Cor. 15:20–24a	In Christ shall all be made alive

* 1 Cor. 15:20–26,
   35–38, 42–44,
   50, 53–58
	Death is swallowed in victory

1 Cor. 15:35–44	The natural body and the spiritual body
1 Cor. 15:50–57	We shall all be changed
* 2 Cor. 4:16–5:1	Visible things are temporary, invisible things eternal
2 Cor. 5:1–10	From God we have a house not made with hands
Eph. 1:11–2:1, 4–10	Saved by grace through faith
Phil. 3:7–11	Knowing him and the power of his resurrection
Phil. 3:20–21	Our citizenship is in heaven
Col. 3:1–17	Set your minds on the things that are above
* 1 Thess. 4:13–18	The comfort of Christ's coming
2 Tim. 2:8–13	If we died with him, we shall also live with him
Heb. 2:14–18	Christ was tested in every way
Heb. 11:1–3, 13–16; 12:1–2	Faith, the pilgrimage, the cloud of witnesses
1 Peter 1:3–9	Without seeing Christ, you love him
1 Peter 3:18–22; 4:6	Christ's ministry to the spirits in prison
1 John 3:1–3	We are children of God
Rev. 7:2–3, 9–17	These are they who have come out of the great tribula-tion
Rev. 14:1–3, 6–7, 12–13	Rest for the saints
* Rev. 21:1–4, 22–25; 22:3–5	A new heaven and a new earth
Rev. 22:1–5	The Lord God will be their light

For those whose faith is unknown:

Rom. 2:12–16	The law written on the heart
* Rom. 14:7–9, 10c–12	None of us live to ourselves

GOSPELS

Matt. 5:1–12a	The Beatitudes
Matt. 11:25–30	Hidden from the wise, revealed to infants
Matt. 25:1–13	Wise and foolish bridesmaids
Matt. 25:31–46	The Last Judgment
Luke 7:11–17	Jesus raises the son of the widow of Nain
Luke 18:15–17	We enter the kingdom only as children
*Luke 23:33, 39–43	Today you will be with me in Paradise
John 3:16–21	God so loved the world
John 5:24–29	Whoever hears and believes has eternal life
John 6:37–40	Anyone who comes to me I will never drive away
John 6:47–58	Whoever believes in me has eternal life
*John 11:17–27	I am the resurrection and the life
John 11:38–44	Lazarus raised from the dead
*John 14:1–6, 25–27	Let not your hearts be troubled

At the loss of a child:

*Matt. 18:1–5, 10	The greatest in the kingdom of heaven
*Mark 10:13–16	Let the children come to me

For those whose faith is unknown:

Matt. 25:31–46	As you did it to one of the least of these

Scripture Readings

All readings are from the New Revised Standard Version of the Bible.

Old Testament

1   *Job 19:23–27*

O that my words were written down!
> O that they were inscribed in a book!
O that with an iron pen and with lead
> they were engraved on a rock forever!
For I know that my Redeemer lives,
> and that at the last he will stand upon the earth;
and after my skin has been thus destroyed,
> then in my flesh I shall see God,
whom I shall see on my side,
> and my eyes shall behold, and not another.
> My heart faints within me!

2   *Ecclesiastes 3:1–15*

For everything there is a season, and a time for every matter under heaven:

> a time to be born, and a time to die;
> a time to plant, and a time to pluck up what is planted;
> a time to kill, and a time to heal;
> a time to break down, and a time to build up;
> a time to weep, and a time to laugh;
> a time to mourn, and a time to dance;
> a time to throw away stones, and a time to gather stones together;
> a time to embrace, and a time to refrain from embracing;
> a time to seek, and a time to lose;
> a time to keep, and a time to throw away;
> a time to tear, and a time to sew;
> a time to keep silence, and a time to speak;
> a time to love, and a time to hate;
> a time for war, and a time for peace.

What gain have the workers from their toil? I have seen the business that God has given to everyone to be busy with. He has made everything suitable for its time; moreover he has put a sense of past and future into their minds, yet they cannot find out what God has done from the beginning to the end. I know that there is nothing better for them than to be happy and enjoy themselves as long as they live; moreover, it is God's gift that all should eat and drink and take pleasure in all their toil. I know that whatever God does endures forever; nothing can be added to it, nor anything taken from it; God has done this, so that all should stand in awe before him. That which is, already has been; that which is to be, already is; and God seeks out what has gone by.

Comfort, O comfort my people, says your God.
Speak tenderly to Jerusalem,
    and cry to her
that she has served her term,
    that her penalty is paid,
that she has received from the LORD's hand
    double for all her sins.

A voice cries out:
"In the wilderness prepare the way of the LORD,
    make straight in the desert a highway for our God.
Every valley shall be lifted up,
    and every mountain and hill be made low;
the uneven ground shall become level,
    and the rough places a plain.
Then the glory of the LORD shall be revealed,
    and all people shall see it together,
    for the mouth of the LORD has spoken."

A voice says, "Cry out!"
    And I said, "What shall I cry?"
All people are grass,
    their constancy is like the flower of the field.
The grass withers, the flower fades,
    when the breath of the LORD blows upon it;
    surely the people are grass.
The grass withers, the flower fades;
    but the word of our God will stand forever.
Get you up to a high mountain,
    O Zion, herald of good tidings;
lift up your voice with strength,
    O Jerusalem, herald of good tidings,
    lift it up, do not fear;
say to the cities of Judah,
    "Here is your God!"
See, the LORD God comes with might,
    and his arm rules for him;
his reward is with him,
    and his recompense before him.
He will feed his flock like a shepherd;
    he will gather the lambs in his arms,
and carry them in his bosom,
    and gently lead the mother sheep.

4   *Isaiah 40:28–31*

Have you not known? Have you not heard?
The LORD is the everlasting God,
 the Creator of the ends of the earth.
He does not faint or grow weary;
 his understanding is unsearchable.
He gives power to the faint,
 and strengthens the powerless.
Even youths will faint and be weary,
 and the young will fall exhausted;
but those who wait for the LORD shall renew their strength,
 they shall mount up with wings like eagles,
they shall run and not be weary,
 they shall walk and not faint.

5   *Isaiah 65:17–25*

For I am about to create new heavens
 and a new earth;
the former things shall not be remembered
 or come to mind.
But be glad and rejoice forever
 in what I am creating;
for I am about to create Jerusalem as a joy,
 and its people as a delight.
I will rejoice in Jerusalem,
 and delight in my people;
no more shall the sound of weeping be heard in it,
 or the cry of distress.
No more shall there be in it
 an infant that lives but a few days,
 or an old person who does not live out a lifetime;
for one who dies at a hundred years will be considered a youth,
 and one who falls short of a hundred will be considered accursed.
They shall build houses and inhabit them;
 they shall plant vineyards and eat their fruit.
They shall not build and another inhabit;
 they shall not plant and another eat;
for like the days of a tree shall the days of my people be,
 and my chosen shall long enjoy the work of their hands.
They shall not labor in vain,
 or bear children for calamity;
for they shall be offspring blessed by the LORD—
 and their descendants as well.

Before they call I will answer,
  while they are yet speaking I will hear.
The wolf and the lamb shall feed together,
  the lion shall eat straw like the ox;
  but the serpent—its food shall be dust!
They shall not hurt or destroy
  on all my holy mountain, says the LORD.

PSALMS

For another translation of the psalms see pages 611–783.

6   *Psalm 23*

The LORD is my shepherd, I shall not want.
  He makes me lie down in green pastures;
he leads me beside still waters;
  he restores my soul.
He leads me in right paths
  for his name's sake.

Even though I walk through the darkest valley,
  I fear no evil;
for you are with me;
  your rod and your staff—
  they comfort me.

You prepare a table before me
  in the presence of my enemies;
you anoint my head with oil;
  my cup overflows.
Surely goodness and mercy shall follow me
  all the days of my life,
and I shall dwell in the house of the LORD
  my whole life long.

7   *Psalm 46:1–5, 10–11*

God is our refuge and strength,
  a very present help in trouble.
Therefore we will not fear, though the earth should change,
  though the mountains shake in the heart of the sea;
though its waters roar and foam,
  though the mountains tremble with its tumult.

There is a river whose streams make glad the city of God,
    the holy habitation of the Most High.
God is in the midst of the city; it shall not be moved;
    God will help it when the morning dawns.
"Be still, and know that I am God!
    I am exalted among the nations,
    I am exalted in the earth."
The LORD of hosts is with us;
    the God of Jacob is our refuge.

8   *Psalm 90:1–10, 12*

LORD, you have been our dwelling place
    in all generations.
Before the mountains were brought forth,
    or ever you had formed the earth and the world,
from everlasting to everlasting you are God.

You turn us back to dust,
    and say, "Turn back, you mortals."
For a thousand years in your sight
    are like yesterday when it is past,
    or like a watch in the night.

You sweep them away; they are like a dream,
    like grass that is renewed in the morning;
in the morning it flourishes and is renewed;
    in the evening it fades and withers.

For we are consumed by your anger;
    by your wrath we are overwhelmed.
You have set our iniquities before you,
    our secret sins in the light of your countenance.

For all our days pass away under your wrath;
    our years come to an end like a sigh.
The days of our life are seventy years,
    or perhaps eighty, if we are strong;
even then their span is only toil and trouble;
    they are soon gone, and we fly away.

So teach us to count our days
    that we may gain a wise heart.

Bless the LORD, O my soul,
   and all that is within me,
   bless his holy name.
Bless the LORD, O my soul,
   and do not forget all his benefits—
who forgives all your iniquity,
   who heals all your diseases,
who redeems your life from the Pit,
   who crowns you with steadfast love and mercy,
who satisfies you with good as long as you live
   so that your youth is renewed like the eagle's.

The LORD works vindication
   and justice for all who are oppressed.
He made known his ways to Moses,
   his acts to the people of Israel.
The LORD is merciful and gracious,
   slow to anger and abounding in steadfast love.
He will not always accuse,
   nor will he keep his anger forever.
He does not deal with us according to our sins,
   nor repay us according to our iniquities.
For as the heavens are high above the earth,
   so great is his steadfast love toward those who fear him;
as far as the east is from the west,
   so far he removes our transgressions from us.
As a father has compassion for his children,
   so the LORD has compassion for those who fear him.
For he knows how we were made;
   he remembers that we are dust.

As for mortals, their days are like grass;
   they flourish like a flower of the field;
for the wind passes over it, and it is gone,
   and its place knows it no more.
But the steadfast love of the LORD is from everlasting to everlasting
   on those who fear him,
   and his righteousness to children's children,
to those who keep his covenant
   and remember to do his commandments.

The LORD has established his throne in the heavens,
and his kingdom rules over all.
Bless the LORD, O you his angels,
you mighty ones who do his bidding,
obedient to his spoken word.
Bless the LORD, all his hosts,
his ministers that do his will.
Bless the LORD, all his works,
in all places of his dominion.
Bless the LORD, O my soul.

10   *Psalm 121*

I lift up my eyes to the hills—
from where will my help come?
My help comes from the LORD,
who made heaven and earth.

He will not let your foot be moved;
he who keeps you will not slumber.
He who keeps Israel
will neither slumber nor sleep.

The LORD is your keeper;
the LORD is your shade at your right hand.
The sun shall not strike you by day,
nor the moon by night.

The LORD will keep you from all evil;
he will keep your life.
The Lord will keep
your going out and your coming in
from this time on and forevermore.

11   *Psalm 130*

Out of the depths I cry to you, O LORD.
LORD, hear my voice!
Let your ears be attentive
to the voice of my supplications!

If you, O LORD, should mark iniquities,
LORD, who could stand?
But there is forgiveness with you,
so that you may be revered.

I wait for the LORD, my soul waits,
   and in his word I hope;
my soul waits for the LORD
   more than those who watch for the morning,
   more than those who watch for the morning.

O Israel, hope in the LORD!
   For with the LORD there is steadfast love,
   and with him is great power to redeem.
It is he who will redeem Israel
   from all its iniquities.

12   *Psalm 139:1–12*

O LORD, you have searched me and known me.
You know when I sit down and when I rise up;
   you discern my thoughts from far away.
You search out my path and my lying down,
   and are acquainted with all my ways.
Even before a word is on my tongue,
   O LORD, you know it completely.
You hem me in, behind and before,
   and lay your hand upon me.
Such knowledge is too wonderful for me;
   it is so high that I cannot attain it.

Where can I go from your spirit?
   Or where can I flee from your presence?
If I ascend to heaven, you are there;
   if I make my bed in Sheol, you are there.
If I take the wings of the morning
   and settle at the farthest limits of the sea,
even there your hand shall lead me,
   and your right hand shall hold me fast.
If I say, "Surely the darkness shall cover me,
   and the light around me become night,"
even the darkness is not dark to you;
   the night is as bright as the day,
   for darkness is as light to you.

13   *Romans 8:14–23, 31–39*

For all who are led by the Spirit of God are children of God. For you did not receive a spirit of slavery to fall back into fear, but you have received a spirit of adoption. When we cry, "Abba Father!" it is that very Spirit bearing witness with our spirit that we are children of God, and if children, then heirs, heirs of God and joint heirs with Christ—if, in fact, we suffer with him so that we may also be glorified with him.

I consider that the sufferings of this present time are not worth comparing with the glory about to be revealed to us. For the creation waits with eager longing for the revealing of the children of God; for the creation was subjected to futility, not of its own will but by the will of the one who subjected it, in hope that the creation itself will be set free from its bondage to decay and will obtain the freedom of the glory of the children of God. We know that the whole creation has been groaning in labor pains until now; and not only the creation, but we ourselves, who have the first fruits of the Spirit, groan inwardly while we wait for adoption, the redemption of our bodies.

What then are we to say about these things? If God is for us, who is against us? He who did not withhold his own Son, but gave him up for all of us, will he not with him also give us everything else? Who will bring any charge against God's elect? It is God who justifies. Who is to condemn? It is Christ Jesus, who died, yes, who was raised, who is at the right hand of God, who indeed intercedes for us. Who will separate us from the love of Christ? Will hardship, or distress, or persecution, or famine, or nakedness, or peril, or sword? As it is written,

> "For your sake we are being killed all day long;
> we are accounted as sheep to be slaughtered."

No, in all these things we are more than conquerors through him who loved us. For I am convinced that neither death, nor life, nor angels, nor rulers, nor things present, nor things to come, nor powers, nor height, nor depth, nor anything else in all creation, will be able to separate us from the love of God in Christ Jesus our Lord.

14   *Romans 14:7–9, 10b–12*

We do not live to ourselves, and we do not die to ourselves. If we live, we live to the Lord, and if we die, we die to the Lord; so then, whether we live or whether we die, we are the Lord's. For to this end Christ died and lived again, so that he might be Lord of both the dead and the living.

We will all stand before the judgment seat of God. For it is written,

> "As I live, says the Lord, every knee shall bow to me,
> and every tongue shall give praise to God."

So then, each of us will be accountable to God.

Christ has been raised from the dead, the first fruits of those who have died. For since death came through a human being, the resurrection of the dead has also come through a human being; for as all die in Adam, so all will be made alive in Christ. But each in his own order: Christ the first fruits, then at his coming those who belong to Christ. Then comes the end, when he hands over the kingdom to God the Father, after he has destroyed every ruler and every authority and power. For he must reign until he has put all his enemies under his feet. The last enemy to be destroyed is death.

Someone will ask, "How are the dead raised? With what kind of body do they come?" Fool! What you sow does not come to life unless it dies. And as for what you sow, you do not sow the body that is to be, but a bare seed, perhaps of wheat or of some other grain. But God gives it a body as he has chosen, and to each kind of seed its own body.

So it is with the resurrection of the dead. What is sown is perishable, what is raised is imperishable. It is sown in dishonor, it is raised in glory. It is sown in weakness, it is raised in power. It is sown a physical body, it is raised a spiritual body. If there is a physical body, there is also a spiritual body.

What I am saying, brothers and sisters, is this: flesh and blood cannot inherit the kingdom of God, nor does the perishable inherit the imperishable.

For this perishable body must put on imperishability, and this mortal body must put on immortality. When this perishable body puts on imperishability, and this mortal body puts on immortality, then the saying that is written will be fulfilled:

"Death has been swallowed up in victory."
"Where, O death, is your victory?
Where, O death, is your sting?"

The sting of death is sin, and the power of sin is the law. But thanks be to God, who gives us the victory through our Lord Jesus Christ.

Therefore, my beloved, be steadfast, immovable, always excelling in the work of the Lord, because you know that in the Lord your labor is not in vain.

We do not lose heart. Even though our outer nature is wasting away, our inner nature is being renewed day by day. For this slight momentary affliction is preparing us for an eternal weight of glory beyond all measure, because we look not at what can be seen but at what cannot be seen; for what can be seen is temporary, but what cannot be seen is eternal.

For we know that if the earthly tent we live in is destroyed, we have a building from God, a house not made with hands, eternal in the heavens.

But we do not want you to be uninformed, brothers and sisters, about those who have died, so that you may not grieve as others do who have no hope. For since we believe that Jesus died and rose again, even so, through Jesus, God will bring with him those who have died. For this we declare to you by the word of the Lord, that we who are alive, who are left until the coming of the Lord, will by no means precede those who have died. For the Lord himself, with a cry of command, with the archangel's call and with the sound of God's trumpet, will descend from heaven, and the dead in Christ will rise first. Then we who are alive, who are left, will be caught up in the clouds together with them to meet the Lord in the air; and so we will be with the Lord forever. Therefore encourage one another with these words.

Then I saw a new heaven and a new earth; for the first heaven and the first earth had passed away, and the sea was no more. And I saw the holy city, the new Jerusalem, coming down out of heaven from God, prepared as a bride adorned for her husband. And I heard a loud voice from the throne saying,

> "See, the home of God is among mortals.
> He will dwell with them as their God;
> they will be his peoples,
> and God himself will be with them;
> he will wipe every tear from their eyes.
> Death will be no more;
> mourning and crying and pain will be no more,
> for the first things have passed away."

I saw no temple in the city, for its temple is the Lord God the Almighty and the Lamb. And the city has no need of sun or moon to shine on it, for the glory of God is its light, and its lamp is the Lamb. The nations will walk by its light, and the kings of the earth will bring their glory into it. Its gates will never be shut by day—and there will be no night there.

Nothing accursed will be found there any more. But the throne of God and of the Lamb will be in it, and his servants will worship him; they will see his face, and his name will be on their foreheads. And there will be no more night; they need no light of lamp or sun, for the Lord God will be their light, and they will reign forever and ever.

19   *Matthew 18:1–5, 10*

The disciples came to Jesus and asked, "Who is the greatest in the kingdom of heaven?" He called a child, whom he put among them, and said, "Truly I tell you, unless you change and become like children, you will never enter the kingdom of heaven. Whoever becomes humble like this child is the greatest in the kingdom of heaven. Whoever welcomes one such child in my name welcomes me.

"Take care that you do not despise one of these little ones; for, I tell you, in heaven their angels continually see the face of my Father in heaven."

20   *Mark 10:13–16*

People were bringing little children to him in order that he might touch them; and the disciples spoke sternly to them. But when Jesus saw this, he was indignant and said to them, "Let the little children come to me; do not stop them; for it is to such as these that the kingdom of God belongs. Truly I tell you, whoever does not receive the kingdom of God as a little child will never enter it." And he took them up in his arms, laid his hands on them, and blessed them.

21   *Luke 23:33, 39–43*

When they came to the place that is called The Skull, they crucified Jesus there with the criminals, one on his right and one on his left. One of the criminals who were hanged there kept deriding him and saying, "Are you not the Messiah? Save yourself and us!" But the other rebuked him, saying, "Do you not fear God, since you are under the same sentence of condemnation? And we indeed have been condemned justly, for we are getting what we deserve for our deeds, but this man has done nothing wrong." Then he said, "Jesus, remember me when you come into your kingdom." He replied, "Truly I tell you, today you will be with me in Paradise."

22   *John 11:17–27*

When Jesus arrived, he found that Lazarus had already been in the tomb four days. Now Bethany was near Jerusalem, some two miles away, and many of the Jews had come to Martha and Mary to console them about their brother. When Martha heard that Jesus was coming, she went and met him, while Mary stayed at home. Martha said to Jesus, "Lord, if you had been here, my brother would not have died. But even now I know that God will give you whatever you ask of him." Jesus said to her, "Your brother will rise again." Martha said to him, "I know that he will rise again in the resurrection on the last day." Jesus said to her, "I am the resurrection and the life. Those who believe in me, even though they die, will live, and everyone who lives and believes in me will never die. Do you believe this?" She said to him, "Yes, Lord, I believe that you are the Messiah, the Son of God, the one coming into the world."

23 *John 14:1–6, 25–27*

"Do not let your hearts be troubled. Believe in God, believe also in me. In my Father's house there are many dwelling places. If it were not so, would I have told you that I go to prepare a place for you? And if I go and prepare a place for you, I will come again and will take you to myself, so that where I am, there you may be also. And you know the way to the place where I am going." Thomas said to him, "Lord, we do not know where you are going. How can we know the way?" Jesus said to him, "I am the way, and the truth, and the life. No one comes to the Father except through me.

"I have said these things to you while I am still with you. But the Advocate, the Holy Spirit, whom the Father will send in my name, will teach you everything, and remind you of all that I have said to you. Peace I leave with you; my peace I give to you. I do not give to you as the world gives. Do not let your hearts be troubled, and do not let them be afraid."

PASTORAL
LITURGIES

MINISTRY WITH THE SICK

SENTENCES OF SCRIPTURE

The following sentences may be used as calls to worship, or as introductions to prayer. An appropriate sentence may be selected and left with the person at the end of a visit.

1   *Deut. 33:27a*

The eternal God is your dwelling place,
and underneath the everlasting arms.

2   *Josh. 1:9b*

Be strong and courageous;
do not be frightened or dismayed,
for the Lord your God is with you
wherever you go.

3   *Ps. 23:1, 4b*

The Lord is my shepherd, I shall not want.
For you are with me;
Your rod and your staff, they comfort me.

4   *Ps. 27:1*

The Lord is my light and my salvation;
whom shall I fear?
The Lord is the stronghold of my life;
of whom shall I be afraid?

5   *Ps. 27:5*

For God will hide me in a shelter
in the day of trouble;
God will conceal me under the cover of a tent;
and will set me high on a rock.

6   *Ps. 46:1*

God is our refuge and strength,
a very present help in trouble.

7   *Ps. 46:10*

Be still, and know that I am God!

8   *Ps. 102:1, 2*

Hear my prayer, O Lord;
let my cry come to you.
Do not hide your face from me
in the day of my distress.
Incline your ear to me;
answer me speedily in the day when I call.

9   *Ps. 124:8*

Our help is in the name of the Lord,
who made heaven and earth.

10   *Isa. 26:3*

Those of steadfast mind you keep in peace—
in peace because they trust in you.

11   *Isa. 40:31*

Those who wait for the Lord
shall renew their strength,
they shall mount up with wings like eagles,
they shall run and not be weary,
they shall walk and not faint.

12   *Isa. 41:10*

Do not fear, for I am with you,
do not be afraid, for I am your God;
I will strengthen you, I will help you,
I will uphold you with my victorious right hand.

13   *Matt. 11:28*

Come to me,
all you that are weary
and are carrying heavy burdens,
and I will give you rest.

14   *Mark 10:14b*

Let the children come to me,
do not hinder them;
for to such belongs the kingdom of God.

15   *John 6:35*

I am the bread of life.
Whoever comes to me will never be hungry,
and whoever believes in me will never be thirsty.

16   *John 11:25, 26*

I am the resurrection and the life.
Those who believe in me,
even though they die, will live,
and everyone who lives and believes in me
will never die.

17   *John 14:1*

Do not let your hearts be troubled.
Believe in God, believe also in me.

18   *John 14:27*

Peace I leave with you;
my peace I give to you.
I do not give to you as the world gives.
Do not let your hearts be troubled,
and do not let them be afraid.

19   *John 16:33*

I have said this to you,
so that in me you may have peace.
In the world you face persecution.
But take courage;
I have conquered the world!

20   *Rom. 8:18*

I consider that the sufferings of this present time
are not worth comparing
with the glory about to be revealed to us.

21   *2 Cor. 1:4ab, 5*

God consoles us in all our affliction,
so that we may be able
to console those who are in any affliction.
For just as the sufferings of Christ are abundant for us,
so also our consolation is abundant through Christ.

22   *2 Cor. 12:9a*

My grace is sufficient for you,
for power is made perfect in weakness.

23   *1 Peter 1:3*

Blessed be the God and Father of our Lord Jesus Christ,
by whose great mercy
we have been born anew to a living hope
through the resurrection of Jesus Christ from the dead.

24   *Rev. 3:20*

Behold, I stand at the door and knock;
if you hear my voice and open the door,
I will come in to you and eat with you,
and you with me.

SCRIPTURE READINGS

LIST OF SUGGESTED READINGS

The following readings are particularly appropriate for use in pastoral care. An asterisk * indicates that the text of that particular reading is included on pages 974–987.

OLD TESTAMENT

1 Kings 19:4–8	Elijah's despair in the wilderness
Job 5:7–11	God sets on high those who are lowly
Job 7:11–21	Job complains to God
Eccl. 3:1–15	For everything there is a season
Isa. 26:1–4	God will keep them in perfect peace
* Isa. 35	The desert shall rejoice and blossom
Isa. 38	Hezekiah's prayer in distress
Isa. 40:1–11	Comfort my people
* Isa. 40:28–31	Those who wait for the Lord shall renew their strength
Isa. 43:1–3a, 18–19, 25	When you pass through the waters
Isa. 52:13–53:12	Surely he has borne our infirmities
* Isa. 61:1–4	The spirit of the Lord God is upon me

PSALMS

For another translation of the psalms see pages 611–783.

* Ps. 6:2–4, 6–9	Lord, heal me, for my soul is struck with terror
* Ps. 22:1–2, 14–15, 19, 22–24	My God, why have you forsaken me?
* Ps. 23	The Lord is my shepherd
* Ps. 27:1, 4–9a, 13–14	The Lord is my light and my salvation
Ps. 31:1–3, 5, 7, 16, 19, 24	In you, O Lord, I seek refuge
Ps. 34:1–10, 17–19, 22	O magnify the Lord with me
Ps. 39:4–5, 12	Lord, let me know my end
* Ps. 42:1–5	As a deer longs for flowing streams
Ps. 46:1–5, 10–11	A very present help in trouble
Ps. 51:1–12, 15–17	Create in me a clean heart, O God
Ps. 63:1–8	In the shadow of your wings I sing for joy

* Ps. 69:1–3, 13–14a,
    15–17, 29–30,
    32–34   Save me, for the waters come up to my neck
  Ps. 71:1–3, 5–6,
    8–9, 14–16   Do not cast me off in the time of old age
  Ps. 77   I cry to God to hear me
* Ps. 86:1–7, 11–13,
    15–16   In the day of my trouble I call on you
  Ps. 90:1–10, 12   The eternity of God and human transitoriness
  Ps. 91   My refuge and my fortress, my God, in whom I trust
* Ps. 103:1–5   Bless the Lord, O my soul
  Ps. 116:1–9   When I was brought low, the Lord saved me
* Ps. 121   I lift up my eyes to the hills
* Ps. 130   Out of the depths I cry to you, O Lord
  Ps. 137:1–6   By the rivers of Babylon
* Ps. 139:1–18,
    23–24   You have searched me and known me
  Ps. 143:1–2,
    5–6, 10   Give ear to my supplications

NEW TESTAMENT

* Matt. 5:1–12a   The Beatitudes
  Matt. 8:14–17   Jesus and Peter's mother–in–law
* Matt. 10:1, 5a, 7–8a;
  Mark 6:12–13   Jesus calls disciples and sends them out
* Matt. 11:2–5   Go and tell John what you hear and see
* Matt. 11:28–30   All who are weary and are carrying heavy burdens
  Mark 6:53–56   Healing in Gennesaret
* Mark 10:13–16   Let the children come to me
  Mark 15:24–34   My God, why have you forsaken me?
  Luke 4:31–37   The man with an unclean spirit
* Luke 4:40   Jesus lays hands on the sick and heals them
* Luke 5:12–16   A leper is cleansed
  Luke 5:17–26   Paralytic carried by four men
  Luke 7:2–10   The centurion's servant
  Luke 8:26–35   The demoniac(s) at Gadara
* Luke 8:43–48   The woman with hemorrhages
  Luke 9:37–43a   Epileptic boy
  Luke 13:10–17   Woman bent double for eighteen years
  Luke 17:11–19   The ten lepers
  Luke 18:35–43   Blind Bartimaeus
  John 3:16–17   God so loved the world

John 4:46–54	The royal official's son
John 5:2–18	Sick man at pool of Beth-zatha
John 9:1–7	Who sinned . . . that he was born blind?
John 10:11–18	I am the good shepherd
*John 14:1–6, 25–27	Let not your hearts be troubled
*Acts 3:1–10	The lame man at the temple gate
Romans 5:1–11	Hope does not disappoint
*Romans 8:14–23	Present sufferings are not worth comparing with the glory to be revealed
*Romans 8:26–28	The Spirit helps us in our weakness
*Romans 8:31–39	If God is for us, who is against us?
*Romans 12:1, 2	Present your bodies as a living sacrifice
1 Cor. 12:24b–27	The members may have the same care for one another
2 Cor. 1:3–7	Sharing in sufferings and in comfort
2 Cor. 4:16–18	Visible things are temporary, invisible things eternal
Phil. 2:25–30	Epaphroditus' illness
*Phil. 4:4, 6–9	Rejoice in the Lord always; have no anxiety
Heb. 2:14–18	Christ was tested in every way
*Heb. 4:14–16; 5:7–9	Christ learned obedience through what he suffered
*James 5:13–16	Is anyone among you suffering?
*1 Peter 1:3–9	Born anew to a living hope
1 John 3:1–3	We are children of God
1 John 4:16–19	There is no fear in love
Rev. 21:1–7	God will wipe away every tear

Scripture Readings

All readings are from the New Revised Standard Version of the Bible.

Old Testament

1   *Isaiah 35*

The wilderness and the dry land shall be glad,
   the desert shall rejoice and blossom;
like the crocus it shall blossom abundantly,
   and rejoice with joy and singing.
The glory of Lebanon shall be given to it,
   the majesty of Carmel and Sharon.
They shall see the glory of the LORD,
   the majesty of our God.

Strengthen the weak hands,
   and make firm the feeble knees.
Say to those who are of a fearful heart,
   "Be strong, do not fear!
Here is your God.
   He will come with vengeance,
with terrible recompense.
   He will come and save you."

Then the eyes of the blind shall be opened,
   and the ears of the deaf unstopped;
then the lame shall leap like a deer,
   and the tongue of the speechless sing for joy.
For waters shall break forth in the wilderness,
   and streams in the desert;
the burning sand shall become a pool,
   and the thirsty ground springs of water;
the haunt of jackals shall become a swamp,
   the grass shall become reeds and rushes.

A highway shall be there,
   and it shall be called the Holy Way;
the unclean shall not travel on it,
   but it shall be for God's people;
   no traveler, not even fools, shall go astray.
No lion shall be there,
   nor shall any ravenous beast come up on it;
they shall not be found there,
   but the redeemed shall walk there.

And the ransomed of the LORD shall return,
    and come to Zion with singing;
everlasting joy shall be upon their heads;
    they shall obtain joy and gladness,
    and sorrow and sighing shall flee away.

2   *Isaiah 40:28–31*

Have you not known? Have you not heard?
The LORD is the everlasting God,
    the Creator of the ends of the earth.
He does not faint or grow weary;
    his understanding is unsearchable.
He gives power to the faint,
    and strengthens the powerless.
Even youths will faint and be weary,
    and the young will fall exhausted;
but those who wait for the LORD shall know their strength,
    they shall mount up with wings like eagles,
they shall run and not be weary,
    they shall walk and not faint.

3   *Isaiah 61:1–4*

The spirit of the Lord GOD is upon me,
    because the LORD has anointed me;
he has sent me to bring good news to the oppressed,
    to bind up the brokenhearted,
to proclaim liberty to the captives,
    and release to the prisoners;
to proclaim the year of the LORD's favor,
    and the day of vengeance of our God;
    to comfort all who mourn;
to provide for those who mourn in Zion—
    to give them a garland instead of ashes,
the oil of gladness instead of mourning,
    the mantle of praise instead of a faint spirit.
They will be called oaks of righteousness,
    the planting of the LORD, to display his glory.
They shall build up the ancient ruins,
    they shall raise up the former devastations;
they shall repair the ruined cities,
    the devastations of many generations.

For another translation of the psalms see pages 611–783.

4   *Psalm 6:2–4, 6–9*

Be gracious to me, O LORD, for I am languishing;
   O LORD, heal me, for my bones are shaking with terror.
My soul also is struck with terror,
   while you, O LORD—how long?

Turn, O LORD, save my life;
   deliver me for the sake of your steadfast love.

I am weary with my moaning;
   every night I flood my bed with tears;
   I drench my couch with my weeping.
My eyes waste away because of grief;
   they grow weak because of all my foes.

Depart from me, all you workers of evil,
   for the LORD has heard the sound of my weeping.
The LORD has heard my supplication;
   the LORD accepts my prayer.

5   *Psalm 22:1–2, 14–15, 19, 22–24*

My God, my God, why have you forsaken me?
   Why are you so far from helping me, from the words of my groaning?
O my God, I cry by day, but you do not answer;
   and by night, but find no rest.

I am poured out like water,
   and all my bones are out of joint;
my heart is like wax;
   it is melted within my breast;
my mouth is dried up like a potsherd,
   and my tongue sticks to my jaws;
   you lay me in the dust of death.
But you, O LORD, do not be far away!
   O my help, come quickly to my aid!

I will tell of your name to my brothers and sisters;
   in the midst of the congregation I will praise you:
You who fear the LORD, praise him!
   All you offspring of Jacob, glorify him;
   stand in awe of him, all you offspring of Israel!

For he did not despise or abhor
  the affliction of the afflicted;
he did not hide his face from me,
  but heard when I cried to him.

6   *Psalm 23*

The LORD is my shepherd, I shall not want.
  he makes me lie down in green pastures;
He leads me beside still waters;
  he restores my soul.
He leads me in right paths
  for his name's sake.

Even though I walk through the darkest valley,
  I fear no evil;
for you are with me;
  your rod and your staff—
  they comfort me.

You prepare a table before me
  in the presence of my enemies;
you anoint my head with oil;
  my cup overflows.
Surely goodness and mercy shall follow me
  all the days of my life,
and I shall dwell in the house of the LORD
  my whole life long.

7   *Psalm 27:1, 4–9a, 13–14*

The LORD is my light and my salvation;
  whom shall I fear?
The LORD is the stronghold of my life;
  of whom shall I be afraid?

One thing I asked of the LORD,
  that I will seek after:
to live in the house of the LORD
  all the days of my life,
to behold the beauty of the LORD,
  and to inquire in his temple.

For he will hide me in his shelter
  in the day of trouble;
he will conceal me under the cover of his tent;
  he will set me high on a rock.

Now my head is lifted up
    above my enemies all around me,
and I will offer in his tent
    sacrifices with shouts of joy;
I will sing and make melody to the LORD.

Hear, O LORD, when I cry aloud,
    be gracious to me and answer me!
"Come," my heart says, "seek his face!"
    Your face, LORD, do I seek.
    Do not hide your face from me.

I believe that I shall see the goodness of the LORD
    in the land of the living.
Wait for the LORD;
    be strong, and let your heart take courage;
    wait for the LORD!

8   *Psalm 42:1–5*

As a deer longs for flowing streams,
    so my soul longs for you, O God.
My soul thirsts for God,
    for the living God.
When shall I come and behold
    the face of God?
My tears have been my food
    day and night,
while people say to me continually,
    "Where is your God?"

These things I remember,
    as I pour out my soul:
how I went with the throng,
    and led them in procession to the house of God,
with glad shouts and songs of thanksgiving,
    a multitude keeping festival.
Why are you cast down, O my soul,
    and why are you disquieted within me?
Hope in God; for I shall again praise him,
    my help and my God.

9   *Psalm 69:1–3, 13–14a, 15–17, 29–30, 32–34*

Save me, O God,
    for the waters have come up to my neck.
I sink in deep mire,
    where there is no foothold;

I have come into deep waters,
    and the flood sweeps over me.
I am weary with my crying;
    my throat is parched.
My eyes grow dim
    with waiting for my God.

But as for me, my prayer is to you, O LORD.
    At an acceptable time, O God,
    in the abundance of your steadfast love, answer me.
With your faithful help rescue me
    from sinking in the mire;

Do not let the flood sweep over me,
    or the deep swallow me up,
    or the Pit close its mouth over me.

Answer me, O LORD, for your steadfast love is good;
    according to your abundant mercy, turn to me.
Do not hide your face from your servant,
    for I am in distress—make haste to answer me.

But I am lowly and in pain;
    let your salvation, O God, protect me.

I will praise the name of God with a song;
    I will magnify him with thanksgiving.

Let the oppressed see it and be glad;
    you who seek God, let your hearts revive.
For the LORD hears the needy,
    and does not despise his own that are in bonds.

Let heaven and earth praise him,
    the seas and everything that moves in them.

10   *Psalm 86:1–7, 11–13, 15–16*

Incline your ear, O LORD, and answer me,
    for I am poor and needy.
Preserve my life, for I am devoted to you;
    save your servant who trusts in you.
You are my God; be gracious to me, O LORD,
    for to you do I cry all day long.
Gladden the soul of your servant,
    for to you, O LORD, I lift up my soul.
For you, O LORD, are good and forgiving,
    abounding in steadfast love to all who call on you.

Give ear, O LORD, to my prayer;
　　listen to my cry of supplication.
In the day of my trouble I call on you,
　　for you will answer me.

Teach me your way, O LORD,
　　that I may walk in your truth;
　　give me an undivided heart to revere your name.
I give thanks to you, O LORD my God, with my whole heart,
　　and I will glorify your name forever.
For great is your steadfast love toward me;
　　you have delivered my soul from the depths of Sheol.

But you, O LORD, are a God merciful and gracious,
　　slow to anger and abounding in steadfast love and faithfulness.
Turn to me and be gracious to me;
　　give your strength to your servant;
　　save the child of your serving girl.

11   *Psalm 103:1–5*

Bless the LORD, O my soul,
　　and all that is within me,
　　bless his holy name.
Bless the LORD, O my soul,
　　and do not forget all his benefits—
who forgives all your iniquity,
　　who heals all your diseases,
who redeems your life from the Pit,
　　who crowns you with steadfast love and mercy,
who satisfies you with good as long as you live
　　so that your youth is renewed like the eagle's.

12   *Psalm 121*

I lift up my eyes to the hills—
　　From where will my help come?
My help comes from the LORD,
　　who made heaven and earth.

He will not let your foot be moved;
　　he who keeps you will not slumber.
He who keeps Israel
　　will neither slumber nor sleep.

The LORD is your keeper;
　　the LORD is your shade at your right hand.
The sun shall not strike you by day,
　　nor the moon by night.

The LORD will keep you from all evil;
   he will keep your life.
The LORD will keep
   your going out and your coming in
   from this time on and forevermore.

13   *Psalm 130*

Out of the depths I cry to you, O LORD.
   LORD, hear my voice!
Let your ears be attentive
   to the voice of my supplications!

If you, O LORD, should mark iniquities,
   LORD, who could stand?
But there is forgiveness with you,
   so that you may be revered.

I wait for the LORD, my soul waits,
   and in his word I hope;
my soul waits for the LORD
   more than those who watch for the morning,
   more than those who watch for the morning.

O Israel, hope in the LORD!
   For with the LORD there is steadfast love,
   and with him is great power to redeem.
It is he who will redeem Israel
   from all its iniquities.

14   *Psalm 139:1–18, 23–24*

O LORD, you have searched me and known me.
You know when I sit down and when I rise up;
   you discern my thoughts from far away.
You search out my path and my lying down,
   and are acquainted with all my ways.
Even before a word is on my tongue,
   O LORD, you know it completely.
You hem me in, behind and before,
   and lay your hand upon me.
Such knowledge is too wonderful for me;
   it is so high that I cannot attain it.

Where can I go from your spirit?
   Or where can I flee from your presence?
If I ascend to heaven, you are there;
   if I make my bed in Sheol, you are there.

SCRIPTURE READINGS—MINISTRY WITH THE SICK / 981

If I take the wings of the morning
    and settle at the farthest limits of the sea,
even there your hand shall lead me,
    and your right hand shall hold me fast.
If I say, "Surely the darkness shall cover me,
    and the light around me become night,"
even the darkness is not dark to you;
    the night is as bright as the day,
    for darkness is as light to you.

For it was you who formed my inward parts;
    you knit me together in my mother's womb.
I praise you, for I am fearfully and wonderfully made.
    Wonderful are your works;
that I know very well.
    My frame was not hidden from you,
when I was being made in secret,
    intricately woven in the depths of the earth.
Your eyes beheld my unformed substance.
In your book were written
    all the days that were formed for me,
    when none of them as yet existed.
How weighty to me are your thoughts, O God!
    How vast is the sum of them!
I try to count them—they are more than the sand;
    I come to the end—I am still with you.

Search me, O God, and know my heart;
    test me and know my thoughts.
See if there is any wicked way in me,
    and lead me in the way everlasting.

New Testament

15   *Matthew 5:1–12a*

When Jesus saw the crowds, he went up the mountain; and after he sat down, his disciples came to him. Then he began to speak, and taught them, saying:

"Blessed are the poor in spirit, for theirs is the kingdom of heaven.

"Blessed are those who mourn, for they will be comforted.

"Blessed are the meek, for they will inherit the earth.

"Blessed are those who hunger and thirst for righteousness, for they will be filled.

"Blessed are the merciful, for they will receive mercy.

"Blessed are the pure in heart, for they will see God.

"Blessed are the peacemakers, for they will be called children of God.

"Blessed are those who are persecuted for righteousness' sake, for theirs is the kingdom of heaven.

"Blessed are you when people revile you and persecute you and utter all kinds of evil against you falsely on my account. Rejoice and be glad, for your reward is great in heaven."

16   *Matthew 10:1, 5a, 7–8a; Mark 6:12–13*

Jesus summoned his twelve disciples and gave them authority over unclean spirits, to cast them out, and to cure every disease and every sickness. These twelve Jesus sent out with the following instructions: "As you go, proclaim the good news, 'The kingdom of heaven has come near.' Cure the sick." So they went out and proclaimed that all should repent. They cast out many demons, and anointed with oil many who were sick and cured them.

17   *Matthew 11:2–5*

When John heard in prison what the Messiah was doing, he sent word by his disciples and said to him, "Are you the one who is to come, or are we to wait for another?" Jesus answered them, "Go and tell John what you hear and see: the blind receive their sight, the lame walk, the lepers are cleansed, the deaf hear, the dead are raised, and the poor have good news brought to them."

18   *Matthew 11:28–30*

Come to me, all you that are weary and are carrying heavy burdens, and I will give you rest. Take my yoke upon you, and learn from me; for I am gentle and humble in heart, and you will find rest for your souls. For my yoke is easy, and my burden is light.

19   *Mark 10:13–16*

People were bringing little children to [Jesus] in order that he might touch them; and the disciples spoke sternly to them. But when Jesus saw this, he was indignant and said to them, "Let the little children come to me; do not stop them; for it is to such as these that the kingdom of God belongs. Truly I tell you, whoever does not receive the kingdom of God as a little child will never enter it." And he took them up in his arms, laid his hands on them, and blessed them.

20   *Luke 4:40*

As the sun was setting, all those who had any who were sick with various kinds of diseases brought them to him; and he laid his hands on each of them and cured them.

21   *Luke 5:12–16*

Once, when [Jesus] was in one of the cities, there was a man covered with leprosy. When he saw Jesus, he bowed with his face to the ground and begged him, "Lord, if you choose, you can make me clean." Then Jesus stretched out his hand, touched him, and said, "I do choose. Be made clean." Immediately the leprosy left him. And he ordered him to tell no one. "Go," he said, "and show yourself to the priest, and, as Moses commanded, make an offering for your cleansing, for a testimony to them." But now more than ever the word about Jesus spread abroad; many crowds would gather to hear him and to be cured of their diseases. But he would withdraw to deserted places and pray.

22   *Luke 8:43–48*

Now there was a woman who had been suffering from hemorrhages for twelve years; and though she had spent all she had on physicians, no one could cure her. She came up behind him and touched the fringe of his clothes, and immediately the hemorrhage stopped. Then Jesus asked, "Who touched me?" When all denied it, Peter said, "Master, the crowds surround and press in on you." But Jesus said, "Someone touched me; for I noticed that power had gone out from me." When the woman saw that she could not remain hidden, she came trembling; and falling down before him, she declared in the presence of all the people why she had touched him, and how she had been immediately healed. He said to her, "Daughter, your faith has made you well; go in peace."

23   *John 14:1–6, 25–27*

"Do not let your hearts be troubled. Believe in God, believe also in me. In my Father's house there are many dwelling places. If it were not so, would I have told you that I go to prepare a place for you? And if I go and prepare a place for you, I will come again and will take you to myself, so that where I am, there you may be also. And you know the way to the place where I am going." Thomas said to him, "Lord, we do not know where you are going. How can we know the way?" Jesus said to him, "I am the way, and the truth, and the life. No one comes to the Father, except through me.

"I have said these things to you while I am still with you. But the Advocate, the Holy Spirit, whom the Father will send in my name, will teach you everything, and remind you of all that I have said to you. Peace I leave with you; my peace I give to you. I do not give to you as the world gives. Do not let your hearts be troubled, and do not let them be afraid."

One day Peter and John were going up to the temple at the hour of prayer, at three o'clock in the afternoon. And a man lame from birth was being carried in. People would lay him daily at the gate of the temple called the Beautiful Gate so that he could ask for alms from those entering the temple. When he saw Peter and John about to go into the temple, he asked them for alms. Peter looked intently at him, as John did, and said, "Look at us." And he fixed his attention on them, expecting to receive something from them. But Peter said, "I have no silver or gold, but what I have I give you; in the name of Jesus Christ of Nazareth, stand up and walk." And he took him by the right hand and raised him up; and immediately his feet and ankles were made strong. Jumping up, he stood and began to walk, and he entered the temple with them, walking and leaping and praising God. All the people saw him walking and praising God, and they recognized him as the one who used to sit and ask for alms at the Beautiful Gate of the temple; and they were filled with wonder and amazement at what had happened to him.

25 *Romans 8:14–23*

For all who are led by the Spirit of God are children of God. For you did not receive a spirit of slavery to fall back into fear, but you have received a spirit of adoption. When we cry, "Abba! Father!" it is that very Spirit bearing witness with our spirit that we are children of God, and if children, then heirs, heirs of God and joint heirs with Christ—if, in fact, we suffer with him so that we may also be glorified with him.

I consider that the sufferings of this present time are not worth comparing with the glory about to be revealed to us. For the creation waits with eager longing for the revealing of the children of God; for the creation was subjected to futility, not of its own will but by the will of the one who subjected it, in hope that the creation itself will be set free from its bondage to decay and will obtain the freedom of the glory of the children of God. We know that the whole creation has been groaning in labor pains until now; and not only the creation, but we ourselves, who have the first fruits of the Spirit, groan inwardly while we wait for adoption, the redemption of our bodies.

26 *Romans 8:26–28*

Likewise the Spirit helps us in our weakness; for we do not know how to pray as we ought, but that very Spirit intercedes with sighs too deep for words. And God, who searches the heart, knows what is the mind of the Spirit, because the Spirit intercedes for the saints according to the will of God. We know that all things work together for good for those who love God, who are called according to his purpose.

What then are we to say about these things? If God is for us, who is against us? He who did not withhold his own Son, but gave him up for us all, will he not with him also give us everything else? Who will bring any charge against God's elect? It is God who justifies. Who is to condemn? It is Christ Jesus, who died, yes, who was raised, who is at the right hand of God, who indeed intercedes for us. Who will separate us from the love of Christ? Will hardship, or distress, or persecution, or famine, or nakedness, or peril, or sword? As it is written,

> "For your sake we are being killed all day long;
>   we are counted as sheep to be slaughtered."

No, in all these things we are more than conquerors through him who loved us. For I am convinced that neither death, nor life, nor angels, nor rulers, nor things present, nor things to come, nor powers, nor height, nor depth, nor anything else in all creation, will be able to separate us from the love of God in Christ Jesus our Lord.

28 *Romans 12:1, 2*

I appeal to you therefore, brothers and sisters, by the mercies of God, to present your bodies as a living sacrifice, holy and acceptable to God, which is your spiritual worship. Do not be conformed to this world, but be transformed by the renewing of your minds, so that you may discern what is the will of God—what is good and acceptable and perfect.

29 *Philippians 4:4, 6–9*

Rejoice in the Lord always; again I will say, Rejoice.

Do not worry about anything, but in everything by prayer and supplication with thanksgiving let your requests be made known to God. And the peace of God, which surpasses all understanding, will guard your hearts and your minds in Christ Jesus.

Finally, beloved, whatever is true, whatever is honorable, whatever is just, whatever is pure, whatever is pleasing, whatever is commendable, if there is any excellence, and if there is anything worthy of praise, think about these things. Keep on doing the things that you have learned and received and heard and seen in me, and the God of peace will be with you.

30 *Hebrews 4:14–16; 5:7–9*

Since, then, we have a great high priest who has passed through the heavens, Jesus, the Son of God, let us hold fast to our confession. For we do not have a high priest who is unable to sympathize with our weaknesses, but we have one who in every respect has been tested as we are, yet without sin. Let us therefore approach the throne of grace with boldness, so that we may receive mercy and find grace to help in time of need.

In the days of his flesh, Jesus offered up prayers and supplications, with loud cries and tears, to the one who was able to save him from death, and he was heard because of his reverent submission. Although he was a Son, he learned obedience through what he suffered; and having been made perfect, he became the source of eternal salvation for all who obey him. . . .

31   *James 5:13–16*

Are any among you suffering? They should pray. Are any cheerful? They should sing songs of praise. Are any among you sick? They should call for the elders of the church, and have them pray over them, anointing them with oil in the name of the Lord. The prayer of faith will save the sick, and the Lord will raise them up; and anyone who has committed sins will be forgiven. Therefore confess your sins to one another, and pray for one another, so that you may be healed. The prayer of the righteous is powerful and effective.

32   *1 Peter 1:3–9*

Blessed be the God and Father of our Lord Jesus Christ! By his great mercy he has given us a new birth into a living hope through the resurrection of Jesus Christ from the dead, and into an inheritance that is imperishable, undefiled, and unfading, kept in heaven for you, who are being protected by the power of God through faith for a salvation ready to be revealed in the last time. In this you rejoice, even if now for a little while you have had to suffer various trials, so that the genuineness of your faith—being more precious than gold that, though perishable, is tested by fire—may be found to result in praise and glory and honor when Jesus Christ is revealed. Although you have not seen him, you love him; and even though you do not see him now, you believe in him and rejoice with an indescribable and glorious joy, for you are receiving the outcome of your faith, the salvation of your souls.

PRAYERS

These prayers may be used in visiting the sick and in the services that follow. They may also suggest language or themes for extemporary prayer when that form of prayer is more suitable. Other suitable prayers may be found on pages 830–833.

1

For the sick

Lord of all health,
you are the source of our life
and our fulfillment in death.
Be for N. now
comfort in the midst of pain,
strength to transform weakness,
and light to brighten darkness,
through Christ our Lord.   **Amen.**   [836]

2

For healing

By your power, great God,
our Lord Jesus healed the sick
and gave new hope to the hopeless.
Though we cannot command or possess your power,
we pray for those who want to be healed
(especially for N.).
Mend their wounds, soothe fevered brows,
and make broken people whole again.
Help us to welcome every healing as a sign that,
though death is against us,
you are for us,
and have promised renewed and risen life
in Jesus Christ the Lord.   **Amen.**   [837]

3

For parent(s) of a sick child

Merciful God,
Enfold N. [*name of child*] in the arms of your love.
Comfort N., N. [parent(s)] in their anxiety.
Deliver *them* from despair,
give *them* patience to endure
and guide *them* to choose wisely for N. [*name of child*],
in the name of him who welcomed little children,
even Jesus Christ our Lord.   **Amen.**   [838]

4

For those experiencing tragedy

Out of the darkness we cry to you, O God.
Enable us to find in Christ
the faith to trust your care
even in the midst of pain,
so that we may not walk alone
through the valley of the shadow of death,
through Christ our Lord.   **Amen.**   [839]

5

For a sick child

Jesus, friend of little children,
bless N. with your healing love
and make *him/her* well.   **Amen.**   [840]

6

For the sick and those giving care

Faithful Healer of the sick,
in your loving mercy,
embrace N. in *her/his* time of need.
Guide the nurses, doctors
and others who attend *her/him*.
Use their skills
to restore N. to health and joy
for the service of Christ our Savior.   **Amen.**   [841]

7

For those who work for healing

God of compassion,
who in Jesus Christ healed the sick,
bless all who continue your work of healing.
Enhance their skills, and deepen their understanding,
that through their ministry
those who suffer may be restored to fullness of health,
for the sake of Christ our Lord.   **Amen.**   [842]

8

For those in medical services

Merciful God,
your healing power is everywhere about us.
Strengthen those who work among the sick;
give them courage and confidence in everything they do.

Encourage them when their efforts seem futile
or when death prevails.
Increase their trust in your power
even to overcome death and pain and crying.
May they be thankful for every sign of health you give,
and humble before the mystery of your healing grace;
through Jesus Christ our Lord. **Amen.** [843]

9

For one in emotional distress

Merciful God,
you give us the grace that helps in time of need.
Surround N. with your steadfast love
and lighten *his/her* burden.
By the power of your Spirit,
free *him/her* from distress
and give *him/her* a new mind and heart made whole
in the name of the risen Christ. **Amen.** [844]

10

For one in emotional distress

God of life,
deliver your servant N.
from distress and loneliness.
Give *her/him* your peace,
and fill *her/him* with your Holy Spirit.
Lift *her/him* from despair
to claim the life you offer in Jesus Christ,
in whose name we pray. **Amen.** [845]

11

For those in mental distress

Mighty God,
in Jesus Christ you deal with spirits that darken our minds
and set us against ourselves.
Give peace to those who are torn by conflict,
cast down, or lost in worlds of illusion.
By your power,
drive from our minds demons that shake confidence
and wreck love.
Tame unruly forces within us,
and bring us to your truth,
so that we may accept ourselves
as your beloved children in Jesus Christ. **Amen.** [846]

12

For one who has attempted suicide

Gracious God,
your Son came among us not to condemn but to save.
He taught us that nothing can separate us from your love.
Release us from the fear that we are worthless,
and stay our hands from self-destruction.
Uphold N. with your love.
Fill *him/her* with hope
and with trust in your guidance,
that your power may make *him/her* new
through the grace of our Lord Jesus Christ.   **Amen.**   [847]

13

For one who is anxious

Merciful God,
in Jesus Christ we have your promise of peace.
Receive N., who seeks your help.
Assure *her/him* that you are near.
Fill *her/him* with your Spirit,
cast out *her/his* anxiety and fear,
and help *her/him* to rely on the strength you provide,
through Jesus Christ our Lord.   **Amen.**   [848]

14

For someone who is old

God of grace and hope,
we thank you for life, love, and good memories,
for the gift of age,
and for the wisdom that comes from experience.
We bless you for your constant presence,
for with you there is fullness of joy.
Give us the courage and faith
to accept life as it comes,
confident that the future is yours
and that we belong to you forever;
through Jesus Christ our Lord.   **Amen.**   [849]

15

For those in coma or unable to communicate

Eternal God,
you have known us before we were here
and will continue to know us after we are gone.
Touch N. with your grace and presence.
As you give your abiding care,
assure *him/her* of our love and presence.
Though we are unable to respond to each other,
assure *him/her* that our communion together remains secure,
and that your love for *him/her* is unfailing.
In Christ, who came through to us, we pray. **Amen.** [850]

16

For an Alzheimer's disease patient

God of compassion,
you have borne our griefs
and carried our sorrows.
Preserve your covenant of peace
with your servant N., in *his/her* distress.
Although the pain of *his/her* forgetfulness is great,
we rejoice that you remember *him/her* always in your grace.
Supply *his/her* every need
according to the riches of your glory in Christ Jesus. **Amen.** [851]

17

For those giving care to a patient with Alzheimer's disease

God, our refuge and strength,
our present help in time of trouble,
care for those who tend the needs of N.
Strengthen them in body and spirit.
Refresh them when weary;
console them when anxious;
comfort them in grief;
and hearten them in discouragement.
Lord of peace, be with us all,
and give us peace at all times
and in every way. **Amen.** [852]

18

For those suffering with AIDS

O God,
your compassion is unbounded,
and your mercy is endless.
You know what we need before we ask;
you understand our anxieties and fears.
Reassure N., of your love that never ends.
Calm *his/her* troubled mind,
and renew hope within *him/her*.
Help *him/her* rely upon your strength,
trusting you to restore confidence in your never-failing grace.
Grant wisdom and compassion
to doctors and nurses that attend *him/her*.
Give *his/her* family and friends
assurance of your presence and power;
through Jesus Christ our Lord.   **Amen.**   [853]

19

For use when a life-support system is withdrawn

God of compassion and love,
you have breathed into us the breath of life
and have given us the exercise of our minds and wills.
In our frailty we surrender all life to you from whom it came,
trusting in your gracious promises;
through Jesus Christ our Lord.   **Amen.**   [854]

20

For parents after the birth of a stillborn child
or the death of a newly born child

Merciful God,
you strengthen us by your power and wisdom.
Be gracious to N. and N. in their grief,
and surround them with your unfailing love;
that they may not be overwhelmed by their loss,
but have confidence in your goodness,
and courage to meet the days to come;
through Jesus Christ our Lord.   **Amen.**   [855]

An Outline of Holy Communion with Those Unable to Attend Public Worship

Call to Worship
[Doxology, Psalm, Hymn, or Spiritual]
Confession and Pardon
Scripture Reading and Brief Sermon
[Psalm, Hymn, or Spiritual]
Invitation to the Lord's Table
Great Thanksgiving
Lord's Prayer
Breaking of the Bread
Communion
Prayer After Communion
Blessing

An Outline of Holy Communion with Those Unable to Attend Public Worship: With Option of Laying On of Hands (and Anointing)

Call to Worship
[Doxology, Psalm, Hymn, or Spiritual]
Confession and Pardon
Scripture Reading and Brief Sermon
[Psalm, Hymn, or Spiritual Song]
Laying On of Hands and Anointing with Oil
    Thanksgiving and Invocation
    Laying On of Hands [and Anointing with Oil]
    Prayer
[Psalm, Hymn, or Spiritual]
Invitation to the Lord's Table
Great Thanksgiving
Lord's Prayer
Breaking of the Bread
Communion
Prayer After Communion
Blessing

Holy Communion with Those Unable to Attend Public Worship

This service is for the celebration of the Lord's Supper with those who are homebound, in a hospital or nursing home, or in other circumstances that prevent them from attending public worship. The service may be used with individuals or with groups of persons, and may be expanded or abbreviated depending upon the circumstances.

The minister shall be accompanied by one or more members of the congregation authorized by the session to represent the church.

CALL TO WORSHIP

The minister greets the people:

The peace of the Lord be always with you.

The people answer:

And also with you.

The minister then continues, using one or more of the following:

1   *Matt. 11:28, 29*

Jesus says:
Come to me,
all you that are weary and are carrying heavy burdens,
and I will give you rest.
Take my yoke upon you, and learn from me;
for I am gentle and humble in heart,
and you will find rest for your souls.

I am the bread of life.
Whoever comes to me will never be hungry,
and whoever believes in me will never be thirsty.
Everything that the Father gives me will come to me,
and anyone who comes to me I will never drive away.

3 *Matt. 18:20*

For where two or three are gathered in my name,
I am there among them.

4 *Matt. 5:6*

Blessed are those who hunger and thirst for righteousness,
for they will be filled.

5 *Rev. 3:20*

Behold! I stand at the door and knock;
if you hear my voice and open the door,
I will come in to you and eat with you,
and you with me.

DOXOLOGY, PSALM, HYMN, OR SPIRITUAL

A doxology, psalm, hymn, or spiritual may be sung or said.

CONFESSION AND PARDON

CALL TO CONFESSION

The minister calls the people to confess their sins:

In the Lord's Supper,
Christ is present by the power of the Holy Spirit,
and offers us his body, broken for our sake,
and his blood, shed for the forgiveness of our sins.

As we prepare to receive this great gift,
let us confess our sin
and hear the promise of forgiveness.

A brief period of silence may be observed for examination of conscience.

Confession of Sin

All confess their sin, using the following prayer:

**Merciful God,
we confess that we have sinned against you
in thought, word, and deed,
by what we have done,
and by what we have left undone.
We have not loved you
with our whole heart and mind and strength;
we have not loved our neighbors as ourselves.**

**In your mercy forgive what we have been,
help us amend what we are,
and direct what we shall be,
so that we may delight in your will
and walk in your ways,
to the glory of your holy name.**   [49]

Declaration of Forgiveness

The minister declares the assurance of God's forgiving grace, using one of
the following:

1

The mercy of the Lord
is from everlasting to everlasting.
I declare to you, in the name of Jesus Christ,
you are forgiven.

May the God of mercy,
who forgives you all your sins,
strengthen you in all goodness,
and by the power of the Holy Spirit
keep you in eternal life.

Amen.

2   *Rom. 8:34; 2 Cor. 5:17*

Hear the good news!
Who is in a position to condemn?
Only Christ,
and Christ died for us,
Christ rose for us,
Christ reigns in power for us,
Christ prays for us.

Anyone who is in Christ
is a new creation.
The old life has gone;
a new life has begun.

Know that you are forgiven
and be at peace.
Amen.

SCRIPTURE READING AND BRIEF SERMON

A scripture lesson is read and briefly interpreted.

PSALM, HYMN, OR SPIRITUAL

A psalm, hymn, or spiritual may be sung.

LAYING ON OF HANDS

The laying on of hands and anointing with oil may be included here, as
provided for in the service for wholeness (pp. 1019–1021).

INVITATION TO THE LORD'S TABLE

The minister says:

Luke 24:30, 31

According to Luke,
when our risen Lord was at table with his disciples,
he took the bread, and blessed and broke it,
and gave it to them.
Then their eyes were opened
and they recognized him.

GREAT THANKSGIVING

The following dialogue may be used, according to the circumstances:

The Lord be with you.

And also with you.

Lift up your hearts.

We lift them to the Lord.

Let us give thanks to the Lord our God.

It is right to give our thanks and praise.

The minister says:

Holy God, we praise you.
Let the heavens be joyful,
and the earth be glad.

We bless you for creating the whole world,
for your promises to your people Israel,
and for Jesus Christ in whom your fullness dwells.

Born of Mary, he shares our life.
Eating with sinners, he welcomes us.
Guiding his children, he leads us.
Visiting the sick, he heals us.
Dying on the cross, he saves us.
Risen from the dead, he gives new life.
Living with you, he prays for us.

According to the circumstances, the following may be included:

Therefore we praise you,
joining our voices with choirs of angels
and with all the faithful of every time and place,
who forever sing to the glory of your name:

**Holy, holy, holy Lord, God of power and might,
heaven and earth are full of your glory.
Hosanna in the highest.**

**Blessed is he who comes in the name of the Lord.
Hosanna in the highest.**

With thanksgiving we take this bread and this cup
and proclaim the death and resurrection of our Lord.
Receive our sacrifice of praise.

Pour out your Holy Spirit upon us
that this meal may be
a communion in the body and blood of our Lord.

Make us one with Christ
and with all who share this feast.

Unite us in faith,
encourage us with hope,
inspire us to love,
that we may serve as your faithful disciples
until we feast at your table in glory.

We praise you, eternal God,
through Christ your Word made flesh,
in the holy and life-giving Spirit,
now and forever.   [121]

Amen.

LORD'S PRAYER

The minister invites all present to say the Lord's Prayer.

And now, with the confidence of the children of God,
let us pray:

All pray together.

Or

Our Father in heaven,
hallowed be your name,
your kingdom come,
your will be done,
on earth as in heaven.
Give us today our daily bread.
Forgive us our sins
as we forgive those who sin against us.
Save us from the time of trial
and deliver us from evil.
For the kingdom, the power,
  and the glory are yours
now and forever.   Amen.

Our Father, who art in heaven,
hallowed be thy name,
thy kingdom come,
thy will be done,
on earth as it is in heaven.
Give us this day our daily bread;
and forgive us our debts,
as we forgive our debtors;
and lead us not into temptation,
but deliver us from evil.
For thine is the kingdom,
and the power, and the glory,
  forever.   Amen.

BREAKING OF THE BREAD

The minister breaks the bread, saying:

1 Cor. 11:23–26; Luke 22:19–20

The Lord Jesus, on the night of his arrest, took bread,
and after giving thanks to God,
he broke it, and gave it to his disciples, saying:
Take, eat.
This is my body, given for you.
Do this in remembrance of me.

The minister lifts the cup, saying:

In the same way he took the cup, saying:
This cup is the new covenant sealed in my blood,
shed for you for the forgiveness of sins.
Whenever you drink it,
do this in remembrance of me.

Every time you eat this bread and drink this cup,
you proclaim the saving death of the risen Lord,
until he comes.

COMMUNION

The minister and those present receive Communion.

One of the following may be used:

1

In giving the bread:

The body of Christ, given for you.   **Amen.**

In giving the cup:

The blood of Christ, shed for you.   **Amen.**

Or

2

In giving the bread:

The body of Christ, the bread of heaven.   **Amen.**

In giving the cup:

The blood of Christ, the cup of salvation.   **Amen.**

Prayer After Communion

After all have been served, the minister says this or a similar prayer:

Let us pray:

We thank you, O God,
that through Word and Sacrament
you have given us your Son,
who is the true bread from heaven
and food of eternal life.
So strengthen us in your service
that our daily living may show our thanks,
through Jesus Christ our Lord.   [61]

Amen.

Blessing

The minister gives God's blessing to those present, using one of the following, or another blessing (pp. 83–161).

1   *See Num. 6:24–26*

The Lord bless you and keep you.
The Lord be kind and gracious to you.
The Lord look upon you with favor
and give you peace.

Amen.

2   *2 Thess. 3:18*

The grace of our Lord Jesus Christ be with you.

Amen.

AN OUTLINE OF A SERVICE FOR WHOLENESS FOR USE WITH A CONGREGATION

Opening Sentences
Psalm, Hymn, or Spiritual
Confession and Pardon
Doxology, Psalm, Hymn, or Spiritual
Readings from Scripture
Sermon
[Psalm, Hymn, or Spiritual]
Offering of Our Lives to God
Intercession for Healing
Laying On of Hands and Anointing with Oil
    Thanksgiving and Invocation
    Laying On of Hands [and Anointing with Oil]
    Lord's Prayer or Prayer
[Hymn]
Blessing

AN OUTLINE OF A SERVICE FOR WHOLENESS FOR USE WITH A CONGREGATION FOLLOWING THE SERVICE FOR THE LORD'S DAY

When the service for wholeness follows a service including the confession of sin, the reading of scripture, and a sermon, these elements may be omitted and the service for wholeness takes the following form:

Opening Sentences
Psalm, Hymn, or Spiritual
Offering of Our Lives to God
Intercession for Healing
Laying On of Hands and Anointing with Oil
    Thanksgiving and Invocation
    Laying On of Hands [and Anointing with Oil]
    Lord's Prayer or Prayer
[Hymn]
Blessing

AN OUTLINE OF A SERVICE FOR WHOLENESS WITH THE LORD'S SUPPER FOR USE WITH A CONGREGATION

When the celebration of the Lord's Supper is included as a part of the service of wholeness, it follows the laying on of hands and anointing, as indicated below.

Opening Sentences
Psalm, Hymn, or Spiritual
Confession and Pardon
Doxology, Psalm, Hymn, or Spiritual
Readings from Scripture
Sermon
[Psalm, Hymn, or Spiritual]
Offering of Our Lives to God
Intercession for Healing
Laying On of Hands and Anointing with Oil
    Thanksgiving and Invocation
    Laying On of Hands [and Anointing with Oil]
    Prayer
[Hymn]
Invitation to the Lord's Table
Great Thanksgiving
Lord's Prayer
Breaking of the Bread
Communion
Prayer After Communion
Blessing

A SERVICE FOR WHOLENESS
FOR USE WITH A CONGREGATION

This service is for use with a congregation. It may include the celebration of the Lord's Supper (pp. 998–1002). The service may also follow a regular service of worship. If it follows a service including the confession of sin, the reading of scripture, and a sermon, these elements may be omitted here.

OPENING SENTENCES

The people are called to worship in these or similar words from scripture:

Ps. 124:8

Our help is in the name of the Lord,

who made heaven and earth.

One of the following, or another verse from scripture, is said:

1   *Isa. 40:31*

Those who wait for the Lord
shall renew their strength,
they shall mount up with wings like eagles,
they shall run and not be weary,
they shall walk and not faint.

2   *1 Peter 1:3, alt.*

Give praise to God the Almighty,
by whose great mercy
we have been born anew to a living hope
through the resurrection of Jesus Christ from the dead.

3   *2 Cor. 1:4ab, 5*

God consoles us in all our affliction,
so that we may be able
to console those who are in any affliction.
For just as the sufferings of Christ are abundant for us,
so also our consolation is abundant through Christ.

WHEN THIS SERVICE FOLLOWS ANOTHER INCLUDING A
CONFESSION OF SIN, THE READING OF SCRIPTURE, AND
A SERMON, THE SERVICE CONTINUES ON PAGE 1009.

PSALM, HYMN, OR SPIRITUAL

CONFESSION AND PARDON

CALL TO CONFESSION

> The people are called to confession with these or other sentences of scripture that promise God's forgiveness.

Luke 11:9, 10

Jesus said:
Ask and it will be given you;
seek, and you will find;
knock, and it will be opened to you.

For every one who asks receives,
and the one who seeks finds,
and to the one who knocks it will be opened.

Friends in Christ,
God knows our needs before we ask,
and in our asking
prepares us to receive the gift of grace.

Let us open our lives to God's healing presence,
forsaking all that separates us
from God and neighbor.

Let us be mindful not only of personal evil
but also of our communal sins
of family, class, race, and nation.

Let us confess to God whatever has wounded us
or brought injury to others,
that we may receive mercy
and become for each other
ministers of God's grace.

CONFESSION OF SIN

A brief silence may be observed for examination of conscience.

The minister then says:

Let us confess our sin together.

All confess their sin, using one of the following, or another prayer of confession (pp. 53–54, 87–89):

1

Merciful God,
we confess that we have sinned against you
in thought, word, and deed,
by what we have done,
and by what we have left undone.
We have not loved you
with our whole heart and mind and strength;
we have not loved our neighbors as ourselves.

In your mercy forgive what we have been,
help us amend what we are,
and direct what we shall be,
so that we may delight in your will
and walk in your ways,
to the glory of your holy name.   [49]

2

Eternal God,
in whom we live and move and have our being,
whose face is hidden from us by our sins,
and whose mercy we forget in the blindness of our hearts:
Cleanse us from all our offenses,
and deliver us from proud thoughts and vain desires,
that with reverent and humble hearts
we may draw near to you,
confessing our faults,
confiding in your grace,
and finding in you our refuge and our strength;
through Jesus Christ your Son.   [67]

DECLARATION OF FORGIVENESS

The minister declares the assurance of God's forgiving grace:

1

The mercy of the Lord
is from everlasting to everlasting.
I declare to you, in the name of Jesus Christ,
you are forgiven.

May the God of mercy,
who forgives you all your sins,
strengthen you in all goodness,
and by the power of the Holy Spirit
keep you in eternal life.

Amen.

2   *Rom. 8:34; 2 Cor. 5:17*

Hear the good news!
Who is in a position to condemn?
Only Christ,
and Christ died for us,
Christ rose for us,
Christ reigns in power for us,
Christ prays for us.

Anyone who is in Christ
is a new creation.
The old life has gone;
a new life has begun.

Know that you are forgiven
and be at peace.

Amen.

DOXOLOGY, PSALM, HYMN, OR SPIRITUAL

A doxology, psalm, hymn, or spiritual may be sung.

READINGS FROM SCRIPTURE

Before the scriptures are read, a prayer for illumination is said by the
reader (pp. 60, 90–91).

Appropriate selections from the scripture are read.

SERMON

A sermon follows.

IF THE CONFESSION OF SIN, THE READING OF SCRIPTURE, AND THE SERMON ARE OMITTED, THE SERVICE CONTINUES HERE FROM PAGE 1006.

[PSALM, HYMN, OR SPIRITUAL]

OFFERING OF OUR LIVES TO GOD

The minister or another leader says:

Rom. 12:1

I appeal to you therefore,
brothers and sisters,
by the mercies of God,
to present your bodies as a living sacrifice,
holy and acceptable to God,
which is your spiritual worship.

Here all present may ponder in silence all that is happening in their lives, and may, with renewed commitment, offer themselves and their gifts for ministry to the service of Jesus Christ in the world.

INTERCESSION FOR HEALING

The following, or a similar prayer of intercession, is said:

God, our creator,
your will for us and for all your people
is health and salvation:

have mercy on us.

Jesus Christ, Son of God,
you came that we might have life
and have it in abundance:

have mercy on us.

Holy Spirit,
dwelling within us,
you make us temples of your presence:

have mercy on us.

To the triune God,
the source of all love and all life,
let us offer our prayers.

For all who are in need of healing,

> Silence.

Lord, in your mercy,
hear our prayer.

For all who are disabled by injury or illness,

> Silence.

Lord, in your mercy,
hear our prayer.

For all who are troubled by confusion or pain,

> Silence.

Lord, in your mercy,
hear our prayer.

For all whose increasing years bring weariness,

> Silence.

Lord, in your mercy,
hear our prayer.

For all about to undergo surgery,

> Silence.

Lord, in your mercy,
hear our prayer.

For all who cannot sleep,

> Silence.

Lord, in your mercy,
hear our prayer.

For all who practice the healing arts,

Silence.

Lord, in your mercy,
hear our prayer.

Here petitions for specific needs may be offered by the people.

Into your hands, O God,
we commend all for whom we pray,
trusting in your mercy;
through Jesus Christ our Lord. [856]
Amen.

LAYING ON OF HANDS AND ANOINTING WITH OIL

Those desiring the laying on of hands [and anointing with oil] come forward, and bow or kneel. Each may make her or his request known to the minister(s) and/or the elder(s).

THANKSGIVING AND INVOCATION

One of the following, or a similar prayer, is said. (A) is used when all will receive both anointing and the laying on of hands; (B) is used when only the laying on of hands will be received; (C) is used when some will be anointed and others will not.

A

When all are to receive the laying on of hands and anointing:

Gracious God, source of all healing,
in Jesus Christ you heal the sick
and mend the broken.
We bless you for this oil
pressed from the fruits of the earth,
given to us as a sign
of healing and forgiveness,
and of the fullness of life you give.

By your Spirit,
come upon all who are anointed with this oil
that they may receive your healing touch
and be made whole,
to the glory of Jesus Christ our Redeemer.   [857]

Amen.

B

> When all are to receive the laying on of hands, without anointing, one of
> the following is used:

1

Gracious God, source of all healing,
in Jesus Christ you heal the sick and mend the broken.
By your Spirit,
come upon all who receive the laying on of hands,
that they may receive your healing touch
and be made whole,
to the glory of Jesus Christ our Redeemer.   [858]

Amen.

2

Lord and giver of life,
as by your power
the apostles anointed the sick,
and they were healed,
so come, Creator Spirit,
and heal those who now receive the laying on of hands.   [859]

Amen.

C

> When among those to receive the laying on of hands, some are to be
> anointed and others are not:

Gracious God, source of all healing,
in Jesus Christ you heal the sick and mend the broken.
We bless you for this oil pressed from the fruits of the earth,
given to us as a sign of healing and forgiveness,
and of the fullness of life you give.
By your Spirit,
come upon all who receive this ministry of compassion,
that they may receive your healing touch and be made whole,
to the glory of Jesus Christ our Redeemer.   [860]

Amen.

Laying On of Hands

> The minister, and/or elders, lay both hands on the head of each individual and, after a brief silence, say one of the following prayers.

> During the laying on of hands and anointing, the congregation may sing a hymn, psalm, or refrain.

1

N., may the God of all mercy
forgive you your sins,
release you from suffering,
and restore you to wholeness and strength.

Amen.

2

N., may God deliver you from all evil,
preserve you in all goodness,
and bring you to everlasting life;
through Jesus Christ our Lord.

Amen.

3

Spirit of the living God, present with us now,
enter N., in body, mind, and spirit,
and heal *her/him* of all that harms *her/him*.

4

N., may the Lord Christ grant you healing.

Amen.

Anointing with Oil

> If the person is also to be anointed, the minister or elder dips her or his thumb in the oil and makes the sign of the cross on the person's forehead, adding these words:

1

I anoint you with oil,
in the name of the Father,
and of the Son,
and of the Holy Spirit.

Amen.

Or

2

As you are anointed with this oil,
so may God grant you the anointing of the Holy Spirit.

Amen.

LORD'S PRAYER OR PRAYER

If the Lord's Supper is not celebrated, the Lord's Prayer (A) is said. If the
Lord's Supper is celebrated, (B) or a similar prayer is said.

A

If the Lord's Supper does not follow:

And now, with the confidence of the children of God,
let us pray:

All pray together.

Or

Our Father in heaven,
hallowed be your name,
your kingdom come,
your will be done,
on earth as in heaven.
Give us today our daily bread.
Forgive us our sins
as we forgive those who sin against us.
Save us from the time of trial
and deliver us from evil.
For the kingdom, the power,
   and the glory are yours
now and forever.   Amen.

Our Father, who art in heaven,
hallowed be thy name,
thy kingdom come,
thy will be done,
on earth as it is in heaven.
Give us this day our daily bread;
and forgive us our debts,
as we forgive our debtors;
and lead us not into temptation,
but deliver us from evil.
For thine is the kingdom,
and the power, and the glory,
   forever.   Amen.

B

If the Lord's Supper follows:

Mighty God,
you rise with healing in your wings,
to scatter all enemies that assault us.

As we wait in hope for the coming of that day
when crying and pain shall be no more,
help us by your Holy Spirit
to receive your power into our lives
and to trust in your eternal love,
through Jesus Christ our Savior.   [861]

Amen.

> Those who have received the laying on of hands (and anointing) are dismissed with these or similar words.

Go in peace to love and serve the Lord.

HYMN

> A hymn may be sung.

> If the Lord's Supper is to follow, the table may be prepared during the singing of the hymn. The service proceeds with the order for the Lord's Supper, beginning with the invitation to the Lord's table on page 998.

BLESSING

> A blessing, such as one of the following, is given.

See Num. 6:24–26

The Lord bless you and keep you.
The Lord be kind and gracious to you.
The Lord look upon you with favor
and give you peace.

Amen.

> Or

Rom. 15:13

May the God of hope
fill you with all joy and peace in believing,
so that you may abound in hope
by the power of the Holy Spirit.

Amen.

An Outline of a Service for Wholeness for Use with an Individual

Opening Sentences
Prayer
Scripture Reading
Laying On of Hands and Anointing with Oil
   Thanksgiving and Invocation
   Laying On of Hands [and Anointing with Oil]
   Prayer
Blessing

An Outline of a Service for Wholeness with Repentance and Forgiveness for Use with an Individual

Opening Sentences
Prayer
Repentance and Forgiveness
   Invitation to Confession
   Prayer of Confession
   Declaration of Forgiveness
   The Peace
Scripture Reading
Laying On of Hands and Anointing with Oil
   Thanksgiving and Invocation
   Laying On of Hands [and Anointing with Oil]
   Prayer
Blessing

An Outline of a Service for Wholeness with the Lord's Supper for Use with an Individual

Opening Sentences
Prayer
Scripture Reading
Sermon
Laying On of Hands and Anointing with Oil
    Thanksgiving and Invocation
    Laying On of Hands [and Anointing with Oil]
    Prayer
Invitation to the Lord's Table
Great Thanksgiving
Lord's Prayer
Breaking of the Bread
Communion
Prayer After Communion
Blessing

An Outline of a Service for Wholeness with Repentance and Forgiveness and the Lord's Supper for Use with an Individual

Opening Sentences
Prayer
Repentance and Forgiveness
    Invitation to Confession
    Prayer of Confession
    Declaration of Forgiveness
    The Peace
Scripture Reading
Sermon
Laying On of Hands and Anointing with Oil
    Thanksgiving and Invocation
    Laying On of Hands [and Anointing with Oil]
    Prayer
Invitation to the Lord's Table
Great Thanksgiving
Lord's Prayer
Breaking of the Bread
Communion
Prayer After Communion
Blessing

A Service for Wholeness for Use with an Individual

This service is for use in a hospital, home, or nursing home with individuals who are unable to participate in a corporate service of wholeness.

It may be used in relation to the service of repentance and forgiveness (pp. 1023–1024) and/or the celebration of the Lord's Supper (pp. 995–1002).

Except when the Lord's Supper is included, it may be led by a minister, a spiritual director, or another member of the Christian community.

OPENING SENTENCES

The leader says:

Ps. 124:8

Our help is in the name of the Lord,

who made heaven and earth.

The leader continues with one of the following, or another verse from scripture:

1

Isa. 40:31

Those who wait for the Lord
shall renew their strength,
they shall mount up with wings like eagles,
they shall run and not be weary,
they shall walk and not faint.

2

1 Peter 1:3

Give praise to God the Almighty,
by whose great mercy
we have been born anew to a living hope
through the resurrection of Jesus Christ from the dead.

PRAYER

The following or a similar prayer is said.

Let us pray:

God of compassion,
you have given us Jesus Christ, the great physician,
who made the broken whole
and healed the sick.
Touch our wounds, relieve our hurts,
and restore us to wholeness of life,
through the same Jesus Christ our Lord.   [862]

Amen.

When the person wishes to unburden his or her conscience, the service of
repentance and forgiveness (pp. 1023–1024) may be included here.

SCRIPTURE READING

An appropriate passage from scripture may be read (pp. 971–987) and briefly
interpreted.

LAYING ON OF HANDS AND ANOINTING WITH OIL

THANKSGIVING AND INVOCATION

One of the following, or a similar prayer, is said. (A) is used when both
anointing and the laying on of hands will be received; (B) is used when
only the laying on of hands will be received.

A

For use with the laying on of hands with anointing:

Gracious God, source of all healing,
in Jesus Christ you heal the sick
and mend the broken.
We bless you for this oil
pressed from the fruits of the earth,
given to us as a sign
of healing and forgiveness,
and of the fullness of life you give.

By your Spirit,
come upon N., who now receives the anointing with oil,
that *he/she* may receive your healing touch
and be made whole,
to the glory of Jesus Christ our Redeemer.   [857]

Amen.

B

> With the laying on of hands, without anointing, one of the following may
> be used:

1

Gracious God, source of all healing,
in Jesus Christ you heal the sick
and mend the broken.
By your Spirit,
come upon N., who now receives the laying on of hands,
that *she/he* may receive your healing touch
and be made whole,
to the glory of Jesus Christ our Redeemer.   [858]

Amen.

2

Lord and giver of life,
as by your power
the apostles anointed the sick,
and they were healed,
so come, Creator Spirit,
and heal N., who now receives the laying on of hands.   [859]

Amen.

LAYING ON OF HANDS

> The leader lays both hands on the person's head and, following a brief si-
> lence, says one of the following:

1

N., may the God of all mercy
forgive you your sins,
release you from suffering,
and restore you to wholeness and strength.

Amen.

2

N., may God deliver you from all evil,
preserve you in all goodness,
and bring you to everlasting life;
through Jesus Christ our Lord.

Amen.

3

Spirit of the living God, present with us now,
enter N., in body, mind, and spirit,
and heal *her/him* of all that harms *her/him*.

Amen.

4

N., may the Lord Christ grant you healing.

Amen.

ANOINTING WITH OIL

If the person is also to be anointed, the leader dips her or his thumb
in the oil and makes the sign of the cross on the person's forehead,
adding these words:

1

I anoint you with oil
in the name of the Father,
and of the Son,
and of the Holy Spirit.

Or

2

As you are anointed with this oil,
so may God grant you the anointing of the Holy Spirit.

PRAYER

One of the following, or a similar prayer, is then said:

1

Blessed are you, O Lord our God,
Ruler of all creation.
We praise you for the abundance of your blessings.
To those who ask, you give love;
to those who seek, you give faith;
to those who knock, you open the way of hope.
Help us to serve you in the power of the Holy Spirit,
through Jesus Christ our Lord.   [863]

Amen.

2

Mighty God,
you rise with healing in your wings,
to scatter all enemies that assault us.
As we wait in hope for the coming of that day
when crying and pain shall be no more,
help us by your Holy Spirit
to receive your power into our lives
and to trust in your eternal love,
through Jesus Christ our Savior.   [861]

Amen.

If the Lord's Supper is to be celebrated, the service proceeds with
the order for the Lord's Supper, beginning with the invitation to the
Lord's table on page 998.

BLESSING

The following, or another blessing, is given.

Rom. 15:13

May the God of hope
fill you with all joy and peace in believing,
so that you may abound in hope
by the power of the Holy Spirit.

Amen.

A Service of Repentance and Forgiveness for Use with a Penitent Individual

Outline

Invitation to Confession
Prayer of Confession
Declaration of Forgiveness
The Peace

> This service is for use on occasions when a penitent person seeks an unburdening of conscience and asks the counsel of a minister, spiritual director, or other member of the Christian community. The counseling session may conclude with this service.

INVITATION TO CONFESSION

> The minister, spiritual director, or other member of the Christian community invites their confession of sin together, saying:

1 John 1:9

If we confess our sins,
God who is faithful and just
will forgive us our sins
and cleanse us from all unrighteousness.

God, be merciful to me, a sinner.

N., join me in a prayer of confession.

PRAYER OF CONFESSION

> Together they pray this or a similar prayer of confession (pp. 53–54, 87–89):

Merciful God,
we confess that we have sinned against you
in thought, word, and deed,
by what we have done,
and by what we have left undone.
We have not loved you
with our whole heart and mind and strength;
we have not loved our neighbors as ourselves.

In your mercy forgive what we have been,
help us amend what we are,
and direct what we shall be,
so that we may delight in your will
and walk in your ways,
to the glory of your holy name.   [49]

DECLARATION OF FORGIVENESS

> The assurance of God's forgiving grace is declared to the penitent in these or similar words.

The mercy of the Lord
is from everlasting to everlasting.
I declare to you, in the name of Jesus Christ,
you are forgiven.

May the God of mercy,
who forgives you all your sins,
strengthen you in all goodness,
and by the power of the Holy Spirit
keep you in eternal life.

Amen.

THE PEACE

Phil. 4:7

May the peace of God, which passes all understanding,
keep your heart and your mind in Christ Jesus.

Amen.

> A sign of peace may be shared.

PRAYER AT THE TIME OF DEATH

Outline

Greeting
Scripture Sentence
Prayer
Lord's Prayer
Prayers of Commendation
Prayer for Family and Friends
Blessing

When death is near, the pastor and other officers of the church should be notified so that the ministry of the church may be offered to the dying person and the family.

GREETING

The pastor or an elder, deacon, family member, or other member of the community of faith greets those present:

The Lord be with you.

And also with you.

SCRIPTURE SENTENCE

Then one of the following verses from scripture is said:

1   *Rom. 14:8*

If we live, we live to the Lord,
and if we die, we die to the Lord;
so then, whether we live or whether we die,
we are the Lord's.

2   *Ps. 46:1*

God is our refuge and strength,
a very present help in trouble.

Praise be to the God and Father of our Lord Jesus Christ,
the Father of mercies and God of all comfort,
who comforts us in all our sorrows,
so that we can comfort others in their sorrow,
with the consolation we have received from God.

PRAYER

This or a similar prayer is said:

Gracious God, look on N.,
whom you created in your image,
and claimed as your own through baptism.
Comfort *her/him* with the promise of life eternal,
made sure in the death and resurrection of your Son,
Jesus Christ our Lord.   [864]

Amen.

LORD'S PRAYER

All pray together.

Or

**Our Father in heaven,
hallowed be your name,
your kingdom come,
your will be done,
on earth as in heaven.
Give us today our daily bread.
Forgive us our sins
as we forgive those who sin against us.
Save us from the time of trial
and deliver us from evil.
For the kingdom, the power,
  and the glory are yours
now and forever.   Amen.**

**Our Father, who art in heaven,
hallowed be thy name,
thy kingdom come,
thy will be done,
on earth as it is in heaven.
Give us this day our daily bread;
and forgive us our debts,
as we forgive our debtors;
and lead us not into temptation,
but deliver us from evil.
For thine is the kingdom,
and the power, and the glory,
  forever.   Amen.**

PRAYERS OF COMMENDATION

One of the following is said:

1

N., our *sister/brother* in the faith,
we entrust you to God who created you.
May you return to the one who formed us out of the dust of the earth.
Surrounded by the great cloud of witnesses beyond all time and space,
may Christ come to meet you
as you go forth from this life.

May Christ, the Lord of glory,
who was crucified for you,
bring you freedom and peace.

May Christ, the High Priest,
who has forgiven all your sins,
keep you among his people.

May Christ, the Son of God,
who died for you,
show you the glories of his eternal kingdom.

May Christ, the Good Shepherd,
enfold you with his tender care.
May you see your Redeemer face to face
and enjoy the sight of God for ever.   [865]

Amen.

2

Lord Jesus Christ,
deliver your servant N. from all evil,
and set *him/her* free from every bond;
that *he/she* may rest with all your saints
in the joy of your eternal home
for ever and ever.   [866]

Amen.

3

Gracious God,
Sustain with your presence our *sister/brother* N.
Help *her/him* now to trust your goodness
and claim your promise of life everlasting.
Cleanse *her/him* of all sin
and remove all burdens.
Grant *her/him* the sure joy of your salvation,
through Jesus Christ our Lord.   [867]

Amen.

4

Almighty God,
by rising from the grave,
Jesus Christ conquered death
and leads us to eternal life.
Watch over our *brother/sister* N.
Give *him/her* a vision of that home within your love
where pain is gone and death shall be no more;
through Jesus Christ the Lord of life.   [868]

Amen.

5

For use when a life–support system is withdrawn

God of compassion and love,
you have breathed into us the breath of life
and have given us the exercise of our minds and wills.
In our frailty we surrender all life to you from whom it came,
trusting in your gracious promises;
through Jesus Christ our Lord.   [854]

Amen.

The leader then lays his or her hand on the head of the dying person and says:

Depart, O Christian soul, in peace;
in the name of God the Creator who formed you;
in the name of Jesus Christ who redeemed you;
in the name of the Holy Spirit the Comforter who sanctifies you.
In communion with the saints and all the heavenly host,
may you rest in peace,
and dwell forever with the Lord.

Amen.

The leader continues:

Into your hands, O merciful Savior,
we commend your servant N.
Acknowledge, we humbly beseech you,
a sheep of your own fold,
a lamb of your own flock,
a sinner of your own redeeming.
Receive *him/her* into the arms of your mercy,
into the blessed rest of everlasting peace,
and into the glorious company of the saints in light.   [822]

Amen.

The following prayer is then said:

O Lord, support us all the day long,
until the shadows lengthen and the evening comes
and the busy world is hushed,
and the fever of life is over,
and our work is done.
Then, in your mercy, grant us a safe lodging,
and a holy rest, and peace at the last;
through Jesus Christ our Lord.   [504]

Amen.

PRAYER FOR FAMILY AND FRIENDS

One of the following, or a similar prayer, may be said for the family and
friends of the dying. Those present may be invited to offer other prayers.

1

Almighty God, our creator and redeemer,
you are our comfort and strength.
You have given us our *sister/brother* N.
to know and to love in our pilgrimage on earth.
Uphold us now as we entrust *her/him*
to your boundless love and eternal care.
Assure us that not even death
can separate us from your infinite mercy.
Deal graciously with us in our anguish,
that we may truly know your sure consolation
and learn to live in confident hope of the resurrection;
through your Son, Jesus Christ our Lord.   [869]

Amen.

2

Lord God,
look kindly upon us in our sorrow
as this life is taken from us,
and gather our pain into your peace.
Be with us in our grieving, and overcome all our doubts.
Awaken our gratitude for your gifts of love and tenderness.
As we are able to receive them,
teach us the lessons of life that can be learned in death.
We pray through Christ our Lord.   [870]

Amen.

3

Lead, kindly Light,
our only hope in darkness.
Heal the wounds of sorrow and renew our trust in your goodness.
Enable us to be grateful for the ties that bind us to N.
Renew our strength each day to seek your will
and lean upon your mercy.
Keep us ever in the communion of saints
and in the promise of life eternal,
through Christ our Lord.   [871]

Amen.

4

God of compassion,
in sorrow, we receive from you the comfort you alone can give.
Enable us to see that you are always working for our good.
You are our dwelling place, O God,
and underneath us are your everlasting arms.
Assure us of your love
that we may be able to accept what we cannot understand.
Help us to be aware
not only of the shadows of death,
but also of the splendor of life eternal.
Enable us even now to face life with courage;
give us the grace and the strength to go on,
knowing that the great cloud of witnesses surrounds us.
Let the life of N. still inspire us.
Comfort and uphold us,
until we share together the light of your glory
and the peace of your eternal presence;
through Jesus Christ our Lord.   [872]

Amen.

BLESSING

A blessing, such as the following, may be given.

See Num. 6:24–26

The Lord bless you and keep you.
The Lord be kind and gracious to you.
The Lord look upon you with favor
and give you peace.

Amen.

CALENDAR AND
LECTIONARIES

THE SCRIPTURE IN PUBLIC WORSHIP

LECTIONARY FOR SUNDAYS AND FESTIVALS

The lectionary contains scripture readings for each Sunday and festival in a three-year cycle. The texts are taken from the *Common Lectionary* (Revised) prepared by the Consultation on Common Texts. The Consultation is a forum for liturgical renewal among many of the major Christian churches of North America.

Each yearly cycle of readings and psalms begins with the First Sunday of Advent. The Table of Major Celebrations of the Liturgical Calendar (pp. 1096–1097) displays the schedule for using this lectionary.

This lectionary also contains a psalm (or canticle) for each day. Since the psalm serves as a reflection upon the first reading, it is ordinarily not to be regarded as another reading. Given its character as a response, the psalm is most appropriately sung. Musical settings are provided in *The Presbyterian Hymnal*, and in *The Psalter—Psalms and Canticles for Singing*. Also, the texts for the psalms in this book (pp. 611–783) are pointed for singing to simple psalm tones such as those on pages 601–610. When it is not possible to sing the psalms, they may be read responsively or antiphonally.

SUGGESTIONS FOR READING

Readings may be lengthened or shortened when required by the circumstances. The verses contained within parentheses ( ) may be used when a longer reading is desired.

In addition, minor alteration of a reading can assist the hearers to understand the setting and flow of the text.

It is not always clear who is speaking, who is being described, or who is being addressed, particularly in the first verse of some readings. In such instances, the reader—after announcing the reading—may specify who the speaker or audience is. (Example: In reading Matthew 5:21-37, the reader need not begin with the opening words, "You have heard . . . ," but may begin: "Jesus said, 'You have heard . . . ,'" or "Jesus said to the crowds, 'You have heard . . .'")

Nouns occasionally need to be substituted for pronouns when it is unclear to whom the pronoun is referring (Example: In reading Mark 1:40-45, the reader may wish to say: "A leper came to Jesus begging him . . . ," instead of saying, "A leper came to him begging him . . .")

In addition, conjunctions that refer only to what has preceded should be omitted when they are found at the beginning of a reading. (Example: Read "Thanks be to God . . ." at the beginning of 2 Corinthians 5:16-21, instead of "But thanks be to God . . .")

LOCAL ADAPTATIONS OF THE LECTIONARY

The purpose of a lectionary is to provide for a disciplined use of the whole range of scripture in the church's worship. When the sixteenth-century Reformers rejected the use of the lectionary in use in the medieval church, they did not reject the notion that the selection of Bible readings for use in worship should be disciplined and informed by the wisdom of the church. Instead of the medieval lectionary, the Reformers recovered an ancient tradition of reading and preaching through the books of the Bible in course. This principle of selection of scripture passages is called *lectio continua* or continuous reading as distinct from the principle of *lectio selecta* or select reading in which particular readings are always assigned for specific days. Unlike contemporary lectionaries, lectionaries in earlier centuries did not embody the reading of any portion of the Bible in sequence. The Lectionary for Sundays and Festivals in this book embodies a semi-continuous reading of much of the Bible, during Ordinary Time, while embracing a select lectionary for the Christmas and Easter cycles and certain other festivals.

Some may wish to adopt the principle of continuous reading as an alternative to the lectionary contained in this book. In such cases, a book of the Bible (or a portion of a book) is chosen on the basis of its appropriateness for the particular season in the liturgical life of the church. Then chapter by chapter, or verse by verse, the whole message of the chosen book is proclaimed in an orderly manner over a series of weeks or months. The principle of continuous reading provides a responsible alternative to the use of the *Common Lectionary* in liturgical reading of the Bible and in preaching in worship.

Because the principle of continuous reading is already built into the *Common Lectionary* during portions of the liturgical calendar, local adaptations of the principle may also be combined with use of the lectionary in this book. For example, some may wish to use the lectionary in the book during the Christmas and Easter cycles, when the readings are carefully integrated with the meaning of the seasons and the events celebrated. Then, during Ordinary Time, particularly during the time between Pentecost and Advent when the lectionary itself features parallel semi-continuous readings from the Old Testament, the epistles, and the Gospels, some may wish to move to continuous reading of one or more books of the Bible that are particularly appropriate to the life and ministry of a particular congregation.

CALENDAR AND LECTIONARY: SUNDAYS AND FESTIVALS

THE CHRISTMAS CYCLE

ADVENT

Advent is a four-week period in which the church, rejoicing in Christ's first coming, eagerly looks forward to Christ's coming again. Beginning with the Sunday nearest November 30, the season is observed for the four Sundays prior to Christmas. *Liturgical color:* purple or blue.

CHRISTMAS

Christmas is the festival of the birth of Christ, the celebration of the incarnation. Christmas begins on Christmas Eve and ends with Epiphany (January 6), and may include either one or two Sundays. *Liturgical color:* white and gold.

SUNDAY OR FESTIVAL	YEAR A	YEAR B	YEAR C
ADVENT			
1st Sunday of Advent	Isa. 2:1-5	Isa. 64:1-9	Jer. 33:14-16
	Ps. 122	*Ps. 80:1-7, 17-19*	*Ps. 25:1-10*
	Rom. 13:11-14	1 Cor. 1:3-9	1 Thess. 3:9-13
	Matt. 24:36-44	Mark 13:24-37	Luke 21:25-36
2nd Sunday of Advent	Isa. 11:1-10	Isa. 40:1-11	Mal. 3:1-4
	Ps. 72:1-7, 18-19	*Ps. 85:1-2, 8-13*	*Luke 1:68-79*
	Rom. 15:4-13	2 Peter 3:8-15a	Phil. 1:3-11
	Matt. 3:1-12	Mark 1:1-8	Luke 3:1-6
3rd Sunday of Advent	Isa. 35:1-10	Isa. 61:1-4, 8-11	Zeph. 3:14-20
	Ps. 146:5-10	*Ps. 126*	*Isa. 12:2-6*
	or *Luke 1:47-55*	or *Luke 1:47-55*	
	James 5:7-10	1 Thess. 5:16-24	Phil. 4:4-7
	Matt. 11:2-11	John 1:6-8, 19-28	Luke 3:7-18

Sunday or Festival	Year A	Year B	Year C
4th Sunday of Advent	Isa. 7:10-16	2 Sam. 7:1-11, 16	Micah 5:2-5a
	Ps. 80:1-7, 17-19	*Luke 1:47-55 or*	*Luke 1:47-55*
		Ps. 89:1-4, 19-26	*or Ps. 80:1-7*
	Rom. 1:1-7	Rom. 16:25-27	Heb. 10:5-10
	Matt. 1:18-25	Luke 1:26-38	Luke 1:39-45
			(46-55)

CHRISTMAS

Christmas Eve	Isa. 9:2-7	Isa. 9:2-7	Isa. 9:2-7
(Dec. 24)	*Ps. 96*	*Ps. 96*	*Ps. 96*
	Titus 2:11-14	Titus 2:11-14	Titus 2:11-14
	Luke 2:1-14 (15-20)	Luke 2:1-14 (15-20)	Luke 2:1-14 (15-20)
Nativity of Jesus Christ/ Christmas Day (at dawn)	Isa. 62:6-12	Isa. 62:6-12	Isa. 62:6-12
	Ps. 97	*Ps. 97*	*Ps. 97*
	Titus 3:4-7	Titus 3:4-7	Titus 3:4-7
(Dec. 25)	Luke 2:(1-7) 8-20	Luke 2:(1-7) 8-20	Luke 2:(1-7) 8-20
Nativity of Jesus Christ/ Christmas Day	Isa. 52:7-10	Isa. 52:7-10	Isa. 52:7-10
	Ps. 98	*Ps. 98*	*Ps. 98*
	Heb. 1:1-4 (5-12)	Heb. 1:1-4 (5-12)	Heb. 1:1-4 (5-12)
(Dec. 25)	John 1:1-14	John 1:1-14	John 1:1-14

If these readings are not used on Christmas Day, they should be used at some service during the Christmas cycle because of the significance of John's prologue.

1st Sunday after Christmas Day	Isa. 63:7-9	Isa. 61:10–62:3	1 Sam. 2:18-20, 26
	Ps. 148	*Ps. 148*	*Ps. 148*
	Heb. 2:10-18	Gal. 4:4-7	Col. 3:12-17
	Matt. 2:13-23	Luke 2:22-40	Luke 2:41-52
2nd Sunday after Christmas Day	Jer. 31:7-14	Jer. 31:7-14	Jer. 31:7-14
	Ps. 147:12-20	*Ps. 147:12-20*	*Ps. 147:12-20*
	Eph. 1:3-14	Eph. 1:3-14	Eph. 1:3-14
	John 1:(1-9) 10-18	John 1:(1-9) 10-18	John 1:(1-9) 10-18
Epiphany of the Lord (Jan. 6) or Sunday before Epiphany	Isa. 60:1-6	Isa. 60:1-6	Isa. 60:1-6
	Ps. 72:1-7, 10-14	*Ps. 72:1-7, 10-14*	*Ps. 72:1-7, 10-14*
	Eph. 3:1-12	Eph. 3:1-12	Eph. 3:1-12
	Matt. 2:1-12	Matt. 2:1-12	Matt. 2:1-12

ORDINARY TIME

Ordinary Time is divided into two periods. The first period was previously called Sundays after Epiphany, and the second and longer period was referred to as the Sundays after Pentecost. The first period of Ordinary Time begins after Epiphany (January 6) and continues until Ash Wednesday. The Baptism of the Lord is the first Sunday of this period of Ordinary Time, the Transfiguration of the Lord is the last Sunday. Because of the variable date of Easter, this period of Ordinary Time may include from four to nine Sundays. *Liturgical color:* green, except for the Baptism of the Lord and the Transfiguration of the Lord when the color is white.

SUNDAY OR FESTIVAL	YEAR A	YEAR B	YEAR C
Baptism of the Lord *Sun. between Jan. 7 and 13 inclusive*	Isa. 42:1-9 *Ps. 29* Acts 10:34-43 Matt. 3:13-17	Gen. 1:1-5 *Ps. 29* Acts 19:1-7 Mark 1:4-11	Isa. 43:1-7 *Ps. 29* Acts 8:14-17 Luke 3:15-17, 21-22
2nd Sunday in Ordinary Time *Sun. between Jan. 14 and 20 inclusive*	Isa. 49:1-7 *Ps. 40:1-11* 1 Cor. 1:1-9 John 1:29-42	1 Sam. 3:1-10 (11-20) *Ps. 139:1-6, 13-18* 1 Cor. 6:12-20 John 1:43-51	Isa. 62:1-5 *Ps. 36:5-10* 1 Cor. 12:1-11 John 2:1-11
3rd Sunday in Ordinary Time *Sun. between Jan. 21 and 27 inclusive*	Isa. 9:1-4 *Ps. 27:1, 4-9* 1 Cor. 1:10-18 Matt. 4:12-23	Jonah 3:1-5, 10 *Ps. 62:5-12* 1 Cor. 7:29-31 Mark 1:14-20	Neh. 8:1-3, 5-6, 8-10 *Ps. 19* 1 Cor. 12:12-31a Luke 4:14-21
4th Sunday in Ordinary Time *Sun. between Jan. 28 and Feb. 3 inclusive**	Micah 6:1-8 *Ps. 15* 1 Cor. 1:18-31 Matt. 5:1-12	Deut. 18:15-20 *Ps. 111* 1 Cor. 8:1-13 Mark 1:21-28	Jer. 1:4-10 *Ps. 71:1-6* 1 Cor. 13:1-13 Luke 4:21-30
5th Sunday in Ordinary Time *Sun. between Feb. 4 and 10 inclusive**	Isa. 58:1-9a (9b-12) *Ps. 112:1-9 (10)* 1 Cor. 2:1-12 (13-16) Matt. 5:13-20	Isa. 40:21-31 *Ps. 147:1-11, 20c* 1 Cor. 9:16-23 Mark 1:29-39	Isa. 6:1-8 (9-13) *Ps. 138* 1 Cor. 15:1-11 Luke 5:1-11

Sunday or Festival	Year A	Year B	Year C
6th Sunday in	Deut. 30:15-20	2 Kings 5:1-14	Jer. 17:5-10
Ordinary Time	*Ps. 119:1-8*	*Ps. 30*	*Ps. 1*
Sun. between Feb.	1 Cor. 3:1-9	1 Cor. 9:24-27	1 Cor. 15:12-20
*11 and 17 inclusive**	Matt. 5:21-37	Mark 1:40-45	Luke 6:17-26
7th Sunday in	Lev. 19:1-2, 9-18	Isa. 43:18-25	Gen. 45:3-11, 15
Ordinary Time	*Ps. 119:33-40*	*Ps. 41*	*Ps. 37:1-11, 39-40*
Sun. between Feb.	1 Cor. 3:10-11, 16-23	2 Cor. 1:18-22	1 Cor. 15:35-38,
*18 and 24 inclusive**			42-50
	Matt. 5:38-48	Mark 2:1-12	Luke 6:27-38
8th Sunday in	Isa. 49:8-16a	Hos. 2:14-20	Isa. 55:10-13
Ordinary Time	*Ps. 131*	*Ps. 103:1-13, 22*	*Ps. 92:1-4, 12-15*
Sun. between Feb.	1 Cor. 4:1-5	2 Cor. 3:1-6	1 Cor. 15:51-58
*25 and 29 inclusive**	Matt. 6:24-34	Mark 2:13-22	Luke 6:39-49
Transfiguration of	Ex. 24:12-18	2 Kings 2:12	Ex. 34:29-35
the Lord	*Ps. 2 or Ps. 99*	*Ps. 50:1-6*	*Ps. 99*
Sunday preceding	2 Peter 1:16-21	2 Cor. 4:3-6	2 Cor. 3:12–4:2
Lent	Matt. 17:1-9	Mark 9:2-9	Luke 9:28-36
			(37-43)

Except when this Sunday is The Transfiguration of the Lord.

EASTER CYCLE

LENT

Lent is a season of forty weekdays and six Sundays, beginning on Ash Wednesday and culminating in Holy Week. During this season, the church, in joy and sorrow, proclaims, remembers, and responds to the atoning death of Christ. Two distinct periods at the end of Lent are: Holy Week (the week immediately preceding Easter, beginning with Passion/Palm Sunday) and the Three Days (the final three days comprising Maundy Thursday, Good Friday and the Easter Vigil). *Liturgical color:* first five weeks—purple. Passion/Palm Sunday— red and/or purple. Monday, Tuesday, and Wednesday of Holy Week—purple. Maundy Thursday—purple (until church is stripped bare). Good Friday and Saturday in Holy Week—no color since the church remains stripped bare.

Easter is a fifty-day season of seven Sundays, beginning with the Resurrection of the Lord (Easter Day), the festival of Christ's resurrection. Ascension Day, forty days after Easter, is celebrated to affirm that Christ is Lord of all times and places. The Day of Pentecost marks the end of the Easter season. *Liturgical color:* white and gold, except for the Day of Pentecost which is red.

SUNDAY OR FESTIVAL	YEAR A	YEAR B	YEAR C
LENT			
Ash Wednesday	Joel 2:1-2, 12-17 *or* Isa. 58:1-12 *Ps. 51:1-17* 2 Cor. 5:20b–6:10 Matt. 6:1-6, 16-21	Joel 2:1-2, 12-17 *or* Isa. 58:1-12 *Ps. 51:1-17* 2 Cor. 5:20b–6:10 Matt. 6:1-6, 16-21	Joel 2:1-2, 12-17 *or* Isa. 58:1-12 *Ps. 51:1-17* 2 Cor. 5:20b–6:10 Matt. 6:1-6, 16-21
1st Sunday in Lent	Gen. 2:15-17; 3:1-7 *Ps. 32* Rom. 5:12-19 Matt. 4:1-11	Gen. 9:8-17 *Ps. 25:1-10* 1 Peter 3:18-22 Mark 1:9-15	Deut. 26:1-11 *Ps. 91:1-2, 9-16* Rom. 10:8b-13 Luke 4:1-13
2nd Sunday in Lent	Gen. 12:1-4a *Ps. 121* Rom. 4:1-5, 13-17 John 3:1-17	Gen. 17:1-7, 15-16 *Ps. 22:23-31* Rom. 4:13-25 Mark 8:31-38	Gen. 15:1-12, 17-18 *Ps. 27* Phil. 3:17–4:1 Luke 13:31-35
3rd Sunday in Lent	Ex. 17:1-7 *Ps. 95* Rom. 5:1-11 John 4:5-42	Ex. 20:1-17 *Ps. 19* 1 Cor. 1:18-25 John 2:13-22	Isa. 55:1-9 *Ps. 63:1-8* 1 Cor. 10:1-13 Luke 13:1-9
4th Sunday in Lent	1 Sam. 16:1-13 *Ps. 23* Eph. 5:8-14 John 9:1-41	Num. 21:4-9 *Ps. 107:1-3, 17-22* Eph. 2:1-10 John 3:14-21	Josh. 5:9-12 *Ps. 32* 2 Cor. 5:16-21 Luke 15:1-3, 11b-32
5th Sunday in Lent	Ez. 37:1-14 *Ps. 130* Rom. 8:6-11 John 11:1-45	Jer. 31:31-34 *Ps. 51:1-12 or Ps. 119:9-16* Heb. 5:5-10 John 12:20-33	Isa. 43:16-21 *Ps. 126* Phil. 3:4b-14 John 12:1-8

| --- | --- | --- | --- |
HOLY WEEK			
Passion/Palm Sunday (6th Sunday in Lent)	*Liturgy of the Palms:* Matt. 21:1-11 *Ps. 118:1-2, 19-29* *Liturgy of the Passion:* Isa. 50:4-9a *Ps. 31:9-16* Phil. 2:5-11 Matt. 26:14–27:66 *or* Matt. 27:11-54	*Liturgy of the Palms:* Mark 11:1-11 *or* John 12:12-16 *Ps. 118:1-2, 19-29* *Liturgy of the Passion:* Isa. 50:4-9a *Ps. 31:9-16* Phil. 2:5-11 Mark 14:1–15:47 *or* Mark 15:1-39 (40-47)	*Liturgy of the Palms:* Luke 19:28-40 *Ps. 118:1-2, 19-29* *Liturgy of the Passion:* Isa. 50:4-9a *Ps. 31:9-16* Phil. 2:5-11 Luke 22:14–23:56 *or* Luke 23:1-49
Monday of Holy Week	Isa. 42:1-9 *Ps. 36:5-11* Heb. 9:11-15 John 12:1-11	Isa. 42:1-9 *Ps. 36:5-11* Heb. 9:11-15 John 12:1-11	Isa. 42:1-9 *Ps. 36:5-11* Heb. 9:11-15 John 12:1-11
Tuesday of Holy Week	Isa. 49:1-7 *Ps. 71:1-14* 1 Cor. 1:18-31 John 12:20-36	Isa. 49:1-7 *Ps. 71:1-14* 1 Cor. 1:18-31 John 12:20-36	Isa. 49:1-7 *Ps. 71:1-14* 1 Cor. 1:18-31 John 12:20-36
Wednesday of Holy Week	Isa. 50:4-9a *Ps. 70* Heb. 12:1-3 John 13:21-32	Isa. 50:4-9a *Ps. 70* Heb. 12:1-3 John 13:21-32	Isa. 50:4-9a *Ps. 70* Heb. 12:1-3 John 13:21-32

THE THREE DAYS

Maundy Thursday	Ex. 12:1-4 (5-10)	Ex. 12:1-4 (5-10)	Ex. 12:1-4 (5-10)
	11-14	11-14	11-14
	Ps. 116:1-2, 12-19	*Ps. 116:1-2, 12-19*	*Ps. 116:1-2, 12-19*
	1 Cor. 11:23-26	1 Cor. 11:23-26	1 Cor. 11:23-26
	John 13:1-17,	John 13:1-17,	John 13:1-17,
	31b-35	31b-35	31b-35

Good Friday	Isa. 52:13–53:12	Isa. 52:13–53:12	Isa. 52:13–53:12
	Ps. 22	*Ps. 22*	*Ps. 22*
	Heb. 10:16-25	Heb. 10:16-25	Heb. 10:16-25
	or Heb. 4:14-16;	*or* Heb. 4:14-16;	*or* Heb. 4:14-16;
	5:7-9	5:7-9	5:7-9
	John 18:1–19:42	John 18:1–19:42	John 18:1–19:42

EASTER

Easter Vigil	Gen. 1:1–2:4a	Gen. 1:1–2:4a	Gen. 1:1–2:4a
(First Service	*Ps. 136:1-9, 23-26*	*Ps. 136:1-9, 23-26*	*Ps. 136:1-9, 23-26*
of Easter)	Gen. 7:1-5, 11-18;	Gen. 7:1-5, 11-18;	Gen. 7:1-5, 11-18;
	8:6-18; 9:8-13	8:6-18; 9:8-13	8:6-18; 9:8-13
	Ps. 46	*Ps. 46*	*Ps. 46*
	Gen. 22:1-18	Gen. 22:1-18	Gen. 22:1-18
	Ps. 16	*Ps. 16*	*Ps. 16*
	Ex. 14:10-31;	Ex. 14:10-31;	Ex. 14:10-31;
	15:20-21	15:20-21	15:20-21
	Ex. 15:1b-13, 17-18	*Ex. 15:1b-13, 17-18*	*Ex. 15:1b-13, 17-18*
	Isa. 55:1-11	Isa. 55:1-11	Isa. 55:1-11
	Isa. 12:2-6	*Isa. 12:2-6*	*Isa. 12:2-6*
	Prov. 8:1-8, 19-21;	Prov. 8:1-8, 19-21;	Prov. 8:1-8, 19-21;
	9:4b-6	9:4b-6	9:4b-6
	Ps. 19	*Ps. 19*	*Ps. 19*
	Ezek. 36:24-28	Ezek. 36:24-28	Ezek. 36:24-28
	Ps. 42 and 43	*Ps. 42 and 43*	*Ps. 42 and 43*
	Ezek. 37:1-14	Ezek. 37:1-14	Ezek. 37:1-14
	Ps. 143	*Ps. 143*	*Ps. 143*
	Zeph. 3:14-20	Zeph. 3:14-20	Zeph. 3:14-20
	Ps. 98	*Ps. 98*	*Ps. 98*
	Rom. 6:3-11	Rom. 6:3-11	Rom. 6:3-11
	Ps. 114	*Ps. 114*	*Ps. 114*
	Matt. 28:1-10	Mark 16:1-8	Luke 24:1-12

A minimum of three Old Testament readings should be chosen. Ordinarily Exodus 14 will be included.

Sunday or Festival	Year A	Year B	Year C
Resurrection of the Lord/Easter	Acts 10:34-43 *or* Jer. 31:1-6 *Ps. 118:1-2, 14-24* Col. 3:1-4 *or* Acts 10:34-43 John 20:1-18 *or* Matt. 28:1-10	Acts 10:34-43 *or* Isa. 25:6-9 *Ps. 118:1-2, 14-24* 1 Cor. 15:1-11 *or* Acts 10:34-43 John 20:1-18 *or* Mark 16:1-8	Acts 10:34-43 *or* Isa. 65:17-25 *Ps. 118:1-2, 14-24* 1 Cor. 15:19-26 *or* Acts 10:34-43 John 20:1-18 *or* Luke 24:1-12
Easter Evening	Isa. 25:6-9 *Ps. 114* 1 Cor. 5:6b-8 Luke 24:13-49	Isa. 25:6-9 *Ps. 114* 1 Cor. 5:6b-8 Luke 24:13-49	Isa. 25:6-9 *Ps. 114* 1 Cor. 5:6b-8 Luke 24:13-49
2nd Sunday of Easter	Acts 2:14a, 22-32 *Ps. 16* 1 Peter 1:3-9 John 20:19-31	Acts 4:32-35 *Ps. 133* 1 John 1:1–2:2 John 20:19-31	Acts 5:27-32 *Ps. 118:14-29 or Ps. 150* Rev. 1:4-8 John 20:19-31
3rd Sunday of Easter	Acts 2:14a, 36-41 *Ps. 116:1-4, 12-19* 1 Peter 1:17-23 Luke 24:13-35	Acts 3:12-19 *Ps. 4* 1 John 3:1-7 Luke 24:36b-48	Acts 9:1-6 (7-20) *Ps. 30* Rev. 5:11-14 John 21:1-19
4th Sunday of Easter	Acts 2:42-47 *Ps. 23* 1 Peter 2:19-25 John 10:1-10	Acts 4:5-12 *Ps. 23* 1 John 3:16-24 John 10:11-18	Acts 9:36-43 *Ps. 23* Rev. 7:9-17 John 10:22-30
5th Sunday of Easter	Acts 7:55-60 *Ps. 31:1-5, 15-16* 1 Peter 2:2-10 John 14:1-14	Acts 8:26-40 *Ps. 22:25-31* 1 John 4:7-21 John 15:1-8	Acts 11:1-18 *Ps. 148* Rev. 21:1-6 John 13:31-35
6th Sunday of Easter	Acts 17:22-31 *Ps. 66:8-20* 1 Peter 3:13-22 John 14:15-21	Acts 10:44-48 *Ps. 98* 1 John 5:1-6 John 15:9-17	Acts 16:9-15 *Ps. 67* Rev. 21:10, 21:22–22:5 John 14:23-29 *or* John 5:1-9

Sunday or Festival	Year A	Year B	Year C
Ascension of the Lord	Acts 1:1-11	Acts 1:1-11	Acts 1:1-11
	Ps. 47 or *Ps. 93*	*Ps. 47* or *Ps. 93*	*Ps. 47* or *Ps. 93*
	Eph. 1:15-23	Eph. 1:15-23	Eph. 1:15-23
	Luke 24:44-53	Luke 24:44-53	Luke 24:44-53

These readings may be used on the seventh Sunday of Easter.

7th Sunday of Easter	Acts 1:6-14	Acts 1:15-17, 21-26	Acts 16:16-34
	Ps. 68:1-10, 32-35	*Ps. 1*	*Ps. 97*
	1 Peter 4:12-14; 5:6-11	1 John 5:9-13	Rev. 22:12-14, 16-17, 20-21
	John 17:1-11	John 17:6-19	John 17:20-26
Day of Pentecost	Acts 2:1-21	Acts 2:1-21	Acts 2:1-21
	or Num. 11:24-30	*or* Ezek. 37:1-14	*or* Gen. 11:1-9
	Ps. 104:24-34, 35b	*Ps. 104:24-34, 35b*	*Ps. 104:24-34, 35b*
	1 Cor. 12:3b-13	Rom. 8:22-27	Rom. 8:14-17
	or Acts 2:1-21	*or* Acts 2:1-21	*or* Acts 2:1-21
	John 20:19-23	John 15:26-27;	John 14:8-17
	or John 7:37-39	16:4b-15	(25-27)

If the passage from the Old Testament is chosen for the first reading, the passage from Acts is used as the second reading.

ORDINARY TIME

The second period which comprises Ordinary Time begins following Pentecost and continues until Advent. Trinity Sunday is the first Sunday of this period of Ordinary Time, and Christ the King (or, Reign of Christ) is its last Sunday. *Liturgical color:* green, except for Trinity Sunday, All Saints' Day (or first Sunday in November if celebrated on that Sunday), and Christ the King (or Reign of Christ), when the color is white.

SUNDAY OR FESTIVAL	YEAR A	YEAR B	YEAR C
Trinity Sunday	Gen. 1:1–2:4a	Isa. 6:1-8	Prov. 8:1-4, 22-31
	Ps. 8	*Ps. 29*	*Ps. 8*
	2 Cor. 13:11-13	Rom. 8:12-17	Rom. 5:1-5
	Matt. 28:16-20	John 3:1-17	John 16:12-15

If the Sunday between May 24 and 28 inclusive follows Trinity Sunday, the readings for the 8th Sunday in Ordinary Time are used.

9th Sunday in Ordinary Time	Gen. 6:9-22; 7:24; 8:14-19	1 Sam. 3:1-10 (11-20)	1 Kings 18:20-21 (22-29) 30-39
Sun. between May 29 and June 4 inclusive (If after Trinity Sunday)	*Ps. 46*	*Ps. 139:1-6, 13-18*	*Ps. 96*
	Rom. 1:16-17; 3:22b-28 (29-31)	2 Cor. 4:5-12	Gal. 1:1-12
	Matt. 7:21-29	Mark 2:23–3:6	Luke 7:1-10
10th Sunday in Ordinary Time	Gen. 12:1-9	1 Sam. 8:4-11 (12-15) 16-20 (11:14-15)	1 Kings 17:8-16 (17-24)
Sun. between June 5 and 11 inclusive (If after Trinity Sunday)	*Ps. 33:1-12*	*Ps. 138*	*Ps. 146*
	Rom. 4:13-25	2 Cor. 4:13–5:1	Gal. 1:11-24
	Matt. 9:9-13, 18-26	Mark 3:20-35	Luke 7:11-17
11th Sunday in Ordinary Time	Gen. 18:1-15 (21:1-7)	1 Sam. 15:34–16:13	1 Kings 21:1-10 (11-14) 15-21a
Sun. between June 12 and 18 inclusive (If after Trinity Sunday)	*Ps. 116:1-2, 12-19*	*Ps. 20*	*Ps. 5:1-8*
	Rom. 5:1-8	2 Cor. 5:6-10 (11-13) 14-17	Gal. 2:15-21
	Matt. 9:35–10:8 (9-23)	Mark 4:26-34	Luke 7:36–8:3
12th Sunday in Ordinary Time	Gen. 21:8-21	1 Sam. 17:(1a, 4-11, 19-23) 32-49 and	1 Kings 19:1-4 (5-7) 8-15a
Sun. between June 19 and 25 inclusive (If after Trinity Sunday)	*Ps. 86:1-10, 16-17*	*Ps. 9:9-20;* or *1 Sam. 17:57–18:5, 10-16* and *Ps. 133*	*Ps. 42 and 43*
	Rom. 6:1b-11	2 Cor. 6:1-13	Gal. 3:23-29
	Matt. 10:24-39	Mark 4:35-41	Luke 8:26-39
13th Sunday in Ordinary Time	Gen. 22:1-14	2 Sam. 1:1, 17-27	2 Kings 2:1-2, 6-14
Sun. between June 26 and July 2 inclusive	*Ps. 13*	*Ps. 130*	*Ps. 77:1-2, 11-20*
	Rom. 6:12-23	2 Cor. 8:7-15	Gal. 5:1, 13-25
	Matt. 10:40-42	Mark 5:21-43	Luke 9:51-62

SUNDAY OR FESTIVAL	YEAR A	YEAR B	YEAR C
14th Sunday in Ordinary Time *Sun. between July 3 and 9 inclusive*	Gen. 24:34-38, 42-49, 58-67 *Ps. 45:10-17* or *S. of Sol. 2:8-13* Rom. 7:15-25a Matt. 11:16-19, 25-30	2 Sam. 5:1-5, 9-10 *Ps. 48* 2 Cor. 12:2-10 Mark 6:1-13	2 Kings 5:1-14 *Ps. 30* Gal. 6:(1-6) 7-16 Luke 10:1-11, 16-20
15th Sunday in Ordinary Time *Sun. between July 10 and 16 inclusive*	Gen. 25:19-34 *Ps. 119:105-112* Rom. 8:1-11 Matt. 13:1-9, 18-23	2 Sam. 6:1-5, 12b-19 *Ps. 24* Eph. 1:3-14 Mark 6:14-29	Amos 7:7-17 *Ps. 82* Col. 1:1-14 Luke 10:25-37
16th Sunday in Ordinary Time *Sun. between July 17 and 23 inclusive*	Gen. 28:10-19a *Ps. 139:1-12, 23-24* Rom. 8:12-25 Matt. 13:24-30, 36-43	2 Sam. 7:1-14a *Ps. 89:20-37* Eph. 2:11-22 Mark 6:30-34, 53-56	Amos 8:1-12 *Ps. 52* Col. 1:15-28 Luke 10:38-42
17th Sunday in Ordinary Time *Sun. between July 24 and 30 inclusive*	Gen. 29:15-28 *Ps. 105:1-11, 45b* or *Ps. 128* Rom. 8:26-39 Matt. 13:31-33, 44-52	2 Sam. 11:1-15 *Ps. 14* Eph. 3:14-21 John 6:1-21	Hos. 1:2-10 *Ps. 85* Col. 2:6-15 (16-19) Luke 11:1-13
18th Sunday in Ordinary Time *Sun. between July 31 and Aug. 6 inclusive*	Gen. 32:22-31 *Ps. 17:1-7, 15* Rom. 9:1-5 Matt. 14:13-21	2 Sam. 11:26–12:13a *Ps. 51:1-12* Eph. 4:1-16 John 6:24-35	Hos. 11:1-11 *Ps. 107:1-9, 43* Col. 3:1-11 Luke 12:13-21
19th Sunday in Ordinary Time *Sun. between Aug. 7 and 13 inclusive*	Gen. 37:1-4, 12-28 *Ps. 105:1-6, 16-22, 45b* Rom. 10:5-15 Matt. 14:22-33	2 Sam. 18:5-9, 15, 31-33 *Ps. 130* Eph. 4:25–5:2 John 6:35, 41-51	Isa. 1:1, 10-20 *Ps. 50:1-8, 22-23* Heb. 11:1-3, 8-16 Luke 12:32-40

SUNDAY OR FESTIVAL	YEAR A	YEAR B	YEAR C
20th Sunday in Ordinary Time	Gen. 45:1-15	1 Kings 2:10-12; 3:3-14	Isa. 5:1-7
Sun. between Aug. 14 and 20 inclusive	*Ps. 133* Rom. 11:1-2a, 29-32 Matt. 15:(10-20) 21-28	*Ps. 111* Eph. 5:15-20 John 6:51-58	*Ps. 80:1-2, 8-19* Heb. 11:29–12:2 Luke 12:49-56
21st Sunday in Ordinary Time	Ex. 1:8–2:10	1 Kings 8:(1, 6, 10-11) 22-30, 41-43	Jer. 1:4-10
Sun. between Aug. 21 and 27 inclusive	*Ps. 124* Rom. 12:1-8 Matt. 16:13-20	*Ps. 84* Eph. 6:10-20 John 6:56-69	*Ps. 71:1-6* Heb. 12:18-29 Luke 13:10-17
22nd Sunday in Ordinary Time	Ex. 3:1-15	S. of Sol. 2:8-13	Jer. 2:4-13
Sun. between Aug. 28 and Sept. 3 inclusive	*Ps. 105:1-6, 23-26, 45c* Rom. 12:9-21 Matt. 16:21-28	*Ps. 45:1-2, 6-9* James 1:17-27 Mark 7:1-8, 14-15, 21-23	*Ps. 81:1, 10-16* Heb. 13:1-8, 15-16 Luke 14:1, 7-14
23rd Sunday in Ordinary Time	Ex. 12:1-14	Prov. 22:1-2, 8-9, 22-23	Jer. 18:1-11
Sun. between Sept. 4 and 10 inclusive	*Ps. 149* Rom. 13:8-14 Matt. 18:15-20	*Ps. 125* James 2:1-10 (11-13) 14-17 Mark 7:24-37	*Ps. 139:1-6, 13-18* Philemon 1-21 Luke 14:25-33
24th Sunday in Ordinary Time	Ex. 14:19-31	Prov. 1:20-33	Jer. 4:11-12, 22-28
Sun. between Sept. 11 and 17 inclusive	*Ps. 114 or Ex. 15:1b-11, 20-21* Rom. 14:1-12 Matt. 18:21-35	*Ps. 19* James 3:1-12 Mark 8:27-38	*Ps. 14* 1 Tim. 1:12-17 Luke 15:1-10
25th Sunday in Ordinary Time	Ex. 16:2-15	Prov. 31:10-31	Jer. 8:18–9:1
Sun. between Sept. 18 and 24 inclusive	*Ps. 105:1-6, 37-45* Phil. 1:21-30 Matt. 20:1-16	*Ps. 1* James 3:13–4:3, 7-8a Mark 9:30-37	*Ps. 79:1-9* 1 Tim. 2:1-7 Luke 16:1-13

Sunday or Festival	Year A	Year B	Year C
26th Sunday in Ordinary Time *Sun. between Sept. 25 and Oct. 1 inclusive*	Ex. 17:1-7 *Ps. 78:1-4, 12-16* Phil. 2:1-13 Matt. 21:23-32	Esth. 7:1-6, 9-10; 9:20-22 *Ps. 124* James 5:13-20 Mark 9:38-50	Jer. 32:1-3a, 6-15 *Ps. 91:1-6, 14-16* 1 Tim. 6:6-19 Luke 16:19-31
27th Sunday in Ordinary Time *Sun. between Oct. 2 and 8 inclusive*	Ex. 20:1-4, 7-9, 12-20 *Ps. 19* Phil. 3:4b-14 Matt. 21:33-46	Job 1:1; 2:1-10 *Ps. 26* Heb. 1:1-4; 2:5-12 Mark 10:2-16	Lam. 1:1-6 *Lam. 3:19-26* or *Ps. 137* 2 Tim. 1:1-14 Luke 17:5-10
28th Sunday in Ordinary Time *Sun. between Oct. 9 and 15 inclusive*	Ex. 32:1-14 *Ps. 106:1-6, 19-23* Phil. 4:1-9 Matt. 22:1-14	Job 23:1-9, 16-17 *Ps. 22:1-15* Heb. 4:12-16 Mark 10:17-31	Jer. 29:1, 4-7 *Ps. 66:1-12* 2 Tim. 2:8-15 Luke 17:11-19
29th Sunday in Ordinary Time *Sun. between Oct. 16 and 22 inclusive*	Ex. 33:12-23 *Ps. 99* 1 Thess. 1:1-10 Matt. 22:15-22	Job 38:1-7 (34-41) *Ps. 104:1-9, 24, 35c* Heb. 5:1-10 Mark 10:35-45	Jer. 31:27-34 *Ps. 119:97-104* 2 Tim. 3:14–4:5 Luke 18:1-8
30th Sunday in Ordinary Time *Sun. between Oct. 23 and 29 inclusive*	Deut. 34:1-12 *Ps. 90:1-6, 13-17* 1 Thess. 2:1-8 Matt. 22:34-46	Job 42:1-6, 10-17 *Ps. 34:1-8 (19-22)* Heb. 7:23-28 Mark 10:46-52	Joel 2:23-32 *Ps. 65* 2 Tim. 4:6-8, 16-18 Luke 18:9-14
31st Sunday in Ordinary Time *Sun. between Oct. 30 and Nov. 5 inclusive*	Josh. 3:7-17 *Ps. 107:1-7, 33-37* 1 Thess. 2:9-13 Matt. 23:1-12	Ruth 1:1-18 *Ps. 146* Heb. 9:11-14 Mark 12:28-34	Hab. 1:1-4; 2:1-4 *Ps. 119:137-144* 2 Thess. 1:1-4, 11-12 Luke 19:1-10
All Saints' Day *Nov. 1 or may be used 1st Sun. in Nov.*	Rev. 7:9-17 *Ps. 34:1-10, 22* 1 John 3:1-3 Matt. 5:1-12	Isa. 25:6-9 *Ps. 24* Rev. 21:1-6a John 11:32-44	Dan. 7:1-3, 15-18 *Ps. 149* Eph. 1:11-23 Luke 6:20-31˙

Sunday or Festival	Year A	Year B	Year C
32nd Sunday in Ordinary Time *Sun. between Nov. 6 and 12 inclusive*	Josh. 24:1-3a, 14-25 *Ps. 78:1-7* 1 Thess. 4:13-18 Matt. 25:1-13	Ruth 3:1-5; 4:13-17 *Ps. 127* Heb. 9:24-28 Mark 12:38-44	Hag. 1:15b–2:9 *Ps. 145:1-5, 17-21* or *Ps. 98* 2 Thess. 2:1-5, 13-17 Luke 20:27-38
33rd Sunday in Ordinary Time *Sun. between Nov. 13 and 19 inclusive*	Judges 4:1-7 *Ps. 123* 1 Thess. 5:1-11 Matt. 25:14-30	1 Sam. 1:4-20 *1 Sam. 2:1-10* Heb. 10:11-14 (15-18) 19-25 Mark 13:1-8	Isa. 65:17-25 *Isa. 12* 2 Thess. 3:6-13 Luke 21:5-19
Christ the King (or Reign of Christ) *Sun. between Nov. 20 and 26 inclusive*	Ezek. 34:11-16, 20-24 *Ps. 100* Eph. 1:15-23 Matt. 25:31-46	2 Sam. 23:1-7 *Ps. 132:1-12 (13-18)* Rev. 1:4b-8 John 18:33-37	Jer. 23:1-6 *Luke 1:68-79* Col. 1:11-20 Luke 23:33-43

DAILY LECTIONARY

THE DAILY LECTIONARY that follows is arranged in a two-year cycle and provides for reading twice through the New Testament and once through the Old Testament during the two-year cycle. The readings reflect the seasons and festivals of the liturgical year. This lectionary is prepared for use at morning and evening prayer, rather than at the Service for the Lord's Day. The Table of Major Celebrations of the Liturgical Calendar (pp. 1096–1097) displays the schedule for using this lectionary.

The psalms follow a weekly cycle throughout each season, except for the period from Christmas to the Baptism of the Lord, when each day has its own appointed psalms, and Ordinary Time, which follows a four-week cycle of psalms. One of the laudate psalms (Ps. 145–150) is appointed for a particular day in each week for use in morning prayer throughout the year. If circumstances do not allow the singing or reading of both of the appointed psalms, one may be used.

Three readings are provided for each day, although only one or two are normally used in a single service. Ordinarily the Old Testament reading and one of the New Testament readings (Epistle—Year One; Gospel—Year Two) are read in the morning, and the remaining New Testament reading in the evening. Or one reading may be read in the morning and one in the evening. For example, the Old Testament reading may be read in the morning and the Gospel reading in the evening throughout a two-year cycle. In the following two years the epistle reading may be read in the morning and the Gospel reading in the evening.

At certain festivals, some readings are more appropriate for the morning or for the evening. An asterisk (*) indicates that the reading is intended for use in the morning. Two asterisks (**) indicate that the reading is intended for use in the evening. The Old Testament is traditionally read first. When a festival interrupts the sequence of readings (or if the readings in the Lectionary for Sundays and Festivals are used for daily prayer on Sundays and festivals), the daily readings may be reordered or modified to preserve continuity or avoid repetition. Readings for special days, for use in both years, are listed on page 1095.

This lectionary includes some readings from the Apocrypha. Within the Reformed tradition, the Apocryphal books are not recognized as part of the canon of Holy Scripture and are not considered authoritative for doctrine. Nevertheless, the Apocryphal books may be instructive. Selections from the Old Testament are provided as alternatives to the readings from the Apocrypha for use when canonical readings are preferred or when the Apocrypha is not accessible.

DAILY LECTIONARY

DAY	PSALM	YEAR 1	YEAR 2
1st Week of Advent			
Sunday	*Morning:* Ps. 24; 150	Isa. 1:1-9	Amos 1:1-5, 13–2:8
	Evening: Ps. 25; 110	2 Peter 3:1-10	1 Thess. 5:1-11
		Matt. 25:1-13	Luke 21:5-19
Monday	*Morning:* Ps. 122; 145	Isa. 1:10-20	Amos 2:6-16
	Evening: Ps. 40; 67	1 Thess. 1:1-10	2 Peter 1:1-11
		Luke 20:1-8	Matt. 21:1-11
Tuesday	*Morning:* Ps. 33; 146	Isa. 1:21-31	Amos 3:1-11
	Evening: Ps. 85; 94	1 Thess. 2:1-12	2 Peter 1:12-21
		Luke 20:9-18	Matt. 21:12-22
Wednesday	*Morning:* Ps. 50; 147:1-11	Isa. 2:1-4	Amos 3:12–4:5
		1 Thess. 2:13-20	2 Peter 3:1-10
	Evening: Ps. 53; 17	Luke 20:19-26	Matt. 21:23-32
Thursday	*Morning:* Ps. 18:1-20; 147:12-20	Isa. 2:5-22	Amos 4:6-13
		1 Thess. 3:1-13	2 Peter 3:11-18
	Evening: Ps. 126; 62	Luke 20:27-40	Matt. 21:33-46
Friday	*Morning:* Ps. 102; 148	Isa. 3:1–4:1	Amos 5:1-17
	Evening: Ps. 130; 16	1 Thess. 4:1-12	Jude 1-16
		Luke 20:41–21:4	Matt. 22:1-14
Saturday	*Morning:* Ps. 90; 149	Isa. 4:2-6	Amos 5:18-27
	Evening: Ps. 80; 72	1 Thess. 4:13-18	Jude 17-25
		Luke 21:5-19	Matt. 22:15-22

Day	Psalm	Year 1	Year 2
2nd Week of Advent			
Sunday	*Morning:* Ps. 24; 150	Isa. 5:1-7	Amos 6:1-14
	Evening: Ps. 25; 110	2 Peter 3:11-18	2 Thess. 1:5-12
		Luke 7:28-35	Luke 1:57-68
Monday	*Morning:* Ps. 122; 145	Isa. 5:8-17	Amos 7:1-9
	Evening: Ps. 40; 67	1 Thess. 5:1-11	Rev. 1:1-8
		Luke 21:20-28	Matt. 22:23-33
Tuesday	*Morning:* Ps. 33; 146	Isa. 5:18-25	Amos 7:10-17
	Evening: Ps. 85; 94	1 Thess. 5:12-28	Rev. 1:9-16
		Luke 21:29-38	Matt. 22:34-46
Wednesday	*Morning:* Ps. 50; 147:1-11	Isa. 6:1-13	Amos 8:1-14
	Evening: Ps. 53; 17	2 Thess. 1:1-12	Rev. 1:17–2:7
		John 7:53–8:11	Matt. 23:1-12
Thursday	*Morning:* Ps. 18:1-20; 147:12-20	Isa. 7:1-9	Amos 9:1-10
	Evening: Ps. 126; 62	2 Thess. 2:1-12	Rev. 2:8-17
		Luke 22:1-13	Matt. 23:13-26
Friday	*Morning:* Ps. 102; 148	Isa. 7:10-25	Hag. 1:1-15
	Evening: Ps. 130; 16	2 Thess. 2:13–3:5	Rev. 2:18-29
		Luke 22:14-30	Matt. 23:27-39
Saturday	*Morning:* Ps. 90; 149	Isa. 8:1-15	Hag. 2:1-9
	Evening: Ps. 80; 72	2 Thess. 3:6-18	Rev. 3:1-6
		Luke 22:31-38	Matt. 24:1-14
3rd Week of Advent			
Sunday	*Morning:* Ps. 24; 150	Isa. 13:1-13	Amos 9:11-15
	Evening: Ps. 25; 110	Heb. 12:18-29	2 Thess. 2:1-3, 13-17
		John 3:22-30	John 5:30-47

The readings below are interrupted after December 17 in favor of the readings identified by date in the 4th Week of Advent.

Monday	*Morning:* Ps. 122; 145	Isa. 8:16–9:1	Zech. 1:7-17
	Evening: Ps. 40; 67	2 Peter 1:1-11	Rev. 3:7-13
		Luke 22:39-53	Matt. 24:15-31

DAY	PSALM	YEAR 1	YEAR 2
Tuesday	*Morning:* Ps. 33; 146	Isa. 9:2-7	Zech. 2:1-13
	Evening: Ps. 85; 94	2 Peter 1:12-21	Rev. 3:14-22
		Luke 22:54-69	Matt. 24:32-44
Wednesday	*Morning:* Ps. 50; 147:1-11	Isa. 9:8-17 2 Peter 2:1-10a	Zech. 3:1-10 Rev. 4:1-8
	Evening: Ps. 53; 17	Mark 1:1-8	Matt. 24:45-51
Thursday	*Morning:* Ps. 18:1-20; 147:12-20	Isa. 9:18–10:4 2 Peter 2:10b-16	Zech. 4:1-14 Rev. 4:9–5:5
	Evening: Ps. 126; 62	Matt. 3:1-12	Matt. 25:1-13
Friday	*Morning:* Ps. 102; 148	Isa. 10:5-19	Zech. 7:8–8:8
	Evening: Ps. 130; 16	2 Peter 2:17-22	Rev. 5:6-14
		Matt. 11:2-15	Matt. 25:14-30
Saturday	*Morning:* Ps. 90; 149	Isa. 10:20-27	Zech. 8:9-17
	Evening: Ps. 80; 72	Jude 17-25	Rev. 6:1-17
		Luke 3:1-9	Matt. 25:31-46

4th Week of Advent

DAY	PSALM	YEAR 1	YEAR 2
December 18	**Sunday** *Morning:* Ps. 24; 150 *Evening:* Ps. 25; 110	Isa. 11:1-9 Eph. 6:10-20 John 3:16-21	Gen. 3:8-15 Rev. 12:1-10 John 3:16-21
December 19	**Monday** *Morning:* Ps. 122; 145 *Evening:* Ps. 40; 67	Isa. 11:10-16 Rev. 20:1-10 John 5:30-47	Zeph. 3:14-20 Titus 1:1-16 Luke 1:1-25
December 20	**Tuesday** *Morning:* Ps. 33; 146 *Evening:* Ps. 85; 94	Isa. 28:9-22 Rev. 20:11–21:8 Luke 1:5-25	1 Sam. 2:1b-10 Titus 2:1-10 Luke 1:26-38
December 21	**Wednesday** *Morning:* Ps. 50; 147:1-11 *Evening:* Ps. 53; 17	Isa. 29:9-24 Rev. 21:9-21 Luke 1:26-38	2 Sam. 7:1-17 Titus 2:11–3:8a Luke 1:39-48a (48b-56)

DAY	PSALM	YEAR 1	YEAR 2
December 22	*Thursday* *Morning:* Ps. 18:1-20; 147:12-20 *Evening:* Ps. 126; 62	Isa. 31:1-9 Rev. 21:22–22:5 Luke 1:39-48a (48b-56)	2 Sam. 7:18-29 Gal. 3:1-14 Luke 1:57-66
December 23	*Friday* *Morning:* Ps. 102; 148 *Evening:* Ps. 130; 16	Isa. 33:17-22 Rev. 22:6-11, l8-20 Luke 1:57-66	Jer. 31:10-14 Gal. 3:15-22 Luke 1:67-80 *or* Matt. 1:1-17
December 24	*Saturday* *Morning:* Ps. 90; 149 *Evening:* Ps. 80; 72	Isa. 35:1-10 Rev. 22:12-17, 21 Luke 1:67-80	Isa. 60:1-6 Gal. 3:23–4:7 Matt. 1:18-25
Christmas Eve	Ps. 132; 114	Isa. 59:15b-21 Phil. 2:5-11	Isa. 59:15b-21 Phil. 2:5-11
Christmas Day	*Morning:* Ps. 2; Laudate Psalm* *Evening:* Ps. 98; 96	Zech. 2:10-13 1 John 4:7-16 John 3:31-36	Micah 4:1-5; 5:2-4 1 John 4:7-16 John 3:31-36
1st Sunday after *Christmas*	[Use psalms appointed for date.]	Isa. 62:6-7, 10-12 Heb. 2:10-18 Matt. 1:18-25	1 Sam. 1:1-2, 7b-28 Col. 1:9-20 Luke 2:22-40
December 26	*Morning:* Ps. 116; Laudate Psalm* *Evening:* Ps. 119:1- 24; Ps. 27	Wisd. of Sol. 4:7-15 *or* 2 Chron. 24:17- 22 Acts 6:1-7 Acts 7:59–8:8	Wisd. of Sol. 4:7-15 *or* 2 Chron. 24:17- 22 Acts 6:1-7 Acts 7:59–8:8
December 27	*Morning:* Ps. 34; Laudate Psalm* *Evening:* Ps. 19; 121	Prov. 8:22-30 1 John 5:1-12 John 13:20-35	Prov. 8:22-30 1 John 5:1-12 John 13:20-35
December 28	*Morning:* Ps. 2; Laudate Psalm* *Evening:* Ps. 110; 111	Isa. 49:13-23 Isa. 54:1-13 Matt. 18:1-14	Isa. 49:13-23 Isa. 54:1-13 Matt. 18:1-14

* *Laudate psalms: Sunday*—Ps. 150; *Monday*—Ps. 145; *Tuesday*—Ps. 146; *Wednesday*—Ps. 147:1-11;
Thursday—Ps. 147:12-20; *Friday*—Ps. 148; *Saturday*—Ps. 149

Day	Psalm	Year 1	Year 2
December 29	*Morning:* Ps. 96; Laudate Psalm* *Evening:* Ps. 132; 97	Isa. 12:1-6 Rev. 1:1-8 John 7:37-52	2 Sam. 23:13-17b 2 John 1-13 John 2:1-11
December 30	*Morning:* Ps. 93; Laudate Psalm* *Evening:* Ps. 89:1-18; 39:19-52	Isa. 25:1-9 Rev. 1:19-20 John 7:53–8:11	1 Kings 17:17-24 3 John 1-15 John 4:46-54
December 31	*Morning:* Ps. 98; Laudate Psalm* *Evening:* Ps. 45; 96	Isa. 26:1-6 2 Cor. 5:16–6:2 John 8:12-19	1 Kings 3:5-14 James 4:13-17; 5:7-11 John 5:1-15
January 1	*Morning:* Ps. 98; Laudate Psalm* *Evening:* Ps. 99; 8	Gen. 17:1-12a, 15-16 Col. 2:6-12 John 16:23b-30	Isa. 62:1-5, 10-12 Rev. 19:11-16 Matt. 1:18-25
2nd Sunday after ***Christmas***	[Use psalms appointed for date.]	Ecclus. 3:3-9, 14-17 *or* Deut. 33:1-5 1 John 2:12-17 John 6:41-47	1 Kings 3:5-14 Col. 3:12-17 John 6:41-47
January 2	*Morning:* Ps. 48; Laudate Psalm* *Evening:* Ps. 9; 29	Gen. 12:1-7 Heb. 11:1-12 John 6:35-42, 48-51	1 Kings 19:1-8 Eph. 4:1-16 John 6:1-14
January 3	*Morning:* Ps. 111; Laudate Psalm* *Evening:* Ps. 107; 15	Gen. 28:10-22 Heb. 11:13-22 John 10:7-17	1 Kings 19:9-18 Eph. 4:17-32 John 6:15-27
January 4	*Morning:* Ps. 20; Laudate Psalm* *Evening:* Ps. 93; 97	Ex. 3:1-5 Heb. 11:23-31 John 14:6-14	Josh. 3:14–4:7 Eph. 5:1-20 John 9:1-12, 35-38
January 5	*Morning:* Ps. 99; Laudate Psalm*	Josh. 1:1-9 Heb. 11:32–12:2 John 15:1-16	Jonah 2:2-9 Eph. 6:10-20 John 11:17-27, 38-44

---

* *Laudate psalms: Sunday*—Ps. 150; *Monday*—Ps. 145; *Tuesday*—Ps. 146; *Wednesday*—Ps. 147:1-11; *Thursday*—Ps. 147:12-20; *Friday*—Ps. 148; *Saturday*—Ps. 149

Day	Psalm	Year 1	Year 2
Eve of Epiphany	Ps. 96; 110	Isa. 66:18-23 Rom. 15:7-13	Isa. 66:18-23 Rom. 15:7-13

Epiphany and following

Epiphany **January 6**	*Morning:* Ps. 72; Laudate Psalm* *Evening:* Ps. 100; 67	Isa. 52:7-10 Rev. 21:22-27 Matt. 12:14-21	Isa. 49:1-7 Rev. 21:22-27 Matt. 12:14-21

The readings for the dated days after the Epiphany are used only until the following Saturday evening.

January 7	*Morning:* Ps. 46 *or* 97; Laudate Psalm* *Evening:* Ps. 27; 93; *or* 114	Isa. 52:3-6 Rev. 2:1-7 John 2:1-11	Deut. 8:1-3 Col. 1:1-14 John 6:30-33, 48-51
January 8	*Morning:* Ps. 46 *or* 47; Laudate Psalm* *Evening:* Ps. 27; 93; *or* 114	Isa. 59:15b-21 Rev. 2:8-17 John 4:46-54	Ex. 17:1-7 Col. 1:15–23 John 7:37-52
January 9	*Morning:* Ps. 46 *or* 47; Laudate Psalm* *Evening:* Ps. 27; 93; *or* 114	Isa. 63:1-5 Rev. 2:18-29 John 5:1-15	Isa. 45:14-19 Col. 1:24–2:7 John 8:12-19
January 10	*Morning:* Ps. 46 *or* 47; Laudate Psalm* *Evening:* Ps. 27; 93; *or* 114	Isa. 65:1-9 Rev. 3:1-6 John 6:1-14	Jer. 23:1-8 Col. 2:8-23 John 10:7-17
January 11	*Morning:* Ps. 46 *or* 47; Laudate Psalm* *Evening:* Ps. 27; 93; *or* 114	Isa. 65:13-16 Rev. 3:7-13 John 6:15-27	Isa. 55:3-9 Col. 3:1-17 John 14:6-14

---

* *Laudate psalms: Sunday*—Ps. 150; *Monday*—Ps. 145; *Tuesday*—Ps. 146; *Wednesday*—Ps. 147:1-11; *Thursday*—Ps. 147:12-20; *Friday*—Ps. 148; *Saturday*—Ps. 149

Day	Psalm	Year 1	Year 2
January 12	*Morning:* Ps. 46 *or* 97; Laudate Psalm*	Isa. 66:1-2, 22-23 Rev. 3:14-22 John 9:1-12, 35-38	Gen. 49:1-2, 8-12 Col. 3:18–4:6 John 15:1-16
Eve of Baptism of the Lord	Ps. 27; 93; *or* 114	Isa. 61:1-9 Gal. 3:23-29; 4:4-7	Isa. 61:1-9 Gal. 3:23-29; 4:4-7

Baptism of the Lord (Sunday between Jan. 7 and 13 inclusive) and following

Day	Psalm	Year 1	Year 2
Baptism of the Lord	*Morning:* Ps. 104; 150 *Evening:* Ps. 29	Isa. 40:1-11 Heb. 1:1-12 John 1:1-7, 19-20, 29-34	Gen. 1:1–2:3 Eph. 1:3-14 John 1:29-34
Monday	*Morning:* Ps. 5; 145 *Evening:* Ps. 82; 29	Isa. 40:12-24 Eph. 1:1-14 Mark 1:1-13	Gen. 2:4-9 (10-15) 16-25 Heb. 1:1-14 John 1:1-18
Tuesday	*Morning:* Ps. 42; 146 *Evening:* Ps. 102; 133	Isa. 40:25-31 Eph. 1:15-23 Mark 1:14-28	Gen. 3:1-24 Heb. 2:1-10 John 1:19-28
Wednesday	*Morning:* Ps. 89:1-18; 147:1-11 *Evening:* Ps. 1; 33	Isa. 41:1-16 Eph. 2:1-10 Mark 1:29-45	Gen. 4:1-16 Heb. 2:11-18 John 1:(29-34) 35-42
Thursday	*Morning:* Ps. 97; 147:12-20 *Evening:* Ps. 16; 62	Isa. 41:17-29 Eph. 2:11-22 Mark 2:1-12	Gen. 4:17-26 Heb. 3:1-11 John 1:43-51
Friday	*Morning:* Ps. 51; 148 *Evening:* Ps. 142; 65	Isa. 42:(1-9) 10-17 Eph. 3:1-13 Mark 2:13-22	Gen. 6:1-8 Heb. 3:12-19 John 2:1-12
Saturday	*Morning:* Ps. 104; 149 *Evening:* Ps. 138; 98	Isa. (42:18-25) 43:1-13 Eph. 3:14-21 Mark 2:23–3:6	Gen. 6:9-22 Heb. 4:1-13 John 2:13-22

DAY	PSALM	YEAR 1	YEAR 2

Week following Sunday between Jan. 14 and 20 inclusive

Sunday
Morning: Ps. 19; 150
Evening: Ps. 81; 113

Isa. 43:14–44:5
Heb. 6:17–7:10
John 4:27-42

Gen. 7:1-10, 17-23
Eph. 4:1-16
Mark 3:7-19

Monday
Morning: Ps. 135; 145
Evening: Ps. 97; 112

Isa. 44:6-8, 21-23
Eph. 4:1-16
Mark 3:7-19a

Gen. 8:6-22
Heb. 4:14–5:6
John 2:23–3:15

Tuesday
Morning: Ps. 123; 146
Evening: Ps. 30; 86

Isa. 44:9-20
Eph. 4:17-32
Mark 3:19b-35

Gen. 9:1-17
Heb. 5:7-14
John 3:16-21

Wednesday
Morning: Ps. 15;
147:1-11
Evening: Ps. 48; 4

Isa. 44:24–45:7
Eph. 5:1-14
Mark 4:1-20

Gen. 9:18-29
Heb. 6:1-12
John 3:22-36

Thursday
Morning: Ps. 36;
147:12-20
Evening: Ps. 80; 27

Isa. 45:5-17
Eph. 5:15-33
Mark 4:21-34

Gen. 11:1-9
Heb. 6:13-20
John 4:1-15

Friday
Morning: Ps.130; 148
Evening: Ps. 32; 139

Isa. 45:18-25
Eph. 6:1-9
Mark 4:35-41

Gen. 11:27–12:8
Heb. 7:1-17
John 4:16-26

Saturday
Morning: Ps. 56; 149
Evening: Ps. 118; 111

Isa. 46:1-13
Eph. 6:10-24
Mark 5:1-20

Gen. 12:9–13:1
Heb. 7:18-28
John 4:27-42

Week following Sunday between Jan. 21 and 27 inclusive

Sunday
Morning: Ps. 67; 150
Evening: Ps. 46; 93

Isa. 47:1-15
Heb. 10:19-31
John 5:2-18

Gen. 13:2-18
Gal. 2:1-10
Mark 7:31-37

Monday
Morning: Ps. 57; 145
Evening: Ps. 85; 47

Isa. 48:1-11
Gal. 1:1-17
Mark 5:21-43

Gen. 14:(1-7) 8-24
Heb. 8:1-13
John 4:43-54

Day	Psalm	Year 1	Year 2
Tuesday	*Morning:* Ps. 54; 146 *Evening:* Ps. 28; 99	Isa. 48:12-21 (22) Gal. 1:18–2:10 Mark 6:1-13	Gen. 15:1-11, 17-21 Heb. 9:1-14 John 5:1-18
Wednesday	*Morning:* Ps. 65; 147:1-11 *Evening:* Ps. 125; 91	Isa. 49:1-12 Gal. 2:11-21 Mark 6:13-29	Gen. 16:1-14 Heb. 9:15-28 John 5:19-29
Thursday	*Morning:* Ps.143; 147:12-20 *Evening:* Ps. 81; 116	Isa. 49:13-23 (24-26) Gal. 3:1-14 Mark 6:30-46	Gen. 16:15–17:14 Heb. 10:1-10 John 5:30-47
Friday	*Morning:* Ps. 88; 148 *Evening:* Ps. 6; 20	Isa. 50:1-11 Gal. 3:15-22 Mark 6:47-56	Gen. 17:15-27 Heb. 10:11-25 John 6:1-15
Saturday	*Morning:* Ps. 122; 149 *Evening:* Ps. 100; 63	Isa. 51:1-8 Gal. 3:23-29 Mark 7:1-23	Gen. 18:1-16 Heb. 10:26-39 John 6:16-27

Week following Sun. between Jan. 28 and Feb. 3 inclusive, except when this Sunday is Transfiguration

Day	Psalm	Year 1	Year 2
Sunday	*Morning:* Ps.108; 150 *Evening:* Ps. 66; 23	Isa. 51:9-16 Heb. 11:8-16 John 7:14-31	Gen. 18:16-33 Gal. 5:13-25 Mark 8:22-30
Monday	*Morning:* Ps. 62; 145 *Evening:* Ps. 73; 9	Isa. 51:17-23 Gal. 4:1-11 Mark 7:24-37	Gen. 19:1-17 (18-23) 24-29 Heb. 11:1-12 John 6:27-40
Tuesday	*Morning:* Ps. 12; 146 *Evening:* Ps. 36; 7	Isa. 52:1-12 Gal. 4:12-20 Mark 8:1-10	Gen. 21:1-21 Heb. 11:13-22 John 6:41-51
Wednesday	*Morning:* Ps. 96; 147:1-11 *Evening:* Ps. 132; 134	Isa. 52:13–53:12 Gal. 4:21-31 Mark 8:11-26	Gen. 22:1-18 Heb. 11:23-31 John 6:52-59
Thursday	*Morning:* Ps. 116; 147:12-20 *Evening:* Ps. 26; 130	Isa. 54:1-10 (11-17) Gal. 5:1-15 Mark 8:27–9:1	Gen. 23:1-20 Heb. 11:32–12:2 John 6:60-71

DAY	PSALM	YEAR 1	YEAR 2
Friday	*Morning:* Ps. 84; 148	Isa. 55:1-13	Gen. 24:1-27
	Evening: Ps. 25; 40	Gal. 5:16-24	Heb. 12:3-11
		Mark 9:2-13	John 7:1-13
Saturday	*Morning:* Ps. 63; 149	Isa. 56:1-8	Gen. 24:28-38, 49-51
	Evening: Ps. 125; 90	Gal. 5:25–6:10	Heb. 12:12-29
		Mark 9:14-29	John 7:14-36

Week following Sun. between Feb. 4 and 10 inclusive, except when this Sunday is Transfiguration

DAY	PSALM	YEAR 1	YEAR 2
Sunday	*Morning:* Ps. 103; 150	Isa. 57:1-13	Gen. 24:50-67
	Evening: Ps. 117; 139	Heb. 12:1-6	2 Tim. 2:14-21
		John 7:37-46	Mark 10:13-22
Monday	*Morning:* Ps. 5; 145	Isa. 57:14-21	Gen. 25:19-34
	Evening: Ps. 82; 29	Gal. 6:11-18	Heb. 13:1-16
		Mark 9:30-41	John 7:37-52
Tuesday	*Morning:* Ps. 42; 146	Isa. 58:1-12	Gen. 26:1-6, 12-33
	Evening: Ps. 102; 133	2 Tim. 1:1-14	Heb. 13:17-25
		Mark 9:42-50	John 7:53–8:11
Wednesday	*Morning:* Ps. 89:1-18; 147:1-11	Isa. 59:1-21	Gen. 27:1-29
		2 Tim 1:15–2:13	Rom. 12:1-8
	Evening: Ps. 1; 33	Mark 10:1-16	John 8:12-20
Thursday	*Morning:* Ps. 97; 147:12-20	Isa. 60:1-22	Gen. 27:30-45
		2 Tim. 2:14-26	Rom. 12:9-21
	Evening: Ps. 16; 62	Mark 10:17-31	John 8:21-32
Friday	*Morning:* Ps. 51; 148	Isa. 61:1-9	Gen. 27:46–28:4, 10-22
	Evening: Ps. 142; 65	2 Tim. 3:1-17	Rom. 13:1-14
		Mark 10:32-45	John 8:33-47
Saturday	*Morning:* Ps. 104; 149	Isa. 61:10–62:5	Gen. 29:1-20
	Evening: Ps. 138; 98	2 Tim. 4:1-8	Rom. 14:1-23
		Mark 10:46-52	John 8:47-59

Day	Psalm	Year 1	Year 2

Week following Sun. between Feb. 11 and 17 inclusive, except when this Sunday is Transfiguration

Sunday	*Morning:* Ps. 19; 150 *Evening:* Ps. 81; 113	Isa. 62:6-12 1 John 2:3-11 John 8:12-19	Gen. 29:20-35 1 Tim. 3:14–4:10 Mark 10:23-31
Monday	*Morning:* Ps. 135; 145 *Evening:* Ps. 97; 112	Isa. 63:1-6 1 Tim. 1:1-17 Mark 11:1-11	Gen. 30:1-24 1 John 1:1-10 John 9:1-17
Tuesday	*Morning:* Ps. 123; 146 *Evening:* Ps. 30; 86	Isa. 63:7-14 1 Tim. 1:18–2:8 (9-15) Mark 11:12-26	Gen. 31:1-24 1 John 2:1-11 John 9:18-41
Wednesday	*Morning:* Ps. 15; 147:1-11 *Evening:* Ps. 48; 4	Isa. 63:15–64:9 1 Tim. 3:1-16 Mark 11:27–12:12	Gen. 31:25-50 1 John 2:12-17 John 10:1-18
Thursday	*Morning:* Ps. 36; 147:12-20 *Evening:* Ps. 80; 27	Isa. 65:1-12 1 Tim. 4:1-16 Mark 12:13-27	Gen. 32:3-21 1 John 2:18-29 John 10:19-30
Friday	*Morning:* Ps. 130; 148 *Evening:* Ps. 32; 139	Isa. 65:17-25 1 Tim. 5:(1-16) 17-22 (23-25) Mark 12:28-34	Gen. 32:22–33:17 1 John 3:1-10 John 10:31-42
Saturday	*Morning:* Ps. 56; 149 *Evening:* Ps. 118; 111	Isa. 66:1-6 1 Tim. 6:(1-5) 6-21 Mark 12:35-44	Gen. 35:1-20 1 John 3:11-18 John 11:1-16

Week following Sun. between Feb. 18 and 24 inclusive, except when this Sunday is Transfiguration

Sunday	*Morning:* Ps. 67; 150 *Evening:* Ps. 46; 93	Isa. 66:7-14 1 John 3:4-10 John 10:7-16	Prov. 1:20-33 2 Cor. 5:11-21 Mark 10:35-45
Monday	*Morning:* Ps. 57; 145 *Evening:* Ps. 85; 47	Ruth 1:1-14 2 Cor. 1:1-11 Matt. 5:1-12	Prov. 3:11-20 1 John 3:18–4:6 John 11:17-29

Day	Psalm	Year 1	Year 2
Tuesday	*Morning:* Ps. 54; 146 *Evening:* Ps. 28; 99	Ruth 1:15-22 2 Cor. 1:12-22 Matt. 5:13-20	Prov. 4:1-27 1 John 4:7-21 John 11:30-44
Wednesday	*Morning:* Ps. 65; 147:1-11 *Evening:* Ps. 125; 91	Ruth 2:1-13 2 Cor. 1:23–2:17 Matt. 5:21-26	Prov. 6:1-19 1 John 5:1-12 John 11:45-54
Thursday	*Morning:* Ps. 143; 147:12-20 *Evening:* Ps. 81; 116	Ruth 2:14-23 2 Cor. 3:1-18 Matt. 5:27-37	Prov. 7:1-27 1 John 5:13-21 John 11:55–12:8
Friday	*Morning:* Ps. 88; 148 *Evening:* Ps. 6; 20	Ruth 3:1-18 2 Cor. 4:1-12 Matt. 5:38-48	Prov. 8:1-21 Philemon 1-25 John 12:9-19
Saturday	*Morning:* Ps. 122; 149 *Evening:* Ps. 100; 63	Ruth 4:1-22 2 Cor. 4:13–5:10 Matt. 6:1-6	Prov. 8:22-36 2 Tim. 1:1-14 John 12:20-26

Week following Sun. between Feb. 25 and 29 inclusive, except when this Sunday is Transfiguration

Day	Psalm	Year 1	Year 2
Sunday	*Morning:* Ps. 108; 150 *Evening:* Ps. 66; 23	Deut. 4:1-9 2 Tim. 4:1-8 John 12:1-8	Prov. 9:1-12 2 Cor. 9:6b-15 Mark 10:46-52
Monday	*Morning:* Ps. 62; 145 *Evening:* Ps. 73; 9	Deut. 4:9-14 2 Cor. 10:1-18 Matt. 6:7-15	Prov. 10:1-12 2 Tim. 1:15–2:13 John 12:27-36a
Tuesday	*Morning:* Ps. 12; 146 *Evening:* Ps. 36; 7	Deut. 4:15-24 2 Cor. 11:1-21a Matt. 6:16-23	Prov. 15:16-33 2 Tim. 2:14-26 John 12:36b-50
Wednesday	*Morning:* Ps. 96; 147:1-11 *Evening:* Ps. 132; 134	Deut. 4:25-31 2 Cor. 11:21b-33 Matt. 6:24-34	Prov. 17:1-20 2 Tim. 3:1-17 John 13:1-20
Thursday	*Morning:* Ps. 116; 147:12-20 *Evening:* Ps. 26; 130	Deut. 4:32-40 2 Cor. 12:1-10 Matt. 7:1-12	Prov. 21:30–22:6 2 Tim. 4:1-8 John 13:21-30

Day	Psalm	Year 1	Year 2
Friday	*Morning:* Ps. 84; 148 *Evening:* Ps. 25; 40	Deut. 5:1-22 2 Cor. 12:11-21 Matt. 7:13-21	Prov. 23:19-21, 29–24:2 2 Tim. 4:9-22 John 13:31-38
Saturday	*Morning:* Ps. 63; 149 *Evening:* Ps. 125; 90	Deut. 5:22-33 2 Cor. 13:1-14 Matt. 7:22-29	Prov. 25:15-28 Phil. 1:1-11 John 18:1-14

Transfiguration (Sunday preceding Lent) and following

Day	Psalm	Year 1	Year 2
Sunday	*Morning:* Ps. 103; 150 *Evening:* Ps. 117; 139	Dan. 7:9-10, 13-14 2 Cor. 3:1-9 John 12:27-36a	Mal. 4:1-6 2 Cor. 3:7-18 Luke 9:18-27
Monday	*Morning:* Ps. 5; 145 *Evening:* Ps. 82; 29	Deut. 6:1-15 Heb. 1:1-14 John 1:1-18	Prov. 27:1-6, 10-12 Phil. 2:1-13 John 18:15-18, 25-27
Tuesday	*Morning:* Ps. 42; 146 *Evening:* Ps. 102; 133	Deut. 6:16-25 Heb. 2:1-10 John 1:19-28	Prov. 30:1-4, 24-33 Phil. 3:1-11 John 18:28-38
Ash Wednesday	*Morning:* Ps. 5; 147:1-11 *Evening:* Ps. 27; 51	Jonah 3:1–4:11 Heb. 12:1-14 Luke 18:9-14	Amos 5:6-15 Heb. 12:1-14 Luke 18:9-14
Thursday	*Morning:* Ps. 27; 147:12-20 *Evening:* Ps. 126; 102	Deut. 7:6-11 Titus 1:1-16 John 1:29-34	Hab. 3:1-10 (11-15) 16-18 Phil. 3:12-21 John 17:1-8
Friday	*Morning:* Ps. 22; 148 *Evening:* Ps. 105; 130	Deut. 7:12-16 Titus 2:1-15 John 1:35-42	Ezek. 18:1-4, 25-32 Phil. 4:1-9 John 17:9-19
Saturday	*Morning:* Ps. 43; 149 *Evening:* Ps. 31; 143	Deut. 7:17-26 Titus 3:1-15 John 1:43-51	Ezek. 39:21-29 Phil. 4:10-20 John 17:20-26

DAY	PSALM	YEAR 1	YEAR 2
1st Week in Lent			
Sunday	*Morning:* Ps. 84; 150	Jer. 9:23-24	Dan. 9:3-10
	Evening: Ps. 42; 32	1 Cor. 1:18-31	Heb. 2:10-18
		Mark 2:18-22	John 12:44-50
Monday	*Morning:* Ps. 119:73-80; 145	Deut. 8:1-20	Gen. 37:1-11
		Heb. 2:11-18	1 Cor. 1:1-19
	Evening: Ps. 121; 6	John 2:1-12	Mark 1:1-13
Tuesday	*Morning:* Ps. 34; 146	Deut. 9:(1-3) 4-12	Gen. 37:12-24
	Evening: Ps. 25; 91	Heb. 3:1-11	1 Cor. 1:20-31
		John 2:13-22	Mark 1:14-28
Wednesday	*Morning:* Ps. 5; 147:1-11	Deut. 9:13-21	Gen. 37:25-36
		Heb. 3:12-19	1 Cor. 2:1-13
	Evening: Ps. 27; 51	John 2:23–3:15	Mark 1:29-45
Thursday	*Morning:* Ps. 27; 147:12-20	Deut. 9:23–10:5	Gen. 39:1-23
		Heb. 4:1-10	1 Cor. 2:14–3:15
	Evening: Ps. 126; 102	John 3:16-21	Mark 2:1-12
Friday	*Morning:* Ps. 22; 148	Deut. 10:12-22	Gen. 40:1-23
	Evening: Ps. 105; 130	Heb. 4:11-16	1 Cor. 3:16-23
		John 3:22-36	Mark 2:13-22
Saturday	*Morning:* Ps. 43; 149	Deut. 11:18-28	Gen. 41:1-13
	Evening: Ps. 31; 143	Heb. 5:1-10	1 Cor. 4:1-7
		John 4:1-26	Mark 2:23–3:6
2nd Week in Lent			
Sunday	*Morning:* Ps. 84; 150	Jer. 1:1-10	Gen. 41:14-45
	Evening: Ps. 42; 32	1 Cor. 3:11-23	Rom. 6:3-14
		Mark 3:31–4:9	John 5:19-24
Monday	*Morning:* Ps. 119:73-80; 145	Jer. 1:11-19	Gen. 41:46-57
		Rom. 1:1-15	1 Cor. 4:8-20 (21)
	Evening: Ps. 121; 6	John 4:27-42	Mark 3:7-19a

Day	Psalm	Year 1	Year 2
Tuesday	*Morning:* Ps. 34; 146	Jer. 2:1-13, 29-32	Gen. 42:1-17
	Evening: Ps. 25; 91	Rom. 1:16-25	1 Cor. 5:1-8
		John 4:43-54	Mark 3:19b-35
Wednesday	*Morning:* Ps. 5;	Jer. 3:6-18	Gen. 42:18-28
	147:1-11	Rom. 1:(26-27)	1 Cor. 5:9–6:11
	Evening: Ps. 27; 51	28–2:11	
		John 5:1-18	Mark 4:1-20
Thursday	*Morning:* Ps. 27;	Jer. 4:9-10, 19-28	Gen. 42:29-38
	147:12-20	Rom. 2:12-24	1 Cor. 6:12-20
	Evening: Ps. 126; 102	John 5:19-29	Mark 4:21-34
Friday	*Morning:* Ps. 22; 148	Jer. 5:1-9	Gen. 43:1-15
	Evening: Ps. 105; 130	Rom. 2:25–3:18	1 Cor. 7:1-9
		John 5:30-47	Mark 4:35-41
Saturday	*Morning:* Ps. 43; 149	Jer. 5:20-31	Gen. 43:16-34
	Evening: Ps. 31; 143	Rom. 3:19-31	1 Cor. 7:10-24
		John 7:1-13	Mark 5:1-20

3rd Week in Lent

Day	Psalm	Year 1	Year 2
Sunday	*Morning:* Ps. 84; 150	Jer. 6:9-15	Gen. 44:1-17
	Evening: Ps. 42; 32	1 Cor. 6:12-20	Rom. 8:1-10
		Mark 5:1-20	John 5:25-29
Monday	*Morning:* Ps. 119:73-	Jer. 7:1-15	Gen. 44:18-34
	80; 145	Rom. 4:1-12	1 Cor. 7:25-31
	Evening: Ps. 121; 6	John 7:14-36	Mark 5:21-43
Tuesday	*Morning:* Ps. 34; 146	Jer. 7:21-34	Gen. 45:1-15
	Evening: Ps. 25; 91	Rom. 4:13-25	1 Cor. 7:32-40
		John 7:37-52	Mark 6:1-13
Wednesday	*Morning:* Ps. 5;	Jer. 8:4-7, 18–9:6	Gen. 45:16-28
	147:1-11	Rom. 5:1-11	1 Cor. 8:1-13
	Evening: Ps. 27; 51	John 8:12-20	Mark 6:13-29
Thursday	*Morning:* Ps. 27;	Jer. 10:11-24	Gen. 46:1-7, 28-34
	147:12-20	Rom. 5:12-21	1 Cor. 9:1-15
	Evening: Ps. 126; 102	John 8:21-32	Mark 6:30-46

DAY	PSALM	YEAR 1	YEAR 2
Friday	*Morning:* Ps. 22; 148	Jer. 11:1-8, 14-17	Gen. 47:1-26
	Evening: Ps. 105; 130	Rom. 6:1-11	1 Cor. 9:16-27
		John 8:33-47	Mark 6:47-56
Saturday	*Morning:* Ps. 43; 149	Jer. 13:1-11	Gen. 47:27–48:7
	Evening: Ps. 31; 143	Rom. 6:12-23	1 Cor. 10:1-13
		John 8:47-59	Mark 7:1-23

4th Week in Lent

DAY	PSALM	YEAR 1	YEAR 2
Sunday	*Morning:* Ps. 84; 150	Jer. 14:1-9 (10-16)	Gen. 48:8-22
	Evening: Ps. 42; 32	17-22	Rom. 8:11-25
		Gal. 4:21–5:1	John 6:27-40
		Mark 8:11-21	
Monday	*Morning:* Ps. 119:73-80; 145	Jer. 16:(1-9) 10-21	Gen. 49:1-28
		Rom. 7:1-12	1 Cor. 10:14–11:1
	Evening: Ps. 121; 6	John 6:1-15	Mark 7:24-37
Tuesday	*Morning:* Ps. 34; 146	Jer. 17:19-27	Gen. 49:29–50:14
	Evening: Ps. 25; 91	Rom. 7:13-25	1 Cor. 11:2-34
		John 6:16-27	Mark 8:1-10
Wednesday	*Morning:* Ps. 5; 147:1-11	Jer. 18:1-11	Gen. 50:15-26
		Rom. 8:1-11	1 Cor. 12:1-11
	Evening: Ps. 27; 51	John 6:27-40	Mark 8:11-26
Thursday	*Morning:* Ps. 27; 147:12-20	Jer. 22:13-23	Ex. 1:6-22
		Rom. 8:12-27	1 Cor. 12:12-26
	Evening: Ps. 126; 102	John 6:41-51	Mark 8:27–9:1
Friday	*Morning:* Ps. 22; 148	Jer. 23:1-8	Ex. 2:1-22
	Evening: Ps. 105; 130	Rom. 8:28-39	1 Cor. 12:27–13:3
		John 6:52-59	Mark 9:2-13
Saturday	*Morning:* Ps. 43; 149	Jer. 23:9-15	Ex. 2:23–3:15
	Evening: Ps. 31; 143	Rom. 9:1-18	1 Cor. 13:1-13
		John 6:60-71	Mark 9:14-29

DAY	PSALM	YEAR 1	YEAR 2
5th Week in Lent			
Sunday	*Morning:* Ps. 84; 150	Jer. 23:16-32	Ex. 3:16–4:12
	Evening: Ps. 42; 32	1 Cor. 9:19-27	Rom. 12:1-21
		Mark 8:31–9:1	John 8:46-59
Monday	*Morning:* Ps. 119:73-80; 145	Jer. 24:1-10	Ex. 4:10-20 (21-26) 27-31
	Evening: Ps. 121; 6	Rom. 9:19-33	1 Cor. 14:1-19
		John 9:1-17	Mark 9:30-41
Tuesday	*Morning:* Ps. 34; 146	Jer. 25:8-17	Ex. 5:1–6:1
	Evening: Ps. 25; 91	Rom. 10:1-13	1 Cor. 14:20-33a, 39-40
		John 9:18-41	Mark 9:42-50
Wednesday	*Morning:* Ps. 5; 147:1-11	Jer. 25:30-38	Ex. 7:8-24
	Evening: Ps. 27; 51	Rom. 10:14-21	2 Cor. 2:14–3:6
		John 10:1-18	Mark 10:1-16
Thursday	*Morning:* Ps. 27; 147:12-20	Jer. 26:1-16 (17-24)	Ex. 7:25–8:19
	Evening: Ps. 126; 102	Rom. 11:1-12	2 Cor. 3:7-18
		John 10:19-42	Mark 10:17-31
Friday	*Morning:* Ps. 22; 148	Jer. 29:1 (2-3) 4-14	Ex. 9:13-35
	Evening: Ps. 105; 130	Rom. 11:13-24	2 Cor. 4:1-12
		John 11:1-27 *or* John 12:1-10	Mark 10:32-45
Saturday	*Morning:* Ps. 43; 149	Jer. 31:27-34	Ex. 10:21–11:8
	Evening: Ps. 31; 143	Rom. 11:25-36	2 Cor. 4:13-18
		John 11:28-44 *or* John 12:37-50	Mark 10:46-52
Holy Week			
Passion/Palm Sunday	*Morning:* Ps. 84; 150	Zech. 9:9-12*	Zech. 9:9-12*
	Evening: Ps. 42; 32	1 Tim. 6:12-16*	1 Tim. 6:12-16*
		or Zech. 12:9–11; 13:1, 7-9**	*or* Zech. 12:9-11; 13:1, 7-9**
		Matt. 21:12-17**	Luke 19:41-48**

*Intended for use in the morning   **Intended for use in the evening

Day	Psalm	Year 1	Year 2
Monday	*Morning:* Ps. 119:73-80; 145	Jer. 11:18-20; 12:1-16 (17)	Lam. 1:1-2, 6-12
	Evening: Ps. 121; 6	Phil. 3:1-14 John 12:9-19	2 Cor. 1:1-7 Mark 11:12-25
Tuesday	*Morning:* Ps. 34; 146	Jer. 15:10-21	Lam. 1:17-22
	Evening: Ps. 25; 91	Phil. 3:15-21 John 12:20-26	2 Cor. 1:8-22 Mark 11:27-33
Wednesday	*Morning:* Ps. 5; 147:1-11	Jer. 17:5-10, 14-17 (18) Phil. 4:1-13	Lam. 2:1-9 2 Cor. 1:23–2:11
	Evening: Ps. 27; 51	John 12:27-36	Mark 12:1-11
Maundy Thursday	*Morning:* Ps. 27; 147:12-20	Jer. 20:7-11 (12-13) 14-18	Lam. 2:10-18
	Evening: Ps. 126; 102	1 Cor. 10:14-17; 11:27-32 John 17:1-11 (12-26)	1 Cor. 10:14-17; 11:27-32 Mark 14:12-25
Good Friday	*Morning:* Ps. 22; 148	Wisd. of Sol. 1:16–2:1, 12-22 *or*	Lam. 3:1-9, 19-33
	Evening: Ps. 105; 130	Gen. 22:1-14 1 Peter 1:10-20 John 13:36-38* *or* John 19:38-42**	1 Peter 1:10-20 John 13:36-38* *or* John 19:38-42**
Holy Saturday	*Morning:* Ps. 43; 149	Job 19:21-27a	Lam. 3:37-58
	Evening: Ps. 31; 143	Heb. 4:1-16* Rom. 8:1-11**	Heb. 4:1-16* Rom. 8:1-11**
Easter Week			
Sunday	*Morning:* Ps. 93; 150	Ex. 12:1-14*	Ex. 12:1-14*
	Evening: Ps. 136; 117	John 1:1-18* *or* Isa. 51:9-11** Luke 24:13-35** *or* John 20:19-23**	John 1:1-18* *or* Isa. 51:9-11** Luke 24:13-35** *or* John 20:19-23**
Monday	*Morning:* Ps. 97; 145	Jonah 2:1-10	Ex. 12:14-27
	Evening: Ps. 124; 115	Acts 2:14, 22-32 John 14:1-14	1 Cor. 15:1-11 Mark 16:1-8

*Intended for use in the morning   **Intended for use in the evening

Day	Psalm	Year 1	Year 2
Tuesday	*Morning:* Ps. 98; 146	Isa. 30:18-26	Ex. 12:28-39
	Evening: Ps. 66; 116	Acts 2:36-41 (42-47)	1 Cor. 15:12-28
		John 14:15-31	Mark 16:9-20
Wednesday	*Morning:* Ps. 99; 147:1-11	Micah 7:7-15	Ex. 12:40-51
		Acts 3:1-10	1 Cor. 15:(29) 30-41
	Evening: Ps. 9; 118	John 15:1-11	Matt. 28:1-16
Thursday	*Morning:* Ps. 47; 147:12-20	Ezek. 37:1-14	Ex. 13:3-10
		Acts 3:11-26	1 Cor. 15:41-50
	Evening: Ps. 68; 113	John 15:12-27	Matt. 28:16-20
Friday	*Morning:* Ps. 96; 148	Dan. 12:1-4, 13	Ex. 13:1-2, 11-16
	Evening: Ps. 49; 148	Acts 4:1-12	1 Cor. 15:51-58
		John 16:1-15	Luke 24:1-12
Saturday	*Morning:* Ps. 92; 149	Isa. 25:1-9	Ex. 13:17–14:4
	Evening: Ps. 23; 114	Acts 4:13-21 (22-31)	2 Cor. 4:16–5:10
		John 16:16-33	Mark 12:18-27

2nd Week of Easter

Day	Psalm	Year 1	Year 2
Sunday	*Morning:* Ps. 93; 150	Isa. 43:8-13	Ex. 14:5-22
	Evening: Ps. 136; 117	1 Peter 2:2-10	1 John 1:1-7
		John 14:1-7	John 14:1-7
Monday	*Morning:* Ps. 97; 145	Dan. 1:1-21	Ex. 14:21-31
	Evening: Ps. 124; 115	1 John 1:1-10	1 Peter 1:1-12
		John 17:1-11	John 14:(1-7) 8-17
Tuesday	*Morning:* Ps. 98; 146	Dan. 2:1-16	Ex. 15:1-21
	Evening: Ps. 66; 116	1 John 2:1-11	1 Peter 1:13-25
		John 17:12-19	John 14:18-31
Wednesday	*Morning:* Ps. 99; 147:1-11	Dan. 2:17-30	Ex. 15:22–16:10
		1 John 2:12-17	1 Peter 2:1-10
	Evening: Ps. 9; 118	John 17:20-26	John 15:1-11
Thursday	*Morning:* Ps. 47; 147:12-20	Dan. 2:31-49	Ex. 16:10-22
		1 John 2:18-29	1 Peter 2:11–3:12
	Evening: Ps. 68; 113	Luke 3:1-14	John 15:12-27

DAY	PSALM	YEAR 1	YEAR 2
Friday	*Morning:* Ps. 96; 148	Dan. 3:1-18	Ex. 16:23-36
	Evening: Ps. 49; 138	1 John 3:1-10	1 Peter 3:13–4:6
		Luke 3:15-22	John 16:1-15
Saturday	*Morning:* Ps. 92; 149	Dan. 3:19-30	Ex. 17:1-16
	Evening: Ps. 23; 114	1 John 3:11-18	1 Peter 4:7-19
		Luke 4:1-13	John 16:16-33

3rd Week of Easter

DAY	PSALM	YEAR 1	YEAR 2
Sunday	*Morning:* Ps. 93; 150	Dan. 4:1-18	Ex. 18:1-12
	Evening: Ps. 136; 117	1 Peter 4:7-11	1 John 2:7-17
		John 21:15-25	Mark 16:9-20
Monday	*Morning:* Ps. 97; 145	Dan. 4:19-27	Ex. 18:13-27
	Evening: Ps. 124; 115	1 John 3:19–4:6	1 Peter 5:1-14
		Luke 4:14-30	Matt. (1:1-17) 3:1-6
Tuesday	*Morning:* Ps. 98; 146	Dan. 4:28-37	Ex. 19:1-16
	Evening: Ps. 66; 116	1 John 4:7-21	Col. 1:1-14
		Luke 4:31-37	Matt. 3:7-12
Wednesday	*Morning:* Ps. 99; 147:1-11	Dan. 5:1-12	Ex. 19:16-25
		1 John 5:1-12	Col. 1:15-23
	Evening: Ps. 9; 118	Luke 4:38-44	Matt. 3:13-17
Thursday	*Morning:* Ps. 47; 147:12-20	Dan. 5:13-30	Ex. 20:1-21
		1 John 5:13-20 (21)	Col. 1:24–2:7
	Evening: Ps. 68; 113	Luke 5:1-11	Matt. 4:1-11
Friday	*Morning:* Ps. 96; 148	Dan. 6:1-15	Ex. 24:1-18
	Evening: Ps. 49; 138	2 John 1-13	Col. 2:8-23
		Luke 5:12-26	Matt. 4:12-17
Saturday	*Morning:* Ps. 92; 149	Dan. 6:16-28	Ex. 25:1-22
	Evening: Ps. 23; 114	3 John 1-15	Col. 3:1-17
		Luke 5:27-39	Matt. 4:18-25

4th Week of Easter

DAY	PSALM	YEAR 1	YEAR 2
Sunday	*Morning:* Ps. 93; 150	Wisd. of Sol. 1:1-15	Ex. 28:1-4, 30-38
	Evening: Ps. 136; 117	*or* Gen. 18:22-33	
		1 Peter 5:1-11	1 John 2:18-29
		Matt. 7:15-29	Mark 6:30-44

DAY	PSALM	YEAR 1	YEAR 2
Monday	*Morning:* Ps. 97; 145	Wisd. of Sol.	Ex. 32:1-20
	Evening: Ps. 124; 115	1:16–2:11, 21-24	
		or Jer. 30:1-9	
		Col. 1:1-14	Col. 3:18–4:6 (7-18)
		Luke 6:1-11	Matt. 5:1-10
Tuesday	*Morning:* Ps. 98; 146	Wisd. of Sol. 3:1-9	Ex. 32:21-34
	Evening: Ps. 66; 116	*or* Jer. 30:10-17	
		Col. 1:15-23	1 Thess. 1:1-10
		Luke 6:12-26	Matt. 5:11-16
Wednesday	*Morning:* Ps. 99;	Wisd. of Sol. 4:16–5:8	Ex. 33:1-23
	147:1-11	*or* Jer. 30:18-22	
	Evening: Ps. 9; 118	Col. 1:24–2:7	1 Thess. 2:1-12
		Luke 6:27-38	Matt. 5:17-20
Thursday	*Morning:* Ps. 47;	Wisd. of Sol. 5:9-23	Ex. 34:1-17
	147:12-20	*or* Jer. 31:1-14	
	Evening: Ps. 68; 113	Col. 2:8-23	1 Thess. 2:13-20
		Luke 6:39-49	Matt. 5:21-26
Friday	*Morning:* Ps. 96; 148	Wisd. of Sol. 6:12-23	Ex. 34:18-35
	Evening: Ps. 49; 138	*or* Jer. 31:15-22	
		Col. 3:1-11	1 Thess. 3:1-13
		Luke 7:1-17	Matt. 5:27-37
Saturday	*Morning:* Ps. 92; 149	Wisd. of Sol. 7:1-14	Ex. 40:18-38
	Evening: Ps. 23; 114	*or* Jer. 31:23-25	
		Col. 3:12-17	1 Thess. 4:1-12
		Luke 7:18-28 (29-30)	Matt. 5:38-48
		31-35	

5th Week of Easter

DAY	PSALM	YEAR 1	YEAR 2
Sunday	*Morning:* Ps. 93; 150	Wisd. of Sol. 7:22–8:1	Lev. 8:1-13, 30-36
	Evening: Ps. 136; 117	*or* Isa. 32:1-8	
		2 Thess. 2:13-17	Heb. 12:1-14
		Matt. 7:7-14	Luke 4:16-30
Monday	*Morning:* Ps. 97; 145	Wisd. of Sol. 9:1, 7-	Lev. 16:1-19
	Evening: Ps. 124; 115	18 *or* Jer. 32:1-15	
		Col. 3:18–4:18	1 Thess. 4:13-18
		Luke 7:36-50	Matt. 6:1-6, 16-18

DAY	PSALM	YEAR 1	YEAR 2
Tuesday	*Morning:* Ps. 98; 146 *Evening:* Ps. 66; 116	Wisd. of Sol. 10:1-4 (5-12) 13-21 *or* Jer. 32:16-25 Rom. 12:1-21 Luke 8:1-15	Lev. 16:20-34 1 Thess. 5:1-11 Matt. 6:7-15
Wednesday	*Morning:* Ps. 99; 147:1-11 *Evening:* Ps. 9; 118	Wisd. of Sol. 13:1-9 *or* Jer. 32:36-44 Rom. 13:1-14 Luke 8:16-25	Lev. 19:1-18 1 Thess. 5:12-28 Matt. 6:19-24
Thursday	*Morning:* Ps. 47; 147:12-20 *Evening:* Ps. 68; 113	Wisd. of Sol. 14:27–15:3 *or* Jer. 33:1-13 Rom. 14:1-12 Luke 8:26-39	Lev. 19:26-37 2 Thess. 1:1-12 Matt. 6:25-34
Friday	*Morning:* Ps. 96; 148 *Evening:* Ps. 49; 138	Wisd. of Sol. 16:15–17:1 *or* Deut. 31:30–32:14 Rom. 14:13-23 Luke 8:40-56	Lev. 23:1-22 2 Thess. 2:1-17 Matt. 7:1-12
Saturday	*Morning:* Ps. 92; 149 *Evening:* Ps. 23; 114	Wisd. of Sol. 19:1-8, 18-22 *or* Deut. 32:34-41 (42) 43 Rom. 15:1-13 Luke 9:1-17	Lev. 23:23-44 2 Thess. 3:1-18 Matt. 7:13-21

6th Week of Easter

DAY	PSALM	YEAR 1	YEAR 2
Sunday	*Morning:* Ps. 93; 150 *Evening:* Ps. 136; 117	Ecclus. 43:1-12, 27- 32 *or* Deut. 15:1-11 1 Tim. 3:14–4:5 Matt. 13:24-34a	Lev. 25:1-17 James 1:2-8, 16-18 Luke 12:13-21
Monday	*Morning:* Ps. 97; 145 *Evening:* Ps. 124; 115	Deut. 8:1-10 *or* Deut. 18:9-14 James 1:1-15 Luke 9:18-27	Lev. 25:35-55 Col. 1:9-14 Matt. 13:1-16

Day	Psalm	Year 1	Year 2
Tuesday	*Morning:* Ps. 98; 146 *Evening:* Ps. 66; 116	Deut. 8:11-20 *or* Deut. 18:15-22 James 1:16-27 Luke 11:1-13	Lev. 26:1-20 1 Tim. 2:1-6 Matt. 13:18-23
Wednesday	*Morning:* Ps. 99; 147:1-11	Baruch 3:24-37 *or* Deut. 19:1-7 James 5:13-18 Luke 12:22-31	Lev. 26:27-42 Eph. 1:1-10 Matt. 22:41-46
Eve of Ascension	Ps. 9; 118	2 Kings 2:1-15 Rev. 5:1-14	2 Kings 2:1-15 Rev. 5:1-14
Ascension Day	*Morning:* Ps. 47; 147:12-20 *Evening:* Ps. 68; 113	Ezek. 1:1-14, 24-28b Heb. 2:5-18 Matt. 28:16-20	Dan. 7:9-14 Heb. 2:5-18 Matt. 28:16-20
Friday	*Morning:* Ps. 96; 148 *Evening:* Ps. 49; 138	Ezek. 1:28–3:3 Heb. 4:14–5:6 Luke 9:28-36	1 Sam. 2:1-10 Eph. 2:1-10 Matt. 7:22-27
Saturday	*Morning:* Ps. 92; 149 *Evening:* Ps. 23; 114	Ezek. 3:4-17 Heb. 5:7-14 Luke 9:37-50	Num. 11:16-17, 24-29 Eph. 2:11-22 Matt. 7:28–8:4

7th Week of Easter

Day	Psalm	Year 1	Year 2
Sunday	*Morning:* Ps. 93; 150 *Evening:* Ps. 136; 117	Ezek. 3:16-27 Eph. 2:1-10 Matt. 10:24-33, 40-42	Ex. 3:1-12 Heb. 12:18-29 Luke 10:17-24
Monday	*Morning:* Ps. 97; 145 *Evening:* Ps. 124; 115	Ezek. 4:1-17 Heb. 6:1-12 Luke 9:51-62	Josh. 1:1-9 Eph. 3:1-13 Matt. 8:5-17
Tuesday	*Morning:* Ps. 98; 146 *Evening:* Ps. 66; 116	Ezek. 7:10-15, 23b-27 Heb. 6:13-20 Luke 10:1-17	1 Sam. 16:1-13a Eph. 3:14-21 Matt. 8:18-27
Wednesday	*Morning:* Ps. 99; 147:1-11 *Evening:* Ps. 9; 118	Ezek. 11:14-25 Heb. 7:1-17 Luke 10:17-24	Isa. 4:2-6 Eph. 4:1-16 Matt. 8:28-34

DAY	PSALM	YEAR 1	YEAR 2
Thursday	*Morning:* Ps. 47; 147:12-20	Ezek. 18:1-4, 19-32	Zech. 4:1-14
		Heb. 7:18-28	Eph. 4:17-32
	Evening: Ps. 68; 113	Luke 10:25-37	Matt. 9:1-8
Friday	*Morning:* Ps. 96; 148	Ezek. 34:17-31	Jer. 31:27-34
	Evening: Ps. 49; 138	Heb. 8:1-13	Eph. 5:1-32
		Luke 10:38-42	Matt. 9:9-17
Saturday	*Morning:* Ps. 92; 149	Ezek. 43:1-12	Ezek. 36:22-27
		Heb. 9:1-14	Eph. 6:1-24
		Luke 11:14-23	Matt. 9:18-26
Eve of Pentecost	Ps. 23; 114	Ex. 19:3-8a, 16-20	Ex. 19:3-8a, 16-20
		1 Peter 2:4-10	1 Peter 2:4-10
Pentecost	*Morning:* Ps. 104; 150	Isa. 11:1-9	Deut. 16:9-12
	Evening: Ps. 29; 33	1 Cor. 2:1-13	Acts 4:18-21, 23-33
		John 14:21-29	John 4:19-26

On the weekdays which follow, the readings are taken from the week which corresponds to the date of Pentecost.

Eve of *Trinity Sunday*	Ps. 125; 90	Ecclus. 42:15-25 *or* Isa. 6:1-8	Ecclus. 42:15-25 *or* Isa. 6:1-8
		Eph. 3:14-21	Eph. 3:14-21
Trinity Sunday	*Morning:* Ps. 103; 150	Ecclus. 43:1-12	Job. 38:1-11; 42:1-5
	Evening: Ps. 117; 139	(27-33) *or* Deut. 6:1-9 (10-15)	
		Eph. 4:1-16	Rev. 19:4-16
		John 1:1-18	John 1:29-34

On the weekdays which follow, the readings are taken from the week which corresponds to the date of Trinity Sunday.

Week following Sunday between May 11 and 16 inclusive, if after Pentecost Sunday

Monday	*Morning:* Ps. 62; 145	Isa. 63:7-14	Ezek. 33:1-11
	Evening: Ps. 73; 9	2 Tim. 1:1-14	1 John 1:1-10
		Luke 11:24-36	Matt. 9:27-34
Tuesday	*Morning:* Ps. 12; 146	Isa. 63:15–64:9	Ezek. 33:21-33
	Evening: Ps. 36; 7	2 Tim. 1:15–2:13	1 John 2:1-11
		Luke 11:37-52	Matt. 9:35–10:4

Day	Psalm	Year 1	Year 2
Wednesday	*Morning:* Ps. 96; 147:1-11	Isa. 65:1-12 2 Tim. 2:14-26	Ezek. 34:1-16 1 John 2:12-17
	Evening: Ps. 132; 134	Luke 11:53–12:12	Matt. 10:5-15
Thursday	*Morning:* Ps. 116; 147:12-20	Isa. 65:17-25 2 Tim. 3:1-17	Ezek. 37:21b-28 1 John 2:18-29
	Evening: Ps. 26; 130	Luke 12:13-31	Matt. 10:16-23
Friday	*Morning:* Ps. 84; 148	Isa. 66:1-6	Ezek. 39:21-29
	Evening: Ps. 25; 40	2 Tim. 4:1-8	1 John 3:1-10
		Luke 12:32-48	Matt. 10:24-33
Saturday	*Morning:* Ps. 63; 149	Isa. 66:7-14	Ezek. 47:1-12
	Evening: Ps. 125; 90	2 Tim. 4:9-22	1 John 3:11-18
		Luke 12:49-59	Matt. 10:34-42

Week following Sunday between May 17 and 23 inclusive, if after Pentecost Sunday

Day	Psalm	Year 1	Year 2
Monday	*Morning:* Ps. 5; 145	Ruth 1:1-18	Prov. 3:11-20
	Evening: Ps. 82; 29	1 Tim. 1:1-17	1 John 3:18–4:6
		Luke 13:1-9	Matt. 11:1-6
Tuesday	*Morning:* Ps. 42; 146	Ruth 1:19–2:13	Prov. 4:1-27
	Evening: Ps. 102; 133	1 Tim. 1:18–2:8	1 John 4:7-21
		Luke 13:10-17	Matt. 11:7-15
Wednesday	*Morning:* Ps. 89:1-18; 147:1-11	Ruth 2:14-23 1 Tim. 3:1-16	Prov. 6:1-19 1 John 5:1-12
	Evening: Ps. 1; 33	Luke 13:18-30	Matt. 11:16-24
Thursday	*Morning:* Ps. 97; 147:12-20	Ruth 3:1-18 1 Tim. 4:1-16	Prov. 7:1-27 1 John 5:13-21
	Evening: Ps. 16; 62	Luke 13:31-35	Matt. 11:25-30
Friday	*Morning:* Ps. 51; 148	Ruth 4:1-22	Prov. 8:1-21
	Evening: Ps. 142; 65	1 Tim. 5:17-22 (23-25)	2 John 1-13
		Luke 14:1-11	Matt. 12:1-14
Saturday	*Morning:* Ps. 104; 149	Deut. 1:1-8	Prov. 8:22-36
	Evening: Ps. 138; 98	1 Tim. 6:6-21	3 John 1-15
		Luke 14:12-24	Matt. 12:15-21

Day	Psalm	Year 1	Year 2
Week following Sunday between May 24 and 28 inclusive, if after Pentecost Sunday			
Sunday	*Morning:* Ps. 19; 150	Deut. 4:1-9	Prov. 9:1-12
	Evening: Ps. 81; 113	Rev. 7:1-4, 9-17	Acts 8:14-25
		Matt. 12:33-45	Luke 10:25-28, 38-42
Monday	*Morning:* Ps. 135; 145	Deut. 4:9-14	Prov. 10:1-12
	Evening: Ps. 97; 112	2 Cor. 1:1-11	1 Tim. 1:1-17
		Luke 14:25-35	Matt. 12:22-32
Tuesday	*Morning:* Ps. 123; 146	Deut. 4:15-24	Prov. 15:16-33
	Evening: Ps. 30; 86	2 Cor. 1:12-22	1 Tim. 1:18–2:15
		Luke 15:1-10	Matt. 12:33-42
Wednesday	*Morning:* Ps. 15; 147:1-11	Deut. 4:25-31	Prov. 17:1-20
	Evening: Ps. 48; 4	2 Cor. 1:23–2:17	1 Tim. 3:1-16
		Luke 15:1-2, 11-32	Matt. 12:43-50
Thursday	*Morning:* Ps. 36; 147:12-20	Deut. 4:32-40	Prov. 21:30–22:6
	Evening: Ps. 80; 27	2 Cor. 3:1-18	1 Tim. 4:1-16
		Luke 16:1-9	Matt. 13:24-30
Friday	*Morning:* Ps. 130; 148	Deut. 5:1-22	Prov. 23:19-21, 29–24:2
	Evening: Ps. 32; 139	2 Cor. 4:1-12	1 Tim. 5:17-22 (23-25)
		Luke 16:10-17 (18)	Matt. 13:31-35
Saturday	*Morning:* Ps. 56; 149	Deut. 5:22-33	Prov. 25:15-28
	Evening: Ps. 118; 111	2 Cor. 4:13–5:10	1 Tim. 6:6-21
		Luke 16:19-31	Matt. 13:36-43
Week following Sunday between May 29 and June 4 inclusive, if after Pentecost Sunday			
Sunday	*Morning:* Ps. 67; 150	Deut. 11:1-12	Eccl. 1:1-11
	Evening: Ps. 46; 93	Rev. 10:1-11	Acts 8:26-40
		Matt. 13:44-58	Luke 11:1-13
Monday	*Morning:* Ps. 57; 145	Deut. 11:13-19	Eccl. 2:1-15
	Evening: Ps. 85; 47	2 Cor. 5:11–6:2	Gal. 1:1-17
		Luke 17:1-10	Matt. 13:44-52

Day	Psalm	Year 1	Year 2
Tuesday	*Morning:* Ps. 54; 146 *Evening:* Ps. 28; 99	Deut. 12:1-12 2 Cor. 6:3-13 (14–7:1) Luke 17:11-19	Eccl. 2:16-26 Gal. 1:18–2:10 Matt. 13:53-58
Wednesday	*Morning:* Ps. 65; 147:1-11 *Evening:* Ps. 125; 91	Deut. 13:1-11 2 Cor. 7:2-16 Luke 17:20-37	Eccl. 3:1-15 Gal. 2:11-21 Matt. 14:1-12
Thursday	*Morning:* Ps. 143; 147:12-20 *Evening:* Ps. 81; 116	Deut. 16:18-20; 17:14-20 2 Cor. 8:1-16 Luke 18:1-8	Eccl. 3:16–4:3 Gal. 3:1-14 Matt. 14:13-21
Friday	*Morning:* Ps. 88; 148 *Evening:* Ps. 6; 20	Deut. 26:1-11 2 Cor. 8:16-24 Luke 18:9-14	Eccl. 5:1-7 Gal. 3:15-22 Matt. 14:22-36
Saturday	*Morning:* Ps. 122; 149 *Evening:* Ps. 100; 63	Deut. 29:2-15 2 Cor. 9:1-15 Luke 18:15-30	Eccl. 5:8-20 Gal. 3:23–4:11 Matt. 15:1-20

Week following Sunday between June 5 and 11 inclusive, if after Pentecost Sunday

Day	Psalm	Year 1	Year 2
Sunday	*Morning:* Ps. 108; 150 *Evening:* Ps. 66; 23	Deut. 29:16-29 Rev. 12:1-12 Matt. 15:29-39	Eccl. 6:1-12 Acts 10:9-23 Luke 12:32-40
Monday	*Morning:* Ps. 62; 145 *Evening:* Ps. 73; 9	Deut. 30:1-10 2 Cor. 10:1-18 Luke 18:31-43	Eccl. 7:1-14 Gal. 4:12-20 Matt. 15:21-28
Tuesday	*Morning:* Ps. 12; 146 *Evening:* Ps. 36; 7	Deut. 30:11-20 2 Cor. 11:1-21a Luke 19:1-10	Eccl. 8:14–9:10 Gal. 4:21-31 Matt. 15:29-39
Wednesday	*Morning:* Ps. 96; 147:1-11 *Evening:* 132; 134	Deut. 31:30–32:14 2 Cor. 11:21b-33 Luke 19:11-27	Eccl. 9:11-18 Gal. 5:1-15 Matt. 16:1-12
Thursday	*Morning:* Ps. 116; 147:12-20 *Evening:* Ps. 26; 130	Ecclus. 44:19–45:5 *or* S. of Sol. 1:1-3, 9-11, 15-16a; 2:1-3a 2 Cor. 12:1-10 Luke 19:28-40	Eccl. 11:1-8 Gal. 5:16-24 Matt. 16:13-20

Day	Psalm	Year 1	Year 2
Friday	*Morning:* Ps. 84; 148 *Evening:* Ps. 25; 40	Ecclus. 45:6-16 *or* S. of Sol. 2:8-13; 4:1-4a, 5-7, 9-11 2 Cor. 12:11-21 Luke 19:41-48	Eccl. 11:9–12:14 Gal. 5:25–6:10 Matt. 16:21-28
Saturday	*Morning:* Ps. 63; 149 *Evening:* Ps. 125; 90	Ecclus. 46:1-10 *or* S. of Sol. 5:10-16; 7:1-2 (3-5) 6-7a (9); 8:6-7 2 Cor. 13:1-14 Luke 20:1-8	Num. 3:1-13 Gal. 6:11-18 Matt. 17:1-13

Week following Sunday between June 12 and 18 inclusive

Day	Psalm	Year 1	Year 2
Sunday	*Morning:* Ps. 103; 150 *Evening:* Ps. 117; 139	Ecclus. 46:11-20 *or* Ex. 6:2-13; 7:1-6 Rev. 15:1-8 Matt. 18:1-14	Num. 6:22-27 Acts 13:1-12 Luke 12:41-48
Monday	*Morning:* Ps. 5; 145 *Evening:* Ps. 82; 29	1 Sam. 1:1-20 Acts 1:1-14 Luke 20:9-19	Num. 9:15-23; 10:29-36 Rom. 1:1-15 Matt. 17:14-21
Tuesday	*Morning:* Ps. 42; 146 *Evening:* Ps. 102; 133	1 Sam. 1:21–2:11 Acts 1:15-26 Luke 20:19-26	Num. 11:1-23 Rom. 1:16-25 Matt. 17:22-27
Wednesday	*Morning:* Ps. 89:1-18; 147:1-11 *Evening:* Ps. 1; 33	1 Sam. 2:12-26 Acts 2:1-21 Luke 20:27-40	Num. 11:24-33 (34-35) Rom. 1:28–2:11 Matt. 18:1-9
Thursday	*Morning:* Ps. 97; 147:12-20 *Evening:* Ps. 16; 62	1 Sam. 2:27-36 Acts 2:22-36 Luke 20:41–21:4	Num. 12:1-16 Rom. 2:12-24 Matt. 18:10-20
Friday	*Morning:* Ps. 51; 148 *Evening:* Ps. 142; 65	1 Sam. 3:1-21 Acts 2:37-47 Luke 21:5-19	Num. 13:1-3, 21-30 Rom. 2:25–3:8 Matt. 18:21-35
Saturday	*Morning:* Ps. 104; 149 *Evening:* Ps. 138; 98	1 Sam. 4:1b-11 Acts 4:32–5:11 Luke 21:20-28	Num. 13:31–14:25 Rom. 3:9-20 Matt. 19:1-12

Day	Psalm	Year 1	Year 2

Week following Sunday between June 19 and 25 inclusive

Sunday	*Morning:* Ps. 19; 150 *Evening:* Ps. 81; 113	1 Sam. 4:12-22 James 1:1-18 Matt. 19:23-30	Num. 14:26-45 Acts 15:1-12 Luke 12:49-56
Monday	*Morning:* Ps. 135; 145 *Evening:* Ps. 97; 112	1 Sam. 5:1-12 Acts 5:12-26 Luke 21:29-36	Num. 16:1-19 Rom. 3:21-31 Matt. 19:13-22
Tuesday	*Morning:* Ps. 123; 146 *Evening:* Ps. 30; 86	1 Sam. 6:1-16 Acts 5:27-42 Luke 21:37–22:13	Num. 16:20-35 Rom. 4:1-12 Matt. 19:23-30
Wednesday	*Morning:* Ps. 15; 147:1-11 *Evening:* Ps. 48; 4	1 Sam. 7:2-17 Acts 6:1-15 Luke 22:14-23	Num. 16:36-50 Rom. 4:13-25 Matt. 20:1-16
Thursday	*Morning:* Ps. 36; 147:12-20 *Evening:* Ps. 80; 27	1 Sam. 8:1-22 Acts 6:15–7:16 Luke 22:24-30	Num. 17:1-11 Rom. 5:1-11 Matt. 20:17-28
Friday	*Morning:* Ps. 130; 148 *Evening:* Ps. 32; 139	1 Sam. 9:1-14 Acts 7:17-29 Luke 22:31-38	Num. 20:1-13 Rom. 5:12-21 Matt. 20:29-34
Saturday	*Morning:* Ps. 56; 149 *Evening:* Ps. 118; 111	1 Sam. 9:15–10:1 Acts 7:30-43 Luke 22:39-51	Num. 20:14-29 Rom. 6:1-11 Matt. 21:1-11

Week following Sunday between June 26 and July 2 inclusive

Sunday	*Morning:* Ps. 67; 150 *Evening:* Ps. 46; 93	1 Sam. 10:1-16 Rom. 4:13-25 Matt. 21:23-32	Num. 21:4-9, 21-35 Acts 17:(12-21) 23-24 Luke 13:10-17
Monday	*Morning:* Ps. 57; 145 *Evening:* Ps. 85; 47	1 Sam. 10:17-27 Acts 7:44–8:1a Luke 22:52-62	Num. 22:1-21 Rom. 6:12-23 Matt. 21:12-22
Tuesday	*Morning:* Ps. 54; 146 *Evening:* Ps. 28; 99	1 Sam. 11:1-15 Acts 8:1b-13 Luke 22:63-71	Num. 22:21-38 Rom. 7:1-12 Matt. 21:23-32

Day	Psalm	Year 1	Year 2
Wednesday	*Morning:* Ps. 65; 147:1-11	1 Sam. 12:1-6 (7-15) 16-25	Num. 22:41–23:12
	Evening: Ps. 125; 91	Acts 8:14-25	Rom. 7:13-25
		Luke 23:1-12	Matt. 21:33-46
Thursday	*Morning:* Ps. 143; 147:12-20	1 Sam. 13:5-18	Num. 23:11-26
		Acts 8:26-40	Rom. 8:1-11
	Evening: Ps. 81; 116	Luke 23:13-25	Matt. 22:1-14
Friday	*Morning:* Ps. 88; 148	1 Sam. 13:19–14:15	Num. 24:1-13
	Evening: Ps. 6; 20	Acts 9:1-9	Rom. 8:12-17
		Luke 23:26-31	Matt. 22:15-22
Saturday	*Morning:* Ps. 122; 149	1 Sam. 14:16-30	Num. 24:12-25
	Evening: Ps. 100; 63	Acts 9:10-19a	Rom. 8:18-25
		Luke 23:32-43	Matt. 22:23-40

Week following Sunday between July 3 and 9 inclusive

Day	Psalm	Year 1	Year 2
Sunday	*Morning:* Ps. 108; 150	1 Sam. 14:36-45	Num. 27:12-23
	Evening: Ps. 66; 23	Rom. 5:1-11	Acts 19:11-20
		Matt. 22:1-14	Mark 1:14-20
Monday	*Morning:* Ps. 62; 145	1 Sam. 15:1-3, 7-23	Num. 32:1-6, 16-27
	Evening: Ps. 73; 9	Acts 9:19b-31	Rom. 8:26-30
		Luke 23:44-56a	Matt. 23:1-12
Tuesday	*Morning:* Ps. 12; 146	1 Sam. 15:24-35	Num. 35:1-3, 9-15, 30-34
	Evening: Ps. 36; 7	Acts 9:32-43	
		Luke 23:56b– 24:11 (12)	Rom. 8:31-39
			Matt. 23:13-26
Wednesday	*Morning:* Ps. 96; 147:1-11	1 Sam. 16:1-13	Deut. 1:1-18
		Acts 10:1-16	Rom. 9:1-18
	Evening: Ps. 132; 134	Luke 24:13-35	Matt. 23:27-39
Thursday	*Morning:* Ps. 116; 147:12-20	1 Sam. 16:14–17:11	Deut. 3:18-28
		Acts 10:17-33	Rom. 9:19-33
	Evening: Ps. 26; 130	Luke 24:36-53	Matt. 24:1-14
Friday	*Morning:* Ps. 84; 148	1 Sam. 17:17-30	Deut. 31:7-13, 24–32:4
	Evening: Ps. 25; 40	Acts 10:34-48	
		Mark 1:1-13	Rom. 10:1-13
			Matt. 24:15-31

Day	Psalm	Year 1	Year 2
Saturday	*Morning:* Ps. 63; 149	1 Sam. 17:31-49	Deut. 34:1-12
	Evening: Ps. 125; 90	Acts 11:1-18	Rom. 10:14-21
		Mark 1:14-28	Matt. 24:32-51

Week following Sunday between July 10 and 16 inclusive

Day	Psalm	Year 1	Year 2
Sunday	*Morning:* Ps. 103; 150	1 Sam. 17:50–18:4	Josh. 1:1-18
	Evening: Ps. 117; 139	Rom. 10:4-17	Acts 21:3-15
		Matt. 23:29-39	Mark 1:21-27
Monday	*Morning:* Ps. 5; 145	1 Sam. 18:5-16	Josh. 2:1-14
	Evening: Ps. 82; 29	(17-27a) 27b-30	
		Acts 11:19-30	Rom. 11:1-12
		Mark 1:29-45	Matt. 25:1-13
Tuesday	*Morning:* Ps. 42; 146	1 Sam. 19:1-18	Josh. 2:15-24
	Evening: Ps. 102; 133	(19-24)	
		Acts 12:1-17	Rom. 11:13-24
		Mark 2:1-12	Matt. 25:14-30
Wednesday	*Morning:* Ps. 89:1-18;	1 Sam. 20:1-23	Josh. 3:1-13
	147:1-11	Acts 12:18-25	Rom. 11:25-36
	Evening: Ps. 1; 33	Mark 2:13-22	Matt. 25:31-46
Thursday	*Morning:* Ps. 97;	1 Sam. 20:24-42	Josh. 3:14–4:7
	147:12-20	Acts 13:1-12	Rom. 12:1-8
	Evening: Ps. 16; 62	Mark 2:23–3:6	Matt. 26:1-16
Friday	*Morning:* Ps. 51; 148	1 Sam. 21:1-15	Josh. 4:19–5:1, 10-15
	Evening: Ps. 142; 65	Acts 13:13-25	Rom. 12:9-21
		Mark 3:7-19a	Matt. 26:17-25
Saturday	*Morning:* Ps. 104; 149	1 Sam. 21:1-23	Josh. 6:1-14
	Evening: Ps. 138; 98	Acts 13:26-43	Rom. 13:1-7
		Mark 3:19b-35	Matt. 26:26-35

Week following Sunday between July 17 and 23 inclusive

Day	Psalm	Year 1	Year 2
Sunday	*Morning:* Ps. 19; 150	1 Sam. 23:7-18	Josh. 6:15-27
	Evening: Ps. 81; 113	Rom. 11:33–12:2	Acts 22:30–23:11
		Matt. 25:14-30	Mark 2:1-12

Day	Psalm	Year 1	Year 2
Monday	*Morning:* Ps. 135; 145	1 Sam. 24:1-22	Josh. 7:1-13
	Evening: Ps. 97; 112	Acts 13:44-52	Rom. 13:8-14
		Mark 4:1-20	Matt. 26:36-46
Tuesday	*Morning:* Ps. 123; 146	1 Sam. 25:1-22	Josh. 8:1-22
	Evening: Ps. 30; 86	Acts 14:1-18	Rom. 14:1-12
		Mark 4:21-34	Matt. 26:47-56
Wednesday	*Morning:* Ps. 15;	1 Sam. 25:23-44	Josh. 8:30-35
	147:1-11	Acts 14:19-28	Rom. 14:13-23
	Evening: Ps. 48; 4	Mark 4:35-41	Matt. 26:57-68
Thursday	*Morning:* Ps. 36;	1 Sam. 28:3-20	Josh. 9:3-21
	147:12-20	Acts 15:1-11	Rom. 15:1-13
	Evening: Ps. 80; 27	Mark 5:1-20	Matt. 26:69-75
Friday	*Morning:* Ps. 130; 148	1 Sam. 31:1-13	Josh. 9:22–10:15
	Evening: Ps. 32; 139	Acts 15:12-21	Rom. 15:14-24
		Mark 5:21-43	Matt. 27:1-10
Saturday	*Morning:* Ps. 56; 149	2 Sam. 1:1-16	Josh. 23:1-16
	Evening: Ps. 118; 111	Acts 15:22-35	Rom. 15:25-33
		Mark 6:1-13	Matt. 27:11-23

Week following Sunday between July 24 and 30 inclusive

Day	Psalm	Year 1	Year 2
Sunday	*Morning:* Ps. 67; 150	2 Sam. 1:17-27	Josh. 24:1-15
	Evening: Ps. 46; 93	Rom. 12:9-21	Acts 28:23-31
		Matt. 25:31-46	Mark 2:23-28
Monday	*Morning:* Ps. 57; 145	2 Sam. 2:1-11	Josh. 24:16-33
	Evening: Ps. 85; 47	Acts 15:36–16:5	Rom. 16:1-16
		Mark 6:14-29	Matt. 27:24-31
Tuesday	*Morning:* Ps. 54; 146	2 Sam. 3:6-21	Judg. 2:1-5, 11-23
	Evening: Ps. 28; 99	Acts 16:6-15	Rom. 16:17-27
		Mark 6:30-46	Matt. 27:32-44
Wednesday	*Morning:* Ps. 65;	2 Sam. 3:22-39	Judg. 3:12-30
	147:1-11	Acts 16:16-24	Acts 1:1-14
	Evening: Ps. 125; 91	Mark 6:47-56	Matt. 27:45-54

Day	Psalm	Year 1	Year 2
Thursday	*Morning:* Ps. 143; 147:12-20	2 Sam. 4:1-12	Judg. 4:4-23
		Acts 16:25-40	Acts 1:15-26
	Evening: Ps. 81; 116	Mark 7:1-23	Matt. 27:55-66
Friday	*Morning:* Ps. 88; 148	2 Sam. 5:1-12	Judg. 5:1-18
	Evening: Ps. 6; 20	Acts 17:1-15	Acts 2:1-21
		Mark 7:24-37	Matt. 28:1-10
Saturday	*Morning:* Ps. 122; 149	2 Sam. 5:22–6:11	Judg. 5:19-31
	Evening: Ps. 100; 63	Acts 17:16-34	Acts 2:22-36
		Mark 8:1-10	Matt. 28:11-20

Week following Sunday between July 31 and Aug. 6 inclusive

Day	Psalm	Year 1	Year 2
Sunday	*Morning:* Ps. 108; 150	2 Sam. 6:12-23	Judg. 6:1-24
	Evening: Ps. 66; 23	Rom. 14:7-12	2 Cor. 9:6-15
		John 1:43-51	Mark 3:20-30
Monday	*Morning:* Ps. 62; 145	2 Sam. 7:1-17	Judg. 6:25-40
	Evening: Ps. 73; 9	Acts 18:1-11	Acts 2:37-47
		Mark 8:11-21	John 1:1-18
Tuesday	*Morning:* Ps. 12; 146	2 Sam. 7:18-29	Judg. 7:1-18
	Evening: Ps. 36; 7	Acts 18:12-28	Acts 3:1-11
		Mark 8:22-33	John 1:19-28
Wednesday	*Morning:* Ps. 96; 147:1-11	2 Sam. 9:1-13	Judg. 7:19–8:12
		Acts 19:1-10	Acts 3:12-26
	Evening: Ps. 132; 134	Mark 8:34–9:1	John 1:29-42
Thursday	*Morning:* Ps. 116; 147:12-20	2 Sam. 11:1-27	Judg. 8:22-35
		Acts 19:11-20	Acts 4:1-12
	Evening: Ps. 26; 130	Mark 9:2-13	John 1:43-51
Friday	*Morning:* Ps. 84; 148	2 Sam. 12:1-14	Judg. 9:1-16, 19-21
	Evening: Ps. 25; 40	Acts 19:21-41	Acts 4:13-31
		Mark 9:14-29	John 2:1-12
Saturday	*Morning:* Ps. 63; 149	2 Sam. 12:15-31	Judg. 9:22-25, 50-57
	Evening: Ps. 125; 90	Acts 20:1-16	Acts 4:32–5:11
		Mark 9:30-41	John 2:13-25

Day	Psalm	Year 1	Year 2

Week following Sunday between Aug. 7 and 13 inclusive

Sunday	*Morning:* Ps. 103; 150 *Evening:* Ps. 117; 139	2 Sam. 13:1-22 Rom. 15:1-13 John 3:22-36	Judg. 11:1-11, 29-40 2 Cor. 11:21b-31 Mark 4:35-41
Monday	*Morning:* Ps. 5; 145 *Evening:* Ps. 82; 29	2 Sam. 13:23-39 Acts 20:17-38 Mark 9:42-50	Judg. 12:1-7 Acts 5:12-26 John 3:1-21
Tuesday	*Morning:* Ps. 42; 146 *Evening:* Ps. 102; 133	2 Sam. 14:1-20 Acts 21:1-14 Mark 10:1-16	Judg. 13:1-15 Acts 5:27-42 John 3:22-36
Wednesday	*Morning:* Ps. 89:1-18; 147:1-11 *Evening:* Ps. 1; 33	2 Sam. 14:21-33 Acts 21:15-26 Mark 10:17-31	Judg. 13:15-24 Acts 6:1-15 John 4:1-26
Thursday	*Morning:* Ps. 97; 147:12-20 *Evening:* Ps. 16; 62	2 Sam. 15:1-18 Acts 21:27-36 Mark 10:32-45	Judg. 14:1-19 Acts 6:15–7:16 John 4:27-42
Friday	*Morning:* Ps. 51; 148 *Evening:* Ps. 142; 65	2 Sam. 15:19-37 Acts 21:37–22:16 Mark 10:46-52	Judg. 14:20–15:20 Acts 7:17-29 John 4:43-54
Saturday	*Morning:* Ps. 104; 149 *Evening:* Ps. 138; 98	2 Sam. 16:1-23 Acts 22:17-29 Mark 11:1-11	Judg. 16:1-14 Acts 7:30-43 John 5:1-18

Week following Sunday between Aug. 14 and 20 inclusive

Sunday	*Morning:* Ps. 19; 150 *Evening:* Ps. 81; 113	2 Sam. 17:1-23 Gal. 3:6-14 John 5:30-47	Judg. 16:15-31 2 Cor. 13:1-11 Mark 5:25-34
Monday	*Morning:* Ps. 135; 145 *Evening:* Ps. 97; 112	2 Sam. 17:24–18:8 Acts 22:30–23:11 Mark 11:12-26	Judg. 17:1-13 Acts 7:44–8:1a John 5:19-29
Tuesday	*Morning:* Ps. 123; 146 *Evening:* Ps. 30; 86	2 Sam. 18:9-18 Acts 23:12-24 Mark 11:27–12:12	Judg. 18:1-15 Acts 8:1-13 John 5:30-47

Day	Psalm	Year 1	Year 2
Wednesday	*Morning:* Ps. 15; 147:1-11	2 Sam. 18:19-33	Judg. 18:16-31
		Acts 23:23-35	Acts 8:14-25
	Evening: Ps. 48; 4	Mark 12:13-27	John 6:1-15
Thursday	*Morning:* Ps. 36; 147:12-20	2 Sam. 19:1-23	Job 1:1-22
		Acts 24:1-23	Acts 8:26-40
	Evening: Ps. 80; 27	Mark 12:28-34	John 6:16-27
Friday	*Morning:* Ps. 130; 148	2 Sam. 19:24-43	Job 2:1-13
	Evening: Ps. 32; 139	Acts 24:24–25:12	Acts 9:1-9
		Mark 12:35-44	John 6:27-40
Saturday	*Morning:* Ps. 56; 149	2 Sam. 23:1-7, 13-17	Job 3:1-26
	Evening: Ps. 118; 111	Acts 25:13-27	Acts 9:10-19a
		Mark 13:1-13	John 6:41-51

Week following Sunday between Aug. 21 and 27 inclusive

Day	Psalm	Year 1	Year 2
Sunday	*Morning:* Ps. 67; 150	2 Sam. 24:1-2, 10-25	Job 4:1-6, 12-21
	Evening: Ps. 46; 93	Gal. 3:23–4:7	Rev. 4:1-11
		John 8:12-20	Mark 6:1-6a
Monday	*Morning:* Ps. 57; 145	1 Kings 1:(1-4) 5-31	Job 4:1; 5:1-11, 17-21, 26-27
	Evening: Ps. 85; 47	Acts 26:1-23	Acts 9:19b-31
		Mark 13:14-27	John 6:52-59
Tuesday	*Morning:* Ps. 54; 146	1 Kings 1:32–2:4 (5-46a) 46b	Job 6:1-4, 8-15, 21
	Evening: Ps. 28; 99	Acts 26:24–27:8	Acts 9:32-43
		Mark 13:28-37	John 6:60-71
Wednesday	*Morning:* Ps. 65; 147:1-11	1 Kings 3:1-15	Job 6:1; 7:1-21
		Acts 27:9-26	Acts 10:1-16
	Evening: Ps. 125; 91	Mark 14:1-11	John 7:1-13
Thursday	*Morning:* Ps. 143; 147:12-20	1 Kings 3:16-28	Job 8:1-10, 20-22
		Acts 27:27-44	Acts 10:17-33
	Evening: Ps. 81; 116	Mark 14:12-26	John 7:14-36
Friday	*Morning:* Ps. 88; 148	1 Kings 5:1–6:1, 7	Job 9:1-15, 32-35
	Evening: Ps. 6; 20	Acts 28:1-16	Acts 10:34-48
		Mark 14:27-42	John 7:37-52

Day	Psalm	Year 1	Year 2
Saturday	*Morning:* Ps. 122; 149 *Evening:* Ps. 100; 63	1 Kings 7:51–8:21 Acts 28:17-31 Mark 14:43-52	Job 9:1; 10:1-9, 16-22 Acts 11:1-18 John 8:12-20

Week following Sunday between Aug. 28 and Sept. 3 inclusive

Day	Psalm	Year 1	Year 2
Sunday	*Morning:* Ps. 108; 150 *Evening:* Ps. 66; 23	1 Kings 8:22-30 (31-40) 1 Tim. 4:7b-16 John 8:47-59	Job. 11:1-9, 13-20 Rev. 5:1-14 Matt. 5:1-12
Monday	*Morning:* Ps. 62; 145 *Evening:* Ps. 73; 9	2 Chron. 6:32–7:7 James 2:1-13 Mark 14:53-65	Job 12:1-6, 13-25 Acts 11:19-30 John 8:21-32
Tuesday	*Morning:* Ps. 12; 146 *Evening:* Ps. 36; 7	1 Kings 8:65–9:9 James 2:14-26 Mark 14:66-72	Job 12:1; 13:3-17, 21-27 Acts 12:1-17 John 8:33-47
Wednesday	*Morning:* Ps. 96; 147:1-11 *Evening:* Ps. 132; 134	1 Kings 9:24–10:13 James 3:1-12 Mark 15:1-11	Job 12:1; 14:1-22 Acts 12:18-25 John 8:47-59
Thursday	*Morning:* Ps. 116; 147:12-20 *Evening:* Ps. 26; 130	1 Kings 11:1-13 James 3:13–4:12 Mark 15:12-21	Job 16:16-22; 17:1, 13-16 Acts 13:1-12 John 9:1-17
Friday	*Morning:* Ps. 84; 148 *Evening:* Ps. 25; 40	1 Kings 11:26-43 James 4:13–5:6 Mark 15:22-32	Job 19:1-7, 14-27 Acts 13:13-25 John 9:18-41
Saturday	*Morning:* Ps. 63; 149 *Evening:* Ps. 125; 90	1 Kings 12:1-20 James 5:7-20 Mark 15:33-39	Job 22:1-4, 21–23:7 Acts 13:26-43 John 10:1-18

Week following Sunday between Sept. 4 and 10 inclusive

Day	Psalm	Year 1	Year 2
Sunday	*Morning:* Ps. 103; 150 *Evening:* Ps. 117; 139	1 Kings 12:21-33 Acts 4:18-31 John 10:31-42	Job 25:1-6; 27:1-6 Rev. 14:1-7, 13 Matt. 5:13-20
Monday	*Morning:* Ps. 5; 145 *Evening:* Ps. 82; 29	1 Kings 13:1-10 Phil. 1:1-11 Mark 15:40-47	Job 32:1-10, 19–33:1, 19-28 Acts 13:44-52 John 10:19-30

Day	Psalm	Year 1	Year 2
Tuesday	*Morning:* Ps. 42; 146 *Evening:* Ps. 102; 133	1 Kings 16:23-34 Phil. 1:12-30 Mark 16:1-8 (9-20)	Job 29:1-20 Acts 14:1-18 John 10:31-42
Wednesday	*Morning:* Ps. 89:1-18; 147:1-11 *Evening:* Ps. 1; 33	1 Kings 17:1-24 Phil. 2:1-11 Matt. 2:1-12	Job 29:1; 30:1-2, 16-31 Acts 14:19-28 John 11:1-16
Thursday	*Morning:* Ps. 97; 147:12-20 *Evening:* Ps. 16; 62	1 Kings 18:1-19 Phil. 2:12-30 Matt. 2:13-23	Job 29:1; 31:1-23 Acts 15:1-11 John 11:17-29
Friday	*Morning:* Ps. 51; 148 *Evening:* Ps. 142; 65	1 Kings 18:20-40 Phil. 3:1-16 Matt. 3:1-12	Job 29:1; 31:24-40 Acts 15:12-21 John 11:30-44
Saturday	*Morning:* Ps. 104; 149 *Evening:* Ps. 138; 98	1 Kings 18:41–19:8 Phil. 3:17–4:7 Matt. 3:13-17	Job 38:1-17 Acts 15:22-35 John 11:45-54

Week following Sunday between Sept. 11 and 17 inclusive

Day	Psalm	Year 1	Year 2
Sunday	*Morning:* Ps. 19; 150 *Evening:* Ps. 81; 113	1 Kings 19:8-21 Acts 5:34-42 John 11:45-57	Job 38:1, 18-41 Rev. 18:1-8 Matt. 5:21-26
Monday	*Morning:* Ps. 135; 145 *Evening:* Ps. 97; 112	1 Kings 21:1-16 1 Cor. 1:1-19 Matt. 4:1-11	Job 40:1-24 Acts 15:36–16:5 John 11:55–12:8
Tuesday	*Morning:* Ps. 123; 146 *Evening:* Ps. 30; 86	1 Kings 21:17-29 1 Cor. 1:20-31 Matt. 4:12-17	Job 40:1; 41:1-11 Acts 16:6-15 John 12:9-19
Wednesday	*Morning:* Ps. 15; 147:1-11 *Evening:* Ps. 48; 4	1 Kings 22:1-28 1 Cor. 2:1-13 Matt. 4:18-25	Job 42:1-17 Acts 16:16-24 John 12:20-26
Thursday	*Morning:* Ps. 36; 147:12-20 *Evening:* Ps. 80; 27	1 Kings 22:29-45 1 Cor. 2:14–3:15 Matt. 5:1-10	Job 28:1-28 Acts 16:25-40 John 12:27-36a

DAY	PSALM	YEAR 1	YEAR 2
Friday	*Morning:* Ps. 130; 148 *Evening:* Ps. 32; 139	2 Kings 1:2-17 1 Cor. 3:16-23 Matt. 5:11-16	Esth. 1:1-4, 10-19 Acts 17:1-15 John 12:36b-43
Saturday	*Morning:* Ps. 56; 149 *Evening:* Ps. 118; 111	2 Kings 2:1-18 1 Cor. 4:1-7 Matt. 5:17-20	Esth. 2:5-8, 15-23 Acts 17:16-34 John 12:44-50

Week following Sunday between Sept. 18 and 24 inclusive

DAY	PSALM	YEAR 1	YEAR 2
Sunday	*Morning:* Ps. 67; 150 *Evening:* Ps. 46; 93	2 Kings 4:8-37 Acts 9:10-31 Luke 3:7-18	Esth. 3:1–4:3 James 1:19-27 Matt. 6:1-6, 16-18
Monday	*Morning:* Ps. 57; 145 *Evening:* Ps. 85; 47	2 Kings 5:1-19 1 Cor. 4:8-21 Matt. 5:21-26	Esth. 4:4-17 Acts 18:1-11 Luke (1:1-4) 3:1-14
Tuesday	*Morning:* Ps. 54; 146 *Evening:* Ps. 28; 99	2 Kings 5:19-27 1 Cor. 5:1-8 Matt. 5:27-37	Esth. 5:1-14 Acts 18:12-28 Luke 3:15-22
Wednesday	*Morning:* Ps. 65; 147:1-11 *Evening:* Ps. 125; 91	2 Kings 6:1-23 1 Cor. 5:9–6:11 Matt. 5:38-48	Esth. 6:1-14 Acts 19:1-10 Luke 4:1-13
Thursday	*Morning:* Ps. 143; 147:12-20 *Evening:* Ps. 81; 116	2 Kings 9:1-16 1 Cor. 6:12-20 Matt. 6:1-6, 16-18	Esth. 7:1-10 Acts 19:11-20 Luke 4:14-30
Friday	*Morning:* Ps. 88; 148 *Evening:* Ps. 6; 20	2 Kings 9:17-37 1 Cor. 7:1-9 Matt. 6:7-15	Esth. 8:1-8, 15-17 Acts 19:21-41 Luke 4:31-37
Saturday	*Morning:* Ps. 122; 149 *Evening:* Ps. 100; 63	2 Kings 11:1-20a 1 Cor. 7:10-24 Matt. 6:19-24	Esth. 9:1-32 Acts 20:1-16 Luke 4:38-44

Week following Sunday between Sept. 25 and Oct. 1 inclusive

DAY	PSALM	YEAR 1	YEAR 2
Sunday	*Morning:* Ps. 108; 150 *Evening:* Ps. 66; 23	2 Kings 17:1-18 Acts 9:36-43 Luke 5:1-11	Hos. 1:1–2:1 James 3:1-13 Matt. 13:44-52

DAY	PSALM	YEAR 1	YEAR 2
Monday	*Morning:* Ps. 62; 145	2 Kings 17:24-41	Hos. 2:2-15
	Evening: Ps. 73; 9	1 Cor. 7:25-31	Acts 20:17-38
		Matt. 6:25-34	Luke 5:1-11
Tuesday	*Morning:* Ps. 12; 146	2 Chron. 29:1-3;	Hos. 2:16-23
	Evening: Ps. 36; 7	30:1 (2-9) 10-27	
		1 Cor. 7:32-40	Acts 21:1-14
		Matt. 7:1-12	Luke 5:12-26
Wednesday	*Morning:* Ps. 96;	2 Kings 18:9-25	Hos. 3:1-5
	147:1-11	1 Cor. 8:1-13	Acts 21:15-26
	Evening: Ps. 132; 134	Matt. 7:13-21	Luke 5:27-39
Thursday	*Morning:* Ps. 116;	2 Kings 18:28-37	Hos. 4:1-10
	147:12-20	1 Cor. 9:1-15	Acts 21:27-36
	Evening: Ps. 26; 130	Matt. 7:22-29	Luke 6:1-11
Friday	*Morning:* Ps. 84; 148	2 Kings 19:1-20	Hos. 4:11-19
	Evening: Ps. 25; 40	1 Cor. 9:16-27	Acts 21:37–22:16
		Matt. 8:1-17	Luke 6:12-26
Saturday	*Morning:* Ps. 63; 149	2 Kings 19:21-36	Hos. 5:1-7
	Evening: Ps. 125; 90	1 Cor. 10:1-13	Acts 22:17-29
		Matt. 8:18-27	Luke 6:27-38

Week following Sunday between Oct. 2 and 8 inclusive

DAY	PSALM	YEAR 1	YEAR 2
Sunday	*Morning:* Ps. 103; 150	2 Kings 20:1-21	Hos. 5:8–6:6
	Evening: Ps. 117; 139	Acts 12:1-17	1 Cor. 2:6-16
		Luke 7:11-17	Matt. 14:1-12
Monday	*Morning:* Ps. 5; 145	2 Kings 21:1-18	Hos. 6:7–7:7
	Evening: Ps. 82; 29	1 Cor. 10:14–11:1	Acts 22:30–23:11
		Matt. 8:28-34	Luke 6:39-49
Tuesday	*Morning:* Ps. 42; 146	2 Kings 22:1-13	Hos. 7:8-16
	Evening: Ps. 102; 133	1 Cor. 11:2 (3-16) 17-22	Acts 23:12-24
		Matt. 9:1-8	Luke 7:1-17
Wednesday	*Morning:* Ps. 89:1-18;	2 Kings 22:14–23:3	Hos. 8:1-14
	147:1-11	1 Cor. 11:23-34	Acts 23:23-35
	Evening: Ps. 1; 33	Matt. 9:9-17	Luke 7:18-35

Day	Psalm	Year 1	Year 2
Thursday	*Morning:* Ps. 97; 147:12-20	2 Kings 23:4-25	Hos. 9:1-9
		1 Cor. 12:1-11	Acts 24:1-23
	Evening: Ps. 16; 62	Matt. 9:18-26	Luke 7:36-50
Friday	*Morning:* Ps. 51; 148	2 Kings 23:36–24:17	Hos. 9:10-17
	Evening: Ps. 142; 65	1 Cor. 12:12-26	Acts 24:24–25:12
		Matt. 9:27-34	Luke 8:1-15
Saturday	*Morning:* Ps. 104; 149	Jer. 35:1-19	Hos. 10:1-15
	Evening: Ps. 138; 98	1 Cor. 12:27–13:3	Acts 25:13-27
		Matt. 9:35–10:4	Luke 8:16-25

Week following Sunday between Oct. 9 and 15 inclusive

Day	Psalm	Year 1	Year 2
Sunday	*Morning:* Ps. 19; 150	Jer. 36:1-10	Hos. 11:1-11
	Evening: Ps. 81; 113	Acts 14:8-18	1 Cor. 4:9-16
		Luke 7:36-50	Matt. 15:21-28
Monday	*Morning:* Ps. 135; 145	Jer. 36:11-26	Hos. 11:12–12:1
	Evening: Ps. 97; 112	1 Cor. 13:(1-3) 4-13	Acts 26:1-23
		Matt. 10:5-15	Luke 8:26-39
Tuesday	*Morning:* Ps. 123; 146	Jer. 36:27–37:2	Hos. 12:2-14
	Evening: Ps. 30; 86	1 Cor. 14:1-12	Acts 26:24–27:8
		Matt. 10:16-23	Luke 8:40-56
Wednesday	*Morning:* Ps. 15; 147:1-11	Jer. 37:3-21	Hos. 13:1-3
		1 Cor. 14:13-25	Acts 27:9-26
	Evening: Ps. 48; 4	Matt. 10:24-33	Luke 9:1-17
Thursday	*Morning:* Ps. 36; 147:12-20	Jer. 38:1-13	Hos. 13:4-8
		1 Cor. 14:26-33a	Acts 27:27-44
	Evening: Ps. 80; 27	(33b-36) 37-40	
		Matt. 10:34-42	Luke 9:18-27
Friday	*Morning:* Ps. 130; 148	Jer. 38:14-28	Hos. 13:9-16
	Evening: Ps. 32; 139	1 Cor. 15:1-11	Acts 28:1-16
		Matt. 11:1-6	Luke 9:28-36
Saturday	*Morning:* Ps. 56; 149	Jer. 52:1-34	Hos. 14:1-9
	Evening: Ps. 118; 111	1 Cor. 15:12-29	Acts 28:17-31
		Matt. 11:7-15	Luke 9:37-50

Day	Psalm	Year 1	Year 2
Week following Sunday between Oct. 16 and 22 inclusive			
Sunday	*Morning:* Ps. 67; 150 *Evening:* Ps. 46; 93	Jer. 29:1, 4-14 *or* Jer. 39:11–40:6 Acts 16:6-15 Luke 10:1-12, 17-20	Ecclus. 4:1-10 *or* Micah 1:1-9 1 Cor. 10:1-13 Matt. 16:13-20
Monday	*Morning:* Ps. 57; 145 *Evening:* Ps. 85; 47	Jer. 44:1-14 *or* Jer. 29:1, 4-14 1 Cor. 15:30-41 Matt. 11:16-24	Ecclus. 4:20–5:7 *or* Micah 2:1-13 Rev. 7:1-8 Luke 9:51-62
Tuesday	*Morning:* Ps. 54; 146 *Evening:* Ps. 28; 99	Lam. 1:1-5 (6-9)10-12 *or* Jer. 40:7–41:3 1 Cor. 15:41-50 Matt. 11:25-30	Ecclus. 6:5-17 *or* Micah 3:1-8 Rev. 7:9-17 Luke 10:1-16
Wednesday	*Morning:* Ps. 65; 147:1-11 *Evening:* Ps. 125; 91	Lam. 2:8-15 *or* Jer. 41:4-18 1 Cor. 15:51-58 Matt. 12:1-14	Ecclus. 7:4-14 *or* Micah 3:9–4:5 Rev. 8:1-13 Luke 10:17-24
Thursday	*Morning:* Ps. 143; 147:12-20 *Evening:* Ps. 81; 116	Ezra 1:1-11 *or* Jer. 42:1-22 1 Cor. 16:1-9 Matt. 12:15-21	Ecclus. 10:1-18 *or* Micah 5:1-4, 10-15 Rev. 9:1-12 Luke 10:25-37
Friday	*Morning:* Ps. 88; 148 *Evening:* Ps. 6; 20	Ezra 3:1-13 *or* Jer. 43:1-13 1 Cor. 16:10-24 Matt. 12:22-32	Ecclus. 11:2-20 *or* Micah 6:1-8 Rev. 9:13-21 Luke 10:38-42
Saturday	*Morning:* Ps. 122; 149 *Evening:* Ps. 100; 63	Ezra 4:7, 11-24 *or* Jer. 44:1-14 Philemon 1-25 Matt. 12:33-42	Ecclus. 15:9-20 *or* Micah 7:1-7 Rev. 10:1-11 Luke 11:1-13
Week following Sunday between Oct. 23 and 29 inclusive			
Sunday	*Morning:* Ps. 108; 150 *Evening:* Ps. 66; 23	Hag. 1:1–2:9 *or* Jer. 44:15-30 Acts 18:24–19:7 Luke 10:25-37	Ecclus. 18:19-33 *or* Jonah 1:1-17a 1 Cor. 10:15-24 Matt. 18:15-20

Day	Psalm	Year 1	Year 2
Monday	*Morning*: Ps. 62; 145 *Evening*: Ps. 73; 9	Zech. 1:7-17 *or* Jer. 45:1-5 Rev. 1:4-20 Matt. 12:43-50	Ecclus. 19:4-17 *or* Jonah 1:17–2:10 Rev. 11:1-14 Luke 11:14-26
Tuesday	*Morning*: Ps. 12; 146 *Evening*: Ps. 36; 7	Ezra 5:1-17 *or* Lam. 1:1-5 (6-9) 10-12 Rev. 4:1-11 Matt. 13:1-9	Ecclus. 24:1-12 *or* Jonah 3:1–4:11 Rev. 11:14-19 Luke 11:27-36
Wednesday	*Morning*: Ps. 96; 147:1-11 *Evening*: Ps. 132; 134	Ezra 6:1-22 *or* Lam. 2:8-15 Rev. 5:1-10 Matt. 13:10-17	Ecclus. 28:14-26 *or* Nahum 1:1-14 Rev. 12:1-6 Luke 11:37-52
Thursday	*Morning*: Ps. 116; 147:12-20 *Evening*: Ps. 26; 130	Neh. 1:1-11 *or* Lam. 2:16-22 Rev. 5:11–6:11 Matt. 13:18-23	Ecclus. 31:12-18, 25–32:2 *or* Nahum 1:15–2:12 Rev. 12:7-17 Luke 11:53–12:12
Friday	*Morning*: Ps. 84; 148 *Evening*: Ps. 25; 40	Neh. 2:1-20 *or* Lam. 4:1-22 Rev. 6:12–7:4 Matt. 13:24-30	Ecclus. 34:1-8, 18-22 *or* Nahum 2:13–3:7 Rev. 13:1-10 Luke 12:13-31
Saturday	*Morning*: Ps. 63; 149 *Evening*: Ps. 125; 90	Neh. 4:1-23 *or* Lam. 5:1-22 Rev. 7:(4-8) 9-17 Matt. 13:31-35	Ecclus. 35:1-17 *or* Nahum 3:8-19 Rev. 13:11-18 Luke 12:32-48

Week following Sunday between Oct. 30 and Nov. 5 inclusive

Day	Psalm	Year 1	Year 2
Sunday	*Morning*: Ps. 103; 150 *Evening*: Ps. 117; 139	Neh. 5:1-9 *or* Ezra 1:1-11 Acts 20:7-12 Luke 12:22-31	Ecclus. 36:1-17 *or* Zeph. 1:1-6 1 Cor. 12:27–13:13 Matt. 18:21-35
Monday	*Morning*: Ps. 5; 145 *Evening*: Ps. 82; 29	Neh. 6:1-19 *or* Ezra 3:1-13 Rev. 10:1-11 Matt. 13:36-43	Ecclus. 38:24-34 *or* Zeph. 1:7-13 Rev. 14:1-13 Luke 12:49-59

DAY	PSALM	YEAR 1	YEAR 2
Tuesday	*Morning:* Ps. 42; 146	Neh. 12:27-31a, 42b-	Ecclus. 43:1-22
	Evening: Ps. 102; 133	47 *or* Ezra 4:7, 11-24	*or* Zeph. 1:14-18
		Rev. 11:1-19	Rev. 14:14–15:8
		Matt. 13:44-52	Luke 13:1-9
Wednesday	*Morning:* Ps. 89:1-18;	Neh. 13:4-22	Ecclus. 43:23-33
	147:1-11	*or* Hag. 1:1–2:9	*or* Zeph. 2:1-15
	Evening: Ps. 1; 33	Rev. 12:1-12	Rev. 16:1-11
		Matt. 13:53-58	Luke 13:10-17
Thursday	*Morning:* Ps. 97;	Ezra 7:(1-10) 11-26	Ecclus. 44:1-15
	147:12-20	*or* Zech. 1:7-17	*or* Zeph. 3:1-7
	Evening: Ps. 16; 62	Rev. 14:1-13	Rev. 16:12-21
		Matt. 14:1-12	Luke 13:18-30
Friday	*Morning:* Ps. 51; 148	Ezra 7:27-28; 8:21-36	Ecclus. 50:1, 11-24
	Evening: Ps. 142; 65	*or* Ezra 5:1-17	*or* Zeph. 3:8-13
		Rev. 15:1-8	Rev. 17:1-18
		Matt. 14:13-21	Luke 13:31-35
Saturday	*Morning:* Ps. 104; 149	Ezra 9:1-15	Ecclus. 51:1-12
	Evening: Ps. 138; 98	*or* Ezra 6:1-22	*or* Zeph. 3:14-20
		Rev. 17:1-14	Rev. 18:1-14
		Matt. 14:22-36	Luke 14:1-11

Week following Sunday between Nov. 6 and Nov. 12 inclusive

DAY	PSALM	YEAR 1	YEAR 2
Sunday	*Morning:* Ps. 19; 150	Ezra 10:1-17	Ecclus. 51:13-22
	Evening: Ps. 81; 113	*or* Neh. 1:1-11	*or* Joel 1:1-13
		Acts 24:10-21	1 Cor. 14:1-12
		Luke 14:12-24	Matt. 20:1-16
Monday	*Morning:* Ps. 135; 145	Neh. 9:1-15 (16-25)	Joel 1:1-13
	Evening: Ps. 97; 112	*or* Neh. 2:1-20	*or* Joel 1:15–2:2
		Rev. 18:1-8	Rev. 18:15-24
		Matt. 15:1-20	Luke 14:12-24
Tuesday	*Morning:* Ps. 123; 146	Neh. 9:26-38	Joel 1:15–2:2 (3-11)
	Evening: Ps. 30; 86	*or* Neh. 4:1-23	*or* Joel 2:3-11
		Rev. 18:9-20	Rev. 19:1-10
		Matt. 15:21-28	Luke 14:25-35

DAY	PSALM	YEAR 1	YEAR 2
Wednesday	*Morning:* Ps. 15; 147:1-11	Neh. 7:73b–8:3, 5-18 *or* Neh. 5:1-19	Joel 2:12-19
	Evening: Ps. 48; 4	Rev. 18:21-24	Rev. 19:11-21
		Matt. 15:29-39	Luke 15:1-10
Thursday	*Morning:* Ps. 36; 147:12-20	1 Macc. 1:1-28 *or* Neh. 6:1-19	Joel 2:21-27
	Evening: Ps. 80; 27	Rev. 19:1-10	James 1:1-15
		Matt. 16:1-12	Luke 15:1-2, 11-32
Friday	*Morning:* Ps. 130; 148	1 Macc. 1:41-63 *or* Neh. 12:27-31a, 42b-47	Joel 2:28–3:8
	Evening: Ps. 32; 139	Rev. 19:11-16	James 1:16-27
		Matt. 16:13-20	Luke 16:1-9
Saturday	*Morning:* Ps. 56; 149	1 Macc. 2:1-28 *or* Neh. 13:4-22	Joel 3:9-17
	Evening: Ps. 118; 111	Rev. 20:1-6	James 2:1-13
		Matt. 16:21-28	Luke 16:10-17 (18)

Week following Sunday between Nov. 13 and 19 inclusive

DAY	PSALM	YEAR 1	YEAR 2
Sunday	*Morning:* Ps. 67; 150	1 Macc. 2:29-43 (44-48) *or* Ezra 7:(1-10) 11-26	Hab. 1:1-4 (5-11) 12–2:1
	Evening: Ps. 46; 93	Acts 28:14b-23	Phil. 3:13–4:1
		Luke 16:1-13	Matt. 23:13-24
Monday	*Morning:* Ps. 57; 145	1 Macc. 2:49-70 *or* Ezra 7:27-28; 8:21-36	Hab. 2:1-4, 9-20
	Evening: Ps. 85; 47	Rev. 20:7-15	James 2:14-26
		Matt. 17:1-13	Luke 16:19-31
Tuesday	*Morning:* Ps. 54; 146	1 Macc. 3:1-24 *or* Ezra 9:1-15	Hab. 3:1-10 (11-15) 16-18
	Evening: Ps. 28; 99	Rev. 21:1-8	James 3:1-12
		Matt. 17:14-21	Luke 17:1-10

Day	Psalm	Year 1	Year 2
Wednesday	*Morning:* Ps. 65; 147:1-11	1 Macc. 3:25-41 *or* Ezra 10:1-17	Mal. 1:1, 6-14
	Evening: Ps. 125; 91	Rev. 21:9-21	James 3:13–4:12
		Matt. 17:22-27	Luke 17:11-19
Thursday	*Morning:* Ps. 143; 147:12-20	1 Macc. 3:42-60 *or* Neh. 9:1-15 (16-25)	Mal. 2:1-16
	Evening: Ps. 81; 116	Rev. 21:22–22:5	James 4:13–5:6
		Matt. 18:1-9	Luke 17:20-37
Friday	*Morning:* Ps. 88; 148	1 Macc. 4:1-25 *or* Neh. 9:26-38	Mal. 3:1-12
	Evening: Ps. 6; 20	Rev. 22:6-13	James 5:7-12
		Matt. 18:10-20	Luke 18:1-8
Saturday	*Morning:* Ps. 122; 149	1 Macc. 4:36-59 *or* Neh. 7:73b–8:3, 5-18	Mal. 3:13–4:6
	Evening: Ps. 100; 63	Rev. 22:14-21	James 5:13-20
		Matt. 18:21-35	Luke 18:9-14

Christ the King or Reign of Christ (Sunday between Nov. 20 and 26) and following

Day	Psalm	Year 1	Year 2
Sunday	*Morning:* Ps. 108; 150	Isa. 19:19-25	Zech. 9:9-16
	Evening: Ps. 66; 23	Rom. 15:5-13	1 Peter 3:13-22
		Luke 19:11-27	Matt. 21:1-13
Monday	*Morning:* Ps. 62; 145	Joel 3:1-2, 9-17	Zech. 10:1-12
	Evening: Ps. 73; 9	1 Peter 1:1-12	Gal. 6:1-10
		Matt. 19:1-12	Luke 18:15-30
Tuesday	*Morning:* Ps. 12; 146	Nahum 1:1-13	Zech. 11:4-17
	Evening: Ps. 36; 7	1 Peter 1:13-25	1 Cor. 3:10-23
		Matt. 19:13-22	Luke 18:31-43
Wednesday	*Morning:* Ps. 96; 147:1-11	Obad. 15-21	Zech. 12:1-10
		1 Peter 2:1-10	Eph. 1:3-14
	Evening: Ps. 132; 134	Matt. 19:23-30	Luke 19:1-10
Thursday	*Morning:* Ps. 116; 147:12-20	Zeph. 3:1-13	Zech. 13:1-9
		1 Peter 2:11-25	Eph. 1:15-23
	Evening: Ps. 26; 130	Matt. 20:1-16	Luke 19:11-27

Day	Psalm	Year 1	Year 2
Friday	*Morning:* Ps. 84; 148	Isa. 24:14-23	Zech. 14:1-11
	Evening: Ps. 25; 40	1 Peter 3:13–4:6	Rom. 15:7-13
		Matt. 20:17-28	Luke 19:28-40
Saturday	*Morning:* Ps. 63; 149	Micah 7:11-20	Zech. 14:12-21
	Evening: Ps. 125; 90	1 Peter 4:7-19	Phil. 2:1-11
		Matt. 20:29-34	Luke 19:41-48

SPECIAL DAYS

Displayed below are special days that are commonly observed in various branches of the ecumenical church. With the exception of All Saints' Day and the civil days New Year's Day and Thanksgiving, they are ordinarily not included in Reformed observance. However, there is value in including them in daily prayer. Their inclusion will recognize the work of God in these biblical events, and express our solidarity with Christians in other traditions. Psalms are those appointed for the day of the week in which a special day falls.

New Year's Eve or Day

Eccl. 3:1-13
Rev. 21:1-6a
Matt. 25:31-46

Presentation of the Lord—Feb. 2

Mal. 3:1-4
Heb. 2:14-18
Luke 2:22-40

Annunciation of the Lord—March 25

Isa. 7:10-14
1 Tim. 3:16
  or Heb. 2:5-10
Luke 1:26-38

Visitation of Mary to Elizabeth—May 31

Isa. 11:1-5 *or* 1 Sam. 2:1-10
Rom. 12:9-16b
Luke 1:39-47

Birth of John the Baptist—June 24

Mal. 3:1-4 *or* Isa. 40:1-11
Luke 1:5-23, 57-67 (68-80) *
Matt. 11:2-19 **

Holy Cross—Sept. 14

Num. 21:4b-9 *or* Isa. 45:21-25
1 Cor. 1:18-24
John 3:13-17 *or* John 12:20-33

All Saints' Day—Nov. 1

Isa. 26:1-4, 8-9, 12-13, 19-21
Rev. 21:9-11, 22-27 (22:1-5)
  or Heb. 11:32–12:2
Matt. 5:1-12

Thanksgiving Day

Deut. 8:1-10 *or* Deut. 26:1-11
Phil. 4:6-20 *or* 1 Tim. 2:1-4
Luke 17:11-19 *or* Matt. 6:25-33

*Intended for use in the morning   **Intended for use in the evening

TABLE OF MAJOR CELEBRATIONS OF THE LITURGICAL CALENDAR

LECTIONARIES		FIRST SUNDAY OF ADVENT	ASH WEDNESDAY	EASTER	ASCENSION	PENTECOST
Sunday Cycle	Daily Cycle					
A	I	November 29, 1992	February 24, 1993	April 11, 1993	May 20, 1993	May 30, 1993
B	II	November 28, 1993	February 16, 1994	April 3, 1994	May 12, 1994	May 22, 1994
C	I	November 27, 1994	March 1, 1995	April 16, 1995	May 25, 1995	June 4, 1995
A	II	December 3, 1995	February 21, 1996	April 7, 1996	May 16, 1996	May 26, 1996
B	I	December 1, 1996	February 12, 1997	March 30, 1997	May 8, 1997	May 18, 1997
C	II	November 30, 1997	February 25, 1998	April 12, 1998	May 21, 1998	May 31, 1998
A	I	November 29, 1998	February 17, 1999	April 4, 1999	May 13, 1999	May 23, 1999
B	II	November 28, 1999	March 9, 2000	April 23, 2000	June 1, 2000	June 11, 2000
C	I	December 3, 2000	February 28, 2001	April 15, 2001	May 24, 2001	June 3, 2001
A	II	December 2, 2001	February 13, 2002	March 31, 2002	May 9, 2002	May 19, 2002
B	I	December 1, 2002	March 5, 2003	April 20, 2003	May 29, 2003	June 8, 2003
C	II	November 30, 2003	February 25, 2004	April 11, 2004	May 20, 2004	May 30, 2004
A	I	November 28, 2004	February 9, 2005	March 27, 2005	May 5, 2005	May 15, 2005
B	II	November 27, 2005	March 1, 2006	April 16, 2006	May 25, 2006	June 4, 2006
C	I	December 3, 2006	February 21, 2007	April 8, 2007	May 17, 2007	May 27, 2007
A	II	December 2, 2007	February 6, 2008	March 23, 2008	May 1, 2008	May 11, 2008
B	I	November 30, 2008	February 25, 2009	April 12, 2009	May 21, 2009	May 31, 2009
C	II	November 29, 2009	February 17, 2010	April 4, 2010	May 13, 2010	May 23, 2010
A	I	November 28, 2010	March 9, 2011	April 24, 2011	June 2, 2011	June 12, 2011
B	II	November 27, 2011	February 22, 2012	April 8, 2012	May 17, 2012	May 27, 2012
C	I	December 2, 2012	February 13, 2013	March 31, 2013	May 9, 2013	May 19, 2013

A	II	December 1, 2013	March 5, 2014	April 20, 2014	May 29, 2014	June 8, 2014
B	I	November 30, 2014	February 18, 2015	April 5, 2015	May 14, 2015	May 24, 2015
C	II	November 29, 2015	February 10, 2016	March 27, 2016	May 5, 2016	May 15, 2016
A	I	November 27, 2016	March 1, 2017	April 16, 2017	May 25, 2017	June 4, 2017
B	II	December 3, 2017	February 14, 2018	April 1, 2018	May 10, 2018	May 20, 2018
C	I	December 2, 2018	March 6, 2019	April 21, 2019	May 30, 2019	June 9, 2019
A	II	December 1, 2019	February 26, 2020	April 12, 2020	May 21, 2020	May 31, 2020
B	I	November 29, 2020	February 17, 2021	April 4, 2021	May 13, 2021	May 23, 2021
C	II	November 28, 2021	March 2, 2022	April 17, 2022	May 26, 2022	June 5, 2022
A	I	November 27, 2022	February 22, 2023	April 9, 2023	May 18, 2023	May 28, 2023
B	II	December 3, 2023	February 14, 2024	March 31, 2024	May 9, 2024	May 19, 2024
C	I	December 1, 2024	March 5, 2025	April 20, 2025	May 29, 2025	June 8, 2025
A	II	November 30, 2025	February 18, 2026	April 5, 2026	May 14, 2026	May 24, 2026
B	I	November 29, 2026	February 10, 2027	March 28, 2027	May 6, 2027	May 16, 2027
C	II	November 28, 2027	March 2, 2028	April 16, 2028	May 25, 2028	June 4, 2028
A	I	December 3, 2028	February 14, 2029	April 1, 2029	May 10, 2029	May 20, 2029
B	II	December 2, 2029	March 6, 2030	April 21, 2030	May 30, 2030	June 9, 2030
C	I	December 1, 2030	February 26, 2031	April 13, 2031	May 22, 2031	June 1, 2031
A	II	November 30, 2031	February 11, 2032	March 28, 2032	May 6, 2032	May 16, 2032
B	I	November 28, 2032	March 2, 2033	April 17, 2033	May 26, 2033	June 5, 2033
C	II	November 27, 2033	February 22, 2034	April 9, 2034	May 18, 2034	May 28, 2034
A	I	December 3, 2034	February 7, 2035	March 25, 2035	May 3, 2035	May 13, 2035
B	II	December 2, 2035	February 27, 2036	April 13, 2036	May 22, 2036	June 1, 2036
C	I	November 30, 2036	February 18, 2037	April 5, 2037	May 14, 2037	May 24, 2037
A	II	November 29, 2037	March 10, 2038	April 25, 2038	June 3, 2038	June 13, 2038
B	I	November 28, 2038	February 23, 2039	April 10, 2039	May 19, 2039	May 29, 2039
C	II	November 27, 2039	February 15, 2040	April 1, 2040	May 10, 2040	May 20, 2040

ACKNOWLEDGMENTS

MATERIAL FROM THE FOLLOWING SOURCES is gratefully acknowledged and is used by permission. Adaptations are by permission of copyright holders. Every effort has been made to determine the ownership of all texts and music used in this resource and to make proper arrangements for their use. The publisher regrets any oversight that may have occurred and will gladly make proper acknowledgment in future editions if this is brought to the publisher's attention.

SCRIPTURE QUOTATIONS

Except as otherwise noted, all scripture quotations are from the New Revised Standard Version of the Bible, copyright © 1989 by the Division of Christian Education of the National Council of the Churches of Christ in the U.S.A., and are used by permission. The following quotations are altered: Ps. 25:1–2; Ps. 27:5; Ps. 29:2–4; Ps. 34:3; Ps. 34:8; Ps. 46:1–3; Ps. 51:17; Ps. 95:1–2; Ps. 96:1–2; Ps. 96:11–13; Ps. 100:1, 2, 4a; Ps. 100:1, 2, 5; Ps. 103:1–2; Ps. 105:1–5; Ps. 106:1; Ps. 116:12–13; Ps. 118:1; Ps. 119:1–2; Ps. 130:5; Ps. 141:2; Isa. 2:4; Isa. 6:3; Isa. 7:14b; Isa. 11:6; Isa. 12:6; Isa. 35:1–2; Isa. 55:11; Isa. 57:15; Isa. 62:4c, 5b; Isa. 103:13; Jer. 31:33–34; Jer. 33:14a, 15; Joel 1:1a; Joel 2:13; Joel 2:28–29; Micah 6:8; Zech. 14:5c, 7; Matt. 5:14–16; Matt. 7:7; Matt. 17:5; Matt. 22:37–40; Matt. 28:19a, 20b; Luke 4:18; Luke 8:15; Luke 9:35; Luke 10:2; Luke 21:36; Luke 24:30–31; John 3:14–15; John 6:63,68; John 8:12; John 10:27–28a; John 11:25–26; John 13:34; John 15:5; John 15:16; John 17:17; Acts 1:8; Acts 20:35b; Rom. 5:5; Rom. 6:3–4; Rom. 8:1, 28, 38, 39; Rom. 11:33, 36; Rom. 12:1; Rom. 15:13; 2 Cor. 1:3–4; 2 Cor. 5:19; 2 Cor. 12:9a; Eph. 1:17–18; Eph. 2:10; Phil. 2:5–11; Phil. 2:13; Phil. 2:15–16; Phil. 3:13–14; Phil. 4:7; Phil. 4:23; Col. 1:15–20; 2 Thess. 3:16; 1 Tim. 1:17; 1 Tim. 6:15–16; 2 Tim. 1:10; Heb. 2:9; Heb. 4:12; Heb. 4:14, 16; Heb. 13:15; Heb. 13:16; Heb. 13:20–21; James 1:18; 1 Peter 2:9; 1 Peter 2:24; 1 Peter 5:10–11; 2 Peter 3:18; 1 John 1:8–9; 1 John 4:7–8; 1 John 4:9; 1 John 4:10; Rev. 1:5–6; Rev. 1:17–18; Rev. 2:7, 11, 17, 29; Rev. 3:6, 13, 22; Rev. 7:9–10; Rev. 14:13; Rev. 19:6–7; Rev. 22:5.

Also: Canticle of David (1 Chron. 29:10–11); Canticle of Miriam and Moses (Ex. 15:1, 2, 11, 13, 17–18); and Christ the Servant (1 Peter 2:21–25).

The following scripture quotations are from the *Revised Standard Version of the Bible*, copyright 1946, 1952, © 1971, 1973 by the Division of Christian Education of the National Council of the Churches of Christ in the U.S.A., and are used by permission: Deut. 33:27; 2 Sam. 22:29, 33; Ps. 139:23–24; Isa. 40:3; Isa. 53:4; Isa. 60:1–3; Matt. 3:2; Matt. 16:16; Mark 10:14b; Luke 2:10–11; Luke 11:9–10; Luke 21:28; John 1:14; John 3:17; John 6:68; Rom. 15:13; 2 Cor. 8:9; Phil. 1:9–10; Phil. 4:7; 1 Tim. 1:15; Heb. 4:16; 2 Peter 3:13; Rev. 4:8; Rev. 5:12. *Altered:* Deut. 7:9; Ps. 86:11–12; Matt. 24:42, 44; Luke 2:14; John 13:34; 1 Cor. 16:13–14; 1 Thess. 5:23; 1 Peter 1:3; Rev. 3:20. *Other:* Canticle of Hannah (1 Sam. 2:1–4, 7, 8).

The following scripture quotations are from the *Good News Bible: The Bible in Today's English Version,* © American Bible Society 1966, 1971, 1976: Ps. 5:2b–3; Isa. 40:31; Ezek. 36:26; *Altered:* Deut. 32:11; Ps. 74:16–17; Lam. 3:22–23; 2 Cor. 4:6; Col. 2:12; 1 Tim. 6:21; Heb. 10:22.

The following scripture quotations are from *The New English Bible* are copyright © The Delegates of the Oxford University Press and The Syndics of the Cambridge University Press 1961, 1970: Rom. 5:8; 1 John 3:23; *Altered:* Ps. 4:8; Rom. 22:33, 36; 1 Cor. 10:16–17; 1 Tim. 1:17; Titus 2:11; 1 Peter 1:3–4.

Scripture quotations from *The New Testament in Modern English*, translated by J. B. Phillips, revised edition, copyright © J. B. Phillips, 1958, 1959, 1960, 1972: Rom. 8:24. *Altered:* 2 Cor. 5:17.

The following scripture quotations are based on more than one translation: Num. 6:24–26 (RSV, TEV); Ps. 85:10–11 (NRSV, TEV, NEB); Ps. 86:5–6 (NRSV, TEV, NEB); Ps. 139:11–12 (TEV, JB NRSV); Dan. 2:22–23 (TEV, NRSV); Matt. 4:23 (RSV, NRSV); Matt. 23:9–10 (RSV, NEB); Matt. 24:42, 44; Matt. 25:34–36 (RSV, NRSV); Luke 11:9 (RSV, NRSV); John 15:15–17 (RSV, NRSV); Rom. 5:8 (RSV, NRSV); Rom. 6:3–5 (NRSV, TEV, NEB); Eph. 3:20–21 (RSV, NRSV); 1 Thess. 4:14, 17–18 (NRSV, NEB, JB, PHI); 1 Tim: 3:16 (RSV, NRSV); 1 Peter 2:24 (RSV, PHI); 1 Peter 2:24 (RSV, NRSV); Rev. 3:10 (RSV, NRSV); Rev. 14:13 (KJV, RSV); Rev. 21:23–24 (TEV, NEB, JB, NRSV). Also: The Beatitudes (Matt. 5:3–12) (NEB, NRSV); A Canticle for Pentecost (John 14:16; 16:13a; 14:26; Acts 2:2, 4a; Rom.8:26) (NEB, NRSV); A Canticle of Creation (Song of the Three Young Men 35–65, 34) (RSV, NEB, BCP); A Canticle of Love (1 John 4:7, 8; 1 Cor. 13:4–10; 12–13) (RSV, NEB, NRSV); A Canticle to the Lamb (Rev. 4:11; 5:9–10, 12, 13) (RSV, BCP); Christ, the Head of All Creation (Col. 1:15–20) (NEB, NRSV); God's Chosen One (Isa. 11:1–4, 6, 9) (RSV, NRSV); Jesus Christ Is Lord (Phil. 2:5c–11) (RSV, NRSV); The Mystery of Our Religion (1 Tim. 3:16; 6:15, 16) (RSV, NRSV); The Spirit of the Lord (Isa. 61:1–3, 10, 11) (NRSV, NEB); The Steadfast Love of the Lord (Lam. 3:22–26) (RSV, NEB).

The following quotations are from the psalter and canticles in *A New Zealand Prayer Book: He Karakia Mihinare o Aotearoa,* © Church of the Province of New Zealand, 1989: Ps. 96:1–2 alt.; Ps. 96:6–7; Ps. 103:8.

The text of the Psalms section (pp. 611–783) and those psalm texts contained in the Daily Prayer section (pp. 491–572) of this book are from *An Inclusive-Language*

Psalter of the Christian People, copyright © 1993 by the Order of St. Benedict, Inc., and published by license of The Liturgical Press, Collegeville, Minnesota, United States of America. All rights reserved.

LITURGICAL TEXTS

The numbers contained in the lists of prayers that follow refer to the numbers at the end of each prayer. The sources noted are the resources from which the texts in this book were taken, or sources cited in them. In many cases the particular text is not original with the source noted, since many liturgical texts that are widely shared are derived from a longer tradition and appear in a number of contemporary service books. In some instances a prayer cited from one service book may have appeared in previous editions. For example, a prayer cited from the *Book of Common Worship* (1946) may also have appeared in the 1932 and 1906 editions. Texts that have been altered are so designated or are marked (alt.).

SUPPLEMENTAL LITURGICAL RESOURCES

The following texts first appeared in one of the trial-use volumes that were published as part of the process for developing this book.

Service for the Lord's Day, Supplemental Liturgical Resource 1, copyright © 1984 The Westminster Press: 48, 56, 77, 103, 112. *Altered:* 100, 115, 121, 130, 792.

Holy Baptism and Services for the Renewal of Baptism, Supplemental Liturgical Resource 2, copyright © 1985 The Westminster Press: 413, 415, 416, 417, 418, 424. Altered: 411, 412, 422, 426.

Christian Marriage, Supplemental Liturgical Resource 3, copyright © 1986 The Westminster Press: 791, 793, 799. *Altered:* 798, 800. *Other texts:* Statement of the Gift of Marriage (alt.).

The Funeral: A Service of Witness to the Resurrection, Supplemental Liturgical Resource 4, copyright © 1986 The Westminster Press: 801, 803, 805, 807, 812, 813, 829, 830, 833. *Altered:* 819, 824, 864, 867, 869, 870, 871.

Daily Prayer, Supplemental Liturgical Resource 5, copyright © 1987 The Westminster Press: 244, 267, 301, 315, 318, 435, 436, 437, 438, 439, 440, 444, 449, 458, 459, 460, 461, 463, 465, 466, 468, 469, 474, 476, 483, 485, 486, 538, 548, 566, 592, 607, 611, 615, 618, 622, 629, 634, 642, 643, 647, 655, 659, 662. *Altered:* 131 (concluding collect), 214, 434, 441, 442, 457, 462, 464, 467, 472, 473, 475, 482, 484, 487, 490, 492, 493, 497, 541, 543, 545, 546, 551, 553, 554, 557, 562, 575, 576, 577, 578, 580, 585, 586, 589, 593, 598, 610, 613, 623, 630, 632, 637, 638, 646, 648, 651, 665.

Services for Occasions of Pastoral Care, Supplemental Liturgical Resource 6, copyright © 1990 Westminster/John Knox Press: 838, 839, 840, 841, 842, 843, 844, 845, 847, 848, 849, 850, 851, 852, 856, 857, 858, 860, 861, 862. *Altered:* 836, 859.

Liturgical Year, Supplemental Liturgical Resource 7, copyright © 1992 Westminster/John Knox Press: 174, 181, 206, 219, 220, 254, 260, 265, 303, 322, 328,

406. *Altered:* 133, 153, 154, 173, 180, 205, 211, 218, 240, 248, 272, 273, 320, 327, 395, 396, 397, 404, 409, 410.

ADDITIONAL PRESBYTERIAN CHURCH (U.S.A.) SOURCES

The Book of Common Worship (Revised), copyright © The Trustees of the Presbyterian Board of Publication and Sabbath-School Work, 1905, 1906, 1932. Used by permission of Westminster/John Knox Press: 46 (alt.).

The Book of Common Worship, copyright, 1946, by The Board of Christian Education of the Presbyterian Church in the United States of America; renewed 1974. Used by permission of Westminster/John Knox Press: *Altered:* 2, 4, 7, 38, 47, 49, 50, 52, 66, 67, 117, 147, 169, 266, 274, 277, 323, 364, 366, 367, 377, 379, 383, 387, 390, 507, 511, 530, 775, 811, 814, 820.

Service for the Lord's Day and Lectionary for the Christian Year, copyright © MCMLXIV The Westminster Press: 126 (alt.).

Book of Common Worship: Provisional Services and Lectionary for the Christian Year, copyright © MCMLXVI W. L. Jenkins. Used by permission of Westminster/John Knox Press: *Altered:* 40, 51, 80, 380.

The Worshipbook: Services, copyright © MCMLXX The Westminster Press: 39, 43, 88, 275, 425, 500, 505, 686, 697, 703, 705, 710, 720, 736, 739, 743, 747, 748, 760, 778, 781, 828. *Altered:* 1, 41, 42, 54, 55, 64, 71, 81, 82, 83, 84, 85, 86, 87, 89, 90, 91, 109, 116, 136, 141, 155, 157, 158, 159, 166, 176, 184, 191, 194, 215, 242, 246, 247, 250, 289, 302, 304, 305, 667, 668, 671, 676, 680, 681, 690, 693, 694, 695, 696, 698, 699, 712, 713, 714, 717, 719, 721, 732, 733, 734, 744, 753, 755, 756, 759, 761, 769, 777, 785, 786, 788, 789, 795, 796, 815, 816, 817, 826, 835, 837, 846. *Other texts:* The charge: "Go into the world in peace . . ."

The Constitution of the Presbyterian Church (U.S.A.), Part I: *Book of Confessions*, copyright © 1991 The Office of the General Assembly, Presbyterian Church (U.S.A.): A Brief Statement of Faith.

INTERNATIONAL COMMISSION ON ENGLISH IN THE LITURGY

Some of the prayers in the Resources for the Liturgical Year are based on prayers in *The Roman Missal*, © 1973, International Committee on English in the Liturgy, Inc., and were adapted for *The Book of Alternative Services of the Anglican Church in Canada*, © 1985 by the General Synod of the Anglican Church in Canada. They are altered and adapted for use in this book with permission of the International Commission on English in the Liturgy and the Anglican Church of Canada.

Eucharistic Prayer A, copyright © 1986, International Commission on English in the Liturgy, Inc. All rights reserved: 118 (alt.).

Eucharistic Prayer of Hippolytus: Text for Consultation, copyright © 1983 International Commission on English in the Liturgy, Inc. All rights reserved: 120 (alt.).

The Liturgy of the Hours: According to the Roman Rite, copyright © 1975, International Commission on English in the Liturgy, Inc. All rights reserved: 502. *Altered:*

151, 217, 314, 471, 481, 491, 514, 534, 552, 558, 564, 579, 581, 582, 583, 587, 588, 595, 596, 599, 602, 620, 624, 644, 661.

Order of Christian Funerals, copyright © 1985, International Commission on English in the Liturgy, Inc.: *Altered:* 818, 834.

Pastoral Care of the Sick, copyright © 1982 International Commission on English in the Liturgy, Inc. All rights reserved: 865 (alt.).

Prayers, copyright © 1983, 1986, 1987, 1988, 1990, 1992, International Commission on English in the Liturgy, Inc. All rights reserved: 140, 143, 146, 156, 160, 193, 293, 297, 348, 351, 371, 386, 400, 403, 407, 450, 451. *Altered:* 167, 223, 280, 296, 339, 368, 374, 389, 448, 517.

The Roman Missal: The Sacramentary, copyright © 1973, International Committee on English in the Liturgy, Inc. All rights reserved. Used by permission of the International Commission on English in the Liturgy, Inc. Excerpts from the English translation: 125 (alt.), 127 (alt.), 268 (alt.). *Other texts:* Acclamations nos. 1, 2, 4 in the great thanksgivings; Easter Proclamation (alt.); Solemn Reproaches of the Cross (alt.)

OTHER SOURCES OF LITURGICAL TEXTS

All Desires Known, by Janet Morley (Ridgefield, Conn.: Morehouse Publishing Co., 1988), copyright © Janet Morley, 1988: 283 (alt.).

Alternative Collects, copyright © 1985, Anglican Church of Australia Trust Corporation. Published by the Anglican Information Office: 402. *Altered:* 238, 357.

The Alternative Service Book 1980, copyright © 1980 by The Central Board of Finance of the Church of England. *Altered:* 114, 144, 164, 168.

The Art of Ministering to the Sick, by Richard C. Cabot and Russell L. Dicks, copyright © 1936 by Macmillan Publishing Company, renewed 1964 by Russell L. Dicks. Reprinted with permission of Macmillan Publishing Company: 515 (alt.).

An Australian Prayer Book, copyright © 1978, The Anglican Church of Australia Trust Corporation: 61 (alt.).

Authorized Services, copyright © 1973 by The Church Hymnal Corporation: 509 (alt.).

Book of Alternative Services of the Anglican Church of Canada, copyright © 1985 General Synod of the Anglican Church of Canada: 519. *Other texts:* Call to Worship "On this day . . ." (Maundy Thursday) (alt.), and Invitation to the Observance of the Lenten Discipline (alt.). Other prayers in this book derived from *The Book of Alternative Services* are of uncertain origin.

The Book of Common Order of the Church of Scotland, copyright © Oxford University Press, 1940: 724 (alt.).

The Book of Common Prayer, according to the use of The Episcopal Church, copyright 1977 by Charles Mortimer Guilbert as custodian: 378, 384, 414, 488, 506, 508, 512, 531, 688, 700, 757, 758, 768, 770, 825. *Altered:* 3, 6, 11, 12, 44, 63, 68, 79, 95, 96, 97, 107, 108, 111, 113, 129, 139, 161, 162, 175, 198, 202, 209, 210, 235, 237, 251, 252, 256, 262, 263, 276, 286, 287, 294, 306, 307, 324, 333, 349, 356,

363, 376, 388, 391, 394, 399, 405, 496, 501, 504, 513, 666, 669, 673, 675, 684, 687, 691, 704, 722, 728, 729, 730, 731, 735, 740, 741, 746, 749, 752, 754, 766, 774, 779, 780, 782, 790, 794, 797, 802, 804, 806, 822, 866. *Other texts:* Acclamation no. 3 in great thanksgivings; Canticle of the Redeemed; Christ Our Passover (alt.); Daily Lectionary, pages 1050–1095 (alt.).

The Book of Common Worship, copyright © The Presbyterian Church in Canada, 1991: 70 (alt.), 106 (alt.).

Book of Worship, copyright © United Church of Christ Office for Church Life and Leadership, 1986: 69, 236. *Altered:* 239, 259, 823, and call to confession, page 1006 (alt.).

A Celebration of Baptism: An Ecumenical Liturgy. Copyright © 1990 by The Consultation on Common Texts. Used by permission of Abingdon Press and The Consultation on Common Texts: All liturgical texts in "Alternative Service for the Sacrament of Baptism" (pp. 419–429), including: 419, 420, 421.

Daily Prayer, by Eric Milner-White and George Wallace Briggs (London: Oxford University Press, 1941): 446 (alt.).

English translations of the following texts, copyright © 1988, English Language Liturgical Consultation (ELLC): Apostles' Creed, Canticle of Mary, Canticle of Simeon, Canticle of Zechariah, "Glory to God in the highest," "Glory to the Father," "Holy, holy, holy Lord," "Jesus, Lamb of God," "Lamb of God, you take away the sin of the world," "Lord, have mercy," Lord's Prayer, Nicene Creed, preface dialogue in the great thanksgivings, "We praise you, O God."

Great thanksgiving F [119] is copyright © 1975 by Marion J. Hatchett, Chairman, The Committee on a Common Eucharistic Prayer.

A Handbook for the Lectionary, by Horace T. Allen, Jr. (Philadelphia: Geneva Press, 1980). Copyright © 1980 The Geneva Press. Used by permission of Westminster/John Knox Press: 138.

Hymn to Christ the Light ("O Radiant Light"), translation © 1979 William G. Storey. All rights reserved.

Liturgy, Journal of the Liturgical Conference, vol. 10, no. 1, copyright © 1992 by The Liturgical Conference, Inc., Silver Spring, Maryland; prayer by Diane Karay Tripp: 495.

Lord Hear Our Prayer, ed. by Thomas McNally and William G. Storey. Copyright © 1978 Ave Maria Press, Notre Dame, Indiana: 784.

Lutheran Book of Worship: Minister's Desk Edition, copyright © 1978, used by permission of Augsburg Fortress: 9, 288, 338, 640, 652, 663, 707, 738, 742, 745. *Altered:* 104, 105, 110, 187, 222, 228, 232, 245, 258, 310, 316, 329, 344, 354, 401, 550, 563, 590, 614, 616, 617, 621, 625, 635, 650, 660, 672, 685, 701. Texts from the Latin Roman Missal as they appear in the *Lutheran Book of Worship:* 165 (alt.), 201 (alt.), 270 (alt.), 292. *Other texts:* Opening sentences for the Service of Light (Evening Prayer); "Worthy is Christ, the Lamb. . . . "

Markings, by Dag Hammarskjöld, translated by Leif Sjöberg and W. H. Auden, copyright © 1964 Alfred A. Knopf, Inc. (New York), and Faber and Faber Ltd. (London): 22.

Martin Luther King, Jr.: A Documentary . . . Montgomery to Memphis, ed. by Flip Schulke (New York and London: W. W. Norton & Co., 1976): 737.

Messale Romano (the Italian Sacramentary), copyright © 1983, Libreria Editrice Vaticana, translations by Fr. Peter Scagnelli used by permission of Liturgy Training Publications: 229, 365. *Altered:* 192, 203, 278, 337, 362, 373.

Morning Praise and Evensong, by William G. Storey, D.M.S., Frank C. Quinn, O.P., and David F. Wright, O.P. Copyright © 1973, Fides Publishers Inc., Notre Dame, Indiana: 456 (alt.).

A New Zealand Prayer Book: He Karakia Mihinare o Aotearoa, © Church of the Province of New Zealand, 1989. Reprinted with permission of the General Secretary: 57, 200, 284, 312, 332, 352, 361, 385, 430, 447. *Altered:* 99, 183, 226, 227, 233, 290, 295, 299, 308, 309, 321, 330, 335, 340, 359, 370, 445, 470. *Also:* Canticle of Judith; Canticle of Penitence; Canticle of Thanksgiving (alt.); The Desert Shall Blossom (alt.); The New Jerusalem (alt.); Seek the Lord (alt.).

1992 Sourcebook for Sundays and Seasons, by G. Thomas Ryan (Chicago: Liturgy Training Publications, 1992): 311 (alt.).

The Occasional Prayers of the 1928 Book Reconsidered, by Eric Milner-White (London: SPCK, 1930): 776.

Occasional Services, copyright © 1982, used by permission of Augsburg Fortress: 854.

Praise God: Common Prayer at Taizé, copyright © 1975 by Les Presses de Taizé. Published by Oxford University Press, 1977. Reprinted by permission of Oxford University Press, Inc. Texts based on the Daily Office of the Community of Taizé: 479. *Altered:* 148, 150, 170, 171, 177, 178, 213, 216, 243, 253, 269, 300, 478, 482.

Praise God in Song, ed. by John Allyn Melloh, S.M., and William G. Storey, texts by John Allyn Melloh, S.M. Copyright © 1979 G.I.A. Publications, Inc., Chicago, Illinois. Altered with permission. All rights reserved: *Altered:* 452, 453, 454, 455, 516, 518.

Praise Him! A Prayerbook for Today's Christians, © 1973 by Ave Maria Press, Notre Dame, Indiana. All rights reserved: 317.

Prayer based on one written by James F. White and Susan J. White and used by permission: 45.

Prayer by John Underwood Stevens, copyright © Louise Coons Stephens: 498.

Prayer by Howard Thurman, from Meditations of the Heart, copyright 1953 by Harper & Row, Publishers, Inc. Used by permission of Ms. Ann Thurman: 24.

Prayers for a New World, ed. by John Wallace Suter. Copyright © 1964 John W. Suter: *Altered:* 15, 702.

Prayers of the Reformers, ed. by Clyde Manschreck, copyright © 1958, Muhlenberg Press. Used by permission of Augsburg Fortress: 709 (alt.).

Prayers of the Spirit, ed. by John Wallace Suter (New York: Harper & Row, 1942): 727 (alt.).

Revised Common Lectionary. Copyright © 1992 by The Consultation on Common Texts (CCT). All rights reserved. Used by permission: The list of readings in the Lectionary for Sundays and Festivals on pages 1035–1048.

SECTION HEADING CROSSES

THE CROSS IS ONE OF THE OLDEST and most universally recognized symbols in Christianity. Those in the *Book of Common Worship* represent a variety of the many forms that have been used throughout history to represent the Christian faith.

 Cross Botonnée
(Preparation for Worship)

 Cross from Fifth-Century
Greek Pottery (Prayers
for Various Occasions)

 Celtic Cross
(Service for the Lord's Day)

 Cross from 4000 B.C.
Near Eastern Pottery
(Marriage)

 Jerusalem Cross
(Resources for the
Liturgical Year)

 Rayed Cross
(The Funeral: A Service of
Witness to the Resurrection)

 Anchored Cross
(Baptism and Reaffirmation
of the Baptismal Covenant)

 Cross Patée
(Pastoral Liturgies)

 Cross Crosslet
(Daily Prayer)

 Cross Cantonnée
(Calendar and
Lectionaries)

 Maltese Cross
(The Psalms)

Illustrations by Aavidar Design Inc.

*This book was designed
and produced by
Creative Publishing Services,
Publications Service,
Presbyterian Church (U.S.A.)
on Macintosh equipment
using Quark XPress.
All text is set in Janson.*